Welcome to
McGraw-Hill Education
ACT DISCARD

*C*ongratulations! You've chosen the ACT guide from America's leading educational publisher. You probably know us from many of the textbooks you used in school. Now we're ready to help you take the next step—and get into the college or university of your choice.

This book gives you everything you need to succeed on the test. You'll get in-depth instruction and review of every topic tested, tips and strategies for every question type, and plenty of practice exams to boost your test-taking confidence.

In addition, in the following pages you'll find:

- **How to Use This Book**: Step-by-step instructions to help you get the most out of your test-prep program.

- **How to Use the Practice Tests**: Tips and strategies to guide your test-taking practice and to help you understand ACT scoring.

- **Your ACT Training Schedule and ACT Emergency Plan**: How to make the best use of your time, even if the test is just days away.

- **50 Top Strategies for Test Day**: Use this list to check your knowledge, or as a last-minute refresher before the exam.

- **Calculator and Speed Reading Tips**: These hints can help you earn high~~~ ~~~~

- **Getting the Most from the Free Online Practice Tests**: Log on to th~ more test-taking practice.

D1378502

ABOUT McGRAW-HILL EDUCATION

This book has been created by McGraw-Hill Education. McGraw-Hill Education is a leading global provider of instructional, assessment, and reference materials in both print and digital form. McGraw-Hill Education has offices in 33 countries and publishes in more than 65 languages. With a broad range of products and services—from traditional textbooks to the latest in online and multimedia learning—we engage, stimulate, and empower students and professionals of all ages, helping them meet the increasing challenges of the twenty-first century knowledge economy.

Learn more. McGraw Hill **Do more.**

How to Use This Book

This book contains general information about the ACT and chapters on each of the test sections. It also contains a Diagnostic Assessment and practice tests. At the end of the book you'll find a discussion of related topics such as choosing a college and an ACT vocabulary list.

Count backward from your ACT test day to determine how much time you have. If you have at least three weeks but preferably twelve to eighteen weeks before test day, you should work through this entire book. You can use the five-step program that follows. If you have less than three weeks, refer to the ACT Emergency Plan on page 5A.

1 Start with the Diagnostic Assessment

The Diagnostic Assessment in Part II of this book is a simulated full-length ACT. Take it as the first step in your test-preparation program. It will help you to pinpoint areas of strength and weakness in your knowledge base and your skill set. After you have scored the Diagnostic Assessment, you should review the parts of the chapters that cover any content areas you found difficult.

2 Learn Test-Taking Strategies

Chapter 2 describes important test-taking strategies that can help you earn extra points. You'll learn about strategic thinking, relaxation techniques, and when to guess if you don't know the answer to a question.

3 Prepare for Each Test Section

Chapters 3–6 cover the four individual sections of the ACT: English, Mathematics, Reading, and Science. Each chapter offers concept reviews and specific strategies for answering the given question type, along with plenty of practice exercises with answers. As you work through these chapters, pay close attention to topics and question types that were particularly difficult for you on the Diagnostic Assessment.

4 Get Ready for the ACT Essay

Chapter 7 provides tips and strategies for the ACT Writing Test, along with information about how your essay will be scored. You'll find typical writing prompts as well as a description of the domain scores to show you what makes a high-scoring ACT essay.

5 Take the Practice Tests

Part IV of this book contains full-length practice ACT tests with complete explanations. Use these tests to check your progress, to gain experience with the ACT format, and to learn to pace yourself to get your highest score.

How to Use the Practice Tests

Take the Diagnostic Assessment Under Realistic Testing Conditions

Time yourself strictly. You need to have an accurate picture of what your performance would be like if test day were today. A good place to take the test is a library; it will be relatively quiet, just like a testing center.

After Your Review, Tackle the Practice Tests

When you have finished your review of the instructional material in Chapters 2–7, start tackling the practice tests in Part IV of this book and on the companion website. Each one is a full-length simulated ACT. These tests contain some variations in style and mix of question types. This approach is intentional so that you can get a taste of all the various formats and styles that can appear on an ACT exam. If you work through all of the material provided, you won't have any surprises on test day.

Review the Explanations as Necessary

There is an explanation for each of the practice questions in this book. You will probably not need to read all of them. Sometimes you can tell right away why you answered a particular question wrong. We have seen countless students smack themselves on the forehead and say, "stupid mistake." We try to refer to these errors as "concentration errors." Everyone makes them from time to time, and you should not worry when they occur. You are likely to focus better on the real test as long as you train properly with the aid of this book. Try to distinguish between concentration errors and any actual holes in your knowledge base. If you have time, read the explanations for any questions that were challenging for you. Sometimes, students answer questions correctly but for the wrong reason, or because they guessed correctly.

Keep Your Score Results in Perspective

ACT scores are sensitive to factors such as fatigue and stress. So don't get worried if you see some variations due to an off day or because the practice test exposed a weakness in your knowledge base or skill set. Just use the information that you gather as a tool to help you improve.

A Note on Scoring the Practice Tests

The scoring tables provided for each test are guides to computing approximate scores. Actual ACT exams are scored from tables that are unique to each test. The actual scale scores depend on factors such as the number of students who take the test, the difficulty level of the items, and the performance of all test takers. This means that "your mileage may vary." Do not get too hung up on your test scores; the idea is to learn something from each practice session and to get used to the "look and feel" of the ACT.

ACT Training Schedule

At least eight weeks before your ACT

▶ Find a quiet place, such as a library, and take the Diagnostic Assessment under actual test conditions. Time yourself strictly. Evaluate your results and pinpoint your areas of strength and weakness. Register for the ACT exam following the procedures described at **www.act.org**.

The first four to six weeks of training

▶ Don't worry about timing. At your leisure, work through the first two ACT practice tests in this book or on the companion website. Think about how the questions and passages are put together and study whatever other sources you need to so that you can fill any holes in your knowledge base. Read Chapters 2–7 in this book.

Two or three weeks before your ACT

▶ Using another practice test, take your first "dress rehearsal" exam on a Saturday morning at 8:00 A.M. Time yourself strictly. Use the results to fine-tune the last part of your training. Review relevant chapters in this book.

One or two weeks before your ACT

▶ Take your second "dress rehearsal" exam. If it doesn't go well, don't get too worried. Try to figure out what went wrong and review the explanations provided and the other relevant portions of this book. There is still time to consolidate your gains and continue to improve. Start planning a fun event for after your ACT exam!

Two to five days before your ACT

▶ Make a practice run to the testing center. Figure out what you are going to wear on test day. Gather your materials together (ticket, ID, pencils, calculator). Adjust your sleep schedule, if necessary, so that you are able to wake up by 7:00 A.M. and be thinking clearly by 8:00 A.M. Confirm your plans for fun after the exam!

The day before your ACT

▶ Rest and relaxation are the order of the day. Do little or no practice or studying. Get some physical activity so that you are better able to sleep and because the endorphins that you release in your brain will help with stress management. Make sure that you take care of your transportation issues and wake-up plan.

Test day!

▶ Get up early. Eat breakfast. Read something to get you "warmed up." Bring your materials. Be on time. Avoid any fellow test takers who are "stress monsters." Remember your game plan for each section. Don't forget to breathe evenly and deeply, and don't tire yourself out with needless physical exertion like tensing up your muscles while taking your ACT. When the test is finished, try not to think about it until you get your score report.

ACT Emergency Plan

If you have only a day or two before your ACT exam, you should take the following steps. They are listed in order of priority so you should do as many of them as you can before your test.

1. Seriously consider rescheduling

The ACT is given several times each year at various locations. Rather than taking your exam with little or no preparation, you should look at the calendar and the ACT website and wait to take your ACT if you can do so and still get the information to your schools of choice before their deadlines.

2. Relax

Even if you don't have enough time to reschedule, you can get some useful information out of this book that will help you to pick up a few points that you might not have gotten otherwise.

3. Take the Diagnostic Assessment

There is a psychological theory called "Test Re-Test" that says that you should do a little bit better on a second ACT than a first ACT, even if you don't do any preparation in between. So make the Diagnostic Assessment your first ACT. Time yourself strictly and do it all in one sitting. Take a 10-minute break after the Mathematics Test.

4. Review the strategies in Chapter 2

Those are the high-yield test-taking strategies that will get you the most extra points on test day.

5. Read through the content chapters

The order should be:
a. Reading (These are the least intuitive strategies.)
b. English (This is the weirdest format of the ACT tests.)
c. Mathematics (Skim through the stuff that you already know. Focus on the material that tends to confuse you. Don't worry about trig at all if you haven't had it in school yet.)
d. Science (Logic and common sense prevail on this test.)

6. Do as many practice questions as you can in your weakest area

Look at the explanations to gain a better understanding of how to approach the questions.

7. Get some sleep

Being well rested will have a bigger impact on your score than staying up all night "cramming." There is a significant skill component on this test. It is not all about knowledge. So you can't learn enough information to guarantee a higher score.

50 Top Strategies for Test Day

When it's almost test day and you've read this book and taken the Practice Tests, make sure you review this page and the pages that follow. Here you'll find 50 essential strategies that can definitely help you earn more points on the ACT. You'll see longer explanations of each strategy, along with examples, in the review portions of this book. The purpose of these pages is to provide a handy, all-in-one, last-minute reminder of these valuable concepts. Use this review to check your test readiness and make sure you're prepared to do your best—and get your best score.

Before the Test

1 Be prepared. Study and practice consistently during your training period. Be organized.

2 Know yourself. Understand your strengths and weaknesses on the ACT.

3 Change bad habits. If you have poor study habits, it took you a while to develop them. Identify these bad habits early so you can make the necessary adjustments.

4 Rest. Get plenty of sleep between practice sessions. Go to bed early the night before the test.

On Test Day

5 Dress comfortably. Wear loose, comfortable, layered clothing. Don't forget your watch.

6 Eat something. Breakfast should be low in sugar and high in protein. Get your normal dose of caffeine, if any.

7 Bring stuff. You need your driver's license, admission ticket, number 2 pencils, a good eraser, and your calculator.

8 Read something. Warm up your brain by reading the newspaper or something similar. Review some practice material.

General Test-Taking Strategies

9   Relax. Don't panic if you are having trouble answering the questions! You do not have to answer all the questions correctly to get a good score. Take a few moments to relax if you are stressed. Put your pencil down, close your eyes, take deep breaths, and clear your mind. When you get back to the test you will feel better.

10   Do the easy stuff first. You do not have to answer the questions from each section in order. It is better to skip the hard ones in each test section and come back to them later. Keep moving so that you don't waste valuable time. If you get stuck, move on!

11   Manage the grid. Do not fill in your "bubble sheet" after every question. Mark your answers in the book and transfer them every one or two pages. Make sure to pay attention to question numbers, especially if you skip a question. Your score depends on what is filled in on the answer sheet.

12   Use the test booklet. The booklet is the only scrap paper you will get. Circle your answer choices, cross out answers you eliminate, and mark questions that you need to come back to later. If you think the answer choice might work, underline it. Do the math! Draw pictures to help you figure out problems and use the space available to write down your calculations.

13   Be aware of time. Pace yourself. Read and work actively through the test. You learned during practice which questions you should focus on and which questions you should come back to later. Use a watch to time yourself. Stay focused. Ignore the environment around you.

14   Guess wisely. There is no scoring penalty on the ACT! Never leave a bubble blank. Eliminate answer choices that you know are wrong. The more you can eliminate, the better your chance of correctly answering the question.

15   Stick with it. Do not second-guess yourself. Your first answer choice is most likely to be correct. If you are not completely comfortable with your first choice, place a question mark next to your answer and come back to it later if you have time. Only change your answer when you are sure that it's wrong.

English Test Strategies

16   Listen to your brain. Read aloud silently. If it sounds right to you, it probably is.

17   Avoid redundancy. Wordiness and redundancy are never rewarded. Usually, the fewer the words that you use, the better.

18   Take DELETE and NO CHANGE seriously. DELETE is a viable answer choice when it eliminates redundant or irrelevant statements. Don't forget to consider the NO CHANGE answer choice. Just because a portion of the passage is underlined does not mean that there is something wrong with it.

19   Try the answer choices. Read each of the choices back into the sentence and then select the one that is grammatically correct and/or clearly expresses the idea.

20   Simplify answer choices. If one part of the answer choice is wrong, the whole answer choice is wrong!

21   Don't make new mistakes. Do not select an answer choice that introduces a new error to the sentence.

22   Match the author. When choosing answer choices, make sure they match the author's strategy and style.

23   Stay organized. Ideas within each essay should flow in a logical sequence.

Math Test Strategies

24 Draw pictures. It really helps to visualize the problem. Your sketches can be quick and a little messy. You should create tables and write out equations too.

25 Think before computing. Look for a way to reason through the problem. Don't just go for your calculator. When you do use your calculator, try to have an idea of what your answer should be.

26 Answer the question that they ask you. Cross out any irrelevant information given in the question. Complete all the steps in the problem—don't quit early.

27 Check the choices. Take a quick peek at the choices as you read the problem. They can provide clues about how to proceed.

28 Test the answers. When trying answer choices, start with the middle value. Because the answers are arranged in order, you can eliminate answer choices based on whether the middle value is too high or too low.

29 Use stand-ins. Use this strategy when you have variables in the question and some of the same variables in the answer choices. Simplify the answer choices by substituting numbers for the variables.

30 Simplify the question. When reading word problems, translate them into mathematical equations and then use substitution.

Reading Test Strategies

31 **Read the question stems first.** When the questions refer to specific lines or words, you may be able to answer the questions right away.

32 **Don't study the passage.** The ACT reading test is in an open-book format. You do not need to memorize the information for a long period of time. Read loosely and only dwell on information that you are sure is important because you need it to answer a question.

33 **Read for the main idea.** The main idea is comprised of topic, scope, and purpose.

34 **Skim the passage.** Do not stop on unfamiliar words the first time through. You may not need to know the meaning of a word to answer the questions. Just try to gain a general understanding of the structure of the passage.

35 **Read and answer the questions.** Paraphrase the question to ensure an understanding of what it is asking you.

36 **Refer back to the passage.** Questions should be answered based on the information in the passage. If a question contains references to specific lines, read a little before and a little after the lines mentioned.

37 **Predict an answer.** After finding relevant information in the passage, try to answer the question in your mind before looking at the answer choices.

38 **Use the process of elimination.** It is reliable but slow. Use it when you cannot predict an answer or your prediction is not listed as an answer choice.

39 **Move around.** Don't be afraid to skip around within the ten-question group that accompanies each passage.

Science Test Strategies

40 Prioritize. Choose passages in the format you like the most and with information that is the least confusing.

41 Think first. Read each question stem, then quickly skim the data presented in the passage to predict an answer. Use common sense to avoid being tricked by distractors.

42 Be "trendy." Note any relationships between variables or trends in the data represented in charts or graphs.

43 Don't be scared by complex vocabulary. The ACT usually defines terms that are absolutely essential to your understanding. Don't waste time trying to pronounce these new terms either.

Writing Test Strategies

44 Carefully read the prompt and perspectives. Be certain you understand the prompt completely.

45 Think about the perspectives. Take the time to formulate your opinion and decide how to analyze the perspectives.

46 Plan your essay. This is the most important stage of the essay-writing process. You can take up to 10 minutes to outline your paper using the scratch paper provided.

47 Be persuasive. Make sure you have compelling reasons and examples to support your position. Place the issue in a broader context.

48 Consider the other side. Be sure to address how someone might challenge or question your position.

49 Write your essay out on the answer pages. Do not worry about the number of examples included in your essay or the length of your essay. Focus on the quality and cohesiveness of your ideas.

50 Review your essay. If you have time at the end, reread your essay. Correct any mistakes in grammar, usage, punctuation, and spelling. Recopy any words that are difficult to read. Make your essay as polished as you can in the time allowed.

Using Your Calculator on the ACT

Here are some handy tips to help you make the best use of your calculator on the ACT Math Test.

Don't Overuse the Calculator

Even though you're allowed to use a calculator, the ACT math section is not a test of your calculator skills. It's a critical thinking test. Top ACT scorers rarely use their calculators, and generally only to check their answers, not to analyze their process. Of course, smart calculator use is occasionally helpful, as the following examples show.

Think Before Computing

ACT math questions test your logical reasoning ability, not just your calculator skills. So think through the problem first before punching in numbers. When using your calculator, be sure you have a good idea of what your answer should look like ahead of time. If the answer you get from your calculator is not at least in your expected ballpark, try again.

Know How to MATH ▶FRAC

Let's say you're solving an ACT math problem about probabilities and you get 34/85 as an answer, but the choices are:

- A. $\dfrac{4}{17}$
- B. $\dfrac{2}{7}$
- C. $\dfrac{2}{5}$
- D. $\dfrac{3}{7}$
- E. $\dfrac{7}{17}$

Did you mess up? No—you just have to simplify. Here, a TI-83 or similar calculator with ▶FRAC might save you time. Type "34/85" and enter, then press the MATH button and then ▶FRAC. Like magic, it will convert the fraction to its lowest terms: 2/5.

Know How to Get a Remainder

Consider this math question: The tables at a wedding reception are set up to accommodate 212 people. There are 24 tables, some seating 8 people and the rest seating 9 people. How many 9-seat tables are there?

Without getting into the details, the answer is simply the remainder when 212 is divided by 24. You could do this by long division, but you can probably do it faster with a calculator:

Enter the division problem and enter: $212 \div 24 = 8.833333\ldots$
Subtract the integer part: $\text{ANS} - 8 = 0.833333\ldots$
Multiply by the original divisor: $\text{ANS} \times 24 = 20$

So the answer is 20. Memorize this handy procedure to streamline "remainder" problems.

Get Fresh Batteries

Even if you don't use your calculator much, you won't be happy if it dies halfway through the ACT. Put in a set of fresh batteries the night before! You might also consider bringing a simple "back-up" calculator, just in case.

Speed Reading for Higher ACT Scores

Learning some basic speed reading techniques can help you to improve your score on the ACT. Speed reading is particularly useful on the ACT Reading Test. On that test, you will need to read and answer questions about four passages, each of about 700–900 words. If you choose to answer all of the questions on the Reading Test, you will have only about eight minutes to work on each of the four passages.

The primary goal of speed reading is to take in as much information as possible in the shortest time possible, while maintaining a high level of comprehension. The first step in becoming a "speed reader" is to determine your baseline reading speed—that is, the speed at which you read comfortably with comprehension. The average person reads at a pace of about 250 words per minute. A realistic goal for you would be 500 to 600 words per minute.

Calculate Your Baseline Reading Speed

First, find a stopwatch or a watch with a second hand. You will need to time yourself for one minute while reading some new material at your typical reading pace—the speed at which you are the most comfortable reading. At the end of the one-minute period, be sure to note where you stopped reading.

For ease of calculation, assume that a "word" is equivalent to 5 units (a unit can be defined as a letter, a space, punctuation, etc.). Count the total lines of text you read, and then count the number of units in each line. Multiply the two values to get your baseline reading speed.

Increase Your Reading Speed

Generally, people read each word separately, one at a time, and the eye stops at individual words. Not only is this inefficient, it is unnecessary. The human brain can comprehend words at almost twice the rate that the human eye can read them in this jerky, stop-and-go process. This type of reading contributes to the tendency of many people to find reading boring; their minds often wander because too much time is spent between words. Increasing the number of words that your eye is able to see when you look at a page is one of the easiest ways to increase your reading speed.

Following are some more specific techniques for improving your overall reading speed.

1 Eliminate all of the "stops" in your reading. By eliminating "stops" you will automatically read faster without losing any comprehension.

2 Turn off your internal narrator. In other words, don't "subvocalize," or read out loud to yourself. This process of speaking the words in your mind will slow you down. NOTE: Some types of reading—the ACT English Test, for example—require you to subvocalize, so be aware of the purpose of your reading.

3 Eliminate regressions. A regression is simply reading what you've already read. Most regressions are subconscious, so you'll really have to pay attention and be focused on your reading to eliminate them.

4 Use your finger while you read. Place your finger below each line of text as you read, and move it along the line of text, following the tip of your finger with your eyes. Practice moving your finger faster and faster while still maintaining comprehension.

5 Read introductory material. The first thing to be aware of is the text before the text. If there is any introductory material, headings, or subheadings, make sure to read and take advantage of them. This supplemental information will serve as signposts on the road to improved understanding of the text. Often, it will provide you with a slight preview of what you are about to read, so that you will approach the passage with some idea of what you can expect to get from it.

6 Focus on main concepts. Spend as little time as possible comprehending individual words, unless they are key concepts. Focus instead on an overall understanding of the author's aims and how the structure of a given piece of writing contributes to those goals. Spending the majority of your time on supporting details is not nearly as efficient as determining the concepts that the author is trying to stress, and then relating the central ideas back to those main points.

7 Don't push it! Once you have achieved some mastery of speed reading, be sure not to overestimate your own rate of comprehension. Try to avoid pushing yourself to the upper limit of your reading speed, as comprehension tends to decrease slightly at that point. You should try to hover slightly below your maximum speed as much as possible, as this gives your brain the greatest opportunity to process the text and make sense of what you are reading.

Practice, Practice, Practice!

You will likely find speed reading quite challenging because you have probably been reading fairly slowly for years. This habit will be hard to break. In fact, without realizing it, you may slow down and speed up multiple times while you read, failing to notice any real improvement in your reading speed or comprehension. It is even possible to see a decrease in both speed and comprehension depending on your level of distraction at the time. Repeated practice is necessary to become a confident speed reader!

McGraw-Hill Education

ACT

ELITE

2021

McGraw-Hill Education

ACT

ELITE

2021

Steven W. Dulan
Amy Dulan

New York   Chicago   San Francisco   Athens   London   Madrid
Mexico City   Milan   New Delhi   Singapore   Sydney   Toronto

1 2 3 4 5 6 7 8 9   LHS   25 24 23 22 21 20 (book alone)
1 2 3 4 5 6 7 8 9   LHS   25 24 23 22 21 20 (Elite)

ISBN   978-1-260-46396-5 (book alone)
MHID   1-260-46396-6

ISBN   978-1-260-46398-9 (Elite)
MHID   1-260-46398-2

e-ISBN 978-1-260-46397-2 (e-book alone)
e-MHID   1-260-46397-4

e-ISBN 978-1-260-46399-6 (e-book Elite)
e-MHID   1-260-46399-0

ACT is a registered trademark of ACT, which was not involved in the production of, and does not endorse, this product.

McGraw-Hill Education products are available at special quantity discounts to use as premiums and sales promotions or for use in corporate training programs. To contact a representative, please visit the Contact Us pages at www.mhprofessional.com.

Contents

About the Authors   ix
Exciting ACT Updates!   xi

PART I   **Getting Started**

CHAPTER 1   Understanding the ACT 3
WHAT IS THE ACT?   3
WHAT IS THE STRUCTURE OF THE ACT?   3
WHO WRITES THE ACT?   4
REGISTERING FOR THE ACT   4
WHY DO ACT EXAMS EXIST?   4
ACT SCORES   5
BIAS ON THE ACT   5
DISABILITIES AND THE ACT   5
TESTING IRREGULARITIES   6
SAT DIFFERENCES AND SIMILARITIES   6

PART II   **ACT Diagnostic Assessment**

ACT Diagnostic Assessment Test 9
ENGLISH TEST   15
MATHEMATICS TEST   27
READING TEST   42
SCIENCE TEST   50
WRITING TEST   60
ANSWER KEY   61
SCORING GUIDE   65
ANSWERS AND EXPLANATIONS   69

PART III   **Strategies and Review**

CHAPTER 2   Strategies to Get Your Best Score . . . 89
THE PSYCHOLOGY OF TESTING   89
STRATEGIC THINKING   91
RELAX TO SUCCEED   91

GETTING READY TO TAKE THE TEST   96

TAKING THE TEST   97

GUESSING ON THE TEST   99

AFTER THE TEST   99

CHAPTER 3   ACT English Test:
Strategies and Concept Review. . . .101

GENERAL STRATEGIES AND TECHNIQUES   102

CONVENTIONS OF STANDARD ENGLISH   104

PRODUCTION OF WRITING AND
KNOWLEDGE OF ENGLISH   107

ACT ENGLISH SKILLS EXERCISES   110

ANSWERS AND EXPLANATIONS   120

PRACTICE QUESTIONS   129

ANSWERS AND EXPLANATIONS   134

CHAPTER 4   ACT Mathematics Test:
Strategies and Concept Review. . . .137

GENERAL STRATEGIES AND TECHNIQUES   139

MATHEMATICS CONCEPT REVIEW   146

ACT MATHEMATICS SKILLS EXERCISES   166

ANSWERS AND EXPLANATIONS   179

PRACTICE QUESTIONS   207

ANSWERS AND EXPLANATIONS   212

CHAPTER 5   ACT Reading Test:
Strategies and Concept Review. . . .217

TIMING   218

GENERAL STRATEGIES AND TECHNIQUES   219

QUESTION TYPES   223

STRATEGIES FOR SPECIFIC QUESTION TYPES   224

ACT READING SKILLS EXERCISES   225

ANSWERS AND EXPLANATIONS   236

PRACTICE QUESTIONS   240

ANSWERS AND EXPLANATIONS   244

CHAPTER 6   ACT Science Test:
Strategies and Concept Review. . . .247

GENERAL STRATEGIES AND TECHNIQUES   248

THE SCIENTIFIC METHOD   252

ACT SCIENCE TEST EXERCISES   253

ANSWERS AND EXPLANATIONS   259

PRACTICE QUESTIONS   261

ANSWERS AND EXPLANATIONS   265

CHAPTER 7 ACT Writing Test:
Strategies and Review 267

    HOW TO PREPARE   269
    THE ESSAY PROMPT   269
    ESSAY WRITING TECHNIQUES   270
    COMMON MISTAKES   273
    ESSAY SCORING   276
    SIMPLIFIED ESSAY SCORING RUBRIC   277
    SAMPLE ESSAY TO SCORE   283
    ACT WRITING SKILLS EXERCISES   284
    ANSWERS AND EXPLANATIONS   289

PART IV **Four Practice Tests**

ACT Practice Tests 293

ACT Practice Test 1 295

    ENGLISH TEST   301
    MATHEMATICS TEST   313
    READING TEST   326
    SCIENCE TEST   334
    WRITING TEST   344
    ANSWER KEY   345
    SCORING GUIDE   349
    ANSWERS AND EXPLANATIONS   353

ACT Practice Test 2 373

    ENGLISH TEST   379
    MATHEMATICS TEST   391
    READING TEST   404
    SCIENCE TEST   412
    WRITING TEST   422
    ANSWER KEY   423
    SCORING GUIDE   427
    ANSWERS AND EXPLANATIONS   431

ACT Practice Test 3 451

    ENGLISH TEST   457
    MATHEMATICS TEST   468
    READING TEST   481
    SCIENCE TEST   489
    WRITING TEST   497
    ANSWER KEY   499
    SCORING GUIDE   503
    ANSWERS AND EXPLANATIONS   507

ACT Practice Test 4 527

    ENGLISH TEST   533
    MATHEMATICS TEST   545
    READING TEST   559
    SCIENCE TEST   567
    WRITING TEST   577
    ANSWER KEY   579
    SCORING GUIDE   583
    ANSWERS AND EXPLANATIONS   587

215 Extra Challenging ACT Questions
Every Top-Scoring Student Should Know 607

PART V   APPENDIXES

APPENDIX 1 What's Next? 787

CHOOSING THE BEST COLLEGE
    OR UNIVERSITY FOR YOU   787
APPLYING TO COLLEGE   791
SUGGESTED HIGH SCHOOL COURSES   794

APPENDIX 2 Grammar and
Punctuation Rules. 795

PUNCTUATION RULES   795
GRAMMAR RULES   800
SENTENCE STRUCTURE RULES   808
COMMONLY MISUSED WORDS   810

APPENDIX 3 ACT Vocabulary List 815

Practice Test Question Index   835

About the Authors

Steve Dulan has been helping students to prepare for success on the ACT and other standardized exams since 1989. He attended the Thomas M. Cooley Law School on a full honors scholarship after achieving a 99th percentile score on his Law School Admission Test (LSAT). In fact, Steve scored in the 99th percentile on every standardized test he has ever taken. While attending law school, Steve continued to teach standardized test prep classes (including ACT, SAT, PSAT, GRE, GMAT, and LSAT) an average of 30 hours each week, and tutored some of his fellow law students in a variety of subjects and in essay exam-writing techniques. Since 1997, Steve has served as president of Advantage Education®, a company dedicated to providing unparalleled test preparation. Thousands of students have benefited from his instruction, coaching, and admissions consulting and have gone on to their colleges of choice. Steve's students have gained admission to some of the most prestigious institutions in the world and received many scholarships of their own. A few of them even beat his ACT score!

Amy Dulan put her analytical skills and nurturing personality to work as an ACT coach after receiving a Psychology degree from Michigan State University in 1991. During forays into the corporate world over the next several years, Amy continued to tutor part-time, eventually helping to found Advantage Education® in 1997. Since then, Amy has worked with thousands of high school students in both a private and classroom setting, helping them to maximize their ACT scores. Her sense of humor and down-to-earth style allow Amy to connect with her students and make learning fun.

The techniques included in this book are the result of Steve and Amy's experiences with students at all ability and motivation levels over many years.

"After working with Steve I was able to crack the ACT and got a 36 composite score! His help made all the difference in getting those last few points for a perfect score!"
C. S. (Student)

"Amy, thanks to you. my daughter was able to get a 35 composite score on her ACT with a perfect 36 on the English test! Thank you for your time and commitment to her success."
J. Q. (Parent)

Exciting ACT Updates!

There are three major changes to ACT that will be available beginning with the September 2020 test date.

ONLINE TESTING

First, the ACT will be available as an **online test** at selected locations.

The sections, question types, timing, and scoring will remain the same. So, all the information and practice material in this book will still be relevant and helpful. The online test may be more comfortable for some students. For others, it might prove more stressful and distracting. Colleges will not know whether you take the online or paper test. This is strictly a matter of personal preference. The scores for online tests will be available as quickly as two days later. This is significantly faster than the paper test and may be helpful for students who are up against application deadlines.

The online test will be given at specified locations on ACT computers. It will not be available for home testing, or on your own laptop, even at a testing center. Scratch paper will be available, and the testing software will include highlighting tools. You will be able to go back and change answers if there is time remaining in the section.

Some students prefer the comfortable environment of working on a computer screen. Others prefer to have the ability to mark on the page with their pencils as they work through the material. We advise you to try both environments before making your decision. *The Official Beginner's Guide for ACT* (a publication of ACT, Inc.) includes access to an online practice test so that you can see for yourself which option is best for you.

SUPERSCORING

Second, ACT will report a **superscore** for those who take more than one ACT. About one-third of all institutions currently allow superscoring. The change is that, now, ACT will automatically report the best score on each of your English, Math, Reading, and Science sections across all of the ACTs you take, and calculate your hypothetical composite score as though each of your best section scores were on the same full ACT. Colleges and universities will still each decide how to handle this information. Some will not consider the superscore in making admission decisions. Be sure to check with the schools and programs you are applying to for more information.

> There is some research showing that superscores are better predictors of college GPA than single-day composite scores. The trend seems to be toward more institutions accepting superscores moving forward.

SECTION RETAKES

Third, if you have taken one complete, or *full battery*, ACT at any time since 2016, you may choose to retake individual sections. You may retake one, two, or three sections as an online test at select locations on any of the seven annual national test dates beginning with September 2020. You may NOT take individual sections as paper-and-pencil exams. In our opinion, this is the most exciting change. It means that, with proper planning, you could take your *full panel* ACT on one day, and then do the writing section as a stand-alone test at a later date without the fatigue that is a major factor for many students. Some students will benefit from the reduced fatigue and stress when retaking only one, two, or three sections rather than an entire ACT exam.

One additional change is that ACT is removing the limit on retakes. In the past, a student could "only" take a lifetime maximum of 12 ACT exams. That limit is being rescinded starting in September of 2020. However, with nearly 50 years combined ACT prep experience, the authors of this book have never met anyone who even came close to the 12-exam limit. We feel that this change is not significant for most test takers.

See: www.act.org/morechoices for more information.

PART I

Getting Started

CHAPTER 1
Understanding the ACT

ACT Structure		
Test	**Number of Questions and Time Allowed**	**Reporting Categories (Content and Skills Tested)**
English	75 Questions 45 Minutes	*Conventions of Standard English* – approximately 40 questions *Production of Writing* – approximately 25 questions *Knowledge of Language* – approximately 10 questions

Math	60 Questions
	60 Minutes
		Preparing for Higher Math – approximately 35 Questions
		
		   • **Number & Quantity**
		   • **Algebra**
		   • **Functions**
		   • **Geometry**
		   • **Statistics & Probability**
		
		Integrating Essential Skills – approximately 25 questions

Reading	40 Questions 35 Minutes	*Key Ideas and Details* – approximately 20 questions *Craft and Structure* – approximately 15 questions *Integration of Knowledge and Ideas* – approximately 5 questions
Science	40 Questions 35 Minutes	*Interpretation of Data* – approximately 20 questions *Evaluation of Models, Inferences, and Results* – approximately 10 questions *Scientific Investigation* – approximately 10 questions
Writing		Optional 40-minute essay.

Understanding the ACT

WHAT IS THE ACT?

Each year, more than 2 million students take the ACT in order to gain entrance into the colleges of their choice. The ACT is a standardized test designed to measure your critical thinking skills and to assess your ability to apply knowledge and logic when solving problems. Your ACT score will be evaluated along with your high school Grade Point Average, involvement in school and extracurricular activities, letters of recommendation, and college application essay. While the ACT is just one factor that is examined during the admissions process, it is essential that you maximize your ACT score so that you can remain competitive among the many other applicants hoping to gain admission.

The authors of the ACT insist that the ACT is an achievement test, meaning that it is designed to measure your readiness for college instruction. There is ongoing debate about how well the ACT accomplishes that mission. What is not debated is that the ACT is not a direct measure of abilities. It is not an IQ test. The ACT is certainly not a measure of your worth as a human being. It is not even a perfect measure of how well you will do in college. Theoretically, each of us has a specific potential to learn and acquire skills. The ACT doesn't measure your natural, inborn ability. If it did, we wouldn't be as successful as we are at raising students' scores on ACT exams.

The ACT actually measures a certain knowledge base and skill set. It is "trainable," meaning that you can do better on your ACT if you work on gaining the knowledge and acquiring the skills that are tested.

WHAT IS THE STRUCTURE OF THE ACT?

The ACT is broken up into four multiple-choice tests and one optional essay task. The multiple-choice tests are called English, Mathematics, Reading, and Science. They are always given in this same order. In fact, there is a lot of predictability when it comes to the ACT. The current exam still has very much in common with ACT exams from past years. This means that we basically know what is going to be on your ACT in terms of question types and content. Refer to the chart on page 2 for more information on the structure of the ACT.

WHO WRITES THE ACT?

There is a company called ACT, Inc. that decides exactly what is going to be on your ACT exam. This group of experts consults with classroom teachers at the high school and college levels. They look at high school and college curricula and they employ educators and specialized psychologists called "psychometricians" (measurers of the mind), who know a lot about the human brain and how it operates under various conditions. We picture them as "evil genius" researchers in white coats somewhere, gleefully rubbing their hands together and trying to think up ways to keep you out of college. Don't fear, however, we are the "good geniuses" trying to get you into the college of your choice. We'll lay out the details of how you will be tested so that you can get yourself ready for the "contest" on test day.

REGISTERING FOR THE ACT

You must register for the ACT in advance. You can't just show up on test day with a number 2 pencil and dive right in. The best source of information for all things ACT is, not surprisingly, the ACT website: **www.act.org**. There is also a very good chance that a guidance counselor, and/or pre-college counselor at your school has an *ACT Registration Packet*, which includes all of the information that you need for your test registration.

WHY DO ACT EXAMS EXIST?

Back in the mid-twentieth century, some people noticed that there was a disturbing trend in college admissions. Most of the people who were entering college came from a fairly small group of people who went to a limited number of high schools. Many had parents who had attended the same colleges. There wasn't much opportunity for students from new families to "break into" the higher education system. Standardized entrance exams were an attempt to democratize the situation and create a *meritocracy*, where admissions decisions were based on achievement and not just social status. The ACT was not the first standardized college entrance exam. It came a little later as an attempt at improving on the older SAT.

Colleges use the ACT for admissions decisions and, sometimes, for advanced placement. It is also used to make scholarship decisions. Since there are variations among high schools around the country, the admissions departments at colleges use the ACT, in part, to help provide a standard for comparison. There are studies that reveal a fair amount of "grade inflation" at some schools. So, colleges cannot rely simply upon grade point averages when evaluating academic performance.

The ACT also measures a certain skill set that is not necessarily measured as part of a Grade Point Average (GPA). We'll dig a little more into that in the individual test chapters.

Amy Says:

One important thing about scores is that you don't have to be perfect to get a good score on the ACT. The truth is that you can miss a fair number of questions and still get a score that places you in the top 1% of all test-takers. In fact, this test is so hard and the time limit is so unrealistic for most test-takers that you can get a score that is at the national average (about a 21) even if you get almost half of the questions wrong.

ACT SCORES

Each of the multiple-choice sections of the ACT is called a Test (English Test, Mathematics Test, Reading Test, and Science Test). Each test is given a score on a scale of 1 to 36. These four "scale scores" are then averaged and rounded according to normal rounding rules to yield a Composite Score. It is this Composite Score that is most often meant when someone refers to your ACT score.

Your actual score report will also refer to detailed results for each test section. These are based on your performance on a subset of the questions on each of these tests. These results will help you to determine your readiness for college-level courses.

BIAS ON THE ACT

Some research suggests that members of different ethnic groups and residents of different states have different average scores on the ACT. The reasons for the different scores are beyond the scope of this book. However, we would like to point out that the differences are small and that the variations among different members of any group are far more substantial than the differences in averages among groups. In other words, if you are a member of a group that does well on the ACT, don't rely on that group membership to guarantee a good score. Conversely, if you are a member of a group with a slightly lower average, don't turn that group membership into a self-fulfilling prophecy. Those students who take the exam seriously and put time and effort into their preparation are the ones who succeed, regardless of ethnicity or state of residence.

Males and females, overall, score about the same. Males tend to do slightly better on Math and Science and females tend to do better on English, Reading, and, it is predicted, Writing. Nevertheless, the gender differences are not significant enough to allow anyone to make score predictions for any one individual. So, as with ethnicity and state of residence, disregard your gender and work hard if you want to maximize your scores.

DISABILITIES AND THE ACT

Some students identify learning and other cognitive disabilities for the first time when they begin to prepare for the ACT. Factors to look out for include extreme anxiety or panic, a marked inability to focus, and major differences in scores between timed and untimed exams.

If any of these warning signs apply to you, it is recommended that you seek assistance from your parents, school counselors, and other professionals who can advise you regarding the screening process for learning disabilities.

If you have a diagnosis from a qualified professional, a law called the Americans with Disabilities Act (ADA) states that reasonable accommodations must be granted that will allow you a level playing field. No discrimination is allowed against anyone who has a legitimate medical condition that affects performance on the ACT.

The most common accommodation is to allow extra time for completion of the exam. Previously, ACT, Inc. would flag score reports of students who were granted extra time. Such is no longer the case. Students with accommodations are not identified to the colleges anymore. Most people see this as a great step forward in fairness under the ADA.

Of course, accommodations are also allowed for physical disabilities. For more information on accommodations for disabilities, contact ACT directly. Be sure to contact ACT very early in the process. You must allow a reasonable length of time for ACT to confirm your diagnosis and for some back and forth discussion regarding proposed accommodations.

TESTING IRREGULARITIES

A "testing irregularity" is basically an accusation of cheating. You can avoid this situation by following all instructions and only working on the section on which you are supposed to be working. This includes marking the answer sheets. Don't go back to a previous section or forward to a later section, either in the test book or on the answer sheet. Do write in the test booklet. We are aware of one student who could have saved himself the time, inconvenience, and expense of a testing irregularity accusation if he had merely shown some work in his test book. If you are accused of a testing irregularity, don't panic. You have certain due process rights. Discuss the matter with your parents and perhaps an attorney as soon as possible so that you can react appropriately.

SAT DIFFERENCES AND SIMILARITIES

The SAT is another standardized college admissions examination. It includes multiple-choice sections and an optional writing test. Some of the material tends to be the same as on the ACT. For instance, the reading comprehension passages are often very similar in structure and content, and some of the math questions are very similar as well.

The SAT is a longer exam overall. The SAT math section has more problems that are really logic questions and less like what you probably learned in your high school math classes. Visit **www.sat.org** for more information.

The vast majority of colleges and universities accept both SAT scores and ACT scores. There are persistent myths that say that schools in certain states either all require the ACT or all require the SAT. These myths simply are not true. Rather than relying upon generalities, you should investigate the colleges in which you are interested and find out for yourself which entrance exams they will accept and whether they have a preference for one or the other.

PART II

ACT Diagnostic Assessment

ACT Diagnostic Assessment Test

ACT Diagnostic Assessment Test

This test will help you to assess your strengths and weaknesses. Take the test under realistic conditions (preferably early in the morning in a quiet location), and allow approximately 3.5 hours for the entire test. Each of the test sections should be taken in the time indicated at the beginning of the sections, and in the order in which they appear. Fill in the bubbles on your answer sheet once you have made your selections.

When you have finished the entire test, check your answers against the Answer Key. Follow the directions on how to score your test, and calculate your score using the Scoring Guide that appears on pages 65 through 67. Then, read the Answers and Explanations, paying close attention to the explanations for the questions that you missed.

Your scores should indicate your performance on the individual test sections, as well as your overall performance on the Diagnostic Test. Once you have identified your areas of strength and weakness, you should review those particular chapters in the book.

ACT DIAGNOSTIC ASSESSMENT TEST
Answer Sheet

ENGLISH

1 (A) (B) (C) (D)	21 (A) (B) (C) (D)	41 (A) (B) (C) (D)	61 (A) (B) (C) (D)
2 (F) (G) (H) (J)	22 (F) (G) (H) (J)	42 (F) (G) (H) (J)	62 (F) (G) (H) (J)
3 (A) (B) (C) (D)	23 (A) (B) (C) (D)	43 (A) (B) (C) (D)	63 (A) (B) (C) (D)
4 (F) (G) (H) (J)	24 (F) (G) (H) (J)	44 (F) (G) (H) (J)	64 (F) (G) (H) (J)
5 (A) (B) (C) (D)	25 (A) (B) (C) (D)	45 (A) (B) (C) (D)	65 (A) (B) (C) (D)
6 (F) (G) (H) (J)	26 (F) (G) (H) (J)	46 (F) (G) (H) (J)	66 (F) (G) (H) (J)
7 (A) (B) (C) (D)	27 (A) (B) (C) (D)	47 (A) (B) (C) (D)	67 (A) (B) (C) (D)
8 (F) (G) (H) (J)	28 (F) (G) (H) (J)	48 (F) (G) (H) (J)	68 (F) (G) (H) (J)
9 (A) (B) (C) (D)	29 (A) (B) (C) (D)	49 (A) (B) (C) (D)	69 (A) (B) (C) (D)
10 (F) (G) (H) (J)	30 (F) (G) (H) (J)	50 (F) (G) (H) (J)	70 (F) (G) (H) (J)
11 (A) (B) (C) (D)	31 (A) (B) (C) (D)	51 (A) (B) (C) (D)	71 (A) (B) (C) (D)
12 (F) (G) (H) (J)	32 (F) (G) (H) (J)	52 (F) (G) (H) (J)	72 (F) (G) (H) (J)
13 (A) (B) (C) (D)	33 (A) (B) (C) (D)	53 (A) (B) (C) (D)	73 (A) (B) (C) (D)
14 (F) (G) (H) (J)	34 (F) (G) (H) (J)	54 (F) (G) (H) (J)	74 (F) (G) (H) (J)
15 (A) (B) (C) (D)	35 (A) (B) (C) (D)	55 (A) (B) (C) (D)	75 (A) (B) (C) (D)
16 (F) (G) (H) (J)	36 (F) (G) (H) (J)	56 (F) (G) (H) (J)	
17 (A) (B) (C) (D)	37 (A) (B) (C) (D)	57 (A) (B) (C) (D)	
18 (F) (G) (H) (J)	38 (F) (G) (H) (J)	58 (F) (G) (H) (J)	
19 (A) (B) (C) (D)	39 (A) (B) (C) (D)	59 (A) (B) (C) (D)	
20 (F) (G) (H) (J)	40 (F) (G) (H) (J)	60 (F) (G) (H) (J)	

MATHEMATICS

1 (A) (B) (C) (D) (E)	16 (F) (G) (H) (J) (K)	31 (A) (B) (C) (D) (E)	46 (F) (G) (H) (J) (K)
2 (F) (G) (H) (J) (K)	17 (A) (B) (C) (D) (E)	32 (F) (G) (H) (J) (K)	47 (A) (B) (C) (D) (E)
3 (A) (B) (C) (D) (E)	18 (F) (G) (H) (J) (K)	33 (A) (B) (C) (D) (E)	48 (F) (G) (H) (J) (K)
4 (F) (G) (H) (J) (K)	19 (A) (B) (C) (D) (E)	34 (F) (G) (H) (J) (K)	49 (A) (B) (C) (D) (E)
5 (A) (B) (C) (D) (E)	20 (F) (G) (H) (J) (K)	35 (A) (B) (C) (D) (E)	50 (F) (G) (H) (J) (K)
6 (F) (G) (H) (J) (K)	21 (A) (B) (C) (D) (E)	36 (F) (G) (H) (J) (K)	51 (A) (B) (C) (D) (E)
7 (A) (B) (C) (D) (E)	22 (F) (G) (H) (J) (K)	37 (A) (B) (C) (D) (E)	52 (F) (G) (H) (J) (K)
8 (F) (G) (H) (J) (K)	23 (A) (B) (C) (D) (E)	38 (F) (G) (H) (J) (K)	53 (A) (B) (C) (D) (E)
9 (A) (B) (C) (D) (E)	24 (F) (G) (H) (J) (K)	39 (A) (B) (C) (D) (E)	54 (F) (G) (H) (J) (K)
10 (F) (G) (H) (J) (K)	25 (A) (B) (C) (D) (E)	40 (F) (G) (H) (J) (K)	55 (A) (B) (C) (D) (E)
11 (A) (B) (C) (D) (E)	26 (F) (G) (H) (J) (K)	41 (A) (B) (C) (D) (E)	56 (F) (G) (H) (J) (K)
12 (F) (G) (H) (J) (K)	27 (A) (B) (C) (D) (E)	42 (F) (G) (H) (J) (K)	57 (A) (B) (C) (D) (E)
13 (A) (B) (C) (D) (E)	28 (F) (G) (H) (J) (K)	43 (A) (B) (C) (D) (E)	58 (F) (G) (H) (J) (K)
14 (F) (G) (H) (J) (K)	29 (A) (B) (C) (D) (E)	44 (F) (G) (H) (J) (K)	59 (A) (B) (C) (D) (E)
15 (A) (B) (C) (D) (E)	30 (F) (G) (H) (J) (K)	45 (A) (B) (C) (D) (E)	60 (F) (G) (H) (J) (K)

READING

1 Ⓐ Ⓑ Ⓒ Ⓓ	11 Ⓐ Ⓑ Ⓒ Ⓓ	21 Ⓐ Ⓑ Ⓒ Ⓓ	31 Ⓐ Ⓑ Ⓒ Ⓓ
2 Ⓕ Ⓖ Ⓗ Ⓙ	12 Ⓕ Ⓖ Ⓗ Ⓙ	22 Ⓕ Ⓖ Ⓗ Ⓙ	32 Ⓕ Ⓖ Ⓗ Ⓙ
3 Ⓐ Ⓑ Ⓒ Ⓓ	13 Ⓐ Ⓑ Ⓒ Ⓓ	23 Ⓐ Ⓑ Ⓒ Ⓓ	33 Ⓐ Ⓑ Ⓒ Ⓓ
4 Ⓕ Ⓖ Ⓗ Ⓙ	14 Ⓕ Ⓖ Ⓗ Ⓙ	24 Ⓕ Ⓖ Ⓗ Ⓙ	34 Ⓕ Ⓖ Ⓗ Ⓙ
5 Ⓐ Ⓑ Ⓒ Ⓓ	15 Ⓐ Ⓑ Ⓒ Ⓓ	25 Ⓐ Ⓑ Ⓒ Ⓓ	35 Ⓐ Ⓑ Ⓒ Ⓓ
6 Ⓕ Ⓖ Ⓗ Ⓙ	16 Ⓕ Ⓖ Ⓗ Ⓙ	26 Ⓕ Ⓖ Ⓗ Ⓙ	36 Ⓕ Ⓖ Ⓗ Ⓙ
7 Ⓐ Ⓑ Ⓒ Ⓓ	17 Ⓐ Ⓑ Ⓒ Ⓓ	27 Ⓐ Ⓑ Ⓒ Ⓓ	37 Ⓐ Ⓑ Ⓒ Ⓓ
8 Ⓕ Ⓖ Ⓗ Ⓙ	18 Ⓕ Ⓖ Ⓗ Ⓙ	28 Ⓕ Ⓖ Ⓗ Ⓙ	38 Ⓕ Ⓖ Ⓗ Ⓙ
9 Ⓐ Ⓑ Ⓒ Ⓓ	19 Ⓐ Ⓑ Ⓒ Ⓓ	29 Ⓐ Ⓑ Ⓒ Ⓓ	39 Ⓐ Ⓑ Ⓒ Ⓓ
10 Ⓕ Ⓖ Ⓗ Ⓙ	20 Ⓕ Ⓖ Ⓗ Ⓙ	30 Ⓕ Ⓖ Ⓗ Ⓙ	40 Ⓕ Ⓖ Ⓗ Ⓙ

SCIENCE

1 Ⓐ Ⓑ Ⓒ Ⓓ	11 Ⓐ Ⓑ Ⓒ Ⓓ	21 Ⓐ Ⓑ Ⓒ Ⓓ	31 Ⓐ Ⓑ Ⓒ Ⓓ
2 Ⓕ Ⓖ Ⓗ Ⓙ	12 Ⓕ Ⓖ Ⓗ Ⓙ	22 Ⓕ Ⓖ Ⓗ Ⓙ	32 Ⓕ Ⓖ Ⓗ Ⓙ
3 Ⓐ Ⓑ Ⓒ Ⓓ	13 Ⓐ Ⓑ Ⓒ Ⓓ	23 Ⓐ Ⓑ Ⓒ Ⓓ	33 Ⓐ Ⓑ Ⓒ Ⓓ
4 Ⓕ Ⓖ Ⓗ Ⓙ	14 Ⓕ Ⓖ Ⓗ Ⓙ	24 Ⓕ Ⓖ Ⓗ Ⓙ	34 Ⓕ Ⓖ Ⓗ Ⓙ
5 Ⓐ Ⓑ Ⓒ Ⓓ	15 Ⓐ Ⓑ Ⓒ Ⓓ	25 Ⓐ Ⓑ Ⓒ Ⓓ	35 Ⓐ Ⓑ Ⓒ Ⓓ
6 Ⓕ Ⓖ Ⓗ Ⓙ	16 Ⓕ Ⓖ Ⓗ Ⓙ	26 Ⓕ Ⓖ Ⓗ Ⓙ	36 Ⓕ Ⓖ Ⓗ Ⓙ
7 Ⓐ Ⓑ Ⓒ Ⓓ	17 Ⓐ Ⓑ Ⓒ Ⓓ	27 Ⓐ Ⓑ Ⓒ Ⓓ	37 Ⓐ Ⓑ Ⓒ Ⓓ
8 Ⓕ Ⓖ Ⓗ Ⓙ	18 Ⓕ Ⓖ Ⓗ Ⓙ	28 Ⓕ Ⓖ Ⓗ Ⓙ	38 Ⓕ Ⓖ Ⓗ Ⓙ
9 Ⓐ Ⓑ Ⓒ Ⓓ	19 Ⓐ Ⓑ Ⓒ Ⓓ	29 Ⓐ Ⓑ Ⓒ Ⓓ	39 Ⓐ Ⓑ Ⓒ Ⓓ
10 Ⓕ Ⓖ Ⓗ Ⓙ	20 Ⓕ Ⓖ Ⓗ Ⓙ	30 Ⓕ Ⓖ Ⓗ Ⓙ	40 Ⓕ Ⓖ Ⓗ Ⓙ

You may wish to remove these sample answer document pages to respond to the practice ACT Writing Test.

Begin WRITING TEST here.

Cut Here

If you need more space, please continue on the next page.

WRITING TEST

_____

_____

_____

_____

_____

_____

_____

_____

_____

_____

_____

_____

_____

_____

_____

_____

_____

_____

_____

_____

_____

_____

_____

_____

END OF THE WRITING TEST

STOP! IF YOU HAVE TIME LEFT OVER, CHECK YOUR WORK ON THIS SECTION ONLY.

2

Cut Here

1 ■ ■ ■ ■ ■ ■ ■ ■ 1

ENGLISH TEST

45 Minutes – 75 Questions

DIRECTIONS: In the passages that follow, some words and phrases are underlined and numbered. In the answer column, you will find alternatives for the words and phrases that are underlined. Choose the alternative that you think is best and fill in the corresponding bubble on your answer sheet. If you think that the original version is best, choose "NO CHANGE," which will always be either answer choice A or F. You will also find questions about a particular section of the passage, or about the entire passage. These questions will be identified by either an underlined portion or by a number in a box. Look for the answer that clearly expresses the idea, is consistent with the style and tone of the passage, and makes the correct use of standard written English. Read the passage through once before answering the questions. For some questions, you should read beyond the indicated portion before you answer.

PASSAGE I

Helen Keller's Light in the Darkness

Helen Keller was born in 1880. Her life begun normally.
<u>   </u>
     1

She was happy, and healthy learning to walk and talk like
<u>   </u>
                  2

her toddler peers. It was not until a high fever robbed her

of sight and hearing just before her second birthday that

her remarkable journey started. Although the exact cause of

Helen's fever was never determined, modern doctors believe

Helen suffered from meningitis. The illness plunged Helen

into a dark silence that most people cannot even imagine

or think of . The Kellers' beloved first-born child was blind
<u>   </u>
    3
and deaf.

     4 Helen wandered around the family's property,

anxious to discover new sensations but unable to understand
<u>   </u>
                5
anything that she experienced. Her resulting tantrums became

more violent as she continued to grow.

1. **A.** NO CHANGE
   B. had began
   C. begins
   D. began

2. **F.** NO CHANGE
   G. happy and healthy, learning to walk and talk
   H. happy, and healthy, learning to walk, and talk,
   J. happy, and healthy learning to walk, and talk

3. **A.** NO CHANGE
   B. to think about
   C. or really think about
   D. DELETE the underlined portion.

4. Which of the following sentences, if added here, would best introduce the new subject of Paragraph 2?
   F. Helen didn't obey her parents.
   G. The next few years were frustrating for Helen and physically and emotionally draining for her family.
   H. Annie Sullivan came to teach Helen.
   J. Helen loved plants and animals, and many different kinds could be found near her home.

5. **A.** NO CHANGE
   B. discover and feel new sensations
   C. feel new sensations about making discoveries
   D. make discoveries and sense new feelings

GO ON TO THE NEXT PAGE.

1 ■ ■ ■ ■ ■ ■ ■ **1**

Feeling sorry for their impaired, daughter Helen's, parents
<u>   </u>
                                          6
allowed the tantrums to occur with no consequences. In a

last-ditch effort to keep the increasingly unmanageable Helen

from being <u>sent up</u> the State Insane Asylum, the Kellers
                7
contacted the Perkins Institute in Boston, Massachusetts.

<u>Primarily just a school for the blind,</u> its staff had once helped
                                   8
a child who was both blind and deaf.

Enter Annie Sullivan, who truly became the "miracle worker"

in Helen's life. <u>Only with self-discipline would Helen</u> be
                                             9
able to overcome her tremendous challenges. Unfortunately,

Helen's parents' constant coddling of their daughter

was undermining Annie's efforts. <u>One's stubbornness is</u>
                                          10

exhausting, but Annie knew that, if <u>channeled; it</u> would
                                          11
be Helen's salvation. In order to work her "miracle," Annie

needed to get Helen away from her parents' pampering.

Annie <u>was given</u> permission to take Helen to live in a little
           12
house on the opposite side of the Kellers' garden. Initially,

Helen continued to fight <u>Annies efforts,</u> but gradually the
                                 13

girl began to behave. Soon, Helen's submission gave way to

trust in Annie. Helen began to comprehend that everything

she touched had a name. Her constant darkness was suddenly

illuminated by this new-found understanding, and her hunger

for knowledge became <u>repressed.</u>
                             14

6. F. NO CHANGE
    G. impaired daughter, Helen's parents
    H. impaired daughter Helens' parents
    J. impaired daughter Helen's, parents

7. A. NO CHANGE
    B. sent to
    C. sent with
    D. sent for

8. F. NO CHANGE
    G. Primarily a blind school,
    H. Just a school for the primarily blind,
    J. For the blind, primarily, this school, along with

9. A. NO CHANGE
    B. Helen, only with her self-discipline, would
    C. Only by including self-discipline, would Helen
    D. Only Helen, with self-discipline, would

10. F. NO CHANGE
    G. One's stubbornness was
    H. Her stubbornness being
    J. Helen's stubbornness was

11. A. NO CHANGE
    B. channeled it
    C. channeled: it
    D. channeled, it

12. F. NO CHANGE
    G. had gave
    H. was giving
    J. gave

13. A. NO CHANGE
    B. Annies' efforts
    C. Annies efforts
    D. Annie's efforts,

14. F. NO CHANGE
    G. excited
    H. insatiable
    J. unfounded

GO ON TO THE NEXT PAGE.

1 ■ ■ ■ ■ ■ ■ ■ ■ 1

For the remainder of her life, Annie Sullivan continued to feed Helen's appetite for learning, providing a constant light in Helen's otherwise impenetrable darkness.

Question 15 asks about the preceding passage as a whole.

15. Suppose the writer was asked to write a brief essay about Helen Keller's professional accomplishments. Would this essay successfully fulfill this goal?
    A. Yes, because the essay focuses on the skill of Annie Sullivan in communicating with Helen.
    B. Yes, because the essay indicates that Helen eventually stopped having tantrums and began learning from Annie Sullivan.
    C. No, because this essay mostly addresses Annie Sullivan's accomplishments concerning Helen.
    D. No, because Helen's disabilities prevented her from having a successful career.

PASSAGE II

The following paragraphs may or may not be in the most logical order. You may be asked questions about the logical order of the paragraphs, as well as where to place sentences logically within any given paragraph.

Holiday Joy (and Chaos)

[1]

Why do the holidays make you feel like a kid again? I'm not talking about the wide-eyed wonder of seeing the tree at Rockefeller Center initially illuminated for the first time.
No, I mean the tantrum-filled, "I want to do it all" attitude of a two-year-old. You begin the season with enthusiasm. You begin thinking about the Christmas season soon after Labor Day, you enthusiastically anticipating the many joys sure to unfold.

[2]

A critical part of the holiday has shopped for gifts.

Not wanting to be rushed with last-minute purchases: you begin your holiday shopping early. In September, you buy the perfect gift for Aunt Susie. You compliment yourself for

16. F. NO CHANGE
    G. illuminated at the initial time.
    H. illuminated for the first time.
    J. firstly illuminated, initially.

17. A. NO CHANGE
    B. enthusiastic
    C. enthusiastically
    D. enthusiasm in

18. F. NO CHANGE
    G. being shopping for gifts.
    H. is shopping for gifts.
    J. for the shopping of gifts.

19. A. NO CHANGE
    B. purchases, you
    C. purchases you
    D. purchases; you

GO ON TO THE NEXT PAGE.

1 ■ ■ ■ ■ ■ ■ ■ ■ 1

thinking ahead. In October, you <u>find</u> just the right gift for
                                    20

Uncle John (who collects ghost figurines). <u>This year you're</u>
                                              21
holiday shopping is going to be a snap!

[3]

Suddenly, it's Thanksgiving. The holiday invitations

begin to arrive. As you mark the dates on the calendar, you

vow that <u>this Christmas, different</u> from those in the past.
          22

You notice a <u>few overlapping events that are scheduled at</u>
                                                      23
<u>the same time,</u> but you're not concerned. You are determined
      23
to enjoy every holiday occasion.

[4]

You calmly begin writing a list that includes names of

family and <u>friends placing</u> checkmarks next to those whose
            24
gifts you've purchased. What's this? You've purchased only

two gifts for fifteen relatives and twelve friends? Suddenly,

the holiday season <u>had became</u> a nightmare. You begin
                     25
making frantic phone calls to obtain wish lists, but to no

avail.

[5]

Now it's November, and the radio stations are playing

Christmas carols. How silly—we have six weeks until

Christmas! There is still plenty of time to find gifts for

everyone on your shopping list.

[6]

26 You rush from store to store. Your eyes dart among

the displays for the perfect gift. Finally, you give up and

purchase 25 generic gift certificates at a department store.

20. F. NO CHANGE
  G. found
  H. will find
  J. have found

21. A. NO CHANGE
  B. This year, your
  C. This year: your
  D. This year you're,

22. F. NO CHANGE
  G. this Christmas will be different
  H. the differences this Christmas would have
  J. a different Christmas it would be

23. A. NO CHANGE
  B. scheduled, overlapping set of events on the schedule,
  C. few overlapping events,
  D. few overlapping events scheduled to occur at the same time,

24. F. NO CHANGE
  G. friends. Placing
  H. friends; placing
  J. friends, placing

25. A. NO CHANGE
  B. has become
  C. becoming
  D. will become

26. Which of the following sentences offers the best introduction to Paragraph 6?
  F. Deciding that you must come up with your own gift ideas, you head to the mall.
  G. Christmas should not be stressful.
  H. Malls have a diverse selection of stores within steps of each other.
  J. Most stores offer gift options for last-minute shoppers.

GO ON TO THE NEXT PAGE.

They are not the most inspired gifts, but you're done

shopping! You <u>trudged home exhausted to</u> begin baking

             ₂₇

cookies. Immediately, your son asks, "What did you get Miss

Jones?" You <u>spring</u> into tears, realizing you forgot not only

        ₂₈

his teacher but seven other people who somehow didn't make

your list. Your son cautiously approaches and gives you a

gentle hug. You feel a glimmer of joy return. You decide to

skip the cookies and get some sleep. As you turn out

the lights, you silently vow to start your shopping earlier

next year!

27. A. NO CHANGE
    B. trudging home, exhausted, to
    C. exhausted trudge home to
    D. trudge home, exhausted, to

28. F. NO CHANGE
    G. erupt
    H. burst
    J. jump

> Questions 29 and 30 ask about the preceding passage as a whole.

29. What function does Paragraph 6 serve in relation to the rest of the essay?
    A. It refers back to the opening sentences of the essay, suggesting that all adults act like toddlers.
    B. It indicates that the narrator will likely succeed in next year's goal of completing her holiday responsibilities early.
    C. It summarizes the essay's main point that Christmas is the most relaxed holiday of the year.
    D. It indicates that, despite the narrator's feelings of being overwhelmed, she may eventually be able to enjoy the holiday.

30. For the sake of unity and coherence of the essay, Paragraph 5 should be placed:
    F. where it is now.
    G. after Paragraph 1.
    H. after Paragraph 2.
    J. after Paragraph 3.

PASSAGE III

Have You No Shame?

    Popular opinion teaches us that guilt is a wasted

emotion. Ironically, this same <u>culture</u> teaches us "No

                      ₃₁

pain, no gain." Although we recognize that physical

fitness may involve occasional discomfort, we are

31. Which choice would most precisely sharpen the focus of this paragraph, in keeping with the way the writer develops the argument in the rest of the essay?
    A. NO CHANGE
    B. physicality
    C. improvement
    D. DELETE the underlined portion.

1 ■ ■ ■ ■ ■ ■ ■ ■ 1

unwilling to accept that society fitness may as well.
                                    32
Despite what we have learned about pain, studies show

that if an exercise hurts, you're probably doing it wrong.

Similarly, if a course of action (or inaction) causes pangs

of guilt, you should start exercising. Nature provides our
        33
bodies with pain receptors to limit injury to ourselves—

if you place your hand on a hot stove, pain prompts

you to remove your hand. Likewise, guilt helps to

stop us from causing or inflicting pain to other people.
                        34
                    Imagine driving through your local business district.

A car is attempting by turning left into your lane. Although
            35
you could safely allow the car to merge, you instead

accelerate so as not to delay your trip another second.

Vehicles these days can stop much more quickly than those
                                    36
in the past. As you drive by, you recognize your neighbor
    36
behind the wheel—the one who watched your dog during

your vacation. You feel an uncomfortable twinge of guilt, and

you find, yourself, driving more courteously for the rest of
    37
your trip.

        Discounting guilt is akin to turning off conscience.

Imagine a society in which no one is in a manner that
                                38
benefits another unless failure to cooperate will result

in legal penalties. Although you may joke that I've just
    39

described rush-hour traffic, I now just have, in fact,
                        40
described sociopathic behavior.

---

32. **F.** NO CHANGE
    G. societal fitness
    H. societal's fitness
    J. societies fitness

33. Which choice best supports the argument that guilt serves a purpose?
    A. NO CHANGE
    B. you should call a psychiatrist.
    C. you should ignore it.
    D. you should change your course of action.

34. **F.** NO CHANGE
    G. stop us from causing unnecessary and grievous pain to other people.
    H. limit emotional injury to others.
    J. limit unnecessary and emotionally grievous injury to others.

35. **A.** NO CHANGE
    B. trying to attempt a turn
    C. trying to attempt to turn
    D. attempting to turn

36. **F.** NO CHANGE
    G. The faster you are traveling, the longer it will take you to stop.
    H. Vehicles today can stop faster than in the past.
    J. DELETE the underlined portion.

37. **A.** NO CHANGE
    B. find yourself, driving,
    C. find yourself driving
    D. find, yourselves, driving

38. **F.** NO CHANGE
    G. acts in
    H. acts as if he is in
    J. performs of and for

39. **A.** NO CHANGE
    B. penalties of a legal nature, which may include fines and/or imprisonment.
    C. fines, imprisonment, or other legal penalties.
    D. penalties of a legal nature.

40. **F.** NO CHANGE
    G. I, myself, just
    H. by just having,
    J. I have,

GO ON TO THE NEXT PAGE.

1 ■ ■ ■ ■ ■ ■ ■ ■ **1**

By definition, guilt is "a feeling of being blame-worthy." Shame is a "feeling of strong regret" or "painful emotion caused by consciousness of guilt." Not surprisingly, an insanity plea stating that the criminal is criminally insane is usually sought when a criminal feels no regret for his actions. So how did guilt get its bad reputation? First, we hate pain, and if we can avoid it, we do. In the case of guilt, however, it is difficult to escape the negativity. Therefore, we decide

the guilt itself—not the action that prompted the guilt—is

wrong. Second, guilt, if improperly managed; can lead to devastation. Guilt should not be ignored, but it should be examined (What caused me to feel guilty?), analyzed (How can I avoid that mistake in the future?), and then released (I move on with new wisdom). Unfortunately, some people spend so much time on the examination that they never move over to the analysis and release. They become crippled by the guilt. The purpose of guilt is not to cause people to withdraw from society but to become better members of it.

41. **A.** NO CHANGE
    B. that he is criminally insane
    C. that he is not of sound mind
    D. DELETE the underlined portion.

42. **F.** NO CHANGE
    G. guilt, so,
    H. guilt, then,
    J. guilt, thereby,

43. **A.** NO CHANGE
    B. guilt, is
    C. guilt: is
    D. guilt. Is

44. **F.** NO CHANGE
    G. managed, which
    H. managed,
    J. managed, it

45. **A.** NO CHANGE
    B. like
    C. on
    D. in time

PASSAGE IV

A Picture of Health

President John F. Kennedy's public image was one of enviable health. Tall and trim, he embodied the tanned, athletic image other men sought. In reality, his "tan" was a symptom of Addison's disease. He had been bedridden for much of his childhood, although he was genuinely athletic, he was forced to watch as healthier children played outside.

46. **F.** NO CHANGE
    G. enviable health, tall
    H. enviable health, but tall
    J. enviable health tall

47. **A.** NO CHANGE
    B. He had been bedridden for much of his life. He was genuinely athletic. He was
    C. Although genuinely athletic, he had been bed-ridden for much of his childhood,
    D. He was a childhood athlete bedridden

GO ON TO THE NEXT PAGE.

1 ■ ■ ■ ■ ■ ■ ■ **1**

Kennedy's ailments <u>began in</u> a two-month
₄₈
hospitalization for scarlet fever at age two. At age thirteen,

he developed colitis. By 1940, he had osteoporosis and

compression fractures in his lower back, and in 1944 he

had his first back surgery. In 1947, Kennedy was officially

diagnosed with Addison's disease, 49 He underwent two

more unsuccessful back surgeries in 1954 and 1955 and took

chronic pain medication from that point until his death in

1963.

By the time Kennedy became president, he

was taking ten to twelve pills every day, including

anti-spasmodics, muscle relaxants, various steroids,

pain medications, and sleeping pills. In addition,

<u>he received anesthetic injections in his back up to six times a day.</u>
₅₀

How did Kennedy hide such significant health problems

from the American people <u>without them seeing it</u>? His
₅₁
best alibi was his appearance: He looked healthy. His well-

being was clear to anyone <u>who</u> saw him, in person or on
₅₂
television.

In addition, he was well-practiced at acting <u>healthy, he was</u>
₅₃

able to hide his <u>crippling pain from all except his doctors</u> and
₅₄
closest relatives. Finally, he was prepared with answers to any

<u>questions for anyone related to his overall health and well-being;</u>
₅₅

48. **F.** NO CHANGE
    G. began by
    H. began for
    J. began with

49. The writer would like to add more detail to help the reader
    to understand the symptoms of Addison's disease. Assum-
    ing all are true, which of the following completions of this
    sentence best achieves this effect?
    A. an auto-immune disorder that has numerous symp-
    toms.
    B. which is rare.
    C. a rare auto-immune disorder characterized by weight
    loss, muscle weakness, fatigue, low blood pressure,
    and darkening of the skin.
    D. which causes a variety of unpleasant symptoms and
    can result in death, often at a very early age.

50. **F.** NO CHANGE
    G. in his back he received anesthetic injections up to six
    times a day.
    H. in his back, up to six times a day, he received anes-
    thetic injections.
    J. up to six times a day in his back, he received anes-
    thetic injections.

51. **A.** NO CHANGE
    B. without their knowledge or noticing it
    C. without noticing them
    D. DELETE the underlined portion.

52. **F.** NO CHANGE
    G. which
    H. that
    J. whom

53. **A.** NO CHANGE
    B. healthy, and he
    C. healthy. As he
    D. healthy; by showing he

54. **F.** NO CHANGE
    G. crippling pain from his doctors, except
    H. pain, which was crippling, from all except his doctors
    J. doctors from his crippling pain

55. **A.** NO CHANGE
    B. related questions about his health;
    C. health-related questions about his well-being;
    D. health-related questions;

GO ON TO THE NEXT PAGE.

for example, he <u>attributes</u> his back problems to old football
                      56
and war injuries.

<u>Perhaps a better question would be why Kennedy was sick.</u>
                      57

The answer is a testimony to Kennedy's incredible strength

and perseverance. A detailed time-line comparison of

his illnesses and treatments with his official decisions

and actions resulted in the following discovery: Neither

his illness <u>and the drugs</u> seemed to have affected his
              58
performance as president.

    By today's standards, Kennedy had medical problems

severe enough to qualify him for federal disability

or retirement. Nevertheless, he not only survived but

<u>performed at the highest level.</u>
              59

56. F. NO CHANGE
   G. attributed
   H. is attributing
   J. was attributed

57. Which of the choices provides the most effective introductory sentence for this paragraph?
   A. NO CHANGE
   B. Perhaps a better question would be whether Kennedy played football.
   C. Perhaps a better question would be whether such an ill man was competent to be president.
   D. Perhaps a better question would be why Kennedy had Addison's disease.

58. F. NO CHANGE
   G. and not the drugs
   H. nor the drugs
   J. and either the drugs

59. A. NO CHANGE
   B. at the highest level, performed.
   C. highly performed at his level.
   D. achieved high performance above his expected level.

Question 60 asks about the preceding passage as a whole.

60. Suppose the writer had been assigned to write a brief essay about Addison's disease and treatment of the disease. Would this essay successfully fulfill the assignment?
   F. Yes, because the essay describes the symptoms of Addison's disease.
   G. Yes, because the essay explains that Addison's disease is treated with steroids.
   H. No, because the essay focuses on President Kennedy's health.
   J. No, because the essay does not describe any symptoms of the disease.

GO ON TO THE NEXT PAGE.

1 ■ ■ ■ ■ ■ ■ ■ ■ 1

PASSAGE V

Warmth in the Arctic

"We're going where?" "To the gateway to the Arctic—
the Land of the Midnight Sun!

We're going traveling to Tromso, Norway!" As the
school year ended, I was looking forward to going home to

Southern California, planned to lifeguard and use my spare
time to surf. Now my friend was proposing that we spend the
summer 250 miles north of the Arctic Circle. Was he nuts?
As I look back, it was the best crazy decision I ever made.

Although the weather in Tromso wasn't hot, it wasn't
particularly cold, either. I occasionally needed a sweater,
but seldom a coat. And, though I didn't develop my
usual summer tan, the warmth of the people of Tromso
more than made up for what the climate did not provide.
Everyone we encountered was eager to help us. 64
                                                63

(1) That summer, my days weren't spent sitting in a
lifeguard chair, spinning a whistle around my finger.
                     65

61. A. NO CHANGE
    B. going and traveling
    C. traveling
    D. traveling on a trip

62. F. NO CHANGE
    G. where I planned
    H. which I planned
    J. in which I planned

63. Given that all are true, which of the choices best illustrates the "warmth" described in the previous sentence?
    A. NO CHANGE
    B. The food in Tromso was delicious.
    C. Most of the people wore fur hats.
    D. Tromso gets very cold in the winter.

64. The writer wishes to include an example of the Tromso residents' treatment of foreigners. Which of the following true sentences, inserted here, would best fulfill that goal?
    F. When we asked for directions, the residents usually provided them.
    G. We had only to glance up from a map to find someone offering (in nearly perfect English) to help us find our way.
    H. My mother is Norwegian, and she is very helpful.
    J. Tromso has more night-time attractions per capita than any other city in Norway, which makes the people very friendly.

65. Which of the following alternatives to the underlined portion would NOT be acceptable?
    A. twirling
    B. flipping
    C. throwing
    D. twisting

GO ON TO THE NEXT PAGE.

(2) Tromso, like other towns, may boast it never sleeps, but for Tromso, it seems to be true. (3) Although I feared that the time would drag, I was pleasantly surprised that it did not. (4) I know I slept less that summer than I ever have; yet, I didn't feel tired.

(5) In fact, my days weren't spent working—or sitting—at all. (6) Whether that was the result of the midnight sun or the

potently rich coffee, I'm not sure. 68

Much of our free time was spent hiking. On a long hike, good boots are essential, especially in preventing blisters. Hiking is so popular in Norway that the government has passed regulations such as the *Friluftsleven* (Outdoor Recreation Act) that allows anyone to hike or ski across wilderness areas, 70 One of our favorite places to hike was on Mount Storsteinen, which is accessible from Tromso by cable car. From the top, we would hike one of the many trails. The views were amazing. I took photos of

many beautiful scenes.

66. **F.** NO CHANGE
G. Residents may boast that they never sleep, but in Tromso, it seems to be true.
H. In other towns, people may boast that it never sleeps, but in Tromso it seems they're true.
J. Towns other than Tromso may boast, but it isn't true that they don't sleep except there.

67. **A.** NO CHANGE
B. besides
C. regardless
D. indeed

68. Which of the following sequences of sentences makes the preceding paragraph most logical?
F. NO CHANGE
G. 2, 3, 1, 5, 4, 6
H. 1, 6, 5, 3, 2, 4
J. 1, 6, 2, 4, 3, 5

69. **A.** NO CHANGE
B. Good boots are essential to preventing blisters, especially on a long hike.
C. My favorite boots are tough and dependable.
D. DELETE the underlined portion.

70. The writer wishes to add a detail to the end of this sentence that will explain how the Act continues to expand hikers' rights. Given that all are true, which of the following statements would most directly accomplish this?
F. adding designated areas as demand increases.
G. even if the areas are unpopulated.
H. despite the difficulties of hiking.
J. including those people who don't enjoy hiking.

71. Which of the descriptions of the photos best creates a vivid image for the reader?
A. NO CHANGE
B. clear mountain lakes, thick birch forests, deep fjords, and the midnight sun.
C. lakes, forests, fjords, and the sun.
D. people and places I had never photographed before.

1 ■ ■ ■ ■ ■ ■ ■ ■ **1**

Now that I'm <u>home,</u> I look forward to returning to
72

Tromso soon. However, next time I am determined to see

<u>Tromsos'</u> sights in the winter. As much as I enjoyed the
73

<u>midnight sun, I am anxious to see the northern lights from</u>
74
<u>Mount Storsteinen,</u>whose vista has been described as world
74

class—exactly as I would describe <u>it's</u> inhabitants.
75

72. **F.** NO CHANGE
    G. home, therefore,
    H. home, for example,
    J. home, on the other hand,

73. **A.** NO CHANGE
    B. Tromsos
    C. Tromsos,
    D. Tromso's

74. **F.** NO CHANGE
    G. sun, the Mount Storsteinen northern lights I am anxious to see,
    H. sun, the northern lights from Mount Storsteinen I am anxious to see,
    J. view of the sun, the northern lights from Mount Storsteinen are something I am anxious to see:

75. **A.** NO CHANGE
    B. the region's
    C. their
    D. some

END OF THE ENGLISH TEST.
STOP! IF YOU HAVE TIME LEFT OVER, CHECK YOUR WORK ON THIS SECTION ONLY.

2 △ △ △ △ △ △ △ △ 2

MATHEMATICS TEST

60 Minutes – 60 Questions

DIRECTIONS: Solve each of the problems in the time allowed, then fill in the corresponding bubble on your answer sheet. Do not spend too much time on any one problem; skip the more difficult problems and go back to them later. You may use a calculator on this test. For this test you should assume that figures are NOT necessarily drawn to scale, that all geometric figures lie in a plane, and that the word *line* is used to indicate a straight line.

---

1. If $4x - 9 = 11$, then $x = ?$
   A. 5
   B. 6
   C. 6.5
   D. 9
   E. 16

2. Consider the following 2 logical statements:

   If the length of $\overline{XY}$ is 4, then the length of $\overline{YZ}$ is 7.

   The length of $\overline{YZ}$ is NOT 7.

   If these statements are both true, then the length of:
   F. $\overline{XY}$ is NOT 4
   G. $\overline{XY}$ is 7
   H. $\overline{YZ}$ is 4
   J. $\overline{YZ}$ is NOT 4
   K. $\overline{YZ}$ is 7

3. If 60% of a given number is 9, then what is 25% of the given number?
   A. 0.66
   B. 1.75
   C. 2.33
   D. 3.75
   E. 6.50

4. Vehicle A averages 16 miles per gallon of gasoline, and Vehicle B averages 35 miles per gallon of gasoline. At these rates, how many more gallons of gasoline does Vehicle A need than Vehicle B to make a 1,120-mile trip?
   F. 32
   G. 38
   H. 46
   J. 63
   K. 70

DO YOUR FIGURING HERE.

GO ON TO THE NEXT PAGE.

2 △ △ △ △ △ △ △ △ **2**

5. The sum of the five consecutive integers below is 390.

$$x - 3$$
$$x - 2$$
$$x - 1$$
$$x$$
$$x + 1$$

What is the value of x?

A. 79
B. 80
C. 81
D. 82
E. 83

DO YOUR FIGURING HERE.

6. If $P = 5a$ and $Q = 3b - 2a$, then what is the value of $P - Q$?

F. $7a + 3b$
G. $3a + 3b$
H. $7a - 3b$
J. $3a - 3b$
K. $5a - 3b$

7. In the figure below, l_1 is parallel to l_2, l_3 is parallel to l_4, and the lines intersect as shown. What is the measure of angle z?

A. $40°$
B. $50°$
C. $60°$
D. $70°$
E. $80°$

8. If $x = 2$, then $-(x^2) + 4x - 3 = ?$

F. 9
G. 5
H. 1
J. -1
K. -7

9. The average of 8 numbers is 6.5. If each of the numbers is decreased by 3, what is the average of the 8 new numbers?

A. 0.0
B. 3.5
C. 4.0
D. 7.5
E. 9.5

GO ON TO THE NEXT PAGE.

2   **2**

10. The expression $5a + 5b$ is equivalent to which of the following?

   F. $5(a - b)$
   G. $10(a + b)$
   H. $5ab$
   J. $5(a + b)$
   K. $10ab$

11. An interior designer charges $25 for each hour that she works on a project, plus a flat $40 project fee. Approximately how many hours of work are included in a $375 bill for a project?

   A. 4.5
   B. 5.8
   C. 9.4
   D. 13.4
   E. 15.0

12. If $\dfrac{8}{x} \ge \dfrac{1}{4}$, what is the largest possible value for x?

   F. $\dfrac{1}{2}$
   G. 4
   H. 16
   J. 24
   K. 32

13. On the clock shown below, what is the number of degrees that the hour hand of the clock moves from 1:00 P.M. to 8:00 P.M.?

   A. 70°
   B. 150°
   C. 210°
   D. 270°
   E. 300°

DO YOUR FIGURING HERE.

GO ON TO THE NEXT PAGE.

2   **2**

14. In the standard (x, y) coordinate plane below, $PQRS$ is a parallelogram. Points P, Q, and S are located on the axes as shown. Which of the following could be the coordinates of point R?

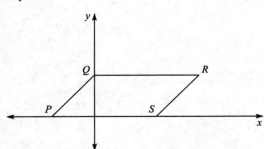

DO YOUR FIGURING HERE.

F. (0, 4)
G. (4, 0)
H. (−3, 0)
J. (6, 4)
K. (6,−4)

15. Which of the following is a factored form of $3x^3y^3 + 3xy$?
A. $3xy(x^2y^2 + 1)$
B. $3(3x^2y^2)$
C. $(3x + 3y)(3x + 3y)$
D. $3x^2y^2(xy)$
E. $3x(x^2y^2 + 3)$

16. A classroom has $(r + s)$ rows of seats and t seats in each row. Which of the following is an expression for the number of seats in the entire classroom?
F. rst
G. $(rs) + (rt)$
H. $t + (rs)$
J. $r + s + t$
K. $(rt) + (st)$

17. The function f is defined as $f(x) = -3x - 3x^2$. What is $f(-3)$?
A. −18
B. −9
C. 9
D. 18
E. 27

18. In a 5-kilometer race, runners recorded times (in minutes : seconds) of 24:04, 22:45, 19:53, and 21:33. What is the difference between the slowest time and the fastest time?
F. 2:23
G. 2:45
H. 4:11
J. 4:51
K. 5:38

GO ON TO THE NEXT PAGE.

2   **2**

19. You are standing in line at the cash register to pay for a watch priced at $12.99. A sales tax of 6% of the $12.99 will be added (rounded to the nearest cent) to the price of the watch. You have 15 one-dollar bills, but how much will you need in coins if you want to have exact change ready?

A. $0.23
B. $0.33
C. $0.53
D. $0.67
E. $0.77

20. For which nonnegative value of x is the expression $\dfrac{1}{16-x^2}$ undefined?

F. 0
G. 4
H. 16
J. 32
K. 256

21. What is the smallest integer greater than $\sqrt{99}$?

A. 3
B. 9
C. 10
D. 11
E. 50

22. Two strips of tape are to be used to seal a box, as shown below. Both strips must go completely around the box. What is the minimum length of tape, in centimeters (cm), required to seal the box?

F. 73 cm
G. 112 cm
H. 120 cm
J. 146 cm
K. 186 cm

DO YOUR FIGURING HERE.

GO ON TO THE NEXT PAGE.

3 1328 00896 5459

2   **2**

DO YOUR FIGURING HERE.

23. Kahla owns 2 bicycle shops (A and B). She stocks 3 brands of biking shorts (X, Y, and Z) in each store. The matrices below show the numbers of each type of biking shorts in each store and the cost for each type of biking short. The value of Kahla's biking short inventory is computed using the costs listed. What is the total value of the biking short inventory for Kahla's 2 stores?

$$\begin{array}{c} & \begin{array}{ccc} X & Y & Z \end{array} \\ \begin{array}{c} A \\ B \end{array} & \left(\begin{array}{ccc} 150 & 200 & 225 \\ 100 & 120 & 175 \end{array} \right) \end{array} \qquad \begin{array}{c} & \text{Cost} \\ \begin{array}{c} X \\ Y \\ Z \end{array} & \left(\begin{array}{c} \$20 \\ \$25 \\ \$30 \end{array} \right) \end{array}$$

   A. $25,000
   B. $20,000
   C. $13,000
   D. $14,750
   E. $10,250

24. Which of the following gives all the solutions of $x^2 + 2x = 8$?
   F. 4 and −2
   G. −4 and 2
   H. −8 and 1
   J. −4 only
   K. −8 only

25. If $(f + g)^2 = 81$ and $fg = 20$, then $f^2 + g^2 = ?$
   A. 1
   B. 9
   C. 41
   D. 81
   E. 100

26. If, for all x, $(x^{4a-3})^2 = x^{10}$, then $a = ?$
   F. $\dfrac{1}{2}$
   G. 1
   H. $\dfrac{13}{4}$
   J. 2
   K. $-\dfrac{15}{6}$

27. For the complex number i such that $i^2 = -1$, what is the value of $i^6 + 3i^4$?
   A. −2
   B. −1
   C. 0
   D. 1
   E. 2

GO ON TO THE NEXT PAGE.

2   △ **2**

28. In the (x, y) coordinate plane, what is the y-intercept of the line $5x - 4y = 7$?

   F. -4

   G. $-\dfrac{7}{4}$

   H. $\dfrac{5}{4}$

   J. $\dfrac{7}{4}$

   K. 7

DO YOUR FIGURING HERE.

29. In the (x, y) coordinate plane, what is the radius of the circle with the equation $(x + 3)^2 + (y - 2)^2 = 10$?

   A. 2

   B. 3

   C. $\sqrt{3}$

   D. $\sqrt{10}$

   E. 10

30. In the right triangle pictured below, l, m, and n are the lengths of its sides. What is the value of $\sin \beta$?

   F. $\dfrac{l}{n}$

   G. $\dfrac{m}{n}$

   H. $\dfrac{n}{l}$

   J. $\dfrac{l}{m}$

   K. $\dfrac{n}{m}$

31. For all nonzero a and b, $\dfrac{(4a^3b)(-5a^5b^3)}{(10a^4b^2)} = ?$

   A. $2a^4b^2$

   B. $-2a^2b^2$

   C. $\dfrac{a^4b^4}{2}$

   D. $\dfrac{9}{b}$

   E. $-2a^4b^2$

GO ON TO THE NEXT PAGE.

2 **2**

DO YOUR FIGURING HERE.

32. In the figure below, 3 parallel lines are crossed by 2 transversals, as shown. The points of intersection and some distances, in inches, are labeled. What is the length, in inches, of x?

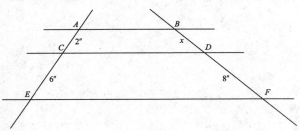

F. 2
G. $\dfrac{8}{3}$
H. 3
J. $\dfrac{4}{3}$
K. 4

33. The figure below shows square $ABCD$ and also shows the circle centered at D with radii $\overline{DC}$ and $\overline{DA}$. If the perimeter of the square is 28 units, what is the area of the circle, in square units?

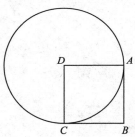

A. 7π
B. 14π
C. 28π
D. 49π
E. 56π

34. Which of the following logical statements identifies the same set as the graph shown below?

F. $x \leq 2$ or $x \geq 4$
G. $x \leq 2$ and $x \geq 4$
H. $x < 2$ or $x > 4$
J. $x \leq 2$ and $x > 4$
K. $x \leq 2$ or $x > 4$

GO ON TO THE NEXT PAGE.

2   **2**

35. A right circular cylinder is shown below, with dimensions given in inches. What is the total surface area of this cylinder, in square inches?

(Note: The total surface area of a cylinder is given by $2\pi r^2 + 2\pi rh$, where r is the radius and h is the height.)

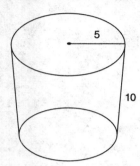

- **A.** $50\,\pi$
- **B.** $100\,\pi$
- **C.** $120\,\pi$
- **D.** $150\,\pi$
- **E.** $200\,\pi$

36. If x and y are real and $\sqrt{4\left(\dfrac{x^2}{3y}\right)} = 1$, then what must be true of the value of y?
- **F.** y must be negative
- **G.** y must be positive
- **H.** y must equal 4
- **J.** y must equal $\dfrac{1}{2}$
- **K.** y may have any value

37. If c is a positive integer that divides evenly into both 64 and 96 but divides evenly into neither 16 nor 20, what should you get when you add the digits in c?
- **A.** 3
- **B.** 5
- **C.** 7
- **D.** 8
- **E.** 10

38. What is the slope of any line parallel to the y-axis in the (x, y) coordinate plane?
- **F.** −1
- **G.** 0
- **H.** 1
- **J.** Undefined
- **K.** Cannot be determined from the given information

GO ON TO THE NEXT PAGE.

2   **2**

39. If point *J* has a nonzero *x*-coordinate and a nonzero *y*-coordinate and the coordinates have the same sign, then point *J* *must* be located in which of the 4 quadrants shown below?

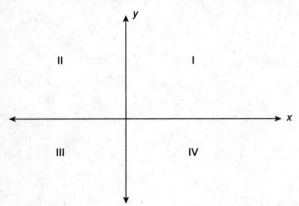

- **A.** I only
- **B.** II only
- **C.** III only
- **D.** I or III only
- **E.** II or IV only

40. The 2 triangles in the rectangle below share a common side. What is $\sin(a - b)$?

(Note: $\sin(a - b) = \sin a \cos b - \cos a \sin b$ for all *a* and *b*.)

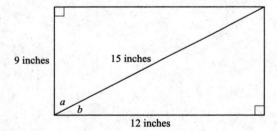

- **F.** $\dfrac{7}{25}$
- **G.** $\dfrac{1}{2}$
- **H.** $\dfrac{3}{5}$
- **J.** 1
- **K.** $\dfrac{25}{9}$

41. A function *F* is defined as follows:

For $x > 0$, $F(x) = x^3 + x^2 - 42x - 29$
For $x < 0$, $F(x) = -x^3 + x^2 + 42x - 29$

What is the value of $F(-2)$?

- **A.** 101
- **B.** 51
- **C.** 0
- **D.** −51
- **E.** −101

DO YOUR FIGURING HERE.

GO ON TO THE NEXT PAGE.

2 △ △ △ △ △ △ △ △ **2**

42. Which of the following calculations will yield an odd integer for any integer n?

F. $4n^2$

G. $3n^2 + 1$

H. $6n^2$

J. $n^2 - 1$

K. $4n^2 - 1$

43. In triangle ABC, the measure of $\angle A$ is $60°$ and the measure of $\angle B$ is $30°$. If $\overline{AB}$ is 8 units long, what is the area, in square units, of triangle ABC?

A. 4

B. $4\sqrt{3}$

C. 8

D. $8\sqrt{3}$

E. $16\sqrt{3}$

44. In the figure below, all distances are in feet and all angles are right angles. A straight line drawn from point W to point Z would be how long, in feet?

F. 1.5

G. 2

H. 4.66

J. 5

K. 7.23

45. A certain rectangle is 4 times as long as it is wide. Suppose the length and width are tripled. The area of the second rectangle is how many times as large as the area of the first?

A. 3

B. 4

C. 9

D. 12

E. 16

46. For what value of b would the following system of equations have an infinite number of solutions?

$$3x + 4y = 14$$

$$6x + 8y = 7b$$

F. 2

G. 4

H. 7

J. 14

K. 28

DO YOUR FIGURING HERE.

GO ON TO THE NEXT PAGE.

2   **2**

47. If $\log_3 x = 2$, then $x = ?$

   A. $\dfrac{1}{\log_9}$

   B. 3

   C. 6

   D. 9

   E. 18^2

DO YOUR FIGURING HERE.

48. When measured from a point on the ground that is a certain distance from the base of a telephone pole, the angle of elevation to the top of the telephone pole is 37°, as shown below. The height of the telephone pole is 24 feet. What is the distance, in feet, to the telephone pole?

24 feet (pole)

37°

distance ?

   F. 24 tan 37°

   G. 24 sin 37°

   H. 24 cos 37°

   J. 24 sec 37°

   K. 24 cot 37°

49. In the parallelogram below, lengths are given in inches. What is the area of the parallelogram, in square inches?

   A. 15

   B. $\sqrt{61}$

   C. 30

   D. $\sqrt{122}$

   E. $2\sqrt{61}$

50. Points A, B, and C are 3 distinct points that lie on the same line. If the length of $\overline{AB}$ is 12 meters and the length of $\overline{BC}$ is 15 meters, then what are all the possible lengths, in meters, for $\overline{AC}$?

   F. 3 only

   G. 27 only

   H. 3 and 27 only

   J. Any number less than 27 or greater than 3

   K. Any number greater than 27 or less than 3

GO ON TO THE NEXT PAGE.

2   **2**

DO YOUR FIGURING HERE.

51. If the right triangle and the rectangle in the figure below have the same area, and indicated lengths are given in centimeters, what is a expressed in terms of b?

A. b
B. $b\sqrt{3}$
C. $b\sqrt{4.5}$
D. $b\sqrt{5}$
E. $b\sqrt{6}$

52. If $6a^4b^3 < 0$, then which of the following CANNOT be true?

F. $b < 0$
G. $b > 0$
H. $a = b$
J. $a < 0$
K. $a > 0$

53. The 1st and 2nd terms of a geometric sequence are p and sp, in that order. What is the 734th term of the sequence?

A. $(sp)^{733}$
B. $(sp)^{734}$
C. $s^{733}p$
D. $s^{734}p$
E. sp^{733}

54. If a system of 2 linear equations in 2 variables has NO solution, and 1 of the equations is graphed in the (x, y) coordinate plane below, which of the following could be the equation of the other line?

F. $y = -2$
G. $y = -4x + 2$
H. $y = -2x - 3$
J. $y = 4x + 2$
K. $y = 4x - 3$

GO ON TO THE NEXT PAGE.

2   △ △ **2**

DO YOUR FIGURING HERE.

55. If $0° \le x \le 90°$ and $\tan x = \dfrac{15}{8}$, then $\cos x =$?

   A. $\dfrac{8}{17}$

   B. $\dfrac{15}{17}$

   C. $\dfrac{17}{8}$

   D. $\dfrac{17}{15}$

   E. $\dfrac{8}{15}$

56. If L, M, and N are real numbers, and if $LMN = 1$, which of the following conditions *must* be true?

   F. $LM = \dfrac{1}{N}$

   G. L, M, and N must all be positive

   H. Either $L = 1$, $M = 1$, or $N = 1$

   J. Either $L = 0$, $M = 0$, or $N = 0$

   K. Either $L < 1$, $M < 1$, or $N < 1$

57. Which of the following is a rational number?

   A. $\dfrac{\sqrt{1}}{\sqrt{2}}$

   B. $\sqrt{2}$

   C. $\sqrt{5}$

   D. $\dfrac{\sqrt{81}}{\sqrt{169}}$

   E. $\sqrt{200}$

58. Which of the following expressions gives the number of distinct permutations of the letters in PEBBLE?

   F. $6!$

   G. $2(4!)$

   H. $\dfrac{4!}{6!}$

   J. $\dfrac{6!}{2!}$

   K. $\dfrac{6!}{(2!)(2!)}$

GO ON TO THE NEXT PAGE.

2   **2**

59. In the figure below, line p has the equation $y = 3x$. Line q is below p, as shown, and q is parallel to p. Which of the following is an equation for q?

DO YOUR FIGURING HERE.

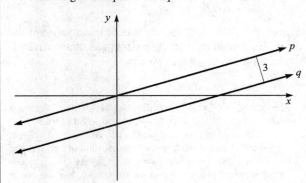

    A. $y = x - 3$
    B. $y = 3x - 3\sqrt{2}$
    C. $y = x - 3\sqrt{2}$
    D. $y = 3x - 3$
    E. $y = 3x + 3$

60. What is the smallest possible value for the product of 2 real numbers that differ by 12?
    F. -36
    G. -27
    H. -11
    J. 0
    K. 13

END OF THE MATHEMATICS TEST.
STOP! IF YOU HAVE TIME LEFT OVER, CHECK YOUR WORK ON THIS SECTION ONLY.

3 ███████████████████████████ **3**

READING TEST

35 Minutes – 40 Questions

DIRECTIONS: This test includes four passages, each followed by ten questions. Read the passages and choose the best answer to each question. After you have selected your answer, fill in the corresponding bubble on your answer sheet. You should refer to the passages as often as necessary when answering the questions.

PASSAGE I

LITERARY NARRATIVE: *"Assimilating in the Promised Land"*

Before she was born, Eui Thi's parents fled the communist rule of North Vietnam to settle in Laos. Although Eui Thi was born in Laos, her family never truly belonged there. While they spoke "the language," it was with a foreign
5 accent. Her father found odd jobs that provided food and shelter for the family, but she never felt at home—and she never felt truly safe.

As the oldest child, ten-year-old Eui Thi's responsibilities were many, but her parents' trust did not include
10 the sharing of adult concerns. Nevertheless, Eui Thi recognized the worried tones of their late-night whispers. As the last U.S. troops evacuated Saigon, the communist enemy was once again too close. Her parents hurriedly packed up the family and fled to Thailand. Suddenly, surrounded by
15 thousands of other refugees, Eui Thi found herself longing for the "stability" of Laos.

Eui Thi now dreamed of going to America. She had heard it called a "melting pot" because people from all over the world lived there; it was the promised land
20 where she would no longer be an outsider! America was huge, with room to run, play, and grow food. She couldn't remember the last time she wasn't hungry.

And then, in October 1975, the word came. Her family was being sent to Iowa. She tried to hide her disap-
25 pointment as she politely asked, "Where is Iowa? I thought we might be going to America." Her parents laughed. "Oh, sweet child—Iowa is in America!" Eui Thi was too excited to feel embarrassed. She was finally going to America.

Weeks later, her family arrived in Iowa. Despite the
30 fact that they had traveled with hundreds of other refugees, her family was suddenly alone with strangers who spoke an unintelligible language. The strangers ushered Eui Thi's family into a car and drove to a house—not just any house—her new home. The strangers walked her to a
35 vast building surrounded by playground equipment. "In a

few days," one said, "you will go to school here." America was all Eui Thi had hoped it would be—and more.

Her zeal quickly faded. On her first day of school, many children pointed, waved, and smiled at her, but she
40 could not understand what they were saying. The friendly strangers had given her clothes for school, but she could plainly see that her clothes were older and more faded than those of the other children. When she voiced this concern to her parents, they scolded her. "We have been given a
45 tremendous gift—a new home in a safe land, school for you children, and a job for your father—and you don't like the clothes these people have provided?" Ashamed, Eui Thi vowed never to share such petty concerns again.

Eui Thi learned quickly, and occasionally wished
50 she hadn't. As she began to understand a few words and phrases, she realized that she was a topic of conversation. She overheard some of the other girls talking about "the funny smells" that wafted from her home. When a child in her brother's class was discovered to have lice, her fam-
55 ily was blamed as the source. Despite the challenges, Eui Thi did her best to dress and act like the other girls, and gradually made a few friends.

Time quickly passed, and soon it was time for Eui Thi's first junior high dance. She was so excited. Dancing
60 was universal! How she had missed the celebratory dancing of the Tai-Dam. When Eui Thi arrived at the dance and her eyes slowly adjusted to the darkness, she realized she knew nothing of *this* kind of dance. Eui Thi silently prayed that no one would ask her to dance. And then, as no one did, she
65 reached a sudden, horrible conclusion. She was from a different world—and there were no other Asians at her school. Everyone else at the dance had fair skin and fine hair, and they had all paired up to dance with each other.

She may have been able to approximate Suzanne
70 Somers' charms, and Farrah Fawcett hairstyles, and even, eventually, American slang, but she would never be the same as the other girls. Although surrounded by other adolescents, Eui Thi was alone. "Some melting pot!" she thought. "Will I ever truly belong?"

GO ON TO THE NEXT PAGE.

3 ████████████████████████████ **3**

1. One of the points suggested in Paragraph 2 regarding Eui Thi's longing for Laos was that:
   A. Laos was now more politically stable.
   B. the threat of communism was no longer present in Laos.
   C. Thailand is closer to Vietnam, making Laos safer by comparison.
   D. feeling like an outsider in Laos was preferable to the chaos of the refugee camp.

2. As it is used in the passage (line 38), the word *zeal* most nearly means:
   F. intensity.
   G. diligence.
   H. happiness.
   J. enthusiasm.

3. The passage most strongly suggests that Eui Thi:
   A. never really wanted to go to America.
   B. distrusts her parents for removing her from her home.
   C. always regretted being the oldest child.
   D. feels like she doesn't belong anywhere.

4. It can reasonably be inferred from Paragraph 2 that Eui Thi's parents were whispering about:
   F. the military conflict in Vietnam.
   G. Eui Thi's lack of close friends.
   H. Eui Thi's lack of appreciation.
   J. the unplanned task of packing.

5. According to the passage, Eui Thi and her family received which of the following upon arriving in America?
   A. A playground
   B. A new house
   C. Fancy clothes
   D. Dance lessons

6. According to the passage, Eui Thi's "the promised land" would include:
   I. a sense of belonging.
   II. room to run.
   III. English lessons.
   IV. adequate food.

   F. I and II only
   G. II and IV only
   H. I, II, and III only
   J. I, II, and IV only

7. The main purpose of the statement in lines 36 and 37 is to:
   A. inform the reader of all that America has to offer.
   B. illustrate the apparent fulfillment of Eui Thi's dreams.
   C. counteract the author's earlier description of the promised land.
   D. provide proof that Eui Thi would live a carefree life from now on.

8. According to the passage, Eui Thi was able to mimic her peers in all aspects EXCEPT:
   F. language.
   G. hairstyle.
   H. culture.
   J. attitude.

9. The dancing at Eui Thi's junior high, as compared to traditional Tai-Dam dancing, was judged in this passage to be:
   A. upbeat and celebratory.
   B. a universal style.
   C. an entirely different style.
   D. dark and exciting.

10. According to the passage, Eui Thi's American school was:
    F. for refugees only.
    G. very far from her home.
    H. within walking distance of her home.
    J. known for its school dances.

GO ON TO THE NEXT PAGE.

3 ████████████████████████████████ **3**

PASSAGE II

SOCIAL SCIENCE: Passage A is adapted from an essay about the American judicial system. Passage B is adapted from an essay about the legal system in Western Europe.

Passage A

American law is an outward expression of the morals and values of the people; this flexibility gives judges the power to adapt the law to the needs and desires of the community. Many have praised the American judicial system because
5　it embodies the idea that the law should do the will of the people. Under this system, the law does not dictate to the citizenry, but rather takes its cues from the populace.

The law can change and adjust to meet the needs of society. The plasticity of this legal system also allows
10　judges to avoid absurd results that might be required if laws were inflexibly and strictly applied. Take, for example, the requirement that a will be signed by two witnesses and notarized. If a will is signed by two witnesses, both of whom are available to testify to the validity of the will and
15　their signatures, there would be no reason for the will to be unenforceable even if it is not notarized. An American judge would likely find that there was no reason to strictly adhere to the legal requirements, and would enforce the will. The one downside to this flexibility is that very few
20　cases are so easily decided, and judges do not always rule in a predictable manner.

A cursory look at the government in America will reveal the foundations of such a variable rule of law. Government is seen as a necessary evil that should have
25　only limited involvement in the daily lives of the people. Americans want a government that interferes in their lives as little as possible—it is controlled by the people and should, at all times, work for the people.

Passage B

In many Western European nations, the law is seen as
30　rigid and not open to interpretation. This rigidity grants a consistency to questions of law that many would argue is absent in other, more flexible systems. The European construction of law provides litigants with a clear picture of how a case will be decided. All parties involved are certain
35　how judges will rule on issues. It is simple that judges will strictly follow the law. This simple fact that the law will not change from one situation to another allows for court systems in Western Europe to process cases efficiently and cuts down on the number of frivolous lawsuits. It is useless
40　for an individual to attempt a case if he knows in advance that the law is not in his favor.

Like any legal system, the Western European format is far from perfect. It arose from a belief that governments are thought of as caretakers, and with this comes potential
45　problems. Though citizens have become accustomed to an unbending, often predictable, code of law, some would assert that this gives the government excessive control over the morals and behaviors of the citizenry. Nevertheless, it can also be remarked that such jurisprudence is
50　freeing; knowing for certain, in advance, whether or not you will be guilty grants a greater degree of protection than other legal systems are able to afford.

Questions 11 – 13 ask about Passage A.

11. Passage A indicates that American law is:
    A. not strictly adhered to.
    B. a necessary evil that interferes with daily living.
    C. adaptable to the needs and desires of the populace.
    D. a cursory representation of rules created by dictators.

12. The author's claim that "American law is an outward expression of the morals and values of the people" (line 1) most likely refers to:
    F. the notion that law-abiding citizens only reside in America.
    G. the idea that laws are established based on the needs of society.
    H. a legal system that will only work within a group of moral people.
    J. a desire of the people to show other countries the value of the American judicial system.

13. As it is used in line 9, "plasticity" most nearly means:
    A. the capacity to be altered.
    B. the ability to remain rigid.
    C. the desires of the citizenry.
    D. the requirement of a signature.

Questions 14 – 16 ask about Passage B.

14. In the first paragraph of Passage B (lines 29–41), the author refers to "frivolous lawsuits" in a manner that:
    F. portrays the Western European legal system as useless.
    G. indicates a positive aspect of the Western European legal system.
    H. defines a legal term prevalent in the Western European legal system.
    J. suggests an improvement to be made to the Western European legal system.

GO ON TO THE NEXT PAGE.

3

3

15. Passage B explains that, in order to prove a case, an individual must:
   A. remain consistent.
   B. know that the law is in his favor.
   C. allow the judge to flexibly interpret the case.
   D. relinquish all control of the case to the Western European court.

16. When the author claims that "such jurisprudence is freeing" (lines 49 – 50), he's most likely referring to the:
   F. idea that people do not have to worry so much about the outcome of a legal case.
   G. notion of citizens remaining innocent until proven guilty in a court of law.
   H. argument against providing free legal services in Western Europe.
   J. predictability of law from one case to another in Western Europe.

Questions 17 – 20 ask about both passages.

---

17. Both Passage A and Passage B indicate that legal systems can be:
   A. imperfect.
   B. inflexible.
   C. imposing.
   D. inefficient.

18. Which of the following questions is central to both passages?
   F. To what extent do flexible legal systems fail citizens?
   G. What types of laws should be avoided in all legal systems?
   H. How have the needs of a society influenced its legal system?
   J. To what extent have individuals reacted negatively to the legal system in their country?

19. With which of the following statements would the authors of both passages be most likely to agree?
   A. Laws should be interpreted in the light of a strict constructionist viewpoint.
   B. There is no legal system that will serve the needs of every citizen flawlessly.
   C. There is no legal system that is not a direct result of societal norms and beliefs.
   D. Laws are meant to conform to the will of the people and should therefore be flexible.

20. Which of the following most accurately describes a way in which the two passages are related to each other?
   F. Passage B expands on details presented in Passage A.
   G. The logic presented in Passage B weakens the claims made in Passage A.
   H. The history suggested in Passage B is proven to be false by the facts in Passage A.
   J. Passage B suggests an alternate framework for discussing the same broad topic as Passage A.

3 ▬▬▬▬▬▬▬▬▬▬▬▬▬▬▬▬▬▬▬▬▬▬▬▬▬▬ **3**

PASSAGE III

HUMANITIES: *"Teen Heartthrob"*

It was 1977 when I first read his name: Shaun Cassidy. I was flipping through the pages of a *Tiger Beat* magazine when my older sister came up behind me and casually pointed at his picture.

5   "He's cute. Isn't he the one who sings that 'Da Doo Ron Ron' song you like?"

    "No, I don't think so," I replied. "I think he's one of the guys on *The Hardy Boys* show I watch on Sunday nights."

10   As my sister walked away, I began reading about Shaun. His older brother was David Cassidy—the one I could remember my sister swooning over in years past. I learned that Shaun Cassidy was, in fact, both the guy on the radio and the guy on *The Hardy Boys*. I became

15 enthralled and quickly developed my first adolescent crush. The walls of my room were soon covered with over 100 images of Shaun's big blue eyes and toothy grin. I became a card-carrying member of The Hardy Boys fan club. His sultry voice serenaded me each night as I drifted

20 off to sleep with his debut album playing on my bright-green record player.

    Although most of my appreciation for Cassidy stemmed from his physical allure, my admiration of his talent was not inappropriate. Like most teen pop stars,

25 his fame as a teenage heartthrob was destined to be short-lived. But his artistic ability was real. After his singing popularity waned and his television show was cancelled, Shaun performed in several other television series and made-for-television movies. Eventually, however, he

30 turned his attention to a new challenge—the theatre.

    By this time, my pubescent crush on this "cute boy" had long since passed. Nevertheless, his name popped out to me occasionally as I scanned the news or glanced through a magazine. In this haphazard way, I casually

35 followed his career through the years. And as I learned of each of his accomplishments, I couldn't help but be pleased for my former idol.

    On and off Broadway, Cassidy continued to develop his acting skills. He soon proved his talent as a stage actor,

40 winning a Critics Circle Award for *The Subject Was Roses* and a Drama-Logue award for his performance in *Diary of a Hunger Strike*. Although he appeared to enjoy performing, the world of television once again beckoned.

    Throughout his television career, Cassidy had been

45 curious about the production side of the business. Despite having occasional questions for the camera crew and others on the technical end, he was especially interested in the responsibilities of the writers, directors, and producers.

    Several years into his stage-acting career, Cassidy's

50 early fascination with the production end of the entertainment industry beckoned, and he felt compelled to learn more. His first foray into the world of television production was naively ambitious. He worked hard as the supervising producer and show developer for a TV series that

55 never aired. After this rude awakening, he decided to learn more about his new craft from more experienced specialists in the entertainment industry.

    As he wrote and co-produced the TV movie *Strays*, Cassidy realized that writing provided a tremendous outlet

60 for his creativity and he spent several of the subsequent years as a television scriptwriter. Later, Cassidy made a second attempt at producing and was far more successful. Although Cassidy occasionally performs on stage and screen (even singing the theme song for one of the televi-

65 sion series he created), he spends most of his time now as a creator and executive producer of television shows for several networks. My youthful admiration of Shaun Cassidy was naive and shallow, but his talent was real and is standing the test of time.

21. Which of the following descriptions most accurately and completely represents this passage?
   A. A thoughtful and heartfelt reminiscence of the singer Shaun Cassidy
   B. A biographical overview of Shaun Cassidy's career since the 1970s
   C. A careful and impartial critique of the singing talent of Shaun Cassidy
   D. A discussion of the author's professional career in relation to that of Shaun Cassidy

22. All of the following aspects of Shaun Cassidy's life were described EXCEPT:
   F. his childhood.
   G. his singing career.
   H. his acting career.
   J. his television writing career.

23. The details in the last paragraph primarily serve to illustrate the:
   A. writer's ability to overcome youthful fantasies.
   B. compelling nature of child stars like Shaun Cassidy.
   C. many innovations of modern television.
   D. progression of Shaun Cassidy's career.

24. The main idea of the last paragraph is that:
   F. Shaun Cassidy is a talented actor.
   G. Shaun Cassidy realized his true passion was behind the camera.
   H. Shaun Cassidy overcame his initial fear of directing.
   J. Shaun Cassidy spends most of his time writing theme songs.

GO ON TO THE NEXT PAGE.

3 ████████████████████████████ **3**

25. It can be inferred from the passage that the writer, in her adolescence, most valued which of the following in a performer?
   A. Physical attractiveness
   B. Professional success
   C. Famous siblings
   D. Writing ability

26. It can be most reasonably concluded from the writer's reference to Cassidy's fame being "destined to be short-lived" that:
   F. many teen performers enjoy longer periods of fame and fortune.
   G. Cassidy had no talent.
   H. most teen performers who rise quickly to fame fall out of favor just as quickly.
   J. teen fans are usually very loyal.

27. According to the passage, in which order did the following events occur in the writer's life?
   I. Recovering from her adolescent crush
   II. Casually following Cassidy's career
   III. Reading about Cassidy in *Tiger Beat*

   A. I, II, III
   B. II, III, I
   C. III, II, I
   D. III, I, II

28. Which of the following best describes the writer's immediate reaction to reading about Cassidy for the first time?
   F. Envy of Cassidy's musical and acting ability
   G. Serious interest in learning about careers in entertainment
   H. Apathy toward entertainers in general
   J. Awe and admiration of the teen idol

29. According to the passage, Cassidy's achievements include all of the following EXCEPT:
   A. operating a camera.
   B. stage acting.
   C. television production.
   D. television writing.

30. The writer states that Shaun Cassidy was:
   F. naive and shallow.
   G. talented and curious.
   H. challenging and inappropriate.
   J. youthful and casual.

GO ON TO THE NEXT PAGE.

3 ████████████████████████████████████ **3**

PASSAGE IV

NATURAL SCIENCE: *"The Need to Succeed"*

After the archeological discoveries of two samples of early humans—the very primitive-appearing Neanderthals and the more modern-looking Cro-Magnons—archeologists throughout the world wondered about the relation-
5 ship between the two. Evidence of Neanderthals is nearly 300,000 years old. Evidence of Cro-Magnon people is about 130,000 years old. Did Cro-Magnons evolve from Neanderthals? Did they co-exist? Did they associate with one another? Why did evidence of Neanderthals' existence
10 stop 30,000 years ago? Although many mysteries still surround these early humans, more is known today than at any other time.

Early understanding of Neanderthals was that they had small brains and could not speak. In fact, their brains
15 were as big as modern humans and they were (at least anatomically) capable of speech. Neanderthals were strong, capable of making basic tools, and, from the beginning, controlled fire. The spearheads they carved even have an aesthetic elegance we can appreciate today.

20 Scientists have argued over two rival theories about the relationship between Neanderthals and modern humans. One theory claims that the descendants of Neanderthals live on to this day; these scientists use the phrase, *"Homo sapiens neanderthalensis."* (*Homo sapiens*
25 is a Latin phrase, meaning "sapient—or intelligent—mankind"). A rival theory hypothesized that Neanderthals were an evolutionary dead end—a species that became extinct about 30,000 years ago; these scientists therefore use the phrase, *"Homo neanderthalensis."* The latter the-
30 ory now appears to be correct. The skulls of Neanderthals and modern human beings differ too much for Neanderthals to be our relatives. In addition, DNA analysis shows that current humans share many genes with early *Homo sapiens* but very few with Neanderthals.

35 So, given that Cro-Magnons (an example of *Homo sapiens sapiens*) did not evolve from Neanderthals, did these two species of early humans ever meet? And why did Neanderthals become extinct? Based on extensive data from sediment cores, archaeological artifacts such as fos-
40 sils and tools, radiometric dating, and climate models, we now have better answers to these questions.

Evidence of Cro-Magnons and Neanderthals overlaps by 100,000 years; they clearly co-existed. In fact, where geography dictated, they occasionally occupied the same
45 cave sites. Whether their associations were always amicable is questionable, but archeologists have found no evidence of violence between the two groups. Instead, a combination of other factors likely conspired against Neanderthals, leading to their ultimate demise.

50 During the time of their co-existence, Neanderthals competed with anatomically modern humans for mutually required resources. This occurred at a time when the increasingly severe cold was affecting not only the early

humans but also the food resources on which they relied.
55 Although Neanderthals tolerated temperatures as cold as zero degrees Fahrenheit, winter temperatures during the last ice age dipped to well below that. To compensate for the reduced temperatures, Neanderthals would have needed significantly more food than normal. Unfortu-
60 nately, the severe cold and the competition of their contemporaries were negatively impacting the availability of food.

Anatomically modern humans were better at dealing with the cold. Early *Homo sapiens* utilized what was then advanced technology in the prehistoric world. They wore
65 warm clothing made of fur and woven materials and lived in enclosed dwellings. They possessed a sophisticated range of weaponry, including bows, arrows, snares, traps, nets, and spears. Their spearheads were carved from a variety of materials, including flint and obsidian. Some of
70 the spears were designed as projectile weapons (javelins), complete with spear throwers to increase effective range. Finally, *Homo sapiens* exhibited the beginnings of communal activity, living, hunting, and fishing in organized groups.

75 Neanderthals, on the other hand, used general-purpose spears—the identical pattern they had used for 100,000 years. These spears, though reasonably effective, required close-range contact with increasingly scant prey. The Neanderthals lacked the innovation skills necessary to
80 survive in a changing world. Adapting to changing conditions, our ancestors used technology to win the prehistoric battle for survival. In essence, the Cro-Magnons won the ultimate "Survivor" contest 30,000 years ago.

31. According to the passage, most scientists now believe that *Homo sapiens*:
A. evolved from *Homo sapiens neanderthalensis.*
B. evolved from *Homo neanderthalensis.*
C. killed off the *Homo neanderthalensis.*
D. is not the same species as *Homo neanderthalensis.*

32. According to the passage, during colder weather, Neanderthals needed:
F. to move to a warmer climate.
G. more food than normal.
H. flint and obsidian.
J. larger caves.

33. According to the passage, DNA testing of Neanderthal remains reveals that:
A. Neanderthals and modern-day humans share very few of the same genes.
B. Neanderthals were genetically similar to Cro-Magnons.
C. Neanderthals and modern-day humans are descended from Cro-Magnons.
D. Neanderthals' brains were as large as the modern human brain.

GO ON TO THE NEXT PAGE.

3 ━━━━━━━━━━━━━━━━━━━━━━━━━━━━━━━━━━ **3**

34. The passage indicates that *Homo neanderthalensis* is:
F. a modern man.
G. an extinct species.
H. a communal hunter.
J. a rival of *Homo sapiens neanderthalensis*.

35. According to the passage, all of the following evidence led to a better understanding of Neanderthals EXCEPT:
A. comparative femur measurements.
B. radiometric dating.
C. sediment cores.
D. climate models.

36. According to the passage, the last evidence of Neanderthals is:
F. about 100,000 years old.
G. about 30,000 years old.
H. 130,000 years old.
J. 300,000 years old.

37. As it is used in line 64, the word *technology* most nearly refers to:
A. technical language.
B. a changing world.
C. competition for food.
D. objects necessary for human survival.

38. According to the passage, some of the weapons used by Cro-Magnons included all of the following EXCEPT:
F. bows and arrows.
G. snares and traps.
H. gill nets.
J. javelins.

39. According to the passage, all of the following factors led to the extinction of the Neanderthals EXCEPT:
A. increasingly cold winters.
B. Cro-Magnons' slaughter of many Neanderthals.
C. Neanderthals' lack of innovation.
D. superior competitors for scarce resources.

40. The passage states that Neanderthals differ from anatomically modern humans in that Neanderthals:
F. lacked critical survival skills.
G. had a very small brain.
H. were incapable of speech.
J. possessed advanced weaponry.

END OF THE READING TEST.
STOP! IF YOU HAVE TIME LEFT OVER, CHECK YOUR WORK ON THIS SECTION ONLY.

4 ◯ ◯ ◯ ◯ ◯ ◯ ◯ **4**

SCIENCE TEST

35 Minutes – 40 Questions

DIRECTIONS: This test includes several passages, each followed by several questions. Read the passage and choose the best answer to each question. After you have selected your answer, fill in the corresponding bubble on your answer sheet. You should refer to the passages as often as necessary when answering the questions. You may NOT use a calculator on this test.

PASSAGE I

Certain types of insects are abundant in each region of the United States. These insects have a profound impact on the *indigenous* (native) plant life that grows in each region. If foreign insects are introduced into a region, the plant life can be devastated. Two experiments were performed to study the effect that foreign insects can have on indigenous plants of a certain region.

Experiment 1

A botanist placed 3 indigenous plant species in a local greenhouse. For 3 weeks no insects were allowed to enter. The amount of plant growth was recorded at the end of 3 weeks. For the next 3-week period, only indigenous insects were allowed near the plants. The plants' growth was recorded again after 6 weeks. In the last 3-week period the native insects were removed, and foreign insects were introduced. The growth of the plants was recorded at the end of the 9-week period. The results are shown in Table 1.

Table 1		
Plant type	**Time frame**	**Total growth (in)**
Big blue stem	0–3 weeks	0.25
	3–6 weeks	0.50
	6–9 weeks	0.25
Fragrant sumac	0–3 weeks	0.15
	3–6 weeks	0.30
	6–9 weeks	0.25
Yaupon	0–3 weeks	1.00
	3–6 weeks	2.00
	6–9 weeks	0.50

Experiment 2

A botanist placed 3 indigenous plant species in a greenhouse as in Experiment 1. This time, foreign insects were introduced from the start of the experiment. The plants' growth was recorded over the same 9-week period. The results are shown in Table 2.

Table 2		
Plant type	**Time frame**	**Total growth (in)**
Big blue stem	0–3 weeks	0.125
	3–6 weeks	0.125
	6–9 weeks	0.100
Fragrant sumac	0–3 weeks	0.025
	3–6 weeks	0.025
	6–9 weeks	0.015
Yaupon	0–3 weeks	0.500
	3–6 weeks	0.500
	6–9 weeks	0.400

Information on the insect types used is given in Table 3.

Table 3	
Insect type	**Indigenous**
Mosquito	Yes
Grasshopper	Yes
Aphid	Yes
Manlid	No
Dragon Fly	No

1. The results of Experiment 2 indicate that all of the plants experienced a decline in growth rate during what time frame?
   A. 0–3 weeks
   B. 3–6 weeks
   C. 6–9 weeks
   D. No decline in growth rate was recorded.

2. According to Table 3, each of the following insects is native to the region studied EXCEPT:
   F. the mosquito.
   G. the dragonfly.
   H. the aphid.
   J. the grasshopper.

GO ON TO THE NEXT PAGE.

4 ◯ ◯ ◯ ◯ ◯ ◯ ◯ **4**

3. According to Experiments 1 and 2, which plant type experienced the most total growth during weeks 6–9?
   A. Big blue stem
   B. Fragrant sumac
   C. Yaupon
   D. Each plant type experienced the same total growth.

4. Based on the experiments, which of the following pairs of insects most likely had the greatest effect on limiting plant growth?
   F. Mantid, Dragonfly
   G. Mosquito, Grasshopper
   H. Grasshopper, Aphid
   J. Aphid, Mosquito

5. Based on the results of Experiments 1 and 2, which of the following statements is most accurate?
   A. Foreign insects have little to no impact on indigenous plant growth.
   B. Native insects can help to increase growth in some plants.
   C. Indigenous plant life is most affected by native insects.
   D. Foreign insects cannot survive in local green-houses.

GO ON TO THE NEXT PAGE.

4 ○ ○ ○ ○ ○ ○ ○ 4

PASSAGE II

Two scientists discuss the possibility of predicting hurricanes and the paths that the hurricanes will take.

Scientist 1

Hurricane prediction can be made in real time based on certain events. For example, winds shift inland and increase in speed up to 2 days before a hurricane makes landfall. The tidal volume can increase by 30% one day before a hurricane makes landfall. Animals are sometimes seen exhibiting strange behavior as far ahead as weeks before a hurricane makes landfall. Certain instruments such as seismographs can detect the ground vibrations that occur while a hurricane is making its way across the ocean. The direction of the vibrations' origin allows the scientific community to predict the path that the hurricane will take. Historical evidence is also a valuable predictive tool.

Scientist 2

Hurricane prediction cannot be made in real time. Shifts in wind speed and direction on shore have not been proven to have any effect on the direction or time of landfall. Only when a hurricane makes landfall can the seismograph be used to determine direction of the hurricane's path. Tidal volume is constantly changing for many different reasons and, therefore, cannot be used as a predictive tool. Previous records of hurricane patterns are a much more accurate way to predict when and where a hurricane will occur. Once enough information has been derived from past hurricanes, predictive measures can be developed.

6. Which of the following ideas about hurricane prediction is implied by Scientist 2?
   F. Present-day predictive tools are not based upon enough past data to be accurate.
   G. Hurricane prediction will never be possible.
   H. Animal behavior is proving itself to be the best possible hurricane predictor available.
   J. Scientific tools are the only things that can predict a hurricane's location and path.

7. A scientific article is published stating that the study of animal behavior is useful in predicting hurricanes. Which of the scientists' viewpoints, if any, is (are) supported by this statement?
   A. Scientist 1
   B. Scientist 2
   C. Both Scientist 1 and Scientist 2
   D. Neither Scientist 1 nor Scientist 2

8. Increased seismic activity has been recorded along the coastline of Florida. With which of the following statements about the finding would Scientist 1 agree?
   F. Tidal volume is likely to decrease by 30%.
   G. A seismograph is only useful for predicting earthquake activity.
   H. Seismic activity has little to do with when or where the hurricane will travel.
   J. A hurricane could be moving across the ocean.

9. Which statement, if true, would support both scientists' viewpoints?
   A. Historical hurricane data has recently been used to predict the path a hurricane will take.
   B. Seismic activity is predictive of both when and where the hurricane will make landfall.
   C. Tidal volume cannot be used as a predictive tool because it is constantly changing.
   D. Tidal volume and wind direction are not accurate or useful predictors of hurricanes.

10. What would be the best way to test the claims made by Scientist 2?
    F. Compare current hurricane data with the past data in the same area.
    G. Monitor seismic activity along the coastline.
    H. Keep a record of the tidal volume before a hurricane makes landfall.
    J. Track animal behavior before the arrival of the hurricane.

11. As they approach land, tropical storms would bring increased winds before the storms attain hurricane status. If early identification of tropical storms could help to predict hurricanes, such information would most likely:
    A. strengthen Scientist 1's viewpoint.
    B. weaken Scientist 1's viewpoint.
    C. weaken the viewpoints of both Scientist 1 and Scientist 2.
    D. have no effect on either scientist's viewpoint.

12. According to Scientist 2, which of the following is a major flaw in Scientist 1's theory on hurricane prediction?
    F. Information gathered from past hurricanes could be useful.
    G. Seismographs are used to monitor the path that a hurricane takes.
    H. Historical data is accurate.
    J. Tidal volume increases can be used to predict hurricanes.

GO ON TO THE NEXT PAGE.

4 ○ ○ ○ ○ ○ ○ ○ **4**

PASSAGE III

One of the primary physical properties of matter is volume. Solids, liquids, and gases, which make up three of the observed states of matter, can easily be recognized by certain physical characteristics, such as volume. The effect of compression (the ability of pressure to alter the volume of matter) is called *compressibility*.

Gases are highly compressible because the volume of gas is very responsive to changes in pressure. A very small change in pressure can considerably alter the volume of a gas. On the other hand, most liquids and solids have a higher density and, therefore, a very low compressibility. Changes in pressure are measured in *atmospheres* (atm).

Figure 1 shows quantities of pressure and volume along an *isotherm*. An isotherm is a line of constant temperature. One can determine the compressibility by noting the relationship between the change in pressure and the change in volume. Portions of the line where large changes in pressure result in only minimal changes in volume signify low compressibility. Portions of the line where small changes in pressure result in a significant change in volume suggest high compressibility.

Divers must be careful to rise slowly in the water, or else nitrogen absorbed into the diver's cells may expand, creating painful and dangerous bubbles. This is called *decompression sickness*, but is more commonly known as "the bends."

Figure 1

Figure 2 shows the air pressure (in atm) at different depths of water in meters (m).

Figure 2

Underwater, pressure can be felt in certain air spaces in the body, such as the lungs, sinuses, and ear canals. Air is a gas with a low density and high compressibility. Therefore, the volume of air inside the body is dependent on the space that contains it. The volume of air in flexible spaces, such as the lungs or sinuses, is reduced or expanded proportionate to the pressure. For example, a diver moving from 10 meters underwater to the surface will have the volume of air in his or her lungs double.

13. According to Figure 2, what is the air pressure at 65 meters below the surface?
    A. 4.5 atm
    B. 5.5 atm
    C. 6.0 atm
    D. 7.0 atm

14. According to the data provided, one could generalize that the volume of air in the lungs:
    F. increases as one moves closer to the surface.
    G. increases as temperature decreases.
    H. increases as the air pressure increases.
    J. increases as one moves deeper underwater.

15. According to the passage, as compared to gases, which of the following statements is true?
    A. Solids have lower compressibility because of their higher density.
    B. Liquids have lower compressibility because of their lower density.
    C. Both liquids and solids have higher compressibility because of their lower density.
    D. Both liquids and solids have lower compressibility because of their lower density.

16. The information provided indicates that compressibility can be a problem when diving. Which of the following statements would best explain why this is true?
    F. Atmospheric pressure is nonexistent below the water's surface.
    G. As you descend underwater, the gas in the body expands quickly.
    H. Moving to the surface causes the gas in the body to expand very quickly.
    J. Moving to the surface causes the gas in the body to compress very quickly.

17. According to Figure 1, compressibility is lowest where:
    A. temperature is lowest and pressure is the lowest.
    B. temperature is highest and pressure is the lowest.
    C. the change in pressure is less than the change in volume.
    D. the change in pressure is greater than the change in volume.

GO ON TO THE NEXT PAGE.

4   **4**

PASSAGE IV

Studies have shown that acid rains damage the skin pigmentation in certain species of salamanders. This results in an inability to change color and be protected from predators. Increased predation accounts for a decrease in the percentage of salamanders that survive to adulthood. Certain species of salamander have developed weather-protective behavior that has an effect on their relative ability to avoid skin damage (Table 1).

Table 1			
Species	Relative ability to avoid acid rain damage	Weather-protective behavior	Exposure to acid rain
A	0.1	None	High
B	0.2	Seeks protection under small plants	Moderate
C	0.2	Seeks protection under tree cover	Moderate
D	0.5	Seeks protection inside trees	Low
E	0.7	Seeks protection inside buildings	None
F	1.0	Seeks protection inside buildings	None
G	1.5	Seeks protection inside buildings	None

Figure 1 shows the percentage of each species that generally survive to adulthood.

Figure 1

18. Based on the information in Figure 1, salamanders from which species are most likely to survive to adulthood despite the presence of acid rain?
F. Species A
G. Species B
H. Species D
J. Species G

19. According to the data in Figure 1, which of the following species showed the greatest difference between survival with no exposure to acid rain and survival with exposure to acid rain?
A. Species B
B. Species C
C. Species E
D. Species G

20. Suppose researchers wanted to conduct additional studies on a different animal to further test their findings. Which of the following should they observe?
F. Fish
G. Squirrel
H. Frog
J. Scorpion

21. According to the information in Table 1, for all of the species shown, as the relative ability to avoid skin damage due to acid rain increases, exposure to acid rain generally:
A. increases only.
B. decreases only.
C. increases then decreases.
D. decreases then increases.

22. Based on the information in Table 1 and Figure 1, the species of salamander with the lowest percentage surviving to adulthood:
F. seeks protection inside trees.
G. seeks protection inside buildings.
H. seeks protection under plants.
J. does not seek protection.

GO ON TO THE NEXT PAGE.

PASSAGE V

Some mountains have been shown to lose rock or sediment due to seasonal snow melting. Figure 1 shows mountain composition, mountain peak section heights in meters (m), and the net change in snowcap lower levels (SCLL) in meters from 1880–1980 along a section of the Rocky Mountains. A net negative change in the SCLL indicates a loss of rock or sediment, and a net positive change indicates a gain of sediment.

Table 1 shows the percentage of the year that a vertical section of the mountain range is exposed to snow melt erosion.

Table 1	
Peak section height (meters)	**Percentage of a year peak section is exposed to snow melt erosion**
0–5	14
5–10	22
10–15	30
15–20	38
20–25	46
25–30	54
30–35	62
35–40	70

Figure 1

GO ON TO THE NEXT PAGE.

4   **4**

23. According to Figure 1, at 13 km along the mountain range, the peak section is composed of:

- **A.** igneous rock and limestone.
- **B.** igneous rock and sandstone.
- **C.** limestone and sandstone.
- **D.** limestone only.

24. At a peak section height of 20 meters, the net change in SCLL is mostly:

- **F.** greater than 20.
- **G.** between −10 and −30.
- **H.** less than −50.
- **J.** between −40 and −50.

25. Based on the information in Table 1, a peak section with a height between 40–45 meters would be exposed to snow melt erosion at approximately what percentage of the year?

- **A.** 28%
- **B.** 56%
- **C.** 78%
- **D.** 92%

26. According to Figure 1, a net change in SCLL is most related to:

- **F.** exposure to rock and sediment.
- **G.** peak section composition.
- **H.** distance along the mountain range.
- **J.** peak section height.

27. According to the information in Table 1, which of the following figures best represents the relationship between the mountain's height and the percentage of the year the mountain is exposed to snow melt erosion?

A.

B.

C.

D.

GO ON TO THE NEXT PAGE.

4   **4**

PASSAGE VI

Microbial flora such as bacteria play an important role in maintaining the digestive tract of animals, where they are called *gut flora*. Bacteria exist in the stomach, duodenum, jejunum, ileum, and colon in different amounts and at different pH levels. Defecation output is a good indicator of digestive tract health. The higher the defecation output, the healthier the digestive tract. A student investigated the effects of creating a bacteria-free environment in a rat's digestive tract.

Experiment 1

The student collected 10 rats to include in the experiment. Five of the rats were given antibiotics to kill all gut flora within their digestive tracts. The remaining 5 rats were not treated with antibiotics. All of the rats were allowed to eat a normal diet. The animals' defecation amounts, measured in feces pellets, and pH levels of the defecation were measured after 5 hours. The results are shown in Table 1.

Table 1

Rat	Antibiotic given	Defecation output (no. of pellets)	pH level
1	Yes	3	6.2
2	Yes	2	6.7
3	Yes	3	6.6
4	Yes	4	6.7
5	Yes	5	6.5
6	No	7	8.0
7	No	9	8.0
8	No	12	8.3
9	No	11	8.5
10	No	10	8.1

Experiment 2

Each of 5 different rats was given an antibiotic to kill all gut flora in the digestive tract. The rats were then given a dose of gut flora 1 hour later. The rats were allowed to eat a normal diet. Each rat's defecation is measured in terms of pH level at 1 hour and again at 5 hours. The pH levels are compared in Table 2.

Table 2

Rat	pH at 1 hour	pH at 5 hours
11	6.5	8.0
12	6.4	7.7
13	6.3	7.5
14	6.6	8.2
15	6.7	8.3

28. Based on Experiment 1, what is the relationship between defecation output and pH level?
   F. As pH level increases, defecation output decreases.
   G. As pH level increases, defecation output increases.
   H. As defecation output increases, pH level decreases.
   J. Both defecation output and pH levels remain the same.

29. In which of the following ways are the designs of Experiments 1 and 2 different?
   A. A dose of gut flora was given to the rats in Experiment 2 and not in Experiment 1.
   B. A normal diet was followed in Experiment 2 and not in Experiment 1.
   C. A control group was established in Experiment 2 and not in Experiment 1.
   D. A smaller population was used in Experiment 1 than in Experiment 2.

30. Which of the following hypotheses about the effects of a bacteria-free digestive tract in a rat is best supported by the results of Experiment 2? If the gut flora is eliminated and then reintroduced, the pH level will:
   F. remain the same.
   G. increase over time.
   H. decrease over time.
   J. increase, and then decrease rapidly.

31. Suppose that Rat 5 was given the gut flora 1 hour after being given the antibiotics. Based on the results in Experiment 2, one would predict that the pH level after 5 hours would be approximately:
   A. 6.3
   B. 6.7
   C. 7.1
   D. 8.0

32. According to the passage, which of the following rats had the highest defecation output?
   F. Rat 3
   G. Rat 6
   H. Rat 8
   J. Rat 10

33. According to the results of both experiments, one can conclude that:
   A. antibiotics kill only microbes that are harmful to the digestive tract.
   B. pH levels in the digestive tract cannot be tested effectively.
   C. gut flora is necessary for the normal functioning of a healthy digestive tract.
   D. the presence of microbes in the digestive tract leads to unhealthy pH levels.

GO ON TO THE NEXT PAGE.

4   **4**

PASSAGE VII

Students performed 3 studies to determine the effect that an object's mass and wind resistance has on the rate that it travels to the ground from a height.

In each study, the students stood on top of a 20-foot bleacher inside the school gymnasium and used an adjustable fan to create wind resistance at a constant rate. The fan was either positioned on the floor, pointing upward, or on the 20-foot bleacher, pointing downward. The objects included a tennis ball, a golf ball, a feather, and a piece of paper.

Study 1

When no wind was blowing, the students dropped a tennis ball and a golf ball at the same time. The times it took for each object to hit the ground were recorded. The same process was followed for the tennis ball and feather, and the golf ball and piece of paper. The students performed the tests 3 times for each group of objects. The results are shown in Table 1.

Table 1	
Object	**Fall time (sec)**
Trial 1: Tennis ball/golf ball Tennis ball/feather Golf ball/paper	2/2 2/13 3/8
Trial 2: Tennis ball/golf ball Tennis ball/feather Golf ball/paper	2/3 2/14 2/9
Trial 3: Tennis ball/golf ball Tennis ball/feather Golf ball/paper	1/1 2/17 3/11

Study 2

With the fan blowing upward, the experiment was repeated. The fan was turned off when the objects reached the ground. The results are shown in Table 2.

Table 2	
Object	**Fall time (sec)**
Trial 1: Tennis ball/golf ball Tennis ball/feather Golf ball/paper	3/3 3/17 4/20
Trial 2: Tennis ball/golf ball Tennis ball/feather Golf ball/paper	4/5 4/15 5/18
Trial 3: Tennis ball/golf ball Tennis ball/feather Golf ball/paper	3/4 2/10 4/14

Study 3

With the fan blowing downward, the students performed the experiment in the same manner. The fan was turned off when the objects reached the ground. The results are recorded in Table 3.

Table 3	
Object	**Fall time (sec)**
Trial 1: Tennis ball/golf ball Tennis ball/feather Golf ball/paper	1/1 1/6 2/5
Trial 2: Tennis ball/golf ball Tennis ball/feather Golf ball/paper	2/3 2/7 2/4
Trial 3: Tennis ball/golf ball Tennis ball/feather Golf ball/paper	4/5 3/6 4/3

34. According to Study 3, which objects differed most in fall time?
    F. Trial 1, Tennis ball/golf ball
    G. Trial 2, Tennis ball/feather
    H. Trial 2, Golf ball/paper
    J. Trial 3, Tennis ball/feather

GO ON TO THE NEXT PAGE.

35. The fall time of the objects was different in Studies 2 and 3. This difference is most likely due to:
   A. wind direction.
   B. settle time.
   C. wind speed.
   D. drop height.

36. Which of the following changes to all three studies would most likely have produced shorter fall times for all of the objects?
   F. Dropping the items from a height of 10 feet
   G. Increasing the speed of the fan
   H. Dropping the items at different times rather than all together
   J. Measuring the times from an adjacent bleacher

37. According to Study 2, which object consistently experienced the most wind resistance?
   A. Golf ball
   B. Paper
   C. Feather
   D. Tennis ball

38. In Study 2 it took the paper longer than the feather to fall. Which of the following is the most likely explanation?
   F. The larger surface area of the paper causes greater wind resistance resulting in longer fall times.
   G. The heavier weight of the paper causes it to fall more quickly than the feather.
   H. The lighter weight of the feather causes it to fall more slowly than the paper.
   J. The smaller surface area of the feather causes greater wind resistance, resulting in longer fall times.

39. Based on the results of all three studies, which object generally had the longest fall time?
   A. Tennis ball
   B. Golf ball
   C. Feather
   D. Paper

40. The students conducted a fourth experiment to test the rate at which each object falls in a partial vacuum. In the partial vacuum, there is no measurable resistance of any kind acting on the objects. What are the most likely results of this experiment?
   F. Each object falls much more slowly in a partial vacuum.
   G. Each object will fall at a nearly identical rate.
   H. The rate of fall will not be affected.
   J. The objects will not fall in a partial vacuum.

END OF THE SCIENCE TEST.
STOP! IF YOU HAVE TIME LEFT OVER, CHECK YOUR WORK ON THIS SECTION ONLY.

WRITING TEST

DIRECTIONS: This test is designed to assess your writing skills. You have forty (40) minutes to plan and write an essay based on the stimulus provided. Be sure to take a position on the issue and support your position using logical reasoning and relevant examples. Organize your ideas in a focused and logical way, and use the English language to clearly and effectively express your position.

When you have finished writing, refer to the Scoring Rubrics discussed in Chapter 7 to estimate your score.

Note: On the actual ACT you will receive approximately 2.5 pages of scratch paper on which to develop your essay, and approximately 4 pages of notebook paper on which to write your essay. We recommend that you limit yourself to this number of pages when you write your practice essays.

Smartphones

The cellular, or wireless, "telephone" has become ubiquitous in our everyday lives. Far from being simply a device for real-time communication, the "smartphone" has replaced several once-common devices and extended the power of the Internet to our pockets and purses. "Apps" (short for "applications") exist for many tasks, including banking and navigation and location services. Certainly, smartphones have created many opportunities and made the lives of many people easier. However, some feel that their prevalence, and our dependence on them, comes at a price. Given the fact that the use of smartphones is only increasing, it is certainly worth examining the implications and their presence in our lives.

PERSPECTIVE ONE	PERSPECTIVE TWO	PERSPECTIVE THREE
What we lose in our increasing dependence on smartphones is direct interaction with the people around us. In the past, people in common spaces such as airports used to converse with one another and learn from one another's perspectives. Now, most people are missing out on many opportunities to interact with people who have experiences and stories that are different from their own.	Smartphones are miracles of modern technology and provide tools that used to be only available to a few people in specific circumstances. We are more connected because of our devices and have more control over our own lives.	We are too dependent on technology. We are losing basic skills and we are sharing far too much information with government, corporations, and each other. Furthermore, the technology is enabling tyrannical governments to suppress their own citizens' desire for freedom.

Essay Task

Write a unified, coherent essay in which you evaluate multiple perspectives on the implications of our reliance on smartphones. In your essay, be sure to:

- analyze and evaluate the perspectives given
- state and develop your own perspective on the issue
- explain the relationship between your perspective and those given

Your perspective may be in full agreement with any of the others, in partial agreement, or wholly different. Whatever the case, support your ideas with logical reasoning and detailed, persuasive examples.

ANSWER KEY

English Test

1. D	21. B	41. D	61. C
2. G	22. G	42. F	62. G
3. D	23. C	43. A	63. A
4. G	24. J	44. H	64. G
5. A	25. B	45. C	65. C
6. G	26. F	46. F	66. G
7. B	27. D	47. C	67. A
8. F	28. H	48. J	68. G
9. A	29. D	49. C	69. D
10. J	30. H	50. F	70. F
11. D	31. A	51. D	71. B
12. F	32. G	52. F	72. F
13. D	33. D	53. B	73. D
14. H	34. H	54. F	74. F
15. C	35. D	55. D	75. B
16. H	36. J	56. G	
17. C	37. C	57. C	
18. H	38. G	58. H	
19. B	39. A	59. A	
20. F	40. J	60. H	

Mathematics Test

1. A	21. C	41. E
2. F	22. K	42. K
3. D	23. A	43. D
4. G	24. G	44. J
5. A	25. C	45. C
6. H	26. J	46. G
7. E	27. E	47. D
8. H	28. G	48. K
9. B	29. D	49. C
10. J	30. F	50. H
11. D	31. E	51. B
12. K	32. G	52. G
13. C	33. D	53. C
14. J	34. K	54. J
15. A	35. D	55. A
16. K	36. G	56. F
17. A	37. B	57. D
18. H	38. J	58. K
19. E	39. D	59. B
20. G	40. F	60. F

Reading Test		**Science Test**	
1. D	21. B	1. C	21. B
2. J	22. F	2. G	22. J
3. D	23. D	3. C	23. A
4. F	24. G	4. F	24. G
5. B	25. A	5. B	25. C
6. J	26. H	6. F	26. J
7. B	27. D	7. A	27. A
8. H	28. J	8. J	28. G
9. C	29. A	9. A	29. A
10. H	30. G	10. F	30. G
11. C	31. D	11. A	31. D
12. G	32. G	12. J	32. H
13. A	33. A	13. C	33. C
14. G	34. G	14. F	34. G
15. B	35. A	15. A	35. A
16. J	36. G	16. H	36. F
17. A	37. D	17. D	37. B
18. H	38. H	18. J	38. F
19. B	39. B	19. B	39. C
20. J	40. F	20. H	40. G

SCORING GUIDE

Your final reported score is your COMPOSITE SCORE. Your COMPOSITE SCORE is the average of all of your SCALE SCORES.

Your SCALE SCORES for the four multiple-choice sections are derived from the Scoring Table on the next page. Use your RAW SCORE, or the number of questions that you answered correctly for each section, to determine your SCALE SCORE. If you got a RAW SCORE of 60 on the English test, for example, you correctly answered 60 out of 75 questions.

Step 1 Determine your RAW SCORE for each of the four multiple-choice sections:

English	_____
Mathematics	_____
Reading	_____
Science	_____

The following Raw Score Table shows the total possible points for each section.

RAW SCORE TABLE	
KNOWLEDGE AND SKILL AREAS	**RAW SCORES**
ENGLISH	75
MATHEMATICS	60
READING	40
SCIENCE	40

Step 2 Determine your SCALE SCORE for each of the four multiple-choice sections using the following Scale Score Conversion Table.

SCALE SCORE	RAW SCORE			
	ENGLISH	MATHEMATICS	READING	SCIENCE
36	75	60	40	39–40
35	74	59	—	38
34	73	57–58	39	37
33	71–72	56	38	36
32	70	55	37	—
31	69	54	—	35
30	68	53	36	34
29	67	52	35	33
28	65–66	51–50	34	32
27	64	48–49	33	31
26	62–63	46–47	32	29–30
25	60–61	44–45	31	27–28
24	58–59	41–43	30	25–26
23	56–57	38–40	29	23–24
22	54–55	35–37	27–28	21–22
21	51–52	31–34	26	20
20	49–50	28–30	24–25	18–19
19	46–48	27	22–23	17
18	43–45	24–26	21	15–16
17	40–42	20–23	19–20	14
16	36–39	16–19	17–18	12–13
15	33–35	12–15	15–16	11
14	30–32	10–11	13–14	10
13	27–29	8–9	11–12	9
12	24–26	6–7	9–10	8
11	21–23	5	8	7
10	19–20	4	6–7	6
9	15–18	—	—	5
8	13–14	3	5	4
7	11–12	—	4	3
6	9–10	2	3	—
5	7–8	—	—	2
4	5–6	1	2	—
3	4	—	—	1
2	2–3	—	1	—
1	0–1	0	0	0

NOTE: Each actual ACT is scaled slightly differently based on a large amount of information gathered from the millions of tests ACT, Inc. scores each year. This scale will give you a fairly good idea of where you are in your preparation process. However, it should not be read as an absolute predictor of your actual ACT score. In fact, on practice tests, the scores are much less important than what you learn from analyzing your results.

If you take the optional Writing Test, you should refer to Chapter 7 for guidelines on scoring your Writing Test Essay.

Step 3 Determine your COMPOSITE SCORE by finding the sum of all your SCALE SCORES for each of the four sections: English, Mathematics, Reading, and Science, and divide by 4 to find the average. Round your COMPOSITE SCORE according to normal rules. For example, $31.2 \approx 31$ and $31.5 \approx 32$.

$$\frac{\qquad}{\substack{\text{ENGLISH} \\ \text{SCALE SCORE}}} + \frac{\qquad}{\substack{\text{MATHEMATICS} \\ \text{SCALE SCORE}}} + \frac{\qquad}{\substack{\text{READING} \\ \text{SCALE SCORE}}} + \frac{\qquad}{\substack{\text{SCIENCE} \\ \text{SCALE SCORE}}} = \frac{\qquad}{\substack{\text{SCALE SCORE} \\ \text{TOTAL}}}$$

$$\frac{\qquad}{\text{SCALE SCORE TOTAL}} \div 4 = \frac{\qquad}{\text{COMPOSITE SCORE}}$$

ANSWERS AND EXPLANATIONS

English Test Explanations

PASSAGE I

1. **The best answer is D.** To maintain parallel structure within this paragraph, you need to use the past tense of the verb *begin*. Notice that Sentences 2 and 3 use past tense main verbs. Sentence 4 also has a clause with the main verb *began*. The verb forms should match tense.

2. **The best answer is G.** The question asks you to identify the correct punctuation surrounding the phrase, *happy and healthy learning to walk and talk.* The phrase contains the main clause, *she was happy and healthy,* and a gerund phrase, *learning to walk and talk like her toddler peers.* Gerund phrases are set apart with a comma. No other commas should be placed within the main clause or the gerund phrase.

3. **The best answer is D.** In order to eliminate the redundancy and clearly express the intended idea, omit the underlined portion.

4. **The best answer is G.** Paragraph 2 illustrates the difficulties faced by both Helen and her parents as they adapted to their new situation. Answer choice G provides the best introduction because it summarizes what is to come while providing enough detail to be complete: Helen is frustrated, and her parents are overwhelmed by her resulting tantrums (they consider sending her to an asylum).

5. **The best answer is A.** The underlined phrase is part of the infinitive clause, meaning, an infinitive form of a verb has to follow the *to*. The other choices are simply more wordy restatements of the original phrase. The most concise selection is answer choice A.

6. **The best answer is G.** The possessive *Helen's* modifies *parents*. Therefore, the two words must not be separated by a comma. A comma is placed after the gerund phrase *Feeling sorry for their impaired daughter* to avoid misunderstanding.

7. **The best answer is B.** This question requires you to use the correct idiom.

8. **The best answer is F.** The sentence as it is written is clear, gives all the necessary information, and is most concise.

9. **The best answer is A.** This question requires you to express the idea clearly and simply. The main idea of the paragraph is Helen's need for self-discipline. Only the original phrase has that emphasis and is grammatically correct. The other answer choices are awkward.

10. **The best answer is J.** The rest of the passage is in the past tense, so to maintain parallel construction, you should use the past tense verb form *was*. Also, the *stubbornness* in question belongs to a particular person: Helen. Therefore, you should restate the antecedent for the sake of clarity.

11. **The best answer is D.** This question asks you to identify the correct punctuation surrounding the phrase *if channeled.* Because it interrupts the sentence between *that* and the clause beginning *it would be...,* it should be set apart by commas.

12. **The best answer is F.** The passive verb construction *was given* implies that Annie is the one who is acting. The context of the passage clearly indicates that it is Helen's parents who act; they are the ones who give permission for Annie and Helen to move to a different house. Since Annie receives the action, the verb phrase must be in the passive voice. Only the original phrase is correct.

13. **The best answer is D.** In this context, *Annies* should be possessive. Therefore, it requires an apostrophe before the *s*: *Annie's*. Furthermore, the phrase *Annie's efforts* ends the first independent clause of the sentence. The second clause, introduced by the conjunction *but,* should be set apart with a comma.

14. **The best answer is H.** The word *insatiable* means "not capable of being satisfied" and is the best word to describe *hunger.*

15. **The best answer is C.** This is a main idea question. The essay focuses on Helen's teacher, Annie Sullivan, and her professional accomplishments in working with Helen.

PASSAGE II

16. **The best answer is H.** The phrase *for the first time* is idiomatic. Answer choice F can be eliminated because it contains redundancy. Answer choices G and J are awkward (not idiomatic) and can be eliminated.

17. **The best answer is C.** The adverb *enthusiastically* correctly modifies the verb *anticipating*. Answer choice A includes the redundant pronoun *you*, which requires a different verb form.

18. **The best answer is H.** Notice that the paragraph uses the words *begin* and *buy*, both of which are present tense. To maintain parallel structure within this paragraph, you need to use a present tense verb; therefore, answer choices G and J can be eliminated. Answer choice F is in present perfect tense. With *a critical*

part of the holiday as the subject of the sentence, this answer choice does not make sense. Answer choice H is best because it uses *is* to equate the two noun phrases *a critical part of the holiday and shopping for gifts.*

19. **The best answer is B.** The phrase *not wanting to be rushed with last-minute purchases* is a gerund phrase and needs to be separated from the main clause by a comma.

20. **The best answer is F.** To maintain parallelism in the paragraph, all of the verb forms must match. The passage states that you "buy" and you "compliment" (present tense). Therefore, you "find" the ghost figurine.

21. **The best answer is B.** *You're* is the contraction of *you are.* Since the sentence already has a main verb, *you're* is grammatically incorrect. The correct form is the possessive pronoun *your.* Also, in this context the introductory phrase *this year* could be set off by a comma or left without punctuation; however, it would never be followed by a colon. Therefore, only answer choice B is correct.

22. **The best answer is G.** This question requires you to express the idea clearly and simply. Only this answer choice is a fully formed clause in standard word order.

23. **The best answer is C.** This choice eliminates the redundancy.

24. **The best answer is J.** Semicolons and periods separate complete sentences. While the first half of this sentence could stand on its own, the second half could not. It does not have a subject or a finite verb in the main clause. The comma is used to separate gerund phrases from the clauses they modify.

25. **The best answer is B.** One way to approach this question is by process of elimination. The sentence as it is written doesn't include a legitimate verb form. So, eliminate answer choice A. The passage has consistently been in the present tense, which means the sentence requires a present verb form. This eliminates answer choice D. Answer choice C does not have tense, so the sentence would be incomplete. This leaves answer choice B, *has become,* which is in the present perfect tense.

26. **The best answer is F.** In this case, the transition is from Paragraph 4 to Paragraph 6. Paragraph 4 ends with the author discovering that she is running out of time to buy gifts and that no one is available to help her. She must solve this problem on her own and act quickly. Answer choice F best captures this sentiment. The choice is supported by the first sentence in Paragraph 6, which emphasizes her frantic shopping.

27. **The best answer is D.** To maintain parallel structure within this paragraph, you need to use a present tense form of the verb *trudge.* Notice that the paragraph uses verbs such as *dart, give up,* and *are,* all of which are present tense. The verb forms should agree, that is, have the same tense.

28. **The best answer is H.** It is idiomatic to use the word *burst* to modify the phrase *into tears.*

29. **The best answer is D.** The passage as a whole describes one person's holiday stress building as it gets closer to Christmas. Paragraph 6 has the story's climax, as the author breaks down as she realizes that she will never finish her tasks in time. A hug from her son helps to remind her of the joy of the season, and she decides to rest instead of doing the next thing on her list. Answer choice D indicates her frustration and her ultimate decision to relax. This best captures the function of Paragraph 6 in relation to the rest of the passage.

30. **The best answer is H.** Paragraph 5 serves as a temporal marker: it tells the reader that, at this point in the narrative, it's the beginning of November with six more weeks before Christmas. Logically, it should be placed after Paragraph 2, with its reference to Halloween, and before Paragraph 3, with its reference to Thanksgiving (late November).

PASSAGE III

31. **The best answer is A.** The paragraph starts with a reference to "popular opinion." The next sentence refers back to that by using the phrase beginning with "this same." That means the sentence needs a subject noun that is a synonym for *popular opinion.* The word *culture* captures that sense accurately.

32. **The best answer is G.** To answer this question, you should first recognize that *physical fitness* is a singular noun phrase. In order to maintain parallel structure within the sentence, you should use *societal fitness,* a singular noun phrase. Eliminate answer choices F and J. The word *societal* is an adjective, describing the noun *fitness,* so it should not show possession. Eliminate answer choice H.

33. **The best answer is D.** The writer is setting up a line of reasoning parallel to that of the preceding sentence; physical exercise is compared to social activity. In both cases, the writer argues that if it hurts, don't do it; you're probably doing something wrong. Answer choice D best completes the parallel relation.

34. The best answer is H. The author states that pain receptors exist to limit physical injury. Guilt, the writer implies, is a psychological pain receptor that helps us "limit injury to others." Repeating the phrase *limit injury* allows the author to emphasize the parallel nature of the processes. The other answer choices either fail to mark the parallel or are too wordy.

35. The best answer is D. The word *attempting* is modifying the verb *turn*. In this usage, *turn* needs to be in the infinitive, that is, the sentence needs to read "attempting to turn."

36. The best answer is J. The focus of the paragraph is social interaction. Information about the time it takes to stop a car is irrelevant and should be deleted.

37. The best answer is C. This question requires you to correctly punctuate the underlined portion. The pronoun *yourself* is the object of the verb *find*, and driving is the verb without tense linked to *yourself*. Therefore, no commas should separate them.

38. The best answer is G. Because *manner* describes a behavior, the sentence requires a verb that denotes action (*acts*), not a state of being (*is*). Answer choices H and J are wordy and can be eliminated.

39. The best answer is A. This question requires you to express the idea clearly and simply. The phrase *legal penalties* is concise and complete. Adding detailed descriptions of those penalties would only distract from the focus of the paragraph, social behavior.

40. The best answer is J. The first clause of the sentence begins with *although*, making it a dependent clause. Therefore, a subject and a verb of the main clause is needed here. Answer choice J is also the most clear, simple option.

41. The best answer is D. The underlined phrase is redundant because it repeats the meaning of *insanity*. It should be omitted.

42. The best answer is F. The transition word *however* suggests a contrast between the idea contained in the preceding sentence and the idea contained in this sentence. This is, in fact, the case, so answer choice F is correct.

43. The best answer is A. Because a hyphen is used earlier in the sentence at the beginning of the phrase, use a hyphen after the phrase as well.

44. The best answer is H. The phrase *if improperly managed* is an interrupting phrase in the sentence and should be set off by commas. The comma at the beginning of the phrase is a clue to the reader to expect a second comma at the end. A semicolon would require a complete sentence preceding it. Eliminate answer choice F. The relative pronoun *which* would create a sentence fragment. Eliminate answer choice G. The pronoun *it* would create a run-on, so eliminate answer choice J.

45. The best answer is C. It is idiomatic to use the phrase *move on* in this context.

PASSAGE IV

46. The best answer is F. Use a period to separate two independent clauses.

47. The best answer is C. This question requires you to express the idea clearly and simply. The focus of this paragraph is the contrast between Kennedy's appearance of health and his actual state of chronic illness. Answer choice C best captures this dynamic. The sentence as written is a run-on, so eliminate answer choice A. Answer choice B has three grammatically correct sentences, but their structure is rigid and plain. It is not the best answer. The word order of answer choice D is awkward, so it can be eliminated.

48. The best answer is J. It is idiomatic to use the phrase "began with" in this context.

49. The best answer is C. The best way to provide more detail is to offer a better description. Paragraph 2 continues from Paragraph 1 by describing in more detail the effects of Addison's disease on Kennedy. A list of the symptoms of the disease would help the reader gain a more complete understanding of the disease.

50. The best answer is F. The sentence is best as written. The clause has standard subject–verb–object word order. The rest of the information follows in logical order. The prepositional phrase *in his back* comes immediately after the noun phrase *anesthetic injections*, which it modifies. The prepositional phrase *up to six times a day* modifies the whole clause and can be placed at the end.

51. The best answer is D. The information given by the phrases in answer choices A, B, and C is already implied in the verb *hide*. Therefore, all these answer choices are redundant and can be eliminated.

52. The best answer is F. Use the subjective pronoun "who." The words "which" and "that" should not be used to refer to a person.

53. The best answer is B. The subject *he* is implied in the second half of this compound sentence. Answer choice B is clear, concise, and grammatically correct. As it is written, the sentence contains a comma splice. Both a period and semicolon must be followed by independent clauses, which is not the case in answer choices C and D.

54. The best answer is F. The question requires you to express the idea clearly and simply. The idea that Kennedy was able to "act healthy" is developed by the sentence, which explains exactly what that means: he was able to hide crippling pain from everyone except his doctors and relatives.

55. The best answer is D. This question requires you to express the idea clearly and simply. Answer choice D is complete and the most concise. The other answer choices are awkward and wordy.

56. The best answer is G. To maintain parallel structure within this paragraph, you need to use the past tense of the verb *attribute*, which is *attributed*. Notice the use of the verbs *was* and *looked*. The verb forms should agree in tense. Furthermore, Kennedy is deceased, so his actions have past tense.

57. The best answer is C. The last two sentences of this paragraph clarify its focus, which is proving that Kennedy's illness did not negatively affect his ability to govern. Answer choice C asks the question that the last two sentences answer. Therefore, it is the best response.

58. The best answer is H. Like the positive pairing *either … or, neither … nor* are usually used together. Therefore, to maintain the parallelism, the underlined portion should be *nor the drugs*.

59. The best answer is A. The sentence as it stands gives us the most important information first: what he did ("performed"), followed by how he did it ("at the highest level"). This order makes logical sense and is the most concise option.

60. The best answer is H. This question requires you to determine the main idea of the passage. Although the passage does describe Addison's disease in some detail, its primary focus is the effect of Addison's disease on President Kennedy. For example, the reader is not told if Kennedy's experience of the disease is common among Addison's sufferers. Likewise, the reader is also not told if treatment has changed since the early 1960s. Therefore, the essay would not be a good general description of Addison's disease and its treatment. Eliminate answer choices F and G. While the essay does describe symptoms of the disease, this is not the main focus, so eliminate answer choice J.

PASSAGE V

61. The best answer is C. The question requires you to avoid redundancy. The word "traveling" implies going on a trip.

62. The best answer is G. The sentence is awkward as written. A relative pronoun could link the two clauses; *where* is best because it refers to a place, *Southern California*.

63. The best answer is A. The author is comparing personal warmth, or genuine friendliness, to the outdoor temperature. She implies that the people of Tromso demonstrate the former. Being helpful is an excellent way to show friendliness.

64. The best answer is G. The passage states that Tromso residents are very helpful to foreigners. This best matches answer choice G. While answer choice F describes polite behavior, it is not as strong an example.

65. The best answer is C. The verbs *twirling, flipping,* and *twisting* are synonyms of *spinning* and could replace *spinning* in the sentence without changing its meaning. The verb *throwing* does not fit the context, and it is NOT acceptable.

66. The best answer is G. This question requires you to express the idea clearly and simply. The current sentence is wordy and redundant (it's unnecessary to repeat *Tromso* in this context). Answer choice G sets up a concise contrast between what residents of other towns claim to do and what residents of Tromso actually do.

67. The best answer is A. The paragraph that follows indicates that, instead of working or sitting, the writer spent much of his time hiking. The phrase *at all* is appropriate here, because it makes a connection between the idea that the writer thought his time in Norway would drag and the fact that his visit was actually very enjoyable.

68. The best answer is G. The best introductory sentence will be one that shows a transition from Paragraph 3 to Paragraph 4. Since Paragraph 3 discusses some of Tromso's attributes (mild weather and friendly people) it makes sense that Paragraph 4 should start out with another of Tromso's characteristics. Sentence 2 does this best. Therefore, the correct sequence of sentences will begin with Sentence 2. Furthermore, there is a strong link between Sentences 1 and 5, and only answer choice G places them together.

69. **The best answer is D.** The sentence introduces the idea of boots and blisters to the paragraph. Since this is not echoed elsewhere, it is irrelevant and should be omitted. Eliminate answer choices B and C for the same reason.

70. **The best answer is F.** The first part of the sentence indicates that hiking is so popular in Norway, that the government passed regulations allowing anyone to hike across wilderness areas. The question stem says *expand hikers' rights*, which mirrors *adding designated areas* in answer choice F.

71. **The best answer is B.** Answer choice B is the only one with descriptive adjectives that help create a vivid image of the "many beautiful scenes." The other answer choices are either too general or contain irrelevant information.

72. **The best answer is F.** The sentence is complete and concise as it stands. The addition of a transition word or phrase is not necessary, so eliminate answer choices G, H, and J.

73. **The best answer is D.** The sentence requires the possessive form of *Tromso*, a singular noun. The correct form adds an apostrophe and an *s* to create *Tromso's*.

74. **The best answer is F.** This question requires you to express the idea clearly and simply.

75. **The best answer is B.** As written, *it's* is the contraction of *it is*. A better choice would be the possessive form *its*. However, the antecedent of *its* would be unclear. (It is not *vista, Mount Storsteinen, northern lights*, or *midnight sun*.) When an antecedent is too distant or unclear, use an expressed noun in possessive form instead, as in answer choice B.

Mathematics Test Explanations

1. **The correct answer is A.** This is a basic algebra problem that requires you to solve for x. Isolate the variable, x, on one side of the equation, as follows:

    $$4x - 9 = 11$$
    $$4x = 20$$
    $$x = 5$$

2. **The correct answer is F.** This kind of statement is called a "conditional." You are told that if the first part is true (XY is 4), then the second part (YZ is 7) will certainly be true. Since the second part is NOT true, you can conclude logically that the first part is also NOT true. Therefore, answer choice F is correct. If XY were equal to 4, then, according to the given statement, YZ would have to be 7. Remember that some ACT mathematics problems require only logic and no computations.

3. **The correct answer is D.** To solve this problem, first set up an equation, as follows, to find the given number (x):

    $$0.6x = 9$$
    $$x = 15$$

    The given number is 15. Next, calculate 25% of 15, as follows:

    $$0.25x = 15$$
    $$x = 3.75$$

4. **The correct answer is G.** The first step in solving this problem is to calculate the amount of fuel needed for each vehicle for the trip, as follows:

    Vehicle A: 1,120 total miles ÷ 16 miles per gallon = 70 gallons

    Vehicle B: 1,120 total miles ÷ 35 miles per gallon = 32 gallons

    Next, find the difference between the gallons required for Vehicles A and B:

    $$70 - 32 = 38$$

5. **The correct answer is A.** To solve this problem, set up an equation, as follows:

    $$(x - 3) + (x - 2) + (x - 1) + x + (x + 1) = 390$$

    Next, simplify the equation and solve for x:

    $$5x - 5 = 390$$
    $$5x = 395$$
    $$x = 79$$

6. **The correct answer is H.** This problem requires you to substitute the values given for P and Q into the equation $P - Q$. The problem states that $P = 5a$ and $Q = 3b - 2a$. Set up the equation as follows, and remember to keep track of the negative sign as you simplify the expression:

    $$P - Q = 5a - (3b - 2a)$$
    $$= 5a - (-2a) - 3b$$
    $$= 5a + 2a - 3b$$
    $$= 7a - 3b$$

7. **The correct answer is E.** The figure in the problem represents 2 parallel lines cut by 2 parallel transversals. The angles created as a result have special properties. Where each of the parallel lines is cut by a transversal, there are 2 pairs of vertical, or opposite, angles. Each angle in the pair is congruent to, or equal to, the other angle in the pair. Therefore, where l_3 intersects l_1 and also where it intersects l_2, two 100° angles are formed; in addition, two 80° angles are formed that are adjacent to the 100° angles, since a straight line measures 180°. The same angles are created where l_4 intersects l_1 and l_2. This means that angle z must equal 80°.

    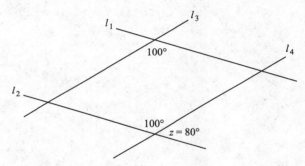

8. **The correct answer is H.** Simply plug 2 in for x wherever x appears in the equation and solve the equation. Don't forget to keep track of the negative signs!

    $$-(2^2) + 4(2) - 3 = -(4) + 8 - 3$$
    $$= 8 - 4 - 3 = 1$$

9. **The correct answer is B.** If the average of 8 numbers is 6.5, then the total of the 8 numbers is $8 \cdot 6.5$, or 52. If each of the 8 numbers is decreased by 3, then the total of the 8 new numbers is $52 - 8(3)$, or $52 - 24$, which is 28. To find the average, divide 28 by 8, to get 3.5.

10. **The correct answer is J.** This question tests your ability to recognize and apply the distributive property of multiplication. According to the distributive property, for any numbers a, b, and c, $c(a + b) = ca + cb$. In this problem, c is 5 so you can factor the expression $5a + 5b$ into $5(a + b)$.

11. The correct answer is D. To solve this problem, first subtract $40 from $375 ($375 - 40 = 335$). Because $40 is a flat fee, it will not figure in the calculations for the number of hours. Set the number of hours to x, multiply by the hourly rate, and solve:

$$25x = 335$$
$$x = 13.4$$

12. The correct answer is K. The easiest way to solve this problem is to plug the answer choices into the inequality and solve. Because the question asks you for the largest possible value of *x*, start with the largest answer choice (note that the answer choices are in ascending order):

$$\frac{8}{32} \geq \frac{1}{4}$$
$$\frac{8}{32} = \frac{1}{4}$$

This satisfies the inequality, so answer choice K, because it is the largest, must be correct.

13. The correct answer is C. In order to solve this problem you must know that there are 360° in a circle, and that the clock shown is divided into 12 segments, 1 for each hour in the day. To calculate the number of degrees that the hour hand moves from 1:00 P.M. to 8:00 P.M. perform the following operations:

360° ÷ 12 = 30°. Each hour in the day is equivalent to 30°.

30° × 7 (the number of hours between 1:00 P.M. and 8:00 P.M.) = 210°

14. The correct answer is J. The first step in choosing the correct answer is to locate point *R* in the coordinate plane. You will see that it is located in the upper-right quadrant, which means that both of the coordinates must be positive. Eliminate answer choices H and K because they both include negative coordinates. You can also eliminate answer choices F and G, because neither of the coordinates of point *R* is zero. That leaves answer choice J as the only possible correct answer.

15. The correct answer is A. This problem requires you to find the Greatest Common Factor. The Greatest Common Factor is $3xy$, because each term has at least 1 factor of 3, 1 factor of *x*, and 1 factor of *y*. When you factor $3xy$ out of $3x^3y^3$ you are left with x^2y^2, and when you factor $3xy$ out of $3xy$, you are left with 1. Therefore, when factored, $3x^3y^3 + 3xy = 3xy(x^2y^2 + 1)$.

16. The correct answer is K. To find the total number of seats in the entire classroom, you must multiply the number of rows, $(r + s)$, by the number of seats in each row, t, using the Distributive Property:

$$(r + s) \cdot t = (r \cdot t) + (s \cdot t)$$

17. The correct answer is A. Simply replace *x* with –3 in the given equation and solve. Be careful to track the negative signs.

$$-3x - 3x^2$$
$$-3(-3) - 3(-3)^2$$
$$9 - 27 = -18$$

18. The correct answer is H. To solve this problem quickly, notice that the slowest time (24 : 04) is just over 24 minutes and the fastest time (19 : 53) is just under 20 minutes. Therefore, the difference between the two times will be around 4 minutes. You can eliminate answer choices F and G because they are too small, and answer choice K because it is too big. Next, convert the times to seconds, as follows:

Slowest time: 24(60) + 4 = 1,444 seconds

Fastest time: 19(60) + 53 = 1,193 seconds

Now subtract to find the difference in seconds: 1,444 − 1,193 = 251. Finally, convert 251 seconds to minutes and seconds: 251 ÷ 60 = 4, remainder 11.

19. The correct answer is E. In order to solve this problem you must first calculate the total cost of the watch, including tax. Since the sales tax is 6%, multiply the price of the watch ($12.99) by 0.06, the decimal equivalent of 6%:

$12.99 × 0.06 = $0.7794

$0.7794 rounded to the nearest cent is $0.78.

Now, add the sales tax to the price of the watch:

$12.99 + $0.78 = $13.77

Based on these calculations, you will need $0.77 in exact change.

20. The correct answer is G. An expression is undefined when the denominator equals 0. Set the denominator equal to 0 and solve for *x*:

$$16 - x^2 = 0$$
$$16 = x^2$$
$$4 = x$$

21. The correct answer is C. To solve this problem, you can use your calculator to determine the square root of 99:

$$\sqrt{99} = 9.9498$$

Clearly, 10 is the smallest integer greater than the square root of 99: 10 > 9.9498. You could also have figured that $\sqrt{99}$ is slightly less than $\sqrt{100}$, which is 10, making 10 the smallest integer greater than the square root of 99.

22. **The correct answer is K.** The key to solving this problem is to recognize that the box has a top and a bottom, plus 4 sides. Because the tape must go completely *around* all 4 sides of the box, you must account for the sides as follows:

$$2(40 \text{ cm}) = 80 \text{ cm (top and bottom, length)}$$

$$2(13 \text{ cm}) = 26 \text{ cm (top and bottom, width)}$$

$$4(20 \text{ cm}) = 80 \text{ cm (four sides, height)}$$

$$80 + 26 + 80 = 186 \text{ cm}$$

23. **The correct answer is A.** The first step in solving this problem is to calculate the value of Kahla's inventory at each price point, as follows:

$$\left. \begin{array}{l} \text{Shop A, Brand X} : 150 \times \$20 = 3{,}000 \\ \text{Shop B, Brand X} : 100 \times \$20 = 2{,}000 \end{array} \right\} = \$5{,}000$$

$$\left. \begin{array}{l} \text{Shop A, Brand Y} : 200 \times \$25 = 5{,}000 \\ \text{Shop B, Brand Y} : 120 \times \$25 = 3{,}000 \end{array} \right\} = \$8{,}000$$

$$\left. \begin{array}{l} \text{Shop A, Brand Z} : 225 \times \$30 = 6{,}750 \\ \text{Shop B, Brand Z} : 175 \times \$30 = 5{,}250 \end{array} \right\} = \$12{,}000$$

Next, find the total value: $\$5{,}000 + \$8{,}000 + \$12{,}000 = \$25{,}000$.

24. **The correct answer is G.** To find the solutions of the expression $x^2 + 2x = 8$, first put it in the correct quadratic form by subtracting 8 from both sides: $x^2 + 2x - 8 = 0$. Now you can factor the polynomial $x^2 + 2x - 8$:

$$(x + \underline{\hspace{1em}})(x - \underline{\hspace{1em}}) = 0$$

Find 2 factors of –8 that, when added together give you 2, and plug them into the solution sets:

$$(x + 4)(x - 2) = 0$$

Now, solve for x:

$$(x + 4) = 0, \text{ so } x = -4$$

$$(x - 2) = 0, \text{ so } x = 2$$

The solutions of $x^2 + 2x = 8$ are –4 and 2.

25. **The correct answer is C.** The key to solving this problem is to recognize that if $(f + g)^2 = 81$, then $f + g$ must equal 9, because 9^2 equals 81. Now, since you are given that $fg = 20$, you need to find 2 numbers that, when added together give you 9, and, when multiplied together give you 20. The only 2 numbers that will satisfy both equations are 4 and 5. Substitute 4 for f and 5 for g in the final equation: $f^2 + g^2 = 4^2 + 5^2 = 16 + 25 = 41$.

26. **The correct answer is J.** When exponents are raised to an exponential power, the rules state that you must multiply the exponents by the power to which they are raised. In this problem, x is raised to the $(4a - 3)$ power. This exponent is then squared, so you should multiply $4a - 3$ by 2: $2(4a - 3) = 8a - 6$. You now have the equation $x^{8a-6} = x^{10}$. Since the coefficients equal (x), the exponents must also be equal, so $8a - 6 = 10$. Solve for a:

$$8a - 6 = 10$$

$$8a = 16$$

$$a = 2$$

27. **The correct answer is E.** The first step in solving this problem is to determine the value of i^6 and $3i^4$. Even though this problem contains a complex number, it is actually a relatively simple exponent problem. You are given that $i^2 = -1$, which means that $i^6 = (i^2)(i^2)(i^2) = (-1)(-1)(-1)$, which equals –1. By the same token, $3i^4 = 3(i^2)(i^2) = 3(-1)(-1)$, which equals 3. Therefore, the value of $i^6 + 3i^4$ is –1 + 3, or 2.

28. **The correct answer is G.** The slope-intercept form for the equation of a line is $y = mx + b$, where m is the slope and b is the y-intercept. Put the given equation in the standard form as follows:

$$5x - 4y = 7$$

$$-4y = -5x + 7$$

$$y = \frac{5x}{4} - \frac{7}{4}$$

Based on this solution, b, the y-intercept, is equal to $-\frac{7}{4}$.

29. **The correct answer is D.** A circle centered at (a, b) with a radius r has the equation $(x - a)^2 + (y - b)^2 = r^2$. Based on this definition, a circle with the equation $(x + 3)^2 + (y - 2)^2 = 10^2$ would have a radius of $\sqrt{10}$. If $r^2 = 10$, then $r = \sqrt{10}$.

30. **The correct answer is F.** The sine of any acute angle is calculated by dividing the length of the side opposite the acute angle by the length of the hypotenuse $\left(\sin = \dfrac{\text{opp}}{\text{hyp}} \right)$. In this problem, the length of the side opposite angle β is l, and the length of the hypotenuse is n. Therefore, the sin of angle β is $\dfrac{l}{n}$.

31. **The correct answer is E.** You should think of this problem as a basic fraction, where $(4a^3b) \times (-5a^5b^3)$ is the numerator and $(10a^4b^2)$ is the denominator. The

first step is to multiply together the 2 elements in the numerator, as follows:

> When multiplying exponents, the rules state that you should add exponents with like coefficients, so $(4a^3b)(-5a^5b^3) = -20a^8b^4$.

To solve a fraction, you simply divide the numerator by the denominator.

> When dividing exponents, the rules state that you should subtract exponents of the same coefficients in the denominator from the exponents of the same coefficients in the numerator, so $-20a^8b^4 \div 10a^4b^2 = -2a^4b^2$.

32. The correct answer is G. Because the 3 lines are parallel, the distances between the points of intersection of each of the transversals are directly proportional. So, the distance from point E to point $C(6'')$ is directly proportional to the distance from point A to point $C(2'')$, and the distance from point F to point $D(8'')$ is proportional to the distance from point D to point $B(x'')$. Set up the following proportion and solve for x:

$$6 : 2 \text{ as } 8 : x$$

$$\frac{6}{2} = \frac{8}{x}$$

$$x = \frac{16}{6}, \text{ which can be simplified to } \frac{8}{3}.$$

33. The correct answer is D. A square is a parallelogram with 4 right angles and 4 sides of the same length. The perimeter of a square is the distance around the square, or the sum of all 4 sides. Since the perimeter is given as 28, the length of each side of the square must be $28 \div 4$, or 7. This means that radii $\overline{DA}$ and $\overline{DC}$ are both equal to 7. The area of a circle is calculated using the formula $A = \pi r^2$. Plug 7 in for r and solve:

$$A = \pi r^2 = \pi(7)^2$$
$$A = \pi 49, \text{ or } 49\pi$$

34. The correct answer is K. According to the graph shown, the number 2 is included, but the number 4 is not included. This means that x must be less than or equal to $2 (x \leq 2)$ and/or x must be greater than $4 (x > 4)$. You can eliminate answer choices F and G, which both indicate that x is greater than or equal to $4 (x \geq 4)$. You can also eliminate answer choice H, which says that x is less than but not equal to $2 (x < 2)$. Now you must decide whether to use *and* or to use *or*. Since the sets do not overlap on the graph, the correct answer is $x \leq 2$ or $x > 4$.

35. The correct answer is D. To solve this problem, substitute the given dimensions into the equation, as follows:

$$\text{Surface area} = 2\pi(5)^2 + 2\pi(5)(10)$$
$$= 2\pi(25) + 2\pi(50)$$
$$= 50\pi + 100\pi$$
$$= 150\pi$$

36. The correct answer is G. Because a negative number cannot have a real square root, the value under a square root sign must be positive. In this problem, the value under the square root sign is $4\left(\dfrac{x^2}{3y}\right)$. Choose values for the answer choices and eliminate those choices that would give you a negative value under the square root sign:

> If y is negative, then $3y$ will be negative, so the value under the square root sign could also be negative. Eliminate answer choice F.

> If y is positive, then $3y$ will be positive. Since the square of a negative number is also positive, even if x is negative, as long as y is positive the value under the square root sign will be positive. Answer choice G will work.

> Answer choices H and J are not true, because you have just determined that y must be positive, which means that, while y *could* be either 4 or $\dfrac{1}{2}$, it could also be some other positive value.

> Answer choice K does not work, because y must be a positive number. By process of elimination, you are left with answer choice G.

37. The correct answer is B. To solve this problem, first list all of the distinct factors of 96: 96, 48, 32, 24, 16, 12, 8, 6, 4, 3, 2, 1. All of these numbers divide evenly into 96. Next, list all of the distinct factors of 64: 64, 32, 16, 8, 4, 2, 1. All of these numbers divide evenly into 64. The only factors that both 96 and 64 have in common are 1, 2, 4, 8, 16, and 32. Since you are told that c is NOT a factor of either 16 or 20, you can eliminate 1, 2, 4, 8, and 16, which factor evenly into either 16 or 20. This leaves you with a value for c of 32. When you add the digits $(3 + 2)$ you get 5.

38. The correct answer is J. The slope of a line is defined as the change in the y-values over the change in the x-values in the standard (x, y) coordinate plane. Slope can be calculated by using the following formula: $\dfrac{(y_1 - y_2)}{(x_1 - x_2)}$. Any line parallel to the y-axis is a vertical line: The x-values do not change (see diagram).

The slope of a vertical line is undefined, answer choice J, because there is no change in x, which means that the denominator $(x_1 - x_2)$ is zero.

39. **The correct answer is D.** If the coordinates of point J are nonzero and have the same sign, they must both either be positive (+, +) or negative (−, −). Therefore, they must be located in either Quadrant I, or Quadrant III, as shown below:

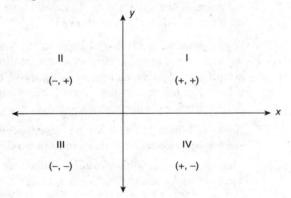

40. **The correct answer is F.** The first step in solving this problem is to calculate the sine and the cosine for both angle a and angle b. The sine of any acute angle is calculated by dividing the length of the side opposite the acute angle by the length of the hypotenuse $\left(\sin = \dfrac{\text{opp}}{\text{hyp}} \right)$. The cosine of any acute angle is calculated by dividing the length of the side adjacent to the acute angle by the hypotenuse $\left(\cos = \dfrac{\text{adj}}{\text{hyp}} \right)$. In this problem, the sin of angle a is $\dfrac{12}{15}$, which reduces to $\dfrac{4}{5}$, and the cos of angle a is $\dfrac{9}{15}$, reduces to $\dfrac{3}{5}$. The sin of angle b is $\dfrac{9}{15}$, or $\dfrac{3}{5}$, and the cos of angle b is $\dfrac{12}{15}$, or $\dfrac{4}{5}$. Now you can plug these values into the equation given in the problem and solve for $\sin(a - b)$:

$$\sin(a - b) = \sin a \cos b - \cos a \sin b$$

$$\sin(a - b) = \left(\dfrac{4}{5} \right)\left(\dfrac{4}{5} \right) - \left(\dfrac{3}{5} \right)\left(\dfrac{3}{5} \right)$$

$$\sin(a - b) = \left(\dfrac{16}{25} \right) - \left(\dfrac{9}{25} \right) = \dfrac{7}{25}$$

41. **The correct answer is E.** To calculate the value of $F(-2)$ where $x < 0$, use the second function. Solve for x:

For $x < 0$, $F(x) = -x^3 + x^2 + 42x - 29$

$-(-2)^3 + (-2)^2 + 42(-2) - 29 =$

$-(-8) + 4 - 84 - 29 =$

$8 + 4 - 113 = -101$

42. **The correct answer is K.** The best approach to this problem is to pick some numbers for n, plug them into the answer choices, and eliminate the answer choices that do not always yield an odd number.

If $n = 1$, then $4n^2 = 4(1)^2 = 4$, which is not odd. Eliminate answer choice F.

If $n = 1$, then $3n^2 + 1 = 3(1)^2 + 1 = 3 + 1 = 4$, which is not odd. Eliminate answer choice G.

If $n = 1$, then $6n^2 = 6(1)^2 = 6$, which is not odd. Eliminate answer choice H.

If $n = 1$, then $n^2 - 1 = (1)^2 - 1 = 0$, which is not odd. Eliminate answer choice J.

If $n = 1$, then $4n^2 - 1 = 4(1)^2 - 1 = 4 - 1 = 3$, which is odd. Try another number: $n = 2$, then $4n^2 - 1 = 4(2)^2 - 1 = 16 - 1 = 15$, which is also odd. Answer choice K will work.

Answer choice K is the only one that will give you an odd number for any value of n.

43. **The correct answer is D.** The area of a triangle is calculated using the formula $A = \dfrac{1}{2}(bh)$, where b is the length of the base, and h is the height. Based on the measures of the angles given, you can draw triangle ABC as shown below:

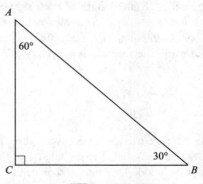

You are given that $\overline{AB}$, the hypotenuse, is 8 units long. Because this is a 30–60–90 triangle, you can calculate the lengths of the base ($\overline{BC}$) and the height ($\overline{AC}$). The relationship between the sides of a 30–60–90 triangle is as follows: The side opposite the 30° angle is equal to $\dfrac{1}{2}$ of the length of the hypotenuse, and the side opposite the 60° angle is equal to $\dfrac{1}{2}$ of the length of the hypotenuse times $\sqrt{3}$. Calculate the lengths of the sides:

$$\text{Side } \overline{BC} \text{ (the base)} = \frac{1}{2}(8)\sqrt{3} = 4\sqrt{3}$$
$$\text{Side } \overline{AC} \text{ (the height)} = \frac{1}{2}(8) = 4$$

Now you can plug these values into the formula for the area of a triangle:

$$A = \frac{1}{2}(4\sqrt{3})(4) = \frac{1}{2}(16\sqrt{3}) = 8\sqrt{3}$$

44. The correct answer is J. The best approach to solving this problem is to draw a picture like the one shown below:

Extend line $\overline{WX}$ through point X to an imaginary point A that is below point Z. Then, when you draw line $\overline{WZ}$, you create a special right triangle (WAZ) with sides of length 3, 4, and 5. Use your knowledge of the special 3–4–5 right triangle to determine $\overline{WZ} = 5$.

45. The correct answer is C. The area of a rectangle is calculated by multiplying the length by the width $(A = w \times l)$. Calculate the area of the first rectangle as follows:

Set the width equal to x, and the length equal to $4x$.

$$A = x(4x) = 4x^2$$

Now calculate the area of the second rectangle:

The length and width are tripled, so the width $= 3x$ and the length $= 12x$
$$A = (3x)(12x) = 36x^2$$

The area of the second rectangle is $36x^2$, which is 9 times greater than the area of the first rectangle $(4x^2)$.

46. The correct answer is G. Systems of equations will have infinite solutions when the equations are equal to each other. The first step in solving this problem is to recognize that the second equation is exactly twice the value of the first equation: $6x = 2(3x)$, $8y = 2(4y)$, so $7b$ must equal $2(14)$. Solve for b:

$$7b = 2(14)$$
$$7b = 28$$
$$b = 4$$

47. The correct answer is D. Logarithms are used to indicate exponents of certain numbers called bases. This problem tells you that log to the base 3 of x equals 2. By definition, $\log_a b = c$ if $a^c = b$. Therefore, $\log_3 x = 2$ if $3^2 = x$. Since $3^2 = 9$, answer choice D is correct.

48. The correct answer is K. The first step in solving this problem is to recognize that the distance from the point on the ground to the telephone pole is equal to the length of the side adjacent to the $37°$ angle, and that the height of the telephone pole is equal to the length of the side opposite the $37°$ angle. The length of the side opposite to any given angle divided by the length of the side adjacent to any given angle is the tangent of that angle. So, in this problem, $\tan 37° = \dfrac{24}{\text{distance}}$. Solve for the distance:

$$\tan 37° = \frac{24}{\text{distance}}$$
$$(\text{distance}) \tan 37° = 24$$
$$\text{distance} = \frac{24}{\tan 37°} = 24\left(\frac{1}{\tan 37°}\right)$$

By definition, cotangent is $\dfrac{1}{\tan}$, so the distance is equal to 24 cot $37°$.

49. The correct answer is C. The area of a parallelogram is calculated by using the formula $A = (b \times h)$, where b is the base and h is the height. The length of the sides, $(\sqrt{61})$, is not relevant in calculating the area. Plug the given values into the formula:

$$A = 6 \times 5$$
$$A = 30$$

50. The correct answer is H. The easiest way to solve this problem is to draw a line and place the given points on the line, as follows:

Based on the line above, one possible length of $\overline{AC}$ is 27. Eliminate answer choices F, J, and K. Since you are left with answer choices G and H, you need to determine if $\overline{AC}$ could also be 3 meters long. Draw another line, and change the order of the points:

Based on this line, another possible length of $\overline{AC}$ is 3, so answer choice H is correct.

51. **The correct answer is B.** Given that both figures have the same area, $\frac{1}{2}(a)(2a) = (b)(3b)$. Therefore, $a^2 = 3b^2$; taking the square root of both sides results in $a = \sqrt{(3b^2)}$ or $a = b\sqrt{3}$.

52. **The correct answer is G.** In this problem, the quantity $6a^4b^3$ is less than zero, which means it must be negative. Since 6 is positive, and a^4 will always be positive, b^3 must be negative. By definition, if you cube a negative number, the result will be negative. Therefore, if b^3 is negative, then b must be negative, or less than zero. This means that b CANNOT be greater than zero, so answer choice G is correct.

53. **The correct answer is C.** In a geometric sequence, the quotient of any 2 successive members or terms of the sequence is a constant. This means that the exponent is 1 larger in each successive element of the progression, because you multiply by the same number each time you move to the next element in the sequence. Here, the second term of the sequence will have an exponent of 1 (sp), the third term of the sequence will have an exponent of 2 (s^2p), the fourth term will have an exponent of 3 (s^3p), and so on. You can see that the exponent of any given term is 1 less than the number of the term. Therefore, the exponent of s of the 734th term must be 733, ($s^{733}p$).

54. **The correct answer is J.** If a system of 2 linear equations in 2 variables has no solution, that means that the lines do not cross each other anywhere in the (x, y) coordinate plane. If the lines do not cross each other, then they must be parallel. Parallel lines have the same slope. The line shown has a positive slope, so you can eliminate answer choice F, which has a slope of zero, and answer choices G and H which have negative slopes. Parallel lines cannot have the same y-intercept, so eliminate answer choice K.

55. **The correct answer is A.** Because angle x is less than 90°, it is an acute angle. The tangent of any acute angle is calculated by dividing the length of the side opposite of the acute angle by the length of the side adjacent to the acute angle $\left(\tan = \frac{\text{opp}}{\text{adj}}\right)$. This means that the length of the side opposite angle x is 15, and the length of the side adjacent to angle x is 8. The cosine of any acute angle is calculated by dividing the length of the side adjacent to the acute angle by the hypotenuse $\left(\cos = \frac{\text{adj}}{\text{hyp}}\right)$. Since you know the lengths of 2 of the sides, you can calculate the hypotenuse by using the Pythagorean Theorem:

> Pythagorean Theorem: $a^2 + b^2 = c^2$, where c is the hypotenuse.

$$8^2 + 15^2 = c^2$$
$$64 + 225 = c^2$$
$$289 = c^2$$
$$\sqrt{289} = c, \text{ so } c = 17$$

The hypotenuse is 17, which means that the cos of angle x is $\frac{8}{17}$.

56. **The correct answer is F.** To solve this problem, first look at the answer choices. You can eliminate answer choice J, because if either L, M, or N were 0, then LMN would equal 0; you are given that $LMN = 1$. Answer choice F must be correct, because $LM = 1/N$ is true when $LMN = 1$ (divide both sides by N). The remaining answer choices could be true, but you can find at least one instance where they do not have to be true.

57. **The correct answer is D.** A number is rational when it can be written as a fraction. Additionally, any square root that is not a perfect root is an *irrational* number. Only answer choice D can be simplified such that it is a rational number:

$$\frac{\sqrt{81}}{\sqrt{169}} = \frac{9}{13}$$

58. **The correct answer is K.** A permutation is distinct when there is no repetition. Because both the letters B and E repeat, you must account for them. Therefore, the number of distinct permutations is 6! (there are six letters in the word) divided by 2! for the two repeating Bs and 2! for the two repeating Es.

59. **The correct answer is B.** The slope-intercept form of the equation of a line is $y = mx + b$, where m is the slope and b is the y-intercept. Parallel lines have the same slope. Since line p has a slope of 3, line q must also have a slope of 3. Eliminate answer choices A and C because the slope is not 3. Now you need to determine the y-intercept. Line q intercepts the y-axis below the origin (0, 0), which means that the y-intercept must be negative. Eliminate answer choice E, which has a positive y-intercept. This leaves answer choices B and D. The distance between lines p and q is 3, as shown in the figure. If you draw a perpendicular line from the origin to line q, you will create a right triangle, with the y-axis as the hypotenuse. Since the hypotenuse is longer than either of the sides, which equal 3, the y-intercept of line q will be greater than 3, so answer choice B must be correct.

60. **The correct answer is F.** If 2 numbers, x and y, differ by 12, that means that $x - y = 12$. Multiplying the 2 numbers, $(x)(y)$, will yield the product. Solve the first

equation for x, then substitute the result for x in the second equation, as follows:

$$x - y = 12$$
$$x = y + 12$$

First equation

$$(y + 12)y \underline{\quad\quad}$$ Second equation

Since one of the answer choices must be the solution to that equation, plug in the answer choices, starting with the smallest value (–36) (note that the answer choices are in ascending order):

$$(y + 12)y = -36$$

$$(y + 12)y + 36 = 0$$

$$y^2 + 12y + 36 = 0$$

$$(y + 6)^2 = 0$$

$$y = -6$$

Now, substitute -6 for y in the first equation and solve for x:

$$x - (-6) = 12$$

$$x = 6$$

Both equations are satisfied, and –36 is the smallest value among the answer choices, so the smallest possible value for the product of 2 real numbers that differ by 12 is –36.

Reading Test Explanations

PASSAGE I

1. **The best answer is D.** Eui Thi's longing for Laos is triggered by the crowding of thousands of other refugees in Thailand. The vast number implies an uncomfortable chaos in the refugee camp. Answer choice D captures Eui Thi's feeling of distress. Furthermore, the paragraph emphasizes the continuing political instability and danger in Laos. The author reinforces that emphasis by putting the word *stability* in quotation marks to show she is using the term ironically.

2. **The best answer is J.** The previous paragraph ends with a description of Eui Thi's hopeful excitement at the idea of living in America and going to a new school. This emotion fades when she realizes the difficulties she will face. The word *enthusiasm* is the best replacement for *zeal* to capture her initial excitement.

3. **The best answer is D.** According to the passage, "Although Eui Thi was born in Laos, her family never truly belonged there." The final sentence of the passage shows that Eui Thi doesn't feel like she belongs in America either. These statements best support answer choice D.

4. **The best answer is F.** The description of Eui Thi's parents' "late-night whispers" is immediately followed by the military situation in Vietnam. The American army has left the Vietnamese capital, and her parents fear the influence of the communists. This information supports answer choice F.

5. **The best answer is B.** The passage states that Eui Thi's family was given a house in America. None of the other answer choices are stated in the passage as something Eui Thi's family received in America.

6. **The best answer is J.** The passage describes Eui Thi's hopes for life in America. She would not be an outsider, meaning she would feel like she belonged there. She would have room to run. And she would have enough to eat so she wouldn't be hungry all of the time. This covers Roman numerals I, II, and IV.

7. **The best answer is B.** According to the passage, "America was all Eui Thi had hoped it would be— and more." At this point, Eui Thi believes that her dreams have come true and that living in America will be a positive experience.

8. **The best answer is H.** The passage indicates that Eui Thi "did her best to dress and act like the other girls" and that she was able to "approximate … charms … hairstyles, and even, eventually, American slang." But, she "was from a different world," and would always be an outsider. This best supports answer choice H.

9. **The best answer is C.** The passage tells the reader that the dancing at Eui Thi's school dance is completely different from the Tai-Dam dancing she was used to. This supports answer choice C. The author doesn't describe the specific differences, which eliminates the other answer choices.

10. **The best answer is H.** In the passage, Eui Thi's sponsors walk her from her house to her new school. This information best matches answer choice H.

PASSAGE II

11. **The best answer is C.** Passage A describes the flexibility and plasticity of the American legal system, which makes answer choice C the best option.

12. **The best answer is G.** According to Passage A, "American law is an outward expression of the morals and values of the people; this flexibility gives judges the power to adapt the law to the needs and desires of the community. Many have praised the American judicial system because it embodies the idea that the law should do the will of the people." This information best supports answer choice G.

13. **The best answer is A.** The context of Passage A shows that the American legal system is flexible and, thereby, able to be altered.

14. **The best answer is G.** Because the passage states that the efficiency of Western European law "cuts down on the number of frivolous lawsuits," the author is indicating that such efficiency is a positive attribute of this type of legal system.

15. **The best answer is B.** According to Passage B, "It is useless for an individual to attempt a case if he knows in advance that the law is not in his favor." This information best supports answer choice B.

16. **The best answer is J.** The context of the last sentence in Passage B indicates that, due to the predictability of law in Western Europe, citizens are afforded greater protection under the law.

17. **The best answer is A.** Passage A suggests that, even though the flexibility of American law can be seen as beneficial, there is still a downside. Likewise, Passage B states that "the Western European format is far from perfect."

18. **The best answer is H.** Only answer choice H is a question that is addressed in both passages. The other answer choices are either beyond the scope of the passages, or only a tenet in one passage and not the other.

19. **The best answer is B.** Because both passages mention potential flaws in the legal systems, it is most likely that the authors would agree that no legal system will serve the needs of every citizen flawlessly.

20. The best answer is J. Each of the passages discusses a different kind of legal system found around the world. Therefore, answer choice J is the best option.

PASSAGE III

21. The best answer is B. Answer choice B captures the descriptive tone of the passage. The passage focuses on all aspects of Cassidy's career from its beginning to the present day.

22. The best answer is F. While the passage highlights the author's childhood interests, it does not discuss Shaun Cassidy's childhood. However, his singing career, acting career, and television writing career are described respectively in the first, second, and third parts of the passage. This supports answer choice F.

23. The best answer is D. The last paragraph discusses Shaun Cassidy's realization that he enjoyed writing, and now primarily spends his time writing and producing, as opposed to acting, which he did when he was younger.

24. The best answer is G. According to the last paragraph, Cassidy "realized that writing provided a tremendous outlet for his creativity," and he "spends most of his time now as a creator and executive producer of television shows for several networks." These details best support answer choice G.

25. The best answer is A. Paragraph 4 describes the author's infatuation with Shaun Cassidy when she was young. Most of her description involves his physical attractiveness. This supports answer choice A.

26. The best answer is H. The sentence states that most teen pop stars have short careers. This supports answer choice H.

27. The best answer is D. Option I is covered in lines 31–32 (where the author's crush is described as "long since passed," or chronologically prior). Option II is covered in lines 34–36, while option III is covered in lines 1–4. So these events happen in the order III, I, II, or answer choice D.

28. The best answer is J. The passage describes the author's immediate reaction to reading about Cassidy for the first time. Her enthusiasm and adolescent crush support answer choice J.

29. The best answer is A. Although the passage mentions that Cassidy had occasional questions for the camera crew, it does not indicate that operating a camera was one of Cassidy's achievements.

30. The best answer is G. The passage states that the author followed Shaun Cassidy's career and "learned of each of his accomplishments." According to the passage, Shaun Cassidy was both curious about and fascinated with "the production end of the entertainment industry." These details and the positive tone of the passage support answer choice G.

PASSAGE IV

31. The best answer is D. The passage tells the reader that our species, *Homo sapiens sapiens*, is not related to *Homo neanderthalensis*. While the last paragraph states that human beings were better able to compete for scarce resources, this does not imply that they actively killed off the Neanderthals. Therefore, the passage supports answer choice D.

32. The best answer is G. The passage tells the reader that the Neanderthals needed more food to survive in colder weather.

33. The best answer is A. The passage states that humans share few genes at all with Neanderthals. This evidence supports the conclusion that Neanderthals are extinct and did not pass on their genetic heritage. Therefore, A is the best answer choice.

34. The best answer is G. The passage indicates that Neanderthals "were an evolutionary dead end," and that they became extinct thousands of years ago.

35. The best answer is A. The passage lists data from radiometric dating (answer choice B), sediment cores (answer choice C), and climate models (answer choice D). Comparative femur measurements is the only one NOT mentioned; therefore, A is the best answer.

36. The best answer is G. The passage states that the last evidence of Neanderthals is from about 30,000 years ago.

37. The best answer is D. The context indicates the types of innovations that helped humans survive the ice age. The wide range, from clothing to weaponry, supports answer choice D.

38. The best answer is H. Although the passage mentions nets, the passage doesn't specify the type. All of the other answer choices are specifically mentioned in the passage.

39. The best answer is B. Cro-Magnons are defined as an early example of modern humans. While the last paragraph states that human beings were better able to compete for scarce resources, this does not imply that they actively killed off the Neanderthals. Therefore, the best answer is B.

40. The best answer is F. According to the passage, "Neanderthals lacked the innovation skills necessary to survive in a changing world." The other answer choices are contradicted in the passage.

Science Test Explanations

PASSAGE I

1. **The correct answer is C.** The results of Experiment 2 are shown in Table 2. While all of the plants grew during each time period, the amount of growth declined after week 6. Therefore, the time frame during which all of the plants began to experience a decline in growth rate was the 6–9 week period, answer choice C.

2. **The best answer is G.** According to the passage, *indigenous* means "native." Therefore, the insect that is NOT native to the region is the dragonfly.

3. **The correct answer is C.** The results of Experiments 1 and 2 are shown in Tables 1 and 2. If you look at the total growth for weeks 6–9, you will see that Yaupon experienced the most growth during weeks 6–9 in both studies.

4. **The correct answer is F.** Based on the results of the experiments, all of the plants experienced the least amount of growth during the time that foreign insects were present in the greenhouse. Table 3 indicates that the mosquito, the grasshopper, and the aphid are all indigenous, or native, insects. Therefore, the mantid, a foreign insect, would have the greatest effect on limiting plant growth.

5. **The correct answer is B.** The results of Experiment 1 show that all of the plants experienced more growth when native insects were present. Therefore, based on these results, you can conclude that, under some circumstances, native insects can help to increase growth in some plants, answer choice B.

PASSAGE II

6. **The correct answer is F.** According to Scientist 2, predictive measures can be developed "once enough information has been derived from past hurricanes." This suggests that Scientist 2 believes that present-day predictive tools are not based on enough past data to be accurate, answer choice F.

7. **The correct answer is A.** Scientist 1 claims, "Animals are sometimes seen exhibiting strange behavior as far ahead as weeks before the hurricane makes landfall." An article stating that animal behavior is useful in predicting hurricanes would support the views of Scientist 1. Scientist 2 does not make any mention of animals, and therefore, this article would not support Scientist 2's view.

8. **The correct answer is J.** According to the passage, Scientist 1 believes that hurricanes making their way across the ocean cause ground vibrations. These vibrations can be detected by seismographs. It makes sense that, if seismic activity has been recorded, Scientist 1 would agree that a hurricane could be moving across the ocean, answer choice J.

9. **The correct answer is A.** Since both scientists agree that historical data is a useful and accurate predictor of hurricanes, it makes sense that both scientists' viewpoints would be supported by the fact that historical hurricane data has recently been used to predict the path of a hurricane. The other answer choices may support one viewpoint or the other, but not both.

10. **The correct answer is F.** Scientist 2 believes that past hurricane data is an accurate way to predict when and where a hurricane will occur. Therefore, comparing current data with past data would be a good way to test whether Scientist 2's claims are realistic. The other answer choices are not supported by the discussion of Scientist 2.

11. **The correct answer is A.** According to the passage, Scientist 1 believes that certain events, such as shifts in wind direction and wind speed, can be used to predict hurricanes. Because tropical storms are often accompanied by increased winds and later classified as hurricanes, Scientist 1's viewpoint is strengthened.

12. **The correct answer is J.** Scientist 1 believes that an increase in tidal volume signals the arrival of a hurricane. Scientist 2 believes that tidal volume can increase for other reasons, so an increase in tidal volume is not a good predictor of hurricanes. According to Scientist 2, then, one major flaw in Scientist 1's viewpoint is the assumption that tidal volume increases only before or during hurricanes, answer choice J.

PASSAGE III

13. **The correct answer is C.** To answer this question, look at Figure 2. Find 65 meters on the *x*-axis, which is depth, and follow it up until you reach the line. Follow that point on the line over to the left until you reach the *y*-axis, which is pressure. The point on the *y*-axis is 6.0 atm, which means that at a depth of 65 meters below the surface, the pressure is 6.0 atm, answer choice C.

14. **The correct answer is F.** The passage states the volume of gas in your lungs is inversely related to the pressure. As a diver moves closer to the surface, the pressure on the air spaces in the body is decreased, meaning that the space inside the lungs increases. Since the volume of a gas, like air, is dependent on the space that contains it, then the volume of air inside the lungs will increase when the space inside the lungs increases, answer choice F.

15. **The correct answer is A.** According to the question, gases have a higher compressibility *because* of their lower densities. The second paragraph of the passage states that gases have low density and high compressibility, whereas solids have high density and low compressibility.

16. **The correct answer is H.** Compressibility is the ability of pressure to alter the volume of matter. Answer H is the only choice that could be a hazard of scuba diving. The remaining answer choices are all false based on the information given in the passage.

17. **The correct answer is D.** According to the passage, portions of the line where large changes in pressure result in only minimal changes in volume signify low compressibility. Therefore, when the change in pressure is greater than the change in volume, compressibility is low, answer choice D.

PASSAGE IV

18. **The correct answer is J.** The *y*-axis indicates the percent of salamanders that survive to adulthood. To determine which species of salamanders is most likely to survive to adulthood, find the tallest bar on the graph—the one that is closest to 100%. Species G is most likely to survive to adulthood, answer choice J.

19. **The correct answer is B.** According to Figure 1, the light-gray bars represent the percent that survive to adulthood when acid rain is present, and the dark-gray bars represent the percent that survive to adulthood when acid rain is not present. To answer the question, find the species that has the biggest difference between the height of the light-gray bar and the dark-gray bar. Species B shows a difference of about 20 percentage points; Species C shows a difference of about 30 percentage points; Species E shows a difference of about 20 percentage points. Species G shows a difference of about 10 percentage points. Therefore, the species with the greatest difference is Species C, answer choice B.

20. **The correct answer is H.** Because both salamanders and frogs are amphibians that live in similar environments and share many features, it makes sense for the researchers to observe frogs.

21. **The correct answer is B.** Information in Table 1 shows that high levels of exposure to acid rain correspond with low relative ability to avoid skin damage. This supports answer choice B.

22. **The correct answer is J.** The first step in answering this question is to look at Figure 1 and notice that Species A has the lowest percentage of survival to adulthood. Next, look at Table 1 and see that Species A does not seek protection, answer choice J.

PASSAGE V

23. **The correct answer is A.** To answer this question, locate 13 km on the "Distance along mountain range" horizontal axis of Figure 1. Then, look at the peak section composition. According to this information, at 13 km along the mountain range, the peak is composed of both igneous rock and limestone, answer choice A.

24. **The correct answer is G.** To answer this question, locate 20 meters on the "peak height" axis of Figure 1. Then, notice that, wherever the peak height is 20 meters, the net change in SCLL is somewhere between –10 and –30, answer choice G.

25. **The correct answer is C.** The data in Table 1 shows that for every increase of 5 meters in height, exposure to snow melt erosion is increased by about 8%. This means that at a height of 40–45 meters, the peak would be exposed about 8% more during the year than if it had a height of 35–40 meters. Based on Table 1, at 35–40 meters, the peak is exposed about 70% of the year. So, at 40–45 meters, it would be exposed approximately 78% of the year, answer choice C.

26. **The correct answer is J.** Figure 1 shows a direct relationship between net SCLL and peak height. At lower heights, the net SCLL is lower; at greater heights, the net SCLL is higher. This information supports answer choice J.

27. **The correct answer is A.** Table 1 shows a direct relationship between the peak section height and the percentage of the year that the peak is exposed to snow melt erosion. As the height goes up, the exposure time goes up. The graph in answer choice A represents this direct relationship.

PASSAGE VI

28. **The correct answer is G.** The results of Experiment 1 are shown in Table 1. Based on the data in Table 1, as pH levels increase, defecation output also increases, answer choice G. Take care with tables and trends. In this case, the data are arranged by rat number, not defecation output or pH level.

29. **The correct answer is A.** According to information in the passage, the rats in Experiment 2 were given a dose of gut flora (microbes) 1 hour into the experiment. No such dose was administered to the rats in Experiment 1. Normal diets were followed by rats in both experiments, so answer choice B can be eliminated. Answer choices C and D contain information that contradicts information given in the passage, so they should be eliminated.

30. **The correct answer is G.** The results of Experiment 2 are shown in Table 2. While you don't know what the pH levels were at the start of the experiment, you can see that the levels were higher after 5 hours than they were after 1 hour. Therefore, based on the results of Experiment 2, you can say that, if all gut flora are eliminated (as was done at the start of the experiment) and then reintroduced (as was done 1 hour into the experiment), the pH level will increase over time, answer choice G.

31. **The correct answer is D.** According to Table 1, Rat 5 had a pH level of 6.5 at 5 hours. This is the same pH level that Rat 11 had at 1 hour, before the gut flora were reintroduced. If Rat 5 were administered the gut flora after 1 hour, it is likely that its pH level would be the same as Rat 11's pH level at 5 hours. Table 2 shows that this level was 8.0, answer choice D.

32. **The correct answer is H.** Table 1 shows defecation output, as measured by number of pellets. The rat with the highest defecation output was Rat 8, which had a defecation output level of 12.

33. **The correct answer is C.** The passage states that, "the higher the defecation output, the healthier the digestive tract." Table 1 shows that rats with a higher defecation output also had pH levels around 8.0 to 8.5. Table 2 shows that after bacteria were reintroduced to the digestive tract, the pH levels increased to around 7.5 to 8.5. These results support the conclusion that bacteria are necessary to the normal functioning of a healthy digestive tract, answer choice C.

PASSAGE VII

34. **The correct answer is G.** The results of Study 3 are shown in Table 3. Look at each answer choice and calculate the differences in Total Time:

   (1) Trial 1, Tennis ball and Golf ball: 0 seconds

   (2) Trial 2, Tennis ball and Feather: 5 seconds

   (3) Trial 2, Golf ball and Paper: 2 seconds

   (4) Trial 3, Tennis ball and Feather: 3 seconds

   The objects which differed most in Total Time were the tennis ball and feather during Trial 2, answer choice G.

35. **The correct answer is A.** Based on the passage, the only difference between Study 2 and Study 3 was the direction that the wind was blowing. This would affect the fall times.

36. **The correct answer is F.** Common sense tells you that dropping an object from a lower height would most likely result in a shorter fall time. Since the objects were dropped from a height of 20 feet, dropping them from a height of 10 feet would most likely produce shorter fall times for all of the objects, answer choice F.

37. **The correct answer is B.** Greater wind resistance is likely to lead to greater fall times. According to data in Table 2, paper consistently took the longest to fall, and therefore, registered the greatest fall times. It is most likely, then, that paper consistently exhibited the most wind resistance.

38. **The correct answer is F.** Since during Study 2 the fan was blowing up at a constant rate, and the paper took longer than the feather to fall, it makes sense that the paper was affected more by the wind from the fan (had greater wind resistance).

39. **The correct answer is C.** In both Study 1 and Study 3, the feather had the longest fall times compared to all other objects. Even though in Study 2 the paper had slightly longer fall times than the feather, overall, the feather took longer to fall over the course of all three studies.

40. **The correct answer is G.** Because there is no measurable resistance of any kind acting on the objects, they will fall at a nearly identical rate. In a vacuum, any object—from a mouse to an elephant—will fall at exactly the same rate.

PART III

Strategies and Review

CHAPTER 2

Strategies to Get Your Best Score

CHAPTER 3

ACT English Test: Strategies and Concept Review

CHAPTER 4

ACT Mathematics Test: Strategies and Concept Review

CHAPTER 5

ACT Reading Test: Strategies and Concept Review

CHAPTER 6

ACT Science Test: Strategies and Concept Review

CHAPTER 7

ACT Writing Test: Strategies and Review

Strategies to Get Your Best Score

Now that you have assessed your strengths and weaknesses, it is time to take a look at some general test-taking strategies that should help you approach the ACT with confidence. We will start by discussing the importance of acquiring the skills necessary to maximize your ACT scores and finish with some tips on how to handle stress before, during, and after the tests. Additional chapters in the book include strategies and techniques specific to each of the ACT sections.

Sometimes, when you look back over a practice test that you took, you can tell right away why you got a particular question wrong. Many students call these errors "stupid mistakes." We suggest that you refer to these errors as "concentration errors." Everyone makes them from time to time, and you should not get overly upset or concerned when they occur. Learn from your mistakes and train yourself to do better by using the techniques in this book. You should note the difference between those concentration errors and any questions that you get wrong because of a lack of understanding or holes in your knowledge base. It is worth reading the explanations for any of the questions that were difficult for you, even if you got them right. Sometimes, students get questions correct for the wrong reasons, or because they simply guessed correctly. While you are practicing, you should mark any questions that you want to recheck and be sure to read the explanations for those questions. In this new edition, we've included expanded explanations for questions that are particularly good examples of certain common question types.

THE PSYCHOLOGY OF TESTING

Cognitive psychologists, the ones who study learning and thinking, use the letters KSA to refer to the basic components of human performance in any activity, from academics to athletics and music to video games. The letters stand for Knowledge, Skills, and Abilities. The ACT measures certain predictable areas of knowledge, and it measures a specific set of skills. You probably already understand this since you are reading this book. In fact, thousands and thousands of students have successfully raised their ACT scores through study and practice. While this book cannot replace four years of high school learning, it can help you acquire the skills necessary for top performance on the ACT.

Steve Says:

Practice enough to recognize "gaps" in your knowledge and internalize important skills.

There is a difference between the way that humans learn knowledge and the way we acquire skills. Knowledge can be learned fairly quickly and is fairly durable, even under stress.

Skills, on the other hand, require repetition in order to perfect. There is an old joke about a tourist in New York City who jumps into the back of a taxicab and asks the driver if he knows how to get to Carnegie Hall. The driver says, "Sure. Practice! Practice! Practice!"

The cabbie's answer was, of course, meant to be humorous. But he was basically correct. Psychologists speak of something called a "perfectly internalized skill," which means that the skill is executed automatically, without any conscious thought.

In our training classes, we often use the example of tying your shoes. If you tied your shoes this morning, it is highly unlikely that you can remember the exact moment of tying them, unless something significant occurred, such as a broken shoelace. The reason that you probably cannot remember actually doing the tying is that, as an adult shoe-tier, you have, by now, perfectly internalized the skill of shoe tying through thousands and thousands of repetitions.

Ideally, you will internalize your response to the various question formats on the ACT so that you do not have to spend time and energy devising plans during the exam. You will just dig right in and be well into your work on each section while some of your less-prepared classmates are still reading the directions and trying to figure out what exactly they are supposed to be doing.

We have included many practice exams in this book for a reason. We want you to do sufficient practice to develop good test-taking skills and, specifically, good ACT-taking skills. As you practice, you should distinguish between practice that is meant to serve as a learning experience and practice that is meant to be a realistic "dress-rehearsal" for your actual ACT.

During practice that is meant to be a learning experience, it is okay to "cheat." You should feel free to turn off the timer and just think about how the questions are put together, stop to look up information in schoolbooks or on the Internet, and examine the explanations in the back of the book. It is even okay to talk to someone about what you are working on during your "learning practice."

However, you need to do some "dry runs," or "dress-rehearsal" practice, too. This is the stage where you time yourself strictly and make sure that you control as many variables as possible in your environment. Some research shows that you will have an easier time repeating your acquired skills and retrieving information from the storage part of your brain if the environment in which you are testing is similar to the environment where you learned the information or acquired the skill. This means getting out of your home and doing your practice tests in an environment that is more like a testing center, such as a library.

So, you learn factual information by studying, and you acquire skills through practice. Of course, there is some overlap between these activities, and it is hoped that you will do some learning while you practice, and vice-versa. In fact, research shows that repetition is important for both information storage and skills acquisition.

Nevertheless, there is a huge difference between knowledge and skills: *Knowing* about a skill, even understanding the skill, is not the same as actually *having* that skill. For example, you may be told all about a skill such as driving a car with a manual (stick-shift) transmission, or playing the piano, or typing on a computer keyboard. You could have the best teacher in the world, possess spectacular learning tools, and pay attention very carefully so that you take in all of the information that is imparted. You might *understand* everything perfectly, but the first few times that you actually attempt the skill, you will probably execute that skill less than perfectly. In fact, the odds are that you will experience some frustration at that point because of the lag between your *understanding* of the skill and your actual ability to *perform* the skill.

Perfecting skills takes practice. You need to do repetitions to "wear in" the pathways in your brain that control each skill. So don't be satisfied with merely reading through this book and saying to yourself, "I get it." You will not reach your full ACT potential unless you put in sufficient time practicing, as well as understanding and learning.

Ideally, you will have several weeks between now and test day. If so, you can use the Training Schedule at the beginning of this book to schedule your preparation. If not, you should use the "ACT Emergency Plan."

Later in this book, we'll go into great detail about the facts that make up the "knowledge base" that is essential for ACT success. First: skills and strategies.

STRATEGIC THINKING

Amy Says:

Do most of your practice under timed conditions so that you can train yourself to relax and learn how to pace yourself.

In college, you are likely to experience stress from things such as family expectations, fatigue, fear of failure, a heavy workload, increased competition, and difficult material. The ACT tries to mimic this stress. The psychometricians (specialized psychologists who study the measurement of various aspects of the mind) who help design standardized tests use what they call "artificial stressors" to help determine how you will respond to that test.

The main stressor that the test-makers use is the time limit. The time limits are set up on the ACT so that most students cannot finish all of the questions in the time allowed.

Another stressor is the element of surprise. If you have practiced sufficiently, there will be few surprises on test day. The ACT is a very predictable exam. In fact, the chart in Chapter 1 tells you how many questions of each type there are.

RELAX TO SUCCEED

One of the worst things that can happen to a test-taker is to panic before or during an exam. Research has shown that there are very predictable and specific results when a person panics for any reason. To panic is to have a set of recognizable symptoms. These symptoms include sweating, shortness of breath, muscle tension, increased heart rate, tunnel vision, nausea, lightheadedness, and even, in extreme cases, loss of consciousness.

These symptoms are the result of chemical changes in the brain that are brought on by some stress stimulus. Interestingly, the stimulus does not have to be external. This means that we can panic ourselves simply by thinking about certain things in certain ways. One common way this occurs is to engage in "what if?" thinking such as: "What if I do badly?" "What if I forget what I've learned?" etc.

In your brain, the stress chemical *epinephrine*, which is more commonly known as *adrenaline*, brings about the symptoms. Adrenaline actually shifts the priorities in your brain. It diverts blood and electrical energy away from some parts of the brain in favor of others. Specifically, it moves the center of your brain activity to the areas that control your body and away from the parts of your brain that are involved in complex thinking.

The set of physical and emotional responses that result from adrenaline's impact on the brain is known as the "fight-or-flight response." It means that you become temporarily more ready to confront physical threats. The side effect of this change is that you are also temporarily less able to think clearly. So, panic makes a person stronger and faster—and also less able to perform the higher-level type of thinking that is rewarded on an ACT exam.

Adrenaline can be useful and even pleasurable in some situations. In fact, it is not a bad thing to have a small amount of adrenaline in your bloodstream while testing due to a healthy amount of excitement about the exam, as it can help sharpen the senses.

The worst case involving adrenaline is often referred to as the "panic spiral," which is basically freaking out because of freaking out. An "overdose" of adrenaline can seriously hurt your chances of scoring well on an exam.

Two of the most important stimuli for the release of adrenaline into the bloodstream are suspense and surprise. This fact is well known to those who design haunted houses and horror movies. Suspense involves the stress that is present during the anticipation phase before an event that involves unknowns. Surprise occurs when you experience something unexpected that you aren't prepared for.

You can control both suspense and surprise by minimizing the unknown factors. The biggest stress-inducing questions involving the ACT are: What do the ACT writers expect of me? Am I prepared? How will I respond to the ACT on test day? If you spend some time and effort answering these questions by studying and practicing under realistic conditions before test day, you'll have a much better chance of controlling your adrenaline levels and handling the exam with no panic.

The psychometricians and other experts who work on the design of ACT exams use "artificial stressors." In other words, they are actually trying to create a certain level of stress in the test-taker. They are doing this because the ACT is supposed to tell college admissions professionals something about how you will respond to the stress of college exams.

The time limit is usually the biggest stressor for test-takers. The first thing to consider is whether you will even attempt all of the questions on each section. On the ACT, a score of 75% correct is considered significantly above average. In fact, if you can get 75% of the questions correct across the board, you'll get about a 27 composite score, which would put you in the top 10% of all scores nationwide. You should do enough practice testing before the big day so that you will know whether you will even attempt all of the questions in each section.

Steve Says:

The goals of your preparation should be to learn about the test, acquire the knowledge and skills that are being measured by the test, and learn about yourself and how you respond to the different aspects of the test.

You should also consider which question types you will attempt and on which ones you will guess. You need to be familiar with the subject matter that is tested on each section of your test. At the beginning of your training period, first work on filling any gaps in your knowledge base. If you know for a fact that a certain topic, like trigonometry, is consistently tested with only a few questions, you may decide to focus your study and practice elsewhere. As you work through this book, you should make a realistic assessment of the best use of your time and energy so that you are concentrating on the areas that will yield the highest score that you can achieve in the amount of time that you have remaining until the exam. This will result in a feeling of confidence on test day, even when you are facing very challenging questions.

Pre-ACT

- **Be prepared.** The old Scout Motto has been repeated for generations for a good reason: It works. The more prepared you feel, the less likely you are to be stressed on test day. Study and practice consistently during your training period. Be organized. Have your supplies and wardrobe ready in advance. Make a practice trip to the test center before your test day.

- **Know yourself.** This means knowing your strengths and weaknesses on the ACT as well as the ways that help you to relax. You will learn about yourself through practice.

- **Get enough rest.** In *Macbeth*, Shakespeare described sleep as the thing that "knits up the ravel'd sleave of care," meaning that the better rested you are, the better things seem. As you get fatigued, you are more likely to look on the dark side of things and worry more. Modern science has confirmed that Shakespeare was correct. Your brain works much better when it is rested. Other research shows that most American teens do not get enough sleep for a variety of reasons. Do what you can to get solid sleep at least two nights before the big day.

- **Eat well.** Excess sugar is bad for stress and for brain function in general. Pouring tons of refined sugar into your system creates biological stress that has an impact on your brain chemistry. Add in some caffeine, as many soda manufacturers do, and you are only magnifying the problem. If you are actually addicted to caffeine, then get your normal dosage.

- **Listen to music.** You cannot listen to music during your ACT exam, so do not listen to it during your practice tests. However, listening to and playing music can be very helpful for pre-test relaxation. Some types of music increase measured brain stress and interfere with clear thinking. Specifically, some rock, hip-hop, and dance rhythms, while great for certain occasions, can have detrimental effects on certain types of brain waves. Other music seems to help to organize brain waves and create a relaxed state that is conducive to learning and skills acquisition.

- **Turn off the screens.** The blue light that comes off of most screens can change your brain chemistry, making it hard to sleep and altering other functions. The ACT is a paper-and-pencil test. It is not taken on a screen. So, any prep done on a screen is definitely second-best. Using paper, pencil, and calculator is the best way to prepare. Remember that, beginning with the September 2020 administration, the ACT will be offered electronically. If you are planning to take advantage of this format, at least some of your practice should be online. Visit www.act.org for more information.

During the ACT

- **Breathe.** When humans get stressed, our breathing tends to get quick and shallow. If you feel yourself tensing up, slow down and take deeper breaths. This will relax you and probably get more oxygen to your brain so that you can think more clearly.

- **Take breaks.** You cannot stay focused intently on your ACT for the entire time that you are in the testing center. You are bound to have distracting thoughts pop into your head or times when you simply cannot process the information at which you are looking. These occurrences are normal. What you should do is close your eyes, clear your mind, and then dig back into the test. This procedure can be accomplished in less than a minute. You could pray, meditate, or simply picture a place or person that helps you to relax. Try visualizing something fun that you have planned for right after your ACT. It is good to have something to look forward to.

- **Stay calm.** Taking an important exam can certainly lead to stress. As part of the process of preparing thousands of students for standardized entrance exams, we have seen a variety of stress reactions. These reactions range from a mild form of nervousness to extreme anxiety that has led to vomiting and fainting in a few cases. Most students deal fairly well with the stress of taking a test. Some students could even be said to be too relaxed in that they don't take the test seriously enough.

- **Have a plan of attack.** The directions printed in this book (both in the chapters and on the Practice Tests) are very similar to the directions that you will find on your ACT. You need to know how you are going to move through each portion of the exam. No time is available to formulate a plan of attack on test day. In fact, you should do enough practice so that you have internalized the skills necessary to do your best on each section without having to stop and think about what to do next.

GETTING READY TO TAKE THE TEST

- **Do some reconnaissance.** Make sure that you know how long it will take to drive to the testing center and where you will park if you are driving yourself. If you are testing in a place that is new to you, try to get into the building between now and test day so that you can get used to the sounds and smells, know where the bathrooms are, and so on.
- **Rest.** You'll need to get some sleep the night before the big day. We recommend exercise the day before so that you can get some good, quality sleep. Research has shown that there is really no such thing as getting too much sleep. So, don't be afraid to go to bed early the night before the test.
- **Wake up early.** Set an alarm and have someone on wake-up duty—either a family member in your house or someone who can call you on the telephone as a back-up plan in case your alarm doesn't go off. You should be at the testing center before 8:00 A.M.
- **Dress comfortably.** Loose, comfortable, layered clothing is best. That way, you can adjust to the temperature of the room. Don't forget your watch. The proctor will give you a five-minute warning near the end of each section, but that is all the timing help you can count on. There may not even be a clock in your testing room.
- **Eat something.** It is a good idea to eat something low in sugar or high in protein on the morning of your test. Get your normal dose of caffeine, if any. This is not the time to experiment.
- **Bring stuff.** You will need your driver's license (or passport), your admission ticket, number 2 pencils, a good eraser or two, and your calculator. You can check the ACT website for up-to-date information regarding which calculators are acceptable. Bring your glasses or contact lenses if you need them. You can bring a snack for the break, but you won't be able to eat or drink while the ACT is in progress.
- **Read something.** "Warm up" your brain by reading a newspaper or something similar so that the ACT isn't the first thing that you read on test day. Review the Top 50 Strategies in the front of this book.

TAKING THE TEST

- **Do the easy stuff first.** Get familiar with the format of each section of the ACT so that you can recognize passages and questions that are likely to give you trouble. Go around those trouble spots rather than through them. It is a much better use of your time and energy to pick up all of the correct answers that you can early on, and then go back and work on the tougher questions that you actually have a legitimate shot at answering correctly. Remember, you don't have to get all of the questions right in order to get a great score on the ACT.

  Although all of the questions on an ACT test are weighted exactly equally to one another, some of the questions are harder than others. Do not be stubborn while there are still other, probably less difficult questions remaining. We often tell students that they should picture their ACT test booklets sitting in a stack in a locked closet somewhere. Your book is there, waiting patiently for you. Within it are some questions that you are probably going to get wrong on test day. So, when you see them, don't be surprised. Just recognize them and work on the easier material first. If time permits, you can always come back and work on the challenging problems in the final minutes before the proctor calls, "Time!"

  This strategy is both a time management and a stress reduction strategy. The idea is to make three or four passes through the test section, always being sure to work on the easiest of whatever material remains.

- **Manage the answer grid.** Avoid the common mistake of marking the answer to each question on your answer document as you finish the question. In other words, you should *not* go to your "bubble sheet" after each question. This is dangerous and wastes time. It is dangerous because you run an increased risk of marking your answer grid incorrectly and perhaps not catching your error until much later. It wastes time because you have to find your place on the answer sheet and then find your place back in the test booklet. The amount of time that is spent marking each question is not great, but it adds up over the course of an entire test section and could cost you the opportunity to get a few more questions done correctly.

  Instead, you should mark your answers in the test booklet and transfer your answers from the test booklet to the answer sheet in groups. Doing this after each passage on English, Reading, and Science is an obvious idea and has the added benefit of helping you to clear your head between passages. This will make it easier to concentrate on the passage at hand rather than possibly still processing memories of the previous passage. On the Mathematics Test, you should fill in some "bubbles" on your answer sheet every two pages or so. On any of the sections, filling in bubbles can be a good activity to keep you busy when you simply need a break to clear your head.

  You are only allowed to work on one section at a time. This includes marking answers on the bubble sheet. So, keep an eye on your time and make sure that you've fully filled in answers for all the questions on the answer sheet before time is up, even if some of them are guesses.

- **Use the test booklet.** An ACT test booklet is meant to be used by one test taker only. Except for the writing test, if you take it, you will not have any scratch paper on test day. You are expected to do all note-taking and figuring on the booklet itself.

- **Be aware of time.** You really don't want it to be a surprise when the proctor yells "Time!" on test day. Therefore, you are going to want to time yourself on test day. You should time yourself during at least some of your practice exams so that you get used to the process and your timepiece. We suggest that you use an analog (dial face) watch. They generally are not set up to give off any annoying beeps that could get you in trouble with your fellow test-takers and your proctor on test day. If you want to avoid the subtracting that comes along with checking the board at the front of the testing room for the time that the proctor wrote down as start and stop times (who wants to do *more* math on ACT day?), you can turn the hands on your watch back from noon (12 o'clock) to allow enough time for the section that you are working on. For instance, if you are working on an ACT Mathematics section, which is 60 minutes long, you can turn your watch back to 11:00 and set it on the desk in front of you. You will be finished when your watch points to 12:00. Similarly, if you are working on a Science section or a Reading section, which is 35 minutes long, set your watch to 11:25 and, again, you will be done at noon. This method has the added benefit of helping you to forget about the outside world while you are testing.

  All that matters during the test is your test. All of life's other issues will have to be dealt with after your test is finished. You might find this mind-set easier to attain if you lose track of what time it is in the "outside world."

- **Don't second-guess yourself.** Most test takers should not change answers once they've made a decision. Their first choices are more likely to be correct. A few people tend to improve their scores when they do correct themselves. You need to find out whether you are an answer changer or not. In other words, if you change an answer, are you more likely to change it *to* the correct answer or *from* the correct answer? You can only learn this fact about yourself by doing practice exams and paying attention to your tendencies.

GUESSING ON THE TEST

Because there is no added scoring penalty for incorrect answers on the ACT, you should never leave a bubble blank on your answer sheet. We counted all of the correct answers on three recent, released ACT exams. We found that the distribution of answers by position on the answer sheet was almost exactly even. This means that there is no position that is more likely to be correct than any other. We use the term "position" when referring to the answer sheet because the letter assigned to the positions change depending on whether you are working on an odd or even question. The odd-numbered questions have answer choices labeled A through D (or A through E on the Mathematics Test), and the even-numbered questions have answer choices that are labeled F through J (or F through K on the Mathematics Test). This system allows you to stay on track on your answer sheet.

Since the answers are distributed fairly evenly across the positions, you should always guess the same position if you are guessing at random. Of course, if you can eliminate a choice or two, or if you have a hunch, then this advice doesn't apply.

Note: Some students worry if they notice long strings of same-position answers on their answer sheets. This arrangement does not necessarily indicate a problem. In analyzing actual, released ACT exams, we counted strings of up to six questions long, whose correct answers were in the same position on the answer sheet.

AFTER THE TEST

Most students find it easier to concentrate on their ACT preparation and on test day if they have a plan for fun right after the test. You should plan something that you can look forward to as a reward to yourself for all of the hard work and effort that you'll be putting into the test. Then, when the going gets tough, you can say to yourself, "If I push through and do my work now, I'll have so much fun right after the exam."

CHAPTER 3

ACT English Test: Strategies and Concept Review

The ACT English Test is designed to measure your ability to understand and interpret the ACT's version of Standard Written English. As you are probably aware, English is a complex language with many variations. Major publications maintain "style sheets" for their employees to use so that they stay consistent over time and between writers. There is no ACT style sheet. But we've looked at every released exam we could for the past 25 years, and we have included in this book the rules that are rewarded by the ACT. Note that there here may be a few differences from the rules that have been taught to you.

Each ACT English Test includes 5 passages with 15 questions each, for a total of 75 multiple-choice questions. The passages cover a variety of subjects, ranging from historical discussions to personal narratives. The questions are divided into three main categories: Conventions of Standard English, Production of Writing, and Knowledge of Language. Conventions of Standard English questions primarily test your basic English usage and grammar skills, while Production of Writing and Knowledge of Language questions test your ability to express an idea clearly and concisely. In this chapter, we'll give you useful strategies and techniques, an overview of the rules of grammar and punctuation that will be tested, as well as a breakdown of the writing skills tested. (You will find all of this information useful on the optional Writing Test also.) At the end of the chapter, you will find some sample practice questions and explanations.

GENERAL STRATEGIES AND TECHNIQUES

Use the following general strategies when tackling the ACT English Test.

Listen to Your Brain

This technique is known as "subvocalization" to psychologists. It means to turn on your internal narrator and "read aloud silently." You can usually trust your ears when answering many of the questions on the English Test. In other words, if it sounds right to you, it probably is. You will recognize when and how to apply basic rules of grammar, even if you don't recall what the specific rule is. You can tap into the part of your brain that controls language processing as you read. That part of your brain "knows" how English is supposed to sound. Let that part of your brain work for you. Remember, the ACT English Test does NOT require you to state a specific rule, only to apply it correctly.

Consider the following example:

> Instead of studying for the exam. The students went to
>
> a movie.
>
> 1

When you read this sentence to yourself, your brain is most likely going to recognize that the first sentence is a fragment. You will probably automatically combine both sentences. On the ACT, look for the answer choice that replaces the period with a comma.

Avoid Redundancy

On the ACT English Test, wordiness and redundancy are never rewarded. Throughout the test, you will be asked to make choices that best express an idea. Usually, the fewer words that you use, the better. Be wary of words that have the same meaning being used in the same sentence. For example, it is not necessary to say "the tiny, little girl smiled at me." Both *tiny* and *little* have the same meaning, so using one or the other is sufficient.

Consider the following example:

> Canadian currency usually looks and appears very
>
> different from its American counterpart.
>
> 2

Because "looks" and "appears" mean the same thing, you can simply pick one of them to make the sentence better.

Take DELETE and NO CHANGE Seriously

You will sometimes see the answer choice "DELETE the underlined portion." Selecting this option will remove the underlined portion from the sentence or paragraph. "DELETE" is a viable answer choice when it eliminates redundant or irrelevant statements. When "DELETE" is given as an answer choice on the ACT, it is correct more than half of the time.

Consider the following example:

> It is important to be cautious and carefully plan your
>
> class schedule each semester.³

While this sentence is grammatically correct, it contains redundancy. The underlined portion is not necessary to the sentence; in fact, the sentence is much more concise and logical without the underlined portion. When DELETE is offered as an answer choice, ask yourself whether or not the underlined portion is relevant and necessary to the general structure of the sentence. If it is not, DELETE may be your best choice.

On the ACT English Test, the first answer choice for almost every question is NO CHANGE. This answer choice should come up about as often as the others do on your answer sheet. Just because a portion of the passage is underlined doesn't mean that there is something wrong with it.

Consider the following example:

> The old man often fished the river that flowed past his
>
> cabin door.⁴

This sentence does not require any changes. On the ACT, the answer choices to a question like this might include a different word, such as the past-form verb *passed*. Your job is to consider grammar, context, and word choice when selecting the best answer and recognize when the sentence is best as written.

Steve Says:

Since there can only be one correct answer for each question, you can eliminate any two choices that mean the same as each other. If you find that two of the choices are synonyms, eliminate them both.

CONVENTIONS OF STANDARD ENGLISH

This area of the ACT English Test addresses punctuation, grammar and usage, and sentence structure. The questions on the actual ACT ask you to apply the rules of Standard Written English to specific sections of the passage, which are usually underlined.

The following strategies and techniques, along with those mentioned on pages 108 through 110, should help you to move quickly and accurately through the Conventions of Standard English questions on the ACT English Test. Review Appendix 2, "Grammar and Punctuation Rules," to brush up on the general rules of Standard Written English.

Try the Answer Choices

Because the test asks you to consider replacing the underlined portion, read each of the choices back into the sentence and select the one that is grammatically correct and/or clearly expresses the idea. If an answer choice creates an error in grammar or sounds awkward and wordy, eliminate it.

Consider the following examples:

> We arrived home three weeks later to witness an incredible
>
>   1
>
> transformation; all of the water damage had been repaired!
>
> 1. **A.** NO CHANGE
>   **B.** by witnessing
>   **C.** for the witnessing of
>   **D.** to the witness of

The best answer is A. This sentence is correct as written. It is in the active voice and correctly uses the infinitive "to witness." Answer choice B suggests that witnessing the transformation was the method by which the author arrived home, which doesn't make sense. Answer choices C and D are awkward when read back into the sentence and do not effectively convey the intended idea. Because answer choice A is clear, concise, and error-free, it is the best choice.

> I removed a picture from the box and placed it in the
>
>   2
>
> photo album.
>
> Which of the following alternatives to the underlined portion would NOT be acceptable?
>
> 2. **F.** box and then placed
>   **G.** box; then I placed
>   **H.** box, placed
>   **J.** box, placing

The best answer is H. When you read each of the answer choices back into the original sentence, the only one that does NOT work is "box, placed." This selection creates an incomplete sentence. The remaining answer choices are grammatically correct and clearly express the intended idea.

Amy Says:

Pay attention to apostrophes—you can often eliminate incorrect answer choices by quickly deciding whether an apostrophe is necessary.

Simplify the Answer Choices

Sometimes you can quickly eliminate incorrect answer choices by showing that one part of an answer choice is incorrect; if one part is wrong, the whole thing is wrong. Simplify the answer choices by focusing on one part at a time.

Consider the following examples:

My English teacher gave us daily quizzes, which angered and confused us. Soon, the

teachers' motives became clear.
　　　1

1. **A.** NO CHANGE
   B. teachers motives
   C. teacher's motives
   D. teacher's motive's

The best answer is C. The first step in answering this question is to determine how many teachers are there. The previous sentence says "My English teacher," so there is only one teacher. Therefore, you can eliminate answer choices A and B, which include the plural form of the noun "teacher." Because both answer choices C and D include the singular possessive form, you can assume that is the correct form of the noun; move on to the word "motives." You simply have to decide whether the plural form or the singular possessive form is correct. In this case, the plural form is best—the teacher has more than one motive—so answer choice C must be correct. The singular possessive form "motive's" is not correct because no possession is indicated.

My dog ran away and lost its collar.
　　　　　　　　　　2

2. **F.** NO CHANGE
   G. lost it's
   H. lost its'
   J. losing it's

The best answer is F. The first step in quickly answering this question is to focus on the pronoun. Because the collar belongs to the dog, the possessive form "its" is correct, and you can eliminate answer choices G and J, which include the contraction of "it is," and answer choice H, which is never correct. (You know that s' generally indicates plural possession; "it" is a singular pronoun and can never show plural possession.) By simplifying the answer choices you are able to quickly and accurately select the correct answer. Additionally, if you knew for certain that "its" was correct, a quick glance at the answer choices would reveal that answer choice F was the only viable option.

Don't Make New Mistakes

Because this test is timed, your tendency might be to rush through some of the seemingly more simple Usage and Mechanics questions. Be careful not to select an answer choice that introduces a new error to the sentence.

Consider the following examples:

While they're, he had as one of his counselors Steve, his friend's older brother.
　　　　1

1. A. NO CHANGE
　B. they're
　C. there,
　D. there, he had as

The best answer is D. Because "they're" is the contraction of "they are," you can eliminate answer choices A and B. You might have been tempted to select the shortest, most concise answer, which would be answer choice C. However, this choice creates a sentence fragment.

Attending a large university has taught me to understand and appreciate differently cultures from my own.
　　　　　2

2. F. NO CHANGE
　G. cultures different then
　H. cultures different from
　J. cultures differently by

The best answer is H. The context of the sentence suggests a contrast between the writer's culture and those cultures that are different. Be careful not to misread answer choice G and select it—"then" indicates a time, not a contrast. Answer choices F and J are awkward and use the adverb "differently" to modify the verbs "understand" and "appreciate," instead of the adjective "different" to modify the noun "cultures."

PRODUCTION OF WRITING AND KNOWLEDGE OF ENGLISH

This area of the ACT English Test addresses writing strategy, organization, style, and word choice. These questions assess your ability to make choices about the effectiveness and clarity of a word, phrase, sentence, or paragraph. You may also be asked about the English passage as a whole. Many of these questions are referred to by a number in a box. The following is more information on the three main skills tested by these questions: Strategy, Organization, and Style:

Strategy: *The choices made and methods used by an author when composing or revising an essay.*

The ACT English Test measures your ability to recognize several areas of writing strategy, including the flow of ideas; the appropriateness and purpose of both the passage and elements of the passage; and the effectiveness of opening, transitional, and closing sentences.

Take a look at the following sample Strategy question:

Horseback riding requires less skill than many people think. Granted, not just anyone can hop onto the back of a horse and maneuver the animal around a racetrack or jumping course, but many people can sit comfortably in a saddle for a short period of time while a horse calmly walks along a wooded trail. ⬚1

1. The writer wishes to add information here that will further support the point made in the preceding sentence. Which of the following sentences will do that best?

    A. Saddles are designed for specific purposes, such as pleasure riding, barrel racing, and roping.
    B. Each year, thousands of people who have never before been on a horse enjoy guided, one-hour trail rides.
    C. Even experienced riders enjoy the peace and tranquility of a ride through the woods after a long day of training.
    D. Former racehorses are often used as trail horses when they retire from the track.

1. The best answer is B. To correctly answer this question, you must first determine the point made in the preceding sentence. The main point of the sentence is that many people, even if they are not skilled at horseback riding, can ride at a slow pace for a short period of time. Answer choice B best supports that idea by providing information about the large number of first-time riders who enjoy relatively short trail rides.

> **Organization:** *Developing logical sequences, categorizing elements, ranking items in order, identifying main ideas, making connections, writing introductions and conclusions, and resolving problems within an essay.*

Organization questions on the ACT English Test are designed to test issues related to the organization of ideas within a passage, the most logical order of sentences and paragraphs, and the relevance of statements made within the context of the passage.

The following is an example of an Organization question:

[1] Prior to this, my mother had stated that she and my dad would only be staying with me for three days. [2] As adults, we often have mixed feelings about a visit from our parents—while we are happy to see them, we also hope that their stay is for a definite and short period of time. [3] My parents recently planned a trip to my neck of the woods, and I prepared my humble home for their arrival. [4] They showed up on the appointed day and my mother announced that they would stay for a full week.

2. Which of the following sequences of sentences will make this paragraph most logical?
   F. NO CHANGE
   G. 1, 4, 3, 2
   H. 2, 3, 4, 1
   J. 4, 3, 2, 1

2. The best answer is H. The best approach to this type of question is to determine which sentence should come first. The first sentence of a paragraph usually introduces the topic of the paragraph. In this case, the sentence that provides us with information about the topic of the paragraph is sentence [2]. Therefore, the first sentence in the logical sequence of this paragraph is sentence [2]. Because the only answer choice that places sentence [2] in the first position is answer choice H, that must be the correct choice. By positioning one sentence at a time you will be able to eliminate answer choices until only the correct one remains.

Style: *The author's presentation of the written word, usually either formal or informal.*

Good writing involves effective word choice as well as clear and unambiguous expression. The ACT English Test requires you to recognize and eliminate redundant material, understand the tone of the passage, and make sure that the ideas are expressed clearly and succinctly.

The following Style questions focus on these issues:

> While <u>having the appearance</u> to be a simple game, checkers is actually quite
> ₃
> complicated. Mathematically there are about 500 quintillion possible ways to win the
> game. Despite this, checkers continues to be mostly a fun game for those who play it,
> even at the competitive level. <u>Checkers was first played in the twelfth century.</u> Some of
> ₄
> the classic moves used in competitions have names like the Goose Walk, Duffer's Delight,
> and the Boomerang. With names like these, it seems <u>that even a serious game</u> has its own
> sense of humor.   5
>
> **3. A.** NO CHANGE
> **B.** appearing
> **C.** appearing that
> **D.** appearances show it
>
> **4. F.** NO CHANGE
> **G.** First played in the twelfth century was checkers.
> **H.** Checkers was originally from the twelfth century.
> **J.** DELETE the underlined portion.
>
> **5. A.** NO CHANGE
> **B.** crucial that a serious game
> **C.** that such a serious game
> **D.** in all seriousness, a game

3. The best answer is B. By replacing the underlined portion with each answer choice you can see that the best way to express this idea is simply with the word *appearing*, answer choice B. Remember to trust the way that things "sound," and go for the shortest, most simple way to say something.

4. The best answer is J. Although the sentence as it is used is grammatically correct, it does not fit the context of the paragraph. In other words, it is irrelevant information and should be omitted; answer choice J is correct.

5. The best answer is A. This question asks you to look at the choice and function of the words in the sentence. The tone of the paragraph is informational, yet informal. A word like *crucial* does not fit the context; therefore, answer choice B should be eliminated. Answer choices C and D do not really fit the context of the paragraph either. The sentence as it is written fits best within the style and tone of the passage, so answer choice A is correct.

ACT ENGLISH SKILLS EXERCISES

The next few pages contain exercises designed to help you apply the concepts generally tested on the ACT English Test and the ACT Writing Test. The general rules of grammar and punctuation are covered in Appendix 2. Be sure to review this information if you struggle with the ACT English skills exercises presented here.

Following this exercise section are simulated ACT English questions, which will allow you to become familiar with the format and types of questions you will see on your actual ACT test.

Using Commas

In the sentences below, add commas where needed.

1. Seagulls sand crabs and starfish are just a few of the species that you might see while vacationing in New Smyrna Beach Florida.

2. "Traci studied piano for three or four years" Andrew said.

3. Ashley Smith a well-known defense attorney retired yesterday.

4. Todd enjoys singing in the shower but when asked to sing in public he always declines.

5. Hey what are you doing?

6. "Well" Justin said "Carmen has written a very good paper."

7. The new roller coaster ride in my opinion wasn't very exciting.

8. After nearly ten years of hard work Rana finally landed her dream job.

9. My mother a fiery woman can be heard yelling at the neighbor boys from nearly a mile away.

10. I thoroughly enjoyed the show and I would encourage anyone to see it.

Using Apostrophes

In the sentences below, underline the correct word in the choices given in parentheses.

1. Though the choice is not (theirs, their's), (their, they're) not afraid to move to a new town.

2. (Whose, Who's) likely to become the football (teams', team's) captain this year?

3. My (mother and father's, mother's and father's) favorite vacation spot is Gulf Shores, Alabama.

4. I know what (your, you're) intentions are, Alex, and (your, you're) not going to get away with this.

5. (It's, Its, Its') a shame that (it's, its, its') once smooth and brilliant surface is now rough and dull.

6. I think the jackets are (theirs, their's).

7. Although change can be difficult, (it's, its, its') often more harmful than helpful to limit new experiences.

8. It was only a matter of minutes before the (girl's, girls') dog had trampled their clothes.

9. I am unsure if this baking pan is (ours, our's) or (yours, your's).

10. Do you know (who's, whose) jacket this is?

Using Colons and Semicolons

In the sentences below, insert colons or semicolons as needed.

1. For the holidays, I am making soft, chewy cookies sweet, decadent chocolates and miniature yellow cupcakes.

2. Molly is always complaining about how cold her car is in the morning maybe she should purchase an electric car starter.

3. I had everything I needed for a full night of studying coffee, chips, cookies, earphones, and my book bag.

4. Jacob is graduating today he is excited.

5. *Time Travel What's it all About?*

In the sentences below, decide whether a colon or a semicolon is needed. Circle the best choice.

6. We began the long trip to California on Monday (: ;) after six fast food meals and two hotel rooms, we finally reached Los Angeles.

7. My stubborn parents have left us no choice (; :) we're going to elope!

8. Today we're going to the beach (: ;) tomorrow we're going to the zoo.

9. Cake flour is best for baking foods such as cakes and cookies (: ;) its low gluten content makes for soft and light products.

10. I have everything I need for a day of snow-filled fun (: ;) hat, gloves, scarf, snow pants, jacket, boots, shovel, and sled.

Using Parentheses and Dashes

In the following sentences, the parentheses and dashes may or may not be in their correct locations. If a sentence is correct and, therefore, needs no change, circle "CORRECT." If a sentence is incorrect, rewrite the sentence with the parentheses and/or dashes in their correct locations. Remember, it's only necessary to change the *location* of the parentheses or dashes, not the punctuation itself (i.e., DO NOT replace the parentheses with dashes, or the dashes with parentheses).

1. Not only did Andy earn the Most Valuable Player Award as a Junior and Senior (quite an achievement), but he was also nominated as "Most Likely to Succeed." CORRECT

    _____

    _____

2. The car almost two decades old made strange noises—as it drove—down the road. CORRECT

    _____

    _____

3. We went to (Lansing) the state capital to learn about Michigan's history. CORRECT

    _____

    _____

4. Mrs. Thornton—a most gentle woman—always bandaged our cuts and scrapes. CORRECT

    _____

    _____

5. The middle school students were suspended on Tuesday the first day of the marking period (for cheating on a science test). CORRECT

    _____

    _____

Subject/Verb Agreement

In the sentences below, underline the verb in parentheses that maintains proper subject and verb agreement.

1. While Jenny wants many expensive things, she (are saving, is saving) her graduation money to pay for college.

2. Every day, Mark (finds, have found) strange things in his desk.

3. Each of the Girl Scouts (has, have) a collection of patches representing different services.

4. Rock climbing, like most extreme sports, (are, is) not without risk.

5. As of this coming Tuesday, Emily (have worked, will have worked) at the ice cream shop for six years.

6. Neither of the boys (has, have) any pets.

7. From what I understand, people can (win, winning) only by completely eliminating their opponents.

8. The author's poems (use, uses) a plethora of similes, metaphors, and personification.

9. When it comes to choosing a mayor, the public (play, plays) a key role.

10. Congress (is, are) in emergency session this week.

Nouns and Pronouns

In the sentences below, underline the word or phrase in the parentheses that best completes the sentence.

1. Jordan responds to a snow day much like any other young boy; (he, they) jumps up and down with excitement.

2. If a student wants to succeed in college, (you, he or she) must be willing to study for several hours each day.

3. I rarely eat at that restaurant, because (it, they) (has, have) poor service.

4. The book was on the table, but now (it, the book) is gone.

5. Leonardo da Vinci was an artist (that, who) created great art.

6. It was Rachel (who, whom) offered the young child a coat.

7. Everyone must at least try (his or her, their) hand at knitting.

8. Neither Nathan nor Jacob will be giving (his, their) speech today.

9. After much deliberation, Danielle told Helen that she would have to expose (her, Helen's) cheating problem.

10. It's best to take the furniture out of the living room in order to clean (it, the furniture).

Run-on Sentences

In the space provided, rewrite each run-on sentence below as one or more complete sentences.

1. In just two days, my family is leaving for Florida the worst part is that they're not taking me I'll be alone while they're soaking up the sun and playing in the sand this isn't fair.

    _____

    _____

    _____

2. High school was a busy time of life for me there was school, sports, student council, and friends although I was very busy, I was also quite happy.

    _____

    _____

    _____

3. Some people hate the winter I, on the other hand, really enjoy winter there's nothing better than playing in the snow on a crisp, cold day, and then coming inside to a warm fire and have a hot cup of chocolate.

    _____

    _____

    _____

4. I think the hardest part about being a college student is figuring out what you want to do for the rest of your life not only do you have to settle on a career path, but you also have to figure out how to pursue your chosen career and where to live once you've decided which job to accept.

    _____

    _____

    _____

5. Learning to drive a vehicle is not as easy as it seems many teenagers have a difficult time driving because it's both a new and nerve-wracking experience but like all new things, the more you drive, the easier it gets.

    _____

    _____

    _____

Sentence Fragments

In the space provided, rewrite the fragments below, using them to form complete sentences.

1. I have a hard time meeting new people. Because I am shy.

    _____

    _____

    _____

2. I am involved in many extracurricular activities. Including basketball, student council, and drama club.

    _____

    _____

    _____

3. Some people are very good at art. As Hillary is, for example.

    _____

    _____

    _____

4. I'm not sure if she understood my frustration. Because instead of trying to help, she just laughed at me!

    _____

    _____

    _____

5. Make sure you have everything you need in your backpack for school. Books, pencils, paper, a calculator, and your lunch.

    _____

    _____

Misplaced Modifiers

In each of the sentence pairs below, one sentence uses a modifier correctly, while the other sentence uses a modifier incorrectly. Locate the correct sentence, and place a "C" in the space provided.

1. _____ She was knitting a scarf for her friend that was warm.

   _____ She was knitting a warm scarf for her friend.

2. _____ At school, Catherine invited me to her birthday party.

   _____ Catherine invited me to her birthday party at school.

3. _____ The Smallville police reported one stolen car.

   _____ One car was reported to the Smallville police that was stolen.

The sentences below include misplaced modifiers. Rewrite the sentences so that the modifier is in the correct place.

4. The teacher compiled material into a review sheet for the students covered in class.

   _____

   _____

   _____

5. The lunch staff served hot dogs to the students on food trays.

   _____

   _____

   _____

6. We returned the tool to the hardware store that stopped working.

   _____

   _____

   _____

Parallelism

In each of the sentence pairs below, one sentence has parallelism while the other sentence includes faulty parallelism. Locate the correct sentence in each pair, and place a "C" in the space provided.

1. _____ Nina is intelligent, motivated, and she is hardworking.

    _____ Nina is intelligent, motivated, and hardworking.

2. _____ She had three life goals: to skydive, to bungee jump, and to scuba dive.

    _____ She had three life goals: to skydive, to go bungee jumping, and a scuba diver.

3. _____ Coach Smith rewarded her team for working hard and going the distance during practice.

    _____ Coach Smith rewarded her team for their hard work and for going the distance during practice.

The sentences below include faulty parallelism. Rewrite them to correct the faulty parallelism.

4. During the summer, I enjoy biking, rollerblading, and to swim laps in the pool.

    _____

    _____

    _____

5. In recent years, more tourists visited museums in Italy than France.

    _____

    _____

    _____

6. My five-year-old brother loves to draw circles and squares, as well as tracing triangles and stars.

    _____

    _____

    _____

Redundancy

The sentences below may or may not contain problems of redundancy. Place a "C" next to the sentence that expresses the idea most clearly and concisely and does NOT include redundancy.

1. _____ The accident happened last year, having occurred on a cold and stormy night.

   _____ The accident happened last year and occurred on a cold and stormy night.

   _____ The accident happened last year on a cold and stormy night.

   _____ The accident happened last year, having occurred, on a cold and stormy night.

2. _____ I think maybe I might go with friends to the movie theater.

   _____ I might go with friends to the movie theater.

   _____ Maybe I might go with friends to the movie theater.

   _____ I think, maybe, I might go with friends to the movie theater.

3. _____ In a few months, after waiting a while, I will move out of my parents' house and get my own place, in due course.

   _____ In a few months, after waiting a while, I will move out of my parents' house.

   _____ In a few months, I will move out of my parents' house and get my own place.

   _____ After waiting a while, I will move out of my parents' house and get my own place, in due time after a few months.

4. _____ Alexander Graham Bell is widely recognized for his inventing and creation of the telephone.

   _____ Alexander Graham Bell is widely recognized for his invention, which was the creation of the telephone.

   _____ Alexander Graham Bell is widely recognized for his invention, that is, the creation of the telephone.

   _____ Alexander Graham Bell is widely recognized for inventing the telephone.

5. _____ One day, while playing in the woods, my cousin happened upon an old, abandoned house.

   _____ One day, while playing in the woods, my cousin accidentally stumbled up against an old, abandoned house.

   _____ One day, while playing in the woods, my cousin unintentionally without planning discovered an old, abandoned house.

   _____ One day, while playing in the woods, my cousin unintentionally happened upon an old, abandoned house.

Wordiness/Awkward Sentence Construction

The sentences below may have a problem with wordiness or awkward construction. Place a "C" next to the sentence that expresses the idea most clearly and concisely and is NOT wordy.

1. _____ It is unfortunate that the plan did not succeed in accomplishing its objective.

   _____ It is unfortunate that the plan did not accomplish its objective.

   _____ Unfortunately, the plan did not succeed in its objective.

   _____ Unfortunately, the plan failed.

2. _____ The achievement, his gold medal in the 2000 Olympic Games, is the one for which he is most widely remembered.

   _____ The achievement for which he is most widely remembered is his gold medal in the 2000 Olympic Games.

   _____ His 2000 Olympic Games gold medal achievement is his most popular point of remembrance.

   _____ He will be remembered for his achievement most widely of winning a gold medal in the 2000 Olympic Games.

3. _____ While my brother may try to argue otherwise, he and my dad are equally strong.

   _____ My dad and brother, though they may argue, considering their weight, are equal in strength.

   _____ While my brother may argue otherwise, he and my dad are the same when strength is considered.

   _____ While my brother may argue otherwise, he and my dad are equally dominant in terms of strength.

4. _____ My brother has attained the age of eighteen years.

   _____ My brother attained the age of eighteen years.

   _____ My brother has reached eighteen years of age.

   _____ My brother is eighteen years old.

5. _____ Through their training, nurses see patients' needs.

   _____ When patients need things, nurses are training to notice it.

   _____ Nurses are trained in order to recognize a lack of something by patients.

   _____ Nurses are trained to recognize patients' needs.

ANSWERS AND EXPLANATIONS

The answers and explanations indicate correct grammar use and the best way to express an idea. You might come up with slightly different corrections for some of the exercises, which is fine as long as the rules of grammar are being followed.

Using Commas

1. Seagulls, sand crabs, and starfish are just a few of the species that you might see while vacationing in New Smyrna Beach, Florida.

     Explanation: Commas are needed when separating three or more words, phrases, or clauses written in a series. A comma is also needed to set off geographical names.

2. "Traci studied piano for three or four years," Andrew said.

     Explanation: A comma is needed to separate a quote from the rest of the sentence.

3. Ashley Smith, a well-known defense attorney, retired yesterday.

     Explanation: Commas are needed to set off an appositive from the rest of the sentence.

4. Todd enjoys singing in the shower, but when asked to sing in public, he always declines.

     Explanation: First, a comma is needed when connecting two independent clauses with a conjunction. Second, a comma is needed to separate introductory material (*when asked to sing in public*) from its main clause (*he always declines*).

5. Hey, what are you doing?

     Explanation: A comma is needed to set off interjections from the rest of the sentence.

6. "Well," Justin said, "Carmen has written a very good paper."

     Explanation: Commas are needed to separate a quote from the rest of the sentence.

7. The new roller coaster ride, in my opinion, wasn't very exciting.

     Explanation: Commas are needed to set off parenthetical expressions from the rest of the sentence.

8. After nearly ten years of hard work, Rana finally landed her dream job.

     Explanation: A comma is needed to set off introductory words and phrases from the rest of the sentence.

9. My mother, a fiery woman, can be heard yelling at the neighbor boys from nearly a mile away.

> **Explanation:** Commas are needed to set off an appositive from the rest of the sentence.

10. I thoroughly enjoyed the show, and I would encourage anyone to see it.

> **Explanation:** A comma is needed when connecting two independent clauses with a conjunction

Using Apostrophes

1. Though the choice is not (<u>theirs</u>, their's), (their, <u>they're</u>) not afraid to move to a new town.

> **Explanation:** The possessive pronoun "theirs" is needed in the first blank and the conjunction "they're" is needed in the second blank. The word *their's* does not exist, and *their* is the possessive determiner, not a subject/verb contraction.

2. (Whose, <u>Who's</u>) likely to become the football (teams', <u>team's</u>) captain this year?

> **Explanation:** The contraction of "who is" is needed in the first blank in order to fill the subject and verb positions. The singular possessive form "team's" is correct. (There is only one captain, so only one team.) The form "teams'" is the plural possessive.

3. My (<u>mother and father's</u>, mother's and father's) favorite vacation spot is Gulf Shores, Alabama.

> **Explanation:** Because "mother and father" share the favorite vacation spot, the ownership is given to the last person listed, which is "father."

4. I know what (<u>your</u>, you're) intentions are, Alex, and (your, <u>you're</u>) not going to get away with this.

> **Explanation:** Possession is shown with "your" in the first blank. The conjunction of "you are" is needed in the second blank, making "you're" the best choice.

5. (<u>It's</u>, Its, Its') a shame that (it's, <u>its</u>, its') once smooth and brilliant surface is now rough and dull.

> **Explanation:** The contraction of "It is" is needed for the first blank, making "It's" the best choice. Possession is needed in the second blank, so "its" is the best choice. The word *its'* does not exist; however, nearly every ACT we have seen uses it as an answer choice at least once. It is never correct.

6. I think the jackets are (<u>theirs</u>, their's).

    Explanation: Possession is shown with "theirs." The word "their's" does not exist.

7. Although change can be difficult, (<u>it's</u>, its, its') often more harmful than helpful to limit new experiences.

    Explanation: The contraction of "it is" is needed, so "it's" is the best choice.

8. It was only a matter of minutes before the (girl's, <u>girls'</u>) dog had trampled their clothes.

    Explanation: Because the third-person, plural possessive determiner *their* is used later in the sentence, the possessive form of the plural noun "girls" is needed, making "girls'" the best choice.

9. I am unsure if this baking pan is (<u>ours</u>, our's) or (<u>yours</u>, your's).

    Explanation: The possessive pronouns *ours* and *yours* are needed. The words *our's* and *your's* do not exist.

10. Do you know (who's, <u>whose</u>) jacket this is?

    Explanation: Possession is indicated with *whose*, making it the best choice. The contraction *who's* is formed of the subject or relative pronoun *who* and the verb *is*.

Using Colons and Semicolons

1. For the holidays, I am making soft, chewy cookies; sweet, scrumptious chocolates; and miniature yellow cupcakes.

    Explanation: Use semicolons to separate items containing commas in a list.

2. Molly is always complaining about how cold her car is in the morning; maybe she should purchase an electric car starter.

    Explanation: Use a semicolon to join two related independent clauses.

3. I had everything I needed for a full night of studying: coffee, chips, cookies, earphones, and my book bag.

    Explanation: Use a colon to introduce a list.

4. Jacob is graduating today; he is excited.

    Explanation: Use a semicolon to join two related, independent clauses.

5. *Time Travel: What's it all About?*

      Explanation: Use a colon to join related clauses when one clause is dependent on, and helps to explain, the other.

6. We began the long trip to California on Monday; after six fast food meals and two hotel rooms, we finally reached Los Angeles.

      Explanation: Use a semicolon to join two related, independent clauses.

7. My stubborn parents have left us no choice; we're going to elope!

      Explanation: Use a semicolon to join two related independent clauses.

8. Today we're going to the beach; tomorrow we're going to the zoo.

      Explanation: Use a semicolon to join two related, independent clauses.

9. Cake flour is best for baking foods such as cakes and cookies; its low gluten content makes for soft and light products.

      Explanation: Use a semicolon to join two related, independent clauses.

10. I have everything I need for a day of snow-filled fun: hat, gloves, scarf, snow pants, jacket, boots, shovel, and sled.

      Explanation: Use a colon to introduce a list.

Using Parentheses and Dashes

1. CORRECT

      Explanation: Parentheses are used to set off material secondary to the meaning of the text as a whole. In this case, "quite an achievement" is not essential to the meaning of the text, making the original sentence correct.

2. The car—almost two decades old—made strange noises as it drove down the street.

      Explanation: Dashes are used to give special emphasis to certain phrases or clauses. Here, the writer is emphasizing the significantly old age of the car.

3. We went to Lansing (the state capital) to learn about Michigan's history.

      Explanation: Parentheses are used to set apart information that is secondary or not essential to the meaning of the sentence. Here, the fact that Lansing is the capital of Michigan is secondary information. Many readers would know this fact already.

4. CORRECT

> **Explanation:** Dashes are used to give special emphasis to certain phrases or clauses. Here, the writer is emphasizing the appositive *a most gentle woman* by using dashes instead of commas.

5. The middle school students were suspended on Tuesday (the first day of the marking period) for cheating on a science test.

> **Explanation:** Parentheses are used to set apart information that is secondary or not essential to the meaning of the sentence. Here, the fact that the particular Tuesday was the first day of the marking period is a secondary detail. The reason that the students were suspended (*for cheating on a science test*) is important information that should not be enclosed in parentheses.

Subject/Verb Agreement

1. While Jenny wants many expensive things, she <u>is saving</u> her graduation money to pay for college.

> **Explanation:** *Jenny* is a singular subject, so the auxiliary verb (a form of *be* in the progressive tenses) must also be singular: *is*.

2. Every day, Mark <u>finds</u> strange things in his desk.

> **Explanation:** *Mark* is a third person, singular subject, so the verb must also be third person, singular: *finds*.

3. Each of the Girl Scouts (<u>has</u>) a collection of patches representing different services.

> **Explanation:** "Each of the Girl Scouts" refers to each individual Girl Scout, which makes the subject singular. Therefore, the verb must also be singular, which makes "has" the best choice.

4. Rock climbing, like most extreme sports, <u>is</u> not without risk.

> **Explanation:** *Rock climbing* is a singular subject, so the verb must also be singular: *is*. Be careful not to be distracted by nouns (as the plural *sports* is here) that come between subject and verb, and which have different grammatical number.

5. As of this coming Tuesday, Emily <u>will have worked</u> at the ice cream shop for six years.

> **Explanation:** This sentence refers to an action that began in the past and is ongoing relative to a time in the future (*this coming Tuesday*). Therefore, the future perfect tense is appropriate.

6. Neither of the boys <u>has</u> any pets.

> **Explanation:** The indefinite pronoun *neither* is singular; therefore, the singular verb form *has* is appropriate.

7. From what I understand, people can <u>win</u> only by completely eliminating their opponents.

> **Explanation:** The verb *can* must be followed by the bare form of a verb.

8. The author's poems <u>use</u> a plethora of similes, metaphors, and personification.

> **Explanation:** "Poems" is the plural subject, so the verb must also be plural, which makes "use" the correct choice.

9. When it comes to choosing a mayor, the public <u>plays</u> a key role.

> **Explanation:** "The public" is the singular subject, so the verb must also be singular, which makes "plays" the correct choice.

10. Congress <u>is</u> in emergency session this week.

> **Explanation:** In American English, and therefore for the purposes of the ACT, nouns are considered singular or plural based on their morphology (how they appear, for example, with an *s* at the end).

In other forms of English, nouns are considered singular or plural based on semantics, that is, whether they describe a single unit or a cumulative body of countable things. This means that for the ACT, *Congress* is singular. Therefore, the singular verb form *is* is correct. Outside the United States, in some English-speaking countries, *Congress* (just like, for example, *parliament, Team Canada, the rock band*) would be considered plural because it implies a group of people.

Nouns and Pronouns

1. **He**—"Jordan" is the singular antecedent.
2. **He or she**—The subject of the first clause, *a student*, is the antecedent of the subject pronoun(s) of the next clause. *A student* is third person; therefore, the second person pronoun *you* cannot be used.
3. **It has**—the "restaurant" is a singular antecedent.
4. **The book**—in order to avoid ambiguity between "the book" and "the table," restate the appropriate antecedent.
5. **Who**—use the relative pronoun "who" when referring to a person.
6. **Who**—The relative pronoun is in subject position: *Rachel* offered the young child a coat. Therefore, *who* is correct. The relative pronoun *whom* is used in object position.
7. **His or her**—the indefinite pronoun "everyone" is singular.
8. **His**—Nouns conjoined with *or* or *nor* take singular verbs and are represented by singular pronouns.
9. **Helen's**—in order to avoid ambiguity, restate the appropriate antecedent.
10. **The furniture**—in order to avoid ambiguity between whether the living room or the furniture's cleaning is discussed, use an expressed noun phrase instead of a pronoun.

Run-on Sentences

Following are examples of corrections to the run-on sentences in this section. You might have come up with other corrections. Refer to the part of this book that discusses run-on sentences if you need assistance.

1. In just two days, my family is leaving for Florida. The worst part is that they're not taking me! I'll be alone while they're soaking up the sun and playing in the sand. This isn't fair.

2. High school was a busy time of life for me. There was school, sports, student council, and friends. Although I was very busy, I was also quite happy.

3. Some people hate the winter. I, on the other hand, really enjoy winter; here's nothing better than playing in the snow on a crisp, cold day, and then coming inside to a warm fire and a cup of hot chocolate.

4. I think the hardest part of being a college student is figuring out what you want to do for the rest of your life. Not only do you have to settle on a career path, but you also have to figure out how to pursue your chosen career and where to live once you've decided on a job.

5. Learning to drive a vehicle is not as easy as it seems. Many teenagers have a difficult time driving because it's both a new and nerve-wracking experience. But, like all new things, the more you drive, the easier it gets.

Sentence Fragments

Following are examples of corrections to the sentence fragments in this section.

1. I have a hard time meeting new people because I am shy.

   Explanation: The phrase "because I am shy" is a dependent clause and cannot stand alone.

2. I am involved in many extracurricular activities, including basketball, student council, and drama club.

   Explanation: The phrase "including basketball, student council, and drama club" is not a clause and cannot stand alone.

3. Some people are very good at art, as Hillary is, for example.

   Explanation: The phrase "as Hillary is" is a dependent clause that cannot stand alone.

4. I'm not sure if she understood my frustration, because instead of trying to help, she just laughed at me!

   Explanation: "Because" should link the first sentence with the second dependent clause using a comma. Use a semicolon to join two related independent clauses.

5. Make sure you have everything you need for school in your backpack: books, pencils, paper, a calculator, and your lunch.

   Explanation: Use a colon to introduce a list.

Misplaced Modifiers

Following are examples of corrections to the misplaced modifiers in this section. The key is to place the modifier next to the word or phrase that it is intended to modify.

1. The correct sentence is, "She was knitting a warm scarf for her friend."
2. The correct sentence is, "At school, Catherine invited me to her birthday party."
3. The correct sentence is, "The Smallville police reported one stolen car."
4. The correct sentence is, "The teacher compiled material covered in class into a review sheet for the students."
5. The correct sentence is, "The lunch staff served hot dogs on food trays to the students."
6. The correct sentence is, "We returned the tool that stopped working to the hardware store."

Parallelism

Following are examples of corrections to the sentences including faulty parallelism in this section.

1. The correct sentence is, "Nina is intelligent, motivated, and hardworking."

   Explanation: The adjectives "intelligent, motivated, and hardworking" all clearly and correctly modify "Nina."

2. The correct sentence is, "She had three life goals: to skydive, to bungee jump, and to scuba dive."

   Explanation: All three of the goals are in the bare form of the verb.

3. The correct sentence is, "Coach Smith rewarded her team for working hard and going the distance during practice."

   Explanation: The verbs "working" and "going" have the same (gerund) form.

4. The correct sentence is, "During the summer, I enjoy biking, rollerblading, and swimming laps in the pool."

   Explanation: The verbs (biking, rollerblading, swimming) must all have the same form in order to maintain parallelism.

5. The correct sentence is, "In recent years, more tourists visited museums in Italy than in France."

   Explanation: The sentence means that more people visited museums in Italy than museums in France. Therefore, *France* cannot stand alone in the sentence, and it should be replaced by *museums in France* or simply *in France*.

6. The correct sentence is, "My five-year-old brother loves to draw circles and squares, as well as trace triangles and stars." OR "My five-year-old brother loves drawing circles and squares, as well as tracing triangles and stars."

> **Explanation:** Verbs should have parallel form when used in series. Here, either the infinitive forms (omitting the *to* the second time) or the gerund forms are appropriate.

Redundancy

Following are the sentences that are NOT redundant.

1. The accident happened last year on a cold and stormy night.
2. I might go with friends to the movie theater.
3. In a few months, I will move out of my parents' house and get my own place.
4. Alexander Graham Bell is widely recognized for inventing the telephone.
5. One day, while playing in the woods, my cousin happened upon an old, abandoned house.

Wordiness/Awkward Sentence Construction

Following are the sentences that are NOT wordy or awkward.

1. Unfortunately, the plan failed.
2. The achievement for which he is most widely remembered is his gold medal in the 2000 Olympic Games.
3. While my brother may try to argue otherwise, he and my dad are equally strong.
4. My brother is eighteen years old.
5. Nurses are trained to recognize patients' needs.

PRACTICE QUESTIONS

Following are simulated ACT English passages and questions, along with explanations for all of the questions. Carefully read the directions, apply the information from this chapter, and attempt all of the questions.

DIRECTIONS: In the passages that follow, some words and phrases are underlined and numbered. In the answer column, you will find alternatives for the words and phrases that are underlined. Choose the alternative that you think is best and circle it. If you think that the original version is best, choose "NO CHANGE," which will always be either answer choice A or F. You will also find questions about a particular section of the passage or about the entire passage. These questions will be identified by a number or numbers in a box. Read the passage through once before answering the questions. An Answer Key and Detailed Explanations are included at the end of this section.

PASSAGE I

Scientific Solutions

Humans can be a remarkably optimistic—and often ingenuous—group. Each new scientific discovery has the ability to inspire hopes (and rumors) that the breakthrough will be the solution to some of society's woes. One discovery may give rise to expectations of ending cancer or world hunger, while another may prove to be a veritable fountain of youth.

A classic example is the story of what happened following the discovery of radioactivity.

About a century ago, the husband and wife team of Marie and Pierre Curie discovered the power of radioactivity. Over the course of the next several years, other scientists sought to harness this power to benefit society. Soon, the radioactive elements radium and uranium were were being used to treat cancer and generate electricity, respectively. People were excited to see what other remarkable capabilities these radioactive elements might possess. They were especially eager to see how the discovery might benefit them personally. When traditional science failed to meet this immediate desire, shrewd entrepreneurs readily filled the void.

1. Which of the following alternatives to the underlined portion would NOT be acceptable?
   A. hunger. Another
   B. hunger, and another
   C. hunger. Because another
   D. hunger; another

2. F. NO CHANGE
   G. power in
   H. power to
   J. power for
   See Expanded Explanation on page 134!

3. A. NO CHANGE
   B. are
   C. was
   D. is

4. F. NO CHANGE
   G. apprehensive
   H. unwilling
   J. frightened
   See Expanded Explanation on page 134!

GO ON TO THE NEXT PAGE.

For example, during the 1920s, an era of, flappers
                                          5
and racoon coats several businesses began selling "radium
                5
water," claiming that the product had various curative

powers. Some of these businesses were eventually revealed

as frauds, whereas they falsely claimed their products
        6
contained radium. The money wasted by the patrons of

these businesses was nothing compared to the suffering

experienced by consumers of Radithor a
                                   7
drinkable solution that actually contained radium. This
      7

product, it was insidious in its results, was purported
      8

to help cure symptoms: of rheumatism, gout, syphilis,
                        9
anemia, epilepsy, multiple sclerosis, and sexual impotence.

One advertisement went so far as to claim that insanity and

mental retardation could be cured, stating: "Science to Cure

All the Living Dead ... the new plan to close up the insane

asylums and wipe out illiteracy."

Over 400,000 bottles of Radithor were produced

before the hazardous dangers of the radium water became
          10
apparent. One of the biggest fans of Radithor was a

millionaire playboy named Eben M. Byers. Purchasing the

product by the case, Byers consumed over 1,000 bottles of

the solution between 1928 and 1930. Eventually, Byers'
                                       11

teeth began to fall out, and which the bones of his jaws
                        12
began to deteriorate. As Byers became increasingly ill,

5. A. NO CHANGE
   B. 1920s—an era of flappers and raccoon coats—
   C. 1920s. An era of, flappers and raccoon coats
   D. 1920s; an era of flappers, and raccoon coats,

   See Expanded Explanation on page 134!

6. F. NO CHANGE
   G. frauds,
   H. frauds, so
   J. frauds because

7. A. NO CHANGE
   B. Radithor a drinkable solution,
   C. Radithor, a drinkable solution
   D. Radithor, a drinkable, solution

8. F. NO CHANGE
   G. product, which was
   H. product that was being
   J. product, which being

9. A. NO CHANGE
   B. symptoms of rheumatism,
   C. symptoms of; rheumatism
   D. symptoms of rheumatism:

10. F. NO CHANGE
   G. perilous
   H. risky
   J. DELETE the underlined portion.

11. A. NO CHANGE
   B. However,
   C. Still,
   D. Similarly,

12. F. NO CHANGE
   G. that
   H. and
   J. DELETE the underlined portion.

GO ON TO THE NEXT PAGE.

he was finally diagnosed with radiation poisoning. While

‾‾‾‾‾‾‾‾‾‾‾‾‾‾‾‾‾‾‾‾‾‾‾‾‾‾‾‾‾‾‾‾
13

Byers lay dying in the hospital, even his breath was found

to be radioactive. At the time of Byers' death, radiation

poisoning was a relatively new phenomenon, primarily seen

among makers of radium-dial watches who was licking his

‾‾‾‾‾‾‾‾‾‾‾‾‾
14

paint brushes to exact a fine tip. Nevertheless, Byers' highly

publicized death swiftly led to the laws that regulate the use

‾‾‾‾‾‾‾‾‾‾‾‾‾‾‾‾
15

and sale of radium and other radioactive elements.

13. The writer would like to indicate that at this point, Byers became aware of the cause of his illness. Given that all the choices are true, which one best accomplishes the writer's goal?
- **A.** NO CHANGE
- **B.** the doctors struggled to cure him.
- **C.** he realized his penchant for Radithor would likely kill him.
- **D.** his faith in his physicians continued to falter.

14. F. NO CHANGE
- **G.** had licked his
- **H.** licked their
- **J.** licks his

15. A. NO CHANGE
- **B.** regulation of
- **C.** regulatory laws of
- **D.** legal regulation and laws relating to

PASSAGE II

Where's the "Play" When Children Play Sports?

According to health experts, over the past thirty years

the childhood obesity rate in the United States has more than

tripled for some of them aged six to eleven, and has doubled

‾‾‾‾‾‾‾‾‾‾‾‾‾
16

for younger children and adolescents. Approximately nine

million children over the age of six are currently considered

obese. One of the primary causes of the epidemic is

inactivity: even though more young children participate in

‾‾‾‾‾‾‾‾‾‾‾‾‾‾‾‾‾‾‾‾‾‾‾‾
17

organized sports than in the leaner days of decades past.

This apparent paradox has two possible explanations.

The first is that without participating in organized sports,

today's children would be even more overweight. With

families eating more high-fat, less nutritious convenience

foods, this is certain possible.

‾‾‾‾‾‾‾‾‾‾‾‾‾‾‾‾
18

Another likely explanation is that organized sports

inadvertently discourage children from spontaneous physical

activity, or "free play." Thirty years ago, most childrens,

‾‾‾‾‾‾‾‾‾
19

first experience with organized games was in school gym

classes. By school age, children had already participated in

neighborhood "pick-up" games where the focus was

16. F. NO CHANGE
- **G.** them
- **H.** children
- **J.** DELETE the underlined portion.

17. A. NO CHANGE
- **B.** inactivity even though, more
- **C.** inactivity, even though more
- **D.** inactivity; even though, more

18. F. NO CHANGE
- **G.** this is most certainly a distinct possibility.
- **H.** this is a possibility.
- **J.** possibly, this could happen.

19. A. NO CHANGE
- **B.** children's
- **C.** childrens
- **D.** children

GO ON TO THE NEXT PAGE.

on fun. They have played catch for hours, ran until they
                    20
were breathless, and developed strategies for how to win

"kick the can." They groaned with disappointment when the

streetlights came on, indicating that it was time to run home

for dinner. It never occurred to the children that they were

acquiring skills. They were just playing.
              21

    By the time they were old enough to participate in

organized sports, these children had learned the most critical

skills from their peers. They knew how to run, throw, catch,

and hit a ball. They previously learned that playing fair,
                        22
being a team player, and displaying good sportsmanship

were critical if they wanted to be invited to play again. Being

allowed to play on a team was a privilege for adolescents, not

a drudgery they had to endure. 23

    The professionals who study the recent phenomenon of

obese children in the United States offer additional

support for the value of "free play." Despite this, many
                                    24
doctors and psychologists today are concerned that the

complex rules in organized sports may confuse a young

child, and a child's bones and muscles may not be ready for

what a sport demands. As a final irony, one of the reasons
                      25
families are consuming so much fattening processed

food is a result of rushing their young children from one
                            26

planned, scheduled, and coached sport to another.
                                      27

---

20. F. NO CHANGE
   G. Playing
   H. They're going to play
   J. They played

21. Which of the following alternatives to the underlined portion would NOT be acceptable?
   A. skills; they
   B. skills they
   C. skills, for they
   D. skills, as they

22. F. NO CHANGE
   G. also
   H. instead
   J. conversely

23. The writer is considering deleting the phrase "not a drudgery they had to endure" from the preceding sentence. Should the phrase be kept or deleted?
   A. Kept, because it emphasizes the positive attitude children had toward "free play" thirty years ago.
   B. Kept, because it is relevant to the essay's focus on the importance of sportsmanship.
   C. Deleted, because the essay proves that "free play" was not considered a privilege thirty years ago.
   D. Deleted, because this level of detail is not consistent with the essay's description of "free play."

24. F. NO CHANGE
   G. However
   H. In fact
   J. Alternatively

25. A. NO CHANGE
   B. If
   C. Whether
   D. To

26. F. NO CHANGE
   G. they're
   H. there
   J. this

27. A. NO CHANGE
   B. practices and/or games of one type of organized sport
   C. organized sport
   D. sport (the organized type)

GO ON TO THE NEXT PAGE.

Should parents send their children out to play
28

with the instruction to come home when the streetlights
28

come on? Of course not. Should they refuse to allow their
28

six-year-olds to learn soccer because they aren't old enough?

No. What parents can do is look for children's sports

programs that focus on fun rather than winning. Programs for

young children should be one third instruction and two thirds

free play. Rather than running from one planned activity

to another, parents should devote part of each weekend to

"family play," participating in activities the whole family can

enjoy, such as hiking, swimming or cross-country skiing.
29

When possible, they should invite a few other families to join

in the fun and play an unorganized game of kickball at the

local park.

28. If the writer were to delete the question and answer at the beginning of the final paragraph, the paragraph would primarily lose:
   F. details about the health implications of childhood obesity.
   G. an explanation of why children become obese.
   H. a tone of nostalgia for times passed.
   J. clarification of the risks twenty-first century parents should reasonably take.

29. A. NO CHANGE
   B. enjoy such as hiking swimming or
   C. enjoy; such as hiking, swimming or
   D. enjoy: such as hiking swimming, or

Question 30 asks about the preceding passage as a whole.

---

30. Suppose the writer had intended to write an essay about children's health worldwide. Would this essay accomplish the writer's goal, and why?
   F. Yes, because it discusses the national epidemic of childhood obesity and encourages parents to sign up their children for organized sports.
   G. Yes, because it discusses the impact of sports on children's health.
   H. No, because it discusses only two possible explanations for childhood obesity in the United States only.
   J. No, because it does not discuss the impact of convenience foods on obesity.

END OF THE ENGLISH TEST.
STOP! IF YOU HAVE TIME LEFT OVER, CHECK YOUR WORK ON THIS SECTION ONLY.

ANSWERS AND EXPLANATIONS

PASSAGE I

1. The best answer is C. You must be careful not to select answer choices that create incomplete sentences. *Because another is anticipated to be a veritable fountain of youth* is an incomplete sentence, so answer choice C is NOT acceptable.

EXPANDED EXPLANATION

2. The best answer is F. This question type is often challenging, especially for multilingual students. An *idiom* is a word combination or phrase specific to a language that doesn't necessarily follow grammatical rules but has become widely used by fluent speakers of that language. (Idioms can also be colloquial expressions unique to a language, such as "raining cats and dogs"; however, the ACT does not test you on these types of idioms.) The best way to think of idioms is as "common usage." Many of these types of questions on the ACT involve the use of prepositions. While more than one preposition may fit in terms of meaning, ACT rewards those students who know which ones are the most common in each instance. In order to do well on these questions, students must be familiar with more than just the basic rules of English. Remember that ACT tests American standard written English. The best way to become familiar with common acceptable usages for the ACT is to work extensively with ACT material.

In this question, NO CHANGE is the credited response. NO CHANGE is always a possible choice on the Sentence Correction questions. It comes up as the correct answer about as often as the other choices. We've noticed that some students have a tendency to over-choose or under-choose "NO CHANGE." The best approach is to test the choices by reading each of them into the sentence and "listening" to them. When working on these questions, turn on the "internal narrator" in your head. (This is often called "subvocalization.") Note that there is really no grammatical reason that answer choice G "power in" is wrong. Radioactivity certainly has power in it. However, it's more common to refer to the "power of radioactivity."

3. The best answer is A. The plural subject *elements* requires the plural verb *were*. Because the action took place in the past, it is appropriate to use the simple past tense.

EXPANDED EXPLANATION

4. The best answer is F. When answering this question, you must look for clues in the parts of the sentence that are not underlined and compare the answer choices to each other. "Eager," the NO CHANGE answer, is definitely a positive word. Notice that all of the other choices are negative words. In many cases, simply labeling each choice as "positive," "negative," or "neutral" is all that you need to choose the correct answer. The last phrase of the sentence, ". . . benefit them personally," shows that the underlined word should be a positive word. Since the only positive word available as a choice is "eager," NO CHANGE is correct for this one.

EXPANDED EXPLANATION

5. The best answer is B. This question highlights that while there is general agreement on the rules of Standard Written English, variations on some usages are still subject to debate. I've been in the room when a punctuation argument broke out between English professors. I was surprised at the depth of passion involved and the fact that when it was all over, they both had to admit that there will probably never be complete agreement on all the rules. As a result, most major publications develop what is called a "style sheet" for their writers so that the publication is consistent on the rules it follows. The actual style sheet for ACT isn't available to us. But we can derive it from studying past exams. One of the more controversial aspects of ACT's style (for English teachers and professors, at least) is the use of pairs of dashes, called em dashes, for parenthetical expressions. Answer choice B is credited here because the descriptive phrase about the clothing fashions of the period can be removed from the sentence without changing its meaning. So, the dashes are acting as parentheses.

When working on this type of problem, exaggerate the pauses at commas. In this sentence, answer choice A is incorrect because the comma after "of" breaks up the phrase for no reason. Answer choice C is incorrect because it turns the first part of the sentence into a fragment by adding the period after "1920s." (Hint: ACT generally punishes those who "over comma" more than those who "under comma.") Answer choice D is incorrect in a way that fools many test-takers. The semicolon is incorrect because it is being used as a "super comma" that leads off a list separated by commas. ACT does not recognize this use of the semicolon and only credits a semicolon when it joins two closely related independent clauses. In other words, a semicolon is only correct on the ACT when it could be replaced by a period and a capital letter.

6. **The best answer is J.** The conjunction *because* implies that the rest of the sentence will explain why the businesses were revealed as frauds. *Whereas* suggests a contradiction, and *so* implies that the sentence will explain what happened as a result of the businesses being revealed as frauds. Eliminate answer choice H. If you do not use a conjunction at all, as in answer choice G, the sentence does not make sense.

7. **The best answer is C.** The phrase *a drinkable solution that actually contained radium* is an appositive, which should always be set off by commas. The other answer choices make the sentence awkward and confusing.

8. **The best answer is G.** The clause *which was insidious in its results* is a nonrestrictive clause that should be set apart from the sentence using commas. The other answer choices make the sentence awkward and confusing.

9. **The best answer is B.** Because the preposition *of* is used, no colon or other punctuation is needed to introduce the list; only commas are needed to separate the items in the series.

10. **The best answer is J.** The words *hazardous, perilous,* and *risky* all have similar meanings. They can't all be correct, so these choices should be eliminated. Since *dangerous* implies *hazard, peril,* and *risk,* including these words in the sentence would be redundant.

11. **The best answer is A.** The adverb *eventually* correctly implies the passage of time. This fits with the context of the passage. The other answer choices are not supported by the context of the passage.

12. **The best answer is H.** Independent clauses (especially highly related ones) can be combined using a comma and the conjunction *and*.

13. **The best answer is C.** The paragraph suggests that Radithor, which contained radium, was the cause of Byers' illness. Only answer choice C shows that Byers recognized that his overconsumption of Radithor was what made him sick and eventually led to his death.

14. **The best answer is H.** There is more than one radium dial watch maker, so you must use the plural pronoun *their.* The other answer choices contain the singular pronoun *his* and should be eliminated.

15. **The best answer is B.** The meaning of *law* implies *regulation*; therefore, it would be redundant to use them together as in answer choices A, C, and D.

PASSAGE II

16. **The best answer is H**. Using the word *children* adds clarity to this sentence. Answer choices F and G should be eliminated because they contain ambiguous pronouns—it is unclear to whom the pronoun *them* refers. Omitting the underlined portion makes the sentence awkward.

17. **The best answer is C.** It is necessary to separate the two main ideas of this sentence with a comma; no other punctuation is needed.

18. **The best answer is H.** This question tests your ability to select the clearest and most concise answer choice. Answer choice F incorrectly uses the adjective "certain" to modify the verb "possible." Answer choices G and J are wordy.

19. **The best answer is B.** Since *children* is a plural noun, it is not correct to add an *s'*. Therefore, answer choice A should be eliminated. In this sentence, the children "possess" the "first experience"— it is theirs. So, you must use the possessive form of *children*, which is children's, answer choice B.

20. **The best answer is J.** You need to maintain parallel verb tense with the sentence. Since the children "ran" and "developed," both simple past tense, you should use the simple past-tense verb *played*. By including the word *have* in answer choice F, the tense becomes present perfect, which is not consistent with the rest of the sentence.

21. **The best answer is B.** It does not make sense that children would practice "skills they were just playing"—you don't "play" skills. The only selection that would NOT be acceptable is answer choice B, so it is correct.

22. **The best answer is G.** The word *also* correctly suggests that the children learned about "playing fair, being a team player, and displaying good sportsmanship" at the same time that they were learning "critical skills from their peers." The other answer choices do not fit the context of the sentence because they are signals of contrast, which is not appropriate here.

23. The best answer is A. The preceding paragraph indicates that, thirty years ago, children often participated in "free play" before they became involved in organized sports. In fact, the paragraph indicates that children enjoyed this "free play," which is likely the primary reason they engaged in such play.

24. The best answer is H. This paragraph goes on to provide more information supporting the idea that children should engage in "free play" instead of organized sports. *However* and *alternatively* suggest a contrast that doesn't exist.

25. The best answer is A. The adverb *as* is used here to introduce a sentence, thereby giving the statement emphasis. It is not idiomatic to use *if* or *for* in this context, so eliminate answer choices B and D. *Whether* implies that something may or may not happen, which is not supported by the context, so eliminate answer choice C.

26. The best answer is F. The plural possessive determiner *their* agrees with the plural noun *families*. *They're* is the contraction of *they are*, and *there* refers to a location. These words are not appropriate in this sentence, so eliminate answer choices G and H. The demonstrative determiner this is singular and does not agree with the plural noun *children*, so eliminate answer choice J.

27. The best answer is C. The best way to express the idea is with the phrase *organized sport*. The other answer choices are too wordy or awkward.

28. The best answer is J. The opening sentences serve to clarify what the author suggests parents should and should not do to encourage healthy activity in their children. The other answer choices are not supported by the passage and should be eliminated.

29. The best answer is A. Commas must be used to separate items in a list. Furthermore, neither a semicolon nor a colon should be used before the phrase *such as*.

30. The best answer is H. The first step in answering this question is to decide if the essay fulfilled the writer's goal. Since the essay is about children in the United States only, it would not fulfill the goal of writing an essay about children's health worldwide. Eliminate answer choices F and G. The essay does discuss the impact of convenience foods, answer choice J, so eliminate it.

CHAPTER 4

ACT Mathematics Test: Strategies and Concept Review

The ACT Mathematics Test is designed to test your ability to reason mathematically, to understand basic mathematical terminology, and to recall basic mathematical formulas and principles. You will have 60 minutes to answer the 60 questions on the ACT Mathematics Test. You should be able to solve problems and apply relevant mathematics concepts in the following areas:

Preparing for Higher Math

This category has five subcategories designed to assess a student's current mathematical learning.

- **Number & Quantity**
  Real and complex number systems
  Integer and rational exponents
  Vectors
  Matrices

- **Algebra**
  Linear expressions
  Polynomials
  Radicals
  Exponential relationships

- **Functions**
  Function definition, notation, representation, and application
  Linear, radical, piecewise, polynomial, and logarithmic functions

- **Geometry**
  Congruence, similarity relationships, surface area
  Volume measurements
  Triangles and circles
  Trigonometric ratios
  Equations of conic sections

- **Statistics & Probability**
  Center and spread of distributions
  Data collection methods
  Bivariate data
  Probabilities

Integrating Essential Skills

This category includes four subcategories designed to assess a student's problem solving, critical reasoning, and strategic thinking ability.

- **Rates and percentages**
- **Proportional relationships**
- **Area, surface area, and volume**
- **Average and median**

Modeling

Questions in this category assess a student's ability to understand, interpret, and evaluate models that represent actual, real-world situations You will see a variety of content areas tested in this category.

GENERAL STRATEGIES AND TECHNIQUES

Use the following general strategies when tackling the ACT Mathematics Test.

Draw Pictures

It really helps sometimes to visualize the problem. This strategy should not take a lot of time and can prevent careless errors. Your sketches can be quick and even a little messy. Sometimes they give you a picture; sometimes you have to just make your own.

Consider the following example:

In the xy-coordinate plane, point P is at $(2, 3)$, point R is at $(8, 3)$, and point S is at $(8, 6)$. What is the area of triangle PRS?

A. 4.5
B. 9
C. 13.5
D. 18
E. 27

The area of a triangle is $\frac{1}{2}$ (base) (height). To solve this problem it might be helpful to draw a diagram, as shown below:

The line segment PR is 6 units long (because the distance between x-coordinates is 6 units), and it is the base of the right triangle. The line segment RS is 3 units long, and it is the height of the right triangle. Using this information, the area of triangle PRS is $\frac{1}{2}$ (6)(3), or 9.

Think Before Computing

Most of the calculations are fairly simple and actually will not require the use of a calculator. In fact, the ACT test writers are just as likely to test your logical reasoning ability or your ability to follow directions as they are to test your ability to punch information into your calculator. If you do use your calculator, be sure that you have a good idea of what your answer should look like ahead of time. If the answer you get from your calculator is not at least in your expected ballpark, try again.

Consider the following example:

If $b - c = 2$, and $a + c = 16$, then $a + b = ?$
A. 8
B. 14
C. 16
D. 18
E. 32

To solve this problem, first recognize that $(b - c) + (a + c) = a + b$. This is true because the c values cancel each other out, leaving you with $b + a$, which is equivalent to $a + b$. Therefore, $a + b$ must equal $2 + 16$, or 18.

Alternatively, you could solve the first equation for c and substitute the solution into the second equation, as follows:

$$b - c = 2$$
$$c = b - 2$$

$$a + c = 16$$
$$a + (b - 2) = 16$$
$$a + b = 18$$

Answer the Question That They Ask You

If the problem requires three steps to reach a solution and you only completed two of the steps, it is likely that the answer you arrived at will be one of the choices. However, it will not be the correct choice! Don't quit early—reason your way through the problem so that it makes sense. Keep in mind, though, that these questions have been designed to take an average of 1 minute each to complete. They do not involve intensive calculations.

Consider the following example:

The rectangular garden shown in the figure has a stone border 2 feet in width on all sides. What is the area, in square feet, of that portion of the garden that *excludes* the border?

6 ft

12 ft

A. 4
B. 16
C. 40
D. 56
E. 72

This problem is asking for the area of the middle portion of the garden. To solve this problem, perform the following calculations, and remember that the border goes around the entire garden. First, subtract the border width from the length of the garden:

$12 - 2(2) = 8$

Next, subtract the border width from the width of the garden:

$6 - 2(2) = 2$

The area (length × width) of the portion of the garden that excludes the border is 8×2, or 16.

If you only accounted for the border along one length and one width of the garden, you would have gotten answer choice C. Answer choice D is the area of the border around the garden. Answer choice E is the area of the entire garden, including the stone border.

Check the Choices

Take a quick peek at the choices as you read the problem for the first time. They can provide valuable clues about how to proceed. For example, you may be able to substitute answer choices for variables in a given equation.

Consider the following example:

If $0 < pr < 1$, then which of the following CANNOT be true?

A. $p < 0$ and $r < 0$

B. $p < -1$ and $r < 0$

C. $p < -1$ and $r < -1$

D. $p < 1$ and $r < 1$

E. $p < 1$ and $r < 0$

At first glance, you might think that you don't have enough information to solve this problem. However, if you recognize that pr must be a positive fraction since it lies between 0 and 1, you can work your way through the answer choices and eliminate those that could be true:

Answer choice A: If both p and r were less than 0, their product would be positive. It's possible for pr to be a positive fraction because both p and r could be negative fractions, so eliminate answer choice A.

Answer choice B: If p were −1 and r were also a negative number their product would be positive. It's possible for pr to be a positive fraction because r could be a negative fraction, so eliminate answer choice B.

Answer choice C: If both p and r were less than −1, then pr would be greater than 1, so this statement cannot be true, and answer choice C is correct.

Answer choice D: If both p and r were less than 1, their product could be positive. It's possible for pr to be a positive fraction because both p and r could be negative fractions, so eliminate answer choice D.

Answer choice E: If p were less than 1, p could be a positive fraction. If r were greater than 0, it would be a positive number, and it's possible for pr to be a positive fraction; eliminate answer choice E.

Test the Answers

Sometimes the quickest way to answer an ACT math question is to try the answer choices that they give you. Each question on the ACT Mathematics Test has five answer choices, and the numerical choices are arranged in ascending or descending order. This means that if you are "trying out" answer choices, it makes sense to try the middle value (choice C or choice H) first. If the middle value is too small, you can eliminate the other two smaller choices. And, if it is too large, you can eliminate the other two larger choices.

Consider the following example:

Which of the following is a value of x for which $(x-3)(x+3)=0$?
A. 2
B. 3
C. 5
D. 6
E. 7

One approach to answering this question is to try the answer choices. Start with answer choice C:

$$(5-3)(5+3)=(2)(8)=16$$

Answer choice C results in an answer that is too big. Because answer choices D and E are both larger than answer choice C, they will result in answers that are greater than 16. Therefore, you can eliminate answer choices C, D, and E, simply by trying answer choice C. Now try answer choice B:

$$(3-3)(3+3)=(0)(6)=0; \text{ answer choice B is correct.}$$

Use "Stand-Ins"

You can sometimes simplify your work on a given problem by using actual numbers as "stand-ins" for variables. This strategy works when you have variables in the question and some of the same variables in the answer choices.

You can simplify the answer choices by substituting actual numbers for the variables. If you use this strategy, remember that numbers on the ACT can be positive or negative and are sometimes whole numbers and sometimes fractions. You should also be careful not to use 1 or 0 as your stand-ins because they can create "identities," which can lead to more than one seemingly correct answer choice.

Consider the following example:

> If a and b are positive consecutive odd integers, where $b > a$, which of the following is equal to $b^2 - a^2$?
> A. $2a$
> B. $4a$
> C. $2a + 2$
> D. $2a + 4$
> E. $4a + 4$

You are given that both a and b are positive consecutive odd integers, and that b is greater than a. Pick two numbers that fit the criteria: $a = 3$ and $b = 5$. Now, substitute these numbers into $b^2 - a^2 : 5^2 = 25$ and $3^2 = 9$; therefore, $b^2 - a^2 = 16$. Now, plug the value that you selected for a into the answer choices until one of them yields 16, as follows:

$2(3) = 6$; eliminate answer choice A.
$4(3) = 12$; eliminate answer choice B.
$2(3) + 2 = 8$; eliminate answer choice C.
$2(3) + 4 = 10$; eliminate answer choice D.
$4(3) + 4 = 16$; answer choice E is correct.

Simplify the Question

Some ACT questions appear quite difficult at first glance, but after careful review, turn out to be pretty straightforward questions. They often include formulas and equations, etc., and ask you to solve for a variable.

Consider the following example:

Each student's project in an art class is given a point score by the teacher and by each of the other students in the class. A student's project grade, g, is determined by the formula $g = \dfrac{3t+s}{3+n}$, where t is the score the teacher gives, s is the sum of the scores the students give, and n is the number of students in the class. What is t in terms of g, s, and n?

A. $t = g - n - s$

B. $t = 3\left(\dfrac{s}{n}\right)$

C. $t = gn + g - s$

D. $t = \dfrac{gn - s}{3}$

E. $t = \dfrac{3g + gn - s}{3}$

To solve this problem, let the answer choices guide you. Note that each answer choice is a solution for t, so all you need to do is solve the given formula for t, as follows:

$$g = \frac{3t+s}{3+n}$$

$$g(3 + n) = 3t + s$$

$$3g + gn = 3t + s$$

$$3g + gn - s = 3t$$

$$\frac{3g + gn - s}{3} = t$$

MATHEMATICS CONCEPT REVIEW

This section serves as a review of the mathematical concepts tested on the ACT. Familiarize yourself with the basic mathematical concepts included here and be able to apply them to a variety of math problems.

Pre-Algebra

The Pre-Algebra (seventh- or eighth-grade level) questions test basic algebraic concepts such as:

1. Operations Using Whole Numbers, Fractions, and Decimals
2. Square Roots
3. Exponents
4. Scientific Notation
5. Ratios, Proportions, and Percent
6. Linear Equations with One Variable
7. Absolute Value
8. Simple Probability

Operations Using Whole Numbers, Decimals, and Fractions

The ACT Mathematics Test will require you to add, subtract, multiply, and divide whole numbers, fractions, and decimals. When performing these operations, be sure to keep track of negative signs and line up decimal points in order to eliminate careless mistakes.

The following are some simple rules to keep in mind regarding whole numbers, fractions, and decimals:

1. Ordering is the process of arranging numbers from smallest to greatest or from greatest to smallest. The symbol > is used to represent "greater than," and the symbol < is used to represent "less than." To represent "greater than or equal to," use the symbol ≥; to represent "less than or equal to," use the symbol ≤.

2. The Commutative Property of Multiplication is expressed as $a \times b = b \times a$, or $ab = ba$.

3. The Distributive Property of Multiplication is expressed as $a(b + c) = ab + ac$.

4. The order of operations for whole numbers can be remembered by using the acronym **PEMDAS**:

   P First, do the operations within the **parentheses**, if any.

   E Next, do the **exponents**.

   MD Next, do the **multiplication** and **division**, in order from left to right.

   AS Finally, do the **addition** and **subtraction**, in order from left to right.

5. When a number is expressed as the product of two or more numbers, it is in factored form. *Factors* are all of the numbers that will divide evenly into one number.

6. A number is called a *multiple* of another number if it can be expressed as the product of that number and a second number. For example, the multiples of 4 are 4, 8, 12, 16, etc., because $4 \times 1 = 4, 4 \times 2 = 8, 4 \times 3 = 12, 4 \times 4 = 16$, etc.

7. The Greatest Common Factor (GCF) is the largest integer that will divide evenly into any two or more integers. The Least Common Multiple (LCM) is the smallest integer into which any two or more integers will divide evenly. For example, the Greatest Common Factor of 24 and 36 is 12, because 12 is the largest integer that will divide evenly into both 24 and 36. The Least Common Multiple of 24 and 36 is 72, because 72 is the smallest integer into which both 24 and 36 will divide evenly.

8. Multiplying and dividing both the numerator and the denominator of a fraction by the same nonzero number will result in an equivalent fraction.

9. When multiplying fractions, multiply the numerators to get the numerator of the product, and multiply the denominators to get the denominator of the product. For example, $\dfrac{3}{5} \times \dfrac{7}{8} = \dfrac{21}{40}$.

10. To divide fractions, multiply the first fraction by the reciprocal of the second fraction. For example, $\dfrac{1}{3} \div \dfrac{1}{4} = \dfrac{1}{3} \times \dfrac{4}{1}$, which equals $\dfrac{4}{3}$.

11. When adding and subtracting like fractions, add or subtract the numerators and write the sum or difference over the denominator. So, $\dfrac{1}{8} + \dfrac{2}{8} = \dfrac{3}{8}$, and $\dfrac{4}{7} - \dfrac{2}{7} = \dfrac{2}{7}$.

12. When adding or subtracting unlike fractions, first find the Lowest Common Denominator. The Lowest Common Denominator is the smallest integer into which all of the denominators will divide evenly. For example, to add $\dfrac{3}{4}$ and $\dfrac{5}{6}$, find the smallest integer into which both 4 and 6 will divide evenly. That integer is 12, so the Lowest Common Denominator is 12. Multiply $\dfrac{3}{4}$ by $\dfrac{3}{3}$ to get $\dfrac{9}{12}$, and multiply $\dfrac{5}{6}$ by $\dfrac{2}{2}$ to get $\dfrac{10}{12}$. Now add the fractions: $\dfrac{9}{12} + \dfrac{10}{12} = \dfrac{19}{12}$, which can be simplified to $1\dfrac{7}{12}$.

13. *Place value* refers to the value of a digit in a number relative to its position. Moving left from the decimal point, the values of the digits are 1's, 10's, 100's, etc. Moving right from the decimal point, the values of the digits are 10ths, 100ths, 1000ths, etc.

14. When converting a fraction to a decimal, divide the numerator by the denominator.

Square Roots

A square root is written $\sqrt{n}$, and is the nonnegative value a that fulfills the expression $a^2 = n$. For example, the square root of 25 would be written as $\sqrt{25}$, which is equivalent to 5^2, or 5×5. A number is considered a perfect square when the square root of that number is a whole number. So, 25 is a perfect square because the square root of 25 is 5.

Exponents

When a whole number is multiplied by itself, the number of times it is multiplied is referred to as the *exponent*. As shown above with square roots, the exponent of 5^2 is 2 and it signifies 5×5. Any number can be raised to any exponential value. For example, $7^6 = 7 \times 7 \times 7 \times 7 \times 7 \times 7 = 117,649$.

Scientific Notation

When numbers are very large or very small, scientific notation is used to shorten them. To form the scientific notation of a number, the decimal point is moved until it is placed after the first nonzero digit from the left in the number. For example, 568,000,000 written in scientific notation would be 5.68×10^8, because the decimal point was moved 8 places to the left. Likewise, 0.0000000354 written in scientific notation would be 3.54×10^{-8}, because the decimal point was moved 8 places to the right.

Ratio, Proportion, and Percent

A *ratio* is the relation between two quantities expressed as one divided by the other. For example, if there are 3 blue cars and 5 red cars, the ratio of blue cars to red cars is $\frac{3}{5}$, or 3:5. A *proportion* indicates that one ratio is equal to another ratio. For example, if the ratio of blue cars to red cars is $\frac{3}{5}$, and there are 8 total cars, you could set up a proportion to calculate the percent of blue cars, as follows:

3 cars is to 8 cars as x percent is to 100 percent

$$\frac{3}{8} = \frac{x}{100}; \text{ solve for } x$$

$$8x = 300$$

$$x = 37.5\%$$

A *percent* is a fraction whose denominator is 100. The fraction $\frac{55}{100}$ is equal to 55%.

Linear Equations with One Variable

In a linear equation with one variable, the variable cannot have an exponent or be in the denominator of a fraction. An example of a linear equation is $2x + 13 = 43$. The ACT Mathematics Test will most likely require you to solve for x in that equation. Do this by isolating x on the left side of the equation, as follows:

$$2x + 13 = 43$$
$$2x = 43 - 13$$
$$2x = 30$$
$$x = \frac{30}{2}, \text{ or } 15$$

One common ACT example of a linear equation with one variable is in questions involving speed of travel. The basic formula to remember is Rate × Time = Distance. The question will give you two of these values and you will have to solve for the remaining value.

Absolute Value

The absolute value of a number is notated by placing that number inside two vertical lines. For example, the absolute value of 10 is written as follows: |10|. Absolute value can be defined as the numerical value of a real number without regard to its sign. This means that the absolute value of 10, |10|, is the same as the absolute value of –10, |–10|, in that they both equal 10. Think of it as the distance from –10 to 0 on the number line and the distance from 0 to 10 on the number line: both distances equal 10 units.

Simple Probability

Probability is used to measure how likely an event is to occur. It is always between 0 and 1; an event that will definitely not occur has a probability of 0, whereas an event that will certainly occur has a probability of 1. To determine probability, divide the number of outcomes that fit the conditions of an event by the total number of outcomes. For example, the chance of getting heads when flipping a coin is 1 out of 2, or $\frac{1}{2}$. There are two possible outcomes (heads or tails) but only one outcome (heads) that fits the conditions of the event. Therefore, the probability of the coin toss resulting in heads is 0.5, or 50%.

When two events are independent, meaning the outcome of one event does not affect the other, you can calculate the probability of both occurring by multiplying the probabilities of each of the events together. For example, the probability of flipping three heads in a row would be $\frac{1}{2} \times \frac{1}{2} \times \frac{1}{2}$, or $\frac{1}{8}$. The ACT Mathematics Test will assess your ability to calculate simple probabilities in everyday situations.

Elementary Algebra

The Elementary Algebra (eighth- or ninth-grade level) questions test elementary algebraic concepts such as:

1. Functions
2. Polynomial Operations and Factoring Simple Quadratic Expressions
3. Linear Inequalities with One Variable
4. Properties of Integer Exponents and Square Roots

Functions

A function is a set of ordered pairs where no two of the ordered pairs has the same x-value. In a function, each input (x-value) has exactly one output (y-value). An example of this relationship would be $y = x^2$. Here, y is a function of x, because for any value of x there is exactly one value of y. However, x is not a function of y, because for certain values of y there is more than one value of x. The *domain* of a function refers to the x-values, while the *range* of a function refers to the y-values. If the values in the domain corresponded to more than one value in the range, the relation is not a function. The following is an example of a function question that may appear on the ACT Mathematics Test:

For the function $f(x) = x^2 - 3x$, what is the value of $f(5)$?

Solve this problem by substituting 5 for x wherever x appears in the function:

$$f(x) = x^2 - 3x$$
$$f(5) = (5)^2 - (3)(5)$$
$$f(5) = 25 - 15$$
$$f(5) = 10$$

Polynomial Operations and Factoring Simple Quadratic Expressions

A polynomial is the sum or difference of expressions like $2x^2$ and $14x$. The most common polynomial takes the form of a simple quadratic expression, such as $2x^2 + 14x + 8$, with the terms in decreasing order. The standard form of a simple quadratic expression is $ax^2 + bx + c$, where a, b, and c are whole numbers. When the terms include both a number and a variable, such as x, the number is called the *coefficient*. For example, in the expression $2x$, 2 is the coefficient of x.

The ACT Mathematics Test will often require you to evaluate, or solve a polynomial by substituting a given value for the variable, as follows:

For $x = -2$, $2x^2 + 14x + 8 = ?$

$$2(-2)^2 + 14(-2) + 8$$
$$2(4) + (-28) + 8$$
$$8 - 28 + 8$$
$$= -12$$

You will also be required to add, subtract, multiply, and divide polynomials. To add or subtract polynomials, simply combine like terms, as in the following examples:

$$(2x^2 + 14x + 8)$$
$$+(3x^2 + 5x + 32)$$
$$\overline{5x^2 + 19x + 40}$$

and

$$(8x^2 + 11x + 23)$$
$$-(7x^2 + 3x + 13)$$
$$\overline{x^2 + 8x + 10}$$

To multiply polynomials, use the distributive property to multiply each term of one polynomial by each term of the other polynomial. Following are some examples:

$$(3x)(x^2 + 4x - 2) = (3x^3 + 12x^2 - 6x)$$

Remember the **FOIL** Method whenever you see this type of multiplication: multiply the **F**irst terms, then the **O**utside terms, then the **I**nside terms, then the **L**ast terms.

$$(2x^2 + 5x)(x - 3) =$$

First terms $(2x^2)(x) = 2x^3$
Outside terms: $(2x^2)(-3) = -6x^2$
Inside terms: $(5x)(x) = 5x^2$
Last terms: $(5x)(-3) = -15x$

Now put the terms in decreasing order:

$$2x^3 + (-6x^2) + 5x^2 + (-15x) = 2x^3 - 1x^2 - 15x$$

You may also be asked to find the factors or solution sets of certain simple quadratic expressions. A factor or solution set takes the form $(x \pm \text{some number})$. Simple quadratic expressions will usually have two of these factors or solution sets. Remember that the standard form of a simple quadratic expression is $ax^2 + bx + c$. To factor the equation, find two numbers that when multiplied together will give you c and when added together will give you b.

The ACT Mathematics Test includes questions similar to the following:

What are the solution sets for $x^2 + 9x + 20$?

Follow these steps to solve:

$$x^2 + 9x + 20 = 0$$
$$(x + \underline{\quad})(x + \underline{\quad}) = 0$$

5 and 4 are two numbers that when multiplied together give you 20, and when added together give you 9.

$(x + 5)(x + 4)$ are the two solution sets for $x^2 + 9x + 20$

Linear Inequalities with One Variable

Linear inequalities with one variable are solved in almost the same manner as linear equations with one variable: by isolating the variable on one side of the inequality. Remember, though, that when multiplying one side of an inequality by a negative number, the direction of the sign must be reversed.

The ACT Mathematics Test will include questions similar to those that follow:

For which values of x is $3x + 4 > 2x + 1$?

Follow these steps to solve:

$3x + 4 > 2x + 1$

$3x - 2x > 1 - 4$

$x > -3$

For which values of x is $6x - 32 < 10x + 12$?

Follow these steps to solve:

$6x - 32 < 10x + 12$

$6x - 10x < 32 + 12$

$-4x < 44$

Now, since you have to divide both sides by -4, remember to reverse the inequality sign: $x > -11$.

Properties of Integer Exponents

The ACT Mathematics Test will assess your ability to multiply and divide numbers with exponents. The following are the rules for operations involving exponents:

- $(x^m)(x^n) = x^{(m+n)}$
- $(x^m)^n = x^{mn}$
- $(xy)^m = (x^m)(y^m)$

- $\left(\dfrac{x}{y}\right)^m = \dfrac{x^m}{y^m}$

- $x^0 = 1$, when $x \neq 0$

- $x^{-m} = \dfrac{1}{x^m}$, when $x \neq 0$

- $\dfrac{a}{x^{-m}} = ax^m$, when $x \neq 0$

Intermediate Algebra

The Intermediate Algebra (ninth- or tenth-grade level) questions test intermediate algebraic concepts such as:

1. Quadratic Formula
2. Radical and Rational Expressions
3. Inequalities and Absolute Value Equations
4. Sequences
5. Systems of Equations
6. Logarithms
7. Roots of Polynomials
8. Matrices

Quadratic Formula

The quadratic formula is expressed as $x = \dfrac{-b \pm \sqrt{(b^2 - 4ac)}}{2a}$. This formula finds solutions to quadratic equations of the form $ax^2 + bx + c = 0$. It is the method that can be used in place of factoring for more complex polynomial expressions. The quantity $b^2 - 4ac$ is called the *discriminant* and can be used to determine quickly at what kind of answer you should arrive. If the discriminant is 0, then there is only one solution. If the discriminant is positive, then there are two real solutions. If the discriminant is negative, then you will have two complex solutions of the form $(a + bi)$, where a and b are real numbers and i is the imaginary number defined by $i^2 = -1$.

Radical and Rational Expressions

The nth root of a given quantity is indicated by the radical sign, $\sqrt{}$. For example, $\sqrt{9}$ is considered a radical, and 9 is the *radicand*. The following rules apply to computations with radical signs:

- $\sqrt{a}$ means the "square root of a," $\sqrt[3]{a}$ means the "cube root of a," etc.
- $\sqrt{a} \times \sqrt{b} = \sqrt{(ab)}$
- $\sqrt[n]{a^n} = a$
- $\sqrt[n]{\sqrt[m]{a}} = \sqrt[mn]{a}$

A *rational number* is a number that can be expressed as a ratio of two integers. Fractions are rational numbers that represent a part of a whole number. To find the square root of a fraction, simply divide the square root of the numerator by the square root of the denominator. If the denominator is not a perfect square, rationalize the denominator by multiplying both the numerator and the denominator by a number that would make the denominator a perfect square.

Consider the following example:

$$\sqrt{\frac{1}{3}} =$$

$$\frac{\sqrt{1}}{\sqrt{3}} = \frac{\sqrt{1}}{\sqrt{3}} \times \frac{\sqrt{3}}{\sqrt{3}} = \frac{\sqrt{3}}{3}$$

Inequalities and Absolute Value Equations

An inequality with an absolute value will be in the form of $|ax + b| > c$, or $|ax + b| < c$. To solve $|ax + b| > c$, first drop the absolute value and create two separate inequalities with the word OR between them. To solve $|ax + b| < c$, first drop the absolute value and create two separate inequalities with the word AND between them. To remember this, think of the inequality sign that is being used in the equation. If it is a "greatOR" than sign, use OR. If it is a "less 'thAND'" sign, use AND. The first inequality will look just like the original inequality without the absolute value. For the second inequality, you must switch the inequality sign and change the sign of c.

To solve $|x + 3| > 5$, first drop the absolute value sign and create two separate inequalities with the word OR between them:

$x + 3 > 5$ OR $x + 3 < -5$. Then solve for x:

$x > 2$ OR $x < -8$.

To solve $|x + 3| < 5$, first drop the absolute value sign and create two separate inequalities with the word AND between them:

$x + 3 < 5$ AND $x + 3 > -5$. Then solve for x:

$x < 2$ AND $x > -8$.

Sequences

An arithmetic sequence is one in which the difference between consecutive terms is the same. For example, 2, 4, 6, 8..., is an arithmetic sequence where 2 is the common difference. In an arithmetic sequence, the nth term can be found using the formula $a_n = a_1 + (n - 1)d$, where d is the common difference.

A geometric sequence is one in which the ratio between two terms is constant. For example, $\frac{1}{2}, 1, 2, 4, 8...$, is a geometric sequence where 2 is the common ratio. With geometric sequences, you can find the nth term using the formula $a_n = a_1(r)^{n-1}$, where r is the common ratio.

Systems of Equations

The most common type of system of equations question tested on the ACT Mathematics Test involves two equations and two unknowns. Solve this system of equations as follows:

$4x + 5y = 21$

$5x + 10y = 30$

If you multiply the top equation by –2, you will get:

$$-8x - 10y = -42$$

Now, you can add the like terms of the two equations together, and solve for x:

$$(-8x + 5x) = -3x$$

$$(-10y + 10y) = 0$$

$$-42 + 30 = -12$$

$$-3x = -12$$

Notice that the two y-terms cancel each other out. Solving for x, you get $x = 4$. Now, choose one of the original two equations, plug 4 in for x, and solve for y:

$$4(4) + 5y = 21$$

$$16 + 5y = 21$$

$$5y = 5$$

$$y = 1$$

Logarithms

Logarithms are used to indicate exponents of certain numbers called *bases*, where $\log_a b = c$, if $a^c = b$. For example, $\log_2 16 = 4$, which means the log to the base 2 of 16 is 4, because $2^4 = 16$.

The following is the kind of logarithm problem you are likely to see on the ACT Mathematics Test:

Which of the following is the value of x that satisfies $\log_x 9 = 2$?
  Follow these steps to solve:

  $\log_x 9 = 2$ means the log to the base x of $9 = 2$.
  So, x^2 must equal 9, and x must equal 3.

Roots of Polynomials

When given a quadratic equation, $ax^2 + bx + c = 0$, you may be asked to find the roots of the equation. This means you need to find what value(s) of x make the equation true. You may either choose to factor the quadratic equation or you may choose to use the quadratic formula. For example, use factoring to find the roots of $x^2 + 6x + 8 = 0$:

$$x^2 + 6x + 8 = 0$$

$$(x + 4)(x + 2) = 0;\text{ solve for } x$$

$$x + 4 = 0 \text{ and } x + 2 = 0, \text{ so } x = -4 \text{ and } x = -2$$

The roots of $x^2 + 6x + 8 = 0$ are $x = -4$ and $x = -2$. Using the quadratic formula will yield the same solution.

Matrices

A matrix is used to organize data in columns and rows. The dimensions of a matrix refer to the number of rows and columns of a given matrix. For example, a 2x3 matrix, as shown below, has two rows and three columns:

$$\begin{bmatrix} 2 & 4 & 6 \\ 1 & 4 & 7 \end{bmatrix}$$

You can add and subtract matrices if each matrix has the same dimensions. Simply add or subtract the numbers that are in the same spot. For example:

$$\begin{bmatrix} 2 & 4 & 6 \\ 1 & 4 & 7 \end{bmatrix} + \begin{bmatrix} 3 & 1 & 2 \\ 8 & 5 & 1 \end{bmatrix} = \begin{bmatrix} 5 & 5 & 8 \\ 9 & 9 & 8 \end{bmatrix}$$

You can also multiply matrices. When you multiply a matrix by a number, you multiply every element in the matrix by the same number. For example:

$$a\begin{bmatrix} 5 & 5 & 8 \\ 9 & 9 & 8 \end{bmatrix} = \begin{bmatrix} 5a & 5a & 8a \\ 9a & 9a & 8a \end{bmatrix}$$

You might also be asked to calculate the determinant of a 2x2 matrix. The formula for calculating the determinant is:

Matrix A: $\begin{bmatrix} a & b \\ c & d \end{bmatrix}$

Determinant A: $ad - bc$

There may be one or two matrix questions on your ACT.

Vectors

By definition, a vector has both magnitude (size) and direction. A vector is depicted using an arrow. The length of the line shows its magnitude and the arrowhead points in the direction.

You can add two vectors by joining them head-to-tail:

You can also subtract vectors by first reversing the direction of the vector you want to subtract, then adding the vectors by joining them head-to-tail:

You will likely see one or two vector questions on your ACT.

Coordinate Geometry

The Coordinate Geometry (Cartesian Coordinate Plane) questions test coordinate geometry concepts such as:

1. Number Line Graphs
2. Equation of a Line
3. Slope
4. Parallel and Perpendicular Lines
5. Distance and Midpoint Formulas

Number Line Graphs

The most basic type of graphing is graphing on a number line. For the most part, you will be asked to graph inequalities. Below are four of the most common types of problems you will be asked to graph on the ACT Mathematics Test:

If the inequality sign specifies "greater than or equal to" (≥), or "less than or equal to" (≤), you would use a closed circle instead of an open circle on the designated number or the number line.

Equation of a Line

There are three forms used to write an equation of a line. The standard form of an equation of a line is in the form $Ax + By = C$. This can be transformed into the slope-intercept form of $y = mx + b$, where m is the slope of the line and b is the y-intercept (that is, the point at which the graph of the line crosses the y-axis). The third form is point-slope form, which is $(y - y_1) = m(x - x_1)$, where m is the slope and (x_1, y_1) is a given point on the line. The ACT Mathematics Test will often require you to put the equation of a line into the slope-intercept form to determine either the slope or the y-intercept of a line as follows:

What is the slope of the line given by the equation $3x + 7y - 16 = 0$?
  Follow these steps to solve:

$3x + 7y - 16 = 0$; isolate y on the left side of the equation.

$7y = -3x + 16$

$y = -\dfrac{3}{7}x + \dfrac{16}{7}$

The slope of the line is $-\dfrac{3}{7}$.

Slope

The slope of a line is the grade at which the line increases or decreases. Commonly defined as "rise over run," the slope is a value that is calculated by taking the change in y-coordinates divided by the change in x-coordinates for any two given points on a line. The formula for slope is $m = \dfrac{(y_2 - y_1)}{(x_2 - x_1)}$ where (x_1, y_1) and (x_2, y_2) are the two given points. For example, if you are given $(3, 2)$ and $(5, 6)$ as two points on a line, the slope would be $m = \dfrac{6-2}{5-3} = \dfrac{4}{2} = 2$. A positive slope means the graph of the line will go up and to the right. A negative slope means the graph of the line will go down and to the right. A horizontal line has slope 0, and a vertical line has undefined slope.

Parallel and Perpendicular Lines

Two lines are parallel if and only if they have the same slope. Two lines are perpendicular if and only if the slope of either of the lines is the negative reciprocal of the slope of the other line. To illustrate, if the slope of line a is 5, then the slope of line b must be $-\dfrac{1}{5}$ for lines a and b to be perpendicular.

Distance and Midpoint Formulas

To find the distance between two points on a coordinate graph, use the formula $\sqrt{([x_2 - x_1]^2 + [y_2 - y_1]^2)}$, where (x_1, y_1) and (x_2, y_2) are the two given points. For instance, the distance between $(3, 2)$ and $(7, 6)$ is $\sqrt{([7-3]^2 + [6-2]^2)} = \sqrt{4^2 + 4^2} = \sqrt{(16+16)} = \sqrt{(32)} = \sqrt{(16)(2)} = 4\sqrt{2}$.

Note: This formula is based on the Pythagorean Theorem and if you can't remember it on test day, just draw a right triangle on your test booklet and proceed from there.

To find the midpoint of a line given two points on the line, use the formula $\left(\dfrac{x_1 + x_2}{2}, \dfrac{y_1 + y_2}{2}\right)$. For example, the midpoint between $(5, 4)$ and $(9, 2)$ is $\left(\dfrac{5+9}{2}, \dfrac{4+2}{2}\right) = (7, 3)$.

Plane Geometry

Plane Geometry questions test plane geometry concepts such as:

1. Properties and Relations of Plane Figures
   a. Triangles
   b. Circles
   c. Rectangles
   d. Parallelograms
   e. Trapezoids
2. Angles, Parallel Lines, and Perpendicular Lines
3. Perimeter, Area, and Volume

Properties and Relations of Plane Figures

Triangles

A triangle is a polygon with three sides and three angles. If the measure of all three angles in the triangle are the same and all three sides of the triangle are the same length, then the triangle is an *equilateral* triangle. If the measure of two of the angles and two of the sides of the triangle are the same, then the triangle is an *isosceles* triangle.

The sum of the interior angles in a triangle is always 180°. If the measure of one of the angles in the triangle is 90° (a right angle), then the triangle is a right triangle, as shown below.

Some right triangles have unique relationships between the angles and the lengths of the sides. These are called *special right triangles*. It may be helpful to remember the following information:

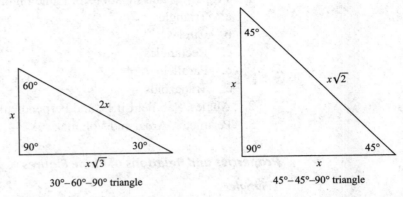

30°–60°–90° triangle   45°–45°–90° triangle

The perimeter of a triangle is the sum of the lengths of the sides. The area of a triangle is $A = \dfrac{1}{2}$ (base)(height). For any right triangle, the Pythagorean Theorem states that $a^2 + b^2 = c^2$, where a and b are legs (sides) and c is the hypotenuse.

Circles

The equation of a circle centered at the point (h, k) is $(x - h)^2 + (y - k)^2 = r^2$, where r is the radius of the circle. The radius of a circle is the distance from the center of the circle to any point on the circle. The diameter of a circle is twice the radius. The formula for the circumference of a circle is $C = 2\pi r$, and the formula for the area of a circle is $A = \pi r^2$.

Rectangles

A rectangle is a polygon with two pairs of congruent, parallel sides and four right angles. The sum of the angles in a rectangle is always 360°. The perimeter of a rectangle is $P = 2l + 2w$, where l is the length and w is the width. The area of a rectangle is $A = lw$. The lengths of the diagonals of a rectangle are congruent, or equal. A square is a special rectangle where all four sides are of equal length, as shown here:

Parallelograms

A parallelogram is a polygon with four sides and four angles that are NOT right angles. A parallelogram has two sets of congruent sides and two sets of congruent angles.

Again, the sum of the angles of a parallelogram is 360°. The perimeter of a parallelogram is $P = 2l + 2w$. The area of a parallelogram is $A =$ (base)(height). The height is the distance from top to bottom. A rhombus is a special parallelogram with four congruent sides.

Trapezoids

A trapezoid is a polygon with four sides and four angles. The bases of the trapezoid (top and bottom) are never the same length. The sides of the trapezoid can be the same length (isosceles trapezoid), or they may not be. The perimeter of the trapezoid is the sum of the lengths of the sides. The area of a trapezoid is $A = \dfrac{1}{2}$ (Base$_1$ + Base$_2$) (Height). Height is the distance between the bases. (The diagonals of an isosceles trapezoid have a unique feature. When the diagonals of a trapezoid intersect, the ratio of the top of the diagonals to the bottom of the diagonals is the same as the ratio of the top base to the bottom base.)

Angles, Parallel Lines, and Perpendicular Lines

Angles can be classified as acute, obtuse, or right. An acute angle is any angle less than 90°. An obtuse angle is any angle that is greater than 90° and less than 180°. A right angle is an angle that is 90°.

When two parallel lines are cut by a perpendicular line, right angles are created, as follows:

When two parallel lines are cut by a transversal, the angles created have special properties. Each of the parallel lines cut by the transversal has four angles surrounding the intersection that are matched in measure and position with a counterpart at the other parallel line. The vertical (opposite) angles are congruent, and the adjacent angles are supplementary; that is, the sum of the two supplementary angles is 180°.

Note: Almost every ACT ever administered has a diagram similar to the one above as part of at least one math question.

Perimeter, Area, and Volume

These formulas are not provided for you on test day. You should make your best effort to memorize them.

Perimeter

The formulas for calculating the perimeter of shapes that appear on the ACT Mathematics Test are as follows:

Triangle: Sum of the Sides

Rectangle and Parallelogram: $2l + 2w$

Square: $4s$ (s is Length of Side)

Trapezoid: Sum of the Sides

Circle (Circumference): $2\mu r$

Area

The formulas for calculating the area of shapes that appear on the ACT Mathematics Test are as follows:

Triangle: $\frac{1}{2}$ (Base)(Height)

Rectangle and Square: (Length)(Width)

Parallelogram: (Base)(Height)

Trapezoid: $\frac{1}{2}$ (Base$_1$ + Base$_2$)(Height)

Circle: πr^2

Volume

The formulas for calculating the volume of basic three-dimensional shapes that appear on the ACT Mathematics Test are as follows:

Rectangular Box and Cube: (Length)(Width)(Height)

Sphere: $\frac{4}{3} \pi r^3$

Right Circular Cylinder: $\pi r^2 h$ (h is the height)

Right Circular Cone: $\frac{1}{3} \pi r^2 h$ (h is the height)

Prism: (Area of the Base)(Height)

Trigonometry

There are typically only four trigonometry questions on the ACT Mathematics Test. If you have never taken trigonometry in school, you may still be able to learn enough here to get by on at least a couple of the four questions. (Even if you NEVER learn trigonometry, don't worry; four questions are not likely to seriously affect your score.) The questions test the basic trigonometric ratios (which are related to right triangles, as shown below).

Basic Trigonometric Concepts

The hypotenuse is the side that is opposite the right angle. Sometimes the graph or diagram shown in the question will have the triangle rotated, so make sure that you know where the right angle is and, of course, the hypotenuse, which is directly opposite the right angle.

SOHCAHTOA

SINE (sin) = **O**pposite/**H**ypotenuse (SOH)
COSINE (cos) = **A**djacent/**H**ypotenuse (CAH)
TANGENT (tan) = **O**pposite/**A**djacent (TOA)

$$\sin \alpha = \frac{z}{y}$$

$$\sin \beta = \frac{x}{y}$$

$$\cos \alpha = \frac{x}{y}$$

$$\cos \beta = \frac{z}{y}$$

$$\tan \alpha = \frac{z}{x}$$

$$\tan \beta = \frac{x}{z}$$

Advanced Trigonometric Concepts

Note: The following information will be extremely confusing and intimidating for anyone who has never heard of it before. This information is included only as a review for those readers who have had a trigonometry class. The rest of you should just guess on the two or three questions that might include these concepts.

The secant, cosecant, and cotangent can be found as follows:

$$\text{SEC(secant)} = \frac{1}{\text{COS}} \quad \text{CSC(cosecant)} = \frac{1}{\text{SIN}} \quad \text{COT(cotangent)} = \frac{1}{\text{TAN}}$$

Remember the following Pythagorean Identities:

$$\sin^2 \theta + \cos^2 \theta = 1$$

$$1 + \tan^2 \theta = \sec^2 \theta$$

$$1 + \cot^2 \theta = \csc^2 \theta$$

Remember the following Trigonometric Identities:

$$\sin(-\theta) = -\sin \theta \quad \cos(-\theta) = \cos \theta \quad \tan(-\theta) = -\tan \theta$$

$$\csc(-\theta) = -\csc \theta \quad \sec(-\theta) = \sec(\theta) \quad \cot(-\theta) = -\cot \theta$$

$$\left.\begin{array}{l} \sin(\alpha + \beta) = \sin \alpha \cos \beta + \sin \beta \cos \alpha \\ \sin(\alpha - \beta) = \sin \alpha \cos \beta - \sin \beta \cos \alpha \\ \cos(\alpha + \beta) = \cos \alpha \cos \beta - \sin \alpha \sin \beta \\ \cos(\alpha - \beta) = \cos \alpha \cos \beta + \sin \alpha \sin \beta \end{array}\right\} \text{Addition and Subtraction Formulas}$$

$$\left.\begin{array}{l} \sin 2\theta = 2 \sin \theta \cos \theta \\ \cos 2\theta = \cos^2 \theta - \sin^2 \theta = 1 - 2\sin^2 \theta = 2\cos^2 \theta - 1 \end{array}\right\} \text{Double-angle Formulas}$$

$$\left.\begin{array}{l} \sin^2 \theta = \frac{(1 - \cos^2)}{2} \quad \cos^2 \theta = \frac{(1 + \cos^2 \theta)}{2} \end{array}\right\} \text{Half-angle Formulas}$$

Radians

To change from degrees to radians, multiply the number of degrees by $\frac{\pi}{180}$. For example, $120°$ is $\frac{120\pi}{180}$ $\frac{2\pi}{3}$ radians. Conversely, to change from radians to degrees, multiply the number of radians by $\frac{180}{\pi}$.

ACT MATHEMATICS SKILLS EXERCISES

The next few pages contain exercises designed to help you apply the concepts generally tested on the ACT Mathematics Test. Following this section are simulated ACT Mathematics questions, which will allow you to become familiar with the format and types of questions you'll see on your actual ACT test. You might want to get some scratch paper before starting this section.

Basic Operations

These questions will test your knowledge of operations using whole numbers, fractions, and decimals.

Insert the correct operator in the blanks below.

1. $108 \_\_ 9 = 12$

2. $7 \_\_ 2 = 3.5$

3. $\dfrac{1}{4} \_\_ \dfrac{3}{8} = \dfrac{5}{8}$

Answer the following questions.

4. What is the greatest common factor of 48 and 72?

5. What is the lowest common denominator of $\dfrac{5}{8}$ and $\dfrac{3}{4}$?

Solve the following equations.

6. $\dfrac{(96-21)}{15} + 11 = \_\_\_\_$

7. $3(27 + 2 - 3) = \_\_\_\_$

8. $\dfrac{1}{3} + \dfrac{3}{7} = \_\_\_\_$

9. $231.2 - 198.7 = \_\_\_\_$

10. $0.25 \times \dfrac{1}{5} = \_\_\_\_$

Exponents and Square Roots

These questions will test your knowledge of operations using square roots.

Solve the following problems.

1. $5^2 = $ _____

2. $\sqrt{36} \div \sqrt{4} = $ _____

3. Express 3×3 as a square: _____

4. $7^2 - 3^2 = $ _____

5. $\sqrt{64} \times 2^2 = $ _____

Properties of Integer Exponents

These questions will test your knowledge of operations involving integer exponents.

Solve the following problems.

1. $x^3 \times x^6 = $ _____

2. $(3^2)^3 = $ _____

3. $\left(\dfrac{5}{3}\right)^3 = $ _____

4. $137^0 = 5$ _____

5. $(y \times z)^2 = $ _____

Fill in the blanks below with the correct number.

1. 2 raised to the power of _____ $= 8$.

2. $3^3 = $ _____

3. _____$^4 = 81$

4. $125 = 5$ _____

5. $(2^4)^2 = $ _____

Scientific Notation

These questions will test your knowledge of operations using scientific notation.

Fill in the blanks below with the correct number.

1. $423,700,000 = 4.237 \times 10$ to the power of _____

2. $3.76 \times 10^5 =$ _____

3. $(2.50 \times 10^4) \div (1.25 \times 10^3) =$ _____

4. $6.47 \times 10^{-5} =$ _____

5. $(4.2 \times 10^3) \times (1.8 \times 10^{-6}) =$ _____

Ratio, Proportion, and Percent

These questions will test your knowledge of operations involving ratio, proportion, and percent.

Answer the following questions.

1. _____ is 30% of 20.

2. $\dfrac{39}{78} = \dfrac{x}{6}$. Solve for x.

3. As an assistant analyst for the Department of Natural Resources, you were asked to analyze samples of river water. A 2-liter sample of water contained about 24 of a particular organism and a 4-liter sample of water contained about 48 such organisms. At this rate, how many of the organisms would you expect to find in a 10-liter sample of water from the same river? _____

4. If 20% of x equals 16, then $x =$ ____.

5. Jim scored 95 points in 5 basketball games for his school. At this rate, how many points will he have scored by the end of the 12-game season?

Linear Equations with One Variable

These questions will test your knowledge of linear equations involving one variable.

Solve the following equations.

1. $3x - 17 = 46$. Solve for x.

2. $\dfrac{x}{4} = -6$. Solve for x.

3. If $x = 15$, then $4x -$ ____ $= 42$.

4. Two trains running on parallel tracks are 600 miles apart. One train is moving east at a speed of 90 mph, while the other is moving west at 75 mph. How long will it take for the two trains to pass each other?

5. $3(x - 4) = 5x - 20$. Solve for x.

Absolute Value

These questions will test your knowledge of operations involving absolute value.

Solve the following equations.

1. If $x = -8$, what is the value of $|x - 6|$?
2. Solve $|4x - 6| = 10$ for x.
3. $|-15| \times |6| = \underline{\hspace{1cm}}$
4. Solve $|6x + 8| = |3x - 7|$ for x.
5. $\dfrac{-32}{|-8|} = \underline{\hspace{1cm}}$

Simple Probability

These questions will test your knowledge of operations involving simple probability.

Answer the following questions.

1. If you roll a single 6-sided die, what is the probability that you will roll an odd number?

2. A company knows that 2.5% of the CD players it makes are defective. If the company produces 300,000 CD players, how many will be defective?

3. When flipping a coin, what is the probability that it will land on tails four times in a row?

4. If the probability that Dave will go to class is 0.7, what is the probability that he will not go to class?

5. There is a bowl with 20 marbles in it (8 blue, 6 red, 3 green, 2 yellow, and 1 orange.) If you reach in and choose one marble at random, what is the probability that it will be red?

Functions

These questions will test your knowledge of operations involving functions.

Answer the following questions.

1. For the function $f(x) = x^2 - 4x + 8$, what is the value of $f(6)$?
2. If $f(x) = x^2$, find $f(x + 1)$.
3. If the function $f(x) = x + 2$, and the function $g(x) = 3x$, what is the function $g(f(x))$?
4. For the function $f(x) = x^4 - \dfrac{3x}{2}$ what is the value of $f(2)$?
5. For the function $f(x) = x^2 + x$, what is the value of $f(-5)$?

Polynomial Operations and Factoring Simple Quadratic Equations

These questions will test your knowledge of operations involving polynomial operations and factoring simple quadratic equations.

Solve the following equations.

1. For $x = 4, 3x^2 - 5x + 9 = $ ____
2. $(5x^3 + 3x - 12) - (2x^3 - 6x + 17) = $ _____
3. $(4x^2 + 2x)(x - 6) = $ _____

Answer the following questions.

4. What are the solution sets for $x^2 + 2x - 48$?
5. $(x - 4)$ and $(2x + 3)$ are the solution sets for what equation?

Linear Inequalities with One Variable

These questions will test your knowledge of operations involving linear inequalities with one variable.

Answer the following questions.

1. For $-5 \leq x < 15, x = $ ____
2. For which values of x is $6x - 3 > 4x + 5$?
3. If $x = 7$, the is $3x + 7$ greater than or less than $5x - 6$?
4. For which values of x is $2x - 5 < -3x + 20$?
5. Solve $-4 \leq x + 3 < 18$ for x.

Quadratic Formula

These questions will test your knowledge of operations involving the quadratic formula.

Answer the following questions.

1. Use the quadratic formula to solve the equation $10x^2 + 22x + 12.1 = 0$.
2. Set up the equation $4x^2 - 7x + 3 = 10x^2 + x - 11$ so it can be used in the quadratic formula.
3. Solve the equation $4x^2 + x - 5 = 0$ using the quadratic formula.
4. Which values of a, b, and c will you use in the quadratic formula for the equation $18x - 117 + 4x^2 = 0$? (Place an "X" next to the correct answer.)
    ____$18, -117, 4$
    ____$-117, 4, 18$
    ____$4, 18, -117$
    ____$4, 18, 117$
5. Solve the equation $(2x + 4)^2 = 0$ using the quadratic formula.

Radical and Rational Expressions

These questions will test your knowledge of operations involving radical and rational expressions.

Solve the following problems.

1. $\sqrt{12} \times \sqrt{3} = ?$

2. $\sqrt{\dfrac{2}{5}} = ?$

3. $\sqrt[3]{27} = ?$

4. $\sqrt{2x^4} \times \sqrt{8y^2} = ?$

5. $\sqrt[7]{11^{14}} = ?$

Inequalities and Absolute Value Equations

These questions will test your knowledge of operations involving inequalities and absolute value equations.

Answer the following questions.

1. For $|7x - 13| < 22,$ which one of the following is true? (Place an "X" next to the correct answer.)

    ___ $7x - 13 > 22$ OR $7x - 13 < -22$

    ___ $7x - 13 < 22$ AND $7x - 13 > -22$

    ___ $-7x - 13 < 22$ AND $-7x - 13 > -22$

    ___ $7x + 13 > 22$ OR $7x + 13 < -22$

2. If $|x + 8| > 15,$ what is/are the possible values of x?

3. If $|2x + 3| < 21,$ what is/are the possible values of x?

4. For $|5x - 6| > 29,$ which one of the following is true? (Place an "X" next to the correct answer.)

    ___ $5x - 6 > 29$ OR $5x - 6 < -29$

    ___ $5x - 6 < 29$ AND $5x - 6 > -29$

    ___ $-5x - 6 < 29$ AND $-5x - 6 > -29$

    ___ $5x + 6 > 29$ OR $5x + 6 < -29$

5. If $\left| -\dfrac{1}{4}x + 3 \right| > 5,$ what is/are the possible values of x?

Sequences

These questions will test your knowledge of operations involving sequences.

Answer the following questions.

1. Find the 3rd term of the arithmetic sequence: $a_n = 3 + (n-1)(2)$.

2. Write a formula for the nth term of the arithmetic sequence $-8, -2, 4, 10,...$

3. In the geometric sequence: $\dfrac{1}{4}, 1, 4, 16,...$, what is the 6th term?

4. Which of the following represents the formula to find the 8th term of the arithmetic sequence 7, 13, 19, 25,...? (Place an "X" next to the correct answer.)

   ___ $13 + (8-1)(19)$

   ___ $25(7)^{19-13}$

   ___ $7(6)^{8-1}$

   ___ $7 + (8-1)(6)$

5. Write a formula for the nth term of the geometric sequence 25, -5, 1, $-\dfrac{1}{5},...$

Systems of Equations

These questions will test your knowledge of operations involving systems of equations.

Solve the following systems of equations.

1. $\begin{cases} x - 2y = 14 \\ x - 4y = -8 \end{cases}$

2. $\begin{cases} 4x - 2y = 6 \\ -6x + 5y = 7 \end{cases}$

3. $\begin{cases} 3x - y = 18 \\ 4x = 24 - 6y \end{cases}$

4. $\begin{cases} 8(y + x) = 12 \\ 4x - 3y = -22 \end{cases}$

5. $\begin{cases} 4x - y = 63 \\ 3y + x = 6 \end{cases}$

Logarithms

These questions will test your knowledge of operations involving logarithms.

Solve the following problems.

1. What is the value of x that satisfies $\log_x 27 = 3$?

2. If $\log_x 625 = 4$, what is the value of x? (Place an "X" next to the correct answer.)
   ___ 4
   ___ 5
   ___ 7
   ___ 19

3. $\log_3 729 =$?

4. If $\log_x 196 = 2$, then $x =$___?

5. If $\log_7 x = 3$, what is the value of x? (Place an "X" next to the correct answer.)
   ___ 5
   ___ 64
   ___ 216
   ___ 343

Roots of Polynomials

These questions will test your knowledge of operations involving roots of polynomials.

Answer the following questions.

1. Find the roots of $2x^2 + 9x - 35$ by factoring.

2. Find the roots of $x^2 + 2x - 3$ by factoring.

3. What polynomial equation has the solutions $x = 6$ and $x = -2$?

4. Solve for x by factoring the polynomial equation $x^2 - 8x + 16$.

5. Find the roots of $-x^2 + 3x + 40$ by factoring.

Number Line Graphs

These questions will test your knowledge of operations involving number line graphs.

Answer the following questions.

1. On a number line, what is the distance between –5 and 3?
2. What is the midpoint of the two points in the below graph?

3. The below graph represents which values for x? (Place an "X" next to the correct answer.)

___ $x > -3$ AND $x < 6$

___ $x \geq -3$ AND $x \leq 6$

___ $x \geq -3$ OR $x < 6$

___ $x \geq -3$ AND $x < 6$

4. The below graph represents the solution to which inequality? (Place an "X" next to the correct answer.)

___ $|2x - 10| < 6$

___ $|2x + 10| < 6$

___ $|2x - 10| > 6$

___ $|-2x + 10| > 6$

5. The below graph represents which values for x? (Place an "X" next to the correct answer.)

___ $x \geq 2$ OR $x < -6$

___ $x \geq 2$ AND $x < -6$

___ $x \geq -6$ OR $x < 2$

___ $x \geq -6$ AND $x > 2$

Equation of a Line and Slope of a Line

These questions will test your knowledge of operations involving the equation of a line and the slope.

Answer the following questions.

1. What is the y-intercept of the line with the equation $2y = 4x + 12$?

2. What is the slope of the line with the equation $3y = -2x + 5$?

3. What is the slope of the line $x = 4$?

4. What is the equation of a line parallel to $y = 4x - 12$ and crossing the y-axis at 3?

5. What is the equation of a line perpendicular to $3x = 2 - y$ with the y-intercept 8?

Distance and Midpoint Formulas

These questions will test your knowledge of operations involving distance and midpoint formulas.

Answer the following questions.

1. What is the distance between the points (3, −4) and (9, 4)?

2. What is one possible value for y if the distance between the two points (2, 8) and (−6, y) is 17?

3. What is the midpoint between (12, 5) and (10, −7)?

4. Solve for x if the midpoint between the two points (x, 1) and (−2, −3) is (5, −1).

5. What is the distance between the points (0, 5) and (5, 0)?

Properties and Relations of Plane Figures

These questions will test your knowledge of operations involving plane figures.

Answer the following questions.

1. What is the hypotenuse of a right triangle with a base of 9 cm and an area of 54 cm²?

2. What is the area of a circle with a circumference of 14π inches?

3. If one of the angles of a parallelogram measures 35°, what is the sum of the remaining angles?

4. A trapezoid has one base of 8 ft, a height of 3 ft, and an area of 30 ft², what is the length of the other base?

5. A polygon with four sides and four right angles has one side of 6 mm. If the area is 42 mm², would the polygon be considered a square or a rectangle?

Angles, Parallel Lines, and Perpendicular Lines

These questions will test your knowledge of operations involving angles, parallel lines, and perpendicular lines.

Answer the following questions.

1. What is the measure of the angle that is supplementary to a 40° angle?

2. What is the measure of the angle that is supplementary to a 25° angle?

3. In the figure below, line *n* is parallel to line *m*, and line *p* is parallel to line *o*. What is the measure of angle *θ*?

4. In the figure below, line *x* is parallel to line *y*. What is the measure of angle *a*?

5. In the figure below, line *t* is parallel to line *u*, and line *v* is perpendicular to line *u*. What is the measure of angle *a*?

Perimeter, Area, and Volume

These questions will test your knowledge of operations involving perimeter, area, and volume.

Answer the following questions.

1. You are applying fertilizer to your backyard. The rectangular yard measures 40 feet wide and 70 feet long. You use 6 pounds of fertilizer to treat 700 square feet. The fertilizer comes in 8-pound bags. How many bags of fertilizer will you need to complete the job?

2. John is building a circular fence around his circular pool. The pool is 26 feet in diameter. If John wants to have 4 feet of space between the edge of the pool and the fence, what is the area that will be enclosed by the fence? ($\pi = 3.14$)

3. Tiffany inflates a beach ball. If the diameter of the ball is 0.6 m, what is the volume?

4. A cylindrical can of pineapple juice contains 350 cm^3 of liquid. If the can is $\dfrac{14}{\pi}$ cm tall, what is the diameter?

5. A cube has an edge length of 5 in; what is the volume of the cube?

Trigonometry

These questions will test your knowledge of operations involving trigonometry.

Answer the following questions.

1. In the triangle below, what is sin a?

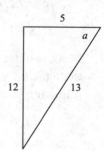

2. If cos $a = \dfrac{4}{5}$, what is tan a?

3. Convert 60° into radians.

4. Convert $\dfrac{3\pi}{4}$ radians into degrees.

5. If sec $a = \dfrac{13}{5}$, what is sin a?

Translating Word Problems

These questions will test your ability to locate relevant mathematical information in word problems.

Place an "X" next to the correct expression in the questions below.

1. Tom had 6 books. He gave 2 to his sister and then purchased 3 more at the bookstore. Which of the following mathematical expressions is equivalent to the number of books that Tom has now?

    ___ $6 - 2 + 3$

    ___ $6 + 2 - 3$

    ___ $6(2 + 3)$

    ___ $6(2 - 3)$

2. Juan walked 3 more miles than Rebecca. Rebecca walked 4 times as far as William. William walked 2 miles. Which of the following mathematical expressions is equivalent to the number of miles Juan walked?

    ___ $3 \times 4 \times 2$

    ___ $(2 + 4) \times 3$

    ___ $4(2) + 3$

    ___ $4 + 3 + 2$

3. Tina goes to the store to purchase some CDs and DVDs. CDs cost $15 and DVDs cost $18. Which of the following expressions gives the total amount of money, in dollars, Tina will pay for purchasing 2 of the CDs and d of the DVDs?

    ___ $15 + d$

    ___ $30 + 18d$

    ___ $18 + d + 30$

    ___ $d(18 + 15)$

4. Mark is older than Frank, but younger than David. If m, f, and d represent the ages, in years, of Mark, Frank, and David, respectively, which of the following is true?

    ___ $d < f < m$

    ___ $f < m < d$

    ___ $d < m < f$

    ___ $f < d < m$

5. Kathy was twice as old as Jim 2 years ago. Today, Jim is j years old. In terms of j, how old was Kathy 2 years ago?

    ___ $2(j - 2)$

    ___ $2j - 2$

    ___ $2(j + 2)$

    ___ $j(2 + 2)$

ANSWERS AND EXPLANATIONS

Basic Operations

1. In order for 12 to be the result of this equation, you must divide 108 by 9. Insert the ÷ symbol in the blank.

2. To reach an answer of 3.5, you must divide 7 by 2. Insert the ÷ symbol in the blank.

3. One way to solve this problem is to look for the Lowest Common Denominator (LCD). The smallest number that both 4 and 8 divide evenly into is 8, so the fraction $\frac{3}{8}$ does not need to be changed. The fraction $\frac{1}{4}$ is equivalent to $\frac{2}{8}$, $\frac{2}{8}$ plus $\frac{3}{8}$ equals $\frac{5}{8}$, so insert the + symbol in the blank.

4. The Greatest Common Factor (GCF) is the largest number that divides evenly into any two or more numbers. List the factors of 48 and 72, then select the largest factor that they have in common:

48	72
1×48	1×72
2×24	2×36
3×16	3×24
4×12	4×18
6×8	6×12
	8×9

Based on this list, the GCF is 24.

5. The LCD is the smallest number into which all of the denominators will divide evenly. For this problem, you must find the smallest number into which 8 and 4 will divide evenly. Since 4 will divide evenly into 8 $\left(\frac{8}{4} = 2\right)$, 8 is your LCD. You can now change $\frac{3}{4}$ to $\frac{6}{8}$ by multiplying both the numerator and denominator by 2 (the amount of times 4 goes into 8).

6. You must first complete the mathematics within the parentheses $(96 - 21 = 75)$. Next, do any multiplication or division in the problem, from left to right. Here, you have 75 divided by 15, which equals 5. Finally, do any addition or subtraction in the problem, from left to right: 5 plus 11 gives us an answer of 16.

7. You must first do the operations within the parentheses $(27 + 2 - 3 = 26)$. Now multiply the value from the parentheses by 3: 3 times $26 = 78$.

8. You must first find the LCD for the two fractions involved. The denominators are 3 and 7. The smallest number into which both of these can divide evenly is 21. Convert each denominator to 21 by multiplying $\frac{1}{3}$ by $\frac{7}{7}$ and $\frac{3}{7}$ by $\frac{3}{3}$. This gives you $\frac{7}{21} + \frac{9}{21}$, which equals $\frac{16}{21}$.

9. This is a simple subtraction problem. To solve this without a calculator, line up the decimal points and subtract, remembering to "borrow" and "carry," as follows:

$$\begin{array}{r} 231.2 \\ -198.7 \\ \hline 32.5 \end{array}$$

10. First convert $\frac{1}{5}$ to a decimal, which is 0.2. Then multiply 0.25 by 0.2, which gives you an answer of 0.05. Another way to solve this is to first convert 0.25 to a fraction, which is $\frac{1}{4}$. When multiplying the two fractions, you first multiply the numerators, and then the denominators, giving you $\frac{1}{20}$. Because this is equivalent to 0.05, either answer will be correct.

Square Roots

1. 5^2 simply means 5 times 5, which equals 25.
2. Find the square roots before you do the division. The square root of 36 is 6, and the square root of 4 is 2. Next divide 6 by 2, which equals 3.
3. "3 times 3" can be stated as "3 squared." The proper way to write this is 3^2.
4. Both numbers are raised to the power of 2 (they are squared). You must first find these squares before you do your subtraction. 7 squared is 49, and 3 squared is 9. So, your answer is 49 – 9, which equals 40.
5. This problem requires you to find a square root of a number as well as a number squared. The square root of 64 is 8, and 2 squared equals 4. Your answer is 8 times 4, which is 32.

Properties of Integer Exponents

1. According to the rule $x^m \times x^n = x^{(m-n)}$; therefore, add the exponents together. $x^3 \times x^6$ is equal to x^{3+6}, or x^{3+6}, or x^9.
2. A rule regarding exponents states that $(x^m)^n = x^{mn}$. Applying this rule gives you $(3^2)^3$, which yields 3^6. 3 to the 6th power is 729.
3. The exponent is distributed to both the numerator and the denominator, creating $\frac{5^3}{3^3}$, or $\frac{125}{27}$.
4. The answer to this problem is 1. For any value x where $x \neq 0, x^0 = 1$.
5. One of the rules regarding exponents tells you that $(xy)^m = x^m \times y^m$. Applying the rule gives you the following:

$$y^2 \times z^2, \text{ or } y^2 z^2$$

Exponents

1. The power that a number is raised to is equivalent to the number of times you multiply that number by itself: $2 \times 2 \times 2$ is equal to 8, so the answer is 2 raised to the power of 3 (2^3).

2. 3^3, or 3 to the 3rd power, means you must multiply $3 \times 3 \times 3$, which equals 27.

3. You must find a number that, when raised to the power of 4, equals 81. Because 81 is a perfect square (9×9, or $9^2 = 81$), and 9 is a perfect square, (3×3, or $3^2 = 9$), you can simply square 3^2 to arrive at 81: $(3^2)^2 = 3^4$.

4. $5^3 = 5 \times 5 \times 5$,, which gives you 125.

5. When raising an exponent to another power, multiply the exponents ($4 \times 2 = 8$). So, the answer is 2^8, or 256.

Scientific Notation

1. When dealing with scientific notation, the power of 10 indicates the number of spaces you must move the decimal place, either to the right (for a positive value), or to the left (for a negative value). To turn 4.237 into 423,700,000, you must move the decimal place 8 spaces to the right. Therefore, 10 needs to be raised to the power of 8 (10^8).

2. To solve this problem, you must simply move the decimal point the number of times indicated by the power of 10. Since you are given 10^5, you know that you must move the decimal point 5 spaces to the right because the exponent is a positive number. This gives you an answer of 376,000.

3. This problem can be set up as $\left(\dfrac{2.50}{1.25}\right) \times \left(\dfrac{10^4}{10^3}\right)$. The first half $\left(\dfrac{2.50}{1.25}\right)$ gives you 2. When dividing like bases, you subtract your exponents ($4 - 3 = 1$). You are left with 2×10^1. Since 10 to the 1st power is 10, the multiplication leaves you with an answer of 20.

4. You are given a negative value for the power to which 10 is raised (–5). This means that you must move the decimal point 5 spaces to the left to get your answer, which is .0000647.

5. You can set this problem up as $(4.2 \times 1.8) \times (10^3 \times 10^{-6})$. The first half of the equation (4.2×1.8) gives you 7.56. When multiplying like bases, you add your exponents: $3 + (-6) = -3$. Therefore, you are left with 7.56×10^{-3}, which can be expressed as 0.00756.

Ratio, Proportion, and Percent

1. To solve this problem, you can set up a proportion. You are looking for a number that is 30% of 20. The proportion looks like $\dfrac{x}{20} = \dfrac{30}{100}$, because the unknown number is equivalent to 30 out of the 100 parts of the whole (20). To solve, you cross-multiply, leaving you with $100x = 600$. Divide both sides by $100 : x = 6$.

2. You are given a proportion to solve. To find the answer, cross-multiply, giving you $78x = 234$. Dividing both sides by 78 will give you the answer $x = 3$.

3. To answer this question you must determine the ratio of organisms to liter of river water. The problem states that a 2-liter sample of water contained about 24 organisms, and a 4-liter sample of water contained about 48 organisms. Upon closer examination of this information you will see that the ratio of organism to water is the same in each sample. Therefore, you can set up a ratio using one sample:

    2 liters of water yields 24 organisms.

    This can be expressed as 2 to 24, or 2:24, which can be reduced to 1:12. For every 1 liter of water you will see 12 organisms. Therefore, 10 liters of water will contain 120 organisms.

4. You need to set up a proportion. You are given that 20% of x is equal to 16, and you want to find the value of x. The proportion looked like this:

    $$\frac{16}{x} = \frac{20}{100}$$

    After cross-multiplying, you are left with $20x = 1,600$. After dividing both sides by 20, you have the answer: $x = 80$.

5. Once again, you need to use a proportion to solve this problem. You know that Jim scored 95 points in 5 games, and you want to find out how many points he will score in a total of 12 games. Your proportion will look like this:

    $$\frac{95}{5} = \frac{x}{12}$$

    Cross-multiplying will leave you with $5x = 1,140$. Divide both sides by 5, and you get your answer, $x = 228$. If Jim continues to score at this rate, he will score a total of 228 points by the end of the season (12 games).

Linear Equations with One Variable

1. First isolate the unknown number (the variable) on one side. To do this, you add 17 to both sides, giving you $3x = 63$. Next, you divide both sides by 3 to get the x alone. This gives you the answer: $x = 21$.

2. Multiply both sides by 4 to get rid of the fraction and leave the x on its own. This gives you $x = -24$.

3. You are given the value of x, and you are looking for a missing number in the equation. If $x = 15$, then $4x = 60$. So you are left with the equation $60 - $ (some number) $= 42$. Subtract 60 from both sides to get 18.

4. This is a standard Rate × Time = Distance problem. Since the two trains start 600 miles apart, you know that their combined distance traveled must equal 600. Using the R × T = D formula, you can say that (Rate of Train 1 × Time of Train 1) + (Rate of Train 2 × Time of Train 2) = 600. You know how fast the trains are moving, and their total distance, but you do not know the time, so solve for T. Train 1 travels at 90 mph for T hours, while Train 2 travels at 75 mph for T hours. Your equation will look like this:

$$90T + 75T = 600$$

$$165T = 600$$

$$T = 3.64 \text{ hours}$$

5. First do the multiplication on the left side of the equation. This gives you $3x - 12 = 5x - 20$. Next, you need to group the like terms together. To do this, subtract $3x$ from both sides, and add 20 to both sides. This leaves you with $8 = 2x$. Dividing both sides by 2 will give you the answer: $x = 4$.

Absolute Value

1. First do the subtraction within the absolute value lines, $(-8-6=-14)$. Absolute value is the numerical value of a real number without regard to its sign. Therefore, the absolute value of –14 is 14.

2. To solve this problem, you need to set up two equations:

   $4x-6=10$, and $4x-6=-10$. You then solve both for x.

   $$4x=16, \text{ and } 4x=-4$$

   $$x=4, \text{ and } x=-1$$

3. In order to perform the multiplication in this problem, you must first find the absolute value of both numbers. The absolute values of –15 and 6 are 15 and 6, respectively. The answer is 15×6, which equals 90.

4. To find the possible answers for x in this problem, you must set up two equations:

   $$6x+8=3x-7, \text{ and } 6x+8=-(3x-7)$$

   First, you need to distribute the minus sign in the second equation, giving you $6x+8=-3x+7$.
   You then solve both for x:

   $$3x=-15, \text{ and } 9x=-1$$

   $$x=-5, \text{ and } x=-\frac{1}{9}$$

5. First find the absolute value of the denominator. The absolute value of –8 is 8. Now you can perform the division. –32 divided by 8 gives you an answer of –4.

Simple Probability

1. On a 6-sided die, there are 3 even and 3 odd numbers. Therefore, the probability that you will roll an odd number is 3 out of 6, or $\frac{3}{6}$. This can be reduced to $\frac{1}{2}$, or .5

2. If 2.5% of the CD players produced by this company are defective, then the number of defective devices out of 300,000 can be determined by multiplication $0.025 \times 300,000 = 7,500$.

3. When flipping a coin, there are only two possible outcomes: heads or tails. Therefore, each side has a probability of $\frac{1}{2}$, or .5, of landing facing up. The chances of the coin landing on tails four times in a row can be expressed as $\frac{1}{2} \times \frac{1}{2} \times \frac{1}{2} \times \frac{1}{2}$, or $\left(\frac{1}{2}\right)^4$. The final answer is $\frac{1}{16}$.

4. In this question, you can look at probability as a percentage. The probability that Dave will go to class is 0.7, or 70%. Therefore, the probability that he will NOT go to class is 100% − 70%, or 30%, which is equivalent to 0.3. Either answer is correct.

5. There are a total of 20 marbles in the bowl, 6 of which are red. If one marble is selected at random, the probability that it will be red is $\frac{6}{20}$ (the # of red marbles/the total # of marbles). This can be reduced to $\frac{3}{10}$.

Functions

1. To solve, substitute 6 for x in the function:

    $f(6) = 6^2 - 4(6) + 8$

    $f(6) = 36 - 24 + 8$

    $f(6) = 20$

2. To solve, substitute $(x+1)$ for x in the function:

    $f(x+1) = (x+1)^2$

    $(x+1)(x+1)$

    $x^2 + x + x + 1$

    $x^2 + 2x + 1$

3. The problem gives $g(x) = 3x$ and $f(x) = x+2$ and asks for $g(f(x))$. The function $g(f(x))$ means that all of the x values in $g(x)$ are replaced with $f(x)$, as follows:

    $g(f(x)) = 3(f(x))$

    $g(f(x)) = 3(x+2)$

    $g(f(x)) = 3x+6$

4. To solve, substitute 2 for x in the function:

    $f(2) = 2^4 - \dfrac{3(2)}{2}$

    $f(2) = 16 - \dfrac{6}{2}$

    $f(2) = 16 - 3$

    $f(2) = 13$

5. To solve, substitute –5 for x in the function:

    $f(-5) = (-5)^2 + (-5)$

    $f(-5) = 25 - 5$

    $f(-5) = 20$

Polynomial Operations and Factoring Simple Quadratic Equations

1. To solve the equation, substitute 4 for x:

   $3(4^2) - 5(4) + 9$

   $3(16) - 20 + 9$

   $48 - 20 + 9 = 37$

2. To add or subtract polynomials, combine like terms (remember to keep track of the negative signs!):

   $(5x^3 + 3x - 12) - (2x^3 - 6x + 17)$
   $(5x^3 - 2x^3) + (3x + 6x) - (17 - 12)$
   $3x^3 + 9x - 29$

3. Use the distributive property to multiply each term of one polynomial by each term of the other (remember to use the FOIL method).

   $(4x^2 + 2x)(x - 6)$

   First terms: $(4x^2)(x) = 4x^3$

   Outside terms: $(4x^2)(-6) = -24x^2$

   Inside terms: $(2x)(x) = 2x^2$

   Last terms: $(2x)(-6) = -12x$

   Now place the terms in decreasing order:

   $4x^3 - 24x^2 + 2x^2 - 12x$

   $4x^3 - 22x^2 - 12x$

4. Find two numbers whose product is −48 and sum is 2. The only possible numbers are 8 and −6. Therefore, the solution sets are $(x - 6)$ and $(x + 8)$.

5. The solution sets are given, so multiply the two sets together to find the original equation, using the FOIL method:

   $(x - 4)(2x + 3)$

   $2x^2 + 3x - 8x - 12$

   $2x^2 - 5x - 12$

Linear Inequalities with One Variable

1. The inequality states that x must be greater than or equal to -5 AND less than 15. Therefore, x could be any number equal to or greater than -5, and also less than -15.

2. Solve this problem algebraically, as follows:

    $$6x - 4x > 5 - (-3)$$
    $$2x > 8$$
    $$x > 4$$

    x must be greater than 4 for this inequality to be true.

3. The value of x is given, so substitute 7 for x and calculate the value of both sides:

    $$3(7) + 7 = 28 \text{ and } 5(7) - 6 = 29$$

    The less than sign ($<$) is used because 28 is less than 29.

4. Once again, the first step in solving this problem is isolating the variable on one side of the inequality:

    $$-5 - 20 < -3x - 2x$$
    $$-25 < -5x$$
    $$5 > x$$

    It is important to remember that when dealing with inequalities, multiplying or dividing by a negative number involves reversing the sign. In this case, both sides were divided by -5, so the sign changes from $<$ to $>$.

5. To solve this problem, subtract 3 from both sides of the inequality and isolate x:

    $$-4 - 3 \leq x < 18 - 3$$
    $$-7 \leq x < 15$$

    x is greater than or equal to -7 and it is less than 15.

Quadratic Formula

1. The quadratic formula is $x = -b \pm \dfrac{\sqrt{(b^2 - 4ac)}}{2a}$

    The first step in solving this problem is to substitute the numbers from the equation into the quadratic formula (keep in mind that the equation is in the form of $ax^2 + bx + c$).

    $$x = \frac{-22 \pm \sqrt{(22^2) - 4(10)(12.1)}}{2(10)}$$

    Next, simplify the problem to find the value of 22^2, which is 484.

    $$x = \frac{-22 \pm \sqrt{(484) - 4(10)(12.1)}}{2(10)}$$

    Next, do the rest of the multiplication, as follows:

    $$x = \frac{-22 \pm \sqrt{484 - 484}}{20}$$

    The square root of 484−484 is simply 0, so you can disregard it for the rest of the problem. You are left with:

    $$x = \frac{-22}{20} \text{ which simplifies to } \frac{-11}{10}.$$

    Because the $\pm$ does not give separate answers, there is only one answer to the problem:

    $$x = -\frac{11}{10}, \text{ or } -1.1.$$

2. $(4x^2 - 7x + 3) - (10x^2 + x - 11) = 0$

    $$4x^2 - 7x + 3 - 10x^2 - x + 11 = 0$$

    $$-6x^2 - 8x + 14 = 0$$

    Multiply the entire equation by −1:

    $$6x^2 + 8x - 14 = 0$$

3. For this problem, $a = 4, b = 1,$ and $c = -5.$ Substitute these numbers into the quadratic formula to get:

$$x = \frac{-1 \pm \sqrt{(1^2) - 4(4)(-5)}}{2(4)}$$

$$x = \frac{-1 \pm \sqrt{81}}{8}$$

The square root of 81 is 9, so you now have:

$$x = \frac{-1 \pm 9}{8}$$

Because of the $\pm$ sign, you have two possible answers. Find them by making two separate equations:

$$x = \frac{8}{8} \text{ and } x = -\frac{10}{8}$$

Simplifying these two answers, you have your solutions: $x = 1$ and $x = -\frac{5}{4}.$

4. The first thing you must do is rearrange the equation to fit the format $ax^2 + bx + c = 0.$ After doing this, the equation will be $4x^2 + 18x - 117.$ Therefore, the values for a, b, and c, respectively, are 4, 18, and –117.

5. First, use FOIL to create a trinomial equation.

$$(2x + 4)^2 = 0$$

$$(2x + 4)(2x + 4) = 0$$

$$4x^2 + 8x + 8x + 16 = 0$$

$$4x^2 + 16x + 16 = 0$$

Now use $a = 4, b = 16,$ and $c = 16$ in the quadratic formula, as follows:

$$x = \frac{-16 \pm \sqrt{(16^2) - 4(4)(16)}}{2(4)}$$

$$x = \frac{-16 \pm \sqrt{(16^2) - (16)(16)}}{8}$$

$$x = \frac{-16 \pm \sqrt{0}}{8}$$

$$x = \frac{-16}{8}$$

$$x = -2$$

Radical and Rational Expressions

1. In this problem, you are dealing with radicals. When it comes to radicals, an important rule to remember is that $\sqrt{a} \times \sqrt{b} = \sqrt{(ab)}$. Applying that rule to this question, you see that $\sqrt{12} \times \sqrt{3} = \sqrt{36}$. The square root of 36 is 6.

2. By rule, $\sqrt{(a/b)} = \sqrt{a}/\sqrt{b}$. Therefore, $\sqrt{2/5} - \sqrt{2}/\sqrt{5}$. Eliminate the radical in the denominator by multiplying the quantity by itself and repeating this multiplication on the numerator:

$$\left(\frac{\sqrt{2}}{\sqrt{5}}\right) \times \left(\frac{\sqrt{5}}{\sqrt{5}}\right)$$

$$= \frac{\sqrt{2} \times \sqrt{5}}{5}$$

$$= \frac{\sqrt{2 \times 5}}{5}$$

$$= \frac{\sqrt{10}}{5}$$

3. This question shows what is called a "cube root." The cube root of a number, x, is the number which raised to the third power gives x. This problem asks you to find the cube root of 27. Since $3 \times 3 \times 3$ is equal to 27, the cube root of 27 is 3.

4. To answer this question, you must first multiply the two parts of the equation, as follows:

$$\sqrt{2x^8} \times \sqrt{8y^2} = \sqrt{16x^4y^2}$$

You can simplify this in order to find the square root:

$$\sqrt{4^2(x^2)^2 y^2}$$

Now that the problem is set up like this, the square root is clear:

$$\sqrt{4^2(x^2)^2 y^2} = \sqrt{4^2} \times \sqrt{(x^2)^2} \times \sqrt{y^2}$$

$$= 4 \times x^2 \times y$$

$$= 4x^2 y$$

5. The rule used in this problem is. $\sqrt[n]{a^m} = a^{(m/n)}$.

Therefore, $\sqrt[7]{11^{14}} = (11^{14})^{1/7} = 11^2 = 121$.

Inequalities and Absolute Value Equations

1. Since the inequality deals with an absolute value, $|7x - 13|$ will always be a positive number. For the inequality to be true, $7x - 13$ must be between the values of -22 AND 22. OR does not work here because the value must meet both the requirement of being larger than -22 as well as the requirement of being smaller than 22. If the absolute value is greater, use OR. If the absolute value is less than, use AND.

2. To solve this problem, you must first drop the absolute value sign, and then create two separate inequalities, in the form of $ax + b = c$. The first inequality looks just like the original, while for the second one, you must switch the inequality sign and the sign of c, as follows:

$$x + 8 > 15 \qquad\qquad x + 8 < -15$$
$$x > 7 \qquad\qquad\qquad x < -23$$

It is impossible for a value to be greater than 7 AND less than -23. Therefore, use OR.

$$x > 7 \text{ OR } x < -23.$$

3. To solve this problem, you must drop the absolute value sign first, and then create two separate inequalities of the form $ax + b = c$. The first inequality looks just like the original, while for the second one, you must switch the inequality sign and the sign of c, as follows:

$$2x + 3 < 21 \qquad\qquad 2x + 3 > -21$$
$$2x < 18 \qquad\qquad\quad 2x > -24$$
$$x < 9 \qquad\qquad\quad\ \ x > -12$$

x must be less than 9 AND greater than -12. Unlike the previous problem, a number can meet both of these rules: $x < 9$ AND $x > -12$.

4. To solve this problem, you must drop the absolute value sign first, and then create two separate inequalities, of the form $ax + b = c$. The first inequality looks just like the original, while for the second one, you must switch the inequality sign and the sign of c. A value cannot be both greater than 29 and less than -29, so OR must be used. Set up the two inequalities to find that $5x - 6 > 29$ OR $5x - 6 < -29$.

5. To solve this problem, create two separate inequalities, as follows:

$$-\frac{1}{4}x + 3 > 5 \qquad\qquad -\frac{1}{4}x + 3 < -5$$
$$-\frac{1}{4}x > 2 \qquad\qquad\quad -\frac{1}{4}x < -8$$
$$x < -8 \qquad\qquad\qquad x > 32$$

Because you multiplied both sides of each inequality by -4, you need to change the direction of the sign. Since x cannot be both less than -8 and greater than 32, OR is used: $x < -8$ OR $x > 32$.

Sequences

1. In order to solve this problem, it is crucial to know the formula for arithmetic sequences. This formula is $a_n = a_1 + (n-1)d$, where a_n is the particular term you are trying to find, a_1 is the first number in the sequence, and d is the common difference. This particular problem has already given you most of the information that you need. All that you have to do is substitute 3 for n, as you are looking for the 3rd term:

$$a_3 = 3 + (3-1)2$$
$$a_3 = 3 + (2)2$$
$$a_3 = 3 + 4$$
$$a_3 = 7$$

2. This question asks you to write your own formula for the sequence. You will need the first term in the sequence, as well as the common difference. The first number is −8, and noticing that you jump from −8, to −2, and then to 4, it is clear that the common difference is 6. Your formula should look like this:

$$a_n = -8 + (n-1)6$$

3. In this problem, you are dealing with a geometric sequence. These sequences have a formula that looks like this: $a_n = a_1(r)^{n-1}$. Here, r is the constant ratio. Looking at the sequence, it goes from $\frac{1}{4}$, to 1, to 4, and then to 16. This indicates that you must multiply by 4 each time; therefore 4 is the constant ratio. To find the 6th term in this sequence, you must set up the following formula:

$$a_6 = \frac{1}{4}(4)^{6-1}$$

$$a_6 = \frac{1}{4}(4)^5$$

$$a_6 = \frac{1}{4}(1024)$$

$$a_6 = 256$$

4. First of all, you need to find an answer that is similar to the formula used for an arithmetic sequence: $a_n = a_1 + (n-1)d$. Looking at the choices, you can eliminate the second and third because they are formulas for a geometric sequence. In the sequence you are given, the first term is 7, and the common difference is 6. Therefore, the correct answer is $7(8-1)(6)$.

5. Here, you are asked to write your own formula once again. However, this time it is for a geometric sequence. The first term is 25, and you must also find the common ratio. To get from 25 to −5, you must divide by −5. This also works to get from −5 to 1, so the common ratio is −1/5. Your formula should look like this:

$$a_n = 25\left(-\frac{1}{5}\right)^{n-1}$$

Systems of Equations

1. When solving systems of equations, the best thing to do first is to isolate one of the variables. In this problem, you can do so by changing the sign on the bottom equation:

    $$x - 2y = 14$$
    $$-x + 4y = 8$$

    Add the two equations together:

    $$2y = 22$$

    $$y = 11$$

    Choose one of the original equations and substitute 11 for y. Solve for x.

    $$x - 2(11) = 14$$

    $$x - 22 = 14$$

    $$x = 36$$

    It is always a good idea to test your answers by substituting x and y values into both of the original equations.

2. This problem is a little trickier than the first, as you cannot simply change the sign of one of the equations to isolate one of the variables. In this situation, you have to make the coefficients the same through multiplication. Since you know that 4 and 6 both go into 12, use the x term. Multiply the top equation by 3, and the bottom by 2:

    $$12x - 6y = 18$$

    $$-12x + 10y = 14$$

    Add the two equations together:

    $$4y = 32$$

    $$y = 8$$

    Finally, choose one of the original equations, substitute 8 for y, and solve for x.

    $$4x - 2(8) = 6$$

    $$4x - 16 = 6$$

    $$4x = 22$$

    $$x = \frac{22}{4}, \text{ or } \frac{11}{2}$$

3. The first step is rearranging the equations to align like terms:

    $$3x - y = 18$$

    $$4x + 6y = 24$$

    Multiply the top equation by 6 and add the equations:

    $$18x - 6y = 108$$
    $$+4x + 6y = 24$$
    $$\overline{22x = 132}$$
    $$x = 6$$

Now choose one of the original equations, substitute 6 in for x, and solve for y:

$$3(6) - y = 18$$

$$18 - y = 18$$

$$-y = 0$$

$$y = 0$$

4. First, distribute the 8 through the parentheses to get $8y + 8x = 12$. You can then multiply the second equation by –2 to isolate one of the variables, and rearrange the equations to line up the like terms:

$$8x + 8y = 12$$

$$-8x + 6y = 44$$

Add the equations together:

$$14y = 56$$

$$y = 4$$

Now choose one of the original equations, substitute 4 for y, and solve for x.

$$8(x + 4) = 12$$

$$8x + 8(4) = 12$$

$$8x + 32 = 12$$

$$8x = -20$$

$$x = -\frac{20}{8}$$

$$x = -\frac{5}{2}$$

5. First, line up the like terms in both equations:

$$4x - y = 63$$

$$x + 3y = 6$$

Multiply the top equation by 3 and add the equations.

$$12x - 3y = 189$$

$$x + 3y = 6$$

$$13x = 195$$

$$x = 15$$

Now substitute 15 for x in one of the equations.

$$x + 3y = 6$$

$$15 + 3y = 6$$

$$3y = -9$$

$$y = -3$$

Logarithms

1. $\log_x 27 = 3$ means the log to the base x of $27 = 3$. This means that x^3 must equal 27, and therefore x must equal 3.

2. By definition, $\log_a b = c$, if $a^c = b$. In this question, you are asked to find the value of a. You are given the values of b and c, so your equation should look like this:

    $$x^4 = 625$$

    You need to find a number that, when raised to the 4th power, equals 625. Test the answer choices: $4^4 = 256, 7^4 = 2401, 5^4 = 625$. Therefore, the correct answer is 5. You could immediately eliminate 7 after finding that 7^4 is already substantially larger than 625.

3. To solve, turn the logarithm into an equation with an exponent:

    $$3^x = 729$$

    Test some values for x:

    $$3^2 = 9$$
    $$3^3 = 27$$
    $$3^4 = 81$$
    $$3^5 = 243$$
    $$3^6 = 729$$

    Therefore, log 3 (729) = 6.

4. By definition, $\log_x 196 = 2$ means the log to the base x of $196 = 2$. This means that x^2 must equal 196. To find the answer, you can simply take the square root of 196, which is 14.

5. By definition, if $\log_7 x = 3$, then $7^3 = x$. Therefore, $x = 343$.

Roots of Polynomials

1. To solve this problem by factoring, you can start with a $2x$ on one side, and an x on the other:

    $$(2x + / - \underline{\quad})(x + / - \underline{\quad})$$

    These two missing numbers must add up to 9 (keep in mind that one of them is being multiplied by 2), and also must multiply to give –35. The only possible factors of 35 are 1, 5, 7, and 35. In looking at the problem, 5 and 7 seem like the most logical choices. You can try a few different combinations, but you should come up with:

    $$(2x - 5)(x + 7)$$

    To find the roots, set each quantity equal to 0:

    $$2x - 5 = 0, x + 7 = 0$$
    $$2x = 5, x = -7$$
    $$x = \frac{5}{2} \text{ and } x = -7$$

2. To solve this problem, begin with an x in both factors:

$$(x + / - \text{\_\_\_})(x + / - \text{\_\_\_})$$

The two missing numbers must have a sum of 2 and a product of –3. 3 is only divisible by 1 and 3, and the sum must be 2, so 3 is positive and 1 is negative.

$$(x - 1)(x + 3)$$
$$x - 1 = 0, x + 3 = 0$$
$$x = 1 \text{ and } x = -3$$

3. For this problem, you will have to work backward; you are already given the roots, and are being asked to find the equation to which they belong. Since the roots given are 6 and –2, you can write out $x - 6 = 0$ and $x + 2 = 0$. Now, to find the original equation, you must multiply these two quantities:

$$(x - 6)(x + 2)$$
$$x^2 - 6x + 2x - 12$$
$$x^2 - 4x - 12$$

4. To solve this problem, start with x in each of the factors:

$$(x + / - \text{\_\_\_})(x + / - \text{\_\_\_})$$

The sum of the missing numbers must be –8, and the product must be 16. Therefore, the numbers must both be –4.

$$(x - 4)(x - 4)$$

This can also be written $(x - 4)^2$. Solve for x:

$$x - 4 = 0$$
$$x = 4$$

5. Since the a value is –1, start with x and $-x$ in the factors.

$$(x + / - \text{\_\_\_})(-x + / - \text{\_\_\_})$$

The sum must be 3 and the product must be 40, but remember that for the sum, one of the numbers is being multiplied by –1. In this case, 8 and 5 are the correct values:

$$(x + 5)(-x + 8)$$
$$x + 5 = 0 \text{ and } -x + 8 = 0$$
$$x = -5 \text{ and } x = 8$$

Number Line Graphs

1. The answer is 8. Distance is always positive and can be shown as absolute value: $|-5-3| = 8$. You can also draw a number line, label –5 and 3, and see that the distance between those two points is 8.

2. The midpoint is simply the point that is exactly halfway between the two points given. It can be thought of as an average. This value can be determined using the following formula:

$$\text{Midpoint} = \frac{1}{2}(x_1 + x_2)$$

$$\text{Midpoint} = \frac{1}{2}(-3 + 2)$$

$$\text{Midpoint} = \frac{1}{2}(-1)$$

$$\text{Midpoint} = -\frac{1}{2}$$

3. The answer is $x \geq -3$ AND $x < 6$. AND is used because the bold line is connecting the two points. If there were a space, OR would be used. This eliminates the third choice. Open circles signify > or < and closed circles signify $\geq$ or $\leq$. This eliminates the first and second choices.

4. First, determine the values of x. Since both circles are open, > and < are used. Also, there is a space between the two points, so OR will be used. In the end, you have $x < 2$ OR $x > 6$. Now it is simply a matter of substituting the x values into the equations and determining which one is correct. The third choice, $|2x - 10| > 6$, is the correct answer.

5. There is a space between the two points, so use OR. This eliminates the second and fourth answer choices. The third choice is incorrect because the graph does not show a bold line for values greater than –6. Also, the open circle means < or > needs to be used, as the values do not include –6. The first choice, $x \geq 2$ OR $x < -6$, is correct.

Equation of a Line and Slope of a Line

1. First, rearrange the equation into the slope-intercept form by isolating y. In this case, you divide by 2:

$$y = 2x + 6$$

In the slope-intercept formula, $y = mx + b, b$ is the y-intercept. Because $b = 6$, the y-intercept is $(0, 6)$.

2. Rearrange the equation into the slope-intercept form by isolating y. In this case, you divide by 3:

$$y = \frac{2}{3}x + 5$$

You know that in the slope-intercept formula, $y = mx + b, m$ is the slope.

Because $m = -\frac{2}{3}$, the correct answer is $-\frac{2}{3}$.

3. This equation represents a vertical line; the y-intercept is 0, so the line is parallel to the y-axis. A vertical line has an undefined slope. This is because slope is equivalent to "rise over run." If the "run" is 0, the slope must be undefined because 0 cannot divide into anything.

4. Remember that in the slope-intercept form $y = mx + b, m$ is the slope and b is the y-intercept. In addition, parallel lines have the same slope; therefore, the slope of both lines (m) is 4. You are given that the y-intercept (the point at which the line crosses the y-axis) is 3. The equation of the line will be $y = 4x + 3$.

5. First, rearrange the equation into slope-intercept form, by subtracting $3x$ and $-y$ from both sides:

$$y = -3x + 2$$

For two lines to be perpendicular, their slopes must be negative reciprocals.

The negative reciprocal of -3 is $\frac{1}{3}$. The problem also states that the perpendicular line has a y-intercept of 8. If you substitute $\frac{1}{3}$ for m and 8 for b in the slope-intercept equation, you get $y = \frac{1}{3}x + 8$.

Distance and Midpoint Formulas

1. The distance formula is: Distance $= \sqrt{(x_2 - x_1)^2 + (y_2 - y_1)^2}$.

    You can substitute the given values of x and y into the formula to solve for the distance, as follows:

    $$\text{Distance} = \sqrt{(3-9)^2 + (-4-4)^2}$$

    $$\text{Distance} = \sqrt{(6)^2 + (8)^2}$$

    $$\text{Distance} = \sqrt{36 + 64}$$

    $$\text{Distance} = \sqrt{100}$$

    $$\text{Distance} = 10$$

2. You can use the distance formula $\{\text{Distance} = \sqrt{(x_2 - x_1)^2 + (y_2 - y_1)^2}\}$ to solve this problem:

    $$17 = \sqrt{(-6-2)^2 + (y-8)^2}$$

    Square both sides.

    $$289 = (-8)^2 + (y-8)^2$$

    $$289 = (64) + (y-8)^2$$

    $$225 = (y-8)^2$$

    Take the square root of both sides.

    $$15 = y - 8$$

    $$23 = y$$

    The following equation is also correct:

    $$17 = \sqrt{(2-(-6))^2 + (8-y)^2}$$

    Square both sides.

    $$289 = (2+6)^2 + (8-y)$$

    $$289 = 64 + (8-y)$$

    $$225 = (8-y)$$

    Take the square root of both sides.

    $$15 = (8-y)$$

    $$7 = -y$$

    $$-7 = y$$

3. Use the midpoint equation to solve this problem. First solve for the x-coordinate, which is half the distance between 12 and 10:

$$x_m = \frac{(x_2 + x_1)}{2}$$

$$x_m = \frac{(10 + 12)}{2}$$

$$x_m = \frac{22}{2}$$

$$x_m = 11$$

Do the same for y_m, which is half the distance between 5 and –7:

$$y_m = \frac{(y_2 + y_1)}{2}$$

$$y_m = \frac{(5 + -7)}{2}$$

$$y_m = -\frac{2}{2}$$

$$y_m = -1$$

Therefore, the midpoint is (11, –1).

4. You only have to solve for the x-coordinate because you are given the y-coordinate:

$$x_m = \frac{(x_2 + x_1)}{2}$$

$$5 = \frac{(-2 + x_1)}{2}$$

$$10 = -2 + x_1$$

$$12 = x_1$$

5. Use the distance formula: Distance $= \sqrt{(x_2 - x_1)^2 + (y_2 - y_1)^2}$ to solve this problem:

$$\text{Distance} = \sqrt{(x_2 - x_1)^2 + (y_2 - y_1)^2}$$

$$\text{Distance} = \sqrt{(5 - 0)^2 + (0 - 5)^2}$$

$$\text{Distance} = \sqrt{(5)^2 + (-5)^2}$$

$$\text{Distance} = \sqrt{(25 + 25)}$$

$$\text{Distance} = \sqrt{50}$$

$$\text{Distance} = \sqrt{25 \times 2} = \sqrt{25} \times \sqrt{2} = 5\sqrt{2}$$

Properties and Relations of Plane Figures

1. The area of a triangle and the length of one of the legs of a right triangle are given. However, you need the length of both legs to use the Pythagorean Theorem to determine the hypotenuse. Since you have the area, start there.

   For a right triangle, Area $= \frac{1}{2}$ (base) × (height). You are given the base and area, so solve for the height:

   $$54 = \frac{1}{2}(9) \times (\text{height})$$

   $$54 = 4.5(\text{height})$$

   $$12 = \text{height}$$

   Now you know the lengths of the two legs of the right triangle and can use the Pythagorean Theorem $(a^2 + b^2 = c^2)$ to calculate the hypotenuse:

   $$9^2 + 12^2 = c^2$$

   $$81 + 144 = c^2$$

   $$225 = c^2$$

   $15 = c$. The hypotenuse is 15 cm.

2. The formula for the area of a circle is: area $= \pi r^2$. The formula for the circumference of a circle is: $C = 2\pi r$. Since you are given the circumference, you can use that to find the radius, r, and then use the radius to find the area:

   $$14\pi = 2\pi r$$

   $$14 = 2r$$

   $$r = 7$$

   Now substitute r into the equation for area:

   $$\text{Area} = \pi(7^2)$$

   Area $= 49\pi$. The area of the circle is 49π in^2.

3. A parallelogram's angles add up to $360° : 360° - 35° = 325°$.

4. The equation for the area of a trapezoid is: area $= \dfrac{1}{2}$ (base$_1$ + base$_2$) (height). Substitute the given variables into the equation and solve for the missing base:

$$30 = \frac{1}{2}(8 + base_2)(3)$$

$$10 = \frac{1}{2}(8 + base_2)$$

$$20 = (8 + base_2)$$

$$base_2 = 12ft$$

5. A square is a special kind of rectangle. All of its sides are equal in length. Since the area of a rectangle is area $= l \times w$, the area of a square would be area $= s^2$ (side squared) because length and width are equal. For this problem, the given side is 6 mm. If the figure were a square, the area would be 36 mm^2. However, the area is said to be 42 mm^2. Therefore the shape is a rectangle and not a square.

Angles, Parallel Lines, and Perpendicular Lines

1. Supplementary angles add together to total 180°. Therefore, the supplementary angle to a 40° angle is a 140° angle.

2. Supplementary angles add together to total 180°. Therefore the supplementary angle to a 25° angle is a 155° angle.

3. The 90° angle marked indicates that the other three angles formed by the intersection of lines p and o each measure 90° also. As line n is parallel to line m, the same four 90° angles are formed at the intersection of lines p and m. Similarly, the angles on line o each measure 90°, too, because lines p and o are parallel. Thus, angle $\theta = 90°$.

4. The transversal crosses two parallel lines, so the angles made at the intersections will be identical. 43° corresponds to the supplementary angle of a on line y. Since 43° and a are supplementary angles, they must add up to 180°. Therefore, the answer is $180° - 43° = 137°$.

5. Since line v is perpendicular to line t, it forms four right angles. The line segment that is unnamed in the diagram dissects one of the right angles. Angle a is one side and 35° is the measurement given for the other side. These two angles add up to $90°: 90° - 35° = 55°$. Therefore, the angle measures 55°.

Perimeter, Area, and Volume

1. The question asks you to determine the number of bags of fertilizer that will cover your rectangular backyard. According to information in the problem, 6 pounds of fertilizer can cover 700 square feet. Begin by calculating the area of the rectangular backyard. The area of a rectangle is determined by multiplying the length (70 feet) by the width (40 feet):

$$70 \times 40 = 2,800$$

The area of the rectangular backyard is 2,800 square feet. The problem states that 6 pounds of fertilizer can cover 700 square feet. Calculate the number of times that 700 will go into 2,800:

$$2,800 \div 700 = 4$$

You will need 4 times 6 pounds of fertilizer to treat 2,800 square feet:

$$4 \times 6 = 24$$

Since you will need a total of 24 pounds of fertilizer to treat the backyard, and each bag of fertilizer weighs 8 pounds, divide 24 by 8 to find the number of bags of fertilizer you will need:

$$24 \div 8 = 3$$

You will need 3 bags of fertilizer to treat a backyard that measures 2,800 square feet.

2. If the pool has a diameter of 26 feet, and the fence needs to be 4 feet away from the edge of the pool, the diameter of the area enclosed by the fence would be $26 + 4 + 4 = 34$ feet. Draw a picture to help visualize the problem:

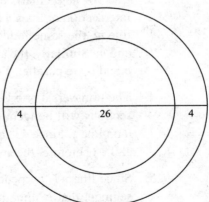

The area of a circle is πr^2. The radius is half of the diameter, so $r = 17$. Substitute 17 for r and 3.14 for π and solve:

$$\text{Area} = (3.14)(17)^2$$

$$\text{Area} = 907.46 \text{ ft}^2$$

3. A beach ball is a sphere, and the formula for the volume of a sphere is: $\left(\dfrac{4}{3}\right)\pi r^3$. The diameter is given as 0.6 m, so the radius is half of that, 0.3 m. Substitute that value into the formula and compute the volume:

$$\text{Volume} = \left(\frac{4}{3}\right)\pi(0.3^3)$$

$$\text{Volume} = \left(\frac{4}{3}\right)\pi(0.027)$$

$$\text{Volume} = 0.036\pi \text{ m}^3, \text{ or approximately } 0.113 \text{ m}^3$$

4. The formula for the volume of a cylinder is $\pi r^2 h$. The question is asking for diameter, so first solve for r, then double it.

$$350 = \pi r^2 \left(\frac{14}{\pi}\right)$$
$$r^2 = 25 \text{ cm}$$
$$r = 5 \text{ cm}$$

Since the radius is 5 cm, the diameter is 10 cm.

5. The equation for the volume of a cube is: s^3. Since we are given an edge, or side (s) of 5, you simply substitute 5 for s. The answer is 125 in³.

Trigonometry

1. Using the mnemonic SOHCAHTOA helps you remember that sine is the ratio of "opposite to hypotenuse." The side opposite of a has a length of 12. The hypotenuse has a length of 13. So, $\sin a = \dfrac{12}{13}$.

2. Using the mnemonic SOHCAHTOA helps you remember that tangent is the ratio of "opposite to adjacent" and cosine is "adjacent over hypotenuse." Since you are given cosine, you know the lengths of two sides of the right triangle. The adjacent leg is 4 and the hypotenuse is 5. Using the Pythagorean Theorem ($a^2 + b^2 = c^2$), you can calculate the length of the opposite leg, and then calculate $\tan a$:

$$a^2 + 4^2 = 5^2$$
$$a^2 + 16 = 25$$
$$a^2 = 9$$
$$a = 3$$

Now you have the adjacent (4) and opposite (3) legs, so $\tan a = \dfrac{3}{4}$.

3. By definition, to convert degrees to radians multiply by $\dfrac{\pi}{180}$:
$$\frac{60\pi}{180} = \frac{\pi}{3}$$

4. To convert radians to degrees $\dfrac{180}{\pi}$:

$$\frac{3\pi}{4} = \left(\frac{180}{\pi}\right)$$

$$= \frac{540\pi}{4\pi}$$

$$= 135$$

5. By definition, secant is the reciprocal of cosine, which is calculated by dividing the length of the adjacent side by the length of the hypotenuse (adj/hyp). Therefore, cos $a = 5/13$, and the length of the side adjacent to the angle is 5, while the length of the hypotenuse is 13. By definition, sine is equivalent to opposite/hypotenuse, so you must use the Pythagorean Theorem $(a^2 + b^2 = c^2)$ to find the length of the side opposite angle a:

$$a^2 + 5^2 = 13^2$$

$$a^2 + 25 = 169$$

$$a^2 = 144$$

$$a = 12$$

Because $a = 12$, the sin of angle $a = \dfrac{12}{13}$.

Translating Word Problems

1. You are given that Tom started out with 6 books. After he gave 2 books to his sister he was left with 6 – 2 books. He then purchased 3 more books, so he now has 6 – 2 + 3 books.

2. To solve this problem, start with William and work backward. William walked 2 miles, and Rebecca walked 4 times as far as William. Therefore, Rebecca walked 4(2) miles. Juan walked 3 more miles than Rebecca, so Juan walked 4(2) + 3 miles.

3. The first step is to calculate the total cost of the CDs: 2(15) = 30. You are given that, in addition to the 2 CDs, Tina also purchases d of the DVDs, each of which costs $18. Therefore, her cost for the DVDs was 18d. Now simply add the terms together to get 30 + 18d.

4. You are given that Mark, m, is older than Frank, f. Therefore, $f < m$. You are also given that Mark, m, is younger than David, d. Therefore, $m < d$. Mark's age is between Frank and David's ages, so $f < m < d$.

5. You are given that Jim is j years old today; therefore, 2 years ago, Jim would have been $j - 2$ years old. At that time, Kathy was twice as old as Jim, or 2($j - 2$).

PRACTICE QUESTIONS

Following are simulated ACT Mathematics questions, along with explanations for all of the questions. Carefully read the directions, apply the information from this chapter, and attempt all of the questions.

DIRECTIONS: The following are problems that are representative of the kinds of questions you will see on the ACT Mathematics Test. Solve each problem and circle the letter of the correct answer. Do not linger over problems that take too much time; come back to them later. You are permitted to use a calculator but remember to use it wisely. The figures are NOT necessarily drawn to scale, all geometric figures lie in a plane, and the word *line* indicates a straight line. Answers and Detailed Explanations are included at the end of this section.

DO YOUR FIGURING HERE.

1. On a real number line, point X has a coordinate of -2 and point Y has a coordinate of 6. What is the length of line segment $\overline{XY}$?
   A. -4
   B. 0
   C. 4
   D. 6
   E. 8

2. Given the right triangle below, how many units long is side AC?

   F. 1
   G. $\sqrt{5}$
   H. 3
   J. $\sqrt{41}$
   K. 9

3. The area of a circle can be approximated by multiplying 3.14 by the radius squared. Which of the following expresses this approximation?
   A. $A \approx (3.14)2r$
   B. $A \approx \dfrac{3.14}{r^2}$
   C. $A \approx \sqrt{3.14r}$
   D. $A \approx 3.14r^2$
   E. $A \approx (3.14r)^2$

4. José has 7 blue shirts and 5 white shirts in one drawer in his dresser. Because he is late for school, he reaches into the drawer and randomly removes a shirt. What is the probability that José removes a white shirt?
   F. 1:12
   G. 1:5
   H. 5:12
   J. 5:7
   K. 7:5

See Expanded Explanation on page 212!

GO ON TO THE NEXT PAGE.

5. Ryan bought a pair of shorts on clearance for $15.75. If the shorts were 30% off, what was the original price of the shorts?
   A. $4.73
   B. $6.75
   C. $20.48
   D. $22.50
   E. $52.50

DO YOUR FIGURING HERE.

6. Stephanie was s years old 5 years ago. How old will she be 4 years from now?
   F. $s+4$
   G. $5(s+4)$
   H. $s+9$
   J. $s-1$
   K. $s+1$

See Expanded Explanation on page 212!

7. What is the sum of the polynomials $4x^2y+2x^2y^3$ and $-2xy+x^2y^3$?
   A. $4x^2y+3x^2y^3-2xy$
   B. $4x^2y+2x^2y^3-2x^2y^3$
   C. $2x^2y+2x^2y^3+xy$
   D. $2x^2-4x^2y^3-2xy^3$
   E. $-2x^2y-2x^2y^3+x^2y^3$

8. If $t=-7$ what is the value of $|t-2|$?
   F. -9
   G. -5
   H. 5
   J. 9
   K. 14

9. For all x, $4-2(x+1)=$?
   A. $2-2x$
   B. $4+x$
   C. $3-2x$
   D. $2x-4$
   E. $4-x$

10. $(x^4)^{15}$ is equivalent to:
    F. x^{11}
    G. x^{19}
    H. x^{60}
    J. $15x^4$
    K. $60x$

11. What is the sum of the 2 solutions to the equation
    $x^2-2x-15=0$?
    A. -8
    B. -2
    C. 2
    D. 8
    E. 15

12. What is the 209th digit after the decimal point in the repeating decimal $0.\overline{76234}$?
    F. 5
    G. 4
    H. 3
    J. 2
    K. 0

GO ON TO THE NEXT PAGE.

13. The admission to Carnival Night at a middle school is $3. The carnival offers many different games in which the students can participate, each costing the same. The graph below shows the total cost per student for admission and games as a function of the number of games purchased.

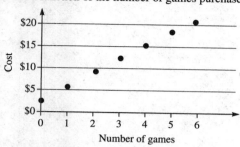

Which of the following is the price of a single game?

F. $1

G. $2

H. $3

J. $4

K. $5

DO YOUR FIGURING HERE.

See Expanded Explanation on page 213!

14. The area of a trapezoid is found by using the equation $\frac{1}{2}h(b_1 + b_2)$, where h is the height and b_1 and b_2 are the lengths of the bases. What is the area of the trapezoid shown below?

F. 18

G. 20

H. 22

J. 30

K. 36

15. For the area of a square to triple, the new side length must be the original side length multiplied by what number?

A. $\sqrt{3}$

B. 2

C. $2\sqrt{3}$

D. 3

E. 9

GO ON TO THE NEXT PAGE.

DO YOUR FIGURING HERE.

16. In the right triangles below, $\overline{PQ}$ is 4 cm, $\overline{QC}$ is 3 cm, $\overline{AB}$ is 8 cm, and $\overline{BP}$ is 5. How long, in cm, is $\overline{AQ}$?

F. 2
G. 3
H. 4
J. 5
K. 6

17. A rectangular classroom is 4 feet longer than it is wide and has an area of 480 square feet. What is the width of the classroom in feet?
A. 12
B. 16
C. 20
D. 24
E. 28

18. In the standard (x, y) coordinate plane, a line has a slope of $\frac{2}{3}$ and passes through $(-1, 1)$. Through which of the following points does this line also pass?
F. $(2, 3)$
G. $(2, 1)$
H. $(2, 2)$
J. $(3, 2)$
K. $(3, 3)$

19. If $\log_x 256 = 4$, then $x = $?
A. 4
B. 16
C. 64
D. $\dfrac{64}{\log_x}$
E. 256^4

20. What is the slope of the line with equation $2x - 3y = 6$?
F. -3
G. -2
H. $\dfrac{2}{3}$
J. 1
K. $\dfrac{3}{2}$

GO ON TO THE NEXT PAGE.

21. $\dfrac{3}{5} \cdot \dfrac{4}{6} \cdot \dfrac{5}{7} \cdot \dfrac{6}{8} \cdot \dfrac{7}{9} = ?$

DO YOUR FIGURING HERE.

- **A.** $\dfrac{1}{2}$
- **B.** $\dfrac{1}{3}$
- **C.** $\dfrac{1}{6}$
- **D.** $\dfrac{3}{8}$
- **E.** $\dfrac{4}{9}$

22. The points, P (1, 2), Q (5, 2), and R (1, −2) in the standard (x, y) coordinate plane are 3 vertices of square $PQRS$. Which of the following points is the fourth vertex, S?
- **F.** (5, −2)
- **G.** (1, 5)
- **H.** (5, −1)
- **J.** (2, −5)
- **K.** (5, 2)

23. The equation $x^2 - 12x + b = 0$ has only 1 solution for x. What is the value of b?
- **A.** 0
- **B.** 3
- **C.** 4
- **D.** 24
- **E.** 36

24. If $0° \le x° \le 90°$ and $\tan x - 1 = 0$, then $x° = ?$
- **F.** 0
- **G.** 15
- **H.** 30
- **J.** 45
- **K.** 60

25. The least common multiple (LCM) of 2 numbers is 108. The greater of the 2 numbers is 54. What is the *maximum* value of the second number?
- **A.** 2
- **B.** 6
- **C.** 18
- **D.** 27
- **E.** 36

END OF THE MATHEMATICS TEST.
STOP! IF YOU HAVE TIME LEFT OVER, CHECK YOUR WORK ON THIS SECTION ONLY.

ANSWERS AND EXPLANATIONS

1. The correct answer is E. You are given that point X is –2 on the number line and point Y is 6 on the number line. Draw a number line and measure the distance between those 2 points:

The distance between point X and point Y on the number line is 8 units, answer choice E.

2. The correct answer is H. To find the length of the sides of a right triangle, use the Pythagorean Theorem: $a^2 + b^2 = c^2$, where c is the hypotenuse, and a and b are the remaining two sides. The hypotenuse is the side opposite the right angle. According to the information given, the hypotenuse is side $\overline{BC}$, which has a length of 5 units. Side $\overline{AB}$ has a length of 4 units, so you must find the length of side $\overline{AC}$. Simply plug the given lengths into the Pythagorean Theorem and solve the equation.

$$4^2 + b^2 = 5^2$$
$$b^2 = 5^2 - 4^2$$
$$b^2 = 25 - 16$$
$$b^2 = 9,$$

so b equals $\sqrt{9}$, or 3, answer choice H.

3. The correct answer is D. The first step in answering this question is to square the radius. The radius squared is equivalent to r^2. Eliminate answer choices A and C, which do not square the radius. Since you are told that you must multiply 3.14 by the radius squared, eliminate answer choice B, which divides 3.14 by the radius squared. You can also eliminate answer choice E, which squares the quantity $(3.14r)$; you are only required to square the radius, r. This leaves $3.14r^2$, answer choice D.

EXPANDED EXPLANATION

4. The correct answer is H. Probability can be expressed as a ratio (commonly known as "odds"). Basically, in this question you are asked to give the odds that José will pull a white shirt out of his drawer if he grabs one without looking at it. Ratios are either "part-to-part" or "part-to-whole." In this case, one single drawer has all of the shirts of both colors in it. Since he is grabbing one shirt out of the entire drawer, you know you must find a "part-to-whole" ratio, not a "part-to-part" ratio. Both answer choices J and K express "part-to-part" (white to blue and blue to white, respectively). So,

---

they can both be eliminated. They are there to trap the unaware test-taker. Both answer choices F and G could be considered "part-to-whole" because F includes 12, which is the total number of shirts in the drawer, and G includes 5, which is the total number of white shirts. However, they are both incorrect because José has a total of 5 white shirts that he could grab out of a total of 12 shirts in the drawer. When we are figuring odds, we are expressing the likelihood of something happening on one try (or trial). Both F and G will fool you if you mistakenly conclude that the ratio must include 1, since he only gets one grab at the shirts. His chance of getting a white shirt on one grab is 5 out of 12 (Number of white shirts: Total number of shirts in the drawer, which is written as 5:12).

5. The correct answer is D. This question asks you to solve for an unknown price. Call the unknown price (the original price) P. Since the shorts were on sale for 30% off, Ryan paid 100% – 30%, or 70% of the original price, P. Multiply P by 0.70, the decimal equivalent of 70%:

$$P \times 0.70 = \$15.75.$$

Set up a proportion to solve for P:

$15.75 is to P as 70% is to 100%

$$\frac{15.75}{P} = \frac{70}{100}; \text{ cross-multiply and solve for } P.$$

$$70P = 1{,}575$$

$$P = \$22.50, \text{ answer choice D.}$$

EXPANDED EXPLANATION

6. The correct answer is H. Although this is a relatively easy question, it is a great example of the fact that word (or "story") problems on ACT Math require translation between two languages: English and Math. Since Stephanie was s years old 5 years ago, she is currently s + 5 years old. The question asks how old she will be 4 years from now. She will be her current age plus 4: (s + 5) + 4, which simplifies to s + 9. If you mistakenly used s for Stephanie's current age and then added four years, you would arrive at answer choice F. If you translated the English to Math incorrectly, or were simply looking for an answer choice that has the same numerals used in the question, you would arrive at answer choice G. (There is usually a "distractor"—that is, an incorrect answer choice—like this one to take advantage of testers who are being lazy or careless.) Answer choices J and K are an opposite pair. Test designers know that testers sometimes assume that one of an opposite pair must be correct. In this case, both are incorrect. However, they jump out to some testers compared to the other answer choices. So, the exam writers do catch some students with this simple trick.

7. **The correct answer is A.** To find the sum of the polynomials, you must add the like terms together. Like terms have the same variables raised to the same powers. The only like terms given in the problem are $2x^2y^3$ and x^2y^3; add them together to get $3x^2y^3$. Therefore, the correct answer is $4x^2y + 3x^2y^3 - 2xy$, answer choice A.

8. **The correct answer is J.** The absolute value of any number is always a positive value. The first step in solving this problem is to perform the math function inside the absolute value signs. Substitute -7 for t in the equation $t - 2$: $-7 - 2 = -9$. Now take the absolute value: The absolute value of -9 is 9, answer choice J.

9. **The correct answer is A.** This is an order of operations question, so the first step is to multiply the quantity in the parenthesis by 2.

$$2(x + 1) = 2x + 2.$$

Next, subtract this quantity from 4, combining like terms and keeping track of the negative sign:

$$4 - (2x + 2) = 4 - 2x - 2$$

Remember to distribute the negative sign.

$$2 - 2x,$$ answer choice A.

10. **The correct answer is H.** When exponents are raised to an exponential power, the rules state that you must multiply the exponents by the power to which they are raised. So, $(x^4)^{15} = x^{(4 \times 15)} = x^{60}$, answer choice H.

11. **The correct answer is C.** The first step in solving this problem is to factor the equation $x^2 - 2x - 15 = 0$. Set up the quantities:

$$(x - \underline{\quad})(x + \underline{\quad}) = 0$$

Find 2 numbers that when multiplied together give you -15, and when added together give you -2. The only numbers that satisfy both operations are -5 and 3.

$$(x - 5)(x + 3) = 0$$
$$x - 5 = 0; x = 5$$
$$x + 3 = 0; x = -3$$

Since the problem asks for the sum of the 2 solutions, add 5 and -3 to get 2, answer choice C.

12. **The correct answer is H.** Notice that there are 5 digits in the repeating decimal (only count the digits after the decimal point). The fifth digit is the number 4, so every place that is a multiple of 5 will be the number 4. Since 210 is a multiple of 5, the 210th digit will be 4. In the repeating decimal, the number 4 always follows the number 3, so the 209th digit will be 3, answer choice H.

EXPANDED EXPLANATION

13. **The correct answer is H.** The figure shows that the price of one game PLUS ADMISSION is just over $5. The total price with price of an additional game is just under $10. And the price of admission with three games is just about right in the middle of $10 and $15. If you didn't have the answer choices as a guide, this information alone would not be enough to come up with a precise answer. But this is a multiple-choice test! So, we can look at the answer choices for some help. Note that the answer choices are all even dollar amounts and they are arranged in ascending order. If you are trying to plug answer choice amounts back into a math problem, it is usually a good idea to start with the middle value. If it is too large, you can eliminate the two larger choices. If it is too small, eliminate the smaller choices. In this case, if you try $3, you can see that it fits the data very well. Admission ($3) + 1 game ($3) = $6, which is just a little more than $5. Similarly, if you plug $3 into the other values on the chart, you can easily see that it works out. So, H is the correct answer. Notice that this problem can seem frustrating at first. The lack of definite dollar amounts on the figure is meant to create anxiety and frustration. But once you realize that the answer choices are all in whole-dollar amounts and far enough apart from one another that only one answer choice can work, it should actually seem fairly straightforward and simple.

14. **The correct answer is K.** You are given the height (4) and the length of b_2 (6). The first step in solving this problem is to calculate the length of b_1. A trapezoid is formed by adding 2 right triangles to opposite ends of a rectangle. Notice how the nonparallel sides both have lengths of 5. Therefore, the two right triangle pieces of the trapezoid are congruent. To find the length of the other leg, use the Pythagorean Theorem with the values given, or simply recognize that the triangles are special-case $3 - 4 - 5$ right triangles. Compute the length of the long base:

$$b_1 = 3 + 6 + 3 = 12$$

Draw a diagram to help visualize the dimensions:

Substitute the values for h, b_1, and b_2 into the equation and calculate the area:

$$\frac{1}{2}(b_1 + b_2)h$$

$$\frac{1}{2}(12 + 6)(4)$$

$$\frac{1}{2}(18)(4)$$

$(9)(4) = 36$, answer choice K.

15. **The correct answer is A.** The area of a square $= s^2$. Translate the question into an equation:

3 times the area equals the side length times some number then squared:

$$3A = (xs)^2$$
$$3A = (s^2)(s^2)$$

Recall the original formula:

$$A = s^2$$

Multiply by 3:

$$3A = 3(s^2)$$

Compare to the new formula:

$$3A = (ss)^2$$
$$3A = (s)(s^2)$$

Thus, $s^2 = 3$

$$s = \sqrt{3}$$

Alternatively, you can use chosen values, such as $s = 1$:

$$A = 1^2$$
$$A = 1$$

The area triples:

$$3 = s^2$$
$$\sqrt{3} = s$$

16. **The correct answer is G.** The best way to solve this problem is to show the given values on the triangle:

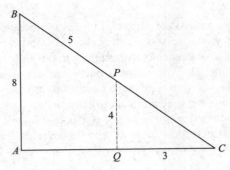

According to information in the problem, both of the triangles are right triangles. Therefore, you can use the Pythagorean Theorem to determine the missing lengths. The first step is to calculate the length of $\overline{PC}$. The Pythagorean Theorem states that $a^2 + b^2 = c^2$, where c is the hypotenuse. Substitute the known values and solve for c:

$$4^2 + 3^2 = c^2$$
$$25 = c^2, \text{ so } c = 5.$$

Therefore, the length of $\overline{PC}$ is 5, and the length of $\overline{BC}$ is $5 + 5$, or 10. Now use the Pythagorean Theorem again to calculate the length of $\overline{AC}$:

$$8^2 + b^2 = 10^2$$
$$64 + b^2 = 100$$
$$b^2 = 36, \text{ so } b = 6$$

Finally, you can calculate the length of $\overline{AQ}$.

$$\overline{AC} = \overline{AQ} + \overline{AC}$$
$$6 = \overline{AQ} + 3$$
$$\overline{AQ} = 3, \text{ answer choice G.}$$

17. **The correct answer is C.** The area of a rectangle = length × width. Since the classroom is 4 feet longer than it is wide, set the width to x feet, and the length to $x + 4$ feet. You are given that the area is equal to 480 square feet. Plug these values into the equation and solve for x:

$$x(x + 4) = 480$$
$$x^2 + 4x = 480$$
$$x^2 + 4x - 480 = 0$$
$$(x + 24)(x - 20) = 0$$
$$x + 24 = 0; x = -24$$
$$x - 20 = 0; x = 20$$

Since the width cannot be a negative number, the width of the classroom must be 20 feet, answer choice C.

18. **The correct answer is F.** The slope of a line is defined as the change in the y-values over the change in the x-values in the standard (x, y) coordinate plane. Slope can be calculated by using the following formula:

$$\frac{(y_1 - y_2)}{(x_1 - x_2)}.$$

Since the slope is $\frac{2}{3}$, for every positive change in 2 along the y-axis, there must be a positive change in 3 along the x-axis. In other words, as you go up 2 in the value of y, you also must go 3 to the right in the value of x. Therefore, the line will pass through the x-coordinate with value $-1 + 3$ or 2, and will pass through the y-coordinate with value $1 + 2$, or 3. That point is (2, 3), answer choice F.

19. **The correct answer is A.** Logarithms are used to indicate exponents of certain numbers called bases. This problem tells you that log to the base x of 4 equals 256. By definition, $\log_a b = c$, if $a^c = b$. So, the question is, when x is raised to the power of 4, you get 256; what is x? By definition, $\log_x 256 = 4$ when $x^4 = 256$. The fourth root of 256 is 4 ($4 \times 4 \times 4 \times 4 = 256$), answer choice A.

20. **The correct answer is H.** The standard form of the equation of a line is $y = mx + b$, where m is the slope. Put the equation in the standard form:

(1) $2x - 3y = 6$

(2) $-3y = -2x + 6$

(3) $y = \frac{2}{3}x - 2$

The slope of the line is $\frac{2}{3}$, answer choice H.

21. **The correct answer is C.** A simple way to solve this problem is to create one fraction, then cancel values that appear in both the numerator and denominator, as follows:

$$\frac{(3)(4)(\cancel{5})(\cancel{6})(\cancel{7})}{(\cancel{5})(\cancel{6})(\cancel{7})(8)(9)} = \frac{(3)(4)}{(8)(9)} = \frac{1}{6}$$

22. **The correct answer is F.** Draw a diagram to help visualize this problem:

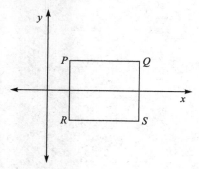

Based on the diagram, point S must have a negative y-coordinate. Eliminate answer choices G and K because they have positive y-coordinates. Since point P is at (1, 2) and point Q is at (5, 2), you know that the distance between the points along the x-axis is 4. A square has 4 sides of equal length, so the distance from point Q to point S must also be 4. Since the y-coordinate of point Q is 2, the y-coordinate of point S must be -2. The only remaining answer choice with a y-coordinate of -2 is answer choice F.

23. **The correct answer is E.** Since the equation $x^2 - 12x + b = 0$ has only 1 solution for x, the equation is a perfect square. This means that $x^2 - 12x + b$ is equivalent to $(x - 6)^2$. Use the FOIL method as follows to solve for b:

$(x - 6)(x - 6) = 0$

First terms: $(x)(x) = x^2$

Outside terms: $(-6)(x) = -6x$

Inside terms: $(-6)(x) = -6x$

Last terms: $(-6)(-6) = 36$

So, $(x - 6)(x - 6) = x^2 - 12x + 36; b$ is 36, answer choice E.

24. **The correct answer is J.** You are given that $\tan x - 1 = 0$, so $\tan x = 1$. By definition, $\tan 45° = 1$, so x must equal 45, answer choice J.

25. **The correct answer is E.** To solve this problem, try the answer choices, starting with the largest number. Since the lowest common denominator is 108, the product of the two numbers must be divisible by 108. $54 \times 36 = 1,944$, which is divisible by 108. Since 36 is the largest of the answer choices, and the question asks for the *maximum* value of the second number, 36 must be the correct answer.

CHAPTER 5

ACT Reading Test: Strategies and Concept Review

The ACT Reading Test has four passages of about 700–900 words each that are each followed by ten questions, for a total of forty questions. The questions can be answered based on information found in the passages. There is virtually no prior knowledge tested on the Reading Test. You will have 35 minutes to complete your work on this section.

The test authors choose subject matter that they think represent the type of material that you will have to read in college. All of the passages on the actual ACT come from material that has been previously published. Therefore, you can rely on the fact that the passages are well edited and will be correct in terms of their grammar, punctuation, and overall structure.

The four passages will be of four different types, as follows:

1. **Literary Narrative** (excerpts from novels and short stories)
2. **Humanities** (passages with topics from arts and literature, often biographies of famous authors, artists, musicians, etc.)
3. **Social Studies** (History, Sociology, Psychology, and other areas of Social Science)
4. **Natural Sciences** (Biology, Chemistry, Physics, etc.)

Questions on the Reading Test will test your skills in identifying Key Ideas and Details, assessing Craft and Structure, and analyzing Integration of Knowledge and Ideas. Use the information and strategies in this chapter to maximize your score on the ACT Reading Test.

TIMING

If you choose to answer all of the questions on the Reading Test, you will have about eight minutes to work on each of the four passages and still have enough time to mark the answers on your answer sheet. For many students, it makes sense to slow down a bit to focus on two or three of the passages and simply guess on the remaining questions. Whether you choose to work on all four of the passages will depend on where you are on the scoring scale. If you get 30 out of the 40 questions correct, you end up with a scaled Reading score of about a 29. (There is minor variation in scaled scores from one exam to the next.) A score of 29 on the Reading Test means that your Reading score would be well within the top 10% of Reading scores nationwide.

The national average ACT Reading Test score is typically around a 20 or 21 on the 36-point scale. This means that the average ACT-taker gets just about exactly one half of the questions correct on the Reading Test. Of course, we recommend that you strive to do your best and we hope that all readers of this book will be well into the above-average range on the ACT. However, it pays to be realistic about what is possible for you on test day. If, after a reasonable amount of practice and study, you are still able to tackle only three of the four passages comfortably within the 35 minutes you are given, you are not in very bad shape. If you can get most of those thirty questions correct, and pick up a few correct answers by guessing on the remaining ten, you could still realistically hope to end up with a top 10% score on the Reading Test.

If you are closer to the average ACT Reading test-taker and find that you are only able to really understand two passages and their accompanying questions in the time allowed, you are still likely to get credit for a few more correct responses by guessing on the remaining twenty questions. In fact, since there are four answer choices for each question, you should predict that you would get about 25% correct when guessing at random. This means that guessing on twenty questions should yield about five correct answers. If you manage to get only 15 correct of the 20 questions that go with the two passages that you work on carefully, you would still have a scale score of approximately 20 or 21.

There are a few factors to consider when deciding which passage(s) you will sacrifice. For example, you should certainly look at the subject matter. Most students have distinct preferences for one or two of the passage types mentioned previously. Conversely, there is probably at least one type of passage that always seems to account for the bulk of the questions that you miss on practice Reading Tests. Always remember to answer every question on your answer sheet, even if you are guessing.

While vocabulary is not tested directly on the ACT, there is certainly an advantage to knowing what the words mean as you try to decipher a passage. We have included a vocabulary list (Appendix 3), which includes words that have appeared on past ACTs and may appear again. Even if none of the words on the list shows up on your exam, you should at least get an idea of the type of words you are likely to see and the level of difficulty that you can expect to find on your test.

Steve Says:

Let your practice testing help you to decide whether to attack all four passages. If you decide to focus on two or three passages on test day, let your practice help guide you when deciding which passages to sacrifice.

GENERAL STRATEGIES AND TECHNIQUES

Use the following general strategies when tackling the ACT Reading Test.

Read the Question Stems First

Once you have decided to attack a specific passage, you should have a plan for *how* to do it. The single most powerful strategy for the Reading Test is to read the *question stems* first. The question stems are the prompts, or stimuli, that appear before the four answer choices. Don't read the answer choices before you read the passage. Most of the answer choices are wrong and, in fact, are referred to by testing professionals as *distractors*. If you read them before you read the passage, you are much more likely to be confused. The questions themselves, though, may contain useful information. You may find that the questions repeatedly refer to specific names or terms. You will find other questions that contain references to the line numbers that are printed down the left side of the passage. These can be very useful in focusing your attention and energy on the parts of the passage that are likely to lead to correct answers to questions.

Don't "Study" the Passage

Probably the biggest mistake that you could make is to read these passages as though you are studying for a test. Unlike most of your previous exams, the ACT Reading Test (and the Science Test also) is in an open-book format. The open-book aspect of the Reading Test means that you should read efficiently. You should not read slowly and carefully as though you will have to remember the information for hours or days. Instead, you should read loosely and only dwell on information that you are sure is important because you need it to answer a question.

The test writers are not interested in whether you can store information for a long period of time and then recall it on an exam day or weeks later. Your reading should be very goal-oriented. If the information you are looking at does not help to answer a question that the test writers find important, then you should not linger over it.

When you study for a test, you probably read carefully so that you don't miss some detail or subtle nuance that is likely to help you to answer an exam question later. You probably reread any part of the material that doesn't make sense immediately. You probably also make connections to your prior knowledge, visualizing as much as you can. If you find a new word, you probably slow down or stop reading and try to figure out what the word means by using context clues. You might also underline or highlight important-looking facts, or make margin notes to help you understand and recall information when you review later.

All of these skills are very useful for the type of reading that you must do when preparing for most exams. However, they are not very useful in the context of the ACT Reading Test. In fact, if you read these passages in the same way that you read when you are studying for a closed-book exam, you are falling into some of the traps that are set by the psychometricians.

The test writers know a lot about how the human mind works. They know about something called *negative transference of learning* that occurs when we have skills that are "adaptive" or useful in our environment. But, when the environment changes, and we keep using our old skills, they can be "maladaptive," or harmful.

So, you should take stock of your current reading habits, compare them to the strategies explained below, and make changes where you must in order to achieve a higher ACT score. Don't feel that you have to give up all of the reading skills that you have acquired thus far in your educational career. However, it is a good idea to add to your "tool box" so that you can adapt your approach to the requirements of the reading "environment" in which you find yourself.

Read for the Main Idea

"Main Idea" has three components: "What?," "What About It?," and "Why did the author write this?" If you can answer these three questions, then you understand the main idea.

Too often, students confuse *topic* with main idea. The topic of a passage only answers the question of "What is the passage about?" If that is all that you notice, you are missing some very important information.

For example, consider a passage that has a topic that we are all at least somewhat familiar with: rain forests. Let's say that you are faced with one passage that is about the ongoing destruction of the rain forests and includes a call for the reader to get involved and help to stop the destruction in some way. "What?" = rain forests. "What About It?" = destruction. "Why?" = to inspire the reader to take action.

Now, say that we keep the same topic, rain forests, but change the other two dimensions: "What About It?" = biodiversity (species variation). "Why?" = to educate the reader. Then we are reading a very different passage. You need all three dimensions of the main idea to understand all that you need to answer the questions correctly.

So, read a little more slowly at the beginning until you get a grip on the main idea. Then, you can skim the rest of the passage.

Skim the Passage

Don't underline. Don't use context clues. When you come to a word or phrase that is unfamiliar, just blow past it. There will be time to come back if you need to. But there is a strong chance that you won't need to bother figuring out exactly what that one word or phrase means in order to answer the bulk of the ten questions that follow the passage. If you waste some of your precious time, you will never get it back. This habit can be hard to break. With perseverance and practice, you will become comfortable with a less-than-perfect understanding of the passage.

The goal at this stage is to develop a general understanding of the structure of the passage so that you can find what you are looking for when you refer back

> **Steve Says:**
>
> The Main Idea ("Big Picture") actually has three parts:
>
> 1. Topic—what is the passage about?
> 2. Scope—what aspect of the topic is being discussed?
> 3. Purpose—why was the passage written?
>
> Identify all three parts to easily answer "Big Picture" questions.

to the passage. You should pay attention to paragraph breaks and quickly try to determine the subtopic for each one. The first sentence is not always the topic sentence. So, don't believe those who say that you can read the first and last sentence of each paragraph and skip the rest of the sentences completely. You are better off skimming over all of the words even if you end up forgetting most of what you read almost immediately.

Remember that you can write in your test booklet. So, when you see a topic word, circle it. If you can sum up a paragraph in a word or two, jot it down in the margin. Remember that the idea at this stage is to not waste time. Keep moving through the material.

Read and Answer the Questions

Start at the beginning of each group of questions. Read the question and make sure that you understand it. Paraphrase it if you need to. (This means to put the question into your own words.) If you paraphrase, keep your language simple. Pretend you are "translating" the question to an average eighth grader. If you can make sure that the person you are imagining can understand the question, then you are ready to answer it. Use the following strategies when answering Reading Test questions:

Refer Back to the Passage

Go back to the part of the passage that will probably contain the answer to your question. It is true that some of the questions on the ACT ask you to draw conclusions based on the information that you read. However, even these questions should be answered based on the information in the passage. There will always be some strong hints, or evidence, that will lead you to an answer.

Some of the questions contain references to specific lines of the passage. The trick in those cases is to read a little before and a little after the specific line that is mentioned. At least read the entire sentence that contains the line that is referenced.

Some of the questions don't really tell you where to look for the answer, or they are about the passage as a whole. In these cases, think about what you learned about the passage while you were skimming it. Note the subtopics for the paragraphs, and let them guide you to the part of the passage that contains the information you need.

Don't be afraid to refer back to the passage repeatedly, and don't be reluctant to skip around within the ten-question group that accompanies each of the four passages. In fact, many students report success with a strategy of actually skipping back and forth among passages. This plan will not work for everyone. But if you feel comfortable with it after trying it on practice tests, then we can't think of any reason not to do it on test day.

Predict an Answer

After you have found the relevant information in the passage, try to answer the question in your mind. Do this before you look at the answer choices. Remember: three out of every four answer choices are incorrect. Not only are they incorrect, but they were written by experts to confuse you. They are less likely to confuse you if you have a clear idea of an answer before you read the answer choices. If you can predict an answer for the question, then skim the choices presented and look for your answer. You may have to be a little flexible to recognize it. Your answer may be there dressed up in different words. If you can recognize a restatement of your predicted answer, mark it. The odds that you will manage to predict one of the incorrect answer choices are slim. Mark the question if you are unsure. If there is time, you can come back to it later.

Use the Process of Elimination

The process of elimination is a good tool, although it should not be the only tool in your box. It is reliable but slow. Use it as a backup strategy either when you cannot predict an answer for a question or your prediction is not listed as an answer choice.

It can be hard to break the habit of applying the process of elimination to every question. You likely have "overused" this technique because you have had more than enough time to take tests in the past.

As mentioned previously, the ACT has time limits that are not even realistic for most students. Form some new reading habits by practicing with ACT reading passages under realistic conditions.

QUESTION TYPES

The ACT Reading Test includes the following question types:

1. **Main Idea/Point of View.** These questions may ask about the main idea of the passage or a specific paragraph. They may also ask about the author's point of view or perspective, and the intended audience. Questions 1, 2, and 18 in the Practice Section are examples of main idea/point of view questions.

2. **Specific Detail.** These questions can be as basic as asking you about a fact that is readily found by referring to a part of the passage. Often, specific detail questions are a bit more difficult because they ask you to interpret the information that is referred to. Questions 7, 12, 13, 14, 16, 19, and 20 in the Practice Section are examples of specific detail questions.

3. **Conclusion/Inference.** These questions require the test-taker to put together information from the passage to use it as evidence for a conclusion. You will have to find language in the passage that will lead you to arrive at the inference that the question demands. (To "infer" is to draw a conclusion based on information in the passage.) Questions 4, 5, 9, 10, and 17 in the Practice Section are examples of conclusion/inference questions.

4. **Extrapolation.** These questions ask you to go beyond the passage itself and find answers that are *probably* true based on what you know from the passage. They can be based on the author's tone or on detailed information in the passage. Question 3 in the Practice Section is an example of an extrapolation question.

5. **Vocabulary in Context.** The ACT does not have a separate vocabulary test. However, there are occasional questions that ask what a specific word means from the passage. The context of the passage should lead you to an educated guess even if you don't know the specific word being asked about. Questions 6, 8, 11, and 15 in the Practice Section are examples of vocabulary in context questions.

STRATEGIES FOR SPECIFIC QUESTION TYPES

Practice sufficiently to be able to identify the different question types and apply the appropriate strategies.

Main Idea

Answer according to your understanding of the three components of the main idea that were mentioned previously (What? What About It? and Why?). It is also worth noting that the incorrect choices are usually either too broad or too narrow in scope. You should eliminate the answer choices that focus on a specific part of the passage and also eliminate the choices that are too general and could describe other passages besides the one that you are working on. Answer these questions last.

Specific Detail

Refer back to the passage to find the answer to the question. Use line or paragraph references in the questions, if they are given. Recognize that sometimes the answer choices are paraphrased, so don't just choose the answers that contain words that appeared in the passage. Make sure that the choice you select responds to the question.

Conclusion/Inference

Although you have to do a bit of thinking for these questions, you should be able to find very strong evidence for your answer. If you find yourself creating a long chain of reasoning and including information from outside the passage, stop and reconsider. The ACT rewards short, strong connections between the evidence in the passage and the answer that is credited.

Extrapolation

This question type asks you about what is probably true based on information in the passage. You need to be sensitive to any clues about the author's tone or attitude and any clues about how the characters in the passage feel. Eliminate any choices that are outside the scope of the passage. As with Inference questions above, the ACT rewards concise, strong connections between the passage and the correct answers.

Vocabulary in Context

The ACT only asks a few vocabulary questions, and they are always in the context of a passage. The best way to answer these questions is the simplest way: just read the answer choices back into the sentence mentioned in the question stem and choose the one that changes the meaning of the sentence the least. If you recognize the Latin roots of the words, or if you have knowledge of Italian, Spanish, or French and recognize roots, you can make educated guesses.

ACT READING SKILLS EXERCISES

The next few pages contain exercises designed to help you apply the concepts generally tested on the ACT Reading Test. Following this exercise section are simulated ACT Reading Test questions in format, which will allow you to become familiar with the types of questions you will encounter on your actual ACT Test.

Identify Topic, Scope, and Purpose

State the Topic, Scope, and Purpose of the following paragraphs. Remember: Topic = what; Scope = to what extent; Purpose = why.

1. In Rembrandt's day, many of his fellow painters portrayed their characters much like the idealized gods of Greek and Roman mythology. Rembrandt differed by painting people in a more realistic and humble manner. He used himself, his family members, and even beggars as models. He viewed these people as being just as worthy of being immortalized in art as mythological figures. He also fittingly enhanced his work by the use of *chiaroscuro*, a technique where light striking the figures dramatically contrasts with a dark background. Rembrandt, the man, emulated his paintings through his singular artistic vision of casting light on the darkness of conformity.

Topic: _____

Scope: _____

Purpose: _____

2. In the early 1960s, Dr. Jane Goodall began studying chimpanzees in Tanzania. Before that time, scientists believed that chimpanzees were strict vegetarians. It was Goodall who first reported that meat was a natural part of the chimpanzee diet. In fact, Goodall discovered that chimpanzees are actually very proficient hunters. Individual chimpanzees have been known to hunt and eat more than 150 small animals each year. Some of the chimpanzees' favorite prey are the feral pig, various small antelope species, and the colobus monkey, a dietary staple. In one notable study, the red colobus monkey accounted for more than 80% of the animals eaten by one group of chimpanzees.

Topic: _____

Scope: _____

Purpose: _____

3. Following fad diets has led to healthier lifestyles for some Americans, but these diets often prove unsustainable. The main problem is the tendency to regain the lost weight after regressing to old eating habits. The good news, however, is that as more research is conducted and more diets are shown to fail, a growing number of people are realizing that dieting is not the key to long-term weight loss. It is becoming increasingly hard to ignore the evidence that a lifestyle of sensible eating and exercise is the path to health. Perhaps we are on the cusp of an exciting new era of health and vitality.

Topic: _____

Scope: _____

Purpose: _____

4. In England in the early 1800s, women were jailed simply because their husbands died and left them with a debt that they could not pay. Prison conditions were appalling, and the injustice was heightened by the fact that the women often had to take their children with them. Elizabeth Fry was determined to make a difference for these women and children. She organized a team of women to go visit the prisoners and teach them to sew, which enabled them to earn some money and drastically improve their lives. Fry never gave up on prison reform, and she spearheaded many efforts that had lasting effects.

Topic: _____

Scope: _____

Purpose: _____

5. While manned missions are more costly than unmanned ones, they are also more successful. Robots and astronauts use much of the same equipment in space, but a human is much more capable of calibrating those instruments correctly and placing them in appropriate and useful positions. A computer is often neither as sensitive nor as accurate as a human managing the same terrain or environmental factors. Robots are also not equipped like humans to solve problems as they arise, and they often collect data that is unhelpful or irrelevant. A human, on the other hand, can make instant decisions about what to explore further and what to ignore.

Topic: _____

Scope: _____

Purpose: _____

Locate and Interpret Significant Details

Read the passage below and answer the questions that follow.

Throughout the Abraham Lincoln and Stephen Douglas presidential debates, Stephen Douglas repeatedly criticized Lincoln's "House Divided" speech. In his "House Divided" speech, Lincoln argues that the "Spirit of Nebraska," the alleged right to choose slavery over freedom in territories, had invaded the country and divided it. The North and the South were no longer working together to put slavery on the road to extinction. In fact, by the late 1850s, the South had fully embraced slavery and wanted to expand it. This new attitude toward slavery promoted by Southerners and some Northern Democrats led Lincoln to believe that they wanted to nationalize slavery.

In the Lincoln-Douglas debates, Lincoln stated that the nation was too divided to continue to compromise on slavery. Lincoln began his defense by referring to the actions of the Founding Fathers, who had worked to eradicate slavery. He mentioned the unanimous abolition of the African slave trade, as well as the Northwest Ordinance and the lack of the word "slave" in the Constitution, to show that the Founding Fathers intended slavery to be strangled in the original Southern States. Lincoln argued that the South had moved away from this course of ending slavery. Lincoln also stated that the federal government, through the Missouri Compromise and the Compromise of 1850, had always regulated slavery in the territories. The Missouri Compromise and the Compromise of 1850 were at odds with the new Dred Scott Decision, which denied that Congress had a right to exclude slavery in the states. The Dred Scott Decision also reinforced the idea that African Americans were not citizens and that slaves could be brought into the North without gaining their freedom. The Dred Scott Decision had the effect of undermining Lincoln's Republican platform that sought to repeal the Kansas-Nebraska Act.

Both in the debates and the "House Divided" speech, Lincoln repeatedly questioned the Democrats' involvement in the Dred Scott Decision. Lincoln suggested that a conspiracy might have taken place between President Buchanan, President Pierce, Chief Justice Roger Taney, and other Democrats, such as Stephen Douglas. Lincoln used evidence to show that the Democrats seemed to have known that the Dred Scott Decision was coming. A key piece of evidence is that the Dred Scott Decision was pushed back until after the election of 1856. In addition, the Democrats had drafted legislation in 1850 and 1854 that contained language seeming to predict that Congress would not be able to exclude slavery in the territories because of Constitutional constraints. The Dred Scott Decision cast doubts on the platform of the Democrats. The Democrats had been endorsing a platform of popular sovereignty, which stated that all new states and territories should be able to vote on whether slavery should be allowed within their borders. The Dred Scott Decision reaffirmed for the South that slaves were considered property. Because America's Constitution protects property, exclusion of slavery through unfriendly legislation was unconstitutional.

Lincoln spoke about the Kansas/Nebraska Act and his opinion on the repeal of the Missouri Compromise throughout the debates. He believed that popular sovereignty was contrary to the principle that valued freedom over slavery. The "Spirit of Nebraska" was what prompted Northerners like Douglas to create the Kansas-Nebraska Act that opposed the "Spirit of '76," the hope of the Founding Fathers that slavery would be strangled within the original Southern states over time. Lincoln believed that the battle over slavery could not be won unless the majority opinion actively opposed slavery.

1. What was the "Spirit of Nebraska" and what, according to Lincoln, had it done to America?

   _____

   _____

   _____

2. Identify two of the arguments Lincoln made to show that the Founding Fathers opposed slavery.

   _____

   _____

   _____

3. What did Lincoln's Republican platform seek to repeal?

   _____

   _____

   _____

4. What were the implications of the "popular sovereignty" platform?

   _____

   _____

   _____

5. What reaffirmed that slaves were considered property?

   _____

   _____

   _____

Understand Sequences of Events and Comprehend Cause–Effect Relationships

Read the passage below and answer the questions that follow.

Every day, one takes for granted the ease of finding out the date. This is simplified to such a great degree by following the Gregorian calendar, based on the solar cycle, which keeps track of 365.25 days each year. This has not always been the case, however. In ancient China, the calendar was based on the lunar cycle, and consisted of a repeating 12-year sequence, each named for a different animal.

The origin of the 12 animals is mythological, with the story being passed down from generation to generation. A common telling of the tale recounts a celebration to honor the Jade Emperor; all of the animals were expected to pay tribute to him on the night of the new year and the first 12 to arrive would receive a great distinction.

In order to reach the Imperial Palace, the animals had to cross a fast-moving river. The cunning rat arrived first climbing atop the ox, who was a much stronger swimmer than the rat, and jumping off right before reaching shore, winning the race. The ox received second place, followed shortly thereafter by the tiger—the strength of both animals allowed them to finish quickly. The rabbit, with his agility, followed by jumping from stone to stone across the river. Next came the mighty and majestic dragon, who flew across the river. When asked why he was not first, he replied that he needed to make rain for the people of Earth and was thus delayed. His kindness earned him the fifth place in the cycle. During the dragon's explanation there was a galloping sound, signaling the arrival of the horse. Suddenly, hidden coiled around the leg of the horse, appeared the snake—nearly as cunning as the rat—who darted in front of the horse, taking sixth place. The horse settled for seventh, just as a raft reached the shore with three more animals. The sheep (eighth), the monkey (ninth), and the rooster (tenth) built a raft and traversed the river with combined effort. For this show of teamwork, they were rewarded in the order that they stepped off of the raft. Next to arrive was the dog, who was met with questioning looks. Supposedly the best swimmer, the dog's lateness was due to his taking a bath in the refreshing waters of the river. His vanity nearly cost him the race. Last was the lazy pig, who stopped on the other side of the river for a feast before he attempted to cross. So weighed down by his meal, he arrived only moments before the Emperor declared the race finished.

Missing from this list of animals is the cat. Sadly, he was a victim of the rat's cunning; the day before the race, the rat informed the cat that he would awaken him prior to the race, so as to allow the cat to rest and save its strength for the race. The day of the race arrived, and the cat continued to sleep while the rat took his spot atop the ox. When the cat awoke, the race was finished, and the cat has hated the rat for what it did ever since.

1. Which animal arrived only moments before the race finished?

   _____

2. What two animals traveled with the second- and seventh-place finishers?

   _____

   _____

3. Why didn't the dog win the race?

_____

_____

_____

4. Name one of the animals that traveled with the monkey.

_____

5. Which animal from the passage did not finish the race?

_____

Determine the Meaning of Words, Phrases, and Statements in Context

Underline the word or phrase in parentheses that best fits the context of each paragraph.

1. A nation has a spiritual as well as material, moral as well as physical existence subjected to internal as well as external conditions of health and virtue, greatness and grandeur, which it must in some measure understand and observe, or become (**lethargic, grandiose**) and infirm, stunted in its growth, and end in premature decay and death.

2. Sylvia Plath, American author of the tragic novel *The Bell Jar*, lived a real-life tragedy bearing many similarities to her fictional story. Like the main character in the story, Plath committed suicide shortly after the (**help, demise**) of her marriage to Ted Hughes, an English poet. Even as a young child, Plath's life was fraught with (**emotional distress, joyous occasions**). When she was just eight years old, Plath's father passed away. Years later, as a junior at Smith College, Plath attempted suicide for the first time and failed.

3. A planet can be described as a non-moon, sun-orbiting object that does not generate nuclear fusion and is large enough to be pulled into a spherical shape by its own gravity. In addition, most known planets generally follow a fixed orbital path. Pluto is not a moon, as it does not orbit another planet. Although Pluto's orbital path is (**irregular, certain**) compared to the other planets of the solar system, it undisputedly orbits the sun.

4. Fairfield Porter trained under world-famous art historian Bernard Berenson and spent countless hours in museums and galleries. Porter's renown as an art critic is due in part to his (**knack for, lack of**) responding directly to an artist's work. He found fault with the common talk-based criticism that spoke of art only in reference to its past or to some vague theoretical framework; such (**criticism, commendation**) attempted to shape the future of art and was far too biased for Porter.

5. After reading Betty Smith's A *Tree Grows in Brooklyn* for the third time, it occurred to me why I so enjoy that story. It begins when the main character, Francie Nolan, is an 11-year-old girl living in tenement housing in Brooklyn, New York, in the early 1900s. The story tells of both her struggles and her dreams, painting a picture of both sadness and (**duress, elation**).

Draw Generalizations

Read the passage below and, in the questions that follow, decide if the statements are true or false. True statements will be those most clearly supported by facts from the passage.

Fear is a normal, legitimate response to genuine danger. However, when fear spirals out of control, becoming persistent and irrational, it constitutes a phobia. Phobias affect a significant portion of the American population. Some experts believe that nearly 25% of Americans live with irrational fears that prevent them from performing everyday activities. Phobias, like other anxiety disorders, can greatly affect quality of life. Generally defined as an unrelenting, anomalous, and unfounded fear of an object or situation, phobias are normally developed from a past negative experience or encounter. Alternatively, children can adopt phobias by observing a family member's reaction to specific stimuli. There is also data to suggest genetic factors linked to phobias.

Phobias come in three distinct classes: agoraphobia, social phobia, and specific phobia. Agoraphobics have an intense fear of leaving a safe place, such as their homes, or being in certain wide open or crowded spaces with no escape. Agoraphobia is the most disabling type of phobia, and treatment is generally complicated by the many associated fears a patient might have. The fear of panic attacks caused by agoraphobia is common. Social phobias are fears related to people or social situations. Social phobias can greatly interfere with work responsibilities and personal relationships. Specific phobia is a general category for any phobia other than agoraphobia and social phobia. This class contains the most recognizable set of symptoms, and is often the easiest class of phobias to treat.

Under the heading of specific phobia, there are four categories: situational, environmental, animal, and medical phobias. Over 350 different phobias have been identified across these four categories. Observers often notice symptoms of a person experiencing intense fear. In many cases, a person facing a phobia will show signs of panic, trepidation, and terror. He or she may also exhibit physical signs including rapid heartbeat, shortness of breath, and trembling. Often, one begins to fear a phobic attack and will experience symptoms without the presence of any external stimuli.

Once a person has been diagnosed with agoraphobia, social phobia, or specific phobia, there is a wide range of treatment options available. Recent medical advances have allowed researchers to identify the parts of the brain associated with phobias. The *amygdala* is one such area of the brain under intense study. This almond-shaped bundle of nerve cells located deep within the brain releases excitatory hormones into the bloodstream and is involved in normal fear conditioning; however, if the amygdala becomes overactive, normal fear responses are heightened. The brain chemical oxytocin has been found to quell activity in the amygdala, thereby weakening the production of the excitatory hormones and limiting the amygdala's communication with other areas of the brain that telegraph the fear response. This relationship between oxytocin and the amygdala indicates a potentially powerful treatment for phobias.

Prior to the development of medical treatments, many people suffering from extreme phobias were often forced to meet with behavioral specialists. These specialists believe that the exaggerated fear experienced is an acquired reflex to some benign stimulus. For example, a normal fear resulting from a dangerous stimulus, such as being bitten by a dog, can turn into an irrational fear of all animals. Behavioral specialists attempt to combat irrational fears through repeated exposure to the phobic stimulus. For instance, a *cynophobic* person might be introduced first to a small, nonthreatening dog, and then be repeatedly exposed to larger dogs in controlled situations until the fear eventually disappears.

These behavioral approaches are still very common and show some positive results. One key to the success of behavioral therapy is the emphasis that therapists place on ensuring that their patients know there indeed are others afflicted with the same disorder. Just knowing that they do not suffer alone helps patients to focus on their treatment and reap the rewards of the therapy.

Any acute fear that hampers daily living and causes great emotional and physical stress should be treated. The vast majority of patients respond to treatment, overcoming their fears to enjoy symptom-free lives. Effective and often permanent relief can come from behavior therapy, medication, or a combination of the two.

1. True/False: As many as a quarter of all Americans may be afflicted with phobias that greatly affect their lives.
2. True/False: Agoraphobia can greatly interfere with work responsibilities and personal relationships, but is easier to treat than specific phobia.
3. True/False: Although now quite uncommon, behavioral approaches were, at one time, successful because they allowed patients to hide their fears.
4. True/False: It is possible for people suffering from a phobia to have symptoms of a phobic attack just from thinking about what it is they are afraid of.
5. True/False: Oxytocin has the potential to treat acute fears that hamper daily life.

Analyze the Author's or Narrator's Voice and Method
Read the passage below and answer the questions that follow.

Eli Whitney (1765–1825) invented the cotton gin, an innovative machine that effectively ended the laborious process of removing cotton seeds by hand, enabling farmers of the American South to harvest the crop en masse. Without a cotton gin, even the most experienced worker could process only one pound of cotton per day. Whitney's machine could screen fifty times as much, making the fiber profitable for the first time.

Although Whitney's cotton-cleaning machine was the first of its kind in America, simple devices had been used around the world for centuries to perform the job. For instance, over a millennium ago in India, a device called a *charka* was invented to separate cotton seeds from lint by pulling the crude fibers through a spinning wheel. The machine was not adaptable, however, to the short-staple cotton produced in North America. In order to process the specific type of cotton fiber grown in the American South, a new apparatus had to be constructed.

Whitney recognized the need for a specialized device to separate cotton's sticky seeds from its desirable fibers. He had already designed many useful items during his lifetime (including muskets and the machines to manufacture them), but none impacted the lives of people as dramatically as the cotton gin did. Some credit it alone for transforming the Southern economy. Even small farms could benefit from a hand-cranked gin; larger versions could be tied to a horse or a water wheel. Large cotton plantations throughout the Southern states displaced farmers of other crops. Cotton production was so profitable, in fact, that food crops fell by the wayside, which had a marked effect on every Southern family's larder.

The cotton gin has to its credit the boost to the cotton industry and the resultant expansion of slavery in Southern plantations. A rush of new immigrants to the United States was making labor inexpensive enough that slavery was an increasingly unprofitable undertaking. Enormous cotton plantations tipped the balance, though, by quickly requiring a massive labor force to work land that had theretofore been unplanted. Plantation owners became fierce advocates for slavery. While immigrants wanted work, many were unwilling to perform the arduous tasks of cotton production. Plantation owners relied almost solely on slave labor until its abolition at the end of the Civil War.

Whitney's cotton gin revolutionized agriculture in the United States. The weight of his invention notwithstanding, he struggled to make a profit from it. After receiving a patent for his invention, Whitney and a partner opted to produce as many cotton gins as possible and charge farmers a steep fee to use them. Farmers considered this fee unnecessary and exorbitant, and began manufacturing copies of the cotton gin instead, claiming that their inventions were unique. Because of a loophole in the patent law, many of the lawsuits brought against the farmers by Whitney and his partner were fruitless. The duo finally agreed to license their cotton gins at a reasonable price, preventing the windfall that Whitney had foreseen.

1. In the first paragraph, the author's use of the words "innovative" and "laborious" reveal what about his/her feelings toward the cotton gin?

    _____

    _____

    _____

2. Why does the author discuss the *charka*?

    _____

    _____

    _____

3. How would you describe the author's approach in the third paragraph when discussing the drop in food crop production?

    _____

    _____

    _____

4. Based on the discussion in the fourth paragraph, what might the author's opinion be concerning the effect of the cotton gin on slavery?

_____

_____

_____

5. What does the author's use of the word "exorbitant" in the last paragraph convey about the farmers' feelings toward the fees charged to use cotton gins?

_____

_____

_____

Paraphrase Question Stems

Following are simulated ACT Reading Test question stems. Paraphrase each of the question stems, putting them into your own words, to help reveal your understanding of the actual question being asked.

1. Which of the following statements does NOT describe one of Joe's reactions to the events of the final play of the game?

_____

_____

_____

2. As depicted in the sixth paragraph (lines 42–50), the relationship between the children and their grandfather is best described by which of the following statements?

_____

_____

_____

3. The examples shown in lines 15–21 appear to most undermine the position held by:

_____

_____

_____

4. The passage most strongly suggests that today's controversy over the existence of dark matter was prompted by which of the following?

_____

_____

_____

5. Which of the following best describes the way the last paragraph functions in relation to the passage as a whole?

_____

_____

_____

ANSWERS AND EXPLANATIONS

Identify Topic, Scope, and Purpose

1. Topic: **Rembrandt**
   Scope: **Rembrandt's artistic vision and painting style**
   Purpose: **To inform the reader**

2. Topic: **The chimpanzee diet**
   Scope: **Jane Goodall's discovery, specifically, that chimpanzees hunted and ate meat**
   Purpose: **To inform the reader**

3. Topic: **Fad diets**
   Scope: **Changing your lifestyle is proven to be more effective than dieting**
   Purpose: **To inform and persuade the reader**

4. Topic: **English women jailed in the early 1800s**
   Scope: **One woman's goal to improve prison conditions for women in the 1800s**
   Purpose: **To inform the reader**

5. Topic: **Manned space missions**
   Scope: **Why manned space missions are more successful than unmanned space missions**
   Purpose: **To inform and persuade the reader**

Locate and Interpret Significant Details

1. In the second sentence of the first paragraph, the author states that the Spirit of Nebraska was "the alleged right to choose slavery over freedom in territories" and that, according to Lincoln, it "had invaded the country and divided it."

2. Any two of the following three arguments found in the second paragraph would be correct: Lincoln mentioned "the unanimous abolition of the African slave trade, the Northwest Ordinance and the lack of the word 'slave' in the Constitution, to show that the Founding Fathers intended slavery to be strangled in the original Southern States."

3. At the end of the second paragraph, the author states, "the Dred Scott Decision had the effect of undermining Lincoln's Republican platform that wanted to repeal the Kansas-Nebraska Act."

4. Near the end of the third paragraph the author states that, "the Democrats had been endorsing a platform of popular sovereignty, which stated that all new states and territories should be able to vote on whether slavery should be allowed within their borders." This implies that slavery would continue to spread if the Democratic platform was made law.

5. The second-to-last sentence of Paragraph 3 states specifically that, "The Dred Scott Decision reaffirmed for the South that slaves were considered property."

Understand Sequences of Events and Comprehend Cause–Effect Relationships

1. **Pig**—"Last was the lazy pig, who stopped on the other side of the river for a feast before he attempted to cross, and was so weighed down by his meal that he arrived only moments before the Emperor declared the race to be finished."

2. **Rat and Snake**—"The cunning rat arrived first by climbing atop the ox, who was a much stronger swimmer than the rat, and jumping off of the ox right before reaching shore, winning the race." AND "Suddenly, hidden coiled around the leg of the horse, appeared the snake—nearly as cunning as the rat—who darted in front of the horse taking sixth place. The horse settled for seventh . . ."

3. This cause-and-effect relationship can be found in the passage: "Supposedly the best swimmer, the dog's lateness was due to his taking a bath in the refreshing waters of the river. His vanity nearly cost him the race."

4. **Sheep or Rooster**—"The sheep (eighth), the monkey (ninth), and the rooster (tenth) built a raft and traversed the river with their combined efforts. For this show of teamwork, they were rewarded in the order that they stepped off of the raft."

5. **Cat**—"Missing from this list of animals is the cat. Sadly, he was a victim of the rat's cunning; the day before the race, the rat informed the cat that he would awaken him prior to the race, so as to allow the cat to rest and save its strength for the race. The day of the race arrived, and the cat continued to sleep while the rat took his spot atop the ox. When the cat awoke, the race was finished, and the cat has hated the rat for what it did ever since."

Determine the Meaning of Words, Phrases, and Statements in Context

Paragraph 1: **Lethargic**   The paragraph indicates that there are positive aspects to a nation's existence that must be understood. Failure to understand and observe these conditions would lead to negative consequences; the nation would become ". . . infirm, stunted in growth, and end in premature decay and death." The word "lethargic" means "lazy" or "sluggish," so it is appropriate here.

Paragraph 2: **Demise**   The negative context of the paragraph can be found in words such as "tragic" and "tragedy." The word "demise" means "death" or "end of existence" and it makes sense that both Plath and her main character would commit suicide after the end of a marriage, which can be particularly painful and tragic.

Emotional distress   The negative context of the paragraph is best supported by the phrase "emotional distress." There is nothing in the paragraph to indicate that Plath's life included many "joyous occasions."

Paragraph 3: **Irregular**   The context of the paragraph indicates that there is some controversy surrounding Pluto's classification as a planet and implies that, unlike the other planets in the solar system (all of which orbit the sun on a generally constant path) Pluto has an "irregular" orbit. The word "although" indicates some sort of contrast, which should lead you to this answer.

Paragraph 4: **Knack for**   According to the paragraph, Porter was renowned as an art critic. The word "renowned" means "widely honored" or "famous," both of which point to the quality of Porter's reputation. It makes sense based on the context of the paragraph that Porter had a "knack for" (meaning "talent for") responding directly to an artist's work, as such behavior would add to his acclaim and renown.

Criticism   The sentence begins with, "He found fault with . . ." This best supports the use of the word "criticism." The word "commendation" means "praise," which is not supported by the context.

Paragraph 5: **Elation**   The paragraph indicates that the girl's life was filled with both struggles and dreams; in other words, she had both negative and positive experiences. The word "both" is the context clue, and should lead you to select the word "elation," meaning "great joy," which correctly complements "sadness." These two conflicting emotions parallel "struggles and dreams."

Draw Generalizations

1. **True**   The passage states: "Phobias affect a significant portion of the American population. Some experts believe that nearly 25% of Americans live with irrational fears that prevent them from performing everyday activities. Phobias, like other anxiety disorders, can greatly affect quality of life."

2. **False**   While it is true that agoraphobia can greatly interfere in a person's life, it is not easier to treat than specific phobia. According to the passage, "Agoraphobia is the most disabling type of phobia, and treatment is generally complicated by the many associated fears a patient might have." Moreover, the passage states that specific phobia "is often the easiest class of phobias to treat."

3. **False**   According to the passage, "Behavioral specialists attempt to combat irrational fears through repeated exposure to the phobic stimulus. . . These behavioral approaches are still very common and show some positive results."

4. **True**   The passage states: "Often, one begins to fear a phobic attack and will experience symptoms without the presence of any external stimuli." This suggests that a person with a phobia can manifest symptoms simply from thinking about the phobia and anticipating the fear.

5. **True**   According to the passage, ". . . if the amygdala becomes overactive, normal fear responses are heightened. The brain chemical *oxytocin* has been found to quell activity in the amygdala, thereby weakening the production of the excitatory hormones and limiting the amygdala's communication with other areas of the brain that telegraph the fear response. This relationship between oxytocin and the amygdala indicates a potentially powerful treatment for phobias."

Analyze the Author's or Narrator's Voice and Method

1. The author believes that the cotton gin revolutionized the way cotton was harvested by eliminating much of the human labor involved. This "innovative" machine ended the "laborious" (labor intensive) practice of cleaning the cotton by hand.

2. The author discusses the *charka* to show that, although cotton-cleaning devices are an old concept, Whitney's cotton gin was the first of its kind adapted to the unique types of cotton grown in America.

3. By mentioning the domination of growing cotton over growing food crops, the author is further emphasizing the extent of the impact the cotton gin had on the Southern economy.

4. The author avoids giving an opinion about whether the expansion of slavery was an ethically appropriate step for Southern plantations. Instead, the author shows the cause–effect relationship between the cotton gin and the increase in slavery based on economic factors. The author probably feels that the expansion of slavery was the natural result of expanded cotton farming.

5. The word "exorbitant" means "excessive." The farmers thought that Eli Whitney wanted too much money to license the use of his invention.

Paraphrase Question Stems

Following are examples of effective paraphrases. Yours might be different; the purpose of this exercise is to help you make the question stems easier to handle, thereby increasing your chances of correctly answering the question.

1. Which answer choice is false?
   Explanation: *Locate the part of the passage that discusses Joe's reaction to the last play of the game. The correct answer choice will be the one that is NOT described in this section of the passage. The incorrect answer choices will all mention something about Joe's true reaction.*

2. How do the children and the grandfather feel about each other?
   Explanation: *First, get a general sense of how the people feel about each other. For example: Did the children do something to anger the grandfather? Is the grandfather happy to see his grandchildren? Then, look for the answer choice that has the same general connotation, usually either positive or negative.*

3. Whose position is weakened by the examples in lines 15–21?
   Explanation: *Carefully read the indicated lines, and then decide whose position is weakened, hurt, or rendered false, by those statements.*

4. What caused the controversy surrounding dark matter?
   Explanation: *Locate the section of the passage that includes information about "today's controversy," and note the events leading up to it. There will often be specific language in the passage that is echoed in the correct answer.*

5. What is the purpose of the last paragraph?
   Explanation: *Read the paragraph (in this case) and determine what it does: does it wrap up the story; does it suggest that more work needs to be done; Does it analyze the arguments presented in the passage? Look carefully at the first word in the answer choices once you've determined the general function of the paragraph in question.*

PRACTICE QUESTIONS

Following are simulated ACT Reading Test passages and questions, along with explanations for all of the questions. Carefully read the directions, apply the information from this chapter, and attempt all of the questions.

DIRECTIONS: This practice section includes two passages, each followed by ten questions. Read the passages and choose the best answer to each question. Circle the answer you choose. You should refer to the passages as often as necessary when answering the questions.

PASSAGE I

LITERARY NARRATIVE: *Fear of Success*

"You appear to have a fear of success," her doctor said.

"You mean a fear of failure, don't you?"

"No. A fear of *success*."

5 "You don't know what you're talking about!" she exclaimed as she stormed out of the doctor's office. As she passed the receptionist's desk, she wryly declared, "You can cancel all the rest of my appointments with Dr. Mornington. I'm cured."

10 "Are you sure you want to do that? The doctor has a nine-month waiting list. If you change your mind, you'll have to go to the end of the list."

"Don't worry. I won't be changing my mind. Like I said 'I'm cured.'" She knew the receptionist hadn't
15 missed the sarcasm in her voice.

This exchange had occurred three months ago. She was now beginning to ruefully realize the accuracy of the saying, "The truth hurts."

At first, she had continued to scoff at the doctor's
20 interpretation of her life's worries as a fear of success. The incidents the doctor focused on had been mere errors in judgment—or corrections of past errors. But then, as she tried to justify her own point of view, she began to see the doctor's perspective.

25 In the third grade, she had been caught copying from Bobby Jacobs' test. Most kids made the mistake of cheating at some point in their life. But she had copied from Bobby—a boy who struggled to earn C's. Why?

In high school, as her academic and athletic success
30 was propelling her toward the Ivy League, she brazenly shoplifted some candy in front of the shopkeeper. When confronted, she blatantly lied, even as the evidence was pulled from her pocket and a videotape of the events played and replayed for her. As her best friend paid for the
35 candy and begged for mercy, the store owner shook his head, but let her go.

Her college career was marked with small lapses in judgment, such as the vandalism of a campus bus, but as her Yale graduation approached, she ardently prepared for
40 an interview with a prominent investment banking firm. "The hours are brutal!" she announced to her roommate. "But if I can survive the first two years, I'll be making well over six figures before I'm twenty-five!" She got the job and moved to the company's Atlanta office. She
45 was paid well for the long hours, but she seldom had the opportunity to meet new friends with whom to spend her hard-earned money, and so, twenty-one months into the job, she quit.

For years, she had been applauding herself for mak-
50 ing this wise personal decision. She didn't want to be one of those money-grubbers with no personal life! But what quality of life had she subsequently achieved? She flitted from one career to another, staying in each job just long enough to get out of debt. Each time, she quit to pursue
55 her "true calling."

Her parents continued to let her live in the downstairs apartment of the working-class neighborhood home in which she had grown up. When she was working, she paid them rent; when she was unemployed, she didn't.
60 What did they care? The old house was paid for and they weren't likely to spend the money on themselves. They would probably just save it for her modest inheritance. It was her money either way. Besides, her parents had never really understood her. They had recognized her intelli-
65 gence only when her grade-school teachers had pointed it out. Her dad, a bricklayer by day and an armchair quarterback by night, had been integral in her athletic success, but intellectually, she had passed him by the time she hit high school. Her mom, a school nurse, was ever concerned, yet
70 couldn't understand her daughter's caprice.

So, was the doctor right? Was she afraid of success? Was she afraid of being a misfit in the world outside her working-class neighborhood? Or was she afraid of falling in love, marrying, and having a child like herself? With a
75 heavy sigh, she reached for the phone.

"Hi. I'd like to make an appointment with Dr. Mornington."

"Are you a current patient?"

"No."

80 "The first available appointment is in ten months," came the reply.

GO ON TO THE NEXT PAGE.

1. The passage is written from the point of view of:
   A. an unidentifiable narrator.
   B. the doctor of a very disturbed woman.
   C. a mother confused by her daughter's strange decisions.
   D. a working-class man.

   See Expanded Explanation on page 244!

2. Which of the following best describes the author's approach to presenting the story of the main character's discovery about herself ?
   F. Starting immediately with a statement of the discovery in the character's voice and continuing with scenes that reveal how the discovery came about
   G. Revealing the character's self-awareness through a blend of reflection and scenes from the character's youth and adulthood
   H. Describing the physical details of scenes and summarizing their significance in a concluding statement in the character's voice
   J. Using dialogue in the midst of scenes from the character's youth and adulthood

3. Each of the events from the main character's youth and early adulthood reveal:
   A. the increasing antagonism between the main character and her doctor.
   B. the judgmental attitude of the main character's parents.
   C. the main character's failure to make wise decisions.
   D. the main character's inability to keep a job.

4. According to the passage, Dr. Mornington would most likely analyze the main character's blatant shoplifting as:
   F. an uncontrollable urge.
   G. the mimicry of similar crimes committed by other members of her family.
   H. an example of her brilliance.
   J. evidence of a subconscious wish to be caught.

5. As she is revealed in the shoplifting incident, the main character's best friend can best be characterized as:
   A. jealous.
   B. genuinely concerned.
   C. apathetic and uncaring.
   D. naïve.

   See Expanded Explanation on page 244!

6. As it is used in line 39, the word *ardently* most nearly means:
   F. half-heartedly.
   G. hotly.
   H. enthusiastically.
   J. loyally.

7. The main character's childhood home was:
   A. a working-class neighborhood of an unnamed city.
   B. a wealthy suburb in Connecticut.
   C. Atlanta.
   D. not mentioned in the passage.

8. The use of the phrase "true calling" in line 55 indicates that the main character:
   F. did not believe in working hard.
   G. worked in the telecommunications industry.
   H. was struggling to find her purpose in life.
   J. hated investment banking, but loved her next job.

9. The passage states that the main character's mother "couldn't understand her daughter's caprice." This most nearly means that the main character's mother:
   A. didn't understand the collegiate words that her daughter used.
   B. was concerned about her daughter's need to see a psychologist.
   C. thought her daughter spent too much of her time playing sports.
   D. did not know what caused her daughter's impulsive behavior.

10. Based on the telephone conversation at the end of the passage, it can most reasonably be inferred that:
    F. the main character is ready to trust her doctor and make positive changes in her life.
    G. Dr. Mornington's receptionist is lying about the long wait to meet with the doctor.
    H. the main character will not see Dr. Mornington.
    J. the main character is unwilling to recognize the need for change in her life.

    See Expanded Explanation on page 245!

GO ON TO THE NEXT PAGE.

PASSAGE II

NATURAL SCIENCE: *An Enemy Within*

The human body's defense mechanisms are truly remarkable. When injured, the human body immediately begins to repair itself; when attacked by germs, it increases production of white blood cells to defend itself and fight back
5 against the germs. And, throughout life, the brain and heart never take a break. With an ever-expanding understanding of how the body keeps itself healthy, modern medicine attempts to work with this predictable machine, supplementing the natural defenses where possible.
10 Unfortunately, the machine occasionally malfunctions, and the very cells designed to protect the body instead attack its allies. For example, leukocytes (white blood cells) occasionally increase for no apparent reason, fighting not against germs, but healthy blood cells; this
15 is commonly referred to as *leukemia*. Although certainly not a desired disease, doctors have made tremendous progress toward curing leukemia. Such is not the case for Huntington's Disease (HD).

HD is a devastating, degenerative brain disorder for
20 which there is no cure. The disease results from genetically programmed degeneration of brain cells, called *neurons*, in certain areas of the brain. This degeneration causes uncontrolled movements, loss of intellectual faculties, and emotional disturbance. Early symptoms of
25 Huntington's Disease may affect cognitive ability or mobility and include depression, mood swings, forgetfulness, irritability, clumsiness, involuntary twitching, and lack of coordination. As the disease progresses, concentration and short-term memory diminish and involuntary movements
30 of the head, trunk, and limbs increase. Walking, speaking, and swallowing abilities deteriorate. Eventually, HD sufferers become unable to care for themselves and are totally dependent upon others. Death follows from complications such as choking, infection, or heart failure.

35   HD typically begins in midlife, between the ages of 30 and 45, though onset may occur as early as the age of 2. Children who develop the juvenile form of the disease rarely live to adulthood. HD affects males and females equally and crosses all ethnic and racial boundaries.

40   HD is a familial disease, passed from parent to child through a mutation in the normal gene. Each child of an HD parent has a 50–50 chance of inheriting the HD gene. If a child does not inherit the HD gene, he or she will not develop the disease and cannot pass it to subsequent gen-
45 erations. A person who inherits the HD gene will sooner or later develop the disease. Whether one child inherits the gene has no bearing on whether others will or will not inherit the gene. The rate of disease progression and the age of onset vary from person to person. A genetic
50 test, coupled with a complete medical history and neurological and laboratory tests, help physicians diagnose HD. Presymptomatic testing is available for individuals who are at risk for carrying the HD gene. The test cannot predict when symptoms will begin, and, in the absence of
55 a cure, some individuals "at risk" elect not to take the test. Strangely, in 1 to 3% of individuals with HD, no family history of HD can be found.

Named for Dr. George Huntington, who first described this hereditary disorder in 1872, HD is now recognized as one of the more common genetic disorders.
60 More than a quarter of a million Americans have HD or are "at risk" of inheriting the disease from an affected parent. Since there is no known way to stop or reverse the course of HD, researchers are continuing to study the HD gene with an eye toward understanding how it causes dis-
65 ease in the human body. In the meantime, physicians prescribe a number of medications to help control emotional and movement problems associated with HD.

Until a cure is found, Huntington's Disease affects entire families: physically, emotionally, socially, and eco-
70 nomically. For those afflicted, the gradual loss of capacities is humiliating; the realization that they may have passed the disease along to their offspring is horrifying. For the families, the physical and financial strain of caring for the afflicted is coupled with the realization that they
75 may someday suffer the same fate. Given the current lack of treatment, HD is nothing less than an insidious villain, which lurks within its helpless victims.

11. As it is used in the first paragraph, the word "machine" most nearly means:
    A. the aggregate of human functions.
    B. a coin-operated device.
    C. a highly organized political group.
    D. a newly discovered medical tool.

12. According to the passage, medical researchers have made tremendous progress in their ability to cure:
    F. leukemia.
    G. Huntington's Disease.
    H. most types of cancer.
    J. white blood cells.

13. According to the passage, all of the following are examples of symptoms of Huntington's Disease EXCEPT:
    A. difficulty swallowing.
    B. forgetfulness.
    C. frequent rashes.
    D. involuntary twitching.

14. The symptoms of Huntington's Disease begin when:
    F. white blood cells multiply too quickly.
    G. leukocytes attack other cells.
    H. brain cells are cured.
    J. neurons degenerate.

15. As it is used in the passage, the word *juvenile* (line 37) most nearly means:
    A. young.
    B. emotionally immature.
    C. insecure.
    D. occurring in childhood.

GO ON TO THE NEXT PAGE.

16. According to the passage, Huntington's Disease occurs in:
    F. individuals of European descent only.
    G. people who carry the HD gene only.
    H. adults between the ages of thirty and forty-five only.
    J. all people with leukemia.

17. According to the passage, if someone carries the Huntington's Disease gene:
    A. he or she may never develop symptoms of HD.
    B. he or she will eventually lose some cognitive ability and coordination.
    C. he or she is likely to have unusual physical traits recognizable before the onset of symptoms.
    D. there is no way of knowing it until symptoms begin.

18. What is the main idea of the second paragraph (lines 19–34)?
    F. Early symptoms of HD are difficult to detect.
    G. Genetically programmed brain cells are responsible for most degenerative diseases.
    H. The progressive nature of HD leads to a decline in bodily functions, resulting in death.
    J. HD is a devastating disorder caused by uncontrolled movements and depression.

19. The author of the passage compares HD to:
    A. a fly in the ointment.
    B. an insidious villain with malicious intent.
    C. a monkey wrench in the machine.
    D. a black-widow spider.

20. According to the passage, HD directly affects:
    I.   those who carry the HD gene.
    II. the families of people with HD.
    III. the patients of those who carry the HD gene.
    F. I only
    G. I and II only
    H. II and III only
    J. I, II, and III

END OF THE READING TEST.
STOP! IF YOU HAVE TIME LEFT OVER, CHECK YOUR WORK ON THIS SECTION ONLY.

ANSWERS AND EXPLANATIONS

PASSAGE I

EXPANDED EXPLANATION

1. **The best answer is A.** ACT reading passages always include questions that ask about the "big picture." They ask about the main idea, the overall structure of the passage, a likely source for the material, a good title for the passage, or some other aspect of the passage as a whole. This question asks who tells the story. Looking at the passage for clues, the reader will be frustrated initially because there are no clues as to the identity of the narrator. If you formulate the answer to the question before looking at the answer choices, you'll be immediately drawn to answer choice A: "an unidentifiable narrator." If you've practiced enough to build confidence in your ability to pre-phrase (predict) answers and then choose your answer when you see it among the choices, this question is one that you can knock out quickly. If you aren't able to pre-phrase an answer, you can always fall back on the process of elimination, which is reliable, but slower. In this passage, you can find the characters listed in answer choices B, C, and D. But you won't find any evidence that any of them is the narrator. The process of elimination will lead you to the same correct answer as pre-phrasing will. There is a good chance that you won't predict exactly the same words that are used in the correct answer choice. So, you'll have to recognize the choice that expresses the idea you predicted even if the language is different.

---

2. **The best answer is G.** The main character discovers her character flaws by reflecting on scenes from her life. The passage does not begin with a statement of discovery. Although dialogue is used at the beginning and end of the passage, it is not used throughout, nor does the main character offer a concluding statement of summary at the end.

3. **The best answer is C.** It is clear based on the details in the passage that the main character has a history of making unwise decisions. The antagonism between the main character and her doctor is evident in the opening paragraphs, but there is no mention of the doctor in other scenes of the main character's life. Although the main character's parents may have judged their daughter's actions, it is not central to the story. Finally, although the main character jumped from one career to another, it is also not a factor in all of the scenes.

4. **The best answer is J.** The doctor states that he believes the main character fears success. It follows that the main character would engage in self-destructive acts such as shoplifting to be denied that success. You can assume that if the main character were caught shoplifting, her chances at a successful life might be reduced.

EXPANDED EXPLANATION

5. **The best answer is B.** In many reading questions, the ACT gives line numbers, or at least paragraph references, as guideposts. This question doesn't. The question refers to the "main character's best friend." So, you're tasked with finding a reference to the best friend in order to answer. Rather than reading the passage sequentially from beginning to end and searching for the phrase "best friend," you'll be rewarded for practicing and cultivating the skill of "scanning and spotting." If you can run your eyes over the text and recognize "best friend", you'll then be able to stop and read the last sentence of that paragraph for clues regarding the best friend's motivation. Comparing the friend's actions of paying and begging for mercy on behalf of the narrator to the answer choices will lead you to answer choice B. There is no reason, based on the text, to doubt the friend's motives. So, answer choice A must be eliminated. If the friend were "apathetic and uncaring," as answer choice C states, she certainly wouldn't have paid for the shoplifted candy. "Naïve" (answer choice D) means "inexperienced" or "unsophisticated." There is no evidence in the passage that would allow the reader to draw that conclusion about the friend.

---

6. **The best answer is H.** *Ardent* can mean "hotly," "enthusiastic," or "whole-hearted." The main character "enthusiastically" prepared for her interview because she really wanted the wellpaying job.

7. **The best answer is A.** The main character's first job was in Atlanta, and she attended college in Connecticut, but the main character grew up on a working-class neighborhood. The name of the place is not mentioned.

8. **The best answer is H.** Given that the main character repeatedly went from one job to another, each time thinking she was answering her "true calling," you can infer that she was struggling to find her purpose

in life. The other choices are not supported by evidence in the passage.

9. **The best answer is D**. *Caprice* is defined as "sudden, impulsive, and seemingly unmotivated notions or actions." This definition is supported by the passage. Although the main character was well educated, the passage does not imply that the mother's vocabulary was not equal to that of her daughter's. The passage does not imply that the mother was aware that her daughter saw a psychologist. Nor does it imply that the mother thought her daughter spent too much time playing sports.

EXPANDED EXPLANATION

10. **The best answer is F.** This is an inference question. To *infer* is to conclude from evidence. So, this question type asks you to draw a conclusion based on evidence found in the passage. The question stem leads you to "the end of the passage." Therefore, you know that you'll be searching the last paragraph for clues to the correct answer rather than finding the answer laid out on the page. For these questions, it is usually best to quickly look at the answer choices before referring back to the passage. The last paragraph begins with a series of rhetorical questions that the main character is asking herself. The action that follows is a heavy sigh followed by a phone call. A sigh often indicates resignation or surrender. Calling the doctor indicates that the character is ready to take action to improve her life. There is no evidence at all in the passage that would support answer choice G or H. Answer choices F and J are directly opposite one another. If J were correct, the character would never have reached for the telephone or sighed. F is correct because it is supported by evidence found in the passage.

PASSAGE II

11. **The best answer is A.** Although humans are not routinely referred to as "machines," the routine, predictable functions of the human body can be likened to a machine. The other options are all legitimate definitions of the word "machine," but are inappropriate in this context.

12. **The best answer is F.** The first paragraph clearly states that doctors "have made tremendous progress in successfully curing leukemia. Such is not the case for Huntington's Disease (HD)." The other answer choices are not supported by details in the passage.

13. **The best answer is C.** Difficulty swallowing, forgetfulness, and involuntary twitching are all listed as symptoms of Huntington's Disease. Frequent rashes are not mentioned.

14. **The best answer is J.** According to the second paragraph, HD is the result of the degeneration of neurons (a type of brain cell). *Degenerate* means "to break down."

15. **The best answer is D.** The word *juvenile* can be used to mean any of the answer choices, but in this context, it means "occurring in childhood."

16. **The best answer is G.** The passage states that if someone "does not inherit the HD gene, he or she will not develop the disease." Therefore, you can infer that HD occurs only in those people who carry the gene. The passage does not state that the disease is more prevalent in one racial or ethnic group than another. Although symptoms of HD usually appear between the ages of thirty and forty-five, symptoms can begin at any age. Lastly, HD has nothing to do with leukemia.

17. **The best answer is B.** Anyone with the HD gene will eventually develop HD. Prior to developing symptoms, people with the HD gene do not look any different from people without it. A blood test can determine if someone carries the HD gene, whether or not he or she has symptoms of the disease.

18. **The best answer is H.** The second paragraph discusses some of the devastating symptoms of HD and strongly indicates that the progressive nature of HD leads to a decline in bodily functions, resulting in death.

19. **The best answer is B.** In the last sentence, HD is described as "an insidious villain which lurks within its helpless victims." The other answer choices are not supported by the passage.

20. **The best answer is G.** The passage only mentions the effects of HD on those afflicted with the disease and their families. Roman numeral III is not supported by the passage.

CHAPTER 6

ACT Science Test: Strategies and Concept Review

The ACT Science Test measures the interpretation, analysis, evaluation, reasoning, and problem-solving skills that apply to the study of the natural sciences. The questions require you to recognize and understand the basic concepts related to the information contained within the passages, critically examine the hypotheses developed, and generalize from given information to draw conclusions or make predictions. The ACT Science Test includes several passages, each followed by four to seven multiple-choice questions, for a total of 40 questions. You will have 35 minutes to complete the ACT Science Test. The content areas found in the passages are Biology, Chemistry, Physics, and Earth Sciences. You do not need to have advanced knowledge of these content areas; you only need to be able to interpret the data as it is presented and understand the scientific method and experimental design. All of the information you need to answer the questions is in the passages. Usually, if you've completed two years of science coursework in high school, you will have all of the background knowledge necessary to understand the passages and answer the questions correctly.

You may have to do some math on the ACT Science Test. You are not, however, allowed to use a calculator. Only basic arithmetic computation will be necessary to answer these questions. You can do math scratch work right on your test booklet.

The ACT Science Test has passages in three formats:

1. **Data Representation**   These passages are mostly charts and graphs. The questions ask you to read information from them or spot trends within the data presented.
2. **Research Summaries**   These passages explain the set-up of an experiment or a series of experiments and the results that were obtained.
3. **Conflicting Viewpoints**   These passages are like the Reading Test passages. There are usually two scientists or two students who disagree on a specific scientific point, and each presents an argument defending his or her position while possibly attacking the other, conflicting position.

GENERAL STRATEGIES AND TECHNIQUES

Use the following strategies and techniques to answer the questions on the ACT Science Test more easily.

Prioritize

Given the time limit, you might end up working through only four or five of the six or seven passages. Choose the passages in the format you like most. If you are having a hard time making sense of the passage that you start with, move on to some less confusing material. The best way to know which passages to do first on test day is to practice ahead of time so that you can recognize the passages that are likely to give you the most points for the time that you put in.

Remember that you will likely see three Data Representation passages, three Research Summary passages, and one Conflicting Viewpoints passage. If charts, graphs, tables, and so on create stress for you, look for the Conflicting Viewpoints passage and start with those questions. If you establish a pattern of success, that is, start out by answering questions correctly and building your confidence, then the remaining passages won't seem so overwhelming.

In addition to prioritizing passages, you can choose to do the questions in each passage in any order. For example, many students look for questions that refer directly to the data and answer those questions first. Any questions that ask you to extrapolate information based on the data or introduce new information can be saved for last. This tactic allows you to get a good feel for relationships among the data, thereby simplifying the overall testing process.

> **Steve Says:**
>
> The ACT Science Test is not strictly a science test! It is a critical thinking test, so do not worry if you think you are "not good at science."

Think First

Once you have chosen a passage to attack, take a moment or two to understand the main idea or ideas presented before you dig into the questions. Common sense will help to keep you from being fooled by some of the distractors that are "way off." For instance, if the passage is describing an experiment done with live mammals in a laboratory, and the question asks about temperatures that are likely to result in a certain behavior, you could certainly rule out an answer choice that says, "400° Fahrenheit."

Consider the following example:

Radon gas can seep from the ground into an existing home through many different pathways, such as cracks in the basement floor, drains, sump pumps, or loose-fitting pipes.

Table 1 shows the radon levels in pCi/L for each of three zones, with areas in Zone 1 indicating a High Radon Potential, areas in Zone 2 indicating a Moderate Radon Potential, and areas in Zone 3 indicating a Low Radon Potential.

Table 1	
Zone	**Radon Level (pCi/L)**
3	< 2
2	2 to 4
1	> 4

1. Studies have shown that existing homes in the same zone can have different radon levels. Are these findings consistent with information presented in the passage?
   A. No, because radon levels cannot be measured in existing homes.
   B. No, because radon seeps into all homes in the same way.
   C. Yes, because the occurrence of radon is very rare.
   D. Yes, because radon levels can vary within the same zone.

The correct answer is D. The introductory paragraph and the table both suggest that radon levels can be different—homes with basement cracks might be more likely to have a radon problem than those homes without basement cracks, for example. Logic will tell you that you can eliminate answer choices A and B. Because answer choice C is not supported by details in the passage, it can also be eliminated.

Be "Trendy"

Many of the Science questions reward test-takers who can spot trends in the data presented. When charts or graphs are given, take a moment to figure out which variables are being charted and note any apparent relationships between them. A *direct relationship* is when one variable increases as the other increases. An *inverse relationship* is when one variable decreases as another increases. Sometimes drawing arrows next to the data helps to show a pattern of increase or decrease.

Consider the following example:

The molar heat of fusion (ΔH_{fus}) is the amount of heat necessary to melt (or freeze) 1.00 mole of a substance at a constant pressure.

The following table lists molar heats of fusion, boiling points, and melting points for several elements.

Element	Melting point (°C)	Boiling point (°C)	ΔH_{fus} (kJ/mol)
Calcium	839.00	1,484.00	8.54
Silver	961.92	2,212.00	11.30
Iron	1,535.00	2,750.00	13.80
Nickel	1,453.00	2,732.00	17.46

Note: measured at a pressure of 1 atmosphere (atm).

1. According to the table, as the energy required to melt 1.00 mole of the given elements increases, the melting points:
   A. increase only.
   B. decrease only.
   C. increase then decrease.
   D. neither increase nor decrease.

The correct answer is C. The passage states that, "The molar heat of fusion (ΔH_{fus}) is the amount of heat necessary to melt (or freeze) 1.00 mole of a substance at a constant pressure." According to the table, as the molar heat of fusion increases, the melting point increases from calcium, to silver, to iron, then decreases for nickel. By noticing a trend in the data, the question becomes easier to answer correctly.

Don't Be Intimidated by Complex Vocabulary

There will certainly be language on the Science Test that is new to you. Don't be worried by words that you have never seen before. The ACT usually defines terms that are absolutely essential to your understanding. You can answer questions about some terms without even knowing exactly what they mean as long as you focus on the overall idea of the passage. Never spend time trying to figure out how to pronounce any of the unfamiliar terms that you run across. This is simply a waste of time and energy.

Consider the following example:

The order *Lepidoptera* includes butterflies and moths. Table 1 is a key for identifying some *Lepidoptera* in North America.

Table 1			
Step	**Trait**	**Appearance**	**Result**
1	Body	Slim	Go to step 2
		Fuzzy	Go to step 3
2	Upper Side of Wings	Orange with black markings	*Agraulis vanillae*
		Yellow with markings	Go to step 4
3	Upper Side of Wings	Brown	Go to step 5
		Yellow	Go to step 7
4	Underside of Wings	Silver markings	Go to step 6
		Green marbling	*Anthocharis cethura*
5	Hindwings*	Pronounced spot on wings	Go to step 8
		No pronounced markings	*Citheronia sepulcralis*
		10–15 cm	*Antheraea polyphemus*

* The hindwings are the pair of wings farthest from the head of the butterfly.

1. Table 1 is used to identify animals that belong to which of the following groups?
   A. Birds
   B. Reptiles
   C. Insects
   D. Mammals

The correct answer is C. You are given that "The order *Lepidoptera* includes butterflies and moths. Table 1 is a key for identifying some *Lepidoptera* in North America." Because butterflies and moths are not birds, reptiles, or mammals, they must be insects. Even though you might never have seen the word *Lepidoptera* before, you can still correctly answer the question because the term is defined for you.

The rest of this chapter will provide an overview of the Scientific Method, a brief review of basic scientific concepts, an introduction to the types of questions you will see on the ACT Science Test, and sample questions with explanations.

THE SCIENTIFIC METHOD

The Scientific Method is the process by which scientists attempt to construct an accurate representation of the world. This process is fundamental to scientific investigation and acquisition of new knowledge based upon actual physical evidence and careful observation. The Scientific Method is a means of building a supportable, documented understanding of our world.

The Scientific Method includes four essential elements:

1. Observation
2. Hypothesis
3. Prediction
4. Experiment

During the **observation** phase, the experimenter directly observes and measures the phenomenon that is being studied. Careful notes should be taken and all pertinent data should be recorded so that the phenomenon (the thing observed) can be accurately described.

The experimenter then generates a **hypothesis** to explain the phenomenon. He or she speculates as to the reason for the phenomenon based on the observations made and recorded.

Next, the experimenter makes **predictions** to test the hypothesis. These predictions are tested with scientific experiments designed to either prove or disprove the hypothesis. The Scientific Method requires that any hypothesis either be ruled out or modified if the predictions are clearly and consistently incompatible with experimental results.

If the **experiments** prove the hypothesis, it may come to be regarded as a *theory* or *law of nature*. However, it is possible that new information and discoveries could contradict any hypothesis at any stage of experimentation.

Experimental Design

When scientists design experiments to test their hypotheses, they have to be careful to avoid "confounding of variables." This means that they have to isolate, as much as possible, one variable at a time so that they can reveal the relationships between the variables, if any. An **independent variable** (manipulated by the experimenter) is under the control of the scientist. As the scientist changes the independent variable, it is hoped that the **dependent variable** (observed by the experimenter) will change as a result, and that a relationship can be established. A **control** is an element of the experiment that is not subjected to the same changes in the independent variable as the **experimental** elements are. For instance, if we want to find out how the consumption of sugar impacts the fatigue level of ACT takers, we would need at least a few ACT takers who do not consume any sugar so that we can measure the "baseline" or "natural" fatigue level of ACT takers for comparison to the group who consumes sugar. If there were no control group, we wouldn't be able to say for sure that sugar has any impact on the fatigue level of ACT takers. If all of the test-takers consumed sugar, and if all of them were sleepy, we would face a confounding-of-variables situation because the sleepiness

---

Amy Says:

The passages included on the ACT Science Test have been written with the Scientific Method in mind. You can often use common sense along with a basic understanding of the process to answer many of the questions.

Steve Says:

Sugar *does* cause increased fatigue levels after the initial "sugar buzz" wears off. It is best to avoid it before your ACT exam.

could be caused by any other factor that the group had in common, like the ACT itself!

Some of the ACT Science Passages refer to "studies" rather than experiments. An experiment is an artificial situation that is created by the researcher. A study is characterized by careful, documented observation. Nevertheless, studies can include some of the elements of experiments, such as control groups.

ACT SCIENCE TEST EXERCISES

The next few pages contain exercises designed to help you apply the concepts generally tested on the ACT Science Test. Remember that this test does not require much knowledge of science. You can get a high score by applying logic and common sense to interpreting trends in the data and thinking about the questions being asked.

Exercise 1

You will tackle the ACT Science Test questions with more confidence if you have a basic understanding of the experimental process. The following set of questions will test your knowledge of the best steps to take in setting up an experiment using this process. Write your answers in the space provided.

> Sally decides to enter her school's science fair. She has always loved flowers and wants to incorporate them into her project. In the end, Sally decides to test the effectiveness of different types of plant food (fertilizer) on a certain type of rose bush. Her goal is to determine which fertilizer produces the tallest rose bushes with the greatest number of flowers.

1. Describe how Sally might set up her experiment. Discuss the actions Sally should take to get reliable data.

_____

_____

_____

_____

_____

_____

2. What are the independent and dependent variables in Sally's experiment, and how should she deal with them?

_____

_____

_____

_____

_____

_____

3. What is the best way for Sally to organize, interpret, and present her data?

_____

_____

_____

_____

_____

_____

_____

The results of Sally's experiment are recorded on the graphs below.

Questions 4–7 refer to the following figures. Place an "X" next to the correct answer.

Figure 1

Figure 2

4. Based on Figure 1, which fertilizer affected plant height the most?

    ___ Fertilizer A

    ___ Fertilizer B

    ___ Fertilizer C

    ___ All were equally effective.

5. At 5 weeks, about how much taller, on average, were the plants receiving Fertilizer B compared to those not receiving any fertilizer?

    ___ 15 cm

    ___ 20 cm

    ___ 30 cm

    ___ 35 cm

6. Which of the following statements is supported by the data in both figures?

____ Fertilizer type has little effect on the number of flowers produced.

____ Fertilizer helped the plants to grow taller and produce more flowers.

____ The control group received more fertilizer than any other group.

____ Fertilizer A yielded the tallest plants with the most flowers.

7. During which 2 weeks did Fertilizer B and Fertilizer C yield the same average number of flowers?

____ Weeks 1 and 2

____ Weeks 3 and 4

____ Weeks 4 and 5

____ Weeks 7 and 8

Exercise 2

The ACT Science Test includes data represented in charts, tables, and graphs. Answer the questions below, identifying and explaining general trends in the data.

Questions 1–4 refer to the following table. Write your answers in the spaces provided.

Butterflies Collected					
	Site 1	**Site 2**	**Site 3**	**Site 4**	**TOTAL**
Monday	46	56	54	50	206
Tuesday	43	55	57	49	204
Wednesday	41	54	58	51	204
Thursday	47	54	59	52	212
Friday	52	58	60	53	223
TOTAL	229	277	288	255	1049

1. How many butterflies were collected at Site 3 on Wednesday? _____

2. What is the greatest number of butterflies collected on any one given day?   _____

3. At which site were the fewest butterflies collected on Friday? _____

4. Which site shows a constant increase in the number of butterflies collected daily throughout the week? _____

Questions 5–8 refer to the following graph. Place an "X" next to the correct answer.

5. During which of the following one-year spans were there fewer than 10 electrical impulse events in all?

    ____ 1923–1924

    ____ 1925–1926

    ____ 1926–1927

    ____ 1930–1931

6. Which of the following one-year spans showed the highest number of electrical impulse events overall?

    ____ 1922–1923

    ____ 1923–1924

    ____ 1924–1925

    ____ 1925–1926

7. How many electrical impulse events occurred from 1923 through 1925?

    ____ 6

    ____ 11

    ____ 18

    ____ 25

8. During which year were no electrical impulse events recorded?

    ____ 1922

    ____ 1925

    ____ 1927

    ____ 1928

Questions 9–12 refer to the following figure. Write your answers in the space provided.

9. According to the figure, what percent of the soil sample's volume is composed of sand? _____

10. According to the figure, sand and silt together comprise what percentage of the soil sample? _____

11. Which particle type's volume comprises the least portion of the soil sample volume? _____

12. A certain plant will only grow in soil that is composed of at least 25% silt or clay or a combination of the two. Will this plant grow in the soil sampled? _____

ANSWERS AND EXPLANATIONS

EXERCISE 1

1. Sally must design an experiment that will allow her to evaluate the effectiveness of several different fertilizers. In order to do this, she needs a group of plants for each of the different fertilizers to be used, and an additional control group. The control group should be grown in the absence of any fertilizer: this way Sally can compare the results from the other groups to the control group to measure the effectiveness of the fertilizers. For example, if the control group produces 3 flowers per plant and the Fertilizer A plant produces 6 flowers per plant, Sally will know that Fertilizer A benefited the plant. She should measure the number of flowers per plant and the height of each plant in each group at a set of specific time intervals. More measurements will typically lead to more accurate results.

2. There are several independent variables that must be controlled to conduct an accurate experiment. For example, Sally must account for differences in individual plants, distribution of fertilizer, distribution of water, and exposure to sunlight. In order to control plant type, the same species of plant should be used in each experiment. Having multiple plants per group and averaging data can control the differences in individual plants. Sally should use equal amounts of fertilizer, water, and light for each group. In addition, the plants need to receive the fertilizer, water, and light at the same time each day.

   There are two dependent variables: the number of flowers and the height of the plant. These represent the data she is trying to collect.

3. Sally should first record her data in a table. Tables are ideal for organizing numerical data. In order to better interpret and present her findings to a wide audience, Sally would benefit from a set of graphs. Since the data is a representation of growth and flower number over time, line graphs would work best. With a line graph, Sally can see the progress of a particular fertilizer over time as well as compare its effectiveness to the other fertilizers and the control group.

4. To answer this question, you should look at Figure 1 and compare the plant heights in Week 1 to the plant heights in Week 8. You can see that the line representing the height of the plants that received Fertilizer B is very steep, which indicates the greatest amount of change. The plants that received Fertilizer B grew about 30 centimeters from Week 1 to Week 8.

5. According to Figure 1, the plants that received Fertilizer B had an average height of about 33 centimeters at 5 weeks, whereas the plants in the control group (those not receiving any fertilizer) had an average height of about 13 centimeters at 5 weeks. Therefore, the plants receiving Fertilizer B were, on average, about 20 centimeters taller than the plants receiving no fertilizer.

6. The data in both figures shows that plants receiving fertilizer grew taller on average and produced more flowers on average than did the plants in the control group. This supports the statement that the application of fertilizer yields taller plants with more flowers.

7. To answer this question, find the spot on Figure 2 at which the lines representing Fertilizers B and C intersect; this is the point at which the data is identical. Because the lines intersect at Week 4 and Week 5, those are the weeks during which the plants receiving Fertilizer B and C produced the same average number of flowers.

EXERCISE 2

1. To answer this question, find the column representing Site 3 and follow it down until it intersects with the row representing Wednesday. You will see that 58 butterflies were collected at Site 3 on Wednesday.

2. To answer this question, find the largest number in the table, disregarding the totals because the question asks about a single day. There were 60 butterflies collected on Friday at Site 3, which is more than any other day.

3. To answer this question, find the row representing Friday and then locate the smallest number in the row. Next, look at the heading of the column that corresponds to that small number. The table shows that 52 butterflies were collected at Site 1 on Friday, fewer than from any other site.

4. To answer this question, find the column that shows a continual increase from Monday through Friday in the number of butterflies collected. Only Site 3 fits this criterion. The other sites do not show a constant increase in the number of butterflies collected throughout the week.

5. To quickly answer this question you can look at the graph and note that from 1930 to 1931, there were no electrical impulse events. Because there will never be more than one correct answer, you can assume that each of the other choices includes 10 or more electrical impulse events. Look at the span indicated in each of the answer choices and count the total number of electrical impulse events:

    1923–1924: there were a total of 12 electrical impulse events.
    1925–1926: there were a total of 17 electrical impulse events.
    1926–1927: there were a total of 10 electrical impulse events.
    1930–1931: there were a total of 0 electrical impulse events.

6. Remember to note the number of electrical impulse events represented by each bar on the graph; you cannot simply count the number of bars to find the correct answer to this question. Look at the span indicated in each of the answer choices and count the total number of electrical impulse events:

    1922–1923: there were a total of 3 electrical impulse events.

1923–1924: there were a total of 12 electrical impulse events.
1924–1925: there were a total of 6 electrical impulse events.
1925–1926: there were a total of 17 electrical impulse events.

Therefore, the span from 1925–1926 showed the highest overall number of electrical impulse events.

7. Remember to note the number of electrical impulse events represented by each bar on the graph; you cannot simply count the number of bars to find the correct answer to this question. From 1923–1924, there were a total of 12 electrical impulse events, and from 1924–1925, there were a total of 6 electrical impulse events. Thus, a total of 18 electrical impulse events occurred from 1923 through 1925.

8. According to the graph, between 1927 and 1928 (in other words, during 1927) no electrical impulse events were recorded. You need to look at the entire span of the year, not just at the hash mark that represents the beginning of each year.

9. To answer this question, find the representation of sand on the key. According to the pie chart, sand represents 75% of the soil sample.

10. To answer this question, find the representation of sand and silt on the key. According to the pie chart, sand represents 75% of the soil sample and silt represents 12% of the soil sample. Therefore, together they represent 75% + 12%, or 87% of the soil sample.

11. To answer this question, first find the smallest "slice of the pie." The pie chart shows that 5.5% of the sample is made up of something other than sand, silt, or clay; therefore, you should now look for the next smallest "slice." When you do this, you see that clay makes up only 7.5% of the soil, less than either silt or sand.

12. The plant will not grow in the soil sampled because, according to the pie chart, the total percentage of silt and clay is only 19.5% (12% + 7.5%).

PRACTICE QUESTIONS

Following are simulated ACT Science passages and questions, along with explanations for all of the questions. Carefully read the directions, apply the information from this chapter, and attempt all of the questions. Preceding each of the passages is a description of the passage type.

DIRECTIONS: There are three passages in this Practice section. Each passage is followed by several questions. After reading a passage, choose the best answer to each question. Circle the letter of the answer you choose.

Data Representation

Data Representation passages present scientific information in tables, charts, graphs, and figures similar to those you might find in a scientific journal or other scientific publication. The questions associated with Data Representation passages will ask you to interpret and analyze the data shown in the tables, charts, graphs, and figures. The following is a Data Representation passage and several questions. The answers and explanations are at the end of this chapter.

PASSAGE I

Soybeans have been bred to exhibit a hereditary association of several characteristics: flower color, leaf shape, the color of the *hypocotyls* (the part of the seedling that is below the seed leaf), plant height, and pod length. Some of these characteristics, or traits, are considered *qualitative*, because the trait is influenced by only a few genes. Other traits are considered *quantitative*, because they show continuous variation, and are influenced by a number of genes. Alternative versions of a gene are called *alleles*. The dominant and recessive alleles for each soybean characteristic are displayed in Table 1. Dominant alleles are visible traits that mask all other traits, and they are more likely to be passed along from one generation to the next. Recessive alleles are hidden characteristics that are masked by dominant alleles. A soybean plant may carry a recessive gene, whose traits will show up only in later generations.

Table 1		
	Dominant alleles	**Recessive alleles**
Qualitative traits		white
Flower color	purple	narrow
Leaf shape	round	green
Color of hypocotyls	purple	
Quantitative traits	short	tall
Plant height		short
Pod length	long	

Figure 1 (next page) is an illustration of how some of the genetic traits may be passed from 1 generation of soybean plants to the next. Each parent passes only 1 trait on to successive generations. The plants are numbered consecutively within each generation.

GO ON TO THE NEXT PAGE.

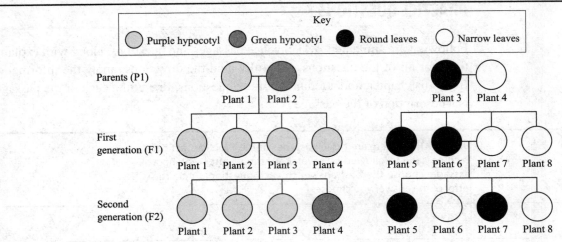

Figure 1

1. Based on Figure 1, what is the relationship between Plant 1 and Plant 2 in the second generation?
   A. Plant 1 is dominant over Plant 2.
   B. Plant 1 is recessive to Plant 2.
   C. Plant 1 and Plant 2 are members of the same generation.
   D. Plant 1 and Plant 2 both have green hypocotyls.

2. In row F2, green hypocotyls appear in the offspring for the first time. Which of the following is the most reasonable explanation for this?
   F. None of the other offspring of generation F2 inherited the gene.
   G. The members of generations P1 and F1 do not carry the gene.
   H. The gene for green hypocotyls is recessive.
   J. The gene for purple hypocotyls is recessive.

   See Expanded Explanation on page 265!

3. Based on Table 1, a soybean with purple flowers and round leaves will most likely:
   A. pass those traits on to later generations.
   B. not be able to pass on qualitative traits.
   C. yield offspring with white flowers and narrow leaves only.
   D. only be able to pass on quantitative traits.

4. According to the passage, plant height is most likely considered a quantitative trait because:
   F. plant height is a recessive characteristic in soybean plants.
   G. all soybean plants are short.
   H. quantitative traits are dominant over qualitative traits.
   J. plant height varies over the lifespan of the soybean plant.

GO ON TO THE NEXT PAGE.

Research Summaries

Research Summary passages provide descriptions of one or more related experiments or studies. The passages usually include a discussion of the design, methods, and results of the experiments or studies. The corresponding questions will ask you to comprehend, evaluate, and interpret the procedures and results. The following is a Research Summary passage and several questions. The answers and explanations are at the end of this chapter.

PASSAGE II

Water pressure influences the rate at which water flows. As water pressure increases, so does the rate of flow. Water pressure can be defined as the amount of force that the water exerts on the container it's in. The more water that is in the container, the greater the water pressure will be. Students conducted the following experiment.

Experiment

Students used push pins to punch holes in an empty, plastic 2-liter bottle. The students created 4 holes, each 1-inch apart, from top to bottom. The pins were left in each hole as it was created. The bottle was filled to the top with water and placed on a table. An 8-inch by 9-inch pan with a piece of blotting paper was placed lengthwise in front of the bottle. A ruler was placed in the pan to measure the spot at which the water stream touched the paper. The students removed the pin nearest the top of the bottle and marked the spot where the water stream touched the paper. The pin was then replaced, the bottle was filled to the top, and the next pin was removed. The spot where the water stream touched the paper was measured. Rate of flow was indicated by the length of the water stream. This was repeated a total of 4 times, once for each pin. The results are recorded in Table 1.

Table 1		
Pin	Position of pin in the bottle	Length of water stream (inches)
A	First (top)	1.5
B	Second	2.0
C	Third	3.0
D	Fourth (bottom)	3.5

5. Based on Table 1, water pressure is greatest:
- **A.** at the top of the full container.
- **B.** at the bottom of the full container.
- **C.** when the water stream is 1.5 inches long.
- **D.** when the water stream is 3.0 inches long.

6. Which of the following is an assumption that the students made prior to beginning the experiment?
- **F.** Water pressure has no effect on the length of the water stream produced.
- **G.** The rate of flow cannot be accurately determined using push pins and plastic bottles.
- **H.** The rate of flow corresponds directly to the length of the water stream produced.
- **J.** Water pressure and rate of flow are the two most important characteristics of water.

See Expanded Explanation on page 265!

7. Which of the following graphs best represents the relationship between water pressure and rate of flow, according to the passage?

A.

B.

C.

D.

8. Based on the results of the experiment, removal of Pin C:
- **F.** created a 3.5-inch water stream.
- **G.** caused the bottle to empty more quickly than did removal of Pin D.
- **H.** increased the total water pressure in the bottle.
- **J.** created a 3-inch water stream.

9. Suppose that the students removed the pins in order, replaced each pin after measuring the water stream, but did not refill the bottle after removing and replacing each pin. According to the passage, the water stream lengths would most likely:
- **A.** be identical to the first experiment.
- **B.** increase for each pin removed.
- **C.** decrease continually after removal of the first pin.
- **D.** be equal for each pin removed.

GO ON TO THE NEXT PAGE.

Conflicting Viewpoints

Conflicting Viewpoints passages provide information on more than one alternative hypothesis or theory related to an observable event or phenomenon. The viewpoints presented are usually inconsistent with one another. Questions associated with Conflicting Viewpoints passages ask you to comprehend, evaluate, and compare differing hypotheses and theories. The following is a Conflicting Viewpoints passage and several questions. The answers and explanations are at the end of this chapter.

PASSAGE III

The idea that complex life exists on planets outside of our solar system has been debated for decades. Two scientists present their viewpoints regarding the possibility of life on planets other than Earth.

Scientist 1

Earth is the only model of planetary life about which we know. Therefore, a determination about what is universal about the formation of life is almost impossible to make. It is highly unlikely that planets with characteristics that enable them to support complex life are also located in zones of solar mass stars that are habitable for complex life. Even if such a planet existed, it is doubtful that a planet outside of our solar system could remain within secure orbits for any real length of time. Even then, if a planet were to be located in a place that could spawn or sustain complex life, that planet might not have the characteristics of Earth that make complex life possible. The factors that enable complex life to exist on Earth include planetary mass and the abundance of water, carbon, and oxygen. These factors are essential for the existence of complex life as we know it. In addition, if one takes into account planetary disasters, the possibility of complex life decreases. Therefore, there is little or no chance for complex life existing or having existed on other planets or worlds.

Scientist 2

Earth has select properties that allow it to sustain complex life. However, it is not impossible that there is another set of characteristics and properties that together are also able to support complex life. Although free oxygen is essential to complex life on Earth and has not been found elsewhere, complex life-forms outside our solar system may use another gas for respiration. In addition, complex or intelligent life may not appear simultaneously. One complex life-form might never discover or know about a life-form that existed before or after the extinction of the first life-form. Studies suggest that 95% of known stars in space appear to have systems very similar to ours. This is very encouraging to those who believe that other complex life currently exists or has existed on planets other than Earth.

10. If the arguments of Scientist 1 are correct, which of the following statements about complex life is most accurate, according to the information in the passage?
   F. The possibility of development or existence of complex life is affected by many factors.
   G. Complex life is dependent on the balance of oxygen, carbon dioxide, and neon gas.
   H. Complex life will most certainly exist if a planet is located in the correct place and has the proper assortment of elements and traits.
   J. It is unlikely that complex life-forms will ever exist on a planet other than Earth, because 95% of star systems are similar to our solar system.

11. Which of the following issues is raised by Scientist 1, but NOT by Scientist 2?
   A. The presence of oxygen is required for complex life to exist on Earth.
   B. Most of the known stars appear to have planetary systems similar to that of Earth.
   C. Planetary disasters could account for the lack of complex life on other planets.
   D. Complex life may not appear simultaneously on planets in different solar systems.

See Expanded Explanation on page 266!

12. Studies have shown that a planet existed that was almost identical to Earth and was located in a place that was conducive to complex life. However, there are no signs that complex life existed. What explanation might Scientist 1 give, based on the information presented in the passage?
   F. Ninety-five percent of the stars near this planet had planetary systems that contained complex life.
   G. Planetary disasters might have eliminated or prevented complex life.
   H. The planet had an overabundance of carbon, oxygen, and water.
   J. The complex life-forms that would have inhabited this planet used another gas for respiration.

13. According to the passage, Scientist 2 would agree with which of the following statements, if true?
   A. Planetary disasters are the primary reason for the existence of complex life on other planets.
   B. Five percent of stars in the universe have systems identical to our own.
   C. Free oxygen is not essential to the existence of complex life on other planets.
   D. All complex life-forms will eventually discover one another.

14. Both Scientist 1 and Scientist 2 would agree with which of the following statements, if true?
   F. Oxygen is necessary for the existence of complex life on Earth.
   G. Planets outside of our solar system are not likely to maintain orbits secure enough for complex life.
   H. Complex life-forms are likely to exist or have existed on other planets.
   J. Complex life-forms are able to easily withstand planetary disasters.

15. Humans on Earth have yet to find another form of complex life on another planet. Scientist 2 would probably account for this by maintaining that:
   A. complex life-forms probably do not exist because other planets do not have the same characteristics and properties as Earth.
   B. complex life may have existed on other planets before the existence of humans on Earth.
   C. complex life has not been found because we have yet to find stars with a system similar to ours.
   D. complex life will only emerge when humans on Earth can survive without water and oxygen.

END OF THE SCIENCE TEST. STOP! IF YOU HAVE TIME LEFT OVER, CHECK YOUR WORK ON THIS SECTION ONLY.

ANSWERS AND EXPLANATIONS

1. **The correct answer is C.** Based on Figure 1, Plant 1 and Plant 2 in row F2 both have purple hypocotyls, so you cannot conclude that one is dominant over the other. Eliminate answer choices A, B, and D. Since row F2 signifies the second generation of plants, both Plant 1 and Plant 2 are members of the same generation, answer choice C.

EXPANDED EXPLANATION

2. **The correct answer is H.** This is an extrapolation question that requires you to choose an answer that is probably true based on the information provided. Essentially, you are asked to draw a conclusion that follows naturally from the given data and definitions. The last sentence of Passage 1 states: "A soybean plant may carry a recessive gene, whose traits will show up only in later generations." Table 1 shows that green hypocotyls are a recessive allele (defined in the passage as "alternative versions of a gene). The question refers us to Figure 1, Row F2, where green hypocotyls appear for the first time. Since recessive genes may control traits that show up in later generations, and there is no green hypocotyl in the F1 row of Figure 1, answer choice H must be correct based on the evidence provided. Note that there is a simple definition of hypocotyl given. However, there is no picture or diagram. You may not have a clear picture in your mind of exactly what a hypocotyl is. The good news is that you don't need to know exactly what it is as long as you can follow the connections provided in the table and figure. As with most of the passages on the ACT Science test, you don't actually need to know much science. You just need to be able to read carefully and apply the information provided to the questions.

3. **The correct answer is A.** According to Table 1, both purple flowers and round leaves are dominant traits. Therefore, it is most likely that these will be passed on to later generations. The other answer choices are not supported by the passage.

4. **The correct answer is J.** According to the passage, a quantitative trait shows "continuous variation." Therefore, it makes the most sense that plant height is considered a quantitative trait because plant height varies over the lifespan of the soybean plant. The other answer choices are not supported by the passage.

5. **The correct answer is B.** The passage states that as "water pressure increases, so does the rate of flow." The passage also indicates that rate of flow corresponds to the length of the water stream. Since the rate of flow was greatest when Pin D was removed, you can conclude that the water pressure was greatest at the bottom of the full container.

EXPANDED EXPLANATION

6. **The correct answer is H.** This is an assumption question. An assumption is an unstated premise (piece of evidence). The way to test answer choices in an assumption question is to negate (state the opposite of) the answer choice. If the opposite of the answer choice does not fit the passage, the design of the experiment, or the data, it is the correct answer choice. The incorrect answer choices in an assumption question are irrelevant. Therefore, their negations will not conflict with the passage. Answer choice H is correct. When we negate the statement, it becomes: "The rate of flow DOES NOT CORRESPOND directly to the length of the water stream produced." If the flow does NOT correspond to the stream length, the entire experiment is illogical because there is no reason to measure the stream lengths. Negating the other answer choices (by finding the main verb of each statement and saying the opposite) gives us statements that either have no effect on the experiment or support the design and results of the experiment.

7. **The correct answer is A.** The passage states that as "water pressure increases, so does the rate of flow." This relationship is indicated by the graph in answer choice A.

8. **The correct answer is J.** Table 1 indicates that the length of the water stream produced when Pin C was removed is 3.0 inches. The other answer choices are not supported by the passage.

9. **The correct answer is C.** According to the passage, the "more water that is in the container, the greater the water pressure will be." This suggests that, if the amount of water in the container is reduced, the water pressure will also be reduced. So, if the students do not replace the water in the container, it is likely that the lengths of the water streams will decrease continually after the first pin is removed.

10. **The correct answer is F.** Scientist 1 argues that a planet's location, security of its orbit, potential for planetary disasters, and surface characteristics affect the probability of complex life existing there. This argument best supports answer choice F.

EXPANDED EXPLANATION

11. **The correct answer is C.** When answering a question like this one on a Conflicting Viewpoints passage that asks about a detail that is discussed in one of the passages but not the other, you should use the process of elimination. Take the answer choices one by one and compare to both scientists' statements. The incorrect answers will either be in both statements or in neither. This is where it pays to have done sufficient practice with ACT passages so that you are good at quick skimming (as opposed to in-depth, linear reading for retention). For example, the key word in answer choice A is "oxygen." Quickly scanning and spotting for the word "oxygen" in both passages shows that both scientists agree that it is vital for complex life on Earth. So, answer choice A must be eliminated. Answer choice B is a point that Scientist 2 makes but Scientist 1 does not. The question is asking for something asserted by Scientist 1 and NOT Scientist 2. So, it must be eliminated. Similarly, answer choice D is a point that is made by Scientist 2; therefore, it must also be eliminated.

12. **The correct answer is G.** Scientist 1 argues that it takes many precise factors together to allow complex life to form. In addition, Scientist 1 says, "if one takes into account planetary disasters, the possibility of complex life decreases." The other answer choices are not supported by the passage.

13. **The correct answer is C.** Scientist 2 says that "it is not impossible that there is another set of characteristics and properties that together are also able to support complex life." Scientist 2 goes on to say that ". . . complex life-forms outside of our solar system may use another gas for respiration." These statements best support answer choice C.

14. **The correct answer is F.** According to the passage, both scientists agree that oxygen is necessary for the existence of complex life on Earth. The other answer choices are supported by either one or the other scientist, but not both, or they are not supported at all by the passage.

15. **The correct answer is B.** Scientist 2 states that "complex or intelligent life may not appear simultaneously. . . . One complex life-form might never discover or know about a life-form that existed before or after the extinction of the first life-form." This statement best supports answer choice B.

CHAPTER 7

ACT Writing Test: Strategies and Review

The ACT Writing Test is optional, meaning that students can choose whether to take it. Make your decision based on the requirements of the colleges and universities to which you plan to apply. Be sure to check with your schools of choice before registering for the ACT. If you take the Writing Test, it will come at the end of the ACT exam. You will have a short break between the ACT multiple-choice sections and the Writing Test.

The Writing Test consists of a "prompt," which is a brief discussion of a topic to which you must respond, and some blank, lined space in which to write your answer. You will have forty minutes to complete the test. The graders are not looking for long essay answers; they are looking for quality essays.

You will receive a total of five scores for your Writing Test: a single subject-level writing score reported on a range of 2–12 and four domain scores. The four domains are "Ideas and Analysis," "Development and Support," "Organization," and "Language Use and Conventions." Each of the four domains is also scored from 2–12. Two professional, trained readers will score your essay on a scale of 1–6 in each of the four writing domains. If the readers' scores disagree by more than one point, a third reader will evaluate the essay and that reader's score will be doubled. The readers are guided by these descriptions of the domains:

Ideas and Analysis: This domain reflects the candidate's ability to engage critically with multiple perspectives and generate relevant ideas.

Development and Support: This domain reflects the ability to construct a sound argument that is well supported by examples.

Organization: This domain reflects the ability to organize and express ideas clearly and with purpose while guiding the reader through discussion.

Language Use and Conventions: This domain reflects the use of language following the rules and conventions of style, grammar, syntax, word choice, and mechanics, including proper punctuation.

If you do not take the Writing Test, your Composite Score (overall multiple-choice score) will not be affected, but the separate English Language Arts (ELA) score will not be reported. Please visit **www.act.org** for more details on the scoring system.

The most important thing to know about this essay is that THERE IS NO CORRECT ANSWER! The readers are looking at the essay as an example of your ability to write a clear, concise, persuasive piece. DO NOT WASTE TIME by trying to figure out which position the test writers want you to choose.

This part of the ACT is designed to measure your writing skills. The test writers specifically choose topics that are probably relevant to high school students, and they even give a couple of different points of view from which to choose. They are looking for essays that have a clear position and support it. The graders will reward you with more points if you stay focused on your main idea throughout your essay and back up your position by giving specific examples and information. You will certainly do well if you have a clear, logical structure and if your language is correct and free of errors in grammar or vocabulary. Don't take any vocabulary risks when writing this essay. If you are not sure what a word means, don't use it. It should go without saying, but remember that you should not fill your essay with slang, jargon, or profanity.

There is a great overlap between the English section of the ACT and the Writing Test. If you can recognize proper English and point out common errors on the multiple-choice portion of the ACT, you should be able to avoid making those same errors on the Writing Test.

The essay prompt gives you three different positions on an issue. Your task is to write an essay in which you develop your perspective on the issue. You may adopt one of the given positions or discuss your own perspective, analyzing the relationships between the given perspectives. You will be given some scratch paper for this part of the ACT. Later in the chapter, we will discuss some specific ideas for the best way to use it. Be certain that you do use it. This is not the time to jump in and start writing a stream-of-consciousness, shoot-from-the-hip answer off the top of your head. Even though you do not have time to do a full first and second draft of this essay, make use of the time that is given to you to do some pre-writing. Be sure that you plan out what you are going to say before you actually start writing out your final answer.

At this point in your ACT testing day, you are likely to be somewhat tired. Try to focus on the fact that you are almost finished, and do what you can to keep your focus for the last thirty minutes. In some cases, this essay will be important to people who make admissions decisions at the institutions to which you are applying.

Amy Says:

Get a "fresh pair" of eyes to review your practice essays. It will not take long for an experienced reader to give you valuable feedback.

HOW TO PREPARE

As was noted earlier in this book, humans acquire skills through practice. Since the Writing Test is a test of your writing skills, you should practice writing in order to score better. Specifically, you should practice the type of writing that is rewarded by the scoring rubric. The best way to make sure that you are on track is to have someone with experience in this area, someone you trust, give you specific feedback on the good and not-so-good parts of your practice essays. You can gain from reading your own essays and comparing them to a rubric. However, writers tend to develop blind spots when it comes to areas that need improvement in their own essays. It is always a good idea to get a fresh set of eyes to review your work. Most high school teachers would be delighted if a student came to them for help on a practice essay. It does not take long for an experienced grader to give feedback that can be immensely valuable to a student.

THE ESSAY PROMPT

The prompt will be a few sentences long and will mention an issue that can cause some disagreement. It will also include three different perspectives on the issue and then instructions to take a position on the issue in your essay. The page following the prompt will be blank on both sides, except for a note that says that anything that you put on those two pages will not be scored. This is the "scratch paper" on which you can jot down whatever notes you want to and do some outlining to help keep yourself on track as you write in your answer document.

Four pages of lined answer space follow the blank pages. You are to confine your response to these four pages. It may not sound like a lot of space, but we have found that the students who write the most and complain about not having enough room to finish are usually spending too much time on irrelevant discussion or have needless repetition in their answers. You may use pencil only. No ink is allowed. You should probably write with a medium pressure since, if you don't press hard enough, your words might not scan. If you press too hard, you will have a hard time keeping your essay neat if you need to erase.

The prompt essentially describes a debate on an issue about which you are likely to have some strong feelings. If you do have strong feelings, you should just stick with your first response to the issue and work from there. If you don't, the fact that ACT will give you three different responses to the issue that other people have had means that you can just choose one of them as your starting point.

ESSAY WRITING TECHNIQUES

Following are the steps that are likely to result in the best essay that you can write. The steps are laid out so that you can perform them one at a time. This is not the time for "multitasking." If you were simply to read the stimulus and then try to write your answer out from the beginning to the end on the lined pages, you would certainly be doing several tasks at once. You would be creating the logical structure of your essay, searching your memory banks for vocabulary words, and anticipating counterarguments at the same time that you would be trying to apply the rules of grammar, punctuation, and spelling correctly, as well as remembering some good, relevant examples to plug into your essay structure. In short, those students who try to write without planning are setting themselves up for a score that is less than their potential because they are trying to do too many things at one time.

Read the Prompt

It is okay to read the prompt over more than once to be certain that you understand it completely. The test booklet is a resource for you to consume, so don't be afraid to underline, circle, and so on. The stimulus is short, so reading carefully will not take up much of your time. However, it may save you from making a mistake in responding to the prompt.

You must know what the task is before you begin. Rushing through this step can cost valuable points and make some of your hard work worthless.

One or two minutes will probably be sufficient time to read the prompt carefully.

Think About the Prompt

If the topic is something that you have thought about or discussed in the past, then you may already have an opinion. If not, then take a short time to formulate your opinion. This is what these essays are really all about: opinion. That is why there is really no correct or incorrect position to take. The test writers are careful to choose topics that have several sides that can be argued successfully.

Plan Your Essay

Your essay should begin with a clear statement of the broader context surrounding the issue. Follow this with a brief synopsis of the issue, then finish with your perspective on the issue.

There is an old saying about effective essays: "Tell them what you are going to tell them. Tell them. Then, tell them what you told them." In other words, you should have a clear introduction, a body, and a conclusion that echoes the introduction. You may choose to do a traditional five-paragraph essay, but it is possible to write a very effective essay with more paragraphs or fewer.

Your outline does not have to include complete sentences. It *does* have to include the ideas that you will put into your final draft. You need to be sure that you have a clear picture of where you are going and how you will get there before you start to write on the answer document.

You will hear some of the other test-takers around you scratching furiously with their pencils from the beginning of the 40-minute period. Sometimes that sound can make you feel like you are falling behind. You are not. Forty minutes is a long time to write two to four pages on a one-paragraph stimulus. The planning stage is the most important stage. Even if you spend 10 minutes on this stage, you will probably still be able to finish on time. Your essay will certainly be better than if you had simply started writing your thoughts with no planning.

Write Your Essay Out on the Answer Pages

You should also remember that there are really four categories of information when you are writing a persuasive essay and the opposing positions are clearly understood:

1. Positive for your position
2. Negative for your position
3. Positive for the opposing positions
4. Negative for the opposing positions

An effective essay uses facts from all four categories. You can think of your position as "correct" and the other positions as "incorrect." When you write a paragraph that is focused on the "correct" side of the issue, you should mention at least one aspect of your choice that may be seen as a negative by some people. Your essay will be much more persuasive if you do not ignore potential problems with your side of the debate. Of course, you should be sure to mention plenty of positive information in order to overcome the potential downside to which you are admitting.

The same technique can be applied to the part of your essay where you discuss opposing positions. You should admit that the other side of the debate has at least one strong point. Then, follow up with enough discussion of the pitfalls associated with the other side of the argument that your side ends up looking like the clear winner.

This is known as dealing with counterarguments, and it is the most effective way of presenting a persuasive written argument. To do this properly requires certain transition words. There are four basic categories of transition words that you will probably have to use:

Contrast: *But, However, On the other hand, Conversely, Although, Even though*, etc.
Similarity: *Likewise, Similarly, Also, Equally*, etc.
Evidence: *Since, Because, In light of, First, Second, Third*, etc.
Conclusion: *Therefore, Thus, As a result, So, It follows that, In conclusion*, etc.

An example of a sentence structure that will allow you to deal with these positive and negative categories of facts follows:

> *The opposition makes a valid point regarding the initial cost of my solution; the truth is that my solution would only cost a few dollars more per user than their option would. Furthermore, it would result in significant maintenance savings over the long run that would more than make up for the slightly higher start-up costs.*

This pair of sentences effectively deals in two ways with the potential objection that the other side might raise. First, it reduces the impact of the higher cost of the author's proposal by pointing out that the difference really is not very large when considered as a cost per user. Then, it points out that the costs will be recaptured in the future through increased savings. In addition, the sentence makes proper use of a semicolon. A semicolon is used correctly when you could erase it and replace it with a period and a capital letter. In other words, the semicolon links two independent clauses, which could stand alone as sentences in their own right. You should use the semicolon when the two sentences are very closely related and are continuing the same thought.

COMMON MISTAKES

There are many common errors that students make on the ACT Writing Test essay. If you know what to avoid, you will not only be a better writer, but, you will have a much easier time on the multiple-choice English Test. Consider the following:

Too General

The scoring rubric awards points for specific examples. Think of the best teachers you have had. They tend to tell you the general concept that they are teaching and then give one or more specific, memorable examples. This strategy works because of the memorable examples.

If you are told that there is no progress without determination and hard work, you might accept the statement as true and you may even remember it. However, you will have a much better chance of fully grasping the idea and remembering it later if you are given a specific example like Thomas Edison, who tried thousands and thousands of different filament materials in his lightbulbs before finally settling on one that gave acceptable light and lasted a reasonable period of time.

Too often, students make broad, general statements in their essays without giving any specific support. Make sure that you provide clear, simple examples of the general statements that you make.

Too Emotional and Opinionated

While it is true that the stimulus will be asking you for an opinion, you should not make the entire essay about your feelings. You should state what your opinion is and then back up your opinion with well-reasoned, logical support. Tell the reader *why* you feel the way you do rather than just telling *how* you feel.

Also, exclamation points are rarely appropriate for a Writing Test essay. Smiley faces or other "emoticons" are never appropriate.

Too Complicated

Many coaches and teachers have suggested that students apply the K.I.S.S. principle. While there is a slightly less polite formulation, we'll explain the K.I.S.S. principle as an acronym for "Keep It Short and Sweet." For example, do not use three words when one will do.

To illustrate, if you want to say, "I do not think that the proposal will work," do not write, "I believe that my feelings on this matter are correct when I state plainly and clearly that the previously proposed solution to this complicated problem will be somewhat less than completely effective as compared to other potential solutions, which have been brought forth concurrently."

The graders are not going to be blown away by your amazing ability to use a dozen words to state a plain idea. They are going to be blown away if you are able to make your point cleanly and clearly.

Amy Says:

Be sure to explain the connection between the examples that you use and your conclusion. Don't assume that the grader will agree with your viewpoint regarding the significance of a given fact.

Risky Vocabulary

If you are not sure what a word means or whether it would be appropriate to use in your essay, don't use it. Many an otherwise wonderful essay has been sunk by a word or two used incorrectly, which made the grader start to question the author's abilities.

For instance, if you were grading an essay that said, "High school students are often *condemned* for their kindness," you might know that the author meant to say, "High school students are often *commended* for their kindness." But you would still have to note the error and take it into account in scoring the essay.

Poor Handwriting

As mentioned previously in the chapter, the grader has to assign a score to your essay that depends on the grader's interpretation of the terms in the rubric. In order to help the grader interpret those terms in your favor when he or she is making judgment calls, you should write or print as neatly as you can. Make it easy for the graders to find the good things about your essay that will allow them to give you all of the points that your hard work deserves.

Shaky Logic

The essay that you must write for the Writing Test is an argument. It is an essay written with the purpose of defending a position. That position is your conclusion, and the support you are offering is evidence for that conclusion. There should be a cause-and-effect relationship between your evidence and your conclusion. In other words, the body of your essay should lead the reader to see the wisdom of your position.

For example, if you are taking the position in your essay that students should be subject to an 11:00 P.M. curfew, do not spend time discussing how you felt about your bedtime when you were seven years old.

Choose relevant examples that are connected to your position in a direct way. One way to do this is to use examples that point out the benefits of your position. For example, "I believe that anyone under the age of 18 should have an 11:00 P.M. curfew on school nights. This is because school starts at 8:00 A.M., which means that most students have to get up at 7:00 A.M., or even earlier. Since students, like everyone, need adequate sleep in order to learn well, an 11:00 P.M. curfew would help students to succeed in school."

While you may disagree with the conclusion of the above argument, you have to admit that there is a cause-and-effect connection between the evidence presented and the position that the author takes.

Unsafe Assumptions

There are two components to an argument: evidence and conclusion.

Evidence leads to conclusions. You need at least two pieces of evidence to support one conclusion. So, if you only give one piece of evidence, you must be making an assumption. Logic professors refer to assumptions as "suppressed premises,"

Steve Says:

Avoid being too familiar, colloquial, or humorous in your response to the prompt. Keep the reader interested, but make sure that the overall tone of the essay is formal.

which is just a fancy way to say, "unstated evidence." If you leave too much of your evidence unstated, your argument starts to get weak.

For example, if an essay says, "Curfews are dangerous because what if I have to be somewhere after 11:00?" The reader immediately starts to wonder, "Where could you have to be? What will you be doing?" There are simply too many unanswered questions. If you happen to agree with the position that the writer is taking, you tend to "help" with the assumptions and provide your own examples and answers to the unanswered questions. You might read the statement above and fill in an example from your own life or one that you would consider plausible. The graders at ACT will not do that extra thinking work for you as they read your essay. You have to be aware of the completeness of your essay and try to minimize the unanswered questions.

Too Conversational

This essay is supposed to be an example of your command of Standard Written English. The fact is that we often let each other "get away with" language in conversation that is simply not correct for Standard Written English. For example, if a friend uses *ain't* or *ya'll* in conversation, we would rarely correct him or her. Similarly, we all tend to use the term *you* when we really are speaking of people in general or people in a certain position, and not referring specifically to the reader or listener.

For example: "*You* could feel the tension in the room when Jeff had a pizza delivered to American History class." The person making that statement should have said, "*I* could feel the tension. . ." or "*We could all* feel the tension."

In general, you should try to leave *you* and *me* out of your essays. It is acceptable to use a personal example and refer to yourself (using "I") once or twice. However, some students get carried away and make the whole essay about themselves. The topics are meant to be relevant to high school students in general and usually refer to a policy matter. The stimulus is not an invitation to write a brief autobiography.

In conversation we often try to be inclusive and gender-neutral. The goal of including everyone is an ideal that this author shares. However, English forces us to use a gender-specific pronoun such as *he* or *she* or *him* or *her*. In conversation, we often ignore the incongruity when someone says, "Whoever forgot *their* umbrella is going to be sorry." The statement should be, "Whoever forgot *his or her* umbrella is going to be sorry."

One way to be inclusive is to alternate between male and female pronouns throughout your piece. This method can create some confusion for your reader. Another method is to use a plural phrasing rather than a singular phrasing: "*Those who forgot their umbrellas* are going to be sorry."

The overall thing to keep in mind is that your essay needs to be a formal document. It is not appropriate to write in the same idiom that you use with friends in informal conversation.

ESSAY SCORING

The ACT graders use a scoring *rubric* when they assign scores to essays. Basically, a rubric is a checklist of characteristics that the grader is supposed to look for when reading your essay. If your essay is more like the one described in the rubric as being a 5 than a 4, the grader will assign your essay a 5. The rubrics are posted on the ACT Web site and listed in ACT publications.

Since everyone knows what is expected, and there is virtually no chance that the grader will know the person who wrote a given essay, the system is reasonably fair. The graders are allowed to give a 6 to an essay that is somewhat less than perfect. The graders know that you have limited time to write, that you are doing this after you have just taken what may be the toughest exam of your life up to now, and that your fatigue and stress levels are likely to be elevated as a result.

Additionally, neatness is not specifically mentioned. However, the colleges to which you are applying will have access to your essay. This means that the people who are deciding on your applications may take your neatness into account. It also may have an impact on the graders as they assign a score to your essay. Since the scale runs from 1 through 6, there are some fine distinctions between a 4 and a 5. That difference could be important to the admissions personnel whom you are trying to impress. Nevertheless, the rubric descriptions of these two scores are very similar to each other. The difference between a 4 and a 5 could hinge on how the grader interprets words like *well-developed* (5) and *adequate* (4) or what exactly makes an error "distracting."

So, make it easy on your grader to interpret those differences in your favor. Keep your essay neat and your handwriting legible. Nothing in the rules prevents you from printing rather than writing in cursive. So, if your printing will be easier for graders and admissions officials to read than your cursive, then by all means print

Refer to the ACT website for a detailed description of the entire rubric and how each point level is described. In general, a 1 or a 2 usually indicates to graders and colleges that the person who wrote the essay either did not put forth a reasonable effort or is probably incapable of handling even basic college writing tasks. A 3 or 4 score means that the grader sees some fairly solid basic skills, but that there is plenty of room for improvement. A 5 or 6 means that the author appears to be ready for challenging college-level work.

Keep in mind that the scores that are assigned by the graders are based on the essay only. The graders do not get to see your ACT multiple-choice scores. They just assign a point value to the essay and move on to the next one. They are not making comments on your worth as a human being or even your intelligence or ability. They are just giving feedback regarding how the essay stacks up to the rubric.

Colleges are likely to make use of the scoring information in different ways. You should do thorough research of the colleges to which you are applying to find out how they interpret ACT results.

SIMPLIFIED ESSAY SCORING RUBRIC

While each of the domains is scored on a scale of 2–12, that score reflects the total of two graders who each score on a scale of 1–6. So, in the following rubric, 6 is the best score available from an individual grader.

Score of 6: Demonstrates Effective Skill

Ideas and Analysis—Critically discusses multiple perspectives. Displays subtlety and precision. Provides context and discusses underlying assumptions.

Development and Support—Integrates skillful reasoning and illustration.

Organization—Unified in purpose and focus. Effectively uses transitions.

Language Use—Skillful and precise word choice. Sentences varied and clear. Effective voice and tone. Any minor errors in grammar, usage, or mechanics do not impair understanding.

Score of 5: Demonstrates Well-Developed Skill

Ideas and Analysis—Productively engages multiple perspectives. Addresses complexities and underlying assumptions.

Development and Support—Mostly integrated, purposeful reasoning and illustration. Capable.

Organization—Mostly controlled by unifying idea. Logical sequencing. Consistent transitions.

Language Use—Precise word choice. Mostly varied sentence structure. Any minor errors in grammar, usage, or mechanics do not impair understanding.

Score of 4: Demonstrates Adequate Skill

Ideas and Analysis—Engages multiple perspectives. Clear in purpose. Analysis recognizes complexity and underlying assumptions.

Development and Support—Clear reasoning and illustration.

Organization—Clear structure. Ideas logically grouped and sequenced. Transitions clarify relationships between ideas.

Language Use—Conveys clarity. Adequate word choice, sometimes precise. Clear sentences with some variety in structure. Appropriate style choices. Errors rarely impede understanding.

Score of 3: Demonstrates Some Developing Skill

Ideas and Analysis—Responds to multiple perspectives. Some clarity of purpose. Limited or tangential context. Somewhat simplistic or unclear.

Development and Support—Mostly relevant, but overly general or simplistic. Reasoning and illustration somewhat repetitious or imprecise.

Organization—Exhibits basic structure. Most ideas logically grouped. Transitions sometimes clarify relationships between ideas.

Language Use—Basic and only somewhat clear. Word choice occasionally imprecise. Little variety in sentence structure. Style and tone not always appropriate. Distracting errors that do not impede understanding.

Score of 2: Demonstrates Weak or Inconsistent Skill

Ideas and Analysis—Weak response to multiple perspectives. Thesis, if any, shows little clarity. Incomplete analysis.

Development and Support—Weak, confused, disjointed. Inadequate reasoning (circular, illogical, unclear).

Organization—Rudimentary structure. Inconsistent and unclear. Misleading transitions.

Language Use—Inconsistent, unclear, imprecise. Sentence structure sometimes unclear. Voice and tone inconsistent and inappropriate. Distracting errors sometimes impede understanding.

Score of 1: Demonstrates Little or No Skill

Ideas and Analysis—Fails to generate an intelligible argument. Unclear or irrelevant attempts at analysis.

Development and Support—Claims lack support. Reasoning and illustration are unclear, irrelevant, or absent.

Organization—Structure lacking. Transitions, if any, fail to connect ideas.

Language Use—Word choice imprecise, incomprehensible. Sentence structure unclear. Errors are pervasive and often impede understanding.

SAMPLE STUDENT RESPONSES

The following is a Sample Writing Prompt and examples of essays representing certain levels of the Scoring Rubric. We have also included an analysis of the scores assigned.

Violence in Video Games

Many people debate whether video game makers should be required to limit the violent content included in their products. There is concern over whether exposure to violence causes violent behavior. Given the prevalence and reach of video games and societal concerns about violent behavior in the real world, it is worth considering the implications of such a requirement.

PERSPECTIVE ONE	PERSPECTIVE TWO	PERSPECTIVE THREE
Human beings are creatures of habit. Exposing one's mind to intense, repeated simulated violence creates a stronger likelihood of actual violence. Desensitization through immersion in lifelike virtual worlds makes actual violence more acceptable to game players.	Game players are well aware that they are merely simulating violence. Violent play was common long before video games were invented. Gamers and their families should be free to decide what is appropriate for them.	All people should be free to decide what media they are exposed to. Attempts to limit access to information tread on the liberty of individuals to make their own choices. Censorship of video games is a dangerous threat to intellectual self-determination.

Essay Task

Write a unified, coherent essay in which you evaluate multiple perspectives on the implications of violence in video games and the suggestion to limit such violence. In your essay, be sure to:

- analyze and evaluate the perspectives given
- state and develop your own perspective on the issue
- explain the relationship between your perspective and those given

Your perspective may be in full agreement with any of the others, in partial agreement, or wholly different. Whatever the case, support your ideas with logical reasoning and detailed, persuasive examples.

Sample Essay—Score of 2

Products with violence shouldn't be limited. Nobody who play games get violent.

If there a choice to play violence games, than you should have it. Its not right to limit information or liberty, being that game players can decide what to play. So what if they make a habit of it. None of my friends are violent and we all play video games.

There is a difference between the real world and the world of video games. And most people know this, like my friends and classmates. We play video games all the time and the violence they say happens because of it is not something we do and I think people will agree with me.

In conclusion, don't limit products with violence. It doesn't work.

Score Analysis:

While the essay writer presents a clear thesis, the argument is not well developed and lacks an appropriate context. There is little support for the writer's position, and the writer fails to provide adequate examples in support of the position. The organization is clear but highly predictable, and it lacks cohesiveness and clear reasoning. The introduction and conclusion are not fully developed. Language is simple and at times inappropriate, with little variation in word choice. While sentence length is somewhat varied, there are too many distracting errors in grammar, usage, and mechanics.

Sample Essay—Score of 4

There is a lot of violence in the world. Some people think it might be caused by exposure to violent video games. I, for one, do not believe that. This is because, even though many people play violent video games for recreation, people know the difference between the real world and video games.

Many kids my age play violent video games, among others. We need something to take our minds off of school and work. My friends who are gamers are not violent as a result of playing video games. In fact, sometimes they play games so much that they are tired and distracted both in and out of school. In my opinion, a person who is tired tends to be non-violent. Also, my friends know the difference between real life and simulated violence, so they don't become desensitized to violence in the real world.

Furthermore, even people who are exposed to simulated violence don't become violent. For example, I see a lot of violence on TV and I play violent video games. Like my friends, this is somewhat a habit, but we are not violent. In fact, violent play was common long before video games were invented. People should be free do decide if they play violent video games or not. If you think that you will lose your freedom of decision, like some people think, then you should not be censored. Censorship can be a threat to freedom, so even if some people become violent by playing violent games, they should still be able to make a choice about playing the games. Limiting the violence in video games will not make an already violent person less violent.

In conclusion, video games should not be required to limit the violent content because we don't become violent just by playing video games. We know the difference between reality and video games, and should be able to make our own choices about whether or not we play a certain kind of video game.

Score Analysis:

The essay writer generates an argument that incorporates multiple perspectives on the given issue. The argument's thesis has a clear purpose and provides a relevant context for analysis of the issue and its perspectives. Development of ideas is mostly specific and logical, with some elaboration. Clear reasoning and examples adequately convey the significance of the argument. The organization of the essay is clear, though predictable. Ideas are presented in a logical sequence, but simple and obvious transitions are used. The introduction and conclusion are clear and generally well developed. Language is competent, with somewhat varied word choice and sentence length. Voice and tone are appropriate. There are a few errors in grammar, usage, and mechanics, but they are not distracting.

Sample Essay—Score of 6

Violence in video games is only one aspect of the larger topic of censorship. There is a concern that the nature of video games is sufficiently different from other media that censorship may be necessary to avoid horrifying real-world violence. Furthermore, since so many who play video games are children and young adults, censorship may be justified considering the impact on their developing brains.

One argument for censorship of video games focuses on the idea of desensitization. The theory seems to be that players are more likely to act upon violent impulses in their real lives after they've been exposed to the simulated violence of the virtual world. However, video games are played by many millions of people of all ages who do not act violently in their daily lives. We all know many people who play video games often. If video games caused violent behavior, we would all be aware of some of them who have committed real violent acts. That does not seem to be the case. I have friends who spend much of their spare time playing violent video games that simulate combat in vivid detail. Not only have I never felt threatened by them, I find them to be warm and caring people in their real lives.

It is important to remember that human beings have been violent since the beginning. A great deal of history consists of the study of war. Weapons have been on the forefront of technological development from the early days civilization up until today. Video games, on the other hand, are a relatively recent development. While it may be true that some gamers have been violent, it strains logic to say that playing video games causes violent behavior. Jack the Ripper is just one example of a person who committed terrible, violent crimes long before the advent of video games. Unless research shows a stronger connection between game play and actual violence beyond mere correlation, it does not seem that censorship is justified.

A very serious concern is the restraint of freedom that comes from all censorship. It is argued that each of us should be free to make our own decisions about the information we expose ourselves to. There have been calls for censorship as each new technology has come along. Our Constitution guarantees freedom of the "press" and, over time, the meaning of "press" has been expanded to include movies, sound recordings, and television, including violent content. Even comic books were censored in their early days. But, eventually, liberty won out and now consumers are free to expose themselves to violent content in all these media. There is no obvious reason to make a special exception for video games.

After considering all the perspectives, my own experiences, and my own knowledge, I am most convinced by Perspectives Two and Three. I stand on the side of liberty and do not believe that video games should be censored. However, I do believe that consumers should be given enough information to make up their own minds before they purchase and play video games. It would not be appropriate to market a game for young children that is described as safe for kids and then includes explicit, violent content. So, I can see the benefit of truth in advertising rules that force video game makers to be honest about the content of their games, even though I believe strongly in freedom of expression. As Perspective Two says, "Gamers and their families should be free to decide what is appropriate for them."

Score Analysis:

This essay makes an argument that critically engages with multiple perspectives on the issue. The author is opposed to censorship, but in favor of truthful descriptions of content. The essay discusses each of the perspectives given in the prompt. The argument employs insightful context and examines implications, complexities, and underlying values and assumptions. The author brings in the idea of "truth in advertising" and the protection of young children. The author links the discussion to the broader topic of censorship and discusses constitutional free speech values. The ideas are developed and follow an integrated line of reasoning. After a short introduction, each perspective is discussed and the ideas are deepened and broadened. Transitions between and within paragraphs strengthen the relationships among ideas. There are very few errors in grammar, usage, and mechanics. Word choice is skillful and precise.

SAMPLE ESSAY TO SCORE

Now that you've had a chance to learn about how the ACT essay is scored, read the following student essay written on the same prompt and generate a score for it. Follow the scoring guidelines on pages 277-278 to decide how you can make the essay better.

As our technology becomes more advanced, more and more teenagers take advantage of it. Playing video games has become increasingly prevalent. Recently, playing violent video games have sparked controversy regarding whether simulated violence is a direct causation of violence in the real world. While many video games do portray realistic scenes of bloodshed, I believe that people are aware of the differences between the virtual world vs the physical world.

While the increase in violent video games has a direct correlation to the increase in crime rates, correlation should not be mistaken for causation. Most people, while playing video games, are able to distinguish the difference between game and reality. This allows them to act logically and not act violently in real life as they would do in a video game. My cousin constantly plays Call of Duty, which is an extremely violent computer game. However, he has never acted violently against anyone even though he is always immersed in a game focused on killing.

Furthermore, video games should be encouraged among teens as it provides an accessible platform to hone their problem solving skills. Many video games such as soccer and basketball related ones don't include any violence at all. Instead, these games allow teens to learn essential skills such as teamwork and patience that are applicable in the real world. According to a friend, simulating soccer scenarios in video games not only allows him to improve his own technique, but also builds his confidence and character. Sometimes, movies and tv news display acts of violence far more gruesome than the ones seen in video games. Also, the bloodshed portrayed in some historical films is far more disturbing than the violence I've witnessed in video games.

In conclusion, with the increase in violence in video games and the controversy surrounding them, many people overlook the benefits brought on by video games. Therefore, I believe that content in video games should not be limited, because playing video games does not cause violence in the real world.

ACT WRITING SKILLS EXERCISES

The next few pages contain exercises designed to help you write more effectively. The ACT English Exercises in Chapter 3 will also help you to improve your writing. Remember to practice your writing skills sufficiently before test day.

Correcting Sentences

Place an "X" next to the sentence that is grammatically correct and is the most clear and concise.

1. ____ The debate is going on about whether or not Miss Kern's final exam is fair in its assessment of student's abilities.

    ____ There is an ongoing debate about whether Miss Kern's final exam fairly assesses students' abilities.

    ____ There is an ongoing debate about whether Miss Kern's final exam is fairly assessing of students' abilities or not.

    ____ There is a debate ongoing about whether the final exam given by Miss Kern fairly assesses students' abilities or not.

    ____ Whether or not Miss Kern's final exam is a fair assessing of students' abilities is an ongoing debate.

2. ____ Some people might be surprised to learn that, prior to 2015, *To Kill a Mockingbird* was the only published novel of Harper Lee.

    ____ Some people might be surprised to learn that *To Kill a Mockingbird* was Harper Lee's only novel that was published.

    ____ Some people might be surprised to learn that *To Kill a Mockingbird* was Harper Lee's only published novel.

    ____ Some people might be surprised to learn that *To Kill a Mockingbird* was the novel that was the only one of Harper Lee ever published.

    ____ Some people might be surprised to learn that *To Kill a Mockingbird* was the only novel published by Harper Lee.

3. ____ When the school board needs to make an important decision, a committee is selected, and they assist in the process.

    ____ When the school board needs to make an important decision, they select a committee and they assist in the process.

    ____ When the school board needs to make an important decision, they assist in the process by electing a committee to decide.

    ____ When the school board needs to make an important decision, a committee it selects to assist in the process.

    ____ When the school board needs to make an important decision, it selects a committee to assist in the process.

4. ____ Having carefully prepared for her debate, the failure of the audience in understanding her argument's main points frustrated Kathy.

____ Having carefully prepared for her debate, the audience's failure to understand the main points of her argument was a frustration to Kathy.

____ Having carefully prepared for her debate, Kathy's frustration at the audience's failure to understand her argument's main points.

____ Having carefully prepared for her debate, Kathy was frustrated by the audience's failure in understanding the main points of her argument.

____ Having carefully prepared for her debate, Kathy was frustrated by the audience's failure to understand the main points of her argument.

5. ____ It has long been known that, throughout the first several months of life, the human brain grows at a rapid and dramatic pace, producing millions of brain cells.

____ The human brain grows throughout the first several months of life, it has long been known, at a rapid and dramatic pace, producing millions of brain cells.

____ Throughout the first several months of life, it has long been known that the human brain grows at a rapid and dramatic pace, producing millions of brain cells.

____ The human brain grows, it has long been known, throughout the first several months of life at a rapid and dramatic pace, producing millions of brain cells.

____ It has long been known that the human brain, growing throughout the first several months of life at a rapid and dramatic pace, producing millions of brain cells.

Improving Paragraphs

Some parts of the paragraphs below need to be rewritten in order to improve the paragraphs. Place an "X" next to the choice that best improves the structure, development, and organization of the paragraphs. (You will not be asked about all the errors contained within the paragraphs.)

(1)Robert Frost is perhaps one of America's best poets. (2)Maybe the most beloved poet of all time. (3)While Frost is clearly known as a New Englander, he lived his first 11 years in California. (4)Born in 1874, Frost moved east after the death of his father. (5)He attended high school in Massachusetts where he became an avid writer. (6)Though he continued to write during his college years, he never earned a college degree nor did he find much success with publishing his poetry.

(7)At the age of 38, Frost moved to England where he quickly joined the literary circles of English writers. (8)A year later, Frost's first book of poetry, *A Boy's Will*, was successfully published and sold. (9)This started the beginning of Frost's acceptance as a literary giant. (10)Prior to this, Frost had been working at mills and grammar schools; he also ran a farm. (11)Shortly after the publication of Frost's second anthology, *North of Boston*, he and his family reestablished their home in the states.

(12) Frost's literary talent met with great success back in the United States. **(13)**While Frost maintained the family's New Hampshire farm, he also wrote and published prolifically. **(14)**In 1923, Frost earned the first of his four Pulitzer Prizes for his work and was the first poet to read at a presidential inauguration in 1961. **(15)**Probably one of Robert Frost's best known and most often quoted poems is "The Road Not Taken," particularly the last lines: "Two roads diverged in a wood, and I —, I took the one less traveled by, And that has made all the difference."

1. Of the following, which is the best way to revise and combine Sentences 1 and 2?

   ____ Perhaps Robert Frost is one of America's most beloved poets for all time.

   ____ Robert Frost is perhaps one of America's best and most beloved poets.

   ____ One of America's best and most beloved poets is perhaps Robert Frost.

   ____ Robert Frost, one of America's best poets, is perhaps the most beloved.

   ____ The beloved American poet Robert Frost is perhaps the best of all times.

2. Of the following, which is the best way to phrase sentence 6?

   ____ NO CHANGE.

   ____ He continued to write during college while he never earned a degree and didn't publish his poetry.

   ____ While he wrote during his college years, he wasn't published and received no degree.

   ____ Going to college did not earn him a degree nor did he get his writings published.

   ____ Although he continued to attend college and write, he did not earn a degree and his works were not published.

3. A strategy the writer uses within the third paragraph is to

   ____ write a poem about the essay's subject.

   ____ use poetic vocabulary to enhance the essay.

   ____ quote directly from the work being discussed.

   ____ contrast the works of two American authors.

   ____ make an emotional plea.

(1)We had assembled all our gear, especially remembering the camera, and were ready to head out. (2)We were finally going to take that ghost town tour. (3)To Rhyolite, Nevada we were going. (4)Rhyolite, once a thriving gold-mining center, was now a small set of abandoned buildings and ruins. (5)We loaded up the dog and backpack into the car and happily set off with smiles on our faces.

(6)Driving up into the foothills where Rhyolite is situated, a visitor can immediately spot one of the few intact structures. (7)This is the Tom Kelly house, built of nearly 50,000 beer and medicine bottles stuck into clay. (8)It is clear that this home was once considered to be a rather magnificent edifice with its glass windows and wide-sweeping front porch. (9)Out in the expansive yard are fine displays of rusted farm tools. (10)Crude glass mosaic art forms are scattered about. (11)A curator of sorts sits on a chair just outside the bottle house, with a cat in her lap, just waiting to enlighten the next visitor about Rhyolite's many charms. (12)**The** scruffy cat does not like to lie on the lady's lap. (13)The house itself is locked tight, due to what the cat lady describes as "pilferers.'

(14)I take my tiny new digital camera out of the backpack, longing to capture Rhyolite's quaintness forever, only to discover the camera's battery pack is dead. (15)This angers my father, who was looking forward to a bit of Rhyolite on his computer desktop. (16)Unfortunately, driving the two miles into Beatty to purchase new batteries is not a solution; this camera is outfitted with a battery pack that requires recharging with its special recharger. (17)My father is further incensed. (18)We spend only a few more minutes exploring the other Rhyolite foundations and then silently get back into the car. (19)We will return to this ghost town another time, and you can be sure we will be carrying two cameras, both freshly charged!

4. Of the following, which is the best way to phrase Sentence 5?

    ____ NO CHANGE.

    ____ We loaded up the dog and the backpack and happily set off in the car with smiles on our faces.

    ____ We had smiles on our faces as we loaded up the dog and the backpack into the car and set off happily.

    ____ As we loaded up the dog and backpack into the car, we had smiles on our faces and happily set off.

    ____ We loaded the dog and backpack into the car and happily set off.

5. Which of the following should be omitted to improve the unity of the second paragraph?

    ____ Sentence 9

    ____ Sentence 10

    ____ Sentence 11

    ____ Sentence 12

    ____ Sentence 13

6. In context, which of the following is the best way to phrase the underlined portion of Sentence 15 (reproduced below)?

   This angers my father, <u>who was looking forward to</u> a bit of Rhyolite on his computer desktop.

   ___ NO CHANGE.

   ___ who had been really looking forward to

   ___ as he had been looking forward to

   ___ who has for a long time been looking forward to

   ___ as he was looking forward to

ANSWERS AND EXPLANATIONS

Correcting Sentences

1. There is an ongoing debate about whether Miss Kern's final exam fairly assesses students' abilities.

   Explanation: This sentence clearly indicates both that the "debate is ongoing" and what the debate is about.

2. Some people might be surprised to learn that *To Kill a Mockingbird* was Harper Lee's only published novel.

   Explanation: The phrase "Harper Lee's only published novel" most clearly and simply expresses the idea. The other answer choices are awkward and unclear.

3. When the school board needs to make an important decision, it selects a committee to assist in the process.

   Explanation: This sentence uses the active voice, and it makes clear who selects the committee and what the committee does. In addition, it correctly identifies the "committee" as a singular noun.

4. Having carefully prepared for her debate, Kathy was frustrated by the audience's failure to understand the main points of her argument.

   Explanation: The clause "Having carefully prepared for her debate" modifies "Kathy." Therefore, "Kathy" should directly follow that descriptive clause.

5. It has long been known that, throughout the first several months of life, the human brain grows at a rapid and dramatic pace, producing millions of brain cells.

   Explanation: The phrase "It has long been known" is a good introduction to the sentence. The rest of the sentence is punctuated correctly and clearly expresses the idea.

Improving Paragraphs

1. Robert Frost is perhaps one of America's best and most beloved poets.

   Explanation: This choice simply and clearly combines the two sentences. There is no ambiguity or awkwardness.

2. NO CHANGE.

   Explanation: The sentence is best as it is written and requires no revision. The other answer choices are wordy and awkward.

3. Quote directly from the work being discussed.

   Explanation: The third paragraph includes direct quotes from Frost's work "The Road Not Taken." None of the other answer choices is supported by the third paragraph.

290 STRATEGIES AND REVIEW
PART III ■ STRATEGIES AND REVIEW

4. We loaded the dog and backpack into the car and happily set off.

   Explanation: It is not necessary to include both the word "happily" and the phrase "with smiles on our faces"; one implies the other.

5. Sentence 12.

   Explanation: Since the second paragraph deals with the appearance of the ghost town upon the author's arrival, the image of the curator is important; however the actions of the cat in her lap do not add to the paragraph. Because Sentence 12 only talks about the cat, it distracts from the paragraph and removing it would improve the unity of the paragraph.

6. NO CHANGE.

   Explanation: The sentence as it is written is clear and concise and effectively expresses the author's intended meaning. The remaining answer choices are unnecessarily awkward and wordy.

PART IV

Four Practice Tests

ACT Practice Test 1

ACT Practice Test 2

ACT Practice Test 3

ACT Practice Test 4

ACT Practice Tests

These simulated tests should help you to evaluate your progress in preparing for the ACT. Take the tests under realistic conditions (preferably early in the morning in a quiet location), and allow approximately 3.5 hours for each entire test. Each of the test sections should be taken in the time indicated at the beginning of the sections, and in the order in which they appear. Fill in the bubbles on your answer sheet once you have made your selections.

When you have finished each test, check your answers against the Answer Key. Follow the directions on how to score your test. Then, read the Explanations, paying close attention to the explanations for the questions that you missed.

ACT PRACTICE TEST 1
Answer Sheet

ENGLISH

1 (A) (B) (C) (D)
2 (F) (G) (H) (J)
3 (A) (B) (C) (D)
4 (F) (G) (H) (J)
5 (A) (B) (C) (D)
6 (F) (G) (H) (J)
7 (A) (B) (C) (D)
8 (F) (G) (H) (J)
9 (A) (B) (C) (D)
10 (F) (G) (H) (J)
11 (A) (B) (C) (D)
12 (F) (G) (H) (J)
13 (A) (B) (C) (D)
14 (F) (G) (H) (J)
15 (A) (B) (C) (D)
16 (F) (G) (H) (J)
17 (A) (B) (C) (D)
18 (F) (G) (H) (J)
19 (A) (B) (C) (D)
20 (F) (G) (H) (J)

21 (A) (B) (C) (D)
22 (F) (G) (H) (J)
23 (A) (B) (C) (D)
24 (F) (G) (H) (J)
25 (A) (B) (C) (D)
26 (F) (G) (H) (J)
27 (A) (B) (C) (D)
28 (F) (G) (H) (J)
29 (A) (B) (C) (D)
30 (F) (G) (H) (J)
31 (A) (B) (C) (D)
32 (F) (G) (H) (J)
33 (A) (B) (C) (D)
34 (F) (G) (H) (J)
35 (A) (B) (C) (D)
36 (F) (G) (H) (J)
37 (A) (B) (C) (D)
38 (F) (G) (H) (J)
39 (A) (B) (C) (D)
40 (F) (G) (H) (J)

41 (A) (B) (C) (D)
42 (F) (G) (H) (J)
43 (A) (B) (C) (D)
44 (F) (G) (H) (J)
45 (A) (B) (C) (D)
46 (F) (G) (H) (J)
47 (A) (B) (C) (D)
48 (F) (G) (H) (J)
49 (A) (B) (C) (D)
50 (F) (G) (H) (J)
51 (A) (B) (C) (D)
52 (F) (G) (H) (J)
53 (A) (B) (C) (D)
54 (F) (G) (H) (J)
55 (A) (B) (C) (D)
56 (F) (G) (H) (J)
57 (A) (B) (C) (D)
58 (F) (G) (H) (J)
59 (A) (B) (C) (D)
60 (F) (G) (H) (J)

61 (A) (B) (C) (D)
62 (F) (G) (H) (J)
63 (A) (B) (C) (D)
64 (F) (G) (H) (J)
65 (A) (B) (C) (D)
66 (F) (G) (H) (J)
67 (A) (B) (C) (D)
68 (F) (G) (H) (J)
69 (A) (B) (C) (D)
70 (F) (G) (H) (J)
71 (A) (B) (C) (D)
72 (F) (G) (H) (J)
73 (A) (B) (C) (D)
74 (F) (G) (H) (J)
75 (A) (B) (C) (D)

MATHEMATICS

1 (A) (B) (C) (D) (E)
2 (F) (G) (H) (J) (K)
3 (A) (B) (C) (D) (E)
4 (F) (G) (H) (J) (K)
5 (A) (B) (C) (D) (E)
6 (F) (G) (H) (J) (K)
7 (A) (B) (C) (D) (E)
8 (F) (G) (H) (J) (K)
9 (A) (B) (C) (D) (E)
10 (F) (G) (H) (J) (K)
11 (A) (B) (C) (D) (E)
12 (F) (G) (H) (J) (K)
13 (A) (B) (C) (D) (E)
14 (F) (G) (H) (J) (K)
15 (A) (B) (C) (D) (E)

16 (F) (G) (H) (J) (K)
17 (A) (B) (C) (D) (E)
18 (F) (G) (H) (J) (K)
19 (A) (B) (C) (D) (E)
20 (F) (G) (H) (J) (K)
21 (A) (B) (C) (D) (E)
22 (F) (G) (H) (J) (K)
23 (A) (B) (C) (D) (E)
24 (F) (G) (H) (J) (K)
25 (A) (B) (C) (D) (E)
26 (F) (G) (H) (J) (K)
27 (A) (B) (C) (D) (E)
28 (F) (G) (H) (J) (K)
29 (A) (B) (C) (D) (E)
30 (F) (G) (H) (J) (K)

31 (A) (B) (C) (D) (E)
32 (F) (G) (H) (J) (K)
33 (A) (B) (C) (D) (E)
34 (F) (G) (H) (J) (K)
35 (A) (B) (C) (D) (E)
36 (F) (G) (H) (J) (K)
37 (A) (B) (C) (D) (E)
38 (F) (G) (H) (J) (K)
39 (A) (B) (C) (D) (E)
40 (F) (G) (H) (J) (K)
41 (A) (B) (C) (D) (E)
42 (F) (G) (H) (J) (K)
43 (A) (B) (C) (D) (E)
44 (F) (G) (H) (J) (K)
45 (A) (B) (C) (D) (E)

46 (F) (G) (H) (J) (K)
47 (A) (B) (C) (D) (E)
48 (F) (G) (H) (J) (K)
49 (A) (B) (C) (D) (E)
50 (F) (G) (H) (J) (K)
51 (A) (B) (C) (D) (E)
52 (F) (G) (H) (J) (K)
53 (A) (B) (C) (D) (E)
54 (F) (G) (H) (J) (K)
55 (A) (B) (C) (D) (E)
56 (F) (G) (H) (J) (K)
57 (A) (B) (C) (D) (E)
58 (F) (G) (H) (J) (K)
59 (A) (B) (C) (D) (E)
60 (F) (G) (H) (J) (K)

READING

1 Ⓐ Ⓑ Ⓒ Ⓓ	11 Ⓐ Ⓑ Ⓒ Ⓓ	21 Ⓐ Ⓑ Ⓒ Ⓓ	31 Ⓐ Ⓑ Ⓒ Ⓓ
2 Ⓕ Ⓖ Ⓗ Ⓙ	12 Ⓕ Ⓖ Ⓗ Ⓙ	22 Ⓕ Ⓖ Ⓗ Ⓙ	32 Ⓕ Ⓖ Ⓗ Ⓙ
3 Ⓐ Ⓑ Ⓒ Ⓓ	13 Ⓐ Ⓑ Ⓒ Ⓓ	23 Ⓐ Ⓑ Ⓒ Ⓓ	33 Ⓐ Ⓑ Ⓒ Ⓓ
4 Ⓕ Ⓖ Ⓗ Ⓙ	14 Ⓕ Ⓖ Ⓗ Ⓙ	24 Ⓕ Ⓖ Ⓗ Ⓙ	34 Ⓕ Ⓖ Ⓗ Ⓙ
5 Ⓐ Ⓑ Ⓒ Ⓓ	15 Ⓐ Ⓑ Ⓒ Ⓓ	25 Ⓐ Ⓑ Ⓒ Ⓓ	35 Ⓐ Ⓑ Ⓒ Ⓓ
6 Ⓕ Ⓖ Ⓗ Ⓙ	16 Ⓕ Ⓖ Ⓗ Ⓙ	26 Ⓕ Ⓖ Ⓗ Ⓙ	36 Ⓕ Ⓖ Ⓗ Ⓙ
7 Ⓐ Ⓑ Ⓒ Ⓓ	17 Ⓐ Ⓑ Ⓒ Ⓓ	27 Ⓐ Ⓑ Ⓒ Ⓓ	37 Ⓐ Ⓑ Ⓒ Ⓓ
8 Ⓕ Ⓖ Ⓗ Ⓙ	18 Ⓕ Ⓖ Ⓗ Ⓙ	28 Ⓕ Ⓖ Ⓗ Ⓙ	38 Ⓕ Ⓖ Ⓗ Ⓙ
9 Ⓐ Ⓑ Ⓒ Ⓓ	19 Ⓐ Ⓑ Ⓒ Ⓓ	29 Ⓐ Ⓑ Ⓒ Ⓓ	39 Ⓐ Ⓑ Ⓒ Ⓓ
10 Ⓕ Ⓖ Ⓗ Ⓙ	20 Ⓕ Ⓖ Ⓗ Ⓙ	30 Ⓕ Ⓖ Ⓗ Ⓙ	40 Ⓕ Ⓖ Ⓗ Ⓙ

SCIENCE

1 Ⓐ Ⓑ Ⓒ Ⓓ	11 Ⓐ Ⓑ Ⓒ Ⓓ	21 Ⓐ Ⓑ Ⓒ Ⓓ	31 Ⓐ Ⓑ Ⓒ Ⓓ
2 Ⓕ Ⓖ Ⓗ Ⓙ	12 Ⓕ Ⓖ Ⓗ Ⓙ	22 Ⓕ Ⓖ Ⓗ Ⓙ	32 Ⓕ Ⓖ Ⓗ Ⓙ
3 Ⓐ Ⓑ Ⓒ Ⓓ	13 Ⓐ Ⓑ Ⓒ Ⓓ	23 Ⓐ Ⓑ Ⓒ Ⓓ	33 Ⓐ Ⓑ Ⓒ Ⓓ
4 Ⓕ Ⓖ Ⓗ Ⓙ	14 Ⓕ Ⓖ Ⓗ Ⓙ	24 Ⓕ Ⓖ Ⓗ Ⓙ	34 Ⓕ Ⓖ Ⓗ Ⓙ
5 Ⓐ Ⓑ Ⓒ Ⓓ	15 Ⓐ Ⓑ Ⓒ Ⓓ	25 Ⓐ Ⓑ Ⓒ Ⓓ	35 Ⓐ Ⓑ Ⓒ Ⓓ
6 Ⓕ Ⓖ Ⓗ Ⓙ	16 Ⓕ Ⓖ Ⓗ Ⓙ	26 Ⓕ Ⓖ Ⓗ Ⓙ	36 Ⓕ Ⓖ Ⓗ Ⓙ
7 Ⓐ Ⓑ Ⓒ Ⓓ	17 Ⓐ Ⓑ Ⓒ Ⓓ	27 Ⓐ Ⓑ Ⓒ Ⓓ	37 Ⓐ Ⓑ Ⓒ Ⓓ
8 Ⓕ Ⓖ Ⓗ Ⓙ	18 Ⓕ Ⓖ Ⓗ Ⓙ	28 Ⓕ Ⓖ Ⓗ Ⓙ	38 Ⓕ Ⓖ Ⓗ Ⓙ
9 Ⓐ Ⓑ Ⓒ Ⓓ	19 Ⓐ Ⓑ Ⓒ Ⓓ	29 Ⓐ Ⓑ Ⓒ Ⓓ	39 Ⓐ Ⓑ Ⓒ Ⓓ
10 Ⓕ Ⓖ Ⓗ Ⓙ	20 Ⓕ Ⓖ Ⓗ Ⓙ	30 Ⓕ Ⓖ Ⓗ Ⓙ	40 Ⓕ Ⓖ Ⓗ Ⓙ

You may wish to remove these sample answer document pages to respond to the practice ACT Writing Test.

Begin WRITING TEST here.

_____

_____

_____

_____

_____

_____

_____

_____

_____

_____

_____

_____

_____

_____

_____

_____

_____

_____

_____

_____

_____

_____

_____

_____

_____

_____

_____

Cut Here

If you need more space, please continue on the next page.

1

WRITING TEST

If you need more space, please continue on the back of this page.

Cut Here

WRITING TEST

If you need more space, please continue on the next page.

Cut Here

WRITING TEST

_____

_____

_____

_____

_____

_____

_____

_____

_____

_____

_____

_____

_____

_____

_____

_____

_____

_____

_____

_____

_____

_____

_____

_____

_____

_____

_____

_____

_____

_____

END OF THE WRITING TEST.
STOP! IF YOU HAVE TIME LEFT OVER, CHECK YOUR WORK ON THIS SECTION ONLY.

4

Cut Here

1 ■ ■ ■ ■ ■ ■ ■ ■ 1

ENGLISH TEST

45 Minutes – 75 Questions

DIRECTIONS: In the passages that follow, some words and phrases are underlined and numbered. In the answer column, you will find alternatives for the words and phrases that are underlined. Choose the alternative that you think is best and fill in the corresponding bubble on your answer sheet. If you think that the original version is best, choose "NO CHANGE," which will always be either answer choice A or F. You will also find questions about a particular section of the passage, or about the entire passage. These questions will be identified by either an underlined portion or by a number in a box. Look for the answer that clearly expresses the idea, is consistent with the style and tone of the passage, and makes the correct use of standard written English. Read the passage through once before answering the questions. For some questions, you should read beyond the indicated portion before you answer.

PASSAGE I

A Focused Intelligence

Aviator Charles A. Lindbergh was undeniably a man of genius. In 1927, he was the first person to complete a successful flight from New York to Paris. Such success was not the result of academic <u>excellence, but the</u> <u>result of ingenuity</u> and determination.

1. A. NO CHANGE
  B. excellence, but the result, of ingenuity,
  C. excellence but the result of, ingenuity
  D. excellence, but the result of, ingenuity

Throughout his childhood and early <u>adulthood being</u> Charles Lindbergh was not interested in erudition. In 1918, with the United States in the throes of World War I, <u>as a result of which</u> Lindbergh eagerly agreed to return to the family farm to grow food for the war effort in exchange for his high school diploma. Though the small Minnesota farm <u>under</u> his care thrived, his passion was not for agriculture, but for things mechanical. When he expressed these interests to his parents, a congressman and a teacher, they encouraged him to obtain a more formal education.

2. F. NO CHANGE
  G. adulthood, he,
  H. adulthood, which was
  J. adulthood,

3. A. NO CHANGE
  B. War I;
  C. War I,
  D. War I, the result was that

4. F. NO CHANGE
  G. beneath
  H. below
  J. supporting

Lindbergh attended the University of Wisconsin <u>to study</u> engineering. However, Lindbergh's penchant for "hands-on" learning, combined with a lack of scholarly discipline and study skills, <u>because of</u> academic probation after barely two years.

5. A. NO CHANGE
  B. and studying
  C. by studying
  D. in which to study

6. F. NO CHANGE
  G. resulted in
  H. as a result of
  J. primarily resulting from

GO ON TO THE NEXT PAGE.

1 ▪ ▪ ▪ ▪ ▪ ▪ ▪ **1**

Realizing that the only practical knowledge he had gained in college was through his participation in the Reserve Officers' Training Corps (R.O.T.C.), Lindbergh dropped out of college, never to return in pursuit of a degree.
                                               ‾‾‾‾‾‾‾‾‾‾‾‾‾‾‾‾‾‾‾‾‾‾‾‾
                                                         7

In 1922, after brief aviation training at the Nebraska Aircraft Corporation, Lindbergh spent two summers traveling from state to state, performing: as a barnstormer, wing
                              ‾‾‾‾‾‾‾‾‾‾‾‾‾‾‾‾‾‾‾‾‾‾‾‾‾‾‾‾‾
                                         8
walker, parachutist, and skydiver. Having found his true

passion as a pilot, Lindbergh enlisted in the Army along with
              ‾‾‾‾‾‾‾‾‾‾‾‾‾‾‾‾
                     9
103 other cadets. Despite his aversion to classroom learning,

he focused his efforts and learned to truly study during
‾‾‾‾‾‾‾‾‾‾
    10
ground school. Failing any one test would have resulted in being "washed out," but Lindbergh passed his tests with

"flying" colors. In 1925, when graduation occurred, only
               ‾‾‾‾‾‾‾‾‾‾‾‾‾‾‾‾‾‾‾‾‾‾‾‾‾‾‾‾‾‾‾‾‾
                            11
eighteen cadets remained, and Lindbergh achieved the highest ranking among all of the members of his class.

Despite his disinterest in formal education, Lindbergh
‾‾‾‾‾‾‾
  12
displayed an enjoyment of learning throughout his life,

seeking out and accepted new challenges. He charted
‾‾‾‾‾‾‾‾‾‾‾‾‾‾‾‾‾‾‾‾‾‾
         13
transcontinental and transoceanic air routes that are still used today. His sister-in-law's fatal heart condition led to his work in the development with surgeon Alexis Carrel
‾‾
                              14
of a perfusion pump, which enabled a damaged heart to
‾‾‾‾‾‾‾‾‾‾‾‾‾‾‾‾‾‾‾
       14

7. **A.** NO CHANGE
   B. return.
   C. return in order to graduate.
   D. return so that he could earn a college degree.

8. **F.** NO CHANGE
   G. performing, as a barnstormer
   H. performing; as a barnstormer,
   J. performing as a barnstormer,

9. **A.** NO CHANGE
   B. pilot. Lindbergh
   C. pilot; Lindbergh
   D. pilot Lindbergh

10. **F.** NO CHANGE
    G. has focused
    H. was focusing
    J. focuses

11. **A.** NO CHANGE
    B. At graduation, which was in 1925,
    C. When he graduated in 1925,
    D. When, in 1925, graduation came

12. **F.** NO CHANGE
    G. In connection to
    H. Due to
    J. Because of

13. **A.** NO CHANGE
    B. sought out and accepting
    C. seeking out and accepting
    D. seeks out and accepts

14. **F.** NO CHANGE
    G. led to his work with surgeon Alexis Carrel in developing a perfusion pump
    H. led to the development of a perfusion pump with his work with surgeon Alexis Carrel
    J. led to the surgeon Alexis Carrel and his work with him to develop a perfusion pump

GO ON TO THE NEXT PAGE.

continue pumping while doctors worked to repair it. 15

15. Which of the following choices (assume all are true) should the writer use here to provide an appropriate conclusion to the essay?
   A. Charles Lindbergh dedicated his efforts to becoming a pilot.
   B. Charles Lindbergh will be best remembered for his trans-Atlantic flight in 1927.
   C. Charles Lindbergh developed a medical device and spent his time traveling the world.
   D. Charles Lindbergh could look back with the wisdom of life's experiences, knowing that he had focused his intelligence in untraditional ways and changed the world.

PASSAGE II

Crude Sophistication

The Vikings of Scandinavia (what is now Norway, Sweden, and Denmark) led what would today be considered a crude existence. In many ways, therefore, they were far more advanced than their contemporaries.
16

17 In fact, to a great extent, Vikings seemed more at home on the ocean than did other European cultures even centuries later.

The Vikings were among the first international

seafaring, traders with purpose-built,
18

wooden trading ships. Vikings sailed from Scandinavia
19
through the Straits of Gibraltar to the eastern Mediterranean. These intrepid explorers also crossed the Atlantic Ocean, settling in Iceland and Greenland. From there, the Vikings

16. The writer wants to emphasize that the Vikings, though crude in many ways, were sophisticated in many others. Which choice does that best?
   F. NO CHANGE
   G. similarly,
   H. however,
   J. to that end,

17. Which of the following sentences, if inserted here, would best illustrate the accomplishments of the Vikings?
   A. Most Vikings were very loyal to family members, even if they did something wrong.
   B. Vikings gained much of their wealth by robbing and plundering, finding easy victims in Christian monasteries.
   C. Vikings traveled far and wide.
   D. Although Christopher Columbus is credited with "discovering" America in 1492, Viking explorers appear to have reached North America much earlier.

18. F. NO CHANGE
   G. seafaring traders: with
   H. seafaring traders, with,
   J. seafaring traders with

19. A. NO CHANGE
   B. trading ships constructed of wooden products.
   C. wooden ships for trading goods.
   D. ships, constructed of wood, for trading.

GO ON TO THE NEXT PAGE.

1 ■ ■ ■ ■ ■ ■ ■ ■ 1

crossed a <u>mostly</u> shorter distance to the North American
      20
continent, where archaeological evidence of their landing has

been found in what is now northern Newfoundland, Canada.

Regardless of whether Vikings arrived <u>first, there</u> distant
                                             21
travel during the ninth to twelfth centuries is quite remarkable.

    Vikings were skillful boatbuilders and sailors. Their

ancient marinas included small river boats, ocean-going

cargo ships, and even warships used to raid their Christian

neighbors. Viking traders sailed <u>around</u> the Baltic sea,
                                     22
obtaining furs and amber.

In Russia, they <u>will meet</u> up and traded goods with Arab
                    23
traders carrying silks and spices.

    Vikings possessed many complicated skills and were

fine craftsmen. For example, their steel sword and ax

blades were <u>heavy and powerful</u>. Similar craftsmanship
               24
was used by leather workers on shoes, harnesses,

and saddlery. Viking women also possessed diverse

<u>skills. Making</u> butter, cheese, and ale, and often weaving
  25
intricate geometric designs into their multi-colored

<u>fabrics (woven fabrics are still used in clothes throughout</u>
                                26
<u>the world today).</u>
        26
    One way in which the Vikings were behind their

contemporaries was in reading and writing. Few Vikings

could read or write, so those who could <u>were considered</u>
                                            27
valuable. Records of brave deeds were etched on large

standing stones called runes. <u>These runes'</u> were made up
                                   28
of sixteen different symbols. Because so few Vikings could

20. F. NO CHANGE
    G. much
    H. most
    J. most of

21. A. NO CHANGE
    B. first, their
    C. first: their
    D. first; they're

22. Which of the following alternatives to the underlined portion would NOT be acceptable?
    F. over
    G. across
    H. into
    J. on

23. A. NO CHANGE
    B. met
    C. would meet
    D. would be meeting

24. Given that all of them are true, which choice supports the
paragraph by giving the most specific details?
    F. NO CHANGE
    G. well made.
    H. often inlaid with intricate designs in silver.
    J. made of steel.

25. A. NO CHANGE
    B. skills; making
    C. skills and included making
    D. skills, including making

26. F. NO CHANGE
    G. fabrics; fabrics like those used in today's clothes.
    H. fabrics—clothes are made from fabrics.
    J. fabrics.

27. A. NO CHANGE
    B. was considering
    C. was considered
    D. considered

28. F. NO CHANGE
    G. These rune's
    H. These runes
    J. They're runes

GO ON TO THE NEXT PAGE.

read, they believed that runes <u>were</u> magical and could be
                    29
used to cast spells. Because they wrote down very little of

their history or beliefs, most of what is known of the Vikings

today is the result of archaeologists' discoveries and 30.

29. **A.** NO CHANGE
    B. had been
    C. were being
    D. was being

30. The writer wants the final statement to reflect information previously provided in the essay. Given that all of the following concluding phrases are true, which one, if inserted here, would do that best?
    F. written records of people who met them, such as their Christian neighbors (and victims) and the Arabs with whom they traded.
    G. other research.
    H. some recovered runes, which were often used by the archaeologists to cast spells and make predictions.
    J. the testimonies of Scandinavian immigrants to America.

PASSAGE III

> The following paragraphs may or may not be in the most logical order. You may be asked questions about the logical order of the paragraphs, as well as where to place sentences logically within any given paragraph.

Everybody Loves Kari

[1]

Kari has always been one of my favorite cousins. We

were allies <u>about</u> the older, bigger cousins in games of
            31
hide-and-seek.

But <u>Kari's appeal</u> isn't specific to me—it's universal!
        32

<u>She has a</u> pretty face and innocent expression make her
    33
irresistible to boys. Her genuine concern for others combined

with her occasional forgetfulness makes her unthreatening

among <u>girls; and her</u> gregarious nature juxtaposed
          34
with a genuine sweetness appeals to adults. Despite her

overwhelming popularity, Kari's congeniality occasionally

31. **A.** NO CHANGE
    B. for
    C. against
    D. despite

32. **F.** NO CHANGE
    G. the appeal of Kari
    H. the appealingness of Kari
    J. Kari's level of appeal

33. **A.** NO CHANGE
    B. She's
    C. It's her
    D. Her

34. **F.** NO CHANGE
    G. girls, so her
    H. girls, with her
    J. girls, and her

GO ON TO THE NEXT PAGE.

1 ■ ■ ■ ■ ■ ■ ■ ■ 1

gets her into trouble. 35

[2]

Girls State provides promising high school juniors the

opportunity of participating on hands-on citizenship training.
                                36

They learn about government by electing each other as public

officials on the local, county, and state levels and then by

carrying out the respective duties of their offices. From each

Girls State convention, two Senators are chosen to continue

on to Girls Nation. Kari was of course chosen, to be one of
                          37

her state's senators.

[3]

At Girls Nation, the schedule was packed from
                        38

morning until night, with one exception: the girls were

allowed one afternoon to sight-see according to their

own agenda. Kari had been sightseeing for about five

minutes when she was meeting a nice, young military
                     39

cadet, who gallantly offered, to show her around the nation's
            40

capital. After a fun (and surprisingly educational) day

together, Kari vowed to write often. Unlike most people

who promises to write, Kari actually does.
              41

[4]

[1] Kari and the cadet were pen pals for several months

until one fateful day when Kari wrote to a girlfriend from

camp. [2] Her letter to her girlfriend was newsy and filled

with many confidences. [3] Kari had attended three proms

35. Which of the following sentences, if added here, would
most effectively signal the essay's shift in focus occurring
at this point?
A. *Congeniality* is defined as "pleasantness," "sociabil-
ity," or "geniality."
B. Take the time she was chosen to represent her home
town at the American Legion Auxiliary Girls State
convention.
C. Kari doesn't get into trouble with the law—just
embarrassing situations like you see on television
comedies.
D. I could give you many examples.

36. F. NO CHANGE
G. by participating in
H. in participation of
J. to participate in

37. A. NO CHANGE
B. was of course chosen:
C. was of, course chosen,
D. was, of course, chosen

38. F. NO CHANGE
G. schedule being
H. scheduling was
J. schedule, it was

39. A. NO CHANGE
B. met
C. had meeted
D. had a meeting with

40. F. NO CHANGE
G. cadet, who, gallantly offered
H. cadet who gallantly offered:
J. cadet, who gallantly offered

41. A. NO CHANGE
B. who promise to write, Kari actually does.
C. Kari actually does write when she promises she'll
write.
D. to whom they promise to write, Kari does it.

GO ON TO THE NEXT PAGE.

1 ■ ■ ■ ■ ■ ■ ■ ■ 1

(with three different boys) that spring, and she had enjoyed herself at each. [4] Her favorite, however, had been with a very cute boy from a town 100 miles away. [5] (How Kari met him is another long story, the details of which she did not omit in her letter to her girlfriend.) 42 [6] The same day, Kari wrote a letter to the cadet. [7] However, out of consideration for the hard-working young man, she omitted information about the many social events she had recently attended. [8] A week later, she received a brief note from the cadet with her letter returned. [9] It said, "I believe you intended the

enclosed letter for another friend." 43 In her haste to send the letters, Kari had inadvertently mixed up the addresses.

Kari and the cadet stopped corresponding.
                    44

42. The writer had considered deleting the italics on the word *not* in the preceding sentence and revising *did not* to read as the contraction *didn't*. If the writer had done this, the sentence would have lost its:

   I. emphasis on the difference between Kari's letter to her girlfriend and her letter to the cadet.

   II. implication that this information was insignificant in the letter.

   III. suggestion that this information would be critical later in the essay.

F. I only
G. III only
H. I and II only
J. I and III only

43. The writer is considering the division of Paragraph 4 into two separate paragraphs. In terms of the logic and coherence of the essay, the best course of action to take would be to:
A. begin a new paragraph with Sentence 3.
B. begin a new paragraph with Sentence 4.
C. begin a new paragraph with Sentence 6.
D. begin a new paragraph with Sentence 7.

44. The writer wishes to add a light note at this point, supporting the essay's sense of completion by tying the ending back to the essay's beginning. Given that all are true, which choice would best accomplish this?
F. NO CHANGE
G. Okay, so *almost* everybody loves Kari!
H. Kari's friend wrote back immediately.
J. The cadet eventually left the military.

Question 45 asks about the preceding passage as a whole.

45. Suppose the writer had been assigned to write an essay describing the many opportunities that Girls State offered to high school juniors. Would this essay successfully fulfill the assignment?
A. Yes, because the essay indicates that Girls State offers many opportunities to high school juniors.
B. Yes, because Kari was selected to be one of her state's senators.
C. No, because the essay proves that Girls State did not provide high school juniors with any opportunities.
D. No, because the essay is a personal recollection of a favorite cousin.

GO ON TO THE NEXT PAGE.

1 ■ ■ ■ ■ ■ ■ ■ **1**

PASSAGE IV

> The following paragraphs may or may not be in the most logical order. You may be asked questions about the logical order of the paragraphs, as well as where to place sentences logically within any given paragraph.

Field of Error

[1]

"Hey, Clint!" I shouted. "Did you know that each stalk of corn only has one ear of corn on it?"

"No way! That seven-foot tall stalk only produces one ear of corn?"

"Really! Isn't that amazing? Get it? A-maize-ing!"

[2]

Have you ever asserted yourself as an expert, only to have your "expertise" challenged and proven wrong? The experience can <u>be, humbling,</u> embarrassing, and seemingly
                       46
never-ending.

[3]

<u>Growing up on a farm in Iowa where I spent my</u>
                               47
<u>evenings, weekends, and summers performing</u>
                       47
<u>menial labor.</u> In the course of doing my chores, I picked
   47
up a few bits of trivia—like the one-ear-of-corn-per-stalk

information. After high school, I went away to <u>college, and</u>
                                               48
took great pains to ensure that I always had summer jobs
lined up that did *not* involve farm labor.

[4]

After college, I moved to the city, where my friends
enjoyed hearing occasional anecdotes and bits of trivia
about life on the farm. <u>Therefore,</u> the truth as I knew it had
                        49
changed.

46. **F.** NO CHANGE
    G. be humbling,
    H. be, humbling
    J. be humbling

47. **A.** NO CHANGE
    B. On a farm in Iowa, I grew up where I spent my evenings, weekends, and summers doing menial labor.
    C. Performing menial labor in the evenings, on weekends and in summers, I grew up on a farm in Iowa where I did those things.
    D. I grew up on a farm in Iowa where I spent my evenings, weekends, and summers performing menial labor.

48. **F.** NO CHANGE
    G. college and
    H. college,
    J. college

49. **A.** NO CHANGE
    B. Unfortunately,
    C. In other words,
    D. Hence,

GO ON TO THE NEXT PAGE.

1   **1**

[5]

Apparently, while I was away at college and beginning my career, genetic engineering had been <u>applied in</u> the field
₅₀
of agriculture, and corn stalks now regularly sported two ears of corn instead of one. <u>I learned this the hard way.</u>
₅₁

[6]

<u>One day,</u> as Clint and his friends were about to tee off,
₅₂

Clint <u>spied</u> a cornfield.
₅₃

54 "Hey guys! I'll bet you ten bucks that not one stalk of corn out there has more than one ear on it." "You're crazy!" they replied. "We'll take that bet!" And so Clint lost ten

dollars and some measure of pride. <u>I on the other hand lost</u>
₅₅

all credibility. <u>It's now much later, ten years later, in fact,</u> and
₅₆

I still cannot see Clint <u>without reminding me</u> of that
₅₇

lost bet. 58

50. **F.** NO CHANGE
    G. applied by
    H. applied with
    J. applied for

51. **A.** NO CHANGE
    B. This, I learned, the hard way.
    C. I learned something like this the hard way.
    D. The hard way is how I learned this.

52. **F.** NO CHANGE
    G. One day in the past
    H. One day long ago
    J. One day, a while back,

53. Which of the following would NOT be an acceptable replacement for the underlined portion?
    A. saw
    B. spotted
    C. noticed
    D. envisioned

54. At this point, the writer would like the reader to imagine the emotion and motivation behind Clint's next words. Which of the following sentences, if added here, would most effectively accomplish this?
    F. "Here's a bet I'm sure to win!" he thought to himself.
    G. "Golfing is a dumb game," he mused.
    H. "I know something about corn," he said.
    J. "There's a cornfield," Clint thought to himself.

55. **A.** NO CHANGE
    B. I, on the other hand lost
    C. I on the other hand, lost,
    D. I, on the other hand, lost

56. **F.** NO CHANGE
    G. Now, after ten long years,
    H. It's been ten years,
    J. Ten long years have gone by,

57. **A.** NO CHANGE
    B. without his reminding me
    C. without being reminded by him
    D. without receiving a reminder from him

58. The writer would like to add an introductory sentence to Paragraph 6 that shows why Clint challenged his friends. Which of the choices does that best?
    F. My childhood friend Clint likes to make small bets with his golfing buddies.
    G. My friend Clint has been to Las Vegas many times.
    H. My friend Clint loves to golf.
    J. My friend Clint has a degree in accounting.

GO ON TO THE NEXT PAGE.

1 ■ ■ ■ ■ ■ ■ ■ ■ 1

> Questions 59 and 60 ask about the preceding passage as a whole.

59. The writer is considering adding the following sentence to the essay, in order to emphasize that she did not intentionally mislead her friends.

> With the exception of occasionally exaggerating some of the "characters" in my stories, I told my friends the truth.

If added, this new sentence would best support and be placed after the first sentence in Paragraph:
A. 2
B. 3
C. 4
D. 5

60. Suppose the writer had been assigned to write an article for a farming magazine that described the impact of genetic engineering on agriculture. Would this essay successfully fulfill the assignment?
F. No, because the essay describes the writer's experience with the repercussions of authoritatively sharing outdated information.
G. No, because the essay focuses on the golf habits of her friend and does not describe genetic engineering in agriculture in detail.
H. Yes, because the essay focuses on how genetic engineering has increased corn yields.
J. Yes, because the essay states that cornstalks now contain two ears of corn where there previously was only one.

PASSAGE V

The Perfect Part-Time Job

Like most college students, I usually needed extra cash. However, I was a bit too discriminating in how I earned that money. Since my parents were paying my tuition, I couldn't very well get a job that interfered with my classes, nor did I want to give up any of my extracurricular activities. Babysitting often fit within these parameters, but it usually didn't pay very well. I scoured the campus papers, only to find that the good jobs were always taken by the time one could call. And then I found it—the perfect part-time job.

61. A. NO CHANGE
    B. in
    C. by
    D. among

62. F. NO CHANGE
    G. I called.
    H. you could call.
    J. you can call.

GO ON TO THE NEXT PAGE.

1 ■ ■ ■ ■ ■ ■ ■ ■ ■ 1

As I left my sociology class one day, I saw the flyer posting nearly outside the door: "Help wanted for Psychology Dissertation Research—Acting Experience Preferred." Normally, I avoided any opportunities in psychology research because it generally involved some form of pain or deprivation for a meager

stipend, which can range from twenty to fifty dollars. Nevertheless, I was intrigued by the

request for acting experience because most of my extracurricular time was spent on stage, so I decided this opportunity warranted a phone call.

As it turned out, I was to be the experimenter; not the subject. And I did not have to inflict any pain. Essentially,

I read the same series of questions to the subjects of the

experiment and providing varied levels of feedback to each subject's answers. In some cases, I would say nothing and simply read the questions. In other cases, I would say things like, "Uh huh," or "Yeah, that happened to me once!" At certain times, I kept my face devoid of emotion and made very little eye contact, while at others, I nodded, smiled, leaned forward, showed concern, and so on in response to the

subject's answers. By combining these verbal, and nonverbal, responses, I played four different roles.

[1] Although the pay was minimal, I found the work exhausting. [2] I would have loved for the experiments to continue, but the research grant money was running low, and the experiments had already yielded definitive results. [3] All too soon, the experiments were completed. [4] To avoid

63. A. NO CHANGE
   B. just posted on the outside of
   C. posted just outside
   D. it was posted just outside

64. F. NO CHANGE
   G. they
   H. it's
   J. being

65. A. NO CHANGE
   B. stipend.
   C. twenty to fifty-dollar stipend.
   D. stipend. These are usually in the twenty to fifty-dollar range.

66. F. NO CHANGE
   G. request for acting experience
   H. requesting acting experience furthermore
   J. request for acting experience, instead

67. A. NO CHANGE
   B. experimenter, not
   C. experimenter: and not
   D. experimenter. Not

68. F. NO CHANGE
   G. subjects with
   H. subjects to
   J. subjects on

69. A. NO CHANGE
   B. various levels of feedback were provided
   C. providing varying levels of feedback
   D. provided varying levels of feedback

70. F. NO CHANGE
   G. so at others
   H. being at others
   J. DELETE the underlined portion.

71. A. NO CHANGE
   B. verbal, and nonverbal
   C. verbal and nonverbal
   D. verbal, and, nonverbal

72. The writer wishes to conclude this sentence with a phrase that would explain why she would have liked the job to continue. Which choice would best accomplish this?
   F. NO CHANGE
   G. fascinating and fun.
   H. about the same as babysitting.
   J. better than nothing.

GO ON TO THE NEXT PAGE.

1 ■ ■ ■ ■ ■ ■ ■ ■ 1

inadvertently skewing the results, I was not allowed to know the researcher's hypothesis ahead of time. [5] When the experiments were complete, my suspicions were confirmed: body language (nonverbal feedback) affects what (and how much) people tell you far more than anything you say. 73

73. For the sake of unity and coherence, Sentence 3 of the last paragraph should be placed:
  A. where it is now.
  B. immediately before Sentence 1.
  C. immediately before Sentence 2.
  D. immediately before Sentence 5.

Questions 74 and 75 ask about the preceding passage as a whole.

---

74. The writer is considering the addition of the following sentence to the essay:

> William James Hall is the building where classes for both the Sociology Department and the Psychology Department are held.

Given that this statement is true, should it be added to the essay, and if so, where?

  F. Yes, at the very beginning, because the sentence effectively introduces the subject of this essay.
  G. Yes, at the beginning of the second paragraph, because the sentence explains why the writer would have seen a psychology flyer outside a sociology classroom.
  H. No, because the information does not add value to this essay about a part-time job.
  J. No, because it is unlikely that any of the students know who William James is.

75. Suppose that the editor of a magazine had assigned the writer to prepare a firsthand account of an undergraduate student majoring in sociology. Does the essay successfully fulfill this assignment?

  A. Yes, because the essay describes what happens when the writer is leaving a sociology class.
  B. Yes, because sociology and psychology are closely linked.
  C. No, because the essay describes a part-time job working on a psychology dissertation research project.
  D. No, because the essay's tone is too formal and too personal for such an assignment.

END OF THE ENGLISH TEST.
STOP! IF YOU HAVE TIME LEFT OVER, CHECK YOUR WORK ON THIS SECTION ONLY.

2 △ △ △ △ △ △ △ △ 2

MATHEMATICS TEST

60 Minutes – 60 Questions

DIRECTIONS: Solve each of the problems in the time allowed, then fill in the corresponding bubble on your answer sheet. Do not spend too much time on any one problem; skip the more difficult problems and go back to them later. You may use a calculator on this test. For this test you should assume that figures are NOT necessarily drawn to scale, that all geometric figures lie in a plane, and that the word *line* is used to indicate a straight line.

---

1. If $2x + 5 = 17$, then $x =$?
   A. 3
   B. 6
   C. 10
   D. 11
   E. 24

DO YOUR FIGURING HERE.

2. Consider the three statements below to be true.

   All horses that run fast are brown.
   Horse A is not brown.
   Horse B runs fast.

   Which of the following statements is true?

   F. Horse B is not brown.
   G. Horse B is brown.
   H. All brown horses run fast.
   J. Horse A runs fast.
   K. Both Horse A and Horse B are brown.

3. How much greater than $x - 2$ is $x + 5$?
   A. 7
   B. 6
   C. 5
   D. 3
   E. 2

4. A group of students sold boxes of greetings cards to raise money. The net amount A, in dollars, raised by selling b boxes of greeting cards is given by the function $A(b) = 4b - 30$. If the students sold 15 boxes of greeting cards, what is the net amount they raised?
   F. $10
   G. $15
   H. $20
   J. $25
   K. $30

GO ON TO THE NEXT PAGE.

2   **2**

DO YOUR FIGURING HERE.

5. A carton of 12 cans of soda is priced at $6.60 now. If the soda goes on sale for 20% off the current price, what will be the price of the carton?
   A. $0.55
   B. $1.32
   C. $5.28
   D. $6.36
   E. $6.40

6. If $a^2 = 64$ and $b^2 = 81$, which of the following CANNOT be the value of $a + b$?
   F. −17
   G. −1
   H. 1
   J. 17
   K. 145

7. In the figure below, B is the midpoint of $\overline{AC}$, $\overline{AC}$ is parallel to $\overline{DG}$, and $\overline{BE}$ is congruent to $\overline{BF}$. What is the measure of angle BFG?

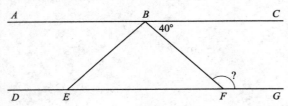

   A. 40°
   B. 80°
   C. 90°
   D. 140°
   E. 180°

8. If $x = -3$, then $x^2 - 6x - 18 = ?$
   F. 9
   G. 0
   H. −9
   J. −27
   K. −45

9. What is the value of $|1 - a|$ if $a = 12$?
   A. −13
   B. −11
   C. 11
   D. 12
   E. 13

10. If $ab = c$, $c = kb$, and $bc \neq 0$, then $k = ?$
   F. 1
   G. $\dfrac{1}{a}$
   H. $a - 1$
   J. a
   K. $a + 1$

GO ON TO THE NEXT PAGE.

2 △ △ △ △ △ △ △ △ **2**

11. $(x^3)^{13}$ is equivalent to:
- **A.** x^{39}
- **B.** x^{16}
- **C.** $3x^{10}$
- **D.** $3x^{13}$
- **E.** $3x^{16}$

DO YOUR FIGURING HERE.

12. If $\dfrac{2}{x} \geq \dfrac{1}{7}$, what is the largest possible value for x?
- **F.** $\dfrac{1}{2}$
- **G.** 7
- **H.** 14
- **J.** 15
- **K.** 28

13. A circle with a circumference of 46π is divided evenly into 12 sectors. What is the total measure, in degrees, of 5 sectors?
- **A.** $46°$
- **B.** $60°$
- **C.** $115°$
- **D.** $150°$
- **E.** $230°$

14. Every day at 7:30 A.M. during one school week, Rachel and Ross counted the number of students who entered the school through the main entrance and recorded the results in the table below. For that school week, what was the average number of students who entered the school through the main entrance?

Day	Number of students
M	450
Tu	427
W	462
Th	433
F	398

- **F.** 427
- **G.** 434
- **H.** 448
- **J.** 453
- **K.** 462

15. Which of the following equations has both $x = -3$ and $x = 6$ as solutions?
- **A.** $(x-6)(x+3) = 0$
- **B.** $(x+6)(x+3) = 0$
- **C.** $(x+6)(x-3) = 0$
- **D.** $(x-6)(x-3) = 0$
- **E.** $x - 6 = x + 3$

GO ON TO THE NEXT PAGE.

2 △ △   △   △   △   △   △   △ **2**

16. For all x, $7 - 2(x - 10) =$?
   F. $5x + 27$
   G. $5x - 27$
   H. $-2x + 27$
   J. $-2x - 13$
   K. $-2x + 3$

17. If 60% of x equals 90, then $x =$?
   A. 5.4
   B. 15
   C. 54
   D. 150
   E. 1,500

18. The price of 1 box of popcorn and 1 drink together is $5.10. The price of 2 boxes of popcorn and 1 drink together is $8.35. What is the cost of 1 drink?
   F. $0.75
   G. $1.85
   H. $2.15
   J. $2.55
   K. $3.25

19. You are standing in line at the cash register to pay for 2 lamps priced at $8.99 each. A sales tax of 7% of the cost of the lamps will be added (rounded to the nearest cent) to the price of the 2 lamps. You have 20 one-dollar bills. How much will you need in coins if you want to have exact change ready?
   A. $0.24
   B. $0.38
   C. $0.62
   D. $0.76
   E. $0.87

20. If $r^3 = 343$, then $3r =$?
   F. 7
   G. 21
   H. 49
   J. 114
   K. 2,229

21. What is the correct order of $\pi, \dfrac{7}{3}$, and $\dfrac{9}{2}$ from least to greatest?
   A. $\dfrac{9}{2} < \pi < \dfrac{7}{3}$
   B. $\dfrac{7}{3} < \pi < \dfrac{9}{2}$
   C. $\pi < \dfrac{9}{2} < \dfrac{7}{3}$
   D. $\pi < \dfrac{7}{3} < \dfrac{9}{2}$
   E. $\dfrac{9}{2} < \dfrac{7}{3} < \pi$

DO YOUR FIGURING HERE.

GO ON TO THE NEXT PAGE.

2   **2**

DO YOUR FIGURING HERE.

22. What number can you add to the numerator and denominator of $\frac{9}{13}$ to get $\frac{3}{4}$?

F. -3

G. $-1\frac{1}{4}$

H. $1\frac{1}{2}$

J. 3

K. 6

23. In the standard (x, y) coordinate plane, what is the slope of the line joining the points $(5, 4)$ and $(2, -7)$?

A. 9

B. $\frac{11}{3}$

C. 1

D. $\frac{3}{11}$

E. $\frac{1}{9}$

24. If p is the greatest prime factor of 38 and f is the greatest prime factor of 100, then $p + f = ?$

F. 7

G. 12

H. 24

J. 29

K. 44

25. If $(t + v)^2 = 289$ and $tv = 30$, then $t^2 + v^2 = ?$

A. -11

B. 1

C. 11

D. 61

E. 229

26. If, for all x, $(x^{3a+5})^4 = x^{44}$, then $a = ?$

F. 1

G. 2

H. $\frac{16}{3}$

J. $\frac{53}{12}$

K. 5

27. Which of the following is a value of x that satisfies $\log_x 16 = 2$?

A. 2

B. 4

C. 8

D. 16

E. 32

28. One endpoint of a line segment in the (x, y) coordinate plane has coordinates $(-2, 9)$. The midpoint of the segment has coordinates $(4, 4)$. What are the coordinates of the other endpoint of the segment?

F. $(-8, 13)$

G. $(-6, 5)$

H. $(2, 13)$

J. $(10, -1)$

K. $(-8, 36)$

GO ON TO THE NEXT PAGE.

2   **2**

29. In the (x, y) coordinate plane, what is the radius of the circle $(x - 4)^2 + (y - 1)^2 = 14$?

A. 7
B. 14
C. $\sqrt{7}$
D. $\sqrt{14}$
E. 296

DO YOUR FIGURING HERE.

30. In the right triangle shown below, $\cos \angle A = ?$

F. $\dfrac{5}{12}$

G. $\dfrac{5}{13}$

H. $\dfrac{12}{13}$

J. $\dfrac{13}{12}$

K. $\dfrac{12}{5}$

31. For all nonzero a and b, $\dfrac{(13a^2b^4)(-8a^3b^5)}{(4a^2b^6)} = ?$

A. $26a^3b^{14}$
B. $-26a^3b^3$
C. $\dfrac{a^3b^3}{-26}$
D. $-26a^4b^9$
E. $\dfrac{-26}{ab}$

32. Which of the following set of three numbers could be the side lengths, in feet, of a right isosceles triangle?

F. $1, 2, 3$
G. $2, 2, 2$
H. $2, 2\sqrt{3}, 4$
J. $1, 2, 2\sqrt{2}$
K. $2, 2, 2\sqrt{2}$

GO ON TO THE NEXT PAGE.

2   **2**

33. In the standard (x, y) coordinate plane, at what point does the line given by the equation $3x + 7y - 2 = 0$ cross the y-axis?

A. $-\dfrac{2}{7}$

B. 0

C. $\dfrac{2}{7}$

D. 2

E. 3

DO YOUR FIGURING HERE.

34. Which of the following logical statements identifies the same set as the graph shown below?

F. $x \geq -4$ and $x < 6$
G. $x > -4$ and $x < 6$
H. $x \geq -4$ or $x < 6$
J. $x \leq -4$ and $x > 6$
K. $x \leq -4$ or $x > 6$

35. What is the perimeter of the figure shown below?

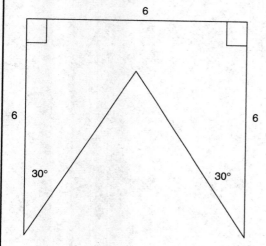

A. 36
B. 30
C. 28
D. 25
E. 24

36. If x and y are real and $\sqrt{3\left(\dfrac{x^3}{2y}\right)} = 4$, then what must be true of the values of x and y?

F. x and y must both be negative
G. x and y must both be positive
H. x and y must both be positive or both be negative
J. x and y must have opposite signs
K. x and y may have any value

GO ON TO THE NEXT PAGE.

2   **2**

37. For all pairs of real numbers A and S where $A = 2S + 9$, $S = ?$

A. $\dfrac{A}{9} + 2$

B. $\dfrac{A}{9} - 2$

C. $9A - 2$

D. $\dfrac{A - 9}{2}$

E. $\dfrac{A + 9}{2}$

38. What is the slope of any line perpendicular to the y-axis in the (x, y) coordinate plane?

F. -1

G. 0

H. 1

J. Undefined

K. Cannot be determined from the given information

39. In the (x, y) coordinate plane, the line with equation $5y = 25x - 50$ crosses the x-axis at the point with coordinates (a, b). What is the value of a?

A. -10

B. -2

C. 0

D. 2

E. 5

40. A right triangle has side lengths as shown below. What is $(\tan \alpha)(\cos \beta)$?

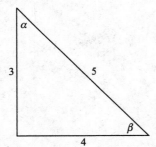

F. $\dfrac{5}{12}$

G. $\dfrac{4}{9}$

H. $\dfrac{15}{20}$

J. $\dfrac{2}{15}$

K. $\dfrac{16}{15}$

DO YOUR FIGURING HERE.

GO ON TO THE NEXT PAGE.

2   **2**

41. Amy can run 3 miles in s minutes. At that pace, how many miles can she run in 50 minutes?

   A. $\dfrac{3s}{50}$

   B. $\dfrac{50s}{3}$

   C. $50\dfrac{s}{3}$

   D. $3(50s)$

   E. $\dfrac{150}{s}$

42. Which of the following inequalities is an equivalent algebraic expression for the statement below?

   3 less than the product of 7 and a number n is less than 38

   F. $7 - 3n < 38$
   G. $35 - 7n < 3$
   H. $38 < 3 - 7n$
   J. $7n - 3 < 38$
   K. $4n < 38$

43. In triangle ABC, the measure of $\angle A$ is 30° and the measure of $\angle B$ is 60°. If $\overline{AB}$ is 16 units long, what is the area, in square units, of triangle ABC?

   A. 16
   B. $16\sqrt{3}$
   C. $32\sqrt{3}$
   D. 256
   E. $256\sqrt{3}$

44. In the standard (x, y) coordinate plane, which of the following lines goes through (0,3) and is perpendicular to $y = 2x + 1$?

   F. $y = -\dfrac{1}{2}x + 3$

   G. $y = \dfrac{1}{2}x + 3$

   H. $y = 2x + 4$
   J. $y = 3x + 1$
   K. $y = 3x + 2$

45. A certain rectangle is 2 times as long as it is wide. Suppose the length is tripled and the width is doubled. The area of the second rectangle is how many times as large as the area of the first?

   A. 2
   B. 3
   C. 6
   D. 9
   E. 12

DO YOUR FIGURING HERE.

GO ON TO THE NEXT PAGE.

2   **2**

46. For what value of z would the following system of equations have an infinite number of solutions?

$$24x - 15y = 108$$
$$72x - 45y = 9z$$

F. 3
G. 9
H. 12
J. 36
K. 108

47. How many prime numbers are there between 36 and 54?
A. 4
B. 5
C. 6
D. 7
E. 8

48. If $\tan A = \dfrac{x}{y}$, $x > 0$, $y > 0$, and $0 < A < 90°$, what is $\sin A$?

F. $\dfrac{x}{y}$

G. $\dfrac{y}{x}$

H. $\dfrac{x}{\sqrt{x^2 + y^2}}$

J. $\dfrac{y}{\sqrt{x^2 + y^2}}$

K. $\dfrac{\sqrt{x^2 + y^2}}{x}$

49. Aishah will create a circle graph to show how she spends her time during a 24-hour day. The size of the sector representing each activity is proportional to the time spent on that activity. Among other activities, Aishah plays the piano for 1.5 hours. How many degrees should the central angle measure in the sector representing playing the piano?
A. 15
B. 22.5
C. 31
D. 48.3
E. 240

DO YOUR FIGURING HERE.

GO ON TO THE NEXT PAGE.

2   **2**

50. Points A, B, and C lie on the same line. If the length of $\overline{AB}$ is 9 meters and the length of $\overline{BC}$ is 11 meters, then what are all the possible lengths, in meters, for $\overline{AC}$?

  F. 20 only
  G. 2 only
  H. 2 and 20 only
  J. Any number less than 2 or greater than 20
  K. Any number greater than 20 or less than 2

51. In the figure shown below, MN is the arc of a circle with center L. If the length of arc MN is 6π, what is the area of sector LMN?

  A. 9π
  B. 36π
  C. 54π
  D. 72π
  E. 108π

52. If $6a^5b^7 < 0$, then which of the following *must* be true?

  F. $a > 0$ and $b > 0$ or $a < 0$ and $b < 0$
  G. $a > 0$ and $b < 0$ or $a < 0$ and $b > 0$
  H. $a = b$
  J. $a < 0$ and $b < 0$
  K. $a > b$

53. Mandy visited 7 patients on her first day as a nurse. Her goal was to visit 3 more patients on each successive day than she had visited the day before. If Mandy met, but did not exceed her goal, how many patients did she visit in all during her first 5 days as a nurse?

  A. 19
  B. 35
  C. 65
  D. 105
  E. 325

54. What is the smallest possible value for the product of 2 real numbers that differ by 8?

  F. 8
  G. 6
  H. −2
  J. −4
  K. −16

DO YOUR FIGURING HERE.

GO ON TO THE NEXT PAGE.

2   △ △ **2**

55. If $0° \leq x \leq 90°$ and $\cos x = \dfrac{4}{5}$, then $\sin x =$?

A. $\dfrac{3}{5}$

B. $\dfrac{3}{4}$

C. $\dfrac{4}{5}$

D. $\dfrac{5}{4}$

E. $\dfrac{4}{3}$

56. For every dollar decrease in price of a set of books, the bookstore sells 1,200 more sets of books per month. The bookstore normally sells 1,750 sets of books per month at $9.50 per set of books. Which of the following expressions represents the number of sets of books sold per month if the cost is reduced by x dollars per set of books?

F. $1,750 + 1,200x$

G. $1,750 - 1,200x$

H. $(9.50 - x)(1,750 + 1,200x)$

J. $9.50 + 1,200x$

K. $1,750 + 9.50x$

57. In a game, 45 marbles numbered 00 through 44 are placed in a box. A player draws 1 marble at random from the box. Without replacing the first marble, the player draws a second marble at random. If the numbers on both marbles drawn have a sum greater than 45 (that is, the sum of Marble 1 and Marble 2 exceeds 45), the player is a winner. If the first marble Martin draws is numbered 17, what is the probability that Martin will be a winner on the next draw?

A. $\dfrac{4}{11}$

B. $\dfrac{16}{46}$

C. $\dfrac{17}{44}$

D. $\dfrac{17}{45}$

E. $\dfrac{16}{43}$

GO ON TO THE NEXT PAGE.

2   △ △ △ △ △ 2

58. Which of the following data sets has the smallest standard deviation?

F. 1, 17
G. 1, 2, 3, 4
H. 2, 2, 3, 6, 6, 8
J. 15, 30, 45
K. 25, 25, 25, 25, 25, 25

59. In the standard (x, y) coordinate plane, the vertices of a square have coordinates $(0, 4)$, $(4, 4)$, $(4, 0)$, and $(0, 0)$. Which of the following is an equation of a circle that is inscribed in the square?

A. $(x+2)^2+(y+2)^2=2$
B. $(x-2)^2+(y-2)^2=2$
C. $(x-2)^2+(y-2)^2=4$
D. $(x+2)^2+(y-2)^2=4$
E. $(x+2)^2+(y+2)^2=8$

60. On Monday, a skirt was priced at $60.00. On Wednesday, the price was reduced by 15%. Two weeks later, the price was further reduced by 20%. What percent of the original price is this last price?

F. 35%
G. 40%
H. 51%
J. 65%
K. 68%

END OF THE MATHEMATICS TEST.
STOP! IF YOU HAVE TIME LEFT OVER, CHECK YOUR WORK ON THIS SECTION ONLY.

3   **3**

READING TEST

35 Minutes – 40 Questions

DIRECTIONS: This test includes four passages, each followed by 10 questions. Read the passages and choose the best answer to each question. After you have selected your answer, fill in the corresponding bubble on your answer sheet. You should refer to the passages as often as necessary when answering the questions.

PASSAGE I

LITERARY NARRATIVE: *This passage is adapted from "The Awakening," by Kate Chopin, originally published in 1899.*

Mrs. Pontellier's eyes were quick and bright; they were a yellowish brown, about the color of her hair. She had a way of turning them swiftly upon an object and holding them there as if lost in some inward maze of contempla-
5   tion or thought. Her eyebrows were a shade darker than her hair. They were thick and almost horizontal, emphasiz-ing the depth of her eyes. She was rather more handsome than beautiful. Her face was captivating by reason of a certain frankness of expression and a contradictory subtle
10   play of features. Her manner was engaging.

Robert LeBruns had a cigar in his pocket which Mr. Pontellier had presented him with, and he was saving it for his after-dinner smoke. This seemed quite proper and natural on his part. In coloring he was not unlike his com-
15   panion. A clean-shaved face made the resemblance more pronounced than it would otherwise have been. There rested no shadow of care upon his open countenance. His eyes gathered in and reflected the light and languor of the summer day.
20   Mrs. Pontellier reached over for a palm-leaf fan that lay on the porch and began to fan herself, while she and Robert chatted incessantly; about the things around them; their amusing adventure out in the water—it had again assumed its entertaining aspect; about the wind, the trees,
25   the people who had gone to the Cheniere; about the chil-dren playing croquet under the oaks, and the Farival twins, who were now performing the overture to "The Poet and the Peasant."

Robert talked a good deal about himself. He was very
30   young, and did not know any better. Mrs. Pontellier talked a little about herself for the same reason. Each was inter-ested in what the other said. Robert spoke of his intention to go to Mexico in the autumn, where fortune awaited him. He was always intending to go to Mexico, but some way

35   never got there. Meanwhile, he held on to his modest posi-tion in the mercantile house in New Orleans, where an equal familiarity with English, French, and Spanish gave him no small value as a clerk and correspondent.

He was spending his summer vacation, as he always
40   did, with his mother at Grand Isle. In former times, before Robert could remember, "the house" had been a summer luxury of the LeBruns. Now, flanked by its dozen or more cottages, which were always filled with exclusive tenants from the "Quartier Francais," it enabled Madame LeBruns
45   to maintain the easy and comfortable existence which appeared to be her birthright.

Mrs. Pontellier talked about her father's Mississippi plantation and her girlhood home in the old Kentucky bluegrass country. She was an American woman, with a
50   small infusion of French which seemed to have been lost in dilution. She read a letter from her sister, who was away in the East, and who had engaged herself to be married. Robert was interested, and wanted to know what manner of girls the sisters were, what the father was like, and how
55   long the mother had been dead.

When Mrs. Pontellier folded the letter it was time for her to dress for the early dinner. "I see Leonce isn't com-ing back," she said, with a glance in the direction whence her husband had disappeared. Robert supposed he was not,
60   as there were a good many New Orleans club men over at Klein's. When Mrs. Pontellier left him to enter her room, the young man descended the steps and strolled over toward the croquet players, where, during the half-hour before dinner, he amused himself with the little Pontellier
65   children, who were very fond of him.

1. When Mrs. Pontellier says "I see Leonce isn't coming back," (lines 57–58) she is expressing her belief that:
    A. she will be having dinner without her husband.
    B. Robert knew her husband wasn't returning.
    C. her husband has left her.
    D. she must go to Klein's for dinner.

GO ON TO THE NEXT PAGE.

2. It can reasonably be inferred from their conversation that Mrs. Pontellier and Robert are:
   F. related to each other.
   G. each married to someone else.
   H. about the same age.
   J. long-time friends.

3. The idea that Robert aspires to gain more wealth and social stature than he currently has is best exemplified by which of the following quotations from the passage?
   A. " … where fortune awaited him."
   B. " … the young man descended the steps and strolled over toward the croquet players …"
   C. " … gave him no small value as a clerk and correspondent."
   D. "Robert talked a good deal about himself."

4. As it is used in paragraph 3, "She and Robert chatted incessantly" most nearly means that:
   F. they each talked about themselves.
   G. they had a long and lively conversation.
   H. they weren't listening to each other.
   J. they both spoke in loud voices.

5. The passage makes it clear that Mrs. Pontellier and her husband:
   A. never spend time together.
   B. do not get along.
   C. enjoy Robert's company.
   D. have children.

6. As it is used to describe Robert in Paragraph 2, the phrase "There rested no shadow of care upon his open countenance" most nearly means that:
   F. his face was well lit.
   G. he was relaxed and carefree.
   H. his sleep habits were poor.
   J. he was feeling stressed.

7. We may reasonably infer from details in the passage that all of the characters in the story are:
   A. poor.
   B. sociable.
   C. lonely.
   D. wealthy.

8. Paragraph 4 indicates that Robert's ambitions are largely:
   F. unfulfilled.
   G. satisfactory.
   H. mundane.
   J. unprecedented.

9. It can be reasonably inferred from information in the passage that:
   A. Robert's mother was better off financially in an earlier time.
   B. Robert is visiting his mother to help her out.
   C. Robert will never go to Mexico.
   D. Robert pretends to be more well-off than he is.

10. The point of view from which the passage is told is best described as that of:
    F. a first person narrator who recounts her experiences with two friends.
    G. a first person narrator who offers insight into characters' thoughts and relates actions from a time she was too young to remember.
    H. a limited third person narrator who relates the thoughts and actions from the perspective of one character.
    J. an omniscient third person narrator who relates the thoughts and actions of more than one character.

GO ON TO THE NEXT PAGE.

3 ████████████████████████████ **3**

PASSAGE II

SOCIAL SCIENCE: *Whales in Inuit Life*

As a result of the overhunting of whales by commercial whaling ships, many whales became endangered—some to the point of near extinction. In response, the motto, "Save the Whales" became a common phrase. The thought
5 of killing this large mammal for human consumption was appalling to many westerners. And so, in 1977, the International Whaling Committee (IWC) imposed a moratorium on all whaling. Almost immediately, a great cry sounded from the Inuit—the indigenous people of the Arctic Circle
10 who rely on the whale for their very survival.

Since about 800 A.D., Inuit whalers have hunted bowhead whales. The whale has many uses, and no part of the animal is wasted. The *baleen* (whalebone) is used to house equipment and insulate boots; the huge vertebrae are used
15 for seats. The stomach and bladder are used for drums. The remainder, including even the tongue, skin, and other organs, are used for food.

This food is surprisingly nutritious. A serving of whale meat is 95% protein. The meat is also rich in iron,
20 niacin, vitamin E, and phosphorus. A favorite snack, *maktaaq* (whale skin) is rich in calcium, selenium, and omega-3 fatty acids. A study of Inuit eating habits found that those who consumed primarily traditional Inuit food (60 to 70% whale meat) were less likely to be obese than
25 Inuit who consumed a more Western diet.

Although the whale itself is prized for the sum of its parts, the process of whaling contributes to the Inuit sense of community. The communal nature of the hunt and the sharing of the whale give the animal a central place
30 in the Inuit cultural and spiritual life. The whole village helps haul in the whale, butcher it, cook it, and distribute it. Sharing the whale throughout the community and with neighboring communities, is an old, respected practice. At the butchering site, the parts of the whale are divided
35 among the whaling crews, with some shares reserved for elders and widows; other parts are saved for festivals, along with meat from seals and fish.

The whaling captain's family and crew feed the whole community after the first successful hunt. At this
40 time of thanksgiving and sharing, the successful crew shares a portion of the catch with the community. In mid-June, at the end of the whaling season, *Naluqatak*, is celebrated. This feast extends throughout the day and features a blanket toss, dancing, and many whale delicacies such as
45 *mikigaq* (fermented whale meat) and other traditional Inuit foods such as fish or caribou soup. This simple celebration is actually indicative of the structure of Inuit relationships.

Family is at the center of Inuit culture, with extended family playing an important role in the lives of each fam-
50 ily member. The relationship of whaling captain to crew often mimics this familial model. Similarly, the traditional blanket toss at *Naluqatak* is symbolic of the whaling

experience. The process requires the coordinated action of many people pulling on a large piece of *ugruk* (seal)
55 skin to toss an individual into the air, thereby creating a communal version of a trampoline. Finally, at *Naluqatak* and at Thanksgiving and Christmas as well, the food of the whale is given to everyone who comes to take part. In this way, tons of whale meat find their way throughout the
60 region all year long.

Because Inuit culture cannot be separated from the environment, the Inuit respect their surroundings. They believe the Arctic animals, land, sea, and weather are all part of the Inuit culture. The Inuit believe that animals are
65 on Earth to provide food and clothing for their survival; to show their respect, they kill only as many animals as they need. Similarly, even though the hunting season for bowhead whales extends from about mid-April to mid-June as the animals migrate down the coast to their summer feeding
70 grounds, many Inuit never hunt beyond the end of May, to avoid the time when calving females are passing through.

The whale provides life, meaning, and identity to the Inuit whalers and their communities. Undoubtedly, prohibiting whaling would endanger Inuit culture far more
75 than the Inuit would ever endanger the whales.

11. According to the passage, the traditional Inuit diet includes all of the following EXCEPT:
   A. *mikigaq.*
   B. *baleen.*
   C. *maktaaq.*
   D. caribou.

12. It's clear from the passage that when imposing the moratorium on whaling, the International Whaling Committee:
   F. was overwhelmed with support from the entire whaling community.
   G. may not have fully considered the impact such a ruling would have on the Inuit.
   H. was appalled by the Inuit's desire to continue hunting whales to extinction.
   J. made the decision based on hundreds of years of scientific research.

13. According to the information presented in the passage, which of the following best describes the relationship between the Inuit and whales?
   A. The Inuit have hunted whales to the point of near extinction.
   B. The Inuit feel that whale hunting is a crime perpetrated by Westerners.
   C. The Inuit worship whales.
   D. The Inuit consider the whales a gift over which they are very protective.

GO ON TO THE NEXT PAGE.

3 ████████████████████████████████ **3**

14. According to the passage, whale meat is nutritionally high in all of the following EXCEPT:
    F. phosphorus.
    G. niacin.
    H. riboflavin.
    J. vitamin E.

15. As it is used in the passage (line 7), the word *moratorium* most nearly means:
    A. a whaling ship.
    B. a common phrase.
    C. a suspension of activity.
    D. the relative incidence of disease.

16. As it is depicted in the passage, *Naluqatak* can best be described as:
    F. a harvest feast.
    G. a pagan celebration.
    H. a whale delicacy.
    J. a solemn ceremony.

17. It can be inferred that the word *coordinated*, as it is used in line 53, primarily refers to:
    A. matching in design, color, and/or texture.
    B. a set of numbers used in specifying a location.
    C. moving together in a smooth, organized way.
    D. athletic and graceful.

18. It can be inferred from the passage that the Inuit perspective toward the elderly is one of:
    F. respect.
    G. pity.
    H. apathy.
    J. condescension.

19. According to the passage, some whalers stop hunting at the end of May because:
    A. that is when the calving females are passing through.
    B. that is when the hunting season officially ends.
    C. they don't want to miss *Naluqatak*.
    D. they have killed their quota of whales by then.

20. It can be inferred from the passage that, in addition to whales, the Inuit also hunt:
    F. penguins.
    G. fox.
    H. moose.
    J. seals.

GO ON TO THE NEXT PAGE.

3 ███████████████████████████████ **3**

PASSAGE III

HUMANITIES: *"Bobby" Jones: Golf Prodigy*

Tiger Woods is often referred to as "the child prodigy of golf." However, eighty years before Woods another youth made headlines in the world of golf. Robert "Bobby" Tyre Jones, Jr. (1902–1971), is described in the *Oxford*
5 *Companion to World Sports and Games* as "probably the greatest player the game has known."

At age fourteen, Bobby became the youngest player ever to enter the U.S. amateur championship. The precocious Jones was known as a temperamental perfectionist,
10 frequently throwing tantrums (as well as balls and clubs). Atlanta sportswriter O. B. "Pop" Keeler became Bobby's friend and publicist. This mentor helped focus Bobby's passion, and he became known as not only a gracious winner and loser but also a remarkably honorable gentleman.

15 After two years on the amateur golf circuit, Jones entered Georgia Tech to earn his degree in mechanical engineering. While there, he continued to play amateur golf and played on his college team. Immediately after graduation, Jones enrolled at Harvard where, since his col-
20 legiate eligibility had been exhausted, he earned a varsity letter as the assistant manager of Harvard's golf team. It is difficult to imagine one of today's professional athletes volunteering to be the assistant manager of a college team!

Perhaps the best story of Jones' sense of fair play
25 comes to us from the 1925 U.S. Open. As he addressed his ball on the long grass on a steep bank near one of the greens, the ball moved. Against official objections, he insisted on adding a penalty stroke to his score. When people remarked on this noble gesture, he replied, "You
30 might as well praise me for not breaking into banks. There is only one way to play this game."

Between 1922 and 1930, Jones was placed first or second in eleven U.S. and British Open championship games. In 1924, he earned his Bachelor of Arts degree
35 from Harvard, with a concentration in English. He then obtained a law degree from Emory University, passing the Georgia bar exam in 1928.

At age twenty-eight, Jones won golf's "Grand Slam" of all four major championships in one year and became
40 the only individual ever to receive two New York City tick-ertape parades. And then, content with his achievements, he retired from competitive golf. Ironically, when Tiger Woods won today's version of the Grand Slam, the fourth win was at the Masters—the golf course (and competition)
45 designed by Bobby Jones. When Tiger Woods entitled his book *How I Play Golf*, it was the same title Bobby Jones had used in his first instructional film series. When Tiger Woods was asked to name his "dream foursome," Woods included Bobby Jones.

50 Sadly, Jones played his last full round of golf in 1948. He suffered from *syringeomyelia*, a rare spinal disease that degenerates the motor and sensory nerves, which confined Jones to a wheelchair. Although the disease filled his later years with pain, Jones stoically managed to continue to
55 enjoy life. When asked how he coped with the painful spinal condition, his reply belied his suffering: "Remember, we play the ball as it lies."

Bobby Jones never had a formal golf lesson in his life
60 and was known to store his golf clubs most winters. Despite this appearance of nonchalance, Jones was a serious athlete whose skill and grace are still emulated by many.

21. The passage suggests that Tiger Woods, when compared to Bobby Jones, is:
A. a poor imitation.
B. similar in many ways.
C. a more talented athlete.
D. eighty years older.

22. It can reasonably be inferred from the second paragraph that "Pop" Keeler could be called:
F. the first sports psychologist.
G. a controlling and manipulative man.
H. a swindler and a crook.
J. a positive force in Jones' life.

23. The passage primarily emphasizes the idea that Jones' golfing success was:
A. the only thing that mattered in his life.
B. the result of extensive lessons.
C. only one highlight of a life well lived.
D. due to constant practice.

24. Within the passage, the main function of the first paragraph is to:
F. provide vivid sensory details about the game of golf.
G. explain how Tiger Woods and Bobby Jones met.
H. identify the book that lists many well-known athletes.
J. introduce a comparison between two young golfers.

25. It can be inferred from the passage that Jones' perspective on higher education was that it:
A. was important to a well-rounded life.
B. was really difficult.
C. was just a way to play more sports.
D. was entirely unnecessary.

26. In the context of the passage, "You might as well praise me for not breaking into banks" (lines 29–31) suggests that Jones:
F. had committed a felony in his temperamental youth.
G. felt the rules of golf were as unbendable as laws against crime.
H. hated to receive praise.
J. thought his admirers were foolish.

GO ON TO THE NEXT PAGE.

3 ████████████████████████████████████ **3**

27. The passage implies that compared to today's professional athletes, Bobby Jones' commitment to being involved in his sport was:
    A. dependent on the sport.
    B. about the same.
    C. lesser.
    D. greater.

28. Details in the passage suggest that *syringeomyelia*:
    F. occurs most often among golfers.
    G. forced Jones to retire at an early age.
    H. gradually left Jones incapacitated.
    J. involves many needles and injections.

29. When Jones commented about playing "the ball where it lies," (lines 56–57) he was referring to:
    A. his penalty stroke at the 1925 U.S. Open.
    B. his debilitating disease.
    C. a fundamental rule of golf.
    D. being honest.

30. Based on the overall tone of the passage, it can be inferred that the author's opinion of Jones is one of:
    F. admiration and respect.
    G. aloof observation.
    H. utter disdain.
    J. apathy and remorse.

GO ON TO THE NEXT PAGE.

3 ▬▬▬▬▬▬▬▬▬▬▬▬▬▬▬▬▬▬▬▬▬▬▬▬▬▬ **3**

PASSAGE IV

NATURAL SCIENCE: The following passages were adapted from essays regarding manned versus unmanned space missions.

Passage A

A robot sent into space to gather information is certainly a valuable tool, but robots are not the complete solution. Even the most technologically advanced robots cannot and should not replace manned missions to outer space.

5 While it is cheaper and less dangerous to launch a computer probe that can gather reams of data, often the information obtained by a machine serves to produce more questions than answers. The space program would be far better off allowing manned missions to follow up on those
10 initial information-gathering robotic ventures.

It is true that manned missions are more costly than unmanned missions, but they are also more successful. Robots and astronauts use much of the same equipment in space, but a human is more capable of calibrating sensi-
15 tive instruments correctly and placing them in appropriate and useful positions. A computer is often neither as sensitive nor as accurate as a human managing the same terrain or environmental factors. Robots are also not as well equipped as humans to solve problems as they arise,
20 and robots often collect data that is unhelpful or irrelevant. A human, on the other hand, can make instant decisions about what to explore further and what to ignore.

While technological advances have allowed mankind to make incredible strides in space exploration, they still
25 cannot match the power and intelligence of the human mind. On-site presence of this biological "supercomputer" is necessary to maintain a space program that truly advances to the next level.

So what is that next level? The vast majority of
30 Americans support government funding of manned space flight, though probably for a variety of reasons. The bottom line is that most of us view outer space as the next great geographic and scientific frontier. Some even believe that soon humans will need another place to live besides
35 Earth.

Passage B

The end of the twentieth century saw many changes in America's space program, probably due in large part to the *Challenger* and *Columbia* Space Shuttle disasters. The tragic deaths of innocent space explorers have shaken
40 support for these endeavors and have caused citizens to question, and some even to reject, the validity of manned space flight. This, coupled with the incredible advances in technological devices, has probably signaled the end of manned space exploration as we know it.

45 We have no reason, however, to lament the end of this chapter of the space program nor to assume that the worlds beyond our Earth will remain unknown and undeveloped. Robotic computers and similar devices continue to evolve and improve. The Mars Pathfinder and rovers
50 have exceeded expectations in providing scientists with important data. With each robot sent into space, not only is valuable information collected, but also the problems the robot encounters are revealed and improvements can be made for future launches.

55 One must admit that humans are hardly suited for life away from planet Earth. People need food, water, and oxygen-rich air, all of which appear to be absent in the broader solar system. This means these necessities would fill a large part of the payload of any manned mission,
60 using up a great deal of the limited space and restricted weight of any spaceship. Once the necessary equipment is on board, the tremendous weight alone becomes a hazard to all of the flight's passengers.

With the rapid improvements in technology, maybe
65 the astronaut is becoming outdated and should be replaced by the robot. After all, no one cries when a computer-driven hunk of metal blows up or disappears. If one more person can be spared from harm in space by applying a technological alternative, how could we not embrace that
70 technology?

Questions 31 – 33 ask about Passage A.

---

31. In line 1, the author of Passage A uses the word "certainly" to indicate:
  A. knowledge about a specific topic.
  B. an opinion over a factual statement.
  C. a rebuttal to the previous statement.
  D. assurance that the statement is accurate.

32. As it is used in line 14, "calibrating" most nearly means:
  F. orbiting.
  G. collecting.
  H. solving.
  J. adjusting.

33. It can be inferred from the passage that the author of Passage A includes the last sentence ("Some even … Earth.") in order to suggest that:
  A. manned space flight is creating a difficult living situation for most humans.
  B. Earth's population growth will increase exponentially because of continued space exploration.
  C. Earth's population is growing to such an extent that the planet might no longer be able to accommodate all of the humans.
  D. scientists are unable to account for the public's reluctance to embrace unmanned space technology, despite the population explosion.

GO ON TO THE NEXT PAGE.

3 ▬▬▬▬▬▬▬▬▬▬▬▬▬▬▬▬▬▬▬▬▬▬▬▬▬ **3**

Questions 34 – 37 ask about Passage B.

34. The author of Passage B mentions the space shuttle disasters most likely to:
   F. promote the idea of continued space exploration.
   G. deny the problems associated with unmanned space exploration.
   H. dismiss the fears held by the public regarding space exploration.
   J. emphasize the serious ramifications of manned space exploration.

35. As it is used in line 45, "lament" most nearly means:
   A. regret.
   B. decide.
   C. oppose.
   D. rejoice.

36. The author of Passage B uses the phrase "computer-driven hunk of metal" (lines 66–67) in order to:
   F. decry the value of machines in space missions.
   G. highlight the lower risk of unmanned space flight.
   H. question hastily prepared unmanned space missions.
   J. foster debate over the role of machines in manned space missions.

37. The question at the end of Passage B primarily draws attention to:
   A. the beauty of life on other planets.
   B. the growing limitations of life on Earth.
   C. the hazards involved with manned space travel.
   D. the knowledge that can be obtained by continuing space exploration.

Questions 38 – 40 ask about both passages.

38. Both passages base their arguments on the assumption that:
   F. technology is the way of the future.
   G. humans and technology are on a collision course.
   H. interest in potential life beyond Earth will continue.
   J. humans have already conquered the "great frontier."

39. What aspect of manned space flight seems to matter a great deal in Passage A, but not in Passage B?
   A. Its marred safety record
   B. Its requirement of life-sustaining provisions like food and water
   C. Its compatibility with sensitive instruments and large amounts of data
   D. Its powerful images showing intrepid explorers expanding human frontiers

40. The authors of both passages agree that:
   F. manned space flight is a thing of the past.
   G. space exploration will continue in some form.
   H. robotics are not reliable enough to be used in the space program.
   J. the government is not doing enough to keep the space program going.

END OF THE READING TEST.
STOP! IF YOU HAVE TIME LEFT OVER, CHECK YOUR WORK ON THIS SECTION ONLY.

SCIENCE TEST

35 Minutes – 40 Questions

DIRECTIONS: This test includes several passages, each followed by several questions. Read the passages and choose the best answer to each question. After you have selected your answer, fill in the corresponding bubble on your answer sheet. You should refer to the passages as often as necessary when answering the questions.

PASSAGE I

Several scientists considered the different environmental factors and their influence on the growth of certain bacteria. The following experiments used *E. coli* bacteria and a controlled temperature to measure the effect of pH levels, nutrients, and growth factors on the number of bacteria produced within a given time period.

Experiment 1

An *E. coli* bacterial colony was placed in each of three petri dishes containing the same nutrient concentration. The pH level of each nutrient concentration was varied according to Table 1. The lids of the petri dishes were replaced and the dishes were left alone. After 6 hours, the percent growth of *E. coli* bacteria was recorded (Table 1).

Table 1

Dish	pH level	Percent growth
1	6	34
2	7	84
3	8	26

Experiment 2

An *E. coli* bacterial colony was placed in each of three petri dishes containing different nutrient concentrations in the form of sugar compounds. The lids of the petri dishes were replaced and the dishes were left alone. After 6 hours, the percent growth of *E. coli* bacteria was recorded (Table 2).

Table 2

Dish	Organic compound	Percent of dry weight	Percent growth overall
1	Glucose Fructose Galactose	50 20 14	26
2	Glucose Fructose Galactose	25 10 7	14
3	Glucose Fructose Galactose	12.5 5 3.5	9

Experiment 3

An *E. coli* bacterial colony was placed in each of three petri dishes with one of three growth factors. Most bacteria, unlike *E. coli*, have two requirements for reproduction: growth factors to synthesize nucleic acids and proteins, and small amounts of different vitamins. Experiment 3 was conducted to ensure that the three growth factors had minimal to no effect on growth. The lids of the petri dishes were replaced and the dishes were left alone. After 6 hours, the percent growth of *E. coli* bacteria was recorded (Table 3).

Table 3

Dish	Growth factors	Percent growth
1	Purines	81
2	Amino acids	79
3	Vitamins	83

GO ON TO THE NEXT PAGE.

1. According to Table 1, what might best contribute to the growth of *E. coli* bacteria?
   A. A pH level above 8
   B. A pH level below 6
   C. A pH level near 7
   D. A pH level above 7

2. According to the results of the 3 experiments, *E. coli* bacteria is different from most bacteria in that:
   F. it does not require growth factors to reproduce.
   G. it does not reproduce if a light source is present.
   H. it does not reproduce if amino acids are not available.
   J. it requires a specific nutrient concentration to reproduce.

3. Which of the following conclusions is strengthened by the results of Experiment 1?
   A. *E. coli* bacteria reproduce most efficiently at a pH level of 7.
   B. *E. coli* bacteria cannot reproduce at a pH level below 8.
   C. *E. coli* bacteria cannot reproduce at a pH level above 6.
   D. *E. coli* bacteria can only reproduce if the pH level is near 7.

4. Bacteria will often reproduce until all of the nutrients available have been depleted. How could the experiment be altered to maximize the length of time that bacteria will reproduce?
   F. Change the observation time from 6 hours to 12 hours.
   G. Regularly resupply each group of bacteria with unlimited nutrients.
   H. Increase the rate of growth by decreasing the pH levels.
   J. Do not test the effect of different nutrient combinations on growth.

5. Which of the following statements is most likely true based on the results of Experiment 2?
   A. Lower levels of nutrient concentrations result in a higher growth percentage of *E. coli*.
   B. Higher levels of nutrient concentrations result in a lower growth percentage of *E. coli*.
   C. Higher levels of nutrient concentrations result in a higher growth percentage of *E. coli*.
   D. Nutrient concentration has no effect on the growth percentage of *E. coli*.

6. The experiments recorded the percent growth that occurred after a 6-hour period. Bacteria often reproduce at a rate that drastically varies from one stage to the next. The best way to study the different stages of growth would be to record the percent growth:
   F. after 2 hours only.
   G. after 4 hours, then again after 6 hours.
   H. after 8 hours only.
   J. every 15 minutes for 3 hours.

GO ON TO THE NEXT PAGE.

4   **4**

PASSAGE II

The San Francisco Bay Area in California has several fault lines that extend throughout the entire region. The Loma Prieta, the Bay Area's last major earthquake, occurred in 1989 along the San Andreas Fault. The Loma Prieta was centered in a mountainous region that was not heavily populated, unlike San Francisco, which lies only 50 miles south. Experts believe that accurate predictions will allow people in populated areas to take the necessary precautions to minimize earthquake damage. Two scientists discuss the probability of the next major earthquake powerful enough to cause widespread damage in the Bay Area.

Scientist 1

The probability of an earthquake occurring in a heavily populated area is extremely difficult to predict. After the massive earthquake of 1906, the rate of powerful, damaging earthquakes in the Bay Area dropped considerably, even though the area is covered with major fault lines. The probability of an earthquake is determined by considering two activities: tectonic plate motions of the Earth's outer shell and the pressure that is released during an earthquake. Global Positioning Systems (GPS) allow scientists to determine the amount of plate motion and the strain it loads onto faults, the first element of predicting quakes easily and with much certainty. The amount of strain, or pressure released, however, is much more difficult to estimate. Scientists currently inspect trenches, analyze data from seismograms, and use historical data to estimate the amount of strain that is released during an earthquake. The main problem is that historical accounts only date back to the 1900s, hardly long enough to illustrate a clear picture of quake activities. Therefore, predictions of the location and the magnitude of an earthquake cannot be made accurately.

Scientist 2

There is a high probability that a major quake will take place within the next 25 years in the Bay Area. Experts can forecast the location and magnitude of an earthquake with a compelling amount of certainty. The probability of an earthquake increases if the strain from plate motion outweighs the amount of pressure released during an actual earthquake. This analysis is complemented with findings from fault line research. The length of fault line ruptures and trenches speak volumes on the magnitude and fault slip of future earthquakes. The 1906 earthquake released over 25 feet of slip, enough to lessen strain in the entire area, thus reducing the frequency and intensity of earthquakes. Because of plate motion, however, strain has been slowly building up. At some point, the equation must balance out again. The only time fault strain is released is during an earthquake, and many populated areas in the Bay Area are near, or even sandwiched between, numerous major fault lines. A damaging earthquake in the near future is inevitable.

7. Which of the following best illustrates the major difference between the two scientists' opinions?
   A. The magnitude of the next earthquake
   B. The location of the next earthquake
   C. The fault line that will erupt
   D. The ability to predict the next earthquake

8. According to Scientist 1, when the probability of an earthquake is calculated, determining the amount of strain released, as compared to determining the strain loaded onto faults from plate motion is:
   F. just as difficult.
   G. more difficult.
   H. slightly less difficult.
   J. virtually impossible.

9. The opinion of Scientist 2 suggests that the strain on a fault increases when:
   A. more pressure is released.
   B. fault slip decreases.
   C. plates shift over time.
   D. the magnitude increases.

10. According to Scientist 1, which of the following statements best illustrates why an earthquake cannot be accurately predicted?
    F. The amount of tectonic plate motion has no influence on the amount of strain put on fault lines.
    G. The amount of strain released during earthquakes has not been recorded for a long enough period of time.
    H. No system is capable of tracking plate motion to an acceptable degree for predicting earthquakes.
    J. No system is capable of measuring the magnitude of an earthquake.

11. A handful of small earthquakes has been recorded in various mountainous regions during the past year. According to Scientist 2, the probability of a large earthquake occurring in those regions would:
    A. decrease because some of the strain was released.
    B. decrease because plate motion ceased.
    C. increase because fault slip would outweigh the strain.
    D. increase because strain has not built up.

GO ON TO THE NEXT PAGE.

12. With which of the following statements would both scientists most likely agree? The San Francisco Bay Area:

F. is not in danger of the possibility of an earthquake.

G. is not populated enough to worry about predicting the next earthquake.

H. has a higher chance of experiencing an earthquake than any other area.

J. has fault lines extending throughout the entire region.

13. The argument made by Scientist 2 would be *strengthened* by which of the following statements about earthquakes, if true?

A. A team of scientists in Ecuador predicts the occurrence of an earthquake near the coast that occurs within days of the date they estimated.

B. A scientist in Alaska announces that the last century's earthquake records are inaccurate and not applicable for current research.

C. An earthquake occurs in the eastern-Mediterranean Sea at a depth of 4.1 kilometers and a magnitude of 5.8.

D. The latest statistics show that the population of Oakland, California, has been slowly declining for the past 12 years.

GO ON TO THE NEXT PAGE.

4   **4**

PASSAGE III

A series of experiments performed by the Italian scientist Alessandro Volta disproved an earlier theory by Luigi Galvani that an electric current was dependent on the presence of animal tissue. Volta also discovered the means of converting chemical energy into electric energy, which is the basis for the modern battery.

Volta's research built from the earlier work of Luigi Galvani, who discovered *galvanism*, a direct electric current produced by chemical reactions. Galvani discovered this phenomenon when he stuck a copper hook through a dead frog and touched the frog's leg with a piece of iron. The dead frog's leg jerked as if it were alive. Galvani believed that an electric fluid present in animal tissue created this movement. Volta used the following experiments to disprove Galvani's theory that an electric fluid was creating the electric current.

Experiment 1

Volta experimented by putting two different metals on his tongue. He experienced pain and concluded that this pain meant that electricity was flowing.

Experiment 2

Volta submerged copper and zinc near each other in an inorganic acidic solution and noted an electrical interaction.

Experiment 3

Volta made a battery cell by placing paper soaked in electrolytes between two different metals and produced a consistent flow of electricity.

Experiment 4

Volta built piles using 30, 40, or 60 layers of metal and separated them with a piece of material dampened by an acid solution. Volta discovered that the intensity of the electric shock was greater when the piles contained 60 layers of metal rather than 30 or 40 layers.

14. Given the results of Experiment 1, which of the following statements best explains why this experiment did not disprove Galvani's earlier theory involving electric fluid?
    F. Galvani used more than 2 metals in his frog experiment to create an electric current.
    G. Volta's tongue is animal tissue and could have contained electric fluid.
    H. Galvani's frog was dead, so it could not feel pain to verify the presence of an electric current.
    J. The surface of Volta's tongue was moist and the dead frog's leg was not.

15. Which of the following was probably thought to be true in designing Experiment 1?
    A. Animal tissue was not needed to produce an electric current.
    B. Two metals were sufficient to produce an electric current.
    C. Pain was the most accurate way to measure the power of an electric current.
    D. A moist surface was not necessary to produce an electric current.

16. The data from this passage best supports the conclusion that:
    F. animal tissues do not contain any fluid that can be used to conduct an electric current.
    G. only copper and zinc will produce an electric current in inorganic solutions.
    H. Galvani did not discover that an electric current is produced by chemical reactions.
    J. more than two pieces or layers of metal can be used to produce an electric current.

17. Which of the following hypotheses is best supported by the results in Experiment 4?
    A. The larger the number of metal layers piled and separated by material dampened in an acidic solution, the greater the intensity of the electric shock.
    B. In order to produce an electric shock, an acidic solution is needed to create the electric current.
    C. The intensity of the electric shock is likely to be dependent on the weight of the individual elements used as well as the density of the elements.
    D. Certain elements create a greater electric shock when combined than others.

18. To test the hypothesis that an acidic solution is always needed to create an electric current, the researcher should determine:
    F. whether the type of acidic solution used in Volta's experiments is present in a dead frog's legs.
    G. whether the tongue and electrolytes contain an acidic solution.
    H. whether all acidic solutions are inorganic in origin.
    J. whether copper or zinc respond to different acidic solutions.

19. Which of the four experiments disproved Galvani's theory that a direct electric current is produced by chemical reactions?
    A. Experiments 2, 3, and 4, because they did not involve animal tissue.
    B. Experiment 1, because it involved living human tissue.
    C. None of the experiments necessarily disprove Galvani's theory that a direct electric current is produced by chemical reactions.
    D. Experiment 3, because Volta created a consistent flow of energy.

GO ON TO THE NEXT PAGE.

4   **4**

PASSAGE IV

A study was conducted to compare the accuracy of two commercially available swimming pool water testing kits (Kit A and Kit B) in determining the levels of chlorine, bromine, and pH in two different water samples. The water samples were kept at a constant temperature of 72°F throughout the entire study. The results include the ideal level or concentration of each chemical and the readings of each kit for two different 100 milliliter (ml) samples of water (Table 1).

Table 1

Chemical	Sample 1	Sample 2
Chlorine (in ppm)		
Ideal	1.0–3.0	1.0–3.0
Kit A	2.40	3.4
KitB	2.10	3.6
Bromine (in ppm)		
Ideal	2.0–4.0	2.0–4.0
Kit A	4.00	3.5
KitB	3.75	3.35
pH		
Ideal	7.4–7.6	7.4–7.6
Kit A	7.40	6.2
KitB	7.90	6.7

The pH scale measures how acidic or basic a substance is on a scale of 0 to 14. Lower numbers indicate increasing acidity, and higher numbers indicate increasing alkalinity (basicity). The ideal pH of a swimming pool is near 7.5. The minimum and maximum pH for a standard swimming pool are 7.2 and 7.8, respectively. Most residential swimming pools, however, have a tendency to drift toward a pH of 8.

The pH level of a sample of water has a tremendous impact on the effectiveness of chlorine. Chlorine is used to destroy contaminants and, at higher levels, is capable of having a bleaching effect on colors and a corrosive effect on surfaces. pH levels are tested using *phenol red*, a dark red powder that is added to a sample and will change the color of the water, depending on the pH. The effectiveness of chlorine at different pH is shown in Figure 1, as a percentage of chlorine's effectiveness at destroying harmful contaminants.

Figure 1

20. Which of the following statements best describes the effectiveness of the chlorine in Sample 2?
   F. The concentration of chlorine in Sample 2 is at an ideal level.
   G. The concentration of chlorine in Sample 2 may be corrosive to surfaces.
   H. The concentration of chlorine in Sample 2 is too weak to destroy contaminants.
   J. The Sample 2 reading of chlorine from Kit A was higher than the reading from Kit B.

21. Which of the following statements is best supported by the results of the study?
   A. The water in Sample 1 only has ideal levels of both chlorine and bromine.
   B. The water in Sample 2 only has ideal levels of both chlorine and bromine.
   C. The water in both Sample 1 and Sample 2 has ideal levels of both chlorine and bromine.
   D. The water in neither Sample 1 nor Sample 2 has ideal levels of both chlorine and bromine.

22. The readings from Kit A of Sample 1 indicate that:
   F. the water from Sample 1 is probably balanced and safe.
   G. the water from Sample 1 is probably harmful to swimmers.
   H. bromine levels are difficult to accurately measure.
   J. Kit B is inferior to Kit A in measuring pH.

23. Another water sample was tested using Kit B. The results indicate that the effectiveness of the chlorine in the sample was just above 80%. What is the estimated pH level of the water sample?
   A. 5.0
   B. 6.5
   C. 7.5
   D. 8.0

24. According to Figure 1, as pH increases:
   F. the presence of harmful contaminants is most likely low.
   G. the presence of harmful contaminants is most likely not affected.
   H. the presence of harmful contaminants is most likely high.
   J. the presence of harmful contaminants cannot be detected.

GO ON TO THE NEXT PAGE.

4   ○ ○   ○ **4**

PASSAGE V

The human body involves a system of many complex processes. For example, it has a specific process for meeting the energy demands of working muscles during exercise. The process by which food molecules (glucose) are broken down in the muscle cells to release energy for work is called *cellular respiration*. There are two types of cellular respiration: *aerobic* (requires oxygen) and anaerobic (does not require oxygen).

When the muscles are working, the body turns *adenosine diphosphate* (ADP) into *adenosine triphosphate* (ATP). ATP is then used as a source of energy, a requirement of muscle contraction. (ATP production is measured in *moles*, a specific unit of measurement.) Figure 1 shows the activity of the two biochemical processes that provide ATP as a function of the intensity of a workout.

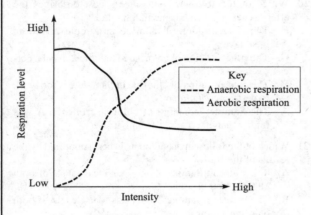

Figure 1

Aerobic respiration produces 18 times more ATP per glucose molecule than does anaerobic respiration. However, the process requires plenty of oxygen and is much more time consuming. Although anaerobic respiration is far less efficient, it is the fastest way to generate ATP. Table 1 shows the sources of glucose that are used during both types of respiration.

Table 1	
Source	**Process**
Liver	Glycogen is broken down into glucose and released into blood
Muscles	Glycogen breaks down into glucose
Intestine	Glycogen is absorbed from food, and transported in the blood
Non-glucose reserves	After glycogen stores are reduced, fatty acids are taken from fat stores; when these are depleted, proteins are used

An individual's fitness level can be determined by measuring the maximum amount of oxygen that can be used in 1 minute of activity per kilogram of body weight, also known as VO2 max. Figure 2 shows the milliliters of oxygen that can be consumed in 1 minute per kilogram of body weight for both females and males at "Poor" and "Excellent" fitness levels.

Figure 2

25. According to Figure 1, as a person's workout intensity increases:
    A. aerobic respiration only increases.
    B. aerobic respiration decreases, then increases sharply.
    C. anaerobic respiration increases, then levels off.
    D. anaerobic respiration decreases, then increases sharply.

26. If an athlete's body produced 2 moles of ATP from anaerobic respiration, how many moles of ATP would have been produced from the same amount of glucose during aerobic respiration?
    F. 36
    G. 34
    H. 18
    J. 16

27. According to the passage, once the glucose from stored glycogen is used, where does the body next obtain sources of energy?
    A. Small intestine
    B. Fat stores
    C. Muscles
    D. Protein

28. As compared to a 50-year-old male in excellent physical condition, a woman of the same age and fitness level consumes approximately how much less oxygen (in milliliters per minute per kilogram, ml/min/kg, body weight)?
    F. 0
    G. 12
    H. 33
    J. 45

29. A 27-year-old female in poor physical condition would consume between:
    A. 25 to 30 milliliters of oxygen per minute.
    B. 33 to 35 milliliters of oxygen per minute.
    C. 37 to 41 milliliters of oxygen per minute.
    D. 47 to 52 milliliters of oxygen per minute.

GO ON TO THE NEXT PAGE.

4   **4**

PASSAGE VI

Cholesterol is a soft, waxy compound that is found in many foods and throughout the entire human body. The body's liver produces cholesterol to form and maintain cell membranes, some hormones, and vitamin D. The liver is also responsible for eliminating cholesterol from the body. Excessive levels of cholesterol in the blood, however, can lead to health problems, including heart disease.

The dietary consumption of specific types of fats is a major factor influencing the levels of low-density lipoprotein cholesterol (LDL), or "bad" cholesterol, and high-density lipoprotein (HDL), or "good" cholesterol. The circulation of too much LDL cholesterol in the blood can lead to buildup in the arteries and subsequently, the development of heart disease. The presence of higher levels of HDL cholesterol helps to protect against the development of heart disease.

Table 1 shows specific types of fats and their effect on cholesterol levels.

Table 1

Type of fat	Effect on cholesterol	
	LDL	HDL
Monounsaturated	Decrease	Increase
Polyunsaturated	Decrease	Increase
Saturated	Increase	Increase
Trans	Increase	Decrease

30. Approximately 75% of the cholesterol in the blood is produced in the body. According to the passage, the remaining 25% of cholesterol that can be found in the blood comes from:
F. diet.
G. LDL.
H. genetics.
J. HDL.

31. If HDL protects against the development of heart disease, which of the following statements is most likely to be true?
A. HDL carries cholesterol to the liver where it can be eliminated.
B. HDL dissolves in the bloodstream and increases total cholesterol levels.
C. HDL becomes "bad" cholesterol after it enters the bloodstream.
D. HDL cholesterol cannot be affected by diet or any other risk factor.

32. According to the passage, which type of fat has the greatest negative net effect on cholesterol levels?
F. Monounsaturated fats
G. Polyunsaturated fats
H. Trans fats
J. Saturated fats

33. According to the following table, which type of cooking oil would most likely be suggested for a person with high cholesterol?

Oil	Saturated	Monounsaturated	Polyunsaturated	Trans
Canola	8	57	35	0
Palm	50	37	13	0
Coconut	87	8	5	0

A. Coconut oil, because it has the least amount of polyunsaturated fats.
B. Palm oil, because it has a good amount of both mono- and polyunsaturated fats.
C. Canola oil, because it has the least amount of saturated fats and a low amount of polyunsaturated fats.
D. Canola oil, because it has the least amount of saturated fats and the most unsaturated fats.

34. Omega-3 fatty acid (found in fish such as mackerel, salmon, sardines, or swordfish) is known for its potential to lower the risk of heart disease. Which of the following best explains why this statement may be true? Omega-3 fatty acid:
F. is a form of saturated fat that increases the levels of both HDL and LDL in the bloodstream.
G. is a form of monounsaturated fat that lowers the level of HDL and increases the level of LDL.
H. is a form of polyunsaturated fat that lowers the level of HDL and increases the level of LDL.
J. is a form of polyunsaturated fat that lowers the level of LDL and increases the level of HDL.

GO ON TO THE NEXT PAGE.

PASSAGE VII

Friction is the resistive force to motion. If an object is moving in one direction, friction is pulling in the opposite direction, allowing an object to stop moving or stay in place. Friction depends mostly on the smoothness of the surfaces that come into contact with an object and the magnitude of force (or weight) of one object on the other. A rough surface, for example, increases friction, making it more difficult for one object to slide over the other.

Some students conducted three experiments to test their hypotheses about the influence of surface material and speed on the force of friction. The students created a ramp and runway from different-sized blocks and two pieces of plywood (Figure 1). They used a toy car to test the effect of friction on the speed and distance that the car was able to travel, once it reached the flat surface. The same car was used in all of the experiments. The students changed the angle (or height) of the ramp in order to change the speed that the car could travel.

Figure 1

Experiment 1

The ramp in this experiment was placed at a 45° angle. The car was placed at the top of the ramp and released. A tape measure was used to determine the distance that the car traveled once it left the ramp until it stopped on different materials that covered the flat surface at the bottom of the ramp. For each material, the experiment was repeated three times and the results are shown in Table 1.

Table 1				
	Distance (in inches)			
Surface	**Trial 1**	**Trial 2**	**Trial 3**	**Avg**
Wax paper	42.00	40.50	43.50	42.00
Plywood	11.00	12.50	11.75	11.75
Carpet	4.25	5.00	5.25	4.83
Asphalt	22.00	23.50	21.75	22.42

Experiment 2

The experiment was repeated with the ramp placed at a 30° angle. The results are shown in Table 2.

Table 2				
	Distance (in inches)			
Surface	**Trial 1**	**Trial 2**	**Trial 3**	**Avg**
Wax paper	32.00	30.00	32.50	31.50
Plywood	7.00	7.50	7.25	7.25
Carpet	3.00	3.25	3.50	3.25
Asphalt	16.00	16.50	17.25	16.58

Experiment 3

The experiment was repeated with the ramp placed at a 15° angle. The results are shown in Table 3.

Table 3				
	Distance (in inches)			
Surface	**Trial 1**	**Trial 2**	**Trial 3**	**Avg**
Wax paper	18.00	20.75	19.75	19.50
Plywood	4.00	3.75	4.00	3.92
Carpet	1.75	2.25	2.00	2.00
Asphalt	10.25	12.75	11.50	11.50

35. In each experiment, the material used affected the force of friction and, as a result, the distance that the car traveled before it came to a stop. Based on the experiments, it is most likely that the stronger the friction, the:
    A. heavier the object as compared to the material.
    B. lighter the object as compared to the material.
    C. longer the distance the car could travel.
    D. shorter the distance the car could travel.

36. Using a smoother surface would most likely:
    F. both decrease friction and increase the distance traveled before the car came to a stop.
    G. both decrease friction and decrease the distance traveled before the car came to a stop.
    H. both increase friction and increase the distance traveled before the car came to a stop.
    J. both increase friction and decrease the distance traveled before the car came to a stop.

GO ON TO THE NEXT PAGE.

37. If each of the following materials was used, as in the experiments, to cover the flat surface at the bottom of the ramp, the friction exerted will likely be the least with which material?
A. Brick
B. Sand
C. Aluminum foil
D. Window screens

38. Which of the following statements best explains why lubricant or oil is used to decrease the friction between two objects?
F. It increases the magnitude of force on each object, making it harder to slide one object past the other.
G. It smoothes the surfaces of both objects, making it easier for one object to slide past the other.
H. It increases the gravitational pull on the objects, making it harder to slide one object past the other.
J. It decreases the weight of each object, making it easier to slide one object past the other.

39. Which variable was kept constant throughout all the experiments?
A. The mass of the car
B. The speed of the car
C. The surface material
D. The angle of the ramp

40. According to the results of the experiments, increasing the ramp's height increased the distance that the car could travel, regardless of the material used. Increasing the height of the ramp:
F. both decreased the speed of the car and increased friction.
G. both decreased the speed of the car and decreased friction.
H. both increased the speed of the car and increased the distance traveled before friction could stop it.
J. both increased the speed of the car and decreased the distance traveled before friction could stop it.

END OF THE SCIENCE TEST.
STOP! IF YOU HAVE TIME LEFT OVER, CHECK YOUR WORK ON THIS SECTION ONLY.

WRITING TEST

DIRECTIONS: This test is designed to assess your writing skills. You have forty (40) minutes to plan and write an essay based on the stimulus provided. Be sure to take a position on the issue and support your position using logical reasoning and relevant examples. Organize your ideas in a focused and logical way, and use the English language to clearly and effectively express your position.

When you have finished writing, refer to the Scoring Rubrics discussed in Chapter 7 to estimate your score.

Note: On the actual ACT you will receive approximately 2.5 pages of scratch paper on which to develop your essay, and approximately 4 pages of notebook paper on which to write your essay. We recommend that you limit yourself to this number of pages when you write your practice essays.

Playing Video Games

Once found only in arcades, video games are now a mainstay of at-home entertainment options for teens. In fact, teenagers have become quite adept at playing video games. One interesting development is that, on one hand, video games have been blamed for increasing violent tendencies in teens and, on the other hand, praised for improving problem solving skills in high school students. Given the potential controversy surrounding teenagers' playing of video games, it is worth examining the implications of the prevalence of video games in the daily lives of teenagers.

PERSPECTIVE ONE	PERSPECTIVE TWO	PERSPECTIVE THREE
Exposing young minds to violence, whether real or virtual, can have a negative impact on how young people view and interact with the world. Violent video games can set a precedent for bad behavior as teenagers mature.	The ability to "think on your feet" and solve problems is put to the test when trying to master a new video game. Teens have a chance to develop this highly transferable skill, which will serve them well in life.	As video games have become more prevalent, actual real-world violence in society has decreased. Millions of consumers of all ages continue to play violent video games and seem to be able to grasp the difference between the game and reality without becoming violent themselves.

Essay Task

Write a unified, coherent essay in which you evaluate multiple perspectives on the implications of teens playing video games. In your essay, be sure to:

- analyze and evaluate the perspectives given
- state and develop your own perspective on the issue
- explain the relationship between your perspective and those given

Your perspective may be in full agreement with any of the others, in partial agreement, or wholly different. Whatever the case, support your ideas with logical reasoning and detailed, persuasive examples.

ANSWER KEY

English Test

1. A	21. B	41. B	61. A
2. J	22. H	42. J	62. G
3. C	23. B	43. C	63. C
4. F	24. H	44. G	64. G
5. A	25. D	45. D	65. B
6. G	26. J	46. G	66. F
7. B	27. A	47. D	67. B
8. J	28. H	48. G	68. F
9. A	29. A	49. B	69. D
10. F	30. F	50. F	70. F
11. C	31. C	51. A	71. C
12. F	32. F	52. F	72. G
13. C	33. D	53. D	73. C
14. G	34. J	54. F	74. H
15. D	35. B	55. D	75. C
16. H	36. J	56. H	
17. D	37. D	57. B	
18. J	38. F	58. F	
19. A	39. B	59. C	
20. G	40. J	60. F	

Mathematics Test

1. B	21. B	41. E
2. G	22. J	42. J
3. A	23. B	43. C
4. K	24. H	44. F
5. C	25. E	45. C
6. K	26. G	46. J
7. D	27. B	47. B
8. F	28. J	48. H
9. C	29. D	49. B
10. J	30. H	50. H
11. A	31. B	51. E
12. H	32. K	52. G
13. D	33. C	53. C
14. G	34. F	54. K
15. A	35. B	55. A
16. H	36. H	56. F
17. D	37. D	57. A
18. G	38. G	58. K
19. A	39. D	59. C
20. G	40. K	60. K

Reading Test

1. A	21. B
2. H	22. J
3. A	23. C
4. G	24. J
5. D	25. A
6. G	26. G
7. B	27. D
8. F	28. H
9. A	29. B
10. J	30. F
11. B	31. D
12. G	32. J
13. D	33. C
14. H	34. J
15. C	35. A
16. F	36. G
17. C	37. C
18. F	38. H
19. A	39. C
20. J	40. G

Science Test

1. C	21. A
2. F	22. F
3. A	23. B
4. G	24. H
5. C	25. C
6. J	26. F
7. D	27. B
8. G	28. G
9. C	29. A
10. G	30. F
11. A	31. A
12. J	32. H
13. A	33. D
14. G	34. J
15. B	35. D
16. J	36. F
17. A	37. C
18. G	38. G
19. C	39. A
20. G	40. H

SCORING GUIDE

Your final reported score is your COMPOSITE SCORE. Your COMPOSITE SCORE is the average of all of your SCALE SCORES.

Your SCALE SCORES for the four multiple-choice sections are derived from the Scoring Worksheet on the next page. Use your RAW SCORE, or the number of questions that you answered correctly for each section, to determine your SCALE SCORE. If you got a RAW SCORE of 60 on the English Test, for example, you correctly answered 60 out of 75 questions.

Step 1 Determine your RAW SCORE for each of the four multiple-choice sections:

English   _____

Mathematics   _____

Reading   _____

Science   _____

The following Raw Score Table shows the total possible points for each section.

RAW SCORE TABLE	
KNOWLEDGE AND SKILL AREAS	RAW SCORES
ENGLISH	75
MATHEMATICS	60
READING	40
SCIENCE	40

Step 2 Determine your SCALE SCORE for each of the four multiple-choice sections using the following Scale Score Conversion Table.

SCALE SCORE	RAW SCORE			
	ENGLISH	MATHEMATICS	READING	SCIENCE
36	75	60	40	39–40
35	74	59	—	38
34	73	57–58	39	37
33	71–72	56	38	36
32	70	55	37	—
31	69	54	—	35
30	68	53	36	34
29	67	52	35	33
28	65–66	51–50	34	32
27	64	48–49	33	31
26	62–63	46–47	32	29–30
25	60–61	44–45	31	27–28
24	58–59	41–43	30	25–26
23	56–57	38–40	29	23–24
22	54–55	35–37	27–28	21–22
21	51–52	31–34	26	20
20	49–50	28–30	24–25	18–19
19	46–48	27	22–23	17
18	43–45	24–26	21	15–16
17	40–42	20–23	19–20	14
16	36–39	16–19	17–18	12–13
15	33–35	12–15	15–16	11
14	30–32	10–11	13–14	10
13	27–29	8–9	11–12	9
12	24–26	6–7	9–10	8
11	21–23	5	8	7
10	19–20	4	6–7	6
9	15–18	—	—	5
8	13–14	3	5	4
7	11–12	—	4	3
6	9–10	2	3	—
5	7–8	—	—	2
4	5–6	1	2	—
3	4	—	—	1
2	2–3	—	1	—
1	0–1	0	0	0

NOTE: Each actual ACT is scaled slightly differently based on a large amount of information gathered from the millions of tests ACT, Inc. scores each year. This scale will give you a fairly good idea of where you are in your preparation process. However, it should not be read as an absolute predictor of your actual ACT score. In fact, on practice tests, the scores are much less important than what you learn from analyzing your results.

If you take the optional Writing Test, you should refer to Chapter 7 for guidelines on scoring your Writing Test Essay.

Step 3 Determine your COMPOSITE SCORE by finding the sum of all your SCALE SCORES for each of the four sections: English, Mathematics, Reading, and Science, and divide by 4 to find the average. Round your COMPOSITE SCORE according to normal rules. For example, 31.2 ≈ 31 and 31.5 ≈ 32.

$$\frac{\quad\quad\quad\quad}{\substack{\text{ENGLISH} \\ \text{SCALE SCORE}}} + \frac{\quad\quad\quad\quad}{\substack{\text{MATHEMATICS} \\ \text{SCALE SCORE}}} + \frac{\quad\quad\quad\quad}{\substack{\text{READING} \\ \text{SCALE SCORE}}} + \frac{\quad\quad\quad\quad}{\substack{\text{SCIENCE} \\ \text{SCALE SCORE}}} = \frac{\quad\quad\quad\quad}{\substack{\text{SCALE SCORE} \\ \text{TOTAL}}}$$

$$\frac{\quad\quad\quad\quad}{\text{SCALE SCORE TOTAL}} \div \;4\; = \frac{\quad\quad\quad\quad}{\text{COMPOSITE SCORE}}$$

ANSWERS AND EXPLANATIONS

English Test Explanations

PASSAGE I

1. **The best answer is A.** Answer choices B, C, and D can be eliminated because of incorrect comma usage. Answer choice B separates the noun *result* from its complement, the prepositional phrase *of ingenuity*. Answer choice C separates the preposition *of* from its object, *ingenuity*. Answer choice D includes an unnecessary comma after *of*.

2. **The best answer is J.** *Charles Lindbergh* is the logical subject of this sentence and should, therefore, be the grammatical subject. The sentence as written, with the gerund *being* before *Charles Lindbergh*, is awkward grammatically and unclear in meaning. Eliminate answer choice F. Answer choice G can be eliminated because it uses the subject pronoun *he* when *Charles Lindbergh* already serves that purpose. Finally, answer choice H can be eliminated because the relative pronoun *which* and the verb *was* would be highly awkward in this position in the sentence.

3. **The best answer is C.** Neither of the introductory prepositional phrases *In 1918* and *with the United States in the throes of World War I* contains a verb, so the main clause begins after these phrases set apart by a comma. Eliminate answer choice B. Answer choices A and D can be eliminated for their awkwardness and wordiness. Answer choice C represents the clearest and most concise answer choice.

4. **The best answer is F.** It is idiomatic to say "under his care."

5. **The best answer is A.** This sentence requires the verb phrase "to study."

6. **The best answer is G.** As written, this sentence is incomplete because it lacks a main verb. Eliminate answer choices F, H, and J because they do not provide a main verb. Only answer choice G contains a verb with tense, the simple past verb, *resulted*.

7. **The best answer is B.** The phrase *in pursuit of a degree* is obvious information considering Lindbergh *dropped out of college*. (You must finish college to earn a degree.) Therefore, eliminate answer choice A. Answer choices C and D are redundant in the same way, and can therefore be eliminated.

8. **The best answer is J.** No punctuation should separate the gerund *performing* from its complement *as a barnstormer, wing walker, parachutist, and skydiver*. Remember that colons and semicolons, in particular, have very specific usages. They should not interrupt the flow of a phrase.

9. **The best answer is A.** The introductory clause *Having found his true passion as a pilot* should be joined to the main clause with a comma.

10. **The best answer is F.** To maintain parallel structure within this sentence, the verb *focused* should agree in tense with the verb *learned*. As this is the case, no change is necessary.

11. **The best answer is C.** This question requires you to choose the most concise answer choice. Although all the answer choices are grammatically correct, answer choice C expresses the meaning in the shortest and clearest way. In addition, using the subject pronoun *he* is appropriate because Lindbergh's name is used in the preceding sentence.

12. **The best answer is F.** *Despite* properly indicates the apparent contradiction between *disinterest in formal education* and *enjoyment of learning*.

13. **The best answer is C.** To describe the manner in which *Lindbergh displayed an enjoyment of learning throughout his life*, the gerund form of the verb is appropriate. Furthermore, the two verbs joined with the conjunction *and* must have parallel form. Therefore, only answer choice C is appropriate here.

14. **The best answer is G.** This question tests your ability to arrange phrases in the clearest order. In this case, the prepositional phrase *with surgeon Alexis Carrel* best modifies the noun *work* and not *development* or *perfusion pump*. The prepositional phrase should immediately follow what it modifies. Therefore, you can eliminate answer choices F and H. Answer choice J is wordy, awkward, and has incorrect meaning, so it can also be eliminated.

15. **The best answer is D.** The focus of the passage is on Lindbergh's intellectual growth and the untraditional ways in which he trained and used his intelligence. Only choice D sums up this message and provides an appropriate conclusion to the essay.

PASSAGE II

16. **The best answer is H.** The second sentence contains a contrast to what comes before. That is, the first sentence says Vikings were crude; the second appears to contradict that by saying they were advanced. The word *however* is the only choice to signal this contrast.

17. **The best answer is D.** Because the new sentence would follow an assertion that the Vikings were advanced, the logical choice would contain an example of some sort of accomplishment. Answer choice D is one such accomplishment, and it mirrors the next sentence, which elaborates on the Vikings' oceangoing superiority compared to *other European cultures even centuries later*, of which Christopher Columbus was a part.

18. **The best answer is J.** The adjective *seafaring* modifies the noun *traders*, so no comma must come between the two words. Eliminate answer choice F. The colon has very specific usages, and cannot be used in this position between a noun (*traders*) and a prepositional phrase (*with … ships*) that modifies it. Eliminate answer choice G. Answer choice H can be eliminated because no comma should separate a preposition (*with*) from its object (*purpose-built, wooden trading ships*).

19. **The best answer is A.** The sentence as it is written is the most concise statement of the information. Therefore, no change is necessary.

20. **The best answer is G.** Use the adjective "much" to modify the noun phrase "shorter distance."

21. **The best answer is B.** The first step in answering this question is to recognize that you must use the possessive determiner *their*, not the contraction of *they are*. Eliminate answer choice D. The phrase "Regardless of whether Vikings arrived first" is not an independent clause. Therefore, it cannot be separated from the rest of the sentence by a semicolon. A colon would be used if what followed were an example or a list. Since it's not, a comma is the only punctuation necessary.

22. **The best answer is H.** It is idiomatic to say *sailed around, sailed over, sailed across*, and *sailed on* the sea in this context. It is not appropriate to say the Vikings *sailed into* the sea to obtain goods.

23. **The best answer is B.** In order to maintain parallel structure, the tense of *meet* has to match the tense of its paired verb, *trade*. Here, the author tells you that, in the past, Vikings traded often with Arabs. Since *met* is the past tense of *meet*, answer choice B is correct.

24. **The best answer is H.** Although all the answer choices have at least some merit, only answer choice H suits the rest of the paragraph. Moreover, the next sentence begins: *Similar craftsmanship* …. Therefore, the underlined portion should speak to the craftsmanship exhibited in Viking sword and ax blades. Answer choice H contains the most specific details about the fineness of the blades.

25. **The best answer is D.** The phrase beginning *Making butter* … is not a complete sentence; it lacks a verb with tense. Therefore, you should not use any form of end punctuation before that phrase. It is appropriate to use a comma.

26. **The best answer is J.** The information included in answer choices F, G, and H is irrelevant. There is no need to further discuss fabrics—it will not add any useful information to the passage.

27. **The best answer is A.** The subject of this clause is *those who could*, which means *those who could read*. It is important to recognize that this whole noun phrase is the subject, and that *could* does not affect the verb that follows. Because the subject is plural and "receives" the action of the verb *consider*, the plural passive-voice construction *were considered* is the best answer.

28. **The best answer is H.** Like periods, semicolons are used to separate independent clauses. *These runes* is not an independent clause. Therefore, the semicolon should be removed. *These runes* is the subject of the sentence and *were* is the verb. So, no punctuation should come between them.

29. **The best answer is A.** In order to maintain parallel structure within the paragraph, this verb needs to be in the simple past tense. It also needs to be plural because the subject, *runes*, is plural. The plural simple past tense of *to be* is *were*. Note that the other main verbs are also in the simple past tense: *was, were, believed, wrote*, and so on.

30. **The best answer is F.** The information given in answer choice F directly reflects the information provided in the third paragraph. Answer choice G is too vague. Answer choice H contradicts information in the last paragraph (the Vikings wrote down little of their history). Answer choice J is not mentioned in the passage.

PASSAGE III

31. **The best answer is C.** It is idiomatic in this context to say *against*.

32. **The best answer is F.** The sentence as written is concise and grammatically correct. No change is needed.

33. **The best answer is D.** The sentence already has a main verb, *make*. Therefore, additional verbs, like *has* or *is* in *She's* and *It's*, are unnecessary.

34. **The best answer is J.** If two related independent clauses are linked by a coordinating conjunction (in this case *and*), a comma is used before the conjunction. The connecting words *so* and *with* are not appropriate.

35. The best answer is B. To answer this question correctly, look ahead to the next paragraph to see what direction the essay is going to take. In this case, the author shifts from a description of Kari to a description of the Girls State convention. Answer choice B not only provides an introduction to the idea of Girls State, but it links Kari to it through her participation in the convention. Answer choice B is an effective transitional sentence.

36. The best answer is J. In English idiom, the noun *opportunity* takes a verb in the infinitive (to + base form) form as its complement (*opportunity to eat / dance / sing / participate / etc.*). It does not take a prepositional phrase as in answer choices F, G, and H.

37. The best answer is D. Answer choices A and C can be eliminated because they would place a comma between the verb phrase *was chosen* and its complement *to be one of her state's senators*. Similarly, answer choice B can be eliminated because the colon cannot interrupt a clause in that way. Besides not having punctuation after *chosen*, answer choice D is best because it correctly sets apart the interrupting phrase *of course* from the passive verb construction *was chosen* using commas.

38. The best answer is F. After the definite determiner *the*, a singular or plural noun phrase may be used. Together, they form the subject of the verb that comes next. In answer choice F, *schedule* and *was* are both singular.

39. The best answer is B. To describe a completed action in the past (meeting a cadet) that interrupted another action (sightseeing), the appropriate sequence of tenses (in either order) is the simple past, which describes completed events, and the past perfect progressive, which emphasizes the duration of an event that was interrupted in the past. Answer choices A and C do not follow this sequence of tenses and, therefore, make the sentence awkward. Answer choice D has a slight difference in meaning (suggesting that perhaps the meeting was planned), and it is not as concise as answer choice B, so eliminate it.

40. The best answer is J. The sentence has the relative subject pronoun *who* beginning the relative clause modifying *cadet*, so it is appropriate to use a comma after *cadet*. No punctuation should be used between the subject *who* and the verb *offered*, so eliminate answer choice G. Similarly, no punctuation should come between the verb *offered* and its complement beginning *to show*; therefore, eliminate answer choices F and H.

41. The best answer is B. Between the similar answer choices A and B, answer choice B is best because the

plural verb *promise* agrees with the plural antecedent *people* of the relative subject pronoun *who*. Answer choice C can be eliminated for wordiness. Answer choice D is awkward in structure and meaning, so it can be eliminated.

42. The best answer is J. Roman numeral II is easy to eliminate; words are italicized to emphasize their significance, not insignificance. Therefore, eliminate answer choice H. Roman numeral I is more subtle, but Sentence 5 makes a distinction between what Kari told her friend and what she told the cadet in the other letter. Roman numeral I makes sense, so eliminate answer choice G. The italics indicate that something significant has been communicated. You can assume (and it turns out to be the case) that this information is significant to what comes next, so Roman numeral III also makes sense.

43. The best answer is C. The first half of the paragraph focuses on Kari's letter to her girlfriend. At Sentence 6, however, the author begins to talk about Kari's letter to the cadet and his response to what he actually received. This shift in focus marks the most appropriate place to begin a new paragraph.

44. The best answer is G. The main idea of this essay is a description of an extremely popular girl who, every now and again, gets in trouble despite herself. Answer choice G reminds the reader that Kari is very popular, while still acknowledging that not everyone feels positively about her. It also says this in a lighthearted way. The other answer choices don't sum up the essay and are much more serious in tone.

45. The best answer is D. The essay reflects the author's personal reminiscence of a cousin, Kari, and includes details about certain events in Kari's life. While the essay mentions Girls State, it is not the main focus of the essay. Therefore, eliminate the two *yes* answer choices, A and B. Answer choice C can be eliminated because the passage does indeed show how Girls State provides opportunities to high school juniors. The focus of the passage is the writer's cousin Kari. Therefore, answer choice D is best.

PASSAGE IV

46. The best answer is G. Commas are used to separate adjectives in a list like this one. However, a comma must not separate the verb *be* from the predicate. Only answer choice G is correct.

47. The best answer is D. The sentence as it is written lacks a main clause, and thus is incomplete. Answer choice D puts the main idea of the sentence first ("I grew up on a farm in Iowa"). The descriptive clause follows, giving additional information. This order is the most concise and logical of any of the answer choices.

48. **The best answer is G.** The verb phrase after the comma (*and took great pains …*) is not an independent clause, meaning it could not stand on its own as a complete sentence. Therefore, a comma should not be used to separate it from the preceding clause.

49. **The best answer is B.** Answer choices A and D (*Therefore and Hence*) indicate that the following sentence is a result of what's come before. In this case, the sentences are not connected causally, so neither answer choice is correct. Also, the last sentence of the paragraph is not a restatement of the previous sentences. Therefore, answer choice C is incorrect. Answer choice B, however, implies that a change has occurred and that this will be significant later in the essay. This implication best matches the sense of the essay.

50. **The best answer is F.** It is idiomatic in this context to say that genetic engineering had been *applied in the field of agriculture* to fully explain why corn stalks now produce two ears of corn instead of one.

51. **The best answer is A.** Answer choice A is written in the active voice, which means that the subject is the one performing the action of the verb. The active voice is almost always better than the passive voice. Answer choice B is also in the active voice, but it has non-standard word order and unnecessary commas.

52. **The best answer is F.** The sentence as it is written is clear and concise. The other answer choices are wordy.

53. **The best answer is D.** The word "envisioned" means "to picture mentally." Because Clint actually saw the cornfield, "envisioned" does not fit the context.

54. **The best answer is F.** Clint's next words refer to gambling—he bets his friends ten dollars based on information given to him by the author. While the information itself is about corn, the implication is that he wouldn't bet ten dollars on that information if he was not sure he would win. Only answer choice F contains this implication.

55. **The best answer is D.** The idiom *on the other hand* is an interrupting phrase, so it must be set apart with commas. Only answer choice D does this correctly.

56. **The best answer is H.** The directions require you to select the answer choice that expresses the idea most clearly and simply. Answer choices F, G, and J are awkward and should be eliminated.

57. **The best answer is B.** Since the gerund *reminding* is associated with Clint, it is correct to use the possessive determiner *his*. The other answer choices are awkward and do not convey the clear meaning of the sentence.

58. **The best answer is F.** Paragraph 6 discusses the bet about the ear of corn that Clint made with his friends. Therefore, it makes sense that Clint challenged his friends because he enjoys making small bets with them. The other answer choices are not specifically supported by the passage.

59. **The best answer is C.** The first sentence in Paragraph 4 includes mention of the author "sharing occasional anecdotes and bits of trivia." It seems most appropriate to insert a sentence here that gives more information about the stories that the author tells. The sentence does not make sense placed elsewhere in the passage.

60. **The best answer is F.** The passage is about making untrue statements and having a difficult time living them down. The passage is not about genetic engineering, so eliminate answer choices H and J. Answer choice F is supported by Paragraph 2.

PASSAGE V

61. **The best answer is A.** It is idiomatic in this context to say *interfered with* to suggest that the author could not take a job that would not allow her to attend classes.

62. **The best answer is G.** In order to maintain parallel structure, pronoun use must be consistent. The rest of the paragraph is in the first-person singular; that is, the story is told from the point of view of the narrator, using the pronoun *I*.

63. **The best answer is C.** Signs, *flyers*, sheets of paper, and so on are *posted*, meaning attached to some vertical surface such as a wall. Answer choice C uses this adjective clearly.

64. **The best answer is G.** The underlined pronoun in this sentence refers back to the noun *opportunities*. Because *opportunities* is plural, its pronoun must be plural, too. Therefore, the pronoun *they* is correct.

65. **The best answer is B.** The focus of the paragraph is how the author found her job. The actual amount of the stipend is irrelevant and should be deleted.

66. **The best answer is F.** Use "because" to indicate the causal relationship. It is not necessary to use a comma.

67. **The best answer is B.** A comma is the simplest punctuation to use here. Eliminate answer choice A because semicolons divide only independent clauses. Eliminate answer choice C because colons can introduce descriptive detail or a list, neither of which is the case here. Eliminate answer choice D because the phrase beginning with *Not* lacks a verb and is thus not a complete sentence.

68. **The best answer is F.** The noun *subjects* refers to the people on which the experiment is being performed. Eliminate answer choices H, which uses the singular noun *subject*, and J, which uses the adjective *subjective*. Of answer choices F and G, only answer choice F is idiomatic, using the correct pronoun *of*.

69. **The best answer is D.** In order to maintain parallel structure, the verb forms must be consistent. In this sentence, the author *read* (a past tense) to the subjects, therefore she must have *provided* (also past tense) varying levels of feedback. Answer choice B is also in the past tense, but it is in the passive voice, which is not consistent with the rest of the sentence.

70. **The best answer is F.** The underlined portion is correct as written. It clearly indicates the contrast between the first and second clauses of the sentence. Omitting the underlined portion creates a comma splice.

71. **The best answer is C.** In this example, *verbal* and *nonverbal* are adjectives modifying the noun *responses*. Because there are only two of them, there is no need to separate them by using commas.

72. **The best answer is G.** The question asks you to find a phrase that would explain why the author would like to continue her work. This implies something positive, like answer choice G ("fascinating and fun"). Answer choices F and J are clearly negative, and the author has already stated that answer choice H, babysitting, is underpaid. Eliminate these answer choices.

73. **The best answer is C.** Sentence 3 describes the end of the experiments. The subject, *experiments*, is obviously plural—this gives us a clue for its proper placement. The paragraph still makes logical sense with Sentence 3 in this new position.

74. **The best answer is H.** This question asks that you identify the main idea of the essay. The main idea is indicated at the end of the first paragraph: a description of "the perfect part-time job." Since this is the case, the additional sentence does not belong anywhere in the passage because it does not contribute meaningful information to the essay. Eliminate answer choices F and G. Answer choice H is the best selection because it responds to the main idea of the passage.

75. **The best answer is C.** This question also relies on identifying the main idea of the essay. The main idea is stated at the end of the first paragraph: a description of "the perfect part-time job." The author's perfect job is in psychology, not sociology. In fact, there is no indication that the author is even a sociology major. Therefore, the essay would not be appropriate for the magazine article because its content is off-topic.

Mathematics Test Explanations

1. **The correct answer is B.** This is a basic Algebra problem that requires you to solve for x. Isolate the variable, x, on one side of the equation, as follows:

$$2x + 5 = 17$$
$$2x = 12$$
$$x = \frac{12}{2} = 6$$

2. **The correct answer is G.** The best way to answer this question is to look at the answer choices given and decide whether each choice is true, based on the 3 statements, or false because it contradicts 1 or more of the 3 statements.

   Answer choice G states that Horse B is brown. Since you know that Horse B also runs fast, and that all horses that run fast are brown, answer choice G must be true, and, therefore is the correct answer.

3. **The correct answer is A.** To solve this problem, find the difference between $x - 2$ and $x + 5$, as follows:

$$(x + 5) - (x - 2)$$
$$= x - x + 5 - (-2)$$
$$= 7$$

4. **The correct answer is K.** To solve this problem, substitute 15 for b in the equation:

$$4(15) - 30$$
$$= 60 - 30$$
$$= 30$$

5. **The correct answer is C.** The price of the carton of soda is currently $6.60, but will be reduced by 20% when it goes on sale. The decimal form of 20% is .20. In order to find the sale price, perform the following operations:

$6.60 (original price)
× .20 (discount percent)
$1.32 (discount amount)

$6.60 (original price)
−$1.32 (discount amount)
$5.28 (sale price)

6. **The correct answer is K.** To find the value of a and b, first find the square root of 64 and 81. Since a negative number squared results in a positive number, consider both the negative and positive values:

$$\sqrt{64} = 8 \text{ or } -8 \text{ and } \sqrt{81} = 9 \text{ or } -9$$

Find all of the possibilities for $a + b$: $-8 + -9 = -17$, $8 + -9 = -1$, $-8 + 9 = 1$, and $8 + 9 = 17$. This means that 145 is NOT a value of $a + b$, so answer choice K is correct.

7. **The correct answer is D.** Triangle BEF is an isosceles triangle with 2 congruent sides, $\overline{BE}$ and $\overline{BF}$, and 2 angles with equal measure, BFE and BEF. $\overline{BF}$ is also the transversal between 2 parallel lines, $\overline{AC}$ and $\overline{DG}$, making angles CBF and BFE alternate interior angles, which are congruent. By definition, if angle CBF is 40°, angle BFE is also 40°. Since there are 180° in a line, angle BFG must equal 180°−40°, or 140°.

8. **The correct answer is F.** Simply substitute −3 for x wherever x appears in the equation and solve the equation. Don't forget to keep track of the negative signs!

$$(-3)^2 - 6(-3) - 18$$
$$= (9) - (-18) - 18$$
$$= 9 + 18 - 18$$
$$= 9 + 0$$
$$= 9$$

9. **The correct answer is C.** In order to solve this problem, you must first substitute the number 12 for the a in $|1 - a|$, so that you get $|1 - 12|$. Then, perform the operation within the vertical lines to get $|-11|$. Since you must disregard the negative sign in order to determine absolute value, the absolute value of −11 is 11.

10. **The correct answer is J.** To solve this problem, substitute kb for c in the first equation and solve for k:

$$ab = kb$$
$$\frac{ab}{b} = k$$
$$a = k$$

11. **The correct answer is A.** According to the law of exponents, $(x^a)^b = x^{(a \times b)}$. So, $(x^3)^{13}$ is equal to $x^{(3 \times 13)}$, or x^{39}.

12. **The correct answer is H.** The easiest way to solve this problem is to plug the answer choices into the inequality and solve. Because the question asks you for the largest possible value of x, start with the largest answer choice (note that the answer choices are in ascending order):

$$\frac{2}{28} \geq \frac{1}{7}; \frac{2}{28} = \frac{1}{14},$$ which is less than $\frac{1}{7}$, so eliminate answer choice K.

Try the next largest number:

$\frac{2}{15} \geq \frac{1}{7}$; $\frac{2}{15} = \frac{1}{7.5}$, which is less than $\frac{1}{7}$, so eliminate answer choice J.

Try the next largest number:

$\frac{2}{14} \geq \frac{1}{7}$; $\frac{2}{14} = \frac{1}{7}$

This satisfies the inequality and is the largest remaining answer choice, so answer choice H must be correct.

13. **The correct answer is D.** There are 360 degrees in a circle. To calculate the number of degrees in 5 of the 12 sectors, perform the following operations:

$360° \div 12 = 30°$. Each sector is equivalent to $30°$.

$30° \times 5$ (the number of sectors) $= 150°$

14. **The correct answer is G.** To solve this problem, calculate the average by first finding the total number of students who entered through the main entrance that week:

$(450 + 427 + 462 + 433 + 398) = 2{,}170$

Next, divide by the number of school days:

$2{,}170 \div 5 = 434$

15. **The correct answer is A.** To solve this problem, set each element of the equations in the answer choices equal to 0 and solve for x, starting with answer choice A:

$(x - 6) = 0$; $x = 6$

$(x + 3) = 0$; $x = -3$

Since this equation has solutions of 6 and -3, answer choice A is correct.

16. **The correct answer is H.** This problem requires you to solve for x. Perform the operations and simplify as much as possible:

First, distribute the -2 to get $-2(x - 10) = -2x - (-20)$; this simplifies to $-2x + 20$.

Then, add the 7 back in to get $7 + (-2x) + 20$, or $-2x + 27$.

17. **The correct answer is D.** The first step in selecting the correct answer to this problem is to recognize that x cannot be less than 90. This means that answer choices A, B, and C can be eliminated. Set up a proportion to calculate the correct answer:

90 is to x as 60% is to 100%.

$\frac{90}{x} = \frac{60}{100}$; cross-multiply and solve for x.

$60x = 9{,}000$

$x = 150$

18. **The correct answer is G.** To solve this problem, calculate the price of 1 box of popcorn and subtract it from the price of 1 box of popcorn and 1 drink.

$8.35 (2 boxes and 1 drink) $-$ \$5.10 (1 box and 1 drink) = \$3.25 (1 box of popcorn)

$5.10 (1 box and 1 drink) $-$ \$3.25 (1 box of popcorn) = \$1.85

The price of 1 drink is \$1.85.

19. **The correct answer is A.** In order to solve this problem you must first calculate the total cost of the lamps, including tax. Since the sales tax is 7%, multiply the price of the 2 lamps ($8.99 $\times$ 2) by 0.07, the decimal equivalent of 7%:

$8.99 \times 2 = \$17.98$

$17.98 \times 0.07 = \$1.2586$

$1.2586 rounded to the nearest cent is \$1.26.

Now, add the sales tax to the price of the lamps:

$17.98 + \$1.26 = \$19.24$

Based on these calculations, you will need \$0.24 in exact change.

20. **The correct answer is G.** To solve this problem, find the cube root of 343, then multiply it by 3:

$r^3 = 343$

$r = 7$

$3r = 21$

You could have quickly eliminated answer choice J because it is too large. Cubing a number typically results in a value greater than the value obtained when multiplying the number by 3. Likewise, you could have eliminated answer choices F and H, because neither 7 nor 49 is divisible by 3.

21. **The correct answer is B.** In order to solve this problem you must know that π is approximately equal to 3.14. The next step is to find the value of the fractions $\frac{7}{3}$ and $\frac{9}{2}$. To do this, divide the numerators by the denominators: $7 \div 3 = 2.33$ and $9 \div 2 = 4.5$. Now, put the values in order from least to greatest: $2.33 < 3.14 < 4.5$, or $\frac{7}{3} < \pi < \frac{9}{2}$.

22. **The correct answer is J.** The question can be solved using the following equation: $\frac{9+x}{13+x} = \frac{3}{4}$.
Cross-multiply to get $4(9+x) = 3(13+x)$. Solve for x:

$$4(9+x) = 3(13+x)$$

$$36+4x = 39+3x$$

$$4x-3x = 39-36$$

$$x = 3$$

23. **The correct answer is B.** The slope of a line is the rise of the line over the run of the line (rise/run). Rise represents the change in y, and run represents the change in x. Two points on the line are given: (5,4) and (2, –7). The y values are 4 and –7, so the change in y is $4 - (-7)$, or 4 + 7, which is 11. The x values are 5 and 2, so the change in x is 5 – 2, or 3. The slope is $\frac{11}{3}$.

24. **The correct answer is H.** To solve this problem, list the prime factors for both 38 and 100:

    Prime factors of 38: 1, 2, 19

    The largest prime factor of 38 (p) is 19, so the correct answer must be greater than 19; eliminate answer choices F and G.

    Prime factors of 100: 1, 2, 5

    The largest prime factor of 100 (f) is 5, so $p+f = 19+5 = 24$.

25. **The correct answer is E.** The key to solving this problem is to recognize that, if $(t+v)^2 = 289$, then $t+v$ must equal 17, because 17^2 equals 289. Now, since you are given that $tv = 30$, you need to find 2 numbers that, when added together give you 17, and when multiplied together give you 30. The only 2 numbers that will satisfy both operations are 15 and 2. Substitute 15 for t and 2 for v in the final equation:

$$15^2 + 2^2$$

$$225 + 4 = 229$$

26. **The correct answer is G.** When exponents are raised to an exponential power, the rules state that you must multiply the exponents by the power to which they are raised. In this problem, x is raised to the $(3a + 5)$ power. This exponent is then raised to the fourth power, so you should multiply $3a + 5$ by 4: $4(3a+5) = 12a+20$. You now have the equation $x^{12a+20} = x^{44}$.

Since the bases are equal (x), the exponents must also be equal, so $12a + 20 = 44$. Solve for a:

$$12a + 20 = 44$$

$$12a = 24$$

$$a = \frac{24}{12} = 2$$

27. **The correct answer is B.** Logarithms are used to indicate exponents of certain numbers called bases. This problem tells you that log to the base x of 16 equals 2. By definition, $\log_a b = c$, if $a^c = b$. So $\log_x 16 = 2$ when $x^2 = 16$. Since the square root of 16 is 4, answer choice B is correct.

28. **The correct answer is J.** To solve this problem you can use the Midpoint Formula. The midpoint of a line, M, is equal to the average of the x-coordinates and the average of the y-coordinates. The formula looks like this:

$$M = \left(\frac{x_1 + x_2}{2}, \frac{y_1 + y_2}{2} \right)$$

You are given 1 point on the line, (–2, 9) and the midpoint of the line (4, 4). Since the midpoint is (4, 4) the average of the x-coordinates is 4, and the average of the y-coordinates is 4. Set up equations to solve for the other endpoint:

$$4 = \frac{-2 + x_2}{2}$$

$$8 = -2 + x_2$$

$$10 = x_2$$

The x-coordinate of the other endpoint is 10. Since only answer choice J includes an x-coordinate of 10, it must be the correct answer. If you solve for the y-coordinate in the same way that you solved for the x-coordinate, you will get $y = -1$.

29. **The correct answer is D.** A circle centered at (a, b) with a radius r, has the equation $(x-a)^2 + (y-b)^2 = r^2$. Based on this definition, a circle with the equation $(x-4)^2 + (y+1)^2 = 14$ would have a radius of $\sqrt{14}$. If $r^2 = 14$, then $r = \sqrt{14}$.

30. **The correct answer is H.** The cosine of any angle is calculated by dividing the length of the side adjacent to the acute angle by the hypotenuse $\left(\cos = \frac{\text{adj}}{\text{hyp}} \right)$,

so the cos $\angle A = \dfrac{12}{x}$. To find the length of the hypotenuse, use the Pythagorean Theorem, $a^2 + b^2 = c^2$:

$$12^2 + 5^2 = c^2$$

$$144 + 25 = 169 = c^2$$

$$\sqrt{169} = \sqrt{c^2}, \text{ so } c = 13$$

The cos of $\angle A = \dfrac{12}{13}$.

31. **The correct answer is B.** You should think of this problem as a basic fraction, where $(13a^2b^4)(-8a^3b^5)$ is the numerator and $(4a^2b^6)$ is the denominator. The first step is to multiply together the 2 elements in the numerator, as follows:

> When multiplying exponents, the rules state that you should add exponents with like bases, so $(13a^2b^4)(-8a^3b^5) = -104a^5b^9$.

To solve a fraction, you simply divide the numerator by the denominator.

> When dividing exponents, the rules state that you should subtract exponents of the same bases in the denominator from the exponents of the same bases in the numerator, so $-104a^5b^9 \div (4a^2b^6) = -26a^3b^3$.

32. **The correct answer is K.** By definition, a right isosceles triangle has 2 sides of equal length, and the hypotenuse is equal to $\sqrt{2}$ times the length of either of the sides (only for a right isosceles triangle). Therefore, a right isosceles triangle could have side lengths equal to 2, 2, and $2\sqrt{2}$, answer choice K.

33. **The correct answer is C.** In the point-slope form of a line, $y = mx + b$, b is the y-intercept. The first step in solving this problem is to put the equation in the point-slope form, as follows:

$$3x + 7y - 2 = 0$$

$$7y = -3x + 2$$

$$y = -\dfrac{3x}{7} + \dfrac{2}{7}$$

As you can see, the y-intercept is $\dfrac{2}{7}$.

34. **The correct answer is F.** According to the graph shown, the number -4 is included, but the number 6 is not included. This means that x must be greater than or equal to -4 ($x \geq -4$) and/or x must be less than 6 ($x < 6$). Since the sets overlap on the graph, the correct answer is $x \geq -4$ and $x < 6$.

35. **The correct answer is B.** You are given that the figure is drawn to scale, so you know that if the square

shown had a bottom, it would also be 6 units (see figure below):

You also know that the angles created by drawing the bottom of the square must be 60° because they are complementary to the 30° shown. Because there are 180° in a triangle, the top angle must also be 60°, thereby creating an equilateral triangle. An equilateral triangle has congruent sides, which means that each side measures 6 units, and the perimeter of the original figure is $6 \times 5 = 30$.

36. **The correct answer is H.** Because a negative number cannot have a square root, the value under a square root sign *must* be positive. In this problem, the value under the square root sign is $3\left(\dfrac{x^3}{2y}\right)$, or $\dfrac{3x^3}{2y}$. Choose values for the answer choices and eliminate those choices that could give you a negative value under the square root sign:

> If x is negative, then x^3 will be negative. If y is also negative, then $2y$ will also be negative, so the value under the square root sign will be positive. Answer choice F will work.

> If x is positive, then x^3 will be positive. If y is also positive, then $2y$ will also be positive, so the value under the square root sign will be positive. Answer choice G will also work. Answer choices J and K are not true, because you have just determined that both x and y must both be either positive or negative.

Since answer choices F and G cannot both be correct, you are left with answer choice H.

37. **The correct answer is D.** The question asks you to solve for S, so perform the following operations:

$$A = 2S + 9$$

$$A - 9 = 2S$$

$$\dfrac{A - 9}{2} = S$$

38. The correct answer is G. Calculate the slope by using the following formula: $\dfrac{(y_1 - y_2)}{(x_1 - x_2)}$. Any line perpendicular to the y-axis is a horizontal line. Because there is no change in y, the numerator ($y_1 - y_2$), is 0. This means that the slope of a horizontal line is 0, answer choice G.

39. The correct answer is D. To solve this problem, recall that wherever a line crosses the x-axis, the y-coordinate is 0. Substitute 0 for y in the equation and solve for x:

$$5 \times 0 = 25x - 50$$

$$0 = 25x - 50$$

$$50 = 25x$$

$$x = 2$$

40. The correct answer is K. To solve this problem, you must calculate the tan α and the cos β. The tangent of any acute angle is calculated by dividing the length of the side opposite the acute angle by the length of the side adjacent to the acute angle $\left(\tan = \dfrac{\text{opp}}{\text{adj}}\right)$. The cosine of any acute angle is calculated by dividing the length of the side adjacent to the acute angle by the hypotenuse $\left(\cos = \dfrac{\text{adj}}{\text{hyp}}\right)$. The tan of angle α is $\dfrac{4}{3}$, and the cos of angle β is $\dfrac{4}{5}$. Now you can substitute these values into the equation given in the problem and solve:

$$(\tan \alpha)(\cos \beta) = \left(\frac{4}{3}\right)\left(\frac{4}{5}\right) = \frac{16}{15}$$

41. The correct answer is E. According to information in the problem, Amy can run 3 miles in s minutes, or $\dfrac{3}{s}$. The question asks you to calculate the distance she can run in 50 minutes. Set up a proportion and solve for x:

$$\frac{3}{s} = \frac{x}{50}$$

$$sx = 150$$

$$x = \frac{150}{s}$$

42. The correct answer is J. To solve this problem, convert the statement into mathematical form. The product of 7 and a number n is equivalent to $7n$. 3 less than $7n$ is equivalent to $7n - 3$. Finally, $7n - 3$ is less than 38, which is expressed mathematically as $7n - 3 < 38$.

43. The correct answer is C. The area of a triangle is calculated using the formula $A = \dfrac{1}{2}(bh)$, where b is the length of the base, and h is the height. Based on the measures of the angles given, you can draw triangle ABC as shown below:

You are given that $\overline{AB}$, the hypotenuse, is 16 units long. Because this is a $30° - 60° - 90°$ triangle, you can calculate the lengths of the height ($\overline{BC}$) and the base ($\overline{AC}$). The relationship between the sides of a $30°$–$60°$–$90°$ triangle is as follows: The side opposite the $30°$ is equal to $\dfrac{1}{2}$ of the length of the hypotenuse, and the side opposite the $60°$ is equal to $\dfrac{1}{2}$ of the length of the hypotenuse times $\sqrt{3}$. Calculate the lengths of the sides:

Side $\overline{AC}$ (the base) $= \dfrac{1}{2}(16\sqrt{3}) = 8\sqrt{3}$

Side $\overline{BC}$ (the height) $= \dfrac{1}{2}(16) = 8$

Now you can substitute these values into the formula for the area of a triangle:

$$A = \frac{1}{2}(8)(8\sqrt{3}) = 4(8\sqrt{3}) = 32\sqrt{3}$$

44. The correct answer is F. Perpendicular lines have negative reciprocal slopes. The equation of the line given is $y = 2x + 1$, so the slope is 2. The slope of a line perpendicular to this line will have a slope equal to $-1/2$. Only answer choice F has a slope equal to $-1/2$, so it must be the correct choice.

45. The correct answer is C. The area of a rectangle is calculated by multiplying the width by the length ($A = w \times l$). Calculate the area of the first rectangle as follows:

Set the width equal to x, and the length equal to $2x$.

$$A = x(2x) = 2x^2$$

Now calculate the area of the second rectangle:

The length is tripled and the width is doubled, so the length $= 3(2x)$ and the width $= 2x$.

$$A = 3(2x)(2x) = 6x(2x) = 12x^2$$

The area of the second triangle is $12x^2$, which is 6 times greater than the area of the first triangle $(2x^2)$.

46. **The correct answer is J.** Systems of equations will have an infinite number of solutions when the equations are equal to each other. The first step in solving this problem is to recognize that the second equation is exactly 3 times the value of the first equation: $72x = 3(24x)$, $45y = 3(15y)$, so $9z$ must equal $3(108)$. Solve for z:

$$9z = 3(108)$$
$$9z = 324$$
$$z = 36$$

47. **The correct answer is B.** A prime number is a number that is only divisible by 1 and itself. If you list all of the numbers between 36 and 54, not including 36 and 54, you will find the prime numbers 37, 41, 43, 47, and 53. There are 5 prime numbers between 36 and 54.

48. **The correct answer is H.** The tangent of any acute angle is calculated by dividing the length of the side opposite the acute angle by the length of the side adjacent to the acute angle $\left(\tan = \dfrac{\text{opp}}{\text{adj}}\right)$. The sine of any acute angle is calculated by dividing the length of the side opposite to the acute angle by the hypotenuse $\left(\sin = \dfrac{\text{opp}}{\text{hyp}}\right)$. If $\tan A = \dfrac{x}{y}$, then $\sin A = \dfrac{x}{\text{hypotenuse}}$. To determine the length of the hypotenuse, use the Pythagorean Theorem, $a^2 + b^2 = c^2$. According to this equation, $a^2 + b^2 = x^2 + y^2$, so $c^2 = x^2 + y^2$, and $c = \sqrt{x^2 + y^2}$. Now that you know the value of the hypotenuse, you can solve for $\sin A$: $\sin A$ is $\dfrac{x}{\sqrt{x^2 + y^2}}$.

49. **The correct answer is B.** To solve this problem, you must first recognize that there are 360 degrees in a circle. Next, set up a ratio to calculate the number of degrees represented by Aishah's time playing the piano:

1.5 is to 24 as x is to 360.

$$\frac{1.5}{24} = \frac{x}{360}$$
$$24x = 540$$
$$x = 22.5$$

50. **The correct answer is H.** The easiest way to solve this problem is to draw a line and place the given points on the line, as follows:

Based on the line above, 1 possible length of AC is 20. Eliminate answer choices G, J, and K. Since you are left with answer choices F and H, you need to determine if AC could also be 2 meters long. Draw another line, and change the order of the points:

(2)

Based on this line, another possible length of AC is 2, so answer choice H must be correct.

51. **The correct answer is E.** To solve this problem, first recall that there are 360 degrees in a circle. The sector shown is equal to 30°, so it is 1/12 of the total circle. Likewise, the arc represents 1/12 of the total circumference of the circle. The formula for the circumference of a circle is $C = 2\pi r$, so the circumference of the circle is $12(6\pi) = 2\pi r$. Solve for r as shown next:

$$12(6\pi) = 2\pi r$$
$$72\pi = 2\pi r$$
$$36 = r$$

You now know that the radius of the circle is 36. The formula for area of a circle is $A = \pi r^2$. Calculate the area of the circle as shown next:

$$A = \pi(36)^2$$
$$A = 1,296\pi$$

Because sector LMN is 1/12 of the total area of the circle, the area of sector LMN is $1,296 \div 12 = 108$.

52. **The correct answer is G.** In this problem, the quantity $6a^5b^7$ is less than 0, which means it must be negative. 6 is positive and a^5 and b^7 can be positive or negative. Since a negative number times a negative number yields a positive number, either a^5 or b^7 must be negative, but not both. Eliminate answer choice F. By definition, if you raise a negative number to an odd numbered power, the result will be negative. Since the problem asks which must be true, answer choice G is correct because it makes either a or b negative, but not both.

53. **The correct answer is C.** The easiest way to solve this problem is to determine the number of patients Mandy visited each day and calculate the total number of visits on all 5 days:

Day 1: 7 visits

Day 2: 7 + 3 = 10 visits

Day 3: 10 + 3 = 13 visits

Day 4: 13 + 3 = 16 visits

Day 5: 16 + 3 = 19 visits

7 + 10 + 13 + 16 + 19 = 65 visits.

54. **The correct answer is K.** If 2 numbers, x and y, differ by 8, that means that $x - y = 8$. Multiplying the 2 numbers, $(x)(y)$, will yield the product. Solve the first equation for x:

$$x - y = 8$$

$$x = y + 8$$

Substitute the result for x in the second equation, as follows:

$$(y + 8)y$$

Since one of the answer choices must be the solution to that equation, plug in the answer choices, starting with the smallest value (note that the answer choices are in descending order):

$$(y + 8)y = -16$$

$$y^2 + 8y = -16$$

$$y^2 + 8y + 16 = 0$$

$$(y + 4)^2 = 0$$

$$y = -4$$

Now, substitute −4 for y in the first equation and solve for x:

$$x - (-4) = 8$$

$$x = 4$$

Since $(4)(-4) = -16$, answer choice K is correct.

55. **The correct answer is A.** Because angle x is less than 90°, it is an acute angle. The cosine of any acute angle is calculated by dividing the length of the side adjacent to the acute angle by the hypotenuse $\left(\cos = \dfrac{\text{adj}}{\text{hyp}} \right)$.

This means that the length of the side adjacent to angle x is 4, and the length of the hypotenuse is 5. The sine of any acute angle is calculated by dividing the length of the side opposite to the acute angle by the hypotenuse $\left(\sin = \dfrac{\text{opp}}{\text{hyp}} \right)$. Since you know the measure of the side adjacent to angle x and the length of the hypotenuse, you can use the Pythagorean Theorem to calculate the length of the side opposite angle x.

Pythagorean Theorem: $a^2 + b^2 = c^2$, where c is the hypotenuse.

$$4^2 + b^2 = 5^2$$

$$16 + b^2 = 25$$

$$b^2 = 9$$

$$b = 3$$

The side opposite angle x is 3, so the sine of angle x is $\dfrac{3}{5}$.

56. **The correct answer is F.** The problem asks for an expression that represents the *number* of sets of books sold, not the *price* of the sets of books sold. One way to understand the problem is to make a table and notice the pattern:

Change in $ per set of books	Number of books sold
Original price of $9.50	1,750 books sold (given in problem)
Decrease by $1.00 = $8.50	1,750 + 1,200(1) books sold
Decrease by $2.00 = $7.50	1,750 + 1,200(2) = 1,750 + 2,400 books sold
Decrease by $3.00 = $6.50	1,750 + 1,200(3) = 1,750 + 3,600 books sold
Decrease by $x = (9.50 − x)	1,750 + 1,200x books sold

57. **The correct answer is A.** The rules of the game state that a player is a winner if 2 marbles drawn have a sum greater than 45. Martin has already drawn the marble numbered 17. In order to win, Martin must draw another marble with a number greater than 28 (17 + 28 = 45). The possible winning marbles are 29, 30, 31 … 44. Therefore, Martin has 16 chances to draw a winning marble. Since he has already drawn one of the 45 marbles and did not put it back, he has 16 chances out of 44 to draw a winning marble. $\dfrac{16}{44}$ can be reduced to $\dfrac{4}{11}$.

58. The correct answer is K. Standard deviation is a measure of how spread out numbers are in a given data set, or how much the numbers in the data set deviate from one another. Because the numbers in answer choice K do not deviate from one another (they are all the same number), the data set has the smallest standard deviation.

59. The correct answer is C. A circle that is inscribed in the square will be contained completely inside the square, and will touch all 4 sides of the square. Draw a picture to help you visualize the problem:

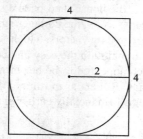

If the vertices, or corners of the square, are at the coordinates given, the length of each of the sides of the square must be 4. This means that the diameter of the circle is 4, and the radius is 2. The equation of a circle centered at (a, b) with a radius r, is $(x-a)^2 + (y-b)^2 = r^2$. Substitute 2 for r and get a value of 4 for r^2. You can eliminate answer choices A, B, and E, which indicate that r^2 is equal to either 2 or 8. Answer choice C matches the standard form of the equation of a circle, so it is the correct choice.

60. The correct answer is K. According to the question, on Wednesday, the original price ($60) was reduced by 15%. This means that the price on Wednesday was 100% −15%, or 85% of $60. Multiply $60 by 0.85, the decimal equivalent of 85%, to get $51. Two weeks later, this price ($51) is further reduced by 20%. Calculate this reduced price:

$100\% - 20\% = 80\%$

$(\$51)\ 0.80 = \$40.80$

Set up a proportion to calculate the percent this price is of the original price:

$40.80 is to $60 as x% is to 100%

$\dfrac{40.80}{60.00} = \dfrac{x}{100}$; cross-multiply and solve for x.

$60x = 4{,}080$

$x = 68$

Reading Test Explanations

PASSAGE I

1. **The best answer is A.** The first sentence of the last paragraph indicates that it was time for Mrs. Pontellier to dress for dinner. She then makes the comment about her husband not returning, so it is most likely that she is expressing her belief that she will be having dinner without her husband, answer choice A.

2. **The best answer is H.** The fourth paragraph indicates that Robert talked a good deal about himself because "he was very young, and did not know any better." The passage goes on to say that "Mrs. Pontellier talked a little about herself for the same reason." You can infer that the two are about the same age, answer choice H.

3. **The best answer is A.** According to the passage, Robert intended to "go to Mexico in the autumn, where fortune awaited him." This suggests that he wanted to seek his fortune in Mexico in order to gain more wealth and social stature than he currently has.

4. **The best answer is G.** The word *incessantly* means "long and uninterrupted." This definition best supports answer choice G. Based on the context of the passage, you could have eliminated answer choices H and J. While it is true that they each talked about themselves, the use of the word *incessantly* suggests that the conversation was long.

5. **The best answer is D.** The only selection that is made clear in the passage about both Mrs. Pontellier and her husband is that they have children, answer choice D. There is no discussion about the way that Mr. Pontellier feels about Robert, or about how Mr. and Mrs. Pontellier get along. While the passage suggests that Mrs. Pontellier will not be having dinner with her husband, the passage does not make it clear that they never spend time together.

6. **The best answer is G.** In order to answer this question, it is necessary to understand the meaning of "countenance," which can be defined as "the face as an indication of mood, emotion, or character." If you did not know the definition, you could infer from the context of the sentence that "countenance" is related to the face, because the author details various characteristics of Robert's face. The phrase "there rested no shadow of care" on Robert's face implies that he seemed carefree and relaxed. Answer choices F and H do not make sense because they refer to the physicality of Robert's face instead of his emotional state. Answer choice J is incorrect because stressed is actually the opposite of displaying "no shadow of care."

7. **The best answer is B.** All of the characters in the story seem to enjoy the company of others, so it makes sense that they are all sociable, answer choice B. The other answer choices are not supported by details in the passage.

8. **The best answer is F.** According to the passage, Robert spoke of his intention to go to Mexico to make his fortune, "but somehow never got there," so he "held on to his modest position." This suggests that his ambitions are unfulfilled.

9. **The best answer is A.** According to the passage, "In former times … 'the house' had been a summer luxury of the LeBruns." Now, the cottages surrounding the house were rented by visitors, which "enabled Madame LeBruns to maintain the easy and comfortable existence which appeared to be her birthright." This suggests that Robert's mother, Madame LeBruns, was better off financially earlier in her life, answer choice A.

10. **The best answer is J.** The narrator is not identified and is not a part of the story. Therefore, the narrator would be considered a third person narrator. Because the story involves a description of the thoughts and actions of more than one character, the narrator would be considered omniscient.

PASSAGE II

11. **The best answer is B.** The passage states that *baleen* is whalebone, which was used for things like storage and insulation, but not for food. All of the other answer choices are mentioned specifically as being part of the Inuit diet.

12. **The best answer is G.** According to the passage, when the moratorium on "all whaling" was imposed, "a great cry sounded from the Inuit," whose lives depended on controlled hunting of whales. This information best supports answer choice G.

13. **The best answer is D.** The Inuit culture is tied to the environment, and the Inuit "believe the Arctic animals … are all part of their culture." They have a great respect for the whales, and hunt only as many animals as they need to survive. This information best supports answer choice D.

14. **The best answer is H.** The passage explicitly states that whale meat is rich in phosphorous, niacin, and vitamin E. Riboflavin is not mentioned.

15. **The best answer is C.** In the first paragraph, the word *moratorium* is used in reference to the International Whaling Committee's response to the overhunting of

whales. Therefore, it makes sense that a moratorium would be a suspension of activity. The other answer choices are not supported by the passage.

16. The best answer is F. According to the passage, *Naluqatak* is a feast that is celebrated at the end of the whaling season. It is a "time of thanksgiving and sharing." Therefore, it can best be described as a harvest feast, answer choice F.

17. The best answer is C. The sixth paragraph indicates that the traditional blanket toss "requires the coordinated action of many people … creating a communal version of a trampoline." The use of the word *coordinated* refers to the organized movement of the people, answer choice C.

18. The best answer is F. A main theme of the passage is the importance of family and community to the Inuit people. It would make sense, then, that the Inuit would respect their elders, answer choice F. The passage also states that the shares of the whale meat are "reserved for elders and widows." The other answer choices are somewhat negative, and do not fit within the context of the passage.

19. The best answer is A. The passage states that "many Inuit never hunt beyond the end of May, to avoid the time when calving females are passing through."

20. The best answer is J. According to the passage, "meat from seals and fish" is saved for festivals. You can conclude that the Inuit also hunt seals, answer choice J.

PASSAGE III

21. The best answer is B. The passage indicates that, like Tiger Woods, Bobby Jones was also a very talented golfer at a young age. Tiger Woods entitled his book, *How I Play Golf*, which was the same title that Bobby Jones used for his instructional film series. These, and other details from the passage, suggest that both of the men were similar in many ways, answer choice B.

22. The best answer is J. The second paragraph states that "Pop" Keeler was a mentor for Bobby, and helped Bobby to become a gracious winner and loser, as well as "a remarkably honorable gentleman." This indicates that "Pop" Keeler was a positive force in Bobby's life, answer choice J.

23. The best answer is C. The passage discusses many accomplishments that Jones made throughout his life, including furthering his education. The passage also

mentions that Jones did not take lessons or practice constantly. Answer choices A, B, and D can be eliminated, because they are not supported by details in the passage.

24. The best answer is J. The first paragraph serves as an introductory paragraph and references the comparison between Tiger Woods and Bobby Jones. The rest of the passage discusses Bobby Jones' many accomplishments and mentions several similarities between Tiger and Bobby.

25. The best answer is A. Since Jones took time away from golfing to earn his college degrees, it is clear that his perspective on higher education was that it was important. The other answer choices are not supported by the passage.

26. The best answer is G. The statement appears in the fourth paragraph, where Jones insisted on following the rules of the game, "adding a penalty stroke to his score." This suggests that he placed as great an emphasis on the rules of golf as he did on the laws against crime.

27. The best answer is D. According to the passage, Bobby Jones "earned a varsity letter as the assistant manager of Harvard's golf team. It is difficult to imagine one of today's professional athletes volunteering to be the assistant manager of a college team!" These details best support the notion that Bobby Jones was more committed than today's professional athletes.

28. The best answer is H. According to the passage, *syringeomyelia* is a rare spinal disease, which eventually confined Jones to a wheelchair. This suggests that the disease gradually left him incapacitated, answer choice H. He had retired from golf years earlier, so answer choice G can be eliminated. The other answer choices are not supported by the passage.

29. The best answer is B. Jones' comment in the seventh paragraph was in response to a question about his debilitating disease.

30. The best answer is F. The overall tone of the passage is very positive, and indicates that the author admired and respected Bobby Jones. The other answer choices are not supported by the passage.

PASSAGE IV

31. The best answer is D. The word "certainly" can be used to indicate assurance. The author likely includes it here to indicate that there is no doubt about the value of robots as information gathering tools.

32. **The best answer is J.** The word "calibrating" can refer to measuring or determining the accuracy of information. The passage suggests that humans would be more useful than robots in adjusting equipment and manipulating data.

33. **The best answer is C.** The context of the passage suggests that one reason "Americans support government funding" of space exploration might be the need for Earth's ever-expanding population to find another place to live.

34. **The best answer is J.** The space shuttle disaster and loss of the astronauts aboard the shuttle was a serious blow to manned space exploration. It is likely the author mentions the accident as a warning about the dangers of sending people into space.

35. **The best answer is A.** The word "lament" means to feel sorrow or regret. The author uses the word to suggest that there is no reason to be sad about the end of manned space exploration because unmanned exploration will continue.

36. **The best answer is G.** The phrase "computer-driven hunk of metal" invokes a sense of detachment, which shows the reader that unmanned space exploration is less dangerous than manned space exploration.

37. **The best answer is C.** The question deals with sparing humans from harm, making it clear that the author believes manned space flight is dangerous and that it is important to "embrace" the notion of astronauts being replaced by robots.

38. **The best answer is H.** An assumption is unstated evidence. While neither of the passages states that interest in potential life beyond Earth will continue, in order for the authors' statements about space exploration to be logical, the continuation of such interest is necessary.

39. **The best answer is C.** According to Passage A, "Robots and astronauts use much of the same equipment in space, but a human is more capable of calibrating sensitive instruments correctly and placing them in appropriate and useful positions." Additionally, "Robots are also not as well equipped as humans to solve problems as they arise, and robots often collect data that is unhelpful or irrelevant." These concerns are not addressed in Passage B.

40. **The best answer is G.** The author of Passage A raises the question, "So what is that next level?" The author of Passage B talks about embracing new technology. Both authors seem to agree that space exploration will continue in some form.

Science Test Explanations

PASSAGE I

1. **The correct answer is C.** Table 1 shows that petri dish 2 had a pH level of 7 and experienced the highest percent growth of *E. coli* bacteria, as compared to petri dishes 1 and 2. Therefore, answer choice C, a pH level near 7, is correct.

2. **The correct answer is F.** The description of Experiment 3 indicates that *most* bacteria, unlike *E. coli*, need certain growth factors and vitamins to reproduce. In addition, the experiment was run to "ensure that the three growth factors have minimal to no effect on growth."

3. **The correct answer is A.** Table 1 shows that *E. coli* bacteria reproduce most efficiently at a pH level of 7, so answer choice A is correct. Answer choice D is not correct because Table 1 shows that *E. coli* can still reproduce at different pH levels, just not as efficiently.

4. **The correct answer is G.** The question states that bacteria often reproduce until all available nutrients have been depleted. By supplying each group of bacteria with unlimited nutrients, the bacteria will reproduce for a longer time.

5. **The correct answer is C.** According to Table 2, petri dish 1, with the highest percent dry weight of the organic compounds (nutrients), yielded the highest percent growth of *E. coli* bacteria. This best supports the statement in answer choice C.

6. **The correct answer is J.** Since the reproduction rate varies drastically from one stage to the next, the best way to study the different growth stages would be to record the growth changes more frequently.

PASSAGE II

7. **The correct answer is D.** The major difference between the scientists' opinions is whether or not earthquakes can be accurately predicted. Scientist 1 believes that predictions cannot be made with accuracy. Scientist 2 believes that accurate predictions can be made about the location and magnitude of the next earthquake.

8. **The correct answer is G.** Scientist 1 claims that Global Positioning Systems can determine the amount of strain that is loaded onto faults from plate motion "easily and with much certainty." On the other hand, Scientist 1 claims that the amount of strain *released* is "much more difficult to estimate."

9. **The correct answer is C.** According to Scientist 2, the movement of the tectonic plates is causing strain to build up. This claim best supports answer choice C.

10. **The correct answer is G.** Scientist 1 states that the main problem in predicting earthquakes is that historical data do not date back far enough to illustrate quake activities clearly. The other answer choices are not supported by the passage.

11. **The correct answer is A.** Scientist 2 claims that an earthquake is caused by the buildup of pressure on a fault line and the only way to release that pressure is through an earthquake. Therefore, if a handful of small earthquakes released some of the pressure along a fault line, there would be a decrease in the probability of another earthquake, answer choice A.

12. **The correct answer is J.** Based on their opinions, the only statement that both scientists would agree with is that the San Francisco Bay Area has fault lines extending through the entire region. Scientist 1 says that the Bay Area is covered with major fault lines and Scientist 2 says that many populated areas in the Bay Area are "near, or even sandwiched between," major fault lines.

13. **The correct answer is A.** Scientist 2 claims that earthquakes can be predicted with much certainty. The only statement that strengthens his claim is answer choice A, which says that the predictions of a group of scientists were accurate.

PASSAGE III

14. **The correct answer is G.** Galvani claimed an electric fluid was present in animal tissue that created an electric current. Volta was trying to prove that you did not need animal tissue or electric fluid to create an electric current. By using his tongue, which is animal tissue, Volta did not disprove Galvani's theory that animal tissue contains electric fluid.

15. **The correct answer is B.** Galvani used two metals in his experiment with the leg of the dead frog. Volta also believed that 2 metals were sufficient to produce an electric current, or he likely would have used a third metal in this experiment. The other answer choices are not supported by the passage.

16. **The correct answer is J.** Volta used several layers of the elements/metals piled on each other, separated by the moist material. We know that he used as many as 60 layers of metal to produce an electric current, which supports answer choice J.

17. **The correct answer is A.** According to Experiment 4, 60 layers of metal produced a greater intensity than 30 or 40 layers. It could be reasonably assumed that the greater the number of layers, the greater the intensity of the electric current.

18. **The correct answer is G.** In Experiment 2, Volta noted an electrical interaction between copper and zinc in an acidic solution. In Experiment 4, he separated layers of metal with material dampened by an acidic solution. If researchers were able to determine that substances used in the other two experiments (the human tongue and paper soaked in electrolytes) also contained an acidic solution, the hypothesis that an acidic solution is needed to create an electric current would be supported.

19. **The correct answer is C.** None of the experiments directly disprove the theory that a direct electric current is produced by chemical reactions. Volta only proved that animal tissue was not needed to produce electric currents. In fact, the first paragraph states that "Volta also discovered the means of converting chemical energy into electric energy which is the basis for the modern battery."

PASSAGE IV

20. **The correct answer is G.** The passage states that high levels of chlorine are capable of having a corrosive effect on surfaces. The chlorine levels in Sample 2 are too high to fall into the ideal range, so it can be inferred that the water from Sample 2 may be corrosive.

21. **The correct answer is A.** According to Table 1, both the chlorine and bromine levels were within the ideal range for Sample 1, regardless of which kit was used. However, for both Kit A and Kit B, chlorine levels for Sample 2 were above the acceptable levels.

22. **The correct answer is F.** According to Table 1, the results from the tests on Sample 1 all fall within the ideal range, which most likely means that the water is balanced and safe for swimmers, answer choice F.

23. **The correct answer is B.** To answer this question, look at Figure 1. Find the point just above 80% on the y-axis and move to the right until you reach the line. Once you reach the line, move down until you arrive at the x-axis. The point on the x-axis that corresponds to this point on the line is a pH of 6.5, answer choice B.

24. **The correct answer is H.** According to the passage, Figure 1 shows the effectiveness of chlorine at different pH as a percentage of chlorine's effectiveness at destroying harmful contaminants. The figure indicates that at a pH of 5, chlorine is 100% effective, while at a pH of 8, chlorine is less than 25% effective. This information best supports the statement that, as pH increases, the presence of harmful contaminants is most likely high.

PASSAGE V

25. **The correct answer is C.** According to Figure 1, anaerobic respiration is represented by the dashed line. The graph shows that, as intensity level increases moving to the right along the x-axis, the dashed line moves in a generally upward direction before leveling off. This indicates that the anaerobic respiration level increases and then levels off, answer choice C.

26. **The correct answer is F.** The passage states that aerobic respiration produces 18 times more ATP than anaerobic respiration. Therefore, if 2 moles of ATP were produced from anaerobic respiration, 36 moles would have been produced during aerobic respiration ($2 \times 18 = 36$).

27. **The correct answer is B.** According to Table 1, the body first uses glycogen stores, then fat stores, and finally protein.

28. **The correct answer is G.** The question is asking you to look at Figure 2 and determine the VO_2 max of a 50-year-old male in "Excellent" physical condition and compare it to a female of the same age and fitness level.

    > Find 50 on the x-axis (Age) and follow it up to the line that corresponds to a male in Excellent condition from the Key. Once you reach the line, move to the left until you reach the y-axis (VO_2 max). This point is at a VO_2 max of approximately 45.

    > Find 50 on the x-axis (Age) again and follow it up to the line that corresponds to a female in excellent condition from the Key. Once you reach the line, move to the left until you reach the y-axis (VO_2 max). This point is at a VO_2 max of approximately 33.

    > 45 (male) − 33 (female) = 12

    The female consumes 12 milliliters less oxygen (per minute per kilogram of body weight), answer choice G.

29. **The correct answer is A.** Look at Figure 2 and find 27 on the x-axis (Age). Follow it up to the line that corresponds to a female in poor physical condition from the Key. Once you reach the line, move to the left until you reach the y-axis (VO_2 max). This point is at a VO_2 max of between 25 and 30, answer choice A.

PASSAGE VI

30. **The correct answer is F.** According to the passage, the body produces all of the cholesterol that it needs. Therefore, cholesterol is found in the body or in particular foods only. It can be inferred that any other cholesterol in the body that was not created there must come from what you eat, answer choice F.

31. **The correct answer is A.** HDL protects against the development of heart disease and is considered "good" cholesterol. Answer choice B says that HDL increases cholesterol levels and answer choice C claims that HDL is "bad" cholesterol, so you can eliminate both of these choices. You know from the passage that answer choice D is also false, so answer choice A must be correct. The passage also states that the liver is responsible for cholesterol from the body.

32. **The correct answer is H.** According to Table 1, trans fats are the only type of fats that increase "bad" LDL cholesterol and decrease "good" HDL cholesterol. Therefore, this type of fat would have the greatest net negative effect on cholesterol levels.

33. **The correct answer is D.** According to Table 1, monounsaturated and polyunsaturated fats are the best for overall cholesterol levels. Saturated and trans fats are the worst for overall cholesterol levels. Based on this information and the data in the question, you can eliminate answer choices A and B. Both palm and coconut oils have high amounts of saturated fats, which increase "bad" cholesterol levels. Canola oil is the best choice, but not because it is low in polyunsaturated fats, which increase "good" cholesterol levels, so answer choice C can also be eliminated. Canola oil is the best choice because it is high in monounsaturated and polyunsaturated fats and low in saturated fats, answer choice D.

34. **The correct answer is J.** According to the question, omega-3 fatty acid is known to lower the risk of heart disease. You know from the passage that high cholesterol levels can cause heart disease, so you can assume that omega-3 fatty acid lowers cholesterol levels. You can also assume that omega-3 fatty acids have lower amounts of "bad" LDL cholesterol and higher amounts of "good" HDL cholesterol. Therefore, lowering the level of "bad" LDL cholesterol and increasing the levels of "good" HDL cholesterol would probably lower the risk of heart disease.

PASSAGE VII

35. **The correct answer is D.** The passage states that friction depends mostly on the smoothness of the surfaces that come into contact with an object. Rough surfaces, like the carpet or driftwood used in the experiments, increase friction because it is harder for the car to travel on these surfaces than on a smoother surface. Therefore, the stronger the friction, the shorter the distance the car can travel, answer choice D.

36. **The correct answer is F.** The passage states that friction depends mostly on the smoothness of the surfaces that come into contact with an object. The smoother the surface, the less friction there will be to stop the car from traveling farther. If the surface is smoother, the friction will be decreased, and the car will be able to travel a longer distance, answer choice F.

37. **The correct answer is C.** According to the passage, friction depends mostly on the smoothness of the surfaces that come into contact with an object. Friction will be the least powerful on a smooth surface, like aluminum foil, answer choice C.

38. **The correct answer is G.** According to the passage, friction depends mostly on the smoothness of the surfaces that come into contact with an object. The smoother the surfaces of the two objects attempting to slide past one another, the less friction there will be to stop or slow the movement. Lubricants or oils cause the surface of an object to become slippery, or smoother, which is why the materials are used to decrease friction, answer choice G. The other answer choices are not supported by the passage.

39. **The correct answer is A.** The passage states that the same car was used in all of the experiments. Therefore, it can be inferred that the mass of the car was kept constant in each experiment, answer choice A.

40. **The correct answer is H.** The passage states that raising the height of the ramp increased the speed that the car could travel, so you can eliminate answer choices F and G. Based on information given in the passage and the results of the experiments, you know that the faster the car traveled, the longer the distance it traveled before friction stopped it. Therefore, increasing the height of the ramp both increased the speed and increased the distance traveled, answer choice H.

ACT PRACTICE TEST 2
Answer Sheet

ENGLISH

1 Ⓐ Ⓑ Ⓒ Ⓓ	21 Ⓐ Ⓑ Ⓒ Ⓓ	41 Ⓐ Ⓑ Ⓒ Ⓓ	61 Ⓐ Ⓑ Ⓒ Ⓓ
2 Ⓕ Ⓖ Ⓗ Ⓙ	22 Ⓕ Ⓖ Ⓗ Ⓙ	42 Ⓕ Ⓖ Ⓗ Ⓙ	62 Ⓕ Ⓖ Ⓗ Ⓙ
3 Ⓐ Ⓑ Ⓒ Ⓓ	23 Ⓐ Ⓑ Ⓒ Ⓓ	43 Ⓐ Ⓑ Ⓒ Ⓓ	63 Ⓐ Ⓑ Ⓒ Ⓓ
4 Ⓕ Ⓖ Ⓗ Ⓙ	24 Ⓕ Ⓖ Ⓗ Ⓙ	44 Ⓕ Ⓖ Ⓗ Ⓙ	64 Ⓕ Ⓖ Ⓗ Ⓙ
5 Ⓐ Ⓑ Ⓒ Ⓓ	25 Ⓐ Ⓑ Ⓒ Ⓓ	45 Ⓐ Ⓑ Ⓒ Ⓓ	65 Ⓐ Ⓑ Ⓒ Ⓓ
6 Ⓕ Ⓖ Ⓗ Ⓙ	26 Ⓕ Ⓖ Ⓗ Ⓙ	46 Ⓕ Ⓖ Ⓗ Ⓙ	66 Ⓕ Ⓖ Ⓗ Ⓙ
7 Ⓐ Ⓑ Ⓒ Ⓓ	27 Ⓐ Ⓑ Ⓒ Ⓓ	47 Ⓐ Ⓑ Ⓒ Ⓓ	67 Ⓐ Ⓑ Ⓒ Ⓓ
8 Ⓕ Ⓖ Ⓗ Ⓙ	28 Ⓕ Ⓖ Ⓗ Ⓙ	48 Ⓕ Ⓖ Ⓗ Ⓙ	68 Ⓕ Ⓖ Ⓗ Ⓙ
9 Ⓐ Ⓑ Ⓒ Ⓓ	29 Ⓐ Ⓑ Ⓒ Ⓓ	49 Ⓐ Ⓑ Ⓒ Ⓓ	69 Ⓐ Ⓑ Ⓒ Ⓓ
10 Ⓕ Ⓖ Ⓗ Ⓙ	30 Ⓕ Ⓖ Ⓗ Ⓙ	50 Ⓕ Ⓖ Ⓗ Ⓙ	70 Ⓕ Ⓖ Ⓗ Ⓙ
11 Ⓐ Ⓑ Ⓒ Ⓓ	31 Ⓐ Ⓑ Ⓒ Ⓓ	51 Ⓐ Ⓑ Ⓒ Ⓓ	71 Ⓐ Ⓑ Ⓒ Ⓓ
12 Ⓕ Ⓖ Ⓗ Ⓙ	32 Ⓕ Ⓖ Ⓗ Ⓙ	52 Ⓕ Ⓖ Ⓗ Ⓙ	72 Ⓕ Ⓖ Ⓗ Ⓙ
13 Ⓐ Ⓑ Ⓒ Ⓓ	33 Ⓐ Ⓑ Ⓒ Ⓓ	53 Ⓐ Ⓑ Ⓒ Ⓓ	73 Ⓐ Ⓑ Ⓒ Ⓓ
14 Ⓕ Ⓖ Ⓗ Ⓙ	34 Ⓕ Ⓖ Ⓗ Ⓙ	54 Ⓕ Ⓖ Ⓗ Ⓙ	74 Ⓕ Ⓖ Ⓗ Ⓙ
15 Ⓐ Ⓑ Ⓒ Ⓓ	35 Ⓐ Ⓑ Ⓒ Ⓓ	55 Ⓐ Ⓑ Ⓒ Ⓓ	75 Ⓐ Ⓑ Ⓒ Ⓓ
16 Ⓕ Ⓖ Ⓗ Ⓙ	36 Ⓕ Ⓖ Ⓗ Ⓙ	56 Ⓕ Ⓖ Ⓗ Ⓙ	
17 Ⓐ Ⓑ Ⓒ Ⓓ	37 Ⓐ Ⓑ Ⓒ Ⓓ	57 Ⓐ Ⓑ Ⓒ Ⓓ	
18 Ⓕ Ⓖ Ⓗ Ⓙ	38 Ⓕ Ⓖ Ⓗ Ⓙ	58 Ⓕ Ⓖ Ⓗ Ⓙ	
19 Ⓐ Ⓑ Ⓒ Ⓓ	39 Ⓐ Ⓑ Ⓒ Ⓓ	59 Ⓐ Ⓑ Ⓒ Ⓓ	
20 Ⓕ Ⓖ Ⓗ Ⓙ	40 Ⓕ Ⓖ Ⓗ Ⓙ	60 Ⓕ Ⓖ Ⓗ Ⓙ	

MATHEMATICS

1 Ⓐ Ⓑ Ⓒ Ⓓ Ⓔ	16 Ⓕ Ⓖ Ⓗ Ⓙ Ⓚ	31 Ⓐ Ⓑ Ⓒ Ⓓ Ⓔ	46 Ⓕ Ⓖ Ⓗ Ⓙ Ⓚ
2 Ⓕ Ⓖ Ⓗ Ⓙ Ⓚ	17 Ⓐ Ⓑ Ⓒ Ⓓ Ⓔ	32 Ⓕ Ⓖ Ⓗ Ⓙ Ⓚ	47 Ⓐ Ⓑ Ⓒ Ⓓ Ⓔ
3 Ⓐ Ⓑ Ⓒ Ⓓ Ⓔ	18 Ⓕ Ⓖ Ⓗ Ⓙ Ⓚ	33 Ⓐ Ⓑ Ⓒ Ⓓ Ⓔ	48 Ⓕ Ⓖ Ⓗ Ⓙ Ⓚ
4 Ⓕ Ⓖ Ⓗ Ⓙ Ⓚ	19 Ⓐ Ⓑ Ⓒ Ⓓ Ⓔ	34 Ⓕ Ⓖ Ⓗ Ⓙ Ⓚ	49 Ⓐ Ⓑ Ⓒ Ⓓ Ⓔ
5 Ⓐ Ⓑ Ⓒ Ⓓ Ⓔ	20 Ⓕ Ⓖ Ⓗ Ⓙ Ⓚ	35 Ⓐ Ⓑ Ⓒ Ⓓ Ⓔ	50 Ⓕ Ⓖ Ⓗ Ⓙ Ⓚ
6 Ⓕ Ⓖ Ⓗ Ⓙ Ⓚ	21 Ⓐ Ⓑ Ⓒ Ⓓ Ⓔ	36 Ⓕ Ⓖ Ⓗ Ⓙ Ⓚ	51 Ⓐ Ⓑ Ⓒ Ⓓ Ⓔ
7 Ⓐ Ⓑ Ⓒ Ⓓ Ⓔ	22 Ⓕ Ⓖ Ⓗ Ⓙ Ⓚ	37 Ⓐ Ⓑ Ⓒ Ⓓ Ⓔ	52 Ⓕ Ⓖ Ⓗ Ⓙ Ⓚ
8 Ⓕ Ⓖ Ⓗ Ⓙ Ⓚ	23 Ⓐ Ⓑ Ⓒ Ⓓ Ⓔ	38 Ⓕ Ⓖ Ⓗ Ⓙ Ⓚ	53 Ⓐ Ⓑ Ⓒ Ⓓ Ⓔ
9 Ⓐ Ⓑ Ⓒ Ⓓ Ⓔ	24 Ⓕ Ⓖ Ⓗ Ⓙ Ⓚ	39 Ⓐ Ⓑ Ⓒ Ⓓ Ⓔ	54 Ⓕ Ⓖ Ⓗ Ⓙ Ⓚ
10 Ⓕ Ⓖ Ⓗ Ⓙ Ⓚ	25 Ⓐ Ⓑ Ⓒ Ⓓ Ⓔ	40 Ⓕ Ⓖ Ⓗ Ⓙ Ⓚ	55 Ⓐ Ⓑ Ⓒ Ⓓ Ⓔ
11 Ⓐ Ⓑ Ⓒ Ⓓ Ⓔ	26 Ⓕ Ⓖ Ⓗ Ⓙ Ⓚ	41 Ⓐ Ⓑ Ⓒ Ⓓ Ⓔ	56 Ⓕ Ⓖ Ⓗ Ⓙ Ⓚ
12 Ⓕ Ⓖ Ⓗ Ⓙ Ⓚ	27 Ⓐ Ⓑ Ⓒ Ⓓ Ⓔ	42 Ⓕ Ⓖ Ⓗ Ⓙ Ⓚ	57 Ⓐ Ⓑ Ⓒ Ⓓ Ⓔ
13 Ⓐ Ⓑ Ⓒ Ⓓ Ⓔ	28 Ⓕ Ⓖ Ⓗ Ⓙ Ⓚ	43 Ⓐ Ⓑ Ⓒ Ⓓ Ⓔ	58 Ⓕ Ⓖ Ⓗ Ⓙ Ⓚ
14 Ⓕ Ⓖ Ⓗ Ⓙ Ⓚ	29 Ⓐ Ⓑ Ⓒ Ⓓ Ⓔ	44 Ⓕ Ⓖ Ⓗ Ⓙ Ⓚ	59 Ⓐ Ⓑ Ⓒ Ⓓ Ⓔ
15 Ⓐ Ⓑ Ⓒ Ⓓ Ⓔ	30 Ⓕ Ⓖ Ⓗ Ⓙ Ⓚ	45 Ⓐ Ⓑ Ⓒ Ⓓ Ⓔ	60 Ⓕ Ⓖ Ⓗ Ⓙ Ⓚ

READING

1 Ⓐ Ⓑ Ⓒ Ⓓ	11 Ⓐ Ⓑ Ⓒ Ⓓ	21 Ⓐ Ⓑ Ⓒ Ⓓ	31 Ⓐ Ⓑ Ⓒ Ⓓ
2 Ⓕ Ⓖ Ⓗ Ⓙ	12 Ⓕ Ⓖ Ⓗ Ⓙ	22 Ⓕ Ⓖ Ⓗ Ⓙ	32 Ⓕ Ⓖ Ⓗ Ⓙ
3 Ⓐ Ⓑ Ⓒ Ⓓ	13 Ⓐ Ⓑ Ⓒ Ⓓ	23 Ⓐ Ⓑ Ⓒ Ⓓ	33 Ⓐ Ⓑ Ⓒ Ⓓ
4 Ⓕ Ⓖ Ⓗ Ⓙ	14 Ⓕ Ⓖ Ⓗ Ⓙ	24 Ⓕ Ⓖ Ⓗ Ⓙ	34 Ⓕ Ⓖ Ⓗ Ⓙ
5 Ⓐ Ⓑ Ⓒ Ⓓ	15 Ⓐ Ⓑ Ⓒ Ⓓ	25 Ⓐ Ⓑ Ⓒ Ⓓ	35 Ⓐ Ⓑ Ⓒ Ⓓ
6 Ⓕ Ⓖ Ⓗ Ⓙ	16 Ⓕ Ⓖ Ⓗ Ⓙ	26 Ⓕ Ⓖ Ⓗ Ⓙ	36 Ⓕ Ⓖ Ⓗ Ⓙ
7 Ⓐ Ⓑ Ⓒ Ⓓ	17 Ⓐ Ⓑ Ⓒ Ⓓ	27 Ⓐ Ⓑ Ⓒ Ⓓ	37 Ⓐ Ⓑ Ⓒ Ⓓ
8 Ⓕ Ⓖ Ⓗ Ⓙ	18 Ⓕ Ⓖ Ⓗ Ⓙ	28 Ⓕ Ⓖ Ⓗ Ⓙ	38 Ⓕ Ⓖ Ⓗ Ⓙ
9 Ⓐ Ⓑ Ⓒ Ⓓ	19 Ⓐ Ⓑ Ⓒ Ⓓ	29 Ⓐ Ⓑ Ⓒ Ⓓ	39 Ⓐ Ⓑ Ⓒ Ⓓ
10 Ⓕ Ⓖ Ⓗ Ⓙ	20 Ⓕ Ⓖ Ⓗ Ⓙ	30 Ⓕ Ⓖ Ⓗ Ⓙ	40 Ⓕ Ⓖ Ⓗ Ⓙ

SCIENCE

1 Ⓐ Ⓑ Ⓒ Ⓓ	11 Ⓐ Ⓑ Ⓒ Ⓓ	21 Ⓐ Ⓑ Ⓒ Ⓓ	31 Ⓐ Ⓑ Ⓒ Ⓓ
2 Ⓕ Ⓖ Ⓗ Ⓙ	12 Ⓕ Ⓖ Ⓗ Ⓙ	22 Ⓕ Ⓖ Ⓗ Ⓙ	32 Ⓕ Ⓖ Ⓗ Ⓙ
3 Ⓐ Ⓑ Ⓒ Ⓓ	13 Ⓐ Ⓑ Ⓒ Ⓓ	23 Ⓐ Ⓑ Ⓒ Ⓓ	33 Ⓐ Ⓑ Ⓒ Ⓓ
4 Ⓕ Ⓖ Ⓗ Ⓙ	14 Ⓕ Ⓖ Ⓗ Ⓙ	24 Ⓕ Ⓖ Ⓗ Ⓙ	34 Ⓕ Ⓖ Ⓗ Ⓙ
5 Ⓐ Ⓑ Ⓒ Ⓓ	15 Ⓐ Ⓑ Ⓒ Ⓓ	25 Ⓐ Ⓑ Ⓒ Ⓓ	35 Ⓐ Ⓑ Ⓒ Ⓓ
6 Ⓕ Ⓖ Ⓗ Ⓙ	16 Ⓕ Ⓖ Ⓗ Ⓙ	26 Ⓕ Ⓖ Ⓗ Ⓙ	36 Ⓕ Ⓖ Ⓗ Ⓙ
7 Ⓐ Ⓑ Ⓒ Ⓓ	17 Ⓐ Ⓑ Ⓒ Ⓓ	27 Ⓐ Ⓑ Ⓒ Ⓓ	37 Ⓐ Ⓑ Ⓒ Ⓓ
8 Ⓕ Ⓖ Ⓗ Ⓙ	18 Ⓕ Ⓖ Ⓗ Ⓙ	28 Ⓕ Ⓖ Ⓗ Ⓙ	38 Ⓕ Ⓖ Ⓗ Ⓙ
9 Ⓐ Ⓑ Ⓒ Ⓓ	19 Ⓐ Ⓑ Ⓒ Ⓓ	29 Ⓐ Ⓑ Ⓒ Ⓓ	39 Ⓐ Ⓑ Ⓒ Ⓓ
10 Ⓕ Ⓖ Ⓗ Ⓙ	20 Ⓕ Ⓖ Ⓗ Ⓙ	30 Ⓕ Ⓖ Ⓗ Ⓙ	40 Ⓕ Ⓖ Ⓗ Ⓙ

You may wish to remove these sample answer document pages to respond to the practice ACT Writing Test.

Begin WRITING TEST here.

_____

_____

_____

_____

_____

_____

_____

_____

_____

_____

_____

_____

_____

_____

_____

_____

_____

_____

_____

_____

_____

_____

_____

_____

_____

_____

_____

Cut Here

WRITING TEST

If you need more space, please continue on the back of this page.

Cut Here

WRITING TEST

Cut Here

3

If you need more space, please continue on the next page.

WRITING TEST

_____

_____

_____

_____

_____

_____

_____

_____

_____

_____

_____

_____

_____

_____

_____

_____

_____

_____

_____

_____

_____

_____

_____

_____

_____

_____

Cut Here

END OF THE WRITING TEST.
STOP! IF YOU HAVE TIME LEFT OVER, CHECK YOUR WORK ON THIS SECTION ONLY.

4

1 ▪ ▪ ▪ ▪ ▪ ▪ ▪ ▪ 1

ENGLISH TEST

45 Minutes – 75 Questions

DIRECTIONS: In the passages that follow, some words and phrases are underlined and numbered. In the answer column, you will find alternatives for the words and phrases that are underlined. Choose the alternative that you think is best and fill in the corresponding bubble on your answer sheet. If you think that the original version is best, choose "NO CHANGE," which will always be either answer choice A or F. You will also find questions about a particular section of the passage, or about the entire passage. These questions will be identified by either an underlined portion or by a number in a box. Look for the answer that clearly expresses the idea, is consistent with the style and tone of the passage, and makes the correct use of standard written English. Read the passage through once before answering the questions. For some questions, you should read beyond the indicated portion before you answer.

PASSAGE I

The following paragraphs may or may not be in the most logical order. You may be asked questions about the logical order of the paragraphs, as well as where to place sentences logically within any given paragraph.

Noh Theater

[1]

Noh is a highly ritualized form of drama that originate in Medieval Japan as a type of play performed
<u>originate in</u>
    1
in front of nobility. Noh theater reached its apex in the fourteenth and fifteenth centuries with the works of a <u>playwright named Kannami and his son Zeami,</u> and it
                                                    2
<u>is remaining largely unchanging.</u>
        3

[2]

There are certain traits that make Noh unique in the Japanese theatrical world. The stage is always sparse, <u>only decorated solely</u> with a painting of a pine tree
        4
as a backdrop. Props are minimal and often symbolic. <u>The fan for example is a staple of Noh theater,</u> and it
                                                        5
usually symbolizes another object. The costumes are

1. **A.** NO CHANGE
   B. original to
   C. originating in
   D. originated in

2. **F.** NO CHANGE
   G. playwright, named Kannami, and his son, Zeami,
   H. playwright named Kannami and his son Zeami;
   J. playwright named Kannami; and his son Zeami,

3. **A.** NO CHANGE
   B. has remained largely unchanged.
   C. will remain unchanging.
   D. will largely remain unchanged.

4. **F.** NO CHANGE
   G. decorated solely
   H. just decorated solely
   J. decorated only solely

5. **A.** NO CHANGE
   B. The fan, for example, is a staple of Noh theater,
   C. The fan for example, is a staple of Noh theater,
   D. The fan, for example is a staple, of Noh theater,

GO ON TO THE NEXT PAGE.

lavish and colorful, and the colors of the costumes are also symbolic. There is a chorus that often narrates, along with instrumentalists who add to the ambience with the unique and otherworldly music <u>it plays.</u>
                                    6

[3]

⑦ If the audience is familiar with Noh, it can

recognize the characters <u>among</u> the stylized masks that
                              8
the actors wear. Certain masks represent certain types of characters and are intended to show specific traits possessed by these characters. The masks are intentionally painted in such a way that the different angles actually look like different facial expressions. ⑨

[4]

<u>Noh theater combines poetry, dance, and music;</u>
                              10

<u>and often deals with supernatural themes.</u> It is a very
                  10
sophisticated and subtle form of drama, and according to legend, possesses something called *yugen*. An approximate English translation of this <u>abstract</u> concept refers to mystery
                                    11
and to what lies beneath the surface.

6. **F.** NO CHANGE.
   G. they play for.
   H. they play.
   J. it will play.

7. Which of the following sentences (assuming all are true) if added here, would best introduce the new subject of Paragraph 3?
   A. In the early days, Noh theater was sponsored by the elite rulers of Japan.
   B. Japanese theater has been popular for centuries.
   C. Masks also play an important role in Noh theater.
   D. There are archetypal characters who show up repeatedly in the repertoire of plays.

8. **F.** NO CHANGE
   G. with
   H. by
   J. for

9. At this point, the writer would like to highlight a very special talent that Noh actors must develop in order to be convincing. Which of the following sentences (assuming all are true) if added here, would most successfully achieve this effect?
   A. The actors wearing them must be skilled at tilting their heads in order to express nuances in emotion.
   B. The masks the actors wear are colorful and detailed and truly works of art.
   C. The actors must learn to express themselves in ways that are often unfamiliar to viewers of Western theater.
   D. Noh actors begin training at a very young age, so by the time they are much older, they have become very accomplished in their trade.

10. **F.** NO CHANGE
    G. Noh theater combines poetry dance and, music, and often deals with supernatural themes.
    H. Noh theater combines poetry, dance and music—and often deals with supernatural themes.
    J. Noh theater combines poetry, dance, and music, and often deals with supernatural themes.

11. Which of the following alternatives for the underlined portion would be LEAST acceptable?
    A. complex
    B. theoretical
    C. representational
    D. summarized

GO ON TO THE NEXT PAGE.

1 ■ ■ ■ ■ ■ ■ ■ ■ **1**

[5]

[1] Most of the plays being performed today are the originals written by Kannami and Zeami, although a few new ones had been written since then. [2] Noh is not the most
12

popular form of theater in Japan today, but it's performers
13
are extremely dedicated, and people still buy tickets to enjoy this classic art form. [3] The fact that it has remained essentially in its original form for over 600 years speak to its
14
incredible beauty, mystique, and lasting elegance.

12. F. NO CHANGE
    G. will have been written
    H. have been wrote
    J. have been written

13. A. NO CHANGE
    B. also its
    C. but its
    D. because it's

14. F. NO CHANGE
    G. will speak
    H. speaks
    J. spoken

Question 15 asks about the preceding passage as a whole.

15. In reviewing her notes, the writer discovers that the following information has been left out of the essay:

    Zeami also wrote a treatise on the methodology of Noh, which is still studied by Noh actors.

    If added to the essay, the sentence would most logically be placed after Sentence:
    A. 2 in Paragraph 2.
    B. 1 in Paragraph 5.
    C. 2 in Paragraph 3.
    D. 3 in Paragraph 5.

PASSAGE II

Calligraphy: Beautiful Writing

[1]

Art takes many forms, including watercolor painting, pencil sketching, photography or sculpture. One
16
lesser known and perhaps less appreciated art form is calligraphy, the elegant script of letters and figures.

16. F. NO CHANGE
    G. photography, sculpture.
    H. photography and to sculpture.
    J. photography, and sculpture.

GO ON TO THE NEXT PAGE.

1 ◼ ◼ ◼ ◼ ◼ ◼ ◼ ◼ **1**

Many modern-day computer fonts are attempts to replicate this ancient art. [17]

The word *calligraphy* is <u>derived from</u> the Greek words
18
kalli, which means "beautiful," and *graphia*, which means
"writing." <u>It is difficult to say from which civilization</u>
19
<u>calligraphy directly emerged</u>, as many ancient peoples
19
relied upon the written word and had some form of written
records. Since the printing press wasn't invented until the
mid-fifteenth century, legible handwriting was an important
and useful skill <u>throughout</u> the known world.
20

Chinese calligraphy <u>date back to</u> nearly 5,000 years.
21
Around 200 B.C., a 3,000-character index was established

<u>for use of</u> Chinese scholars. These scribes
22

<u>having quickly developed</u> their own styles
23

when replicating <u>the characters</u> by varying the
24
thickness of the lines, the amount of ink, and the

types of paper. <u>However,</u> true "artists of script"
25

17. The writer is considering adding the following true statement after the preceding sentence:

> Computer fonts, however, cannot fully replicate the artistry and talent of an accomplished calligrapher.

Would this be a relevant addition to the paragraph?
A. Yes, because the writer goes on to discuss how calligraphy is an art form.
B. Yes, because the passage continues to make references to modern technology.
C. No, because the writer is focusing on calligraphy itself, not on specific calligraphers.
D. No, because computer fonts have nothing to do with the art of calligraphy.

18. F. NO CHANGE
G. derived with
H. derived by
J. derived to

19. A. NO CHANGE
B. It is with difficulty that it is said which civilization calligraphy emerges from,
C. From which civilization calligraphy directly emerged is difficult to say,
D. Which civilization, it is difficult to say, from which calligraphy directly emerged,

20. F. NO CHANGE
G. about
H. from
J. beside

21. A. NO CHANGE
B. dated back to
C. dates back
D. dating back

22. F. NO CHANGE
G. for use in
H. for use with
J. for use by

23. A. NO CHANGE
B. quickly developing
C. quickly developed
D. who have quickly developed

24. F. NO CHANGE
G. a lot of the characters
H. the multitude of characters
J. DELETE the underlined portion

25. A. NO CHANGE
B. Soon,
C. Yet,
D. Otherwise,

GO ON TO THE NEXT PAGE.

1 ■ ■ ■ ■ ■ ■ ■ ■ 1

emerged in Japan and <u>adapted</u> Chinese calligraphy around
                           26

the seventh century, developing their own style, which

included an appreciation <u>for</u> imperfection as well as
                           27

technical ability.

     In Europe, <u>calligraphy was greatly influencing by the</u>
                                                                 28

<u>development of the Church</u> during the Middle Ages.
                           28

Manual recording and duplication of religious texts

demanded an abundance of beautiful handwriting.

A variety of styles soon emerged, including Gothic

calligraphy. In the Gothic style, letters are <u>more spaced close</u>,
                                                29

and lines are much narrower than in other styles.

Because the print takes up less space, less paper

is required.

     Today, calligraphy continues to fascinate both scribes

and art aficionados alike. Modern calligraphy equipment,

such as specialized pens, inks, and paper, <u>makes</u> the art fairly
                                              30

easy to learn.

26. F. NO CHANGE
    G. adapts
    H. adapting
    J. having adapted

27. A. NO CHANGE
    B. with
    C. to
    D. unto

28. F. NO CHANGE
    G. the development of calligraphy greatly influenced
       by the Church
    H. the Church greatly influenced the development of
       calligraphy
    J. calligraphy greatly influenced by the development of
       the Church

29. A. NO CHANGE
    B. close and spaced
    C. more closely spaced
    D. spaced closely

30. F. NO CHANGE
    G. making
    H. make
    J. made by

PASSAGE III

Early American Fur Trappers

     The myth of the early American mountain men <u>paints</u>
                                                            31

a picture of romance, adventure, and intrigue. In reality,

most mountain men were fur traders <u>acting to participate</u>
                                         32

in a tough business that sent them for months at

a time to the vast rivers and mountains of the American

West. For the most part, beaver pelts were the primary

target of these unconventional businessmen, as beaver

31. A. NO CHANGE
    B. paint
    C. by painting
    D. painting

32. F. NO CHANGE
    G. participating
    H. who, acting to participate
    J. choosing to act and participate

GO ON TO THE NEXT PAGE.

1 ■ ■ ■ ■ ■ ■ ■ ■ 1

hats and coats were all the rage in early American towns

and cities. [33]

While some fur trappers and traders traveled alone, many worked together in groups for a particular trading company. The Hudson Bay Company, well-known throughout Europe,

was the world's first and largest fur-trading company. Its
                     ‾‾‾‾‾‾‾‾‾‾‾‾‾‾
                          34

buyers would rendezvous at designated sites in America
                           ‾‾‾‾‾‾‾‾‾‾
                              35
where trappers presented furs in exchange for money or

essential goods. [36]

While the mountain man appear to personify "rugged
                        ‾‾‾‾‾‾‾‾‾
                           37
individualism," he was completely dependent upon his ability

to trap wild animals and, therefore, relied upon consumer

demand in those pelts.
      ‾‾
      38

33. At this point, the writer is considering adding the following sentence:

> While not inexpensive, harvesting beaver pelts directly from North America was far cheaper than importing them from across the ocean.

Would this be a relevant addition to make here?
  A. Yes, because the writer needs to establish that beaver pelts were very expensive.
  B. Yes, because the sentence emphasizes the importance of the American mountain man's contribution.
  C. No, because the paragraph focuses on the American mountain man, not on beaver pelts.
  D. No, because beaver pelts from other countries cost more than those obtained in America.

34. F. NO CHANGE
  G. first and, largest
  H. first and largest;
  J. first, and, largest

35. A. NO CHANGE
  B. designating
  C. designate
  D. and designate

36. Given that all of the following sentences are true, which one should be placed here to offer a logical explanation for why trappers sometimes traded their furs for goods instead of money?
  F. While mountain men were skilled hunters and could capture their own food, they still needed many supplies in order to survive.
  G. Many Indian tribes were willing to trade goods and supplies with the mountain men.
  H. Some mountain men had families back in the cities and towns, so money was important.
  J. Trappers enjoyed trading goods and supplies among themselves, as long as the Hudson Bay Company approved.

37. A. NO CHANGE
  B. appeared to
  C. appear
  D. appears to

38. F. NO CHANGE
  G. by
  H. with
  J. for

GO ON TO THE NEXT PAGE.

1   **1**

While some of the trappers were <u>employing</u> a particular
                                         39
fur company, others chose to be freelancers.

Men <u>hired directly, by a fur company</u> were called
              40
"engagers," and all furs they obtained were

company property <u>and not for personal use</u>.
                                41

The "free-trapper" was the most autonomous of <u>all; he</u>
                                                                42
trapped wherever and with whomever he chose. He also

traded or sold his furs at his own discretion. Although the

free-trappers were considered by their peers to be tough

and hardy <u>because of</u> their ability to endure the hardships
                  43
of mountain living, many of these mountain men

eventually <u>succumb</u> to those hardships.
                  44

39. **A.** NO CHANGE
    B. under the employment of
    C. employed by
    D. DELETE the underlined portion.

40. **F.** NO CHANGE
    G. hired directly, by a fur company
    H. hired directly by a fur company
    J. hired, directly by a fur company

41. **A.** NO CHANGE
    B. that were given directly to the company
    C. and did not belong to them
    D. DELETE the underlined portion.

42. **F.** NO CHANGE
    G. all:
    H. all, he
    J. all he

43. **A.** NO CHANGE
    B. in regards with
    C. because
    D. irregardless of

44. **F.** NO CHANGE
    G. succumbing
    H. will be succumbing
    J. succumbed

Question 45 asks about the preceding passage as a whole.

45. Suppose the writer had intended to write an essay that
    explored the myth of the American mountain man. Would
    this essay successfully fulfill the writer's goal?
    A. No, because the essay focuses on American myths in
        general, not just the myth of the American mountain
        man.
    B. No, because American mountain men did not actually
        exist.
    C. Yes, because the writer explains how the American
        mountain man story is really a myth.
    D. Yes, because the writer discusses the contrast between
        the romantic, mythical side of the mountain man's life
        and the reality of his job.

GO ON TO THE NEXT PAGE.

1 ■ ■ ■ ■ ■ ■ ■ ■ **1**

PASSAGE IV

The Green Bay Packers

In 1919, Curly Lambeau returned home to Green Bay, Wisconsin to playing football at Notre Dame. In a conversation with his friend George Calhoun, he expressed regret at not being able to play football since returning home. Calhoun decides to recommend that Curly start a team in his home town. Excited by the idea, Lambeau convinced his boss at the Indian Packing Company to donate uniforms and the use of an athletic field.

Curly ran ads in the local newspaper, inviting other athletes to join the new team. Only 20 football players joined the team the first year. Although Lambeau named the team the Big Bay Blues, fans and players called the team the Packers.

The conditions under which the Packers played during that first year were a far cry from those enjoyed by modern present-day football teams. They played their games in an empty field behind Hagemeister Brewery. There were no locker rooms, so players normally changed into their uniforms at home before the game. There were no gates or bleachers; so there was no way to charge admission or accurately count attendance.

46. **F.** NO CHANGE
    G. from playing football at Notre Dame.
    H. due to playing football at Notre Dame.
    J. by which to play football at Notre Dame.

47. **A.** NO CHANGE
    B. recommended to him a decision
    C. recommended
    D. gives his recommendation

48. **F.** NO CHANGE
    G. the Packers, they were called by the fans and players of the team.
    H. the team was called the Packers by the fans and the players.
    J. the fans called the team the Packers, the players, too.

49. **A.** NO CHANGE
    B. contemporary
    C. up-to-date
    D. DELETE the underlined portion

50. **F.** NO CHANGE
    G. before the game into their uniforms at home.
    H. uniforms at their home before the game.
    J. into their uniforms, which were at home before the game.

51. **A.** NO CHANGE
    B. gates or bleachers, so there was no way to charge admission
    C. gates, or bleachers, so there was no way to charge admission
    D. gates or bleachers. So there was no way to charge admission

GO ON TO THE NEXT PAGE.

Without fences and stands, the only way by raising money
52

was quite literally to pass a hat around to spectators for
53

donations. 54

In 1920, bleachers were built on one side of
Hagemeister Park, located behind the brewery. The largest
recorded attendance at that location was 6,000 fans for the
game against the Minneapolis Marines on October 23, 1921.

That was the Packers' first official game that was played
55
as part of the new American Professional Football

Association, which is now known as the National

Football League. 56

From their humble beginnings, the Packers have gone

on to win more NFL championships than any other team,

including four Super Bowls. The Packers now play in a

newly renovated stadium being named
57

Lambeau Field after the legendary status of the
58
team's founder. The stadium now seats 72,515—and
58
over 60,000 people are on the waiting list for season

tickets! The team has come a long

52. F. NO CHANGE
G. it raised
H. to raise
J. they could raise any

53. A. NO CHANGE
B. was, quite literally to pass,
C. was quite literally, to pass
D. was, quite literally, to pass

54. The writer is considering changing the first sentence of this paragraph (assuming that if there is an error, it has been fixed). Which sentence would be the best choice?
F. The writer should not replace the sentence.
G. The Packers endured brutal conditions in the first year, all for the love of the game.
H. When the Packers played their first season, professional football was not very popular nationwide.
J. Equipped with a popular new name, the Packers were ready to begin their first season.

55. A. NO CHANGE
B. they played
C. for playing
D. DELETE the underlined portion

56. The writer would like to link the information already presented about the Green Bay Packers to the information in this paragraph. Assuming all are true, which of the following sentences best achieves this effect?
F. Vince Lombardi coached the Packers with great success in the 1960s.
G. The Packers are the only publicly owned team in the NFL.
H. In the 1950s, Curly Lambeau was fired by the Packers as part of an internal power struggle.
J. This historic game marked the beginning of the Green Bay Packers, one of the oldest franchises in professional football.

57. A. NO CHANGE
B. named after
C. named
D. naming

58. F. NO CHANGE
G. after the team's legendary founder.
H. after the legend of the team's founder.
J. after the team founder's legendary status.

GO ON TO THE NEXT PAGE.

1 ■ ■ ■ ■ ■ ■ ■ ■ **1**

way from wearing donated uniforms and passing
                        59
a hat around a nearly empty field.
              59

59. A. NO CHANGE
B. way, from wearing donated uniforms, and passing a hat around a nearly empty field.
C. way from wearing donated uniforms; and passing a hat around a nearly empty field.
D. way from wearing donated uniforms and passing a hat around, a nearly empty field.

Question 60 asks about the preceding passage as a whole.

60. Suppose the writer had been assigned to write a brief essay illustrating the economic influence of the Packers on the city of Green Bay. Would this essay fulfill that assignment?
F. Yes, because the essay indicates that the team relied on a corporate sponsorship to get started.
G. Yes, because the essay indicates that the team has been very successful.
H. No, because the essay primarily focuses on how the team was started and its eventual success.
J. No, because the essay notes that the team relied on donations rather than charging admission.

PASSAGE V

Prepare for the Starfish Inn

"Are we really planning on staying here?" Sophie

asked me incredulously. "I feel like we have no choice!"

I responded. The place in question was the Starfish Inn, a

motel of dubious character on the beach in Jacksonville,

Florida. We ended up here largely of our own
                          61

irresponsibility. It was our freshman year of college,

yet yearning to escape the cold and dreary weather for the
62
sun of spring break, we decided to head south. It was a last-

minute decision; we did not make reservations anywhere.

When we arrived in Florida, we tried to book a room

in a decent, affordable hotel. After visiting six hotels and

finding no vacancy, we stopped at an information booth. A
                          63
kind and helpful woman delivered the discouraging news

61. A. NO CHANGE
B. instead of
C. because of
D. in part of

62. F. NO CHANGE
G. and
H. but
J. where

63. A. NO CHANGE
B. were stopped by
C. had to stop for
D. stopping at

GO ON TO THE NEXT PAGE.

1 ■ ■ ■ ■ ■ ■ ■ ■ ■ 1

that, if we didn't have reservations anywhere, it would be very difficult for us to possess lodging. She recommended
                                          64
that we check a couple of places, but they all seemed far beyond our limited

budget, which was small. Then she said that the Starfish
         65
Inn was reasonably priced, but that she would not want her daughters to stay there!

So there's how we got into our predicament. After
    66
paying the proprietor of the motel, we dragged our

luggage to the room, where we opened the door with
                    67
great trepidation. The room was a starfish-themed
nightmare! Everything was in shades of blue, green,
and turquoise, with real and depicted starfish on nearly
every surface; so the place looked like it hadn't been
                                        68
redecorated since 1975!
        68

[1] With grim determining, we shuffled across the
                  69
somewhat gritty floor to further check out the place. [2] The
couch was threadbare and lumpy and not exactly inviting.
[3] The television was equipped with a rusty, flimsy, antenna
                                              70
that reminded me of the television that my grandpa

kept in his basement workshop. [4] On the down side,
71
however, the small kitchen table was so rickety that I was
afraid to actually use it. [5] On the plus side, the room
did have a kitchenette, so we could save money by cooking
some meals inside. 72

Confronted with all of these problems, Sophie and I
decided we had one option—to make the best of it and

64. Which choice provides the most appropriate image?
   F. NO CHANGE
   G. secure
   H. capture
   J. grab

65. A. NO CHANGE
   B. budget.
   C. budget. Our budget was pretty typical for college students.
   D. budget. I wanted to have enough money left to buy souvenirs.

66. F. NO CHANGE
   G. it's
   H. that's
   J. its

67. A. NO CHANGE
   B. so
   C. we
   D. DELETE the underlined portion.

68. F. NO CHANGE
   G. surface, the place looked like it hadn't been redecorated since 1975!
   H. surface (looking like it hadn't been redecorated since 1975).
   J. surface; the place looked like it hadn't been redecorated since 1975!

69. A. NO CHANGE
   B. determined
   C. determination
   D. determine

70. F. NO CHANGE
   G. with a rusty, flimsy antenna
   H. with a rusty flimsy, antenna
   J. with a rusty flimsy antenna

71. A. NO CHANGE
   B. will keep
   C. in keeping
   D. keep

72. For the sake of unity and coherence, Sentence 5 of this paragraph should be placed:
   F. where it is now.
   G. immediately before Sentence 2.
   H. immediately before Sentence 3.
   J. immediately before Sentence 4.

GO ON TO THE NEXT PAGE.

1 ■ ■ ■ ■ ■ ■ ■ ■ 1

enjoy ourselves! We thought that it was about time to escape the pseudo-undersea atmosphere of the room and enjoy some real ocean views. 73

73. The writer would like to conclude the final paragraph with a sentence that shows the shift in attitude she and her friend Sophie experienced. Which choice would best accomplish this?
   A. I begrudgingly accepted the fact that our motel room was terrible as we headed to the beach.
   B. As the old saying goes: "When life gives you lemons, make lemonade."
   C. We headed to the beach moaning about our crazy motel room.
   D. I decided that my next spring break trip will definitely not be in Florida!

Questions 74 and 75 ask about the preceding passage as a whole.

74. The writer is considering the addition of the following sentence to the essay:

   I couldn't help but be reminded of one of the most fascinating facts about starfish: that if you chop one up, a new starfish will grow from each remaining stump.

   Given that this statement is true, should it be added to the essay, and if so, where?
   F. Yes, at the end of the second paragraph because the lady at the information booth mentioned the Starfish Inn. Adding the sentence would be an effective way for the writer to foreshadow the troubles she and her friend would soon have at the motel.
   G. Yes, at the end of the third paragraph, because the writer had just finished describing the starfish theme of the room.
   H. No, because it is evident that the writer is not interested in scientific facts.
   J. No, because a scientific statement would be out of context in an essay describing the personal experiences of the writer and her friend.

75. Suppose a travel agent hired the writer to write an article warning of the possible hazards of being unprepared for a vacation. Does this essay successfully fulfill the assignment?
   A. Yes, because the first paragraph clearly states that the writer and her friend traveled to Florida.
   B. Yes, because the essay gives an example of what can happen when you don't make reservations before going on vacation.
   C. No, because the essay is primarily intended to be a humorous story about being forced to stay at a dilapidated motel.
   D. No, because the essay concerns college students and does not consider that others may also be unprepared for a vacation.

END OF THE ENGLISH TEST.
STOP! IF YOU HAVE TIME LEFT OVER, CHECK YOUR WORK ON THIS SECTION ONLY.

2   **2**

MATHEMATICS TEST

60 Minutes – 60 Questions

DIRECTIONS: Solve each of the problems in the time allowed, then fill in the corresponding bubble on your answer sheet. Do not spend too much time on any one problem; skip the more difficult problems and go back to them later. You may use a calculator on this test. For this test you should assume that figures are NOT necessarily drawn to scale, that all geometric figures lie in a plane, and that the word *line* is used to indicate a straight line.

1. If $x + 3 = n$, then $2x + 6 = ?$
   A. $n + 3$
   B. $n + 6$
   C. $2n$
   D. $2n + 3$
   E. $2n + 6$

2. The expression $a(b - 2c)$ is equivalent to:
   F. $ab - 2a - 2c$
   G. $ab - 2ac$
   H. $ab - 2bc$
   J. $ab - b - 2c$
   K. $ab - 2b - c$

3. Which 3 numbers should be placed in the blanks below so that the difference between consecutive numbers is the same?

   _____, 3, 10, _____, 24_____

   A. −4, 17, 31
   B. 0, 17, 30
   C. 1, 13, 31
   D. 2, 17, 25
   E. 5, 15, 31

4. Diane bought 1 DVD for $20.00 and 5 others that were on sale for $8.49 each. What was the average price per DVD that she paid for these 6 DVDs?

   F. $\$20.00 + \dfrac{\$8.49}{5}$

   G. $\dfrac{\$20.00 + 5(\$8.49)}{6}$

   H. $\dfrac{\$20.00 + \$8.49}{6}$

   J. $\dfrac{\$20.00 + \$8.49}{2}$

   K. $\dfrac{(\$20.00) + 5(\$8.49)}{2}$

DO YOUR FIGURING HERE.

GO ON TO THE NEXT PAGE.

2   **2**

DO YOUR FIGURING HERE.

5. Roberto needs $18\frac{1}{4}$ feet of lumber for a project. He has $10\frac{1}{2}$ feet of lumber. How many more feet does he need?

   A. $6\frac{7}{8}$

   B. $7\frac{1}{4}$

   C. $7\frac{3}{4}$

   D. $8\frac{1}{3}$

   E. $8\frac{2}{5}$

6. If x is a real number and $3^x = 81$, then $2^x \times 2 = ?$
   F. 4
   G. 8
   H. 16
   J. 32
   K. 64

7. A rectangular garden measures 60 feet by 25 feet. A fence completely encloses the garden. What is the length, in feet, of the fence?
   A. 85
   B. 170
   C. 256
   D. 625
   E. 1,500

8. If $x = -6$, then $-x^2 - 2x + 21 = ?$
   F. −27
   G. −3
   H. 21
   J. 45
   K. 69

9. The formula for the volume of a sphere is $V = \frac{4}{3}\pi r^3$. If the radius, r, of a spherical ball is 2 inches, what is its volume, to the nearest cubic inch?
   A. 8
   B. 19
   C. 25
   D. 34
   E. 96

10. The expression $4c - 2d$ is equivalent to which of the following?
    F. $4(c - 2d)$
    G. $2cd$
    H. $2(c - d)$
    J. $4(c - d)$
    K. $2(2c - d)$

GO ON TO THE NEXT PAGE.

2   **2**

11. For each day on the job, you receive $20.00 plus a fixed amount for each lawn that you mow. Currently you are earning $95.00 per day for mowing 5 lawns. Today you will mow an additional 2 lawns. What will be your new daily earnings?
   A. $50.00
   B. $75.00
   C. $100.00
   D. $125.00
   E. $150.00

DO YOUR FIGURING HERE.

12. Which of the following is a simplified form of $4x + 2x + y - x$?
   F. $3x + y$
   G. $5x + y$
   H. $2(x+2)(x+y)$
   J. $6x - y$
   K. $x(6+y)$

13. When graphed in the standard (x, y) coordinate plane, which of the following equations does NOT represent a line?
   A. $x = 3$
   B. $2y = 7$
   C. $-y = 2x + 1$
   D. $y = \dfrac{3}{4}x$
   E. $x^2 = y - 7$

14. In the figure below, point C is the center of the circle. If $a = 40°$, what is the value of b?

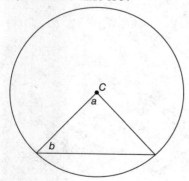

   F. $80°$
   G. $70°$
   H. $60°$
   J. $50°$
   K. $40°$

15. What is the least common multiple of 2, 3, and 9?
   A. 2
   B. 3
   C. 9
   D. 18
   E. 45

GO ON TO THE NEXT PAGE.

2   **2**

DO YOUR FIGURING HERE.

16. If $x = \frac{1}{2}$, then $\frac{1}{x} + \frac{1}{x} - 1 = ?$

   F. −4
   G. 0
   H. 1
   J. 2
   K. 3

17. As shown below, the diagonals of rectangle *MNOP* intersect at the point (5, −1) in the standard (*x*, *y*) coordinate plane. Point *M* is at (−1, −4). Which of the following are the coordinates for point *O*?

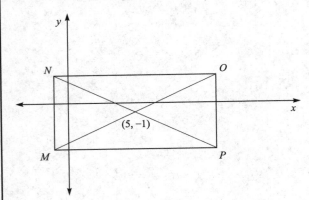

   A. (−6, 2)
   B. (−1, 4)
   C. (9, 3)
   D. (10, −3)
   E. (11, 2)

18. Tony is participating in a charity event and must collect pledges for every mile that he runs in the next 30 days. His friend pledges 9 cents per mile for the first 25 miles that he runs, and 7 cents per mile for each additional mile. Tony's goal is to run 63 miles in the next 30 days. Assuming he meets but does not exceed his goal, what is the total amount Tony should collect from his friend?

   F. $2.25
   G. $4.91
   H. $6.66
   J. $8.33
   K. $10.08

19. If the inequality $|x| > |y|$ is true, then which of the following *must* be true?

   A. $x > 0$
   B. $x < y$
   C. $x = y$
   D. $x \neq y$
   E. $x > y$

GO ON TO THE NEXT PAGE.

2   **2**

20. For which nonnegative value of x is the expression $\dfrac{1}{(100-4x^2)}$ undefined?

    F. 0
    G. 5
    H. 10
    J. 100
    K. 400

21. Given that $x \le 3$ and $x + y \le 7$, what is the LEAST value that y can have?
    A. 0
    B. 3
    C. 4
    D. 7
    E. 10

22. The two squares below have the same dimensions. The vertex of one square is at the center of the other square. What is the area of the shaded region, in square centimeters?

6 cm

    F. 9
    G. 12
    H. 27
    J. 36
    K. 72

23. The lengths of the sides of a triangle are 3, 4, and 5 inches. What is the length, in inches, of the shortest side of a similar triangle that has a perimeter of 36 inches?
    A. 6
    B. 9
    C. 12
    D. 15
    E. 18

24. If $4(a+b)(a-b)=40$ and $a-b=20$, then $a+b=$?
    F. 30
    G. 20
    H. 10
    J. 2
    K. $\dfrac{1}{2}$

DO YOUR FIGURING HERE.

GO ON TO THE NEXT PAGE.

2   **2**

DO YOUR FIGURING HERE.

25. The sum of 3 and 200% of 1 has the same value of which of the following calculations?

   A. 500% of 1
   B. 300% of 3
   C. 200% of 4
   D. 150% of 2
   E. 100% of 3

26. If, for all x, $(x^{7a-2})^3 = x^{57}$, then $a =$?

   F. 2
   G. 3
   H. $\dfrac{31}{5}$
   J. $\dfrac{51}{21}$
   K. 57

27. If 3 times a number n is added to 9, the result is negative. Which of the following gives the possible value(s) for n?

   A. −3 only
   B. 0 only
   C. 6 only
   D. all $n < -3$
   E. all $n > -3$

28. If $\dfrac{3}{5}x = \dfrac{4}{3}$, what is the value of x?

   F. $\dfrac{9}{20}$
   G. $\dfrac{4}{5}$
   H. $\dfrac{5}{4}$
   J. $\dfrac{15}{12}$
   K. $\dfrac{20}{9}$

29. The sum of three numbers is 855. One of the numbers, n, is 50% more than the sum of the other two numbers. What is the value of n?

   A. 155
   B. 214
   C. 513
   D. 570
   E. Cannot be determined from the given information.

GO ON TO THE NEXT PAGE.

2   **2**

30. In the right triangle pictured below, r, s, and t are the lengths of its sides. What is the value of $\tan \alpha$?

DO YOUR FIGURING HERE.

F. $\dfrac{r}{t}$

G. $\dfrac{s}{t}$

H. $\dfrac{t}{r}$

J. $\dfrac{r}{s}$

K. $\dfrac{t}{s}$

31. For all $x > 0$, $\dfrac{1}{x} - \dfrac{3}{4} = ?$

A. $\dfrac{3}{4x}$

B. $3 - 4x$

C. $\dfrac{4}{x} - 3$

D. $\dfrac{3}{x} - \dfrac{4}{x}$

E. $\dfrac{4 - 3x}{4x}$

32. In the figure below, lines m and n are parallel, lines o and p are parallel, and the measure of angle α is 40°. What is the measure of angle β?

F. 40°
G. 50°
H. 110°
J. 140°
K. 180°

33. Which of the following degree measures is equivalent to 4.25 π radians?
A. 270°
B. 360°
C. 594°
D. 765°
E. 945°

GO ON TO THE NEXT PAGE.

2 △ △ △ △ △ △ △ △ **2**

34. Among the points graphed on the number line below, which is the closest to $1\frac{3}{4}$?

DO YOUR FIGURING HERE.

F. A
G. B
H. C
J. D
K. E

35. The sides of a triangle measure $3\sqrt{2}$ meters, 3 meters, and 3 meters. What are the measures of the angles of the triangle, in degrees?
A. $30° - 60° - 90°$
B. $90° - 30° - 30°$
C. $40° - 50° - 90°$
D. $90° - 45° - 45°$
E. $45° - 60° - 90°$

36. What is the median of the data given below?

9, 13, 27, 22, 20, 31, 13

F. 13
G. 19
H. 20
J. 21
K. 22

37. If p is a positive integer that divides both 45 and 60, but divides neither 9 nor 10, what should you get when you add the digits in p?
A. 3
B. 2
C. 5
D. 6
E. 9

38. What is the slope of any line perpendicular to the x-axis in the (x, y) coordinate plane?
F. -1
G. 0
H. 1
J. Undefined
K. Cannot be determined from the given information

39. In the (x, y) coordinate plane, line m is perpendicular to the y-axis and passes through the point $(5, -3)$. Which of the following is an equation for line m?
A. $x = 0$
B. $x = 5$
C. $y = -3$
D. $y = x + 2$
E. $y = x + 8$

GO ON TO THE NEXT PAGE.

2 △ △ △ △ △ △ △ **2**

40. If $\tan \beta = \dfrac{3}{4}$, then $\sin \beta =$?

DO YOUR FIGURING HERE.

   F. $\dfrac{3}{5}$

   G. $\dfrac{3}{4}$

   H. $\dfrac{4}{5}$

   J. $\dfrac{4}{3}$

   K. $\dfrac{5}{4}$

41. What is the product of the mean and the median of the first 5 prime numbers, to the nearest integer?
(Note: 2 is the first prime number.)

   A. 17
   B. 20
   C. 28
   D. 96
   E. 192

42. Which of the following calculations will yield an even integer for any integer n?

   F. $4n^2$
   G. $3n^2 + 1$
   H. $5n^2 - 1$
   J. $3n$
   K. $n^2 - 2n$

43. In triangle CAB, the measure of $\angle A$ is $45°$ and the measure of $\angle B$ is $45°$. If $\overline{AC}$ is 12 units long, what is the perimeter, in units, of triangle CAB?

   A. 36
   B. $36\sqrt{2}$
   C. 72
   D. $24 + 12\sqrt{2}$
   E. $24 + 12\sqrt{3}$

GO ON TO THE NEXT PAGE.

2   △ △ △ △ **2**

> Use the following information to answer questions 44 and 45.

The table below shows the number of households in the town of Potterville, situated in Eaton County, with a high-speed Internet connection for each year from 1999 through 2006.

Year	Number of households	Year	Number of households
1999	152	2003	516
2000	176	2004	647
2001	231	2005	780
2002	422	2006	825

44. Which of the following years had the greatest increase in the number of households with a high-speed Internet connection over the previous year?
    F. 2000
    G. 2002
    H. 2003
    J. 2005
    K. 2006

45. Census data shows that there were approximately 652 households in Eaton County with a high-speed Internet connection in 2000. According to this information, the number of Potterville households with a high-speed Internet connection was approximately what percent of the total number of households in Eaton County with a high-speed Internet connection in 2000?
    A. 15%
    B. 27%
    C. 35%
    D. 50%
    E. 73%

46. What is the largest integer less than $\sqrt{98}$?
    F. 8
    G. 9
    H. 10
    J. 11
    K. 12

2 △ △ △ △ △ △ △ △ 2

47. If $\log_x 169 = 2$, then $x = ?$

A. 2
B. 13
C. 84.5
D. 169
E. 338

DO YOUR FIGURING HERE.

48. Given that $x \begin{bmatrix} 2 & 6 \\ 1 & 4 \end{bmatrix} = \begin{bmatrix} a & 15 \\ b & c \end{bmatrix}$ for some real number x, what is the value of $a + c$?

F. $\dfrac{1}{2}$

G. $\dfrac{15}{2}$

H. 15
J. 30
K. 45

49. What is the area of quadrilateral *WXYZ* if it has vertices with (x, y) coordinates $W(2, 4)$, $X(5, 4)$, $Y(4, 1)$, and $Z(1, 1)$?

A. $\sqrt{17}$
B. 6
C. 9
D. $8\sqrt{2}$
E. 18

50. In the standard (x, y) coordinate plane, if the *x*-coordinate of each point on a line is 3 more than twice the corresponding *y*-coordinate, the slope of the line is:

F. $-\dfrac{1}{2}$

G. $\dfrac{1}{2}$

H. 2
J. 3
K. 6

51. In the (x, y) coordinate plane, what is the radius of the circle having the points $(-4, 4)$ and $(0, -2)$ as endpoints of a diameter?

A. $\sqrt{7}$
B. $2\sqrt{2}$
C. $\sqrt{13}$
D. $2\sqrt{7}$
E. $2\sqrt{13}$

GO ON TO THE NEXT PAGE.

2   **2**

52. If X, Y, and Z are real numbers, and $XYZ = 1$, then which of the following conditions *must* be true?

   F. $XY = \dfrac{1}{Z}$

   G. X, Y, and $Z > 0$

   H. Either $X = 1$, $Y = 1$, or $Z = 1$

   J. Either $X = 0$, $Y = 0$, or $Z = 0$

   K. Either $X < 1$, $Y < 1$, or $Z < 1$

DO YOUR FIGURING HERE.

53. Which of the following expressions gives the number of permutations of 18 objects taken 6 at a time?

   A. $18(6)$

   B. $(18 - 6)!$

   C. $\dfrac{18!}{6!}$

   D. $\dfrac{18!}{(18-6)!}$

   E. $\dfrac{18!}{6!(18-6)!}$

54. The average of a set of 7 integers is 24. When an 8th number is included in the set, the average of the set increases to 31. What is the 8th number?

   F. 31

   G. 55

   H. 80

   J. 168

   K. 217

55. In the figure shown below, $c = ?$

   A. $75°$

   B. $70°$

   C. $65°$

   D. $60°$

   E. Cannot be determined from the information given.

56. The ratio of l to m is 3 to 4, and the ratio of p to m is 1 to 2. What is the ratio of l to p?

   F. 6 to 1

   G. 3 to 8

   H. 3 to 2

   J. 3 to 1

   K. 1 to 1

GO ON TO THE NEXT PAGE.

2 △ △ △ △ △ △ △ △ **2**

57. Jordan has been hired to build a circular wading pool in his neighbor's backyard. The rectangular backyard measures 40 feet wide by 70 feet long. Jordan's neighbors want the pool to be as large as possible, with the edge of the pool at least 4 feet from the edge of the backyard all around. How long should the radius of the pool be, in feet?

A. 16
B. 32
C. 36
D. 40
E. 62

DO YOUR FIGURING HERE.

58. Three distinct lines contained within a plane separate the plane into distinct regions. How many possible distinct regions of the plane may be separated by any 3 such lines?

F. 4, 7, 8
G. 4, 6, 7
H. 3, 6, 7
J. 3, 5, 8
K. 3, 4, 6

59. If the sum of the consecutive integers from -22 to n, inclusive, is 72, then $n =$?

A. 94
B. 74
C. 50
D. 25
E. 23

60. In a set of 13 different numbers, which of the following CANNOT affect the value of the median?

F. Increasing the largest number only.
G. Decreasing the largest number only.
H. Increasing the smallest number only.
J. Increasing each number by 10.
K. Doubling each number.

END OF THE MATHEMATICS TEST.
STOP! IF YOU HAVE TIME LEFT OVER, CHECK YOUR WORK ON THIS SECTION ONLY.

3 **3**

READING TEST

35 Minutes – 40 Questions

DIRECTIONS: This test includes four passages, each followed by ten questions. Read the passages and choose the best answer to each question. After you have selected your answer, fill in the corresponding bubble on your answer sheet. You should refer to the passages as often as necessary when answering the questions.

PASSAGE I

LITERARY NARRATIVE: *Born in Paradise*

Martin spent most of his childhood in a tropical paradise on the island of Barbados. Despite the pleasant climate, Martin's early life was difficult. His father left when Martin was a baby, and his mother, Sheila, worked long
5 hours as a housekeeper at a nearby hotel. Martin was left to be cared for by his teenage brothers. In the best of times, the selfish boys let Martin fend for himself; in the worst of times, they made Martin the target of their pranks. Eventually, Martin's mother recognized his plight and enlisted the
10 help of Martin's grandmother.

Granny loved Martin dearly, but the elderly woman did not have the energy to keep up with a feisty toddler. As often as possible, she took Martin to the rundown neighborhood playground so that he could burn off some of his
15 excess energy. On the endless rainy days of summer, she was often heard to exclaim, "Oh, Martin! What am I gonna do with you?"

To help fill the long, muggy days, Granny began taking Martin to the island's library. There they sat for hours
20 as she slowly read him story after story. When her voice grew tired, young Martin would beg her to teach him to read. "Oh, Martin. You're too young to read, dear," she would reply. But Martin was determined, and his inquisitiveness prevailed. Soon, the symbols on the page took
25 on meaning; as the rainy season ended, Martin begged to continue their library excursions.

"Sheila, Martin is special."

Sheila absently looked up.

"What's that, Mom?"

30 "I said, 'Martin is special!'"

"Oh. Yeah. And, listen, I really appreciate you taking care of him like you have. In a couple of years he can go to school and then it will all be so much easier!"

"I'm not sure it will. When I said he was special I
35 didn't just say it because I'm his grandmother. He's special." She paused and then continued, "You know, he can read."

"It is wonderful the way he likes books and all."

"Have you ever let him read to you?"

40 "Of course! He comes into my room almost every morning and recites his favorite book. He even turns the pages. It's very cute!"

"Sheila! Pay attention! I know you're tired from working long hours, but Martin isn't reciting—he's
45 reading! In all my years I have never seen a four-year-old like him. By next month he'll be reading books that are beyond me!"

Sheila's mother continued: "Honey, the schools here will be too easy for Martin, and you can't afford to send
50 him to one of those fancy international schools. You have got to get to America where they'll have schools for a child like Martin."

"Mom, think what you're saying! I can't just pick up and move to another country! The older boys aren't even
55 finished with school yet, and there's no way they'd leave their friends! Besides, I can't possibly afford to move to America. Do you have any idea how much it costs to live there?"

"Slow down! I'm not telling you to leave today. I'm
60 telling you to start planning and saving. Your older boys will be done with school in a few years. Then they can fend for themselves. Oh, don't give me that look—I'll look after 'em! But you gotta start makin' plans for Martin. Honey, he doesn't like to be bored, and that's gonna be a
65 problem pretty soon. He's a good boy, and he'll behave in these schools while he's still young. But I can't promise that he'll be able to control himself when he realizes he knows more than the teachers! I don't want to see that precious baby wasting his life and getting into trouble!
70 Sweetie, he's got a gift, and you gotta do something with that gift."

Sheila paused for a long moment as she struggled to comprehend all that her mother was telling her. Finally, she sighed. "Okay."

75 "What's that?"

"I said, 'okay.' I trust you. I'll start finding out what I need to do to get Martin and me to America. But I don't know what we're gonna do when we get there!"

"Just work on getting there. You can figure out the
80 rest later."

GO ON TO THE NEXT PAGE.

3 ████████████████████████████████ **3**

1. When Granny says, "I'm not sure it will," (line 34) she is expressing her concern that:
   A. schools in Barbados are dangerous.
   B. Martin is hyperactive and will likely behave poorly in school.
   C. the school will not provide the academic challenge that Martin requires.
   D. life never gets any easier.

2. It can be reasonably inferred from their conversation that Granny believes Sheila is:
   F. not as well-educated as Martin is.
   G. too overworked to recognize Martin's gift.
   H. an incompetent parent.
   J. overly solicitous with her sons.

3. The idea that Martin's mother is unaware of his abilities is best exemplified by which of the following quotations from the passage?
   A. "He even turns the pages. It's very cute!"
   B. "Do you have any idea how much it costs to live there?"
   C. "Mom, think what you're saying!"
   D. "I really appreciate you taking care of him like you have."

4. As it is used in line 33, the word *it* most nearly refers to the:
   F. library excursions.
   G. reading of books.
   H. taking care of Martin.
   J. start of the school year.

5. It can be inferred from the passage that Granny is:
   A. Martin's paternal grandmother.
   B. Sheila's mother-in-law.
   C. Martin's maternal grandmother.
   D. an unknown wealthy benefactor.

6. The passage makes it clear that Martin and his mother:
   F. plan to move to America.
   G. do not get along.
   H. will be alienated from Martin's brothers.
   J. will never see Granny again.

7. You may reasonably infer from the details in the passage that Sheila is:
   A. self-confident.
   B. never going to make friends in America.
   C. negligent in her care of her older sons.
   D. willing to do whatever it takes to help Martin succeed.

8. You may reasonably infer from the passage that Martin's brothers:
   F. attended a school for juvenile delinquents.
   G. often read books to Martin.
   H. were not well-liked in school.
   J. cared more for themselves than for Martin.

9. Within the passage, the main function of the second paragraph is to:
   A. describe the special bond between a grandmother and grandson.
   B. explain the deplorable living conditions of the main characters.
   C. provide evidence of a potential conflict in the story.
   D. introduce a comparison between an old woman and a young child.

10. The title, "Born in Paradise," combined with details presented in the passage implies that:
    F. everyone loves a tropical island.
    G. only natives can attend school in Barbados.
    H. American schools are inferior.
    J. paradise is a relative term.

GO ON TO THE NEXT PAGE.

3 ▬▬▬▬▬▬▬▬▬▬▬▬▬▬▬▬▬▬ **3**

PASSAGE II

SOCIAL SCIENCE: The following passages discuss different battles of the Civil War.

Passage A

The bloodiest single day of war in United States history came when General Robert E. Lee's Confederate Army undertook its first engagement on Northern soil. According to the Antietam National Battlefield, when
5 the fighting had subsided, more than 23,000 soldiers lay dead or wounded, more than all of the dead or wounded Americans in the Revolutionary War, War of 1812, Mexican War, and Spanish-American War combined.

Just a week after his army's victory in the Second
10 Battle of Bull Run, Lee resolved to advance the front into Northern territory. The vast farm fields of western Maryland were ready for harvest, and Lee saw in them an opportunity to nourish his soldiers, replenish his supplies, and turn the residents of the undecided border state to his cause.

15 So with great fanfare, Lee and fellow General "Stonewall" Jackson marched their ragged Army of Northern Virginia across the Potomac River and straight through the Frederick town square. Lee issued the *Proclamation to the People of Maryland* to invite the citizens
20 to join the Southern movement. Soldiers obeyed Lee's order to refrain from violence and pillaging, so for several days the townspeople maintained tacit compliance and sold food, clothes, and shoes to Southern troops. Lee keenly observed, however, that while pleasant, the
25 people of Maryland reserved no sympathy for the Confederate side, so he needed a revised plan.

Forces would divide to take western Maryland and then reform to advance along the railroad toward Harrisburg, Pennsylvania, a crucial Union transport hub.
30 General Jackson led 22,000 troops southwest to Harpers Ferry to engage the 12,000-man Federal fortification. Lee's remaining 18,000 soldiers would march over the mountains 25 miles to Hagerstown and wait for the others. On September 10, 1862, all began their march. No one
35 knew how fateful it would be.

Lee soon realized that the Union was a step ahead. Its Army of the Potomac was reassembled in days instead of the weeks Lee had forecast. In addition, the Harpers Ferry garrison had remained instead of fleeing as Lee had imagined it
40 would upon learning of his advance. Lastly, an enlisted man searching a recently abandoned Confederate camp had recovered a copy of Lee's order detailing the siege of Maryland.

Union General George McClellan moved his forces west through Frederick, and Lee caught word of it. Know-
45 ing the peril his divided troops were in, he ordered men to fortify the paths across the mountains, granting sufficient time to the majority of his soldiers to establish a defensive position near Sharpsburg. Simultaneously, McClellan and his 85,000 men waited along Antietam Creek outside town.
50 By nightfall on September 16, the stage was set for the devastating Battle of Antietam, which would begin at sunrise.

Passage B

The three days of the Battle of Gettysburg, Pennsylvania, constitute the bloodiest fight of the Civil War—50,000 combatants falling dead or wounded or disappearing.
55 Gettysburg is often cited as the last crucial battle of the war before the Confederate surrender. In the intervening two years, the Confederate Army would never again attempt such a grand offensive in the North. On the last day of battle, Union forces anticipated and defused what is now known
60 as Pickett's Charge, the final assault ordered by General Robert E. Lee, leaving Confederate forces in tatters.

Lee approached the third day of Gettysburg with the same strategy as he had the day before. He would divide his forces to attack Federal positions from both the east
65 and the west. Troops under General James Longstreet were to take up the assault on Culp's Hill. However, standing by at dawn, Longstreet and his men unexpectedly suffered a devastating artillery bombardment from Union troops intent on reclaiming the previous day's losses.

70 Lee hastened to revise his plan of attack. Nine brigades were set to attack Federal positions in the center of the line on Cemetery Ridge. The selection of troops for this mission was the first of many Confederate blunders that doomed Pickett's Charge. Confederate General A. P.
75 Hill was ill, so responsibility for his men was passed to General George Pickett, who failed to distinguish between Hill's well-rested men and those who had recently fought in battle. Indeed the battle-fatigued soldiers that made the charge fell into ranks in a thicket behind the cannons.

80 Longstreet initiated the infantry assault under orders from General Lee. The Southern force numbered over 12,000 men across nine brigades to form a mile-long offensive front. The thousand-yard march to within musket range of the Union fortifications was peppered with har-
85 rowing artillery fire. When cannonade became fusillade, the mile of men had narrowed to nearly half. Flanking fire from the left decimated an entire brigade. Forces in the center wheeled to support them but were met with a musket attack from the Eighth Ohio Infantry regiment, which
90 had unexpectedly moved to ambush the Confederate soldiers. The Virginians under General Pickett brought up the rear and retook the fight to the left. Soon, their right flank was exposed to calamitous enfilade fire from the Vermont Brigade. Remaining Confederates succeeded in a partial
95 breech of the center Union line, but reinforcements from the right quickly put down the Southern offensive.

The charge was a massacre. Pickett's brigade commanders, each of his 13 regiment leaders, and nearly half his 12,000 enlisted men fell during the assault. Union
100 dead or wounded numbered fewer than 2,000. Today at Gettysburg, a monument commemorates the "high water mark" of the Confederacy along Cemetery Ridge, for after Pickett's Charge on July 3, 1863, the Army of the South never fully recovered and began the series of retreats and
105 surrenders that concluded the Civil War.

GO ON TO THE NEXT PAGE.

3   **3**

Questions 11 – 13 ask about Passage A.

11. As it is used in line 3, the word "engagement" most nearly means:
    A. match.
    B. commitment.
    C. arrangement.
    D. confrontation.

12. In line 15 the phrase "so with great fanfare" suggests that General Lee was:
    F. broken and despondent.
    G. fatigued from recent battle.
    H. eager to promote his cause.
    J. satisfied with his army's progress.

13. Which statement about the Army of Northern Virginia, if true, would most directly support the view described in lines 20–23?
    A. General Lee was a powerful but often barbaric man.
    B. Soldiers were difficult to control in times of great stress.
    C. Soldiers took great pains to keep their uniforms and equipment tidy.
    D. A rigid chain of command maintained strict order throughout the ranks.

Questions 14 – 17 ask about Passage B.

14. As it is used in line 58, "grand" most nearly means:
    F. haughty.
    G. massive.
    H. wonderful.
    J. extravagant.

15. According to Passage B, Pickett's Charge failed because of which of the following?
    I.   Artillery fire
    II. Infantry charges
    III. Exhausted soldiers
    A. I only
    B. II only
    C. I and II
    D. I, II, and III

16. It can reasonably be inferred from Passage B that the statement "the mile of men had narrowed to nearly half" (line 86) suggests that the Confederate line:
    F. moved within firearms range.
    G. was suffering massive losses.
    H. was easy for Union soldiers to target.
    J. made very slow progress across the field.

17. In lines 101–102, the quotation marks around the phrase "high water mark" serve to:
    A. indicate that this word is used allegorically.
    B. emphasize the limitations of military conquest.
    C. criticize the human preoccupation with expansion.
    D. emphasize the uniqueness of the author's writing.

Questions 18 – 20 ask about both passages.

18. Unlike the author of Passage A, the author of Passage B does which of the following?
    F. Details a specific battle.
    G. Explains a war strategy.
    H. Questions an officer's decision.
    J. Offers an alternative interpretation.

19. Both Passage A and Passage B indicate that the Civil War:
    A. was amicably resolved.
    B. denied certain freedoms to Americans.
    C. resulted in many casualties on both sides.
    D. decided the borders of all fifty states in the Union.

20. Which of the following most accurately describes a way in which the two passages are related to each other?
    F. Passage A introduces a topic that is further detailed in Passage B.
    G. Passage B suggests an alternate framework within which to interpret Passage A.
    H. The history suggested in Passage A is proven to be false by the facts in Passage B.
    J. The evidence presented in Passage B serves to weaken the assertions made in Passage A.

GO ON TO THE NEXT PAGE.

3 ████████████████████████████████ **3**

PASSAGE III

HUMANITIES: *The Passion of Perugino*

I remember feeling slightly disconcerted as I looked up at the unsmiling saints, the Virgin Mary, and even Jesus as I wandered through the hushed halls of the museum. The unworldly experience continues to haunt my memory as I
5 recall the unflinching gazes of Pietro Perugino's subjects staring blankly at me as I admired the power and beauty of the great Italian Renaissance master's most famous works of art. For years, I had studied great artists of the past and present, but not even the breathtaking landscapes of Monet
10 could prepare me for the moment that I was confronted with the genius of one of the least well known artists of the Italian Renaissance. In that moment, my admiration for artists like Renoir and Manet of the French Impressionist Movement, was eclipsed by the austere exquisiteness of
15 these fifteenth-century paintings.

Since that day in the museum, I have gained more knowledge and expertise about the Italian Renaissance movement, and I recognize that Pietro Perugino's work is not beyond critique. His paintings have been described
20 as monotonous and unimaginative because the people portrayed often look alike without any distinguishing features. His paintings lack the ingenuity and fluidity of Sandro Botticelli. Perugino's own pupil, Raphael, could surpass his teacher in creating emotion on the canvas. The
25 genius Michelangelo could evoke dreaminess in his work that creates a feast for the imagination, while keeping minuscule details in perfect perspective. And yet, Pietro Perugino's paintings are still the ones that I see in my mind when I hear the words *Italian Renaissance*.

30 I remember being awestruck as I viewed his fresco *The Delivery of the Keys* (1482) and noticing the elegant simplicity of the painting, which portrayed St. Peter accepting the keys to heaven. The painting should have paled next to the other more dramatic work in the Sistine
35 Chapel, but *The Delivery of the Keys* held its own with its voluminous clouds and elegant gothic buildings in the background. In this piece, Pietro Perugino showed how far art had come since the medieval times. Instead of flat and cardboard-like characters, the subjects in *The Delivery*
40 *of the Keys* display awe, disbelief, and amazement while engrossed in conversation with each other. Perugino also experimented with depth, and he rivaled Leonardo da Vinci in his ability to create a definite background and foreground. *The Delivery of the Keys* boasts a gorgeous
45 mountain landscape that truly appears to be miles away from St. Peter as he accepts the key to eternity.

During our tour of the Sistine Chapel, the guide had shared with us the story of Perugino's life. Perugino would almost starve to death because he forgot to eat or sleep
50 while painting. Rest was never an option for this driven artist. His dedication shined through in his meticulous, yet passionate work. The love that Perugino had for painting shows in the careful detail of works like *The Delivery of the Keys*. In my mind, Perugino's passion for art gives his
55 pieces their distinction and this passion more than makes up for any deficiencies that his critics might find.

I have seen the works of several painters from the Italian Renaissance that are considered far greater than anything created by Perugino. Paintings by Michelangelo,
60 Leonardo da Vinci, and Botticelli are certainly more in demand and enjoy mainstream popularity and acceptance. All of these three artists seemed capable of creating more dramatic and majestic pieces than did Perugino. The work of da Vinci and Michelangelo is seen on postcards and
65 reprinted on cheap posters everywhere because of its universal appeal. Although the brilliance of all of the Italian Renaissance masters is undeniable, the awe-inspiring beauty of Michelangelo's work or the subtle detail of da Vinci's *Mona Lisa* cannot match the simple passion evi-
70 dent in Perugino's paintings. In spite of being more simple and less appealing to the masses, Perugino's paintings reveal raw talent and skill that I have never seen equaled by another artist anywhere in the world.

21. Which of the following descriptions most accurately and completely represents this passage?
   A. A reminiscent and passionate recollection of the narrator's introduction to Perugino's art
   B. An independent critical analysis of Monet, Renoir, and Manet in relation to Perugino
   C. An impartial evaluation of the paintings of Perugino
   D. A thorough biographical outline of Perugino's life

22. All of the following were unmistakably identified as painters in this passage EXCEPT:
   F. Leonardo da Vinci.
   G. Michelangelo.
   H. Botticelli.
   J. Donatello.

23. Which of the following quotations best expresses the main point of the passage?
   A. "Since that day in the museum, I have gained more knowledge and expertise about the Italian Renaissance movement, and I recognize that Pietro Perugino's work is not beyond critique."
   B. "I have seen the works of several painters from the Italian Renaissance that are considered far greater than anything created by Perugino."
   C. "In this piece, Pietro Perugino showed how far art had come since the medieval times."
   D. "In my mind, Perugino's passion for art gives his pieces their distinction and this passion more than makes up for any deficiencies that the critics might find."

GO ON TO THE NEXT PAGE.

3 ■■■■■■■■■■■■■■■■■■■■■■■■ **3**

24. As it is used in the passage (line 22), the word *ingenuity* most nearly means:
    F. resourcefulness.
    G. inventiveness.
    H. quality.
    J. versatility.

25. It can be inferred from the passage that the narrator most highly values which of the following in an artist?
    A. Fluidity and volatility
    B. Unique appearance of subjects
    C. Devotion and passion for art
    D. Classical training from the masters

26. It can be most reasonably concluded from the writer's quote, "In that moment, my admiration for artists like Renoir and Manet of the French Impressionist Movement, was eclipsed by the austere exquisiteness of these fifteenth-century paintings," (lines 12–15) that:
    F. few of the painters of the French Impressionist Movement were as talented as the artists of the Italian Renaissance.
    G. the masters of the Italian Renaissance are more universally accepted than Renoir and Manet.
    H. the narrator believes that the technical skill and creativity of Perugino surpasses that of Renoir and Manet.
    J. the narrator's admiration of Perugino is so great, he or she believes that Perugino's work outshines that of more well-known painters.

27. According to the passage, what are characteristics of Perugino's work?
    I. austerity
    II. showing the passion of the artist
    III. ability to display depth
    IV. abstraction
    A. I, II, III only
    B. I, II only
    C. I, IV only
    D. I, II, IV only

28. Which of the following best describes the narrator's instant reaction upon seeing Perugino's paintings for the first time?
    F. Disbelief in the quality of the work
    G. Unsettled by some of the features of the paintings
    H. Envious of Perugino's genius and artistic ability
    J. Intent on comparing Perugino's work to French Impressionist artists

29. All of the following are a criticism of Perugino's paintings mentioned in the passage EXCEPT:
    A. Perugino's paintings show a lack of imagination.
    B. Perugino's technique in creating depth was not as advanced as Leonardo da Vinci's.
    C. the subjects or people of Perugino's paintings often look alike.
    D. Raphael could create more emotion in his paintings than Perugino.

30. The narrator states his or her opinion about famous artists and their work throughout the passage. All of the following opinions are clearly stated in the passage EXCEPT:
    F. Manet's work is reprinted on postcards and cheap posters because of its popularity.
    G. Leonardo da Vinci and Perugino could both display depth well.
    H. Botticelli's work shows fluidity and ingenuity.
    J. the painting *Mona Lisa* by Leonardo da Vinci shows subtle detail.

GO ON TO THE NEXT PAGE.

3 ▬▬▬▬▬▬▬▬▬▬▬▬▬▬▬▬▬▬▬ **3**

PASSAGE IV

NATURAL SCIENCE: *The Prickly Porcupine*

As we timidly watched the lumbering escape efforts of this oversized rodent, we were struck by its own apparent lack of fear and panic. Then it dawned on us that, unlike most other animals in the wild, the
5   porcupine's mere outward appearance provides more than adequate reason for it rarely to become alarmed or excited. Even knowing that the "shooting-quills" forest legend really is just that, stumbling upon this threatening creature is sure to cause fear and panic
10 only from the human's point of view and not vice versa.

The *Erethizon dorsatum* (Latin for "irritable back") comes equipped with more than 30,000 quills on its back, sides, and tail. Each of these quills con-
15 tains several barbs, or hook-like structures, that can imbed themselves into the flesh of a predator. Rather than throwing their quills, however, porcupines are able to implant them into their would-be attacker when the animal or human gets too close. Porcupines
20 also swing their tails back and forth, slamming quills into their adversaries. Since these quills are hollow, they fill up with the host's blood once imbedded, making them even more difficult to remove. Many a dog has found itself with a noseful or mouthful of porcu-
25 pine quills, which need to be tended to right away. Often, clipping an inch or so off the end of the quills before removing them can aid in their extraction and relieve the excruciating pain.

The porcupine ranks second in size to the beaver
30 among the rodent family. A full-grown porcupine can range anywhere from two to three and a half feet in length and generally weighs between eight and fourteen pounds. However, a porcupine with a plentiful food supply can weigh considerably more. Female
35 porcupines generally give birth once a year to a single offspring. The long, seven-month gestation period ensures a well-developed infant that is nearly ready at birth to take care of itself. Born with soft quills, it takes only a few hours after birth for these quills
40 to harden and be ready for an attack. There are some animals, however, that are able to break down the porcupine's powerful defense system by carefully turning the porcupine over onto its back, exposing its soft and vulnerable underbelly. Bobcats, cougars, and coyotes
45 are especially adept at this technique and pose a major threat to the porcupine.

Porcupines are mostly found in northern and cold climates. They are particularly fond of forested areas, as mature trees provide both food and shelter.

50 During the winter months, porcupines chew almost exclusively on tree bark. As nocturnal animals, porcupines generally sleep high up in a tree during the day, though they also use underground burrows, particularly in the spring while tending their newborns.

55 According to the Yukon Department of Environment, the porcupine has been useful to and appreciated by many. Quills are often used in jewelry- and basket-making, as well as in decorating clothing and shoes. Porcupine meat is even considered to be a tasty meal and fairly easy to
60 obtain. In British Columbia, however, the porcupine has developed a negative reputation due to its appetite for wood, damaging trees and even wooden buildings.

While porcupines can be a source of worry to some people, they are fascinating animals to observe. Because
65 of their incredible defense systems, they take their time to escape a potential enemy, which allows for a great opportunity to view these animals fairly closely. Just don't get too close!

31. The primary purpose of the passage is to:
  A. detail the various ways in which the quills of a porcupine are used by humans.
  B. give a brief overview of the porcupine, its habitat, and the misconceptions associated with it.
  C. prove false the "shooting-quills" legend associated with the porcupine.
  D. detail the safest way to remove porcupine quills from animals such as dogs and beavers.

32. The author calls the porcupine a "threatening creature" (line 9) in the first paragraph because:
  F. it is a timid creature.
  G. it is merely a forest legend.
  H. it becomes alarmed and excited.
  J. it has a frightening appearance.

33. The passage indicates that, unlike some other wild animals, the porcupine:
  A. has a descriptive scientific name.
  B. does not have a defense mechanism.
  C. is not easily frightened.
  D. generally finds plenty of food.

34. According to the author, the porcupine most likely moves slowly because:
  F. its quills add extra weight.
  G. it has no reason to move quickly.
  H. it has no predators.
  J. it has short legs.

GO ON TO THE NEXT PAGE.

3 ▬▬▬▬▬▬▬▬▬▬▬▬▬▬▬▬▬▬▬▬▬▬▬▬ **3**

35. Based on information in the passage, the author feels dogs are especially threatened by porcupines because:
- **A.** dogs are larger than porcupines.
- **B.** dogs are likely to touch porcupines with their noses and mouths.
- **C.** porcupines only attack dogs.
- **D.** porcupines often wander into peoples' backyards.

36. The passage indicates that the Yukon government considers porcupines to be both:
- **F.** scarce and endangered.
- **G.** appreciated and useful.
- **H.** dangerous and unthreatening.
- **J.** feared and disliked.

37. Which of the following quotations best captures the second paragraph's (lines 12–28) main focus?
- **A.** "Each of these quills … can imbed themselves into the flesh of a predator" (lines 14–16).
- **B.** "Rather than throwing their quills" (line 17).
- **C.** "Porcupines also swing their tails" (line 20).
- **D.** "Since these quills are hollow, they fill up with the host's blood" (lines 21–23).

38. The passage indicates that a porcupine turned over on its back would most likely be:
- **F.** safe to approach.
- **G.** killed by predators.
- **H.** unnoticed or ignored.
- **J.** ready to attack.

39. The passage indicates that, if imbedded, a porcupine's quills:
- **A.** can cause death.
- **B.** can be very painful.
- **C.** should be left alone.
- **D.** will eventually fall out on their own.

40. According to the passage, the scientific name for the porcupine means:
- **F.** "prickly animal."
- **G.** "shooting quills."
- **H.** "threatening creature."
- **J.** "irritable back."

END OF THE READING TEST.
STOP! IF YOU HAVE TIME LEFT OVER, CHECK YOUR WORK ON THIS SECTION ONLY.

SCIENCE TEST

35 Minutes – 40 Questions

DIRECTIONS: There are several passages in this test. Each passage is followed by several questions. You should refer to the passages as often as necessary in order to choose the best answer to each question. Once you have selected your answer, fill in the corresponding bubble on your answer sheet.

You may NOT use a calculator on this test.

PASSAGE I

A hurricane is a large, rotating storm centered around an area of very low pressure with strong winds blowing at an average speed in excess of 74 miles per hour. Hurricanes are dangerous natural hazards to people and the environment. However, they are also essential features of the Earth's atmosphere. Hurricanes transfer heat and energy between the equator and the cooler regions toward the poles.

Two meteorologists present their views on hurricane formation.

Meteorologist 1

The most influential factors that turn a storm into a hurricane are a source of very warm, moist air coming from tropical oceans having surface temperatures greater than 26°C, and sufficient spin from the Earth's rotation. The warm ocean heats the air above it, causing a current of very warm, moist air to rise quickly. This creates a center of low pressure at the surface. Trade winds rush in toward the area of low pressure, which force the inward-spiraling winds to whirl upward, releasing heat and moisture. The rotation of the Earth causes the rising column to twist. The rising air cools and quickly produces towering cumulus and cumulonimbus clouds. When the warm water evaporates from the tropical ocean, energy is stored in the water vapor. As the air rises, the majority of the stored energy is released as condensation, resulting in vertically growing cumulonimbus clouds and rain. The hurricane

becomes a self-sustaining heat engine because the release of heat energy warms the air locally and causes a further decrease in pressure. Air rises faster to fill the low-pressure area and more warm, moist air is drawn off the sea. This gives the system additional energy. A hurricane causes major destruction when its path takes it over land, but this also leads to the destruction of the hurricane itself.

Meteorologist 2

Hurricanes start out as a group of storms that begin to rotate when they encounter converging winds. They are not necessarily formed where the surface temperature of the ocean is warm, nor does the Earth's rotation have any bearing on whether storms turn into hurricanes. The converging winds spin the group of storms until they organize into a more powerful spiraling storm. The storm takes the form of a cylinder whirling around an "eye" of relatively still air. The spinning storm heats the surface of the ocean until the warm water turns into water vapor. The water vapor rises very quickly, rotating with the storms and helps to increase the wind speed. The cycle repeats itself and eventually the water vapor is released as condensation, resulting in a tremendous amount of rain. For the hurricane to die, it must reach land. The hurricane causes major destruction when it hits land, but it destroys itself at the same time. Over the past three decades, studies have shown that higher-than-average tropical ocean temperatures did not result in more hurricanes.

GO ON TO THE NEXT PAGE.

4 ◯ ◯ ◯ ◯ ◯ ◯ ◯ 4

1. Assuming that increased levels of atmospheric carbon dioxide (CO_2) cause an increase in air temperatures, which of the following figures best represents the relationship between CO_2 levels and the number of hurricanes, according to Meteorologist 1?

2. Which of the following would Meteorologist 1 suggest leads to an increase in the number of hurricanes, assuming that increased levels of atmospheric CO_2 cause an increase in air temperature?
   F. Decreased levels of atmospheric CO_2
   G. Increased marine life in the oceans
   H. Decreased production and release of particles that increase water temperatures in tropical oceans
   J. Reduced number of forests and trees that help remove CO_2 from the atmosphere during photosynthesis

3. It has been found that nontropical oceans and seas contain higher numbers of marine animals. This results in increased water temperatures at the surface due to the energy that is transferred from the movement of the marine life. However, hurricanes do not occur in these waters. This information would best support the view of:
   A. Meteorologist 1, because hurricanes are mostly self-sustaining.
   B. Meteorologist 1, because increased water temperatures cause hurricanes.
   C. Meteorologist 2, because increased water temperatures do not cause hurricanes.
   D. Meteorologist 2, because there are no converging winds in these waters.

4. According to the hypothesis of Meteorologist 1, which of the following results is expected if global temperatures increase and water temperatures rise?
   F. There will be an increase in the number of hurricanes.
   G. There will be a decrease in the number of hurricanes.
   H. There will be no change in the number of hurricanes.
   J. Hurricanes will be easier to predict.

5. The views of both meteorologists are similar because they imply that:
   A. increased water temperatures alone help create hurricanes.
   B. converging winds are not a necessary component in hurricane formation and duration.
   C. hurricanes become stronger and more destructive with the presence of warm water and water vapor.
   D. there is a correlation between average water temperatures and the number of hurricanes.

6. Meteorologist 2 states that higher:
   F. surface water temperatures cause hurricanes.
   G. surface water temperatures do not cause hurricanes.
   H. wind speeds do not cause hurricanes.
   J. levels of CO_2 cause hurricanes.

7. The hypothesis of Meteorologist 2 could best be tested by:
   A. recording the surface temperature of nontropical oceans and seas over the next 10 years.
   B. recording the surface temperature of tropical oceans and seas over the next 10 years and comparing the data with the number of hurricanes recorded during the same time period.
   C. combining waters with cooler surface temperatures and high converging winds, and recording the data for at least 10 years.
   D. combining waters with warmer surface temperatures and high converging winds, and recording the data for at least 10 years.

GO ON TO THE NEXT PAGE.

4   **4**

PASSAGE II

Gas diffusion occurs when a gas moves from a syringe into a sealed vacuumed area where it can spread widely and thinly throughout the entire vacuumed area. A 50 ml gas sample in a syringe is forced into a sealed vacuumed area. The molecular mass in a.m.u. (atomic mass units), for 6 noble gases, as well as the time required for the gases to completely diffuse throughout the entire 10-cubicfoot (c^3) vacuumed area, are recorded in Table 1. The densities (mass/volume), boiling point (Kelvin, or K), and melting point (Kelvin, or K) are also given.

Table 1					
Noble gas	Diffusion time (sec)	Molecular mass (a.m.u.)	Density (g/cm^3)	Boiling point (K)	Melting point (K)
He	13	4	0.25	5	1
Ne	18	20	1.00	27	25
Ar	28	40	2.00	87	84
Kr	43	84	4.00	120	116
Xe	58	131	6.00	165	161
Rn	73	222	10.0	211	202

Note: Figures are all rounded to the nearest number.

Figure 1 shows a graph of the diffusion time versus the molecular mass of the noble gases.

Figure 1

8. Given the information in Table 1, the difference in diffusion times is greatest between which of the following pairs of noble gases?
   F. He and Kr
   G. Ne and Ar
   H. Kr and Rn
   J. Ne and Xe

9. Based on the passage, what is the relationship between diffusion time and molecular mass?
   A. Diffusion time increases as molecular mass increases.
   B. Diffusion time decreases as molecular mass increases.
   C. Diffusion time stays constant as molecular mass decreases.
   D. Diffusion time stays constant as molecular mass increases.

10. Six vacuumed areas of identical shape and size are placed side by side. Six syringes, each containing 50 milliliters (ml) of one of the noble gases is forced into each vacuumed area. According to the data in Table 1, if these areas are kept under the same conditions, which gas should completely diffuse first?
    F. He
    G. Ne
    H. Ar
    J. Kr

11. A 50-ml sample of Ar gas is allowed to diffuse into a 10-cubic-foot vacuumed area. Given the information in Table 1, what percentage of the vacuumed area will NOT have Ar gas molecules after 14 seconds?
    A. 12.25%
    B. 25%
    C. 50%
    D. 75%

12. According to Table 1, if a vacuumed area of unknown volume is filled with Ne gas, and it takes 54 seconds for this Ne gas to completely diffuse, then the volume of the vacuumed area will be closest to:
    F. 2.5 cubic feet.
    G. 5 cubic feet.
    H. 20 cubic feet.
    J. 30 cubic feet.

GO ON TO THE NEXT PAGE.

4   **4**

PASSAGE III

A study was conducted to determine whether two processes (Process A and Process B) provided reliable data on the content of forest soil samples of varying acidity (acid concentration). The concentrations of several compounds commonly tested for in forest soil samples were measured. The results are presented in Table 1. The results for the processes were compared to estimates obtained using Standard Methods, which provide extremely accurate estimates.

Table 1					
Concentration (mg/L) of :	Acidity of sample (pH level)				
	2	3	4	5	6
Dissolved O_2					
Standard	5.6	5.2	4.6	4.4	3.9
Process A	5.6	5.1	4.4	4.1	3.7
Process B	5.7	5.3	4.7	4.4	4.0
Dissolved CO_2					
Standard	36.5	22.4	10.1	2.2	44.7
Process A	32.4	20.8	11.3	3.4	42.1
Process B	35.6	19.9	9.5	4.4	41.2
Calcium carbonate ($CaCO_3$)					
Standard	23.5	1920	5350	9507	11346
Process A	22.9	1875	5167	8909	12544
Process B	23.7	2002	5454	9589	11543
Dissolved $CaCl_2$					
Standard	78.5	78.8	79.7	81.2	104.4
Process A	73.3	78.2	80.4	85.0	101.2
Process B	66.8	67.8	78.9	89.8	153.2
Dissolved NH_3					
Standard	0.41	0.43	0.88	0.91	0.69
Process A	0.48	0.52	0.68	0.81	0.76
Process B	0.42	0.45	0.86	0.92	0.67

Note: Higher pH levels indicate lower acidity.

13. From the results of the study, one would conclude that at a pH level of 2, Process A is most accurate in measuring the concentration of which of the following compounds, relative to the Standard Method?
    A. Dissolved O_2
    B. Dissolved CO_2
    C. Calcium carbonate
    D. Dissolved $CaCl_2$

14. The data from which of the measurement procedures supports the conclusion that the concentration of calcium carbonate increases as the level of acidity decreases?
    F. Standard Method only
    G. Process A only
    H. Standard Method, Process A, and Process B
    J. The data does not support the conclusion.

15. Is the conclusion that Process A is more accurate than Process B for estimation of NH_3 concentration supported by the results in the table?
    A. Yes, because the estimates using Process A are consistently lower than are the estimates using Process B.
    B. Yes, because the estimates using Process A are more similar to the estimates using the Standard Method than are the estimates using Process B.
    C. No, because the estimates using Process B are more similar to the estimates using the Standard Method than are the estimates using Process A.
    D. No, because the estimates using Process B are consistently higher than the estimates using Process A.

GO ON TO THE NEXT PAGE.

4   **4**

16. Which of the following graphs best represents the relationship between pH level and the concentration of dissolved CO_2 as estimated by Process A?

F.

H.

G.

J.

17. A forest soil sample of unknown acidity was tested using Process A. The concentrations, in milligrams per liter (mg/l), of selected compounds in this sample were: dissolved $O_2 = 5.5$, dissolved $CaCl_2 = 72.1$, and $NH_3 = 0.49$. According to the data in the table, one would predict that the most likely pH level was:

A. 6
B. 5
C. 4
D. 2

GO ON TO THE NEXT PAGE.

4   4

PASSAGE IV

Pesticides are often used to kill and repel fleas and ticks on dogs. Two experiments were designed to measure the effectiveness of different pesticides on fleas and ticks. The pesticides work by making contact with the fleas and ticks during the application and by coating the dogs' skin.

Experiment 1

A biologist tested two types of flea and tick pesticides on flea- and tick-infested dogs. Ten dogs were washed with a shampoo containing 8 oz. of Pesticide A, and 10 other dogs were washed with a shampoo containing 8 oz. of Pesticide B. All dogs weighed between 15 and 20 pounds (lbs) and were noted to have at least 10 visible ticks each. The shampoo volumes were identical. The dogs were then inspected for live fleas and ticks. The total number of remaining fleas and ticks were counted, averaged, and recorded 24 hours after treatment and 48 hours after treatment. The results are shown in Table 1.

Table 1				
	Average count at 24 hrs		Average count at 48 hrs	
	Fleas	Ticks	Fleas	Ticks
Pesticide A	27	5	4	4
Pesticide B	10	11	3	9

Note: The average number of fleas per dog before treatment = 57
The average number of ticks per dog before treatment = 13

Experiment 2

A biologist tested three types of flea and tick shampoos: one containing only Pesticide A, one containing only Pesticide B, and a combination of the shampoos (Pesticide A + B), which contained 50% of Pesticide A and 50% of Pesticide B, on dogs with long and short coats. The experiment was conducted in the same manner as Experiment 1, except fleas and ticks were only counted and averaged after 24 hours. The results are shown in Table 2.

Table 2				
	Average count at 24 hrs		Average count at 24 hrs	
	Long coat		Short coat	
	Fleas	Ticks	Fleas	Ticks
Pesticide A	34	7	26	4
Pesticide B	15	12	9	10
Pesticide A + B	20	10	13	8

Note: The average number of fleas per dog before treatment = 57
The average number of ticks per dog before treatment = 13

Information on average coat length of the dogs in both experiments is given in Table 3.

Table 3	
Coat type	Length (in.)
Long	1.5 ≥ 3.5
Short	0 > 1.5

18. The results of Experiments 1 and 2 indicate that which type of pesticide was most effective in removing fleas?
F. Pesticide A
G. Pesticide B
H. Pesticide A + B
J. Neither pesticide removed fleas.

19. Which scenario would most reduce the number of ticks on a dog?
A. Applying Pesticide B to a dog with a long coat
B. Applying Pesticide A + B to a dog with a short coat
C. Applying Pesticide B to a dog with a short coat
D. Applying Pesticide A to a dog with a short coat

20. Based on the results of Experiment 2, shorter coat length leads to:
F. reduced effectiveness of all pesticides.
G. increased effectiveness of Pesticide A only.
H. increased effectiveness of all pesticides.
J. reduced effectiveness of Pesticide B only.

21. Which of the following best explains why Pesticide A + B did not drastically reduce the number of both fleas and ticks?
A. The two pesticides interfered with each other's effectiveness.
B. The outcome depended on whether the dog had a long or short coat.
C. The pesticides did not remain in sufficient contact with the fleas and ticks.
D. The combined volume of Pesticide A + B was less than that of the other pesticides.

22. Assuming a coat length of 2 inches, what is the average number of ticks per dog 24 hours after application of Pesticide A?
F. 4
G. 7
H. 10
J. 12

GO ON TO THE NEXT PAGE.

4 ○ ○ ○ ○ ○ ○ ○ ○ **4**

PASSAGE V

Radioactive decay is a natural process by which an atom of a radioactive isotope spontaneously decays into another element. The unstable nucleus disintegrates by emitting alpha or beta particles or gamma rays. This process changes the composition of the nucleus and continues to take place until a stable nucleus is reached. *Half-life* is the amount of time it takes for half of the atoms in a sample to decay.

Figure 1 shows the decay from Fluorine 22 to Neon 22.

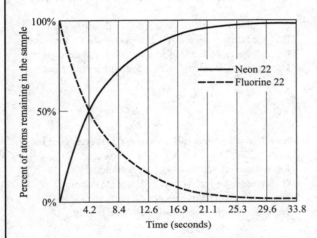

Figure 1

Figure 2 shows the decay from Oxygen 22 to Fluorine 22 to Neon 22.

Figure 2

Table 1 shows the decay products and associated energy in MeV (million electron volts) and velocity, measured as a fraction of the speed of light.

Table 1			
Isotope	Decay product	Energy (MeV)	Particle velocity
Phosphorus 42	Sulfur 42	17.300	0.9995
Nitrogen 22	Oxygen 22	22.800	0.9997
Oxygen 22	Fluorine 22	6.490	0.9973
Fluorine 22	Neon 22	10.818	0.9989

23. According to Figure 1, what is the approximate half-life of Fluorine 22?
    A. 16.9 seconds
    B. 8.4 seconds
    C. 4.2 seconds
    D. 29.6 seconds

24. Based on the passage, radioactive decay:
    F. is stable.
    G. does not occur in nature.
    H. is a natural process.
    J. only occurs in half of the atoms.

25. Based on Table 1, what is the relationship between decay energy and decay particle velocity?
    A. Lower decay energy leads to lower particle velocity.
    B. Lower particle velocity leads to higher decay energy.
    C. Decay energy does not impact particle velocity.
    D. Higher decay energy leads to lower particle velocity.

26. When Cerium 53 decays into Lanthanum 127, the decay energy is 6.100 MeV. According to the data in Table 1, the decay particle velocity is most likely:
    F. greater than the particle velocity of Oxygen 22.
    G. approximately equal to the particle velocity of Flourine 22.
    H. greater than the particle velocity of Nitrogen 22.
    J. approximately equal to the particle velocity of Oxygen 22.

27. Based on Figure 2, at which time do Oxygen 22 and Neon 22 have the same percent of atoms remaining?
    A. 2.2 seconds
    B. 4.5 seconds
    C. 6.7 seconds
    D. 15.7 seconds

28. What statement best explains the meaning of the shape of the Fluorine 22 curve in Figure 1 and the Oxygen 22 curve in Figure 2?
    F. Decay happens at a steady rate regardless of the number of atoms.
    G. Decay starts off slowly and then speeds up.
    H. Decay occurs very quickly at first and slows as the number of atoms is reduced.
    J. The rate of decay is erratic.

GO ON TO THE NEXT PAGE.

4 ○ ○ ○ ○ ○ ○ ○ ○ **4**

PASSAGE VI

A study was conducted on the effects of pesticide exposure on domestic chicken breeds. Some zoologists believe that exposure to pesticides can lead to lower birth rates and increased susceptibility to illness. Table 1 shows the average number of eggs laid, average number of eggs that hatch, and resistance to illness before being exposed to a pesticide for several different domestic chicken breeds.

Table 1			
Chicken breed	Resistance to illness	Average number of eggs laid	Average number of eggs hatched
A	High	10	9
B	High	8	7
C	Medium	11	8
D	Medium	7	5
E	Low	15	9

Figure 1 shows how pesticide exposure affects the chicken's susceptibility to illness.

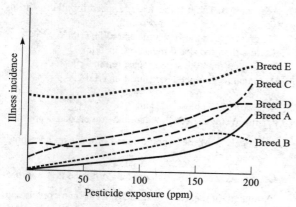

Figure 1

Figure 2 shows the average number of eggs laid and subsequent number of eggs that hatched after exposure to pesticide.

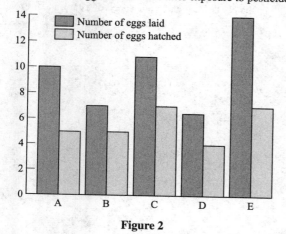

Figure 2

29. Based on the results of the study, if Chicken breed F has a low resistance to illness, approximately how many eggs would you expect to hatch from an average of 20 eggs laid, before pesticide exposure?
   A. 5
   B. 12
   C. 17
   D. 20

30. Based on the information in Figure 1, which breed had the fewest illness incidences at the highest pesticide exposure?
   F. Breed E
   G. Breed C
   H. Breed B
   J. Breed A

31. Based on the data in Figures 1 and 2, which breed is likely to have a higher number of eggs hatch per number of eggs laid, and have a low incidence of illness when exposed to pesticide?
   A. Breed B
   B. Breed A
   C. Breed E
   D. Breed C

32. According to Table 1, what is the relationship between resistance to illness and average number of eggs laid?
   F. The average number of eggs laid remains constant.
   G. There is no direct relationship.
   H. As resistance increases, the average number of eggs laid increases.
   J. As resistance increases, the average number of eggs laid decreases.

33. According to Figure 1, which breed is the least affected by pesticide exposure?
   A. Breed A
   B. Breed B
   C. Breed D
   D. Breed E

34. Based on the passage, which of the following statements is true?
   F. The average number of eggs hatched for all chicken breeds is not affected by pesticide exposure.
   G. Chicken breed C has the lowest resistance to illness.
   H. Chicken breed A had the lowest number of eggs hatch before exposure to pesticide.
   J. The average number of eggs laid by all breeds is not affected by pesticide exposure.

35. According to Table 1, which chicken breed laid the most eggs before pesticide exposure?
   A. E
   B. C
   C. B
   D. A

GO ON TO THE NEXT PAGE.

4   **4**

PASSAGE VII

Some students performed three studies to measure the average speed of a remote-controlled car on different surfaces. Each study was conducted on a fair day with no wind. A 100-foot-long flat surface was marked, and the car's travel time was measured from start to finish with a stopwatch. The car was not modified in any way and the car's batteries were fully charged before each trial.

Study 1

The students placed the car on a smooth asphalt road. One student started the car as the other student started the stopwatch. The student stopped the stopwatch as the car crossed the 100-foot mark. The students calculated the results of three separate trials and averaged the results (see Table 1).

Table 1		
Trial	Time (s)	Speed (ft/s)
1	12	8.33
2	11.3	8.85
3	11.7	8.55
Average:	11.7	8.58

Study 2

The students repeated the procedure used in Study 1, except they placed the car on a rough gravel road. The results are shown in Table 2.

Table 2		
Trial	Time (s)	Speed (ft/s)
1	22.1	4.52
2	21.8	4.59
3	22.4	4.46
Average:	22.4	4.52

Study 3

The students repeated the procedure used in Study 1, except they placed the car on a powdery, dry dirt road. The results are shown in Table 3.

Table 3		
Trial	Time (s)	Speed (ft/s)
1	15.8	6.33
2	16.2	6.17
3	15.7	6.37
Average:	15.9	6.29

36. The highest average speeds resulted from using which surface?
    F. Dirt road
    G. Gravel road
    H. Asphalt road
    J. The speeds remained constant.

37. According to Table 1, the average speed for all three trials is:
    A. greater than the speed measured in Trial 2.
    B. less than the speed measured in Trial 3.
    C. greater than the speed measured in Trial 1.
    D. equal to the speed measured in Trial 2.

38. According to Tables 1, 2, and 3:
    F. the average speed of a car on a gravel road is approximately $\frac{1}{2}$ of the average speed of a car on an asphalt road.
    G. the average speed of a car on a dirt road is $\frac{1}{2}$ approximately of the average speed of a car on a gravel road.
    H. the average speed of a car on an asphalt road is approximately twice the average speed of a car on a dirt road.
    J. the average speed of a car on a gravel road is approximately twice the average speed of a car on a dirt road.

GO ON TO THE NEXT PAGE.

4 ◯ ◯ ◯ ◯ ◯ ◯ ◯ ◯ **4**

39. Based on the passage, the lower average speeds were probably a result of:

   A. human error.
   B. greater friction.
   C. wind resistance.
   D. cloud cover.

40. During which of the following was the travel time of the car the slowest?

   F. Study 1, Trial 2
   G. Study 2, Trial 2
   H. Study 2, Trial 3
   J. Study 3, Trial 2

END OF THE SCIENCE TEST.
STOP! IF YOU HAVE TIME LEFT OVER, CHECK YOUR WORK ON THIS SECTION ONLY.

WRITING TEST

DIRECTIONS: This test is designed to assess your writing skills. You have forty (40) minutes to plan and write an essay based on the stimulus provided. Be sure to take a position on the issue and support your position using logical reasoning and relevant examples. Organize your ideas in a focused and logical way, and use the English language to clearly and effectively express your position.

When you have finished writing, refer to the Scoring Rubrics discussed in Chapter 7 to estimate your score.

Note: On the actual ACT you will receive approximately 2.5 pages of scratch paper on which to develop your essay, and approximately 4 pages of notebook paper on which to write your essay. We recommend that you limit yourself to this number of pages when you write your practice essays.

Seat Belt Laws

Most states currently have laws on the books requiring some or all of the occupants of motor vehicles to fasten their seat belts while the vehicle is in motion. Penalties for operation of a motor vehicle while passengers are unrestrained range from simple fines to potential loss of driving privileges. In many states, there are exceptions for school buses and antique vehicles which were never equipped with seat belts. In some states, a vehicle may not be stopped by law enforcement merely for a seat belt violation, while in other states, officers may stop and ticket a driver for a seat belt violation alone.

PERSPECTIVE ONE	PERSPECTIVE TWO	PERSPECTIVE THREE
Seat belt laws save lives. The statistics show that occupants who are properly restrained are much more likely to survive a serious accident than those who are not. Traffic fatalities nationwide have decreased significantly over the past few decades as seat belt laws have been passed by state after state.	Seat belt laws are an infringement on our basic freedoms. Government does not have the right to force adult citizens to act responsibly simply for their own good. Each individual person is responsible for his or her own safety and society should not be permitted to penalize a person for taking a risk with his or her own body.	Society must bear the medical expenses due to increased injury to individuals who do not use seat belts. Car accidents are still common, even with modern antilock brakes and other similar technologies. In many cases, automobile insurance will not cover treatment for injuries attributable to failure to use safety equipment, leaving all of us to foot the bill.

Essay Task

Write a unified, coherent essay in which you evaluate multiple perspectives on the implications of seat belt laws. In your essay, be sure to:

- analyze and evaluate the perspectives given
- state and develop your own perspective on the issue
- explain the relationship between your perspective and those given

Your perspective may be in full agreement with any of the others, in partial agreement, or wholly different. Whatever the case, support your ideas with logical reasoning and detailed, persuasive examples.

ANSWER KEY

English Test

1. D	21. C	41. D	61. C
2. F	22. J	42. F	62. G
3. B	23. C	43. A	63. A
4. G	24. F	44. J	64. G
5. B	25. B	45. D	65. B
6. H	26. F	46. G	66. H
7. C	27. A	47. C	67. A
8. H	28. H	48. F	68. J
9. A	29. C	49. D	69. C
10. J	30. F	50. F	70. G
11. D	31. A	51. B	71. A
12. J	32. G	52. H	72. J
13. C	33. C	53. D	73. B
14. H	34. F	54. F	74. J
15. B	35. A	55. D	75. C
16. J	36. F	56. J	
17. A	37. B	57. C	
18. F	38. J	58. G	
19. A	39. C	59. A	
20. F	40. H	60. H	

Mathematics Test

1. C	21. C	41. C
2. G	22. H	42. F
3. A	23. B	43. D
4. G	24. K	44. G
5. C	25. A	45. B
6. J	26. G	46. G
7. B	27. D	47. B
8. G	28. K	48. H
9. D	29. C	49. C
10. K	30. J	50. G
11. D	31. E	51. C
12. G	32. J	52. F
13. E	33. D	53. D
14. G	34. K	54. H
15. D	35. D	55. C
16. K	36. H	56. H
17. E	37. D	57. A
18. G	38. J	58. G
19. D	39. C	59. D
20. G	40. F	60. F

Reading Test

1. C	21. A
2. G	22. J
3. A	23. D
4. H	24. G
5. C	25. C
6. F	26. J
7. D	27. A
8. J	28. G
9. C	29. B
10. J	30. F
11. D	31. B
12. H	32. J
13. D	33. C
14. G	34. G
15. D	35. B
16. G	36. G
17. A	37. A
18. F	38. G
19. C	39. B
20. F	40. J

Science Test

1. A	21. A
2. J	22. G
3. C	23. C
4. F	24. H
5. C	25. A
6. G	26. J
7. B	27. B
8. J	28. H
9. A	29. B
10. F	30. H
11. C	31. A
12. J	32. G
13. A	33. D
14. H	34. J
15. C	35. A
16. F	36. H
17. D	37. C
18. G	38. F
19. D	39. B
20. H	40. H

SCORING GUIDE

Your final reported score is your COMPOSITE SCORE. Your COMPOSITE SCORE is the average of all of your SCALE SCORES.

Your SCALE SCORES for the four multiple-choice sections are derived from the Scoring Worksheet on the next page. Use your RAW SCORE, or the number of questions that you answered correctly for each section, to determine your SCALE SCORE. If you got a RAW SCORE of 60 on the English test, for example, you correctly answered 60 out of 75 questions.

Step 1   Determine your RAW SCORE for each of the four multiple-choice sections:

English   _____

Mathematics   _____

Reading   _____

Science   _____

The following Raw Score Table shows the total possible points for each section.

RAW SCORE TABLE	
KNOWLEDGE AND SKILL AREAS	RAW SCORES
ENGLISH	75
MATHEMATICS	60
READING	40
SCIENCE	40

Step 2 Determine your SCALE SCORE for each of the four multiple-choice sections using the following Scale Score Conversion Table.

SCALE SCORE	RAW SCORE			
	ENGLISH	MATHEMATICS	READING	SCIENCE
36	75	60	40	39–40
35	74	59	—	38
34	73	57–58	39	37
33	71–72	56	38	36
32	70	55	37	—
31	69	54	—	35
30	68	53	36	34
29	67	52	35	33
28	65–66	51–50	34	32
27	64	48–49	33	31
26	62–63	46–47	32	29–30
25	60–61	44–45	31	27–28
24	58–59	41–43	30	25–26
23	56–57	38–40	29	23–24
22	54–55	35–37	27–28	21–22
21	51–52	31–34	26	20
20	49–50	28–30	24–25	18–19
19	46–48	27	22–23	17
18	43–45	24–26	21	15–16
17	40–42	20–23	19–20	14
16	36–39	16–19	17–18	12–13
15	33–35	12–15	15–16	11
14	30–32	10–11	13–14	10
13	27–29	8–9	11–12	9
12	24–26	6–7	9–10	8
11	21–23	5	8	7
10	19–20	4	6–7	6
9	15–18	—	—	5
8	13–14	3	5	4
7	11–12	—	4	3
6	9–10	2	3	—
5	7–8	—	—	2
4	5–6	1	2	—
3	4	—	—	1
2	2–3	—	1	—
1	0–1	0	0	0

NOTE: Each actual ACT is scaled slightly differently based on a large amount of information gathered from the millions of tests ACT, Inc. scores each year. This scale will give you a fairly good idea of where you are in your preparation process. However, it should not be read as an absolute predictor of your actual ACT score. In fact, on practice tests, the scores are much less important than what you learn from analyzing your results.

If you take the optional Writing Test, you should refer to Chapter 7 for guidelines on scoring your Writing Test Essay.

Step 3 Determine your COMPOSITE SCORE by finding the sum of all your SCALE SCORES for each of the four sections: English, Mathematics, Reading, and Science, and divide by 4 to find the average. Round your COMPOSITE SCORE according to normal rules. For example, $31.2 \approx 31$ and $31.5 \approx 32$.

ANSWERS AND EXPLANATIONS

English Test Explanations

PASSAGE I

1. **The best answer is D.** The underlined portion must be a verb with tense, or else the sentence would be a fragment. Therefore, eliminate answer choices B and C. Answer choice D, which has past tense, is best because the sentence clearly states that Noh began in *Medieval Japan*, a past time period.

2. **The best answer is F.** This question requires you to select the correct punctuation for the underlined portion. Answer choice G has unnecessary commas. Both answer choice H and answer choice J improperly use semicolons. The comma after *Zeami* is necessary because the two independent clauses are conjoined with *and*.

3. **The best answer is B.** The sentence references a time period in the past (*fourteenth and fifteenth centuries*). To describe an action (in this case, staying unchanged) that began in the past and is ongoing in the present, the present perfect tense is appropriate. Only answer choice B uses this verb tense.

4. **The best answer is G.** The words *only*, *just*, and *solely* all have similar meaning. To avoid redundancy, you should use only one of them in the sentence. Eliminate answer choices F, H, and J.

5. **The best answer is B.** The interrupting phrase *for example* should always be set off by commas when it appears within a sentence. The only answer choice that places a comma before and after *for example* is answer choice B.

6. **The best answer is H.** The noun being replaced by the pronoun in this sentence is *instrumentalists*, which is plural. Therefore, you must use the plural pronoun *they*. Eliminate answer choices F and J. The noun *scores* is the direct object of the verb *play*, so no preposition (*for*) is necessary. Eliminate answer choice G.

7. **The best answer is C.** Paragraph 3 discusses the *stylized masks* worn by the actors to reflect certain characters. The sentence that best introduces this topic is answer choice C.

8. **The best answer is H.** The actors, not the characters that they portray, wear the masks, so you can eliminate answer choice F. The word *with* suggests that the audience is wearing the masks; eliminate answer choice G. In English idiom, someone *recognizes* something or someone *by* some feature or characteristic.

9. **The best answer is A.** This question requires you to select an answer choice that discusses a *unique talent*. Answer choice A explains that *tilting their heads* is a specific skill that must be learned, so it is the best selection. The other answer choices either are too general or they include information about the masks, not the actors.

10. **The best answer is J.** A semicolon must be immediately followed by an independent clause or a phrase that starts with a conjunctive adverb such as *therefore*. Eliminate answer choice F because the semicolon is not followed by an independent clause. The items in a list must be separated by commas if there are three or more items in the list. The only remaining choice with correct comma usage is answer choice J.

11. **The best answer is D.** In context, the adjective *abstract* means *nonspecific* or *somewhat difficult to define and understand*. While an *abstract* is a *summary* of a text, speech, and so on, this definition is not appropriate based on the context.

12. **The best answer is J.** The most important clue indicating the correct tense is the adverb *since*, which denotes a duration of time beginning in the past. Eliminate answer choice G because it refers to the future. In this case, the time period extends to the present. It did not end in the past, so the past perfect tense is not appropriate here. Eliminate answer choice F, which is a present perfect passive-voice construction. In passive constructions, as in H and J, the past participle is used. The past participle of *write* is *written*, not *wrote*, which is the simple past form. Eliminate answer choice H.

13. **The best answer is C.** First, decide whether you should use *its* or *it's*. In this sentence, the noun *Noh theater* is being replaced by the pronoun *it*. The *performers* belong to the theater, so you should use the possessive form of *it*, which is *its*. Eliminate answer choices A and D. There is a contrast suggested in the second half of the sentence, so the correct conjunction is *but*, making answer choice C correct.

14. **The best answer is H.** The *fact* mentioned in this sentence exists now. Second, the subject must agree with the verb. In this sentence, the subject is the long noun clause *the fact that it has remained essentially in its original form for over 600 years*. Although this noun clause ends with a plural noun, the central, controlling noun that determines its grammatical number is *fact*, which is singular. Therefore, a singular verb is needed, *speaks*, answer choice H.

15. The best answer is B. The sentence contains information on Zeami, one of the original playwrights. Zeami is not discussed in either Paragraph 2 or Paragraph 3, so eliminate answer choices A and C. Since you are left with Paragraph 5, decide whether the sentence should be placed after Sentence 1 or Sentence 3. As Sentence 1 mentions Zeami, it would make sense to place the new sentence after Sentence 1.

PASSAGE II

16. The best answer is J. The items in a series must be separated by commas. While answer choice G contains the correct number of commas, it omits the conjunction *and*, which is essential to the sentence.

17. The best answer is A. The preceding sentence mentions computer fonts. It is appropriate to provide a transition into the rest of the passage that is concerned with calligraphy as an art form.

18. The best answer is F. The verb *derive* (here as a past participle in a passive-voice construction) can take as a complement to a prepositional phrase beginning with *from*, in which case it means originate (*from…*). This subject of the sentence, *calligraphy*, has its origins in the two Greek words *kalli* and *graphia*.

19. The best answer is A. The sentence as it is written is clear and concise and in the active voice. The other answer choices are awkward.

20. The best answer is F. This question requires you to best express the idea that legible handwriting was important and useful in many places.

21. The best answer is C. The sentence is describing a general property (the age) of Chinese calligraphy. Therefore, the simple present tense is appropriate. The subject *Chinese calligraphy* is third-person, singular; therefore, the verb must be third-person, singular: *dates*, answer choice C.

22. The best answer is J. This is a passive-voice sentence in which *Chinese scholars* is the agent (who or what does the action of the verb). With active voice, *Chinese scholars* would be the subject. Recall that making sentences passive usually results in moving the subject to the end of the sentence and after the preposition *by*. This is the function of *by* required in this underlined portion. Eliminate answer choices F and H. Next, recognize that *for use by* is idiomatic, whereas *for the use by* is not. Therefore, answer choice J is best. If you cannot recognize that idiom, select answer choice J because it is more concise.

23. The best answer is C. According to the passage, the scribes started using the index around 200 B.C., which is clearly in the past. Therefore, you should use the simple past form of the verb *develop*.

24. The best answer is F. This question requires you to express the idea clearly and concisely. It is mentioned previously in the paragraph that the scribes replicate a 300-character index. Therefore, any reference to quantity is unnecessary.

25. The best answer is B. This question requires you to choose the best conjunctive adverb. A conjunctive adverb can be used to join two independent but related ideas, and is often used at the beginning of a sentence, if that sentence is related to the one directly preceding it. The conjunctive adverbs *however*, *yet*, and *otherwise* suggest a contrast that doesn't exist in this paragraph. It makes sense that soon after the scribes developed their own, individual styles, the scribes would emerge as artists.

26. The best answer is F. The subject of the sentence, true artists of script, "emerged" and "adapted."

27. The best answer is A. It is idiomatic in this context to say *appreciation for*.

28. The best answer is H. This question requires you to express the idea clearly and concisely. First, determine whether it is the *Church* or the *calligraphy* that is being influenced. Based on the context of the passage, it makes sense that the *calligraphy* is being influenced. Eliminate answer choices G and J, which suggest that *calligraphy* influenced the *Church*. It is better to use the active voice, as in answer choice H, which clearly indicates that the *Church* influenced *calligraphy*.

29. The best answer is C. To maintain parallelism within this sentence, the adjective phrase *closely spaced* must be in the comparative form (*more closely spaced*) to match the comparative form *narrower*.

30. The best answer is F. The singular subject *equipment* requires a singular verb. Remember that subject and verb must match in tense.

PASSAGE III

31. The best answer is A. The *myth* that is the subject of this sentence exists in the present, so the simple present tense is appropriate. Eliminate answer choices C and D. The *myth* is singular, so use the singular verb *paints*, answer choice A.

32. The best answer is G. To avoid redundancy, use only the verb *participating* in this sentence. The remaining answer choices are awkward and redundant.

33. The best answer is C. The primary focus of the first paragraph is the mountain man, not the beaver pelts that he harvested. Therefore, the sentence would not be a relevant addition to the paragraph. Answer choice D is not correct because the statement is off-topic.

34. The best answer is F. There is no punctuation required in this phrase that includes two adjectives describing the same noun.

35. The best answer is A. To maintain parallel construction in this sentence, match the verbs "designated" and "presented."

36. The best answer is F. It makes sense that the mountain men would need goods other than the food they captured. (They may have needed clothes, ammunition, cooking utensils, etc.) The other answer choices contain information that is outside the scope of the passage.

37. The best answer is B. It is important to maintain parallelism within the sentence. So, the subject and verb must have the same form. Since the subject, *mountain man*, is singular, the verb must also be singular. Eliminate answer choices A and C. The other verb forms in the sentence, *was* and *relied*, are past tense, so eliminate answer choice D, which includes the present-tense verb *appears*.

38. The best answer is J. This question requires you to recognize that *consumer* is used as the first noun of a compound with the noun *demand*. Any form of the verb *demand* would create an ungrammatical sentence. Therefore, answer choices F, G, and H can be eliminated.

39. The best answer is C. The logical opposite of *freelancers* is being an employee of a firm. Only answer choice C expresses that some trappers were employed by *a particular fur company*.

40. The best answer is H. With commas, provided that all grammar rules are followed, fewer is better. In this sentence, the passive voice verb construction were *called* has the noun phrase *Men hired directly by a fur company* as its subject. The noun *Men* is modified by the past participle phrase *hired directly by a fur company*, so no comma should separate them. Eliminate answer choices F, G, and J.

41. The best answer is D. The sentence already says that the furs were *company property*, so it is not necessary to include any more information about to whom the furs did or did not belong. Answer choices A, B, and C are all redundant and should be eliminated.

42. The best answer is F. A semicolon should be followed by an independent clause that provides more information about the first part of the sentence. The sentence is correct as written. You should not use a comma to separate two main clauses. This is known as a comma splice. Eliminate answer choice H. It is necessary to include some form of punctuation, so eliminate answer choice J. By removing the word *he* in answer choice G, an incomplete sentence is created.

43. The best answer is A. The sentence structure suggests a cause-and-effect relationship. The phrase *because of* provides the proper connection between the effect and the cause. *Irregardless* is not a word and should never be used, so eliminate answer choice D.

44. The best answer is J. The paragraph is in the past tense, therefore it is appropriate to use the past tense verb *succumbed*. The sentence as it is written uses the present tense verb; answer choices G and J use the "-ing" form of the verb, which is incorrect in this context.

45. The best answer is D. This question requires you to determine the main idea of the essay. The essay introduces the concept of the myth of the mountain man, and then goes on to describe the reality of living as a mountain man, which was quite different. Answer choice D best supports the ideas presented in the essay.

PASSAGE IV

46. The best answer is G. It is idiomatic to return home *from* some place.

47. The best answer is C. It is important to maintain parallelism within the paragraph. The verbs *returned, expressed*, and *convinced* are all past tense. Therefore, a past-tense verb should be used in the underlined portion. Eliminate answer choices A and D. Eliminate answer choice B because it is awkward. The simplest way to express the idea conveyed in the sentence is to use *recommended*, answer choice C.

48. The best answer is F. This question requires you to express the idea clearly, concisely, and in the correct word order. First, determine who is the logical subject of the verb *called*. *Fans and players* had their own nickname for the team. Answer choice F is best because it has active voice. Answer choice H has passive voice, so it can be eliminated. Answer choice J is awkward; it, too, can be eliminated.

49. **The best answer is D.** The modifiers *present-day*, *contemporary*, and *up-to-date* all have the same meaning, so none of them can be the correct answer. Since the sentence already includes the word *modern*, it would be redundant to include any of the answer choices. Therefore, omit the underlined portion, answer choice D.

50. **The best answer is F.** This question requires you to express the idea clearly and concisely. Answer choice H suggests that they were already wearing uniforms and had to change into different uniforms at home. This is not supported by information in the paragraph, so eliminate answer choice H. Answer choice G separates the verb *changed* from its prepositional phrase complement *into their uniforms*, so it is somewhat awkward and can be eliminated. Answer choice J is wordy and can be eliminated.

51. **The best answer is B.** In this sentence, *so* is a coordinating conjunction joining two independent clauses. Independent clauses joined with coordinating conjunctions must be separated by a comma placed immediately before the conjunction. Eliminate answer choices A and D. When two nouns are joined with a coordinating conjunction (here, *gates* and *bleachers*), no comma should be used. Therefore, eliminate answer choice C.

52. **The best answer is H.** Idiomatically, the noun *way* can take a verb in the infinitive form (*to* + bare form) as a complement. In this case, that is the clearest and most concise way to express the intended idea.

53. **The best answer is D.** The phrase *quite literally* is an interrupting phrase; therefore, it should be set apart from the sentence using commas.

54. **The best answer is F.** The first sentence as it is written adequately introduces the main idea of the paragraph (the Packers' humble beginnings) and does not need to be replaced. While the conditions under which the Packers played football during the first year were difficult, the paragraph does not support the idea that the conditions were *brutal*, so eliminate answer choice G. The other answer choices are not supported by the context of the paragraph.

55. **The best answer is D.** By definition, a *game* is *played*; therefore, answer choices A, B, and C are redundant and can be eliminated.

56. **The best answer is J.** This question asks you to find a way to *link* information already given in the passage with the information that is to follow. Since the paragraph introduces the *historic game* played at Hagemeister Park and indicates that it was the first game that the Packers played as professionals, answer choice J makes the most sense. The other answer

choices refer specifically to individuals or contain irrelevant information.

57. **The best answer is C.** The adjective *named* is appropriate to precede a building's proper name, here *Lambeau Field*. Answer choice A can be eliminated for wordiness. Answer choices B and D are awkward structurally and logically and can be eliminated.

58. **The best answer is G.** According to the passage, Lambeau Field was *named after* a person named Lambeau. *Founder* in answer choice G correctly and succinctly refers to this man.

59. **The best answer is A.** The verb *come* takes a prepositional object beginning with *from* and is modified by the phrase *a long way*. Therefore, no commas are needed between any of these elements. Eliminate answer choice B. Answer choice C can be eliminated because a semicolon joins dependent clauses. The verb *pass* takes a prepositional indirect object (to whom or to what place the direct object passes). No comma must separate verb from object, so eliminate answer choice D.

60. **The best answer is H.** This question requires you to determine the main idea of the essay. The essay focuses primarily on the beginnings of the Green Bay Packers and some of the team's success and doesn't really have anything to do with any economic influence the team may have had on the city of Green Bay.

PASSAGE V

61. **The best answer is C.** The sentence following the sentence containing the underlined portion explains how the author and her friend ended up at the Starfish Inn. The conjunction *because of* implies that the reason they ended up at the Starfish Inn was their own irresponsibility. Answer choice C is the clearest choice.

62. **The best answer is G.** The coordinate conjunction *and* suggests that, in addition to it being their freshman year of college, the friends wanted to get away for spring break. *Yet* and *but* suggest a contrast that doesn't exist, so eliminate answer choices F and H. The word *where* suggests a specific location; freshman year of college is not a location, so eliminate answer choice J.

63. **The best answer is A.** To maintain parallelism in this paragraph, verbs must have the same form. *Arrived, tried, delivered*, and so on are past forms. Answer choice D has future tense, so eliminate it. Answer choice C is wordy and awkward, so eliminate it. Answer choice B uses the passive voice, and it is awkward in this sentence.

64. The best answer is G. The underlined portion should mean "obtain." This eliminates answer choice F. Answer choices H and J have similar meanings, but they are too literal to be used with *lodging*. Only answer choice G has the correct meaning and is appropriate to use with *lodging* or other services.

65. The best answer is B. The adjective *limited* modifying *budget* implies that the budget is small. Therefore, the sentence as written is redundant. Eliminate answer choice A. The second sentence in each of answer choices C and D is irrelevant to the topic of the passage, so they can be eliminated.

66. The best answer is H. It is idiomatic to use *that's* to refer to the implied reason the girls were in a predicament.

67. The best answer is A. The word *where* indicates a location. The girls dragged their luggage to the room (the location) and then opened the door. Answer choices B and D create incomplete sentences and should be eliminated. Answer choice C creates a comma splice, so it can be eliminated.

68. The best answer is J. This question requires you to select the correct punctuation, while maintaining the meaning of the sentence. A semicolon should be followed by an independent clause, which is the case in answer choice J. Since *The place looked like it hadn't been redecorated since 1975!* is an independent clause, you cannot use a comma. This creates what is called a comma splice, so eliminate answer choice G. No coordinating conjunction (*so*) should be used with a semicolon to join independent clauses. Eliminate answer choice F. Using parentheses as in answer choice H complicates the sentence and takes emphasis away from the writer's exclamatory reaction to the décor of the hotel room.

69. The best answer is C. The adjective *grim* must modify a noun. Answer choices A, B, and D can be eliminated because they are all verb forms.

70. The best answer is G. Rusty and *flimsy* are coordinate adjectives, meaning they modify *antenna* in a similar way. Coordinate adjectives can be separated using *and* or a comma. Answer choices H and J have neither, so eliminate them. However, no comma should come between the modifiers and the noun, so eliminate answer choice F.

71. The best answer is A. The verb *reminded* suggests that the television was *kept* in the past. Eliminate answer choices B (future), C (present emphatic), and D (bare or present plural form).

72. The best answer is J. It makes the most sense to place Sentence 5 immediately before Sentence 4, because Sentence 5 introduces the *kitchenette* and Sentence 4 provides some additional information about the *kitchenette*. The sentence would be inappropriate placed anywhere else in the paragraph.

73. The best answer is B. The writer and her friend are originally very disappointed with the condition of the motel room. However, they decide to *make the best of it and enjoy* themselves. This suggests that they took a bad situation and turned it into a good one. The selection that best acknowledges this shift is answer choice B.

74. The best answer is J. This question requires you to identify the main idea of the essay. The essay is primarily about the difficulties that the friends encountered on their trip and how they ended up staying at a subpar motel. Even though the motel was called the Starfish Inn, any information included in the passage about the animal starfish would be irrelevant.

75. The best answer is C. Although the essay does provide an example of what could go wrong if you don't make reservations before going on vacation, it does not fully discuss possible hazards of being unprepared for a vacation. The essay is a humorous account of being forced to stay at a dilapidated motel, answer choice C.

Mathematics Test Explanations

1. **The correct answer is C.** To answer this question, solve the first equation for x:

$$x + 3 = n$$
$$x = n - 3$$

Next, substitute $n - 3$ for x in the second equation:

$$2(n-3) + 6$$
$$= 2n - 6 + 6$$
$$= 2n$$

2. **The correct answer is G.** This question tests your ability to recognize and apply the distributive property. According to the distributive property, for any numbers a, b, and c, $c(a+b) = ca + cb$. If you distribute the a value, you get $ab - a2c$, or $ab - 2ac$.

3. **The correct answer is A.** The first step in solving this problem is to determine what the difference is between the consecutive numbers. You are given 2 consecutive numbers, 3 and 10, which differ by 7. Think of the numbers as being on a number line. Since the first number must be 7 units from the number 3, and the numbers are in ascending order, the first number must be 7 units to the left of 3 on the number line. Count backwards 7 units from 3 and you will arrive at -4. Since only answer choice A includes -4 in the first blank, answer choice A must be correct.

4. **The correct answer is G.** To find the average price that Diane paid per DVD, you must divide the total dollar amount that Diane paid for the DVDs by the number of DVDs that Diane bought. The total dollar amount that Diane paid for the DVDs can be set up like this:

1 DVD for $20.00 + 5 DVDs for $8.49 each

$20.00 + 5($8.49)

You know from information in the problem that Diane purchased a total of 6 DVDs. Divide the total dollar amount that she paid, $20.00 + 5($8.49), by 6:

$$\frac{\$20.00 + 5(\$8.49)}{6}$$

5. **The correct answer is C.** One way to solve this problem is to convert feet into inches. There are 12 inches in 1 foot, so Roberto needs $(18 \times 12) + 3$, or 219 inches of lumber. He currently has $(10 \times 12) + 6$, or 126 inches of lumber. Therefore, he needs $219 - 126$, or 93 inches of lumber. $93 \div 12 = 7.75$, which is equivalent to $7\frac{3}{4}$ feet.

6. **The correct answer is J.** The first step in solving this problem is to determine the value of x. You know that $3^2 = 9$, and $9^2 = 81$, so 3^4 must equal 81. Therefore, $x = 4$. Now, substitute 4 for x in the second equation and solve: $2^4 = 16$ and $16(2) = 32$.

In addition, because you know that $3^2 = 9$, you know that x must be greater than 2, and you can eliminate answer choices F and G. This process of elimination will help you to narrow down the answer choices if you are not sure how to arrive at the correct answer.

7. **The correct answer is B.** According to the problem, the fence completely encloses the garden. This means that it goes all the way around the garden. Therefore, the length of the fence must be equal to the perimeter of the garden. One formula for calculating the perimeter of a rectangle is $2l + 2w$. Plug the numbers from the problem into this formula:

$$2(60) + 2(25)$$
$$= 120 + 50$$
$$= 170$$

8. **The correct answer is G.** Simply plug -6 in for x wherever x appears in the equation and solve the equation. Don't forget to keep track of the negative signs!

$$-(-6^2) - 2(-6) + 21$$
$$= -(36) - (-12) + 21$$
$$= -36 + 12 + 21$$
$$= -3$$

9. **The correct answer is D.** Substitute the value for the radius given in the problem, 2, into the equation and solve:

$$V = \frac{4}{3}\pi r^3$$
$$V = \frac{4}{3}\pi(2)^3$$
$$V = \frac{4}{3}\pi 8$$
$$V = (8)\left(\frac{4}{3}\right)\pi$$
$$V = \frac{32}{3}\pi$$
$$V = 10.67\pi$$

You also need to know that π is approximately equal to 3.14. Multiply 10.67 by 3.14 and round: $10.67 \times 3.14 = 33.5$, which means that the volume, to the nearest cubic inch, is 34, answer choice D.

10. **The correct answer is K.** This problem tests your ability to recognize and apply the distributive property; however, you must work backward. According to the distributive property, for any numbers a, b, and c, $c(a+b) = ca+cb$. In this problem, since 2 is the common factor for both 4 and 2, you can "factor out" 2. Eliminate answer choices F and J, which have incorrectly factored out 4. Once you factor out 2, the expression will look like this: $2(2c - d)$.

11. **The correct answer is D.** The first step in solving this problem is to calculate the amount of money that you earn each day for mowing lawns:

   $95.00 (total amount earned per day)

   −$20.00 (fixed amount earned per day)

   = $75.00 (amount earned for lawns mowed).

   Next, calculate the amount that you earn per lawn that you mow:

   $75.00 (amount earned for lawns mowed) ÷ 5 (number of lawns mowed) = $15.00 (amount earned per lawn mowed).

   Now determine the amount that you will earn today for mowing the extra lawns:

   2 (additional number of lawns mowed) × $15.00 (amount earned per lawn mowed) = $30.00 (additional income for the day).

   Finally, add this amount to your current daily earnings:

   $95.00 + $30.00 = $125.00

12. **The correct answer is G.** In the expression $4x+2x+y-x$, $4x$, $2x$, and $-x$ are like terms and can be added together:

   $$4x+2x+(-x) = 5x$$

   The term with x and the term with y cannot be added because they contain different variables, so the simplified form of $4x+2x+y-x$ is $5x + y$.

13. **The correct answer is E.** The slope-intercept form of the equation of a line is $y = mx+b$. If y equals 0, and the slope of the line is 1, then $x = 3$ could be the equation of a line, so eliminate answer choice A. Answer choice E is actually the equation for a parabola, which is NOT a line, so answer choice E is correct.

14. **The correct answer is G.** To solve this problem, first recall that the total measure of the interior angles of a triangle is 180°. Also, because the 2 sides of the triangle originating from the center of the circle are each equivalent to the radius of the circle, the sides are congruent. This means that the angles opposite those

sides are also congruent. You can set up an equation like the one shown next to solve for b:

   $$a+2b = 180$$
   $$40+2b = 180$$
   $$2b = 140$$
   $$b = 70$$

15. **The correct answer is D.** The least common multiple of two or more numbers is the smallest number (not zero) that is a multiple of all of the numbers.

   Multiples of 2: ALL even numbers

   Multiples of 3: 3, 6, 9, 12, 15, 18,…

   Multiples of 9: 9, 18,…

   Since 18 is an even number and is the smallest number that is a multiple of both 3 and 9, 18 is the least common multiple of 2, 3, and 9.

16. **The correct answer is K.** To solve this problem, substitute 1/2 for x wherever it appears in the equation:

   $$\frac{1}{\frac{1}{2}} + \frac{1}{\frac{1}{2}} - 1$$

   Remember that $1 \div 1/2$ is equivalent to 1×2.

   $$= 2+2-1$$
   $$= 3$$

17. **The correct answer is E.** The diagonals cross at the midpoint of line MO, which means that point O is as far away from the point $(5, -1)$ as M is. Starting with the x-coordinates, $5-(-1) = 6$, the distance from the midpoint to M on the x-axis. The y-coordinates are $-1 - (-4) = 3$, the distance from the midpoint to M on the y-axis. The coordinates of point O, then, is $x = 5 + 6$, or 11 and $y = -1 + 3$, or 2. Point O is located at $(11, 2)$.

18. **The correct answer is G.** The first step in solving this problem is to calculate the amount of money Tony's friend will donate for the first 25 miles that Tony runs:

   25 miles × $0.09 = $2.25

   Next, calculate the amount of money Tony's friend will donate for the remaining miles:

   63 miles (Tony's goal) – 25 miles = 38 miles
   38 miles × $0.07 = $2.66

   Now, add the 2 amounts together to get the total:

   $2.25 + $2.66 = $4.91

19. **The correct answer is D.** The only instance in which the absolute value of x could possibly be greater than the absolute value of y is when x is not equal to y, answer choice D. If $x = y$, then $|x|$ cannot be greater than $|y|$.

20. **The correct answer is G.** An expression is undefined when the denominator equals 0. Set the denominator equal to 0 and solve for x:

    $$100 - 4x^2 = 0$$
    $$100 = 4x^2$$
    $$25 = x^2$$
    $$5 = x$$

21. **The correct answer is C.** Since $x \leq 3$ and $x + y \leq 7$, the value of y will be at its smallest when the value of x is at its greatest. The greatest possible value for x is 3, therefore, the least possible value for y is 4.

22. **The correct answer is H.** The best approach to this problem is to extend the sides of the shaded square into the nonshaded square, as shown below:

    By doing this you will see that the shaded region is $\frac{3}{4}$ of one of the squares. Since the squares have the same dimensions, calculate the area of the shaded square: Area of a square = side^2. Each side is equal to 6 centimeters, so the area is 6^2, or 36 square centimeters. Multiply the total area of the square, 36, by $\frac{3}{4}$ to get the area of the shaded region: $36 \cdot \frac{3}{4} = \frac{108}{4}$, which is 27, answer choice H. Once you determined that the shaded region was $\frac{3}{4}$ of the total area, 36, you could have eliminated answer choices F and G as being too small, and answer choices J and K as being too big, leaving you with answer choice H.

23. **The correct answer is B.** Similar triangles have the same shape and the same proportions. The perimeter of the first triangle is $3 + 4 + 5$, or 12 inches. You are given that a similar triangle has a perimeter of 36, which is 3 times the perimeter of the first triangle. Therefore, each side in the second triangle must be 3 times the length of the corresponding side in the first

triangle. Since the shortest side of the first triangle is 3 inches, the shortest side of the second triangle must be 3×3, or 9 inches.

24. **The correct answer is K.** This first step in solving this problem is to simplify the equation by dividing both sides by 4:

    $$4(a+b)(a-b) = 40$$
    $$(a+b)(a-b) = 10$$

    Next, substitute 20 for $a - b$ and solve for $a + b$:

    $$(a+b)20 = 10$$
    $$a+b = \frac{10}{20} = \frac{1}{2}$$

25. **The correct answer is A.** To solve this problem, first recognize that 200% of 1 = 2. The sum of 3 and 2 is 5 ($3 + 2 = 5$). Likewise, 500% of 1 = 5, so the sum of 3 and 200% of 1 has the same value as 500% of 1.

26. **The correct answer is G.** When exponents are raised to an exponential power, the rules state that you must multiply the exponents by the power to which they are raised. In this problem, x is raised to the $(7a - 2)$ power. This exponent is then cubed, so you should multiply $7a - 2$ by 3: $3(7a-2) = 21a-6$. You now have the equation $x^{21a-6} = x^{57}$. Since the bases are equal (x), the exponents must also be equal, so $21a - 6 = 57$. Solve for a:

    $$21a - 6 = 57$$
    $$21a = 63$$
    $$a = 3$$

27. **The correct answer is D.** In order for the result to be negative, $3n$ must be less than 9. When you add any negative number larger than 9 to 9, the result will be negative. Therefore, n must be less than −3.

28. **The correct answer is K.** To solve this problem, multiply both sides of the equation by the reciprocal of $\frac{3}{5}$, which is $\frac{5}{3}$:

    $$\left(\frac{5}{3}\right)\left(\frac{3}{5}\right)x = \left(\frac{4}{3}\right)\left(\frac{5}{3}\right)$$
    $$x = \frac{20}{9}$$

29. **The correct answer is C.** This problem contains three variables, and you are given that one of them is n. Let the others be l and m. Since the sum of the three numbers is 855, $l + m + n = 855$. The given statement "n is 50% more than the sum of the other

two numbers" can be represented as $n = 1.5(l + m)$. Convert 1.5 to its decimal equivalent, $\frac{3}{2}$, to get $n = \frac{3}{2}(l + m)$. Multiply both sides of the equation by $\frac{2}{3}$ to get $\frac{2}{3}n = l + m$. Now, substitute $\frac{2}{3}n$ into the original equation for the sum of the three numbers: $\frac{2}{3}n + n = 855$. Since $n = \frac{3}{3}$, when you add the fractions you get $\frac{5}{3}n = 855$, and $n = 513$.

30. **The correct answer is J.** The tangent of any acute angle is calculated by dividing the length of the side opposite the acute angle by the length of the side adjacent to the acute angle $\left(\tan = \dfrac{\text{opp}}{\text{adj}} \right)$. In this problem, the length of the side opposite angle α is r, and the length of the side adjacent to angle α is s. Therefore, the tan of angle α is $\dfrac{r}{s}$.

31. **The correct answer is E.** When you subtract fractions you must first find the common denominator. Multiply the denominators to get $4x$ as the common denominator, then solve for x:

$$\frac{1}{x} - \frac{3}{4}$$

$$= \frac{(4)(1)}{(4)(x)} - \frac{(3)(x)}{(4)(x)}$$

$$= \frac{4}{4x} - \frac{3x}{4x} = \frac{4 - 3x}{4x}$$

32. **The correct answer is J.** The figure in the problem represents 2 parallel lines cut by 2 parallel transversals. The angles created as a result have special properties. Where each of the parallel lines is cut by a transversal, there are 2 pairs of vertical, or opposite angles. Each angle in the pair is congruent to, or equal to, the other angle in the pair. Therefore, where m cuts o and also where it cuts p, two 40° angles are formed, which means that angle $\alpha = 40°$; in addition, two 140° angles are formed that are adjacent to the 40° angles, since a straight line has 180°. So, since the same angles are created where n cuts o and p, and angle β is opposite of the 140° angle that is adjacent to angle α, angle β must be equal to 140°.

33. **The correct answer is D.** Because there are 2π radians in the circumference of every circle and a circle consists of 360°, π radians = 180°. Divide 4.25π radians by π to get 4.25; multiply 4.25(180°) to get the degree measure of the angle, 765°.

34. **The correct answer is K.** In order to solve this problem you must recognize that $1\frac{3}{4}$ is exactly halfway between 1.5 (which equals $1\frac{1}{2}$) and 2 on the number line. This means that the point closest to $1\frac{3}{4}$ on the number line is point E.

35. **The correct answer is D.** By definition, the legs of a 45° − 45° − 90° have the same length, and the hypotenuse is $\sqrt{2}$ times as long as either leg. Since you are given that the length of 2 legs is 3 meters, and the length of the third leg, the hypotenuse, is $3\sqrt{2}$ meters, this must be a 45° − 45° − 90° triangle, answer choice D. Also, since the measure of the angles in a triangle must equal 180°, you can eliminate answer choices B and E.

36. **The correct answer is H.** The median is the middle value in a list that is in either ascending or descending order. Your first step is to put the data in order, as follows:

9, 13, 13, 20, 22, 27, 31

Because the list includes an odd number of values, simply pick the middle value which is 20.

37. **The correct answer is D.** To solve this problem, first list all of the distinct factors of 45: 1, 3, 5, 9, 15, 45. All of these numbers divide evenly into 45. Next, list all of the distinct factors of 60: 1, 2, 3, 4, 5, 6, 10, 12, 15, 30, 60. All of these numbers divide evenly into 60. The only factors that both 45 and 60 have in common are 1, 3, 5, and 15. Since you are told that p is NOT a factor of either 9 or 10, you can eliminate 1, 3, and 5, which factor evenly into either 9 or 10. This leaves you with a value for p of 15. When you add the digits (1 + 5) you get 6.

38. **The correct answer is J.** The slope of a line is defined as the change in the y-values over the change in the x-values in the standard (x, y) coordinate plane. Slope can be calculated by using the following formula: $\dfrac{(y_1 - y_2)}{(x_1 - x_2)}$. Any line perpendicular to the x-axis is a vertical line: The x values do not change (see diagram).

The slope of a vertical line is undefined, answer choice J, because there is no change in x, which means that the denominator $(x_1 - x_2)$ is 0.

39. **The correct answer is C.** To solve this problem, it is helpful to draw a picture like the one shown below:

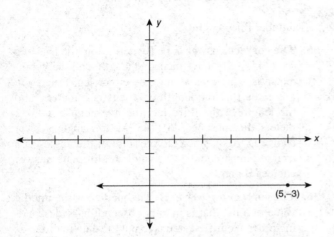

Because you are given that the line is perpendicular to the y-axis, you know that the y-intercept must be -3.

40. **The correct answer is F.** The tangent of any acute angle is calculated by dividing the length of the side opposite the acute angle by the length of the side adjacent to the acute angle $\left(\tan = \dfrac{\text{opp}}{\text{adj}}\right)$. The sine of any acute angle is calculated by dividing the length of the side opposite the acute angle by the hypotenuse $\left(\sin = \dfrac{\text{opp}}{\text{hyp}}\right)$. In this problem, the tangent of angle β is $\dfrac{3}{4}$. This means that the length of the side opposite angle β is 3 units, and the length of the side adjacent to angle β is 4 units. Therefore, by definition, the sine must be 3 units (the length of the side opposite angle β) over some number greater than 4, since the hypotenuse is always the longest side. The only answer choice that will work is $\dfrac{3}{5}$.

41. **The correct answer is C.** The first step in solving this problem is to remember that the median is the middle value in an ordered set of values. List the first five prime numbers, starting with 2:

$$2,3,5,7,11$$

The median is 5. Now, calculate the mean (average):

$$2 + 3 + 5 + 7 + 11 = 28$$

$$28 \div 5 = 5.6$$

The product of the mean and the median of the first five prime numbers is $5 \times 5.6 = 28$.

42. **The correct answer is F.** The best approach to this problem is to pick some numbers for n, substitute them into the answer choices, and eliminate the answer choices that do not always yield an even number:

F: If $n = 1$, then $4n^2 = 4(1)^2 = 4$, which is even. If $n = 2$, then $4n^2 = 4(2)^2 = 16$, another even number. Because you are multiplying n^2 by 4, an even number, the result will always be even. Answer choice F is correct. Check the other answer choices:

G: If $n = 2$, then $3n^2 + 1 = 3(2)^2 + 1 = 12 + 1 = 13$, which is odd. Eliminate answer choice G.

H: If $n = 1$, then $5n^2 = 5(1)^2 = 5$, which is odd. Eliminate answer choice H.

J: If $n = 1$, then $3n = 3(1) = 3$, which is odd. Eliminate answer choice J.

K: If $n = 3$, then $n^2 - 2n = (3)^2 - 2(3) = 3$, which is odd. Eliminate answer choice K.

Answer choice F is the only choice that will always give you an even number for any value of n.

43. **The correct answer is D.** The perimeter of a triangle is calculated by adding together the lengths of all 3 sides. Based on the measures of the angles given, you can draw triangle CAB as shown below:

You are given that $\overline{AC}$, one of the legs, is 12 units long. Because this is a $45° - 45° - 90°$ triangle, the length of the other leg, $\overline{CB}$ is also 12 units long. In a $45° - 45° - 90°$ triangle, the hypotenuse is $\sqrt{2}$ times longer than either leg. Therefore, the length of the hypotenuse is $12\sqrt{2}$. Add together the lengths of all 3 sides to find the perimeter:

$$12 + 12 + 12\sqrt{2} = 24 + 12\sqrt{2}$$

44. The correct answer is G. The best approach to this question is to test each answer choice:

F: The increase from 1999 to 2000 was 176 – 152, or 24.

G: The increase from 2001 to 2002 was 422 – 231, or 191.

H: The increase from 2002 to 2003 was 516 – 422, or 94.

J: The increase from 2004 to 2005 was 780 – 647, or 133.

K: The increase from 2005 to 2006 was 825 – 780, or 45.

The increase from 2001 to 2002 was the greatest, so answer choice G is correct.

45. The correct answer is B. To solve this problem, first look at the table to see that there were 176 households in Potterville that had a high-speed Internet connection in 2000. Next, set up a ratio comparing the number of households to the percent of households, as follows:

176 is to 652 as x% is to 100%

$$\frac{176}{652} = \frac{x}{100}$$

$$17{,}600 = 652x$$

$$26.99 = x$$

The number of Potterville households with a high-speed Internet connection was approximately 27% of the total number of households in Eaton County with a high-speed Internet connection in 2000.

46. The correct answer is G. To solve this problem, note that $9^2 = 81$ and $10^2 = 100$. Since there is no integer between 9 and 10, 9 must be the largest integer *less* than $\sqrt{98}$.

47. The correct answer is B. Logarithms are used to indicate exponents of certain numbers called bases. This problem tells you that log to the base x of 2 equals 169. By definition, $\log_a b = c$ if $a^c = b$. So, the question is, when x is raised to the power of 2, you get 169; what is x? By definition, $\log_x 169 = 2$ when $x^2 = 169$. The square root of 169 is 13.

48. The correct answer is H. To solve this problem, distribute the x and add the corresponding values:

$$\begin{bmatrix} 2x & 6x \\ x & 4x \end{bmatrix} = \begin{bmatrix} a & 15 \\ b & c \end{bmatrix}$$

$$2x + 4x = a + c$$

$$6x = a + c$$

Since $6x$ corresponds to 15, that is the value of $a + c$.

49. The correct answer is C. One way to solve this problem is to plot the points and draw a figure like the one shown below:

After plotting the points, you see that the figure is a parallelogram, whose area is equal to (b)(h). The base is equal to 3, and the height is equal to 3. Therefore, the area is 3×3, or 9.

50. The correct answer is G. You can express the phrase *the x-coordinate is 3 more than twice the corresponding y-coordinate* as follows: $x = 2y + 3$. The slope-intercept form for the equation of a line is $y = mx + b$, where m is the slope. Put the equation in the slope-intercept form:

$$x = 2y + 3$$

$$-2y = -x + 3$$

$$y = \frac{1}{2}x - \frac{3}{2}; \text{ the slope is } \frac{1}{2}.$$

51. The correct answer is C. The length of the diameter is equal to $\sqrt{(4-(-2))^2 + (-4-0)^2}$ or $\sqrt{(36+16)}$, or $\sqrt{52}$, which can be simplified to $2\sqrt{13}$. The radius is then half the length of that diameter, or $\sqrt{13}$.

52. The correct answer is F. If $XYZ = 1$, then Z cannot equal 0. If Z (or X or Y, for that matter) were 0, then XYZ would equal 0. Both sides of the equation can be divided by Z, which gives you $XY = \frac{1}{Z}$, answer choice F. Answer choice G is incorrect because 2 of the values *could* be –1. Answer choice H is incorrect because 2 of the values could be fractions and the third value *could* be a whole number, that, when multiplied by the fractions equals 1.

53. The correct answer is D. The formula for calculating the number of permutations of n objects taken r at a time is $\frac{n!}{(n-r)!}$. Simply plug the given values into the formula.

54. **The correct answer is H.** If the average of 7 integers is 24, then the total must be $7 \cdot 24$, or 168. If the average of 8 integers is 31, then the total must be $8 \cdot 31$, or 248. Since you are adding an 8th integer to the set, the value of the 8th integer will be the difference between 248 and 168: $248 - 168 = 80$, answer choice H.

55. **The correct answer is C.** To solve this problem, first recall that the total measure of the interior angles of a triangle is 180°. It might be helpful to fill in values for the right angles, as shown below:

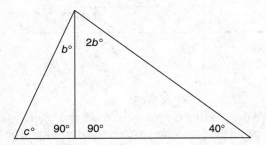

Next, set up an equation to solve for b:

$$2b + 90 + 40 = 180$$

$$2b = 180 - 130$$

$$b = 25$$

Now, set up an equation to solve for c, substituting 25 for b:

$$b + c + 90 = 180$$

$$25 + c + 90 = 180$$

$$b = 180 - 115 = 65$$

56. **The correct answer is H.** You are given that $l/m = \frac{3}{4}$ and $p/m = \frac{1}{2}$. The ratio of l/p is equivalent to $\frac{3}{4} \times \frac{2}{1}$, or $\frac{6}{4}$, which can be reduced to $\frac{3}{2}$.

57. **The correct answer is A.** First, draw the picture of the wading pool according to the information given in the problem, where the distance from the edge of the pool to the edge of the long side of the rectangular region is 4 feet. The distance from the edge of the pool to the edge of the short side of the rectangular region can be anything greater than 4, but it is not necessary to know this distance to solve the problem:

Now you can determine the diameter of the circular pool. The diameter is the maximum distance from 1 point on a circle to another (the dashed line). Since the short side of the rectangular region is 40 feet, and the distance from the edge of the circular pool to each edge of the long sides of the rectangular region is set at 4 feet, the diameter of the circle must be 40 feet $- 2(4$ feet), or 40 feet $- 8$ feet, or 32 feet. The question asks for the radius of the pool, which is $\frac{1}{2}$ of the diameter. $32 \div 2 = 16$.

58. **The correct answer is G.** To solve this problem, start by drawing 3 parallel lines.

This creates 4 distinct regions, so the minimum number of distinct regions must be 4. Eliminate answer choices H, J, and K, which give the minimum number of distinct regions as 3. Now, try drawing 3 lines in other configurations, and you will see that there will always be either 6 or 7 regions:

Therefore, the correct answer is 4, 6, or 7 distinct regions, answer choice G.

59. **The correct answer is D.** To solve this problem, you can apply some logic: because each number between −22 and 22 will cancel each other out, you can start with the next consecutive integer, 23. Now, simply begin adding consecutive integers until you reach 72: 23 + 24 + 25 = 72. Therefore, n must equal 25.

You can also solve this problem mathematically by using the following formula:

$$\frac{(-22+n)(23+n)}{2} = 72$$

By expanding this equation and simplifying it, you can reach the equation $(2n+1)^2 = 2,601$. Therefore, $2n + 1 = 51$ and $n = 25$.

60. **The correct answer is F.** The median is the middle number in an ordered list of numbers. Therefore, the value of the median *can* be changed by increasing each number by 10 or by doubling each number, so eliminate answer choices J and K. Likewise, if you increase the smallest number or decrease the largest number, you could potentially change the order of the numbers in the list, thereby potentially changing the value of the median; eliminate answer choices G and H. However, if you increase the largest number, it will still remain in the last position in the list, so the value of the median will not change.

Reading Test Explanations

PASSAGE I

1. **The best answer is C.** Granny makes this statement in response to Sheila's comment that, once Martin goes to school, "it will all be so much easier." This suggests that Granny was not convinced that school would challenge Martin effectively. The other answer choices are not supported by the passage.

2. **The best answer is G.** During the conversation Granny says, "I know you're tired from working long hours, but Martin isn't reciting—he's reading!" You can infer that Granny believes Sheila is too overworked to recognize Martin's gift, answer choice G.

3. **The best answer is A.** When Martin's mother says, "He even turns the pages. It's very cute!" she indicates that she doesn't actually think that he can read. This is the best example of the idea that she is unaware of his abilities. The other answer choices do not reflect Sheila's ignorance of her son's reading ability.

4. **The best answer is H.** The context indicates that Sheila and Granny are having a discussion about Granny's care of Martin, and that "it" will get easier when Martin starts school.

5. **The best answer is C.** Throughout the passage, Granny is clearly referred to as Martin's grandmother, so answer choice D should be eliminated. It is also made clear that Granny is Sheila's mother. Therefore, since Sheila is Martin's mother, Granny must be Martin's maternal grandmother, answer choice C.

6. **The best answer is F.** At the end of the passage, Martin's mother agrees that she will start finding out how to get to America with Martin. This best supports answer choice F.

7. **The best answer is D.** Sheila states in the passage, "I'll start finding out what I need to do to get Martin and me to America." This suggests that she understands the importance of going to America and will probably do whatever she can to help Martin succeed. The other answer choices are not supported by the details in the passage.

8. **The best answer is J.** The first paragraph states that Martin's brothers are selfish boys, who "let Martin fend for himself" and "made him the target of their pranks." This suggests that Martin's brothers cared more for themselves than they did for Martin. The other answer choices are not supported by the passage.

9. **The best answer is C.** The second paragraph shows the trouble that Granny has taking care of Martin because she is old and lacks the energy to keep up with him. This is a conflict in the story because Granny must now decide upon another course of action. The rest of the story tells about Granny's resolution of this conflict.

10. **The best answer is J.** The first paragraph states that "Martin spent most of his childhood in a tropical paradise" but that his "early life was difficult." The word *paradise* most often refers to a delightful or beautiful place. In this case, however, despite the fact that the island of Barbados contains the natural beauty associated with a paradise, the living conditions were not so delightful. This best supports answer choice J.

PASSAGE II

11. **The best answer is D.** The word "engagement" can refer to an "encounter or a battle." The context of the passage supports answer choice D.

12. **The best answer is H.** The word "fanfare" suggests a "display" of some sort. The passage indicates that Lee wanted to take advantage of an opportunity to advance into Northern territory.

13. **The best answer is D.** According to the passage, "Soldiers obeyed Lee's order to refrain from violence and pillaging, so for several days the townspeople maintained tacit compliance and sold food, clothes, and shoes to Southern troops." These details best support answer choice D.

14. **The best answer is G.** The author uses the word "grand" to describe the large loss of life in the Battle of Gettysburg. "Massive" means "large in scale, amount, or degree," so it is the best choice.

15. **The best answer is D.** The passage mentions "devastating artillery bombardment," "battle fatigued soldiers," and "infantry assault" as reasons for the failure of Pickett's Charge.

16. **The best answer is G.** By using the phrase "mile of men," the author implies that there were many soldiers. When the author says that "the mile of men had narrowed nearly to half," he is indicating that the number of soldiers had been significantly reduced during the battle.

17. **The best answer is A.** Allegory suggests symbolism. Because the author is not speaking of literal water, but instead is using the phrase "high water mark" to refer to the greatest number of Confederate soldiers, he is using the phrase allegorically.

18. **The best answer is F.** Passage A mentions several battles or engagements but does not describe any specific battle, whereas Passage B focuses primarily on a description of the Battle of Gettysburg.

19. The best answer is C. One of the themes throughout both passages is the large loss of life that resulted from the many battles fought during the Civil War.

20. The best answer is F. Passage A introduces the topic of Civil War battles and the great number of casualties that resulted. Passage B expands upon that notion with a description of one particular battle.

PASSAGE III

21. The best answer is A. The narrator states in the introduction that "the unworldly experience continues to haunt my memory as I recall the unflinching gazes of Pietro Perugino's subjects staring blankly at me as I admired the power and beauty of the great Italian Renaissance master's most famous works of art." Although the narrator briefly speaks about the work of other painters in relation to Perugino, this is not the focus of the paragraph. The narrator is also not impartial about the work of Perugino. In fact, the narrator admits that Perugino is one of his favorite painters. The passage also tells very little about Perugino's life outside of his contributions to art. Eliminate answer choices B, C, and D.

22. The best answer is J. The passage does not mention Donatello as a painter. However, all of the other answer choices are explicitly identified as painters in the passage.

23. The best answer is D. Throughout the passage the narrator discussed his or her strong feelings about Perugino's art. The answer choice that best supports this main idea is answer choice D.

24. The best answer is G. *Ingenuity* is another word for *creativity* or *inventiveness*. The narrator is acknowledging that despite his or her admiration for Perugino's work, it lacked the originality of Botticelli.

25. The best answer is C. The narrator states, "Although the brilliance of all of the Italian Renaissance masters is undeniable, the aweinspiring beauty of Michelangelo's work or the subtle detail of da Vinci's *Mona Lisa* cannot match the simple passion evident in Perugino's paintings." Even though Perugino's work may not show some of the technical skill of other Renaissance painters, the narrator believes Perugino's work outshines the more complicated pieces because of his devotion to and passion for his craft.

26. The best answer is J. The use of the word *eclipsed* suggests that the work of Renoir and Manet was overshadowed by Perugino's work.

27. The best answer is A. All of the following quotes appear in the passage: "In that moment, my admiration for artists like Renoir and Manet of the French Impressionist Movement, was eclipsed by the austere exquisiteness of these fifteenth-century paintings," "cannot match the simple passion evident in Perugino's paintings," and "Perugino also experimented with depth, and he rivaled Leonardo da Vinci in his ability to create a definite background and foreground." These statements best support answer choice A. Abstraction is not mentioned in the passage.

28. The best answer is G. The narrator writes, "I remember feeling slightly disconcerted as I looked up at the unsmiling saints, the Virgin Mary, and even Jesus as I wandered through the hushed halls of the museum." *Disconcerted* is a synonym for *unsettled*.

29. The best answer is B. The passage states that "Perugino also experimented with depth, and he rivaled Leonardo da Vinci in his ability to create a definite background and foreground." This suggests that he was as talented as Leonardo da Vinci at creating depth, which is not a criticism.

30. The best answer is F. The passage states that "The work of da Vinci and Michelangelo is seen on postcards and reprinted on cheap posters everywhere because of its universal appeal." The author does not mention Manet in the discussion about postcard and poster reprints.

PASSAGE IV

31. The best answer is B. The passage begins with the author presenting general information about the porcupine and its behavior; this is followed by a discussion of its habitat and concludes by talking about the ways in which porcupines are useful to humans. Answer choice B contains the broadest survey of the information presented within the passage.

32. The best answer is J. The first paragraph states that "the porcupine's mere outward appearance provides more than adequate reason for it rarely to become alarmed or excited." The passage goes on to describe the porcupine as a "threatening creature," which suggests that its appearance is what makes it threatening. The other answer choices are not supported by the passage.

33. The best answer is C. According to the passage, the porcupine, "unlike most other animals in the wild," has a threatening appearance that allows it to remain unexcited in the face of danger. The other answer choices are not supported by details in the passage.

34. **The best answer is G.** The author's statement that "the porcupine's mere outward appearance provides more than adequate reason for it rarely to become alarmed or excited" suggests that the porcupine moves slowly because it has no reason to move quickly, answer choice G.

35. **The best answer is B.** Information in the passage indicates that "a noseful or mouthful of porcupine quills" can cause "excruciating pain." This best supports answer choice B.

36. **The best answer is G.** According to the passage, the Yukon Department of Environment considers the porcupine useful, and believes that it has been and can be "appreciated by many." The passage goes on to give examples of the utility of the porcupine quill. This best supports answer choice G.

37. **The best answer is A.** The topic of the second paragraph is the danger of the porcupine's quills—specifically that these quills can become imbedded and cause serious pain. This idea is best summed up in answer choice A.

38. **The best answer is G.** According to the passage, some animals "are able to break down the porcupine's powerful defense system by carefully turning the porcupine over onto its back, exposing its soft and vulnerable underbelly. Bobcats, cougars, and coyotes are especially adept at this technique and pose a major threat to the porcupine."

39. **The best answer is B.** According to the passage, if a dog gets a noseful or mouthful of quills, it should be "tended to right away," so eliminate answer choice C. The passage goes on to say that extraction of the quills can "relieve the excruciating pain," so it makes sense that imbedded porcupine quills can be very painful, answer choice B.

40. **The best answer is J.** The scientific name for the porcupine is *Erethizon dorsatum*, which is Latin for "irritable back." The other answer choices are mentioned in the passage, but not in reference to the scientific name of the porcupine.

Science Test Explanations

PASSAGE I

1. **The correct answer is A.** Meteorologist 1 believes that the presence of very warm air is one of the things that most influences hurricane formation. Since higher levels of CO_2 increase air temperatures, it is likely that Meteorologist 1 would suggest a direct relationship between CO_2 levels and the number of hurricanes. The graph in answer choice A shows a direct relationship—as CO_2 levels increase, so does the number of hurricanes.

2. **The correct answer is J.** Meteorologist 1 believes that higher air temperatures contribute to hurricane formations. It is given that increased levels of atmospheric CO_2 cause an increase in air temperature. Therefore, reducing the number of forests and trees, which remove CO_2 from the atmosphere, would lead to higher levels of CO_2 in the atmosphere, higher air temperatures, and an increased number of hurricanes.

3. **The correct answer is C.** According to Meteorologist 2, higher water temperatures do not necessarily lead to hurricane formation. Therefore, any evidence suggesting that hurricanes do not occur in areas of the ocean with higher water temperatures would support Meteorologist 2's viewpoint. This best supports answer choice C.

4. **The correct answer is F.** Meteorologist 1 believes that higher air and water temperatures contribute to hurricane formation. Therefore, it is likely that Meteorologist 1 would predict an increase in the number of hurricanes if both air and water temperatures increased. The other answer choices are not supported by Meteorologist 1's viewpoint.

5. **The correct answer is C.** Based on the passage, both meteorologists believe that hurricanes become stronger and more destructive with the presence of warm water and water vapor. While Meteorologist 2 does not believe that higher water temperatures cause hurricanes, the passage indicates that Meteorologist 2 does believe that higher water temperatures increase water vapor levels, which leads to an increase in wind speed.

6. **The correct answer is G.** Meteorologist 2 states that hurricanes "are not necessarily formed where the surface temperature of the ocean is warm," which best supports answer choice G.

7. **The correct answer is B.** Meteorologist 2 suggests that higher water temperatures are not a factor in hurricane formation. A good way to test this theory would be to record surface temperatures of tropical oceans and seas over time, and compare that data with the number of hurricanes recorded during the same time period, answer choice B.

PASSAGE II

8. **The correct answer is J.** To answer this question, calculate the difference in diffusion time between each pair of gases in each answer choice:

    F: He and Kr: 13 and 43; the difference is 30 seconds

    G: Ne and Ar: 18 and 28; the difference is 10 seconds

    H: Kr and Rn: 43 and 73; the difference is 30 seconds

    J: Ne and Xe: 18 and 58; the difference is 40 seconds

    The greatest difference in diffusion time occurs between Ne and Xe, answer choice J.

9. **The correct answer is A.** According to Figure 1 and Table 1, as molecular mass (a.m.u.) increases, diffusion time also increases. The other answer choices are not supported by the data.

10. **The correct answer is F.** According to Table 1, He has the shortest diffusion time; it should completely diffuse first.

11. **The correct answer is C.** According to Table 1, the diffusion time of Ar is 28 seconds. Since 14 is half, or 50%, of 28, it is safe to assume that after 14 seconds, 50% of the vacuumed area will NOT have any Ar gas molecules left, answer choice C.

12. **The correct answer is J.** According to Table 1, in a 10-cubic-foot vacuumed area it takes Ne 18 seconds to diffuse. 18×3 is 54, so the volume of the vacuumed area described in the question is most likely 10×3, or 30 cubic feet, answer choice J.

PASSAGE III

13. **The correct answer is A.** Process A will be most accurate as compared to the Standard Method when the measurements obtained using Process A are similar to the measurements obtained using the Standard Method. If you look at Table 1 you see that, at a pH level of 2, the concentration of dissolved O_2 is identical using both Process A and the Standard Method. Therefore, answer choice A is correct.

14. **The correct answer is H.** The first step in answering this question is to find calcium carbonate on Table 1. Then, see what happens to the concentration levels as you move across the table from left to right. In the Standard Method, Process A, and Process B, the concentration levels all increase significantly as the pH levels increase. Higher pH levels mean lower acidity.

15. **The correct answer is C.** Process B will be more accurate than Process A if the measurements obtained using Process B are similar to the measurements obtained using the Standard Method. Find

NH_3 on Table 1, and compare the results obtained from each method. You will see that, at each pH level, the results obtained using Process B are closer to the results obtained using the Standard Method. Therefore, you can eliminate answer choices A and B, which both say that Process A is more accurate. Answer choice C is most consistent with the data in Table 1, so it is correct.

16. **The correct answer is F.** First, find CO_2 on Table 1, and look at the concentration levels obtained by using Process A. You will see that, from pH levels 2 through 5, there is a gradual reduction in CO_2 concentration, but at a pH level of 6, the CO_2 concentration jumps up dramatically. This is best represented by the graph in answer choice F.

17. **The correct answer is D.** To solve this problem, look at Table 1 and determine the pH level that corresponds the closest to the concentration values given in the problem for Process A. The data best supports answer choice D.

PASSAGE IV

18. **The correct answer is G.** To answer this question, look at Table 1 and Table 2 and determine which pesticide application resulted in the lowest number of fleas remaining. Note that the average number of fleas per dog before treatment in both experiments was 57. In both experiments, application of Pesticide B resulted in fewer fleas than did application of Pesticide A or Pesticide A + B. Therefore, answer choice G is correct.

19. **The correct answer is D.** According to Table 2, dogs with short coats had fewer ticks after all pesticide applications than did dogs with long coats. You can eliminate answer choices A and B. Now, look at Table 2 to determine whether Pesticide A or Pesticide B most reduced the number of ticks on a dog. Since all of the dogs started out with an average of 13 ticks before treatment, and the Pesticide A application resulted in only 4 ticks per dog, while the Pesticide B application resulted in 10 ticks per dog, answer choice D must be correct.

20. **The correct answer is H.** It is clear based on the data in Table 2 that shorter coat length leads to increased effectiveness of all pesticides, answer choice H.

21. **The correct answer is A.** The passage indicates that Pesticide A + B shampoo contained only 50% of each pesticide, while the other shampoos contained 100% of either Pesticide A or Pesticide B. Therefore, the most likely reason for the relative ineffectiveness of Pesticide A + B is that the two pesticides reduced each other's effectiveness, answer choice A. The other answer choices are not supported by the passage.

22. **The correct answer is G.** Based on Table 3, an average coat length of 2 inches would be considered long. On Table 2, find the average number of ticks per dog 24 hours after application of Pesticide A. That number is 7, answer choice G.

PASSAGE V

23. **The correct answer is C.** The passage defines half-life as the "amount of time it takes for half of the atoms in a sample to decay." Locate the line on the graph in Figure 1 that corresponds to Fluorine 22, and find the time at which half, or 50%, of the atoms are remaining in the sample. The half-life of Fluorine 22 is 4.2 seconds, answer choice C.

24. **The correct answer is H.** The passage indicates that radioactive decay is "a natural process by which an atom of a radioactive isotope spontaneously decays into another element." The other answer choices are not supported by details in the passage.

25. **The correct answer is A.** Table 1 indicates that lower decay energy values result in lower particle velocity, answer choice A.

26. **The correct answer is J.** The decay energy of Cerium 53 into Lanthanum 127 (6.100) is closest to the decay energy of Oxygen 22 into Fluorine 22 (6.490). Therefore, it is likely that the particle velocity will be similar to Oxygen 22 as well. This best supports answer choice J.

27. **The correct answer is B.** Oxygen 22 and Neon 22 will have the same percent of atoms remaining at the point where the lines representing each product cross on the graph. When you locate the appropriate lines, you see that they cross at 4.5 seconds, answer choice B.

28. **The correct answer is H.** Both of the curves mentioned in the question show a rather rapid initial decay rate that appears to slow and stabilize as the percentage of atoms remaining is reduced:

This best supports answer choice H.

PASSAGE VI

29. The correct answer is B. Table 1 shows the average number of eggs laid and the average number of eggs hatched before pesticide exposure. Since Breed F has a low resistance to illness, it would probably have a similar eggs hatched to eggs laid ratio as that of Breed E. Since 9 out of 15, or 3 out of 5 of Breed E's eggs hatched, you can assume that the same fraction of Breed F's eggs would hatch: $\frac{3}{5} = \frac{x}{20}$; $x = 12$, answer choice B.

30. The correct answer is H. To answer this question, look at Figure 1 and find the breed that, at the far right end of the figure, has an illness incidence closest to zero. This will be Breed B, answer choice H.

31. The correct answer is A. According to Figure 1, both Breed E and Breed C have a high incidence of illness, so you can eliminate answer choices C and D. Although, according to Figure 2, Breed B lays fewer eggs than does Breed A, more of them hatch. Therefore, Breed B is likely to have a higher number of eggs hatch and have a low incidence of illness.

32. The correct answer is G. According to Table 1, the average number of eggs laid does not seem to be affected by the resistance to illness. Therefore, there is no direct relationship, answer choice G.

33. The correct answer is D. The breed that is least affected by pesticide exposure will likely be the breed that has the most consistent illness incidence both before and after exposure. According to Figure 1, Breed E had a high level of illness before pesticide exposure; illness incidences only increased slightly.

34. The correct answer is J. The only statement that is supported by the passage is that the average number of eggs laid by all breeds is not affected by pesticide exposure. The data in both Table 1 and Figure 2 supports this conclusion.

35. The correct answer is A. According to Table 1, Breed E laid an average of 15 eggs before exposure to pesticide, more than any other breed.

PASSAGE VII

36. The correct answer is H. Based on the data in all 3 tables, the highest average speed was recorded in Table 1. Table 1 shows the results of Study 1, which placed the car on a smooth asphalt road. Therefore, the highest average speeds resulted from using an asphalt road, answer choice H.

37. The correct answer is C. The average speed recorded in Table 1 is 8.58 feet per second. This speed is not greater than the speed recorded in Trial 2 (8.85 ft/s); likewise, it is not less than the speed recorded in Trial 3 (8.55 ft/s); eliminate answer choices A and B. The average speed recorded in Table 1 (8.58 ft/s) is greater than the speed recorded in Trial 1 (8.33 ft/s), so answer choice C must be correct.

38. The correct answer is F. To answer this question, you must remember that Table 1 is associated with an asphalt road, Table 2 is associated with a gravel road, and Table 3 is associated with a dirt road. When you compare the average recorded speed, you will see that the average speed of a car on a gravel road (4.52 ft/s) is approximately half of the average speed of a car on an asphalt road (8.58 ft/s), answer choice F.

39. The correct answer is B. Since the passage indicates that all 3 of the studies were "conducted on a fair day with no wind," you can eliminate answer choices C and D. The studies were also conducted over different ground cover, so the most likely reason for the lower average speeds is greater friction, answer choice B.

40. The correct answer is H. Look at each of the answer choices and compare the travel times:

F: Study 1, Trial 2 = 8.85 ft/s

G: Study 2, Trial 2 = 4.59 ft/s

H: Study 2, Trial 3 = 4.46 ft/s

J: Study 3, Trial 3 = 6.17 ft/s

The slowest travel time was recorded in Study 2, Trial 3, answer choice H.

ACT PRACTICE TEST 3
Answer Sheet

ENGLISH

1 Ⓐ Ⓑ Ⓒ Ⓓ	21 Ⓐ Ⓑ Ⓒ Ⓓ	41 Ⓐ Ⓑ Ⓒ Ⓓ	61 Ⓐ Ⓑ Ⓒ Ⓓ
2 Ⓕ Ⓖ Ⓗ Ⓙ	22 Ⓕ Ⓖ Ⓗ Ⓙ	42 Ⓕ Ⓖ Ⓗ Ⓙ	62 Ⓕ Ⓖ Ⓗ Ⓙ
3 Ⓐ Ⓑ Ⓒ Ⓓ	23 Ⓐ Ⓑ Ⓒ Ⓓ	43 Ⓐ Ⓑ Ⓒ Ⓓ	63 Ⓐ Ⓑ Ⓒ Ⓓ
4 Ⓕ Ⓖ Ⓗ Ⓙ	24 Ⓕ Ⓖ Ⓗ Ⓙ	44 Ⓕ Ⓖ Ⓗ Ⓙ	64 Ⓕ Ⓖ Ⓗ Ⓙ
5 Ⓐ Ⓑ Ⓒ Ⓓ	25 Ⓐ Ⓑ Ⓒ Ⓓ	45 Ⓐ Ⓑ Ⓒ Ⓓ	65 Ⓐ Ⓑ Ⓒ Ⓓ
6 Ⓕ Ⓖ Ⓗ Ⓙ	26 Ⓕ Ⓖ Ⓗ Ⓙ	46 Ⓕ Ⓖ Ⓗ Ⓙ	66 Ⓕ Ⓖ Ⓗ Ⓙ
7 Ⓐ Ⓑ Ⓒ Ⓓ	27 Ⓐ Ⓑ Ⓒ Ⓓ	47 Ⓐ Ⓑ Ⓒ Ⓓ	67 Ⓐ Ⓑ Ⓒ Ⓓ
8 Ⓕ Ⓖ Ⓗ Ⓙ	28 Ⓕ Ⓖ Ⓗ Ⓙ	48 Ⓕ Ⓖ Ⓗ Ⓙ	68 Ⓕ Ⓖ Ⓗ Ⓙ
9 Ⓐ Ⓑ Ⓒ Ⓓ	29 Ⓐ Ⓑ Ⓒ Ⓓ	49 Ⓐ Ⓑ Ⓒ Ⓓ	69 Ⓐ Ⓑ Ⓒ Ⓓ
10 Ⓕ Ⓖ Ⓗ Ⓙ	30 Ⓕ Ⓖ Ⓗ Ⓙ	50 Ⓕ Ⓖ Ⓗ Ⓙ	70 Ⓕ Ⓖ Ⓗ Ⓙ
11 Ⓐ Ⓑ Ⓒ Ⓓ	31 Ⓐ Ⓑ Ⓒ Ⓓ	51 Ⓐ Ⓑ Ⓒ Ⓓ	71 Ⓐ Ⓑ Ⓒ Ⓓ
12 Ⓕ Ⓖ Ⓗ Ⓙ	32 Ⓕ Ⓖ Ⓗ Ⓙ	52 Ⓕ Ⓖ Ⓗ Ⓙ	72 Ⓕ Ⓖ Ⓗ Ⓙ
13 Ⓐ Ⓑ Ⓒ Ⓓ	33 Ⓐ Ⓑ Ⓒ Ⓓ	53 Ⓐ Ⓑ Ⓒ Ⓓ	73 Ⓐ Ⓑ Ⓒ Ⓓ
14 Ⓕ Ⓖ Ⓗ Ⓙ	34 Ⓕ Ⓖ Ⓗ Ⓙ	54 Ⓕ Ⓖ Ⓗ Ⓙ	74 Ⓕ Ⓖ Ⓗ Ⓙ
15 Ⓐ Ⓑ Ⓒ Ⓓ	35 Ⓐ Ⓑ Ⓒ Ⓓ	55 Ⓐ Ⓑ Ⓒ Ⓓ	75 Ⓐ Ⓑ Ⓒ Ⓓ
16 Ⓕ Ⓖ Ⓗ Ⓙ	36 Ⓕ Ⓖ Ⓗ Ⓙ	56 Ⓕ Ⓖ Ⓗ Ⓙ	
17 Ⓐ Ⓑ Ⓒ Ⓓ	37 Ⓐ Ⓑ Ⓒ Ⓓ	57 Ⓐ Ⓑ Ⓒ Ⓓ	
18 Ⓕ Ⓖ Ⓗ Ⓙ	38 Ⓕ Ⓖ Ⓗ Ⓙ	58 Ⓕ Ⓖ Ⓗ Ⓙ	
19 Ⓐ Ⓑ Ⓒ Ⓓ	39 Ⓐ Ⓑ Ⓒ Ⓓ	59 Ⓐ Ⓑ Ⓒ Ⓓ	
20 Ⓕ Ⓖ Ⓗ Ⓙ	40 Ⓕ Ⓖ Ⓗ Ⓙ	60 Ⓕ Ⓖ Ⓗ Ⓙ	

MATHEMATICS

1 Ⓐ Ⓑ Ⓒ Ⓓ Ⓔ	16 Ⓕ Ⓖ Ⓗ Ⓙ Ⓚ	31 Ⓐ Ⓑ Ⓒ Ⓓ Ⓔ	46 Ⓕ Ⓖ Ⓗ Ⓙ Ⓚ
2 Ⓕ Ⓖ Ⓗ Ⓙ Ⓚ	17 Ⓐ Ⓑ Ⓒ Ⓓ Ⓔ	32 Ⓕ Ⓖ Ⓗ Ⓙ Ⓚ	47 Ⓐ Ⓑ Ⓒ Ⓓ Ⓔ
3 Ⓐ Ⓑ Ⓒ Ⓓ Ⓔ	18 Ⓕ Ⓖ Ⓗ Ⓙ Ⓚ	33 Ⓐ Ⓑ Ⓒ Ⓓ Ⓔ	48 Ⓕ Ⓖ Ⓗ Ⓙ Ⓚ
4 Ⓕ Ⓖ Ⓗ Ⓙ Ⓚ	19 Ⓐ Ⓑ Ⓒ Ⓓ Ⓔ	34 Ⓕ Ⓖ Ⓗ Ⓙ Ⓚ	49 Ⓐ Ⓑ Ⓒ Ⓓ Ⓔ
5 Ⓐ Ⓑ Ⓒ Ⓓ Ⓔ	20 Ⓕ Ⓖ Ⓗ Ⓙ Ⓚ	35 Ⓐ Ⓑ Ⓒ Ⓓ Ⓔ	50 Ⓕ Ⓖ Ⓗ Ⓙ Ⓚ
6 Ⓕ Ⓖ Ⓗ Ⓙ Ⓚ	21 Ⓐ Ⓑ Ⓒ Ⓓ Ⓔ	36 Ⓕ Ⓖ Ⓗ Ⓙ Ⓚ	51 Ⓐ Ⓑ Ⓒ Ⓓ Ⓔ
7 Ⓐ Ⓑ Ⓒ Ⓓ Ⓔ	22 Ⓕ Ⓖ Ⓗ Ⓙ Ⓚ	37 Ⓐ Ⓑ Ⓒ Ⓓ Ⓔ	52 Ⓕ Ⓖ Ⓗ Ⓙ Ⓚ
8 Ⓕ Ⓖ Ⓗ Ⓙ Ⓚ	23 Ⓐ Ⓑ Ⓒ Ⓓ Ⓔ	38 Ⓕ Ⓖ Ⓗ Ⓙ Ⓚ	53 Ⓐ Ⓑ Ⓒ Ⓓ Ⓔ
9 Ⓐ Ⓑ Ⓒ Ⓓ Ⓔ	24 Ⓕ Ⓖ Ⓗ Ⓙ Ⓚ	39 Ⓐ Ⓑ Ⓒ Ⓓ Ⓔ	54 Ⓕ Ⓖ Ⓗ Ⓙ Ⓚ
10 Ⓕ Ⓖ Ⓗ Ⓙ Ⓚ	25 Ⓐ Ⓑ Ⓒ Ⓓ Ⓔ	40 Ⓕ Ⓖ Ⓗ Ⓙ Ⓚ	55 Ⓐ Ⓑ Ⓒ Ⓓ Ⓔ
11 Ⓐ Ⓑ Ⓒ Ⓓ Ⓔ	26 Ⓕ Ⓖ Ⓗ Ⓙ Ⓚ	41 Ⓐ Ⓑ Ⓒ Ⓓ Ⓔ	56 Ⓕ Ⓖ Ⓗ Ⓙ Ⓚ
12 Ⓕ Ⓖ Ⓗ Ⓙ Ⓚ	27 Ⓐ Ⓑ Ⓒ Ⓓ Ⓔ	42 Ⓕ Ⓖ Ⓗ Ⓙ Ⓚ	57 Ⓐ Ⓑ Ⓒ Ⓓ Ⓔ
13 Ⓐ Ⓑ Ⓒ Ⓓ Ⓔ	28 Ⓕ Ⓖ Ⓗ Ⓙ Ⓚ	43 Ⓐ Ⓑ Ⓒ Ⓓ Ⓔ	58 Ⓕ Ⓖ Ⓗ Ⓙ Ⓚ
14 Ⓕ Ⓖ Ⓗ Ⓙ Ⓚ	29 Ⓐ Ⓑ Ⓒ Ⓓ Ⓔ	44 Ⓕ Ⓖ Ⓗ Ⓙ Ⓚ	59 Ⓐ Ⓑ Ⓒ Ⓓ Ⓔ
15 Ⓐ Ⓑ Ⓒ Ⓓ Ⓔ	30 Ⓕ Ⓖ Ⓗ Ⓙ Ⓚ	45 Ⓐ Ⓑ Ⓒ Ⓓ Ⓔ	60 Ⓕ Ⓖ Ⓗ Ⓙ Ⓚ

READING

1 (A) (B) (C) (D)
2 (F) (G) (H) (J)
3 (A) (B) (C) (D)
4 (F) (G) (H) (J)
5 (A) (B) (C) (D)
6 (F) (G) (H) (J)
7 (A) (B) (C) (D)
8 (F) (G) (H) (J)
9 (A) (B) (C) (D)
10 (F) (G) (H) (J)

11 (A) (B) (C) (D)
12 (F) (G) (H) (J)
13 (A) (B) (C) (D)
14 (F) (G) (H) (J)
15 (A) (B) (C) (D)
16 (F) (G) (H) (J)
17 (A) (B) (C) (D)
18 (F) (G) (H) (J)
19 (A) (B) (C) (D)
20 (F) (G) (H) (J)

21 (A) (B) (C) (D)
22 (F) (G) (H) (J)
23 (A) (B) (C) (D)
24 (F) (G) (H) (J)
25 (A) (B) (C) (D)
26 (F) (G) (H) (J)
27 (A) (B) (C) (D)
28 (F) (G) (H) (J)
29 (A) (B) (C) (D)
30 (F) (G) (H) (J)

31 (A) (B) (C) (D)
32 (F) (G) (H) (J)
33 (A) (B) (C) (D)
34 (F) (G) (H) (J)
35 (A) (B) (C) (D)
36 (F) (G) (H) (J)
37 (A) (B) (C) (D)
38 (F) (G) (H) (J)
39 (A) (B) (C) (D)
40 (F) (G) (H) (J)

SCIENCE

1 (A) (B) (C) (D)
2 (F) (G) (H) (J)
3 (A) (B) (C) (D)
4 (F) (G) (H) (J)
5 (A) (B) (C) (D)
6 (F) (G) (H) (J)
7 (A) (B) (C) (D)
8 (F) (G) (H) (J)
9 (A) (B) (C) (D)
10 (F) (G) (H) (J)

11 (A) (B) (C) (D)
12 (F) (G) (H) (J)
13 (A) (B) (C) (D)
14 (F) (G) (H) (J)
15 (A) (B) (C) (D)
16 (F) (G) (H) (J)
17 (A) (B) (C) (D)
18 (F) (G) (H) (J)
19 (A) (B) (C) (D)
20 (F) (G) (H) (J)

21 (A) (B) (C) (D)
22 (F) (G) (H) (J)
23 (A) (B) (C) (D)
24 (F) (G) (H) (J)
25 (A) (B) (C) (D)
26 (F) (G) (H) (J)
27 (A) (B) (C) (D)
28 (F) (G) (H) (J)
29 (A) (B) (C) (D)
30 (F) (G) (H) (J)

31 (A) (B) (C) (D)
32 (F) (G) (H) (J)
33 (A) (B) (C) (D)
34 (F) (G) (H) (J)
35 (A) (B) (C) (D)
36 (F) (G) (H) (J)
37 (A) (B) (C) (D)
38 (F) (G) (H) (J)
39 (A) (B) (C) (D)
40 (F) (G) (H) (J)

You may wish to remove these sample answer document pages to respond to the practice ACT Writing Test.

Begin WRITING TEST here.

_____
_____
_____
_____
_____
_____
_____
_____
_____
_____
_____
_____
_____
_____
_____
_____
_____
_____
_____
_____
_____
_____
_____
_____
_____
_____
_____
_____

Cut Here

If you need more space, please continue on the next page.

WRITING TEST

If you need more space, please continue on the back of this page.

2

WRITING TEST

Cut Here

3

If you need more space, please continue on the next page.

WRITING TEST

_____

_____

_____

_____

_____

_____

_____

_____

_____

_____

_____

_____

_____

_____

_____

_____

_____

_____

_____

_____

_____

_____

_____

_____

END OF THE WRITING TEST.

STOP! IF YOU HAVE TIME LEFT OVER, CHECK YOUR WORK ON THIS SECTION ONLY.

4

Cut Here

1 ■ ■ ■ ■ ■ ■ ■ ■ ■ 1

ENGLISH TEST

45 Minutes – 75 Questions

DIRECTIONS: In the passages that follow, some words and phrases are underlined and numbered. In the answer column, you will find alternatives for the words and phrases that are underlined. Choose the alternative that you think is best and fill in the corresponding bubble on your answer sheet. If you think that the original version is best, choose "NO CHANGE," which will always be either answer choice A or F. You will also find questions about a particular section of the passage, or about the entire passage. These questions will be identified by either an underlined portion or by a number in a box. Look for the answer that clearly expresses the idea, is consistent with the style and tone of the passage, and makes the correct use of standard written English. Read the passage through once before answering the questions. For some questions, you should read beyond the indicated portion before you answer.

PASSAGE I

Born to Hunt

I watch his black, leathery nose as it

sporadically quivers, sensing new smells in the air,

<u>desperately trying to identify them.</u> His head remains
            1

<u>perfectly erect, his body,</u> perfectly still. His white tail curls
         2

into the letter "C." He <u>appear</u> to be perfectly balanced, a
                      3
beautiful specimen, poised at the start of the two-track road.

<u>How</u> this adorable canine was a mere twelve weeks old, my
 4
young son already knew the right name was "Hunter."

We had visited the local animal shelter three times in

the previous six months, searching for the perfect boy/dog

chemistry. Disappointed after trial playtimes with several

older animals, we suddenly realized we had yet to visit the

nursery, <u>which was full of playful puppies.</u>
        5

1. **A.** NO CHANGE
   B. trying desperately in identifying them.
   C. desperate in an attempt to identify them.
   D. trying, desperate, to identify them.

2. **F.** NO CHANGE
   G. perfectly erect his body
   H. perfectly, erect his body
   J. perfectly erect his body,

3. **A.** NO CHANGE
   B. appeared
   C. appears
   D. is appearing

4. **F.** NO CHANGE
   G. When
   H. So
   J. For

5. Which choice provides the most specific and precise information?
   A. NO CHANGE
   B. which housed other dogs.
   C. where we saw puppies.
   D. where we hoped to find a puppy.

GO ON TO THE NEXT PAGE.

1 ■ ■ ■ ■ ■ ■ ■ ■ **1**

There he was, a short-haired, pink-skinned, white and
——
6

black spotted angel of a puppy. The bond was instant.

Hunter is his name, and, a hunter is what he aspires to
————————————
7

be. His black, velvet ears are raising and held firmly back as
————
8

he attempts to capture even the slightest of sounds. I know

as I watch him that at any moment he may choose to ignore

the meager training I give him and bound off mindlessly
————
9

into the woods, 100 acres of which he considers his personal
——
10

territory. I could lose him; I know this. Even the neon orange,

bell-adorned collar around his neck is no assurance.

As I stand there watching, marvel at the instincts
——————
11

coursing through his entire being, I know that he, too, is torn
—————————————
12

"Should I pursue the dark but enticing unknowns of the

forest before me, or stay back with the comfort and warmth

of those who care for me?" He turns his head toward me as

I beckon to him, then races back to the yard, grabbing his
—————
13

rubber ball disc in his mouth, bounding into the air as he

runs, happy to be alive .
——————
14

6. **F.** NO CHANGE
   G. were
   H. is
   J. DELETE the underlined portion.

7. **A.** NO CHANGE
   B. is his name; and a hunter
   C. is his name, and a hunter
   D. is his name. And a hunter

8. **F.** NO CHANGE
   G. have risen
   H. are raised
   J. were raised

9. **A.** NO CHANGE
   B. I did give
   C. I once by giving
   D. I gave

10. Which of the following would NOT be an acceptable alter-
    native to the underlined portion?
    F. toward
    G. to
    H. over
    J. through

11. **A.** NO CHANGE
    B. marveling
    C. and marvel
    D. I marveled

12. The underlined portion would best be placed:
    F. where it is now.
    G. after the word *watching*.
    H. after the word *there*.
    J. after the word *as*.

13. Which choice best describes the way the dog returns to the
    writer of the story?
    A. NO CHANGE
    B. comes back
    C. returns
    D. walks

14. If the last part of this sentence was deleted (ending the
    sentence with a period), the paragraph would lose:
    F. the disappointment of the dog's owner.
    G. an understanding of the dog's hunting instincts.
    H. a description of the dog's attitude
    J. an example of dog ownership.

GO ON TO THE NEXT PAGE.

1 ■ ■ ■ ■ ■ ■ ■ ■ 1

Question 15 asks about the preceding passage as a whole.

15. Suppose the writer's goal for this passage was to explain how to train dogs to hunt. Would this essay fulfill the writer's goal?
    A. Yes, because the writer is very accepting of the dog's natural instincts to hunt.
    B. Yes, because the writer knows that, with better training, the dog would be a good hunting dog.
    C. No, because the passage specifically encourages readers not to train dogs to hunt.
    D. No, because the passage restricts its focus to a discussion of a family dog.

PASSAGE II

Don't Fence Me In

One of the first quandaries a new homeowner faces is

the issue, of a fence. Most people are naturally territorial,
          16
at least to some extent, and are inclined to mark off their

boundaries as a statement to their neighbors; it's a way to say,

"Here's my line; don't cross it." However, civilized modern
                            17

society is dictating that this fencing be done in a genial
          18
manner. Excuses are offered to the neighbor: "We need to

keep our dog confined," or "This fence is only necessary for

our children." In reality, fences are most often erected not to

keep loved ones in, but to keep outsiders out.

People also ignore their own privacy, and a solid wood
                   19
fence or concrete wall will certainly accomplish that goal.

Sometimes, however, when someone is on the second or

third level of his home, in this case all the goings-on in his
                         20
neighbor's private backyard are clearly visible.

Rather then constructing a solid screen such as a
      21
fence or wall, some people prefer to take a more subtle

16. F. NO CHANGE
    G. the, issue of
    H. the issue of
    J. the, issue of,

17. Which of the following alternatives to the underlined portion would NOT be acceptable?
    A. their neighbors: it's a way to say,
    B. their neighbors, it's a way to say,
    C. their neighbors. It's a way to say,
    D. their neighbors, as if to say,

18. F. NO CHANGE
    G. dictates
    H. dictated
    J. will be dictating

19. A. NO CHANGE
    B. reject
    C. value
    D. undermine

20. F. NO CHANGE
    G. by this time
    H. for this reason
    J. DELETE the underlined portion.

21. A. NO CHANGE
    B. Rather, than
    C. Rather than
    D. Rather, then,

GO ON TO THE NEXT PAGE.

1 ■ ■ ■ ■ ■ ■ ■ ■ **1**

route and plant trees, shrubs, vines and the like. This
option works well as long as the natural barrier is easy
to maintain year-round. Keep in mind, though, that most
plants require some time to grow. Climbing ivies or
deciduous trees—which lose their foliage—prove to be

ineffective protection of prying eyes and perked ears.
Evergreen trees and shrubs are the best choices for fences

and are better than deciduous trees because they keep their
leaves and needles throughout the year. One must take care,
however, to select species that are suited to their intended
purpose and environment. Planting tall, thin *Cryptomeria*
trees too far apart for example is not a good idea. Plant two
or three rows of the trees rather than a single row of trees
along a property line. When considering how to mark a
property line and create privacy and security, it is important

to be cautious, carefully plan the type of fence you want to
construct, and consider the statement you want to make to

your neighbors'. Privacy fences can take time to come to full

maturity, and more permanent fencing can be costly.

22. **F.** NO CHANGE
    G. trees, shrubs vines, and the like
    H. trees shrubs vines, and the like
    J. trees, shrubs, vines, and the like

23. **A.** NO CHANGE
    B. in that they lose they're foliage
    C. by losing they're foliage
    D. lose their foliage

24. **F.** NO CHANGE
    G. for
    H. toward
    J. against

25. **A.** NO CHANGE
    B. in place of deciduous trees
    C. as opposed to deciduous trees
    D. DELETE the underlined portion.

26. **F.** NO CHANGE
    G. too far apart for, example
    H. too far apart, for example,
    J. too far apart for example,

27. Which of the following creates the most appropriate
    image, based on the context of the passage?
    A. NO CHANGE
    B. fun and enjoyment
    C. relaxation and vacation time
    D. safety and recreation

28. **F.** NO CHANGE
    G. cautiously and
    H. take care to
    J. DELETE the underlined portion.

29. **A.** NO CHANGE
    B. neighbors
    C. neighbor's
    D. neighbors's

30. **F.** NO CHANGE
    G. full of cost
    H. a lot of money
    J. expensive to build

GO ON TO THE NEXT PAGE.

1 ■ ■ ■ ■ ■ ■ ■ ■ 1

PASSAGE III

Maya Angelou

Incredible inner <u>beauty an ingenious</u> gift with words, and
                        31

a golden heart are terms that <u>aptly</u> describe Maya Angelou.
                                  32
Born in 1928 in St. Louis, Missouri, Maya Angelou

experienced a difficult and transient childhood. Much of

<u>what in her young life was</u> is reflected in her first book,
                        33
I Know Why the Caged Bird Sings. As suggested by its title,

this autobiography describes the <u>tumultuous</u> and often
                                    34
frightening aspects of Angelou's teen years, causing the

reader to both sympathize with and marvel at her ability to

cope with, even rise above, many adverse circumstances.

Following one <u>particularly traumatic</u> incident, Maya spent
                        35
the next five years in utter silence, which caused her mother

to send Maya to live in Stamps, Arkansas, with Maya's

grandmother.

As a young woman in Arkansas, Angelou performed

a variety of different jobs, including dancing, singing,

and acting. 36 Angelou went on to become active in the

<u>civil rights movement and</u>, pursued her dream of becoming
                        37
a writer as well. During her lifetime, she wrote many

volumes of poetry and over a dozen books. Since 1981,

Angelou has resided at Wake Forest University where

she is the first Reynolds Professor of American Studies, a

---

31. A. NO CHANGE
   B. beauty; an ingenious
   C. beauty, an ingenious
   D. beauty with an ingenious,

32. F. NO CHANGE
   G. quickly
   H. barely
   J. sparingly

33. A. NO CHANGE
   B. her young life
   C. that which is her young life
   D. that her young life

34. Which of the following alternatives to the underlined portion would NOT be acceptable?
   F. stormy
   G. chaotic
   H. turbulent
   J. booming

35. If the writer of this essay deleted the underlined portion, the essay would primarily lose:
   A. an explanation for Angelou's subsequent behavior.
   B. the essence of the entire passage.
   C. an argument for the writer's point of view.
   D. an unnecessary detail about Angelou's life.

36. Which of the following words from the preceding sentence could be deleted without negatively impacting the grammar and clarity of the sentence?
   F. variety
   G. different
   H. singing
   J. including

37. A. NO CHANGE
   B. civil rights movement and
   C. civil rights, movement, and
   D. civil, rights, movement and

GO ON TO THE NEXT PAGE.

1 ■   ■   ■   ■   ■   ■   ■   ■ **1**

prestigious position. 38 She is one of only two people

ever to have read her own poetry at the inauguration

of a United States President: Bill Clinton.
39

Listening or watching an interview with Maya
40
Angelou is truly a treat. With her deep, throaty voice

and her ability to make words sound like either

blossomed flowers or deafening cannons, Maya Angelou
41

can sense and instill wonder and joy in even the most
42

hardened listener. Angelou has the ability and eliciting
43

emotion in such a way that any listener would become heavy
44
with gratitude for life and hope for humanity.

38. At this point, the writer is considering adding the following true statement:

> The Reynolds Professorship pays well.

Should the writer make this addition here?

F. Yes, because it indicates that Angelou will keep this position for the rest of her life.

G. Yes, because it shows how important the Reynolds professorship appointment is for Angelou's career.

H. No, because it detracts from the points regarding Angelou's difficult childhood.

J. No, because it does not substantially add to the essence of the essay.

39. A. NO CHANGE
B. president; Bill Clinton is his name.
C. president.
D. president known as Bill Clinton.

40. F. NO CHANGE
G. Listening to or watching
H. Listening to or watching with
J. Listening, or watching

41. A. NO CHANGE
B. blossoming flowers
C. blossoms of flowers
D. blossoms and flowers

42. F. NO CHANGE
G. a sense of wonder and joy can instill
H. a sense she can instill of wonder and joy
J. can instill a sense of wonder and joy

43. A. NO CHANGE
B for eliciting
C. to elicit
D. with eliciting

44. F. NO CHANGE
G. this listener has
H. all who listen will have
J. DELETE the underlined portion.

Question 45 asks about the preceding passage as a whole.

45. Suppose the writer had intended to write an essay focusing on Southern poverty. Would this essay successfully fulfill the writer's goal?

A. Yes, because the writer clearly states that Angelou grew up in Arkansas under difficult circumstances.

B. Yes, because the essay discusses Angelou's first book about poverty, *I Know Why the Caged Bird Sings*.

C. No, because the writer's goal is to describe how people can rise above bad situations.

D. No, because the essay's main focus is on the life and accomplishments of Maya Angelou.

GO ON TO THE NEXT PAGE.

1 ■ ■ ■ ■ ■ ■ ■ ■ 1

PASSAGE IV

Summer Visits

[1] Visiting my grandparents every summer was a definite highlight of <u>my youth</u>. [2] Grandma and I would take
___
46

the city bus just to go up the road <u>one mile, to the</u> nearest
___
47

shopping center. [3] That one mile <u>seems as if</u> happy eternity
___
48
to me. [4] There, at the "five-and-dime," Grandma would purchase yards and yards of fabric to take home to my mother. [5] Grandma would let me help choose the material, knowing that much of it would become my new fall school clothes. 49

<u>Before</u> I spent more time with Grandma Ritz,
___
50
I must admit the brief moments with Grandpa Ritz

<u>are truly my most memorable.</u> Grandpa always seemed
___
51

to be in and out, but mostly out. 52 I do remember his over-sized, green chair with its large matching ottoman.

46. **F.** NO CHANGE
    G. the time when I was young.
    H. the summer visits with them.
    J. my young childhood.

47. **A.** NO CHANGE
    B. one mile to the
    C. one mile; to the
    D. one mile: to the

48. **F.** NO CHANGE
    G. seemed
    H. seeming like
    J. seems as

49. The writer is considering adding the following sentence to further describe her mother's talent for sewing:

    > By this time, she had become an excellent seamstress under my grandmother's tutelage.

    The new sentence would best amplify and be placed after Sentence:

    A. 2
    B. 3
    C. 4
    D. 5

50. **F.** NO CHANGE
    G. Except
    H. Because
    J. As for

51. Which of the following choices would NOT be an acceptable alternative for the underlined portion?
    A. are most memorable.
    B. truly are my most memorable.
    C. are the ones I remember most.
    D. being my most memorable.

52. If the writer deleted the phrase *but mostly out* from the preceding sentence, the sentence would primarily lose:
    F. the implication that the writer's grandfather was gone much of the time.
    G. details about the writer's relationship with her grandmother.
    H. a sense of the grandparents' relationship with each other.
    J. an explanation of where the grandfather spent most of his time.

GO ON TO THE NEXT PAGE.

1 ■ ■ ■ ■ ■ ■ ■ ■ ■ **1**

The chair and ottoman was forbidden to all of the
                     53

grandchildren, even when Grandpa was off on one of
           54

his many excursions. Right next to Grandpa's chair was

his cherished bookstand, complete with reading lamp

and reading glasses. I can still picture Grandpa sitting

in that chair in front of his radio (and later a black-

and-white television set), happily reading his favorite

Hemingway novel. Even as a child, Grandpa to me seemed
                     55

like a small man; indeed, he only stood about five and a half
  55

feet tall. Still, Grandpa was a royal king in that chair.
                    56

    My fondest memories are of Grandpa and his fishing

lures. An avid fly-fisherman, Grandpa probably fished every

river within driving distance of his home and made his

own lures. When he wasn't out in his waders somewhere,

he could often be found bent over his garage workbench,

a single lightbulb hanging over his head, putting together
              57

bobbers, colorful feathers, and shiny metal fish bodies.

Occasionally, Grandpa would invite me to accompany him

to the garage, where he would show me how to tie all of the
              58

parts together with a piece of thin fishing wire. He always

assured me that my humble creation would be an asset on his

next fishing expedition. Maybe it would even nab the big one!

    When I became a teenager, my solo summer visits with

my grandparents ended. By then, they were moved out of
                59

the city and into the country, where they purchased acres

and acres of hilly woods. While I never grew to love their

new home as I did the old one, this property became my

53. A. NO CHANGE
   B. were forbidden
   C. are being forbidden
   D. will be forbidden

54. F. NO CHANGE
   G. despite the fact that
   H. including any time when
   J. instead of when

55. A. NO CHANGE
   B. Grandpa, even when I was a child, to me seemed like a small man
   C. Grandpa seemed like a small man to me, even when I was a child
   D. Grandpa seemed to me, even as a child, like a small man

56. F. NO CHANGE
   G. royalty
   H. king
   J. king of royalty

57. The best placement for the underlined portion would be:
   A. where it is now.
   B. after the word *waders*.
   C. after the word *somewhere*.
   D. after the word *feathers*.

58. F. NO CHANGE
   G. he shows
   H. so he would show
   J. as if he could show

59. A. NO CHANGE
   B. they
   C. my grandparents had
   D. it had

GO ON TO THE NEXT PAGE.

Grandpa's sanctuary. He spent nearly every day cleaning out the deadwood, carving walking paths along the creek, and building wooden birdhouses.

Question 60 asks about the preceding passage as a whole.

60. Suppose the writer had intended to write an essay describing the relationship between her grandparents. Would this essay accomplish the writer's goal?
 F. Yes, because the writer clearly describes how important her grandparents were during her childhood.
 G. Yes, because the writer recalls fond memories of both her grandparents.
 H. No, because the essay does not mention the writer's grandparents' relationship with one another.
 J. No, because the writer clearly spent more time with her grandmother than with her grandfather.

PASSAGE V

The Electric Motor Team

In 1834, Thomas Davenport, a poor blacksmith with no formal education, and his wife Emily <u>jointly worked together</u>
                                                     61

to make one of the most <u>misused</u> inventions in the history
                              62
of the world—the electric motor. Thomas was working in Vermont when he heard of an innovative technique used to

<u>efficiently separating iron ore</u> with an electromagnet.
            63
 He was so intrigued, that he convinced his brother

to raise money, and the two of them <u>purchased</u> an
                                          64
electromagnet.

Thomas brought it home and began to experiment with it, first by disassembling it. His wife Emily took a keen interest in the project. Thomas' <u>brother, who witnessed much of their work, said that Emily</u>
        65

---

61. A. NO CHANGE
 B. jointly worked with each other
 C. worked with each other together on a project
 D. worked together

62. Which of the choices would be most appropriate here?
 F. NO CHANGE
 G. justified
 H. important
 J. authoritative

63. A. NO CHANGE
 B. more efficiently separating iron ore
 C. separates iron ore more efficient
 D. separate iron ore more efficiently

64. F. NO CHANGE
 G. purchase
 H. purchasing
 J. to purchase

65. A. NO CHANGE
 B. brother, who witnessed much of their work, said that Emily;
 C. brother who witnessed much of their work, said that Emily
 D. brother, who witnessed, much of their work said that Emily

GO ON TO THE NEXT PAGE.

1 ■ ■ ■ ■ ■ ■ ■ ■ 1

"had a fine education and was as enthusiastic as he was,...
[She] wrote down exactly the way the wire was wound on,
and all about it, from beginning to end." Thomas began work
on his own electromagnet by constructing a core of wires,
                                                        66
but he realized he needed an insulator for the wires. Emily

sacrificed her silk, wedding dress, and tore it into strips.
                                               67
Thomas and Emily then used

these strips of silk torn from her dress to insulate the wires.
                          68
    [1] Thomas was convinced that the improved

electromagnet they built could be accustomed to spin a wheel
                                        69
with attached magnets. [2] Thomas grew very frustrated,
until Emily suggested that mercury might be used as a
conductor. [3] For several months, Thomas could not get it to
work. [4] The wheel would start as the underlying magnets
attracted those on the wheel, but as soon as the underlying
          70
magnets were opposite the magnets on the wheel, the wheel
would stop. [5] There was no way to quickly reverse the
current in the electromagnet before the wheel stopped. [6]
They were trying it, and the wheel turned continuously as
      71

expected. 72

66. Given that all the choices are true, which one most specifically and vividly describes the electromagnetic core?
    F. NO CHANGE
    G. made of tightly wound iron wires
    H. with some wire
    J. like the one he had seen previously

67. **A.** NO CHANGE
    B. silk wedding dress; and tore it into strips.
    C. silk wedding dress and tore it, into strips.
    D. silk wedding dress and tore it into strips.

68. **F.** NO CHANGE
    G. these strips
    H. torn strips of wedding silk from her dress
    J. Emily's strips of silk wedding dress fabric

69. **A.** NO CHANGE
    B. utilized to make it
    C. used to
    D. designed with

70. **F.** NO CHANGE
    G. it
    H. them
    J. these

71. **A.** NO CHANGE
    B. would of tried
    C. try
    D. tried

72. For the sake of the unity and coherence of this paragraph, Sentence 2 should be placed:
    F. where it is now.
    G. after Sentence 4.
    H. after Sentence 5.
    J. after Sentence 6.

GO ON TO THE NEXT PAGE.

1 ■ ■ ■ ■ ■ ■ ■ ■ **1**

[73] After building several more sophisticated models, he finally received the patent for the first electric motor in 1837. Although there was great initial excitement in

the scientific community and the media the electric motor
74

did not gain widespread popularity until after Thomas Davenport's death. However, within forty years of his death, electric motors were being commonly used in

trains and trolleys, and now they are used in thousands of
75

efficient and time-saving machines all over the world.
75

73. Which of the following sentences offers the best introduction to this paragraph?
 A. Emily Davenport's contribution to the electric motor was invaluable.
 B. Building a working electric motor was very difficult and expensive.
 C. Thomas' first application for a patent was rejected at a time when there were no other electrical patents at all.
 D. The U.S. Patent Office was first proposed by Thomas Jefferson.

74. F. NO CHANGE
 G. the scientific community and the media, the electric motor
 H. the scientific community and the media and the electric motor
 J. the scientific community, the media, and the electric motor

75. What function does the underlined portion serve in the essay?
 A. The author is showing that electric motors save time.
 B. The author is showing that modern electric motors are more efficient than the model the Davenports invented.
 C. The author is showing that modern machines have replaced trains and trolleys.
 D. The author is showing that the Davenports' invention directly impacts the modern world.

END OF THE ENGLISH TEST.
STOP! IF YOU HAVE TIME LEFT OVER, CHECK YOUR WORK ON THIS SECTION ONLY.

2 △ △ △ △ △ △ △ △ 2

MATHEMATICS TEST

60 Minutes – 60 Questions

DIRECTIONS: Solve each of the problems in the time allowed, then fill in the corresponding bubble on your answer sheet. Do not spend too much time on any one problem; skip the more difficult problems and go back to them later. You may use a calculator on this test. For this test you should assume that figures are NOT necessarily drawn to scale, that all geometric figures lie in a plane, and that the word *line* is used to indicate a straight line.

DO YOUR FIGURING HERE.

1. At the "Parkway" Bridge, a vehicle must be, at most, 1,500 pounds to cross the bridge. If w represents the car's weight, in pounds, this requirement can be indicated by which of the following inequalities?
   A. $w > 1,500$
   B. $w < 1,500$
   C. $w \geq 1,500$
   D. $w \leq 1,500$
   E. $w \neq 1,500$

2. What is the smallest positive integer that is a multiple of 2, of 6, and of 9?
   F. 12
   G. 17
   H. 18
   J. 56
   K. 112

3. If $\dfrac{z(x+y)^v}{u} = 1$, which of the numbers u, v, x, y, or z CANNOT be 0?
   A. u only
   B. v only
   C. x only
   D. y and z
   E. u and z

4. In a town called Hortonville, exactly 648 of the 2,160 residents have a white house. What percentage of the Hortonville residents does NOT have a white house?
   F. 30%
   G. 50%
   H. 70%
   J. 80%
   K. 90%

5. If $q = -1$ and $s = 3$, what is the value of the expression $\dfrac{(q-s)}{3q}$?
   A. -1
   B. $-\dfrac{2}{3}$
   C. $\dfrac{2}{3}$
   D. $\dfrac{4}{3}$
   E. 4

GO ON TO THE NEXT PAGE.

2   **2**

6. Which of the following expressions is equivalent to $\dfrac{(6p+60)}{6}$?

F. $p + 10$

G. $p + 60$

H. $6p + 10$

J. $11p$

K. $60p$

DO YOUR FIGURING HERE.

7. Given: p and q are parallel lines

s is a transversal crossing lines p and q

o, m, and n are angles

$m + n = 230°$

What is the measure of angle o below?

A. $25°$

B. $65°$

C. $115°$

D. $130°$

E. $140°$

8. The volume of a cylinder is $\pi r^2 h$, where r is the radius of the base of the cylinder and h is the height of the cylinder. What is the volume, in cubic inches, of a cylinder of height 5 inches that has a base of radius 4 inches?

F. 9π

G. 20π

H. 40π

J. 80π

K. 100π

GO ON TO THE NEXT PAGE.

2   **2**

9. What is the value of | 4 − x | if x = 7 ?
   A. −11
   B. −3
   C. 3
   D. 11
   E. 47

DO YOUR FIGURING HERE.

10. In the figure below, where the triangle is created by 3 lines that intersect at the angles indicated, the measure of angle q =?

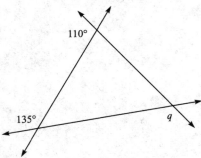

   F. 45°
   G. 65°
   H. 70°
   J. 110°
   K. 115°

11. $(\sqrt{2} - 6)(\sqrt{2} - 4) = ?$
   A. $10\sqrt{2} - 22$
   B. $12\sqrt{2} + 24$
   C. $24 - \sqrt{2}$
   D. $26 - 10\sqrt{2}$
   E. $10 - 11\sqrt{2}$

12. For all real numbers x and y, $(x - 3y)^2 = ?$
   F. $2x - 6y$
   G. $x^2 - 6xy + 9y^2$
   H. $x^2 - 9y^2$
   J. $x^2 - 9x^2 y^2 - 9y^2$
   K. $x^2 + 9xy + 9y$

13. If x is an odd integer greater than 5, what is the next greater odd integer in terms of x?
   A. $x + 2$
   B. $x + 3$
   C. $x + 5$
   D. $3x$
   E. x^2

14. Which of the following has the same graph as $x + 8y = 3$?
   F. $3x + 11y = 6$
   G. $2x + 10y = 5$
   H. $3x + y = 8$
   J. $3x + 24y = 9$
   K. $x - 8y = -3$

GO ON TO THE NEXT PAGE.

2   **2**

15. Anne is 3 times as old as Kyle. If their combined age is 24, how old is Anne?

   A. 24
   B. 18
   C. 12
   D. 9
   E. 6

DO YOUR FIGURING HERE.

16. In the figure below, the 2 intersecting lines *QS* and *PT* form triangles *PRQ* and *SRT*. Lines *PQ* and *ST* are parallel. If angle *P* is 65° and angle *S* is 85°, what is the measure of angle *T*?

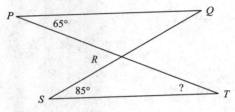

   F. 45°
   G. 55°
   H. 65°
   J. 75°
   K. 85°

17. Carrie has $7 less than does her brother, Steve, who has *d* dollars. Carrie does not spend any money and earns $3. Which of the following is an expression for the amount of money, in dollars, that Carrie has?

   A. $(d-7)+2$
   B. $d+4$
   C. $d-(7+3)$
   D. $d-4$
   E. $d-7$

18. If $0.2a+1.8 = a-2.2$, then $a =$?

   F. 4
   G. 5
   H. 8
   J. 12
   K. 20

19. Of the following, which is the smallest integer, *x*, satisfying the condition that $-\sqrt{8+x}$ is negative?

   A. 2
   B. 3
   C. 4
   D. 5
   E. 6

20. Jennifer cut a ribbon 30 inches long into 2 pieces. The ratio of the lengths of the 2 pieces is 2:3. What is the length, to the nearest inch, of the longer piece?

   F. 5
   G. 6
   H. 12
   J. 15
   K. 18

GO ON TO THE NEXT PAGE.

2   **2**

21. A circle has an area of 49π. What is the diameter of the circle?

   A. 7
   B. 14
   C. 24.5
   D. 49
   E. 153

DO YOUR FIGURING HERE.

22. What is the area, in square centimeters, of the figure shown below?

   F. 21
   G. 24
   H. 34
   J. 40
   K. 84

23. For all positive a, b, and c, $\dfrac{3a^2b^{-4}c^2}{2^{-2}ac^{-2}} = ?$

   A. $\dfrac{3a^3b^4}{4}$

   B. $\dfrac{12a^3}{b^4}$

   C. $\dfrac{3ac^4}{b^4}$

   D. $\dfrac{12ac^4}{b^4}$

   E. $\dfrac{12a^4c}{b^2}$

24. If $\dfrac{3\sqrt{7}}{7} = \dfrac{3\sqrt{7}}{x\sqrt{7}}$ is true, then $x = ?$

   F. 49
   G. 21
   H. 7
   J. $\sqrt{7}$
   K. 1

25. Which of the following gives the complete solution for the quadratic equation $3x^2 = 4x$?

   A. $x = 3$ or $x = \dfrac{3}{4}$

   B. $x = -3$ or $x = -4$

   C. $x = 0$ or $x = \dfrac{3}{4}$

   D. $x = 0$ or $x = \dfrac{4}{3}$

   E. $x = \dfrac{3}{4}$ or $x = \dfrac{3}{4}$

GO ON TO THE NEXT PAGE.

2   **2**

26. In the standard (x, y) coordinate plane, what is the slope of a line containing the points $(3, -8)$ and $(4, 7)$?

F. $-\dfrac{1}{15}$

G. -1

H. $\dfrac{3}{7}$

J. 7

K. 15

DO YOUR FIGURING HERE.

27. In the standard (x, y) coordinate plane, which of the following is an equation of the circle with a center located at $(2, -7)$ and a radius of 5?

A. $(x+2)^2 +(y-7)^2 = 25$

B. $(x-2)^2 +(y+7)^2 = 25$

C. $(x-2)+(y+7) = 5$

D. $(x-7)^2 +(y+2)^2 = 25$

E. $x^2 + y^2 = 25$

28. If $8x^2 - 8x - 6 = (ax - 3)(4x + a)$, what is the value of a?

F. -2

G. 1

H. 2

J. 3

K. 4

29. Which of the following is the slope-intercept form of a line that is perpendicular to $y = -\dfrac{1}{4}x + 1$ in the standard (x, y) coordinate plane and that also contains the point $(0, -5)$?

A. $y = 4x - 5$

B. $y = -\dfrac{1}{4}x$

C. $y = 4x + 5$

D. $y = -\dfrac{1}{4}x - 5$

E. $y = -5x + 4$

30. When baking cookies, the quantity of flour needed is a constant proportion of the number of cookies being made. If 24 cookies require 2 cups of flour, how many cups of flour will 60 cookies require?

F. 2

G. $2\dfrac{1}{4}$

H. 3

J. $4\dfrac{1}{2}$

K. 5

31. What value of p will satisfy the equation $0.1(p + 1,800) = p$?

A. $2,000$

B. $1,620$

C. 800

D. 200

E. 180

GO ON TO THE NEXT PAGE.

32. Which of the following is an equation of the circle shown below?

DO YOUR FIGURING HERE.

 F. $(x-3)^2 + y^2 = 9$
 G. $(x-6)^2 + (y-3)^2 = 9$
 H. $x^2 - (y-6)^2 = 3$
 J. $x^2 + (y+3)^2 = 9$
 K. $(x-3)^2 + (y-3)^2 = 9$

33. Which of the following is the solution statement for the inequality $x + 2(5-x) \le 2x + 3$?

 A. $x \le -7$
 B. $x \ge \dfrac{7}{3}$
 C. $x \ge 3$
 D. $x \le \dfrac{7}{3}$
 E. $x \ge 0$

34. $(4a^4)^4$ is equivalent to:

 F. a
 G. $4a^4$
 H. $16a^8$
 J. $256a^8$
 K. $256a^{16}$

35. Given the parallelogram below, what is the area of the shaded region?

 A. 24
 B. 26
 C. 32
 D. 38
 E. 40

GO ON TO THE NEXT PAGE.

2   **2**

36. What is the only possible solution for x in the equation $\frac{3}{4}x - \frac{3}{8} = \frac{1}{4} + \frac{5}{8}x$?

   F. $\frac{1}{8}$

   G. $\frac{5}{8}$

   H. 3

   J. $\frac{8}{5}$

   K. 5

DO YOUR FIGURING HERE.

37. Two similar isosceles right triangles are shown below. The hypotenuse of the smaller triangle is $2\sqrt{2}$ cm. If the perimeter of the larger triangle is twice that of the smaller triangle, what is the length, in centimeters, of each of the 2 congruent legs of the larger triangle?

   A. 2
   B. $2\sqrt{2}$
   C. $4\sqrt{2}$
   D. 4
   E. $\sqrt{2}$

38. In the figure below, *MNOQ* is a parallelogram and *OPQ* is a right triangle. The side lengths shown are in centimeters. What is the area, in square centimeters, of figure *MNOP*?

   F. 104
   G. 128
   H. 136
   J. 190
   K. 208

GO ON TO THE NEXT PAGE.

2   **2**

39. In the triangle below, sin a =?

DO YOUR FIGURING HERE.

A. $\dfrac{3}{5}$

B. $\dfrac{3}{4}$

C. $\dfrac{4}{5}$

D. $\dfrac{5}{4}$

E. $\dfrac{4}{3}$

40. If $x = -3$ and $x = 5$ are solutions to the equation $(x + m)(x + n) = 0$, then $m + n$ =?

F. −15

G. −8

H. −2

J. 2

K. 8

41. What is the x-coordinate if $(x, 5)$ is on a line that passes through $(-2, -1)$ and $(2, 2)$ in the standard (x, y) coordinate plane?

A. −3

B. 4

C. 5

D. 6

E. 7

42. If $\cos B = \dfrac{15}{17}$ and the $\sin B = \dfrac{8}{17}$, then $\tan B$ =?

F. $\dfrac{8}{15}$

G. $\dfrac{25}{17}$

H. $\dfrac{15}{8}$

J. $\dfrac{17}{15}$

K. $\dfrac{25}{15}$

GO ON TO THE NEXT PAGE.

2 △ △ △ △ △ △ △ △ **2**

43. Which of the following expressions is illustrated in the (x, y) coordinate plane below?

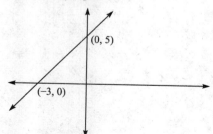

A. $y = \dfrac{5}{3}x + 5$

B. $y = -\dfrac{5}{3}x + 5$

C. $y = \dfrac{3}{5}x - 5$

D. $y = -\dfrac{5}{3}x - 5$

E. $5y - 3x = 0$

44. The noncommon rays of 2 adjacent angles form a straight angle. The measure of one angle is twice the measure of the other angle. What is the measure of the smaller angle?
F. $45°$
G. $55°$
H. $60°$
J. $65°$
K. $90°$

45. How many 3-letter orderings, where no letter is repeated, can be made using the letters of the word PONIES?
A. 6
B. 18
C. 30
D. 120
E. 216

46. Each side of a certain cube has a length of 5 centimeters. What is the volume of the cube, in cubic centimeters?
F. 3^5
G. 4^3
H. 5^3
J. 5^4
K. 6^3

47. What is the distance, in coordinate units, between $3 + 6i$ and $-2 + 3i$ in the complex plane?

A. 5

B. 9
C. $\sqrt{13}$
D. $\sqrt{34}$
E. $\sqrt{65}$

GO ON TO THE NEXT PAGE.

2   **2**

48. Which of the following is a perfect square trinomial?

  F. $4x^2 + 12x + 9$
  G. $9x^2 - 6x + 10$
  H. $2x^2 + 4x + 16$
  J. $9x^2 - 10$
  K. $4x^2 + 16x + 4$

49. Assuming both p and q are negative integers, if $p = 2q$, which of the following *must* be a rational number?

  I. $p + q$

  II. $\dfrac{p}{q}$

  III. $\dfrac{q}{p}$

  A. I only
  B. II only
  C. III only
  D. II and III only
  E. I, II, and III

50. If a and b are positive rational numbers such that $a^{2b} = 3$, then $a^{6b} = ?$

  F. 27
  G. 18
  H. 12
  J. 9
  K. 6

51. If $s = 19 - (5 + r)^3$, for what real value of r will s have its maximum value?

  A. 19
  B. 5
  C. 1
  D. −5
  E. −19

52. The figure below is a regular octagon. What is the measure of 1 of the interior angles of the octagon?

  F. 45°
  G. 60°
  H. 90°
  J. 120°
  K. 135°

DO YOUR FIGURING HERE.

GO ON TO THE NEXT PAGE.

2   **2**

53. The solution set for the equation $2^{x^2+1} = 1$ contains:
   A. 2 imaginary numbers.
   B. 2 positive real numbers.
   C. 1 negative and 1 positive real number.
   D. 1 negative real number only.
   E. 1 real number, which is 0.

DO YOUR FIGURING HERE.

54. In the figure below, lines a and b are parallel and angle measures are as marked. If it can be determined, what is the value of x?

   F. 40
   G. 45
   H. 50
   J. 85
   K. Cannot be determined from the given information

55. Which of the following is (are) equivalent to the mathematical operation $a(b + c)$ for all real numbers a, b, and c?
   I. $ca + ba$
   II. $ab + ac$
   III. $(b + c)a$
   A. I only
   B. II only
   C. III only
   D. I and II only
   E. I, II, and III

56. For values of x where $\sin x$, $\cos x$, and $\tan x$ are all defined,
$$\frac{(\tan x)}{(\sin x)(\cos x)} = ?$$
   F. $\dfrac{1}{\cos^2 x}$
   G. $\cot x$
   H. 1
   J. $\sin^2 x$
   K. $\sec x$

57. What is the solution set for the equation $|x^3| = -x^3$?
   A. All real numbers
   B. All $x \geq 0$
   C. All $x \leq 0$
   D. All odd numbers
   E. Only $x = 1$

GO ON TO THE NEXT PAGE.

2 △ △ △ △ △ △ △ △ **2**

58. For which of the following values of c will there be 2 distinct solutions to the equation $3x^2 + 2x + c = 0$?

F. −1
G. 1
H. 2
J. 3
K. 4

DO YOUR FIGURING HERE.

59. The graph of $y = -2x^2 - 4$ passes through the points $(2, 3a)$ in the standard (x, y) coordinate plane. What is the value of a?

A. 12
B. 4
C. 0
D. −1
E. −4

60. A total of 202 people attended a graduation party. There were 60 tables at which the guests could sit. Some of the tables accommodated 2 people each, and the rest accommodated 4 people each. Assuming all of the tables were filled to capacity and every person got to sit at a table, exactly how many of the tables accommodated 2 people?

F. 3
G. 18
H. 19
J. 20
K. 30

END OF THE MATHEMATICS TEST.
STOP! IF YOU HAVE TIME LEFT OVER, CHECK YOUR WORK ON THIS SECTION ONLY.

3 ▬▬▬▬▬▬▬▬▬▬▬▬▬▬▬▬▬ **3**

READING TEST

35 Minutes – 40 Questions

DIRECTIONS: This test includes four passages, each followed by ten questions. Read the passages and choose the best answer to each question. After you have selected your answer, fill in the corresponding bubble on your answer sheet. You should refer to the passages as often as necessary when answering the questions.

PASSAGE I

LITERARY NARRATIVE: *This passage is adapted from "The Magic Shop," by H. G. Wells, originally published in 1903.*

I had seen the Magic Shop from afar several times; I had passed it once or twice, a shop window of alluring little objects, magic balls, magic hens, wonderful cones, ventriloquist dolls, the basket trick, packs of cards that LOOKED
5 all right, and all that sort of thing, but never had I thought of going in, until one day, almost without warning, Gip hauled me by my finger right up to the window and so conducted himself that there was nothing for it but to take him in. I had not even been sure that the place was there,
10 to tell the truth. It was a modest-sized frontage in Regent Street, between the picture shop and the place where the chicks run about just out of patent incubators, but there it was sure enough.

I had fancied it was down nearer the Circus, or round
15 the corner in Oxford Street, or even in Holborn; always over the way and a little inaccessible it had been, with something of the mirage in its position; but here it was now quite indisputably, 20 and the fat end of Gip's pointing finger made a noise upon the glass. "If I was rich," said
20 Gip, dabbing a finger at the Disappearing Egg, "I'd buy myself that. And that"—which was The Crying Baby, Very Human—"and that," which was a mystery, and called, so a neat card asserted, "Buy One and Astonish Your Friends." "Anything," said Gip, "will disappear under one of those
25 cones. I have read about it in a book. And there, dadda, is the Vanishing Halfpenny—, only they've put it this way up so's we can't see how it's done." Gip, dear boy, inherits his mother's breeding, and he did not propose to enter the shop or worry in any way; only, you know,
30 quite unconsciously he lugged my finger doorward, and he made his interest clear. "That," he said, and pointed to the Magic Bottle. "If you had that?" I said; at which promising inquiry he looked up with a sudden radiance. "I could show it to Jessie," he said, thoughtful as ever of others.

35 "It's less than a hundred days to your birthday, Gibbles," I said, and laid my hand on the door-handle. Gip made no answer, but his grip tightened on my finger, and so we came into the shop. It was no common shop this; it was a magic shop, and all the prancing precedence Gip

40 would have taken in the matter of mere toys was wanting. He left the burden of the conversation to me. It was a little, narrow shop, not very well lit, and the door-bell pinged again with a plaintive note as we closed it behind us. For a moment or so, we were alone and could glance about
45 us. There was a tiger in papier-mâché on the glass case that covered the low counter—a grave, kind-eyed tiger that waggled his head in a methodical manner; there were several crystal spheres, a china hand holding magic cards, a stock of magic fish-bowls in various sizes, and an immod-
50 est magic hat that shamelessly displayed its springs. On the floor were magic mirrors; one to draw you out long and thin, one to swell your head and vanish your legs, and one to make you short and fat; and while we were laughing at these, the shopman came in.

55 At any rate, there he was behind the counter—a curious, sallow, dark man, with one ear larger than the other and a chin like the toe-cap of a boot. "What can we have the pleasure?" he said, spreading his long, magic fingers on the glass case; and so with a start we were aware of
60 him. "I want," I said, "to buy my little boy a few simple tricks." "Legerdemain?" he asked. "Mechanical? Domestic?" "Anything amusing?" said I. "Um!" said the shopman, and scratched his head for a moment as if thinking. Then, quite distinctly, he drew from his head a glass ball.
65 "Something in this way?" he said, and held it out. The action was unexpected. I had seen the trick done at entertainments endless times before—it's part of the common stock of conjurers—but I had not expected it here. "That's good," I said, with a laugh. "Isn't it?" said the shopman.
70 Gip stretched out his disengaged hand to take this object and found merely a blank palm. "It's in your pocket," said the shopman, and there it was! "How much will that be?" I asked. "We make no charge for glass balls," said the shopman politely. "We get them"—he picked one out of his
75 elbow as he spoke—"free." He produced another from the back of his neck, and he laid it beside its predecessor on the counter.

Gip regarded his glass ball sagely, then directed a look of inquiry at the two on the counter, and finally
80 brought his round-eyed scrutiny to the shopman, who smiled. "You may have those too," said the shopman, "and, if you DON'T mind, one from my mouth, SO!" Gip

GO ON TO THE NEXT PAGE.

counseled me mutely for a moment, and then in a profound silence he put away the four balls, resumed my reassuring finger, and nerved himself for the next event.

1. As it is used in the passage (line 14), the word *fancied* most nearly means:
   A. embellished.
   B. imagined.
   C. stated.
   D. pretended.

2. It can be inferred from the passage that the narrator felt the magic shop's location to be:
   F. logical and commonplace.
   G. strange and out of place.
   H. fun and exciting.
   J. warm and inviting.

3. The passage suggests that the narrator first learned about the Magic Shop:
   A. when he had passed it before.
   B. when Gip led him there.
   C. when he was a little boy.
   D. when he moved into the town.

4. The narrator states that Gip "did not propose to enter the shop or worry in any way" in the second paragraph. This description suggests that Gip:
   F. was worried about his mother.
   G. began to have a temper tantrum because he wanted to go into the store.
   H. was not capable of speaking.
   J. was a polite child.

5. The narrator considers the clerk's behavior, as it is described in Paragraph 4, as:
   A. surprising.
   B. frightening.
   C. confusing.
   D. predictable.

6. Gip's reaction to the shopman's first trick can best be described as:
   F. quietly astonished; he takes the glass balls and then goes back to holding his father's hand.
   G. uncomfortably disturbed; he signals to his father that he wishes to leave the shop.
   H. obviously frustrated; he wants to know how the tricks are done.
   J. unamused; he feels the shopman is playing tricks on him.

7. It can be inferred from the passage that the relationship between the narrator and his son is one best characterized by:
   A. misunderstanding.
   B. annoyance.
   C. enjoyment.
   D. patience.

8. It can be reasonably inferred that Gip's feeling about entering the Magic Shop is:
   F. frustration.
   G. anxiety.
   H. uncertainty.
   J. excitement.

9. The description in Paragraph 4 suggests that the shopman's sudden presence causes the narrator and his son to:
   A. stop laughing together.
   B. begin asking endless questions.
   C. leave the shop.
   D. laugh at him.

10. According to the last sentence in the passage, Gip was ready to:
   F. start crying.
   G. make his purchases.
   H. run out of the store.
   J. see the next trick.

GO ON TO THE NEXT PAGE.

3 ▬▬▬▬▬▬▬▬▬▬▬▬▬▬▬▬▬▬▬▬▬▬▬▬▬ **3**

PASSAGE II

SOCIAL SCIENCE: *Alaska, the Beautiful?*

I was a ten-year-old girl in the middle of fifth grade on the day that Alaska garnered the forty-ninth star on the American flag. I clearly remember all the hoopla and celebration. Nearly fifty years later, however, Alaska remains
5 an enigma to me. Having never visited this remote area, I still think of Alaska as little but cold, dark, and desolate, in stark contrast to my image of the golden sunshine and warm breezes of Hawaii, the fiftieth state. At one point in our married life, my husband and I discussed the possibil-
10 ity of pulling up stakes and moving the family to Alaska. A friend of ours had done so several years before and was now earning six digits as a high school principal there. As tempting as it sounded, however, I couldn't get past the idea of living in the vicinity of Siberia, so we never went,
15 not even for a visit with our friend.

So how did this vast and relatively untouched land, a region that is so geographically, and seemingly in all other ways so far removed, become part of the United States? The evolution of this nearly 600,000 square miles of land
20 from U.S. territory to statehood took almost 100 years from beginning to end. In March of 1867, an agreement known as "Seward's Folly" was made between Russia and then Secretary of State William H. Seward to obtain this territory for a mere $7.2 million. As the name of this pact
25 suggests, many people marveled at the apparent stupidity of such a plan. What, after all, did this place called Alaska have to offer the rest of the country?

The Klondike Gold Rush in 1897 was probably the first concrete evidence that Alaska did have something to
30 offer. For over a decade, more than 30,000 miners, fishermen, and trappers entered regions of Alaska, developing a colonial economy in which Alaska's land and water resources were taken out and sold elsewhere. In effect, Alaska's own natural wealth was being stripped for the
35 benefit of a handful of outside entrepreneurs. At this time, Alaska was functioning under the First Organic Act of 1884, which provided the territory with judges, clerks, and marshals. These officials, however, numbered only 13, and so were often not effective. As Alaska's resources were
40 being exploited and public unrest was brewing, Congress passed the Second Organic Act in 1912. This act gave official territory status to Alaska and also appropriated a legislature of eight elected Senators and sixteen elected Members of the House. However, the territory's gover-
45 nor was to be appointed by Congress rather than freely elected, and all acts passed by the local bodies of government were subject to the approval of Congress. The federal government also maintained power over Alaska's vast resources, power that ultimately led to Alaska's statehood.
50 These acts of Congress sealed the concept of Alaska being a part of the United States.

Alaska's first bill requesting statehood was introduced to Congress in 1916. Without a push from Alaska's 58,000 residents, however, the bill was unsuccessful.
55 Ironically, the bombing of Pearl Harbor in the Hawaiian Islands, though thousands of miles away, also brought Alaska into the forefront of national attention. It was two years earlier, in 1940, when Congress had appropriated funds for military bases in Alaska, convinced that Alaska
60 and the nearby Aleutian Island chain were threatened by their proximity to Japan. The bombing of Pearl Harbor and Japanese occupation of two of the islands in the Aleutian chain propelled Congress to provide Alaska with billions of dollars for defense spending and for the con-
65 struction of the Alaska Highway. By 1943, a solid three quarters of Alaska's 233,000 residents were part of the military, changing Alaska forever. After many more years of political wrangling, Alaska finally gained its state-hood on January 3, 1959, due primarily to growing and
70 organized public and political pressure.

At some point in my life I have gained at least some familiarity with every state in the continental United States. And, while never having been to Hawaii, I plan to go there someday soon and dread only the thought
75 of the twelve-hour plane trip. In my head, I'm already enjoying the multitude of fragrant, colorful blossoms, the red-orange sunsets, and the lapping of soft waves on the beach. Alaska, on the other hand, despite glowing reports received from my friend, will probably never mean more
80 to me than the forty-ninth star on the American flag.

11. As it is depicted in the passage, Alaska can most reasonably be characterized as:
   A. an undeveloped territory with few resources.
   B. a region of land that shouldn't be a part of the United States.
   C. a vast, unpopulated region that is difficult to visit.
   D. a desolate region that encountered difficulty in achieving statehood.

12. As it is used in line 5, the word *enigma* most nearly means:
   F. image.
   G. mystery.
   H. picture.
   J. enemy.

13. Based on information in the passage, you can conclude that the author:
   A. is almost 60 years old.
   B. is a young girl.
   C. was born in 1959.
   D. is a resident of Alaska.

GO ON TO THE NEXT PAGE.

3 ████████████████████████████████████ **3**

14. The author uses the statement "The Klondike Gold Rush in 1897 was probably the first concrete evidence that Alaska did have something to offer" (lines 28–30) most nearly to mean that:
   F. gold was first discovered in North America in 1897.
   G. governmental decisions influence economic developments.
   H. before 1897, most people thought Alaska did not have any real value.
   J. miners' lives were made more difficult when they entered Alaska.

15. It can most reasonably be inferred that the author asks the question "So how did this vast and relatively untouched land …?" in Paragraph 2 in order to:
   A. explain why Alaskans were determined to make their territory an official state.
   B. introduce the rest of the information in the paragraph about Alaska's struggle for statehood.
   C. introduce arguments against Alaska's chances at becoming a state.
   D. elaborate on "Seward's Folly."

16. Which of the following statements best describes the author's method of addressing her audience?
   F. She makes an emotional appeal to the reader by describing her childhood.
   G. She describes her personal experiences about her visits to Alaska.
   H. She presents historical background information and personal opinion regarding the topic.
   J. She presents a series of arguments similar to those presented when Alaskans were working toward statehood.

17. It is most reasonable to infer that when the author claims that "Alaska's own natural wealth was being stripped for the benefit of a handful of outside entrepreneurs" in the third paragraph, she means that:
   A. Alaska's benefits to the rest of the country were short-lived.
   B. Native Alaskans were greedy and did not want outsiders to settle there.
   C. Native Alaskans were not reaping the benefits of their own land's resources.
   D. Native Alaskans did not believe in capitalism.

18. As it is used in line 63, the word *propelled* most nearly means:
   F. motivated.
   G. supported.
   H. prospered.
   J. silenced.

19. It can most reasonably be inferred that the author contrasts Alaska and Hawaii throughout the passage in order to:
   A. show how much alike they really are.
   B. encourage the reader to visit Hawaii.
   C. provide a history of Alaska's statehood.
   D. emphasize her personal impressions of each state.

20. According to the author, Alaska's eventual success at gaining statehood can mostly be attributed to:
   F. the public's growing desire to make it happen.
   G. the bombing of Pearl Harbor.
   H. the realization that Alaska had plenty of natural resources.
   J. politicians who forced the issue against the people's wishes.

GO ON TO THE NEXT PAGE.

3   **3**

PASSAGE III

HUMANITIES: *Passage A is adapted from a biography of Ernest Hemingway. Passage B discusses one of Hemingway's best known works.*

Passage A

Ernest Hemingway is one of those rare authors most people know about, whether they have read him or not, because of his sensational publicity and personal invective. He has the distinction of being one of the most famous twentieth-
5 century American writers with his image of ruggedness, confidence, virility, and bravery. He has been regarded less as a writer dedicated to his craft than as a man of action who happened to be afflicted with genius. When he won the Nobel Prize in 1954, *Time* magazine reported
10 the news under *Heroes* rather than *Books*. He wrote about what he knew best: traveling, bullfights, libations, women, wars, big game hunting, deep-sea fishing, and courage. He acquired his expertise through well-reported acts of participation as well as observation: by going to all of the
15 wars of his time, hunting and fishing for great beasts, marrying four times, occasionally getting into fistfights, and drinking to excess.

To a considerable degree, Hemingway was complicit in the formation of his public persona. As a young man
20 living in Chicago and bored by vainglorious drawing room talk about arts and artists, he rejected out of hand the role of the indoor esthete. If he were to become a writer, it was going to be at the opposite pole from Proust and his corklined room! Hemingway had grown up in close con-
25 tact with the outdoors, and throughout his life he pursued the hunting and fishing sports that he had learned from his father. In doing so, Hemingway assuredly took some amusement in confounding public expectations of how a writer should look and conduct himself. After his father's
30 suicide he took on the persona of "Papa Hemingway." It served as a defense, protecting the more complicated person behind the mask. But once the persona took hold, it did not let go, and as a consequence, Hemingway dwindled into celebrity: a person who is famous for being
35 famous, whose personality has been narrowed down to a few instantly recognizable trademarks. The process had the unpropitious effect of confusing Hemingway's work with his life, or rather those components of his life that were lived in open view; it subordinated his literary
40 accomplishment to his personal renown.

Passage B

Ernest Hemingway's novel, *The Sun Also Rises*, has frequently been treated as a novel of the Lost Generation—a group of young American expatriate writers living in Paris who came of age during World War I and established their
45 reputations in the 1920's. They considered themselves "lost" because their inherited values could not operate in the postwar world, and they felt spiritually alienated from a country that they considered hopelessly provincial and emotionally barren. More broadly, the Lost Generation
50 represented the World War I American generation. This approach to *The Sun Also Rises* has become something of a critical cliché. Hemingway described the novel as less about the life of postwar expatriates than about the rhythms of nature as an expression of eternity.

55 Despite its concern with interrogating literary depictions of the relationship between humanity and the natural world, Hemingway's novel has received little eco-critical attention. The *Sun Also Rises* is profoundly concerned with ecological considerations, as the biblical passage of
60 Ecclesiastes echoed in its title would suggest. It presents the main characters as aimless, displaced people without a secure sense of meaning or value and suggests that the characters could find that meaning and value in cultivating a more intimate connection with the natural environment.
65 The novel criticizes conventional depictions of nature and calls for a literature that offers a more complex picture of the connection between humanity and the natural world. It invokes the central elements of pastoral convention: the presentation of city life as complex and of city people as
70 corrupt, the presentation of rural life (and of nature) as somehow more "real" and more simple than life in the city, and the presentation of rural folk as more honest, direct, and virtuous than city dwellers. Literary rural tradition posits a natural world, a green world, to which sophis-
75 ticated urbanites withdraw in search of the lessons of simplicity that only nature can teach. There, amid sylvan groves, meadows, and rural characters—idealized images of countryside existence—the sophisticates attain a critical vision of the good, simple life. The novel pushes the limits
80 of pastoral convention by testing its vision, acknowledging its enduring attraction, and questioning its very construct.

Questions 21–23 ask about Passage A.

---

21. It can reasonably be inferred that the author includes lines 3–10 in order to suggest that Hemingway's "image" and "genius" were both:
  A. easy to achieve.
  B. unnecessary to his success as a writer.
  C. essential to creating his fame and fortune.
  D. important components that helped shape the public's perception of him.

22. All of the following are referred to in Passage A as support of Hemingway's extensive publicity EXCEPT his:
  F. acquisition of a fatherly persona.
  G. Nobel Prize–winning achievements.
  H. reputation as an action-oriented man.
  J. tendency to spend time indoors with society's elite.

GO ON TO THE NEXT PAGE.

3 ▓▓▓▓▓▓▓▓▓▓▓▓▓▓▓▓▓▓▓▓▓▓▓▓▓▓ **3**

23. The author of Passage A describes Hemingway's feelings toward being an "indoor esthete" (line 22) most likely in order to:
    A. emphasize his hatred for that particular social group.
    B. highlight his great sensitivity to the beauty of art and nature.
    C. identify the factors that positively influenced his career as a writer.
    D. describe the forces that caused him to rebel against standard conventions.

Questions 24–26 ask about Passage B.

---

24. In Passage B, the author's attitude toward conventional interpretations of *The Sun Also Rises* (lines 58–60) suggests that:
    F. the post–World War I generation felt that it could not function in society as it was.
    G. literary critics are too focused on a common analysis to examine other viewpoints.
    H. a striking inconsistency between reality and literature exists in Hemingway's novel.
    J. there is a link between the natural world and the themes found in Hemingway's novel.

25. According to Passage B, Hemingway's novel *The Sun Also Rises* has been interpreted in which of the following contexts?
       I. Ecological values
       II. Antiquated belief systems
       III. Traditional pastoral conventions
    A. I only
    B. III only
    C. I and III only
    D. I, II, and III

26. Which individual would best illustrate the attitudes of the characters found in *The Sun Also Rises*?
    F. A writer who feels comfortable in society and in large cities.
    G. A mature person actively rebelling against society in 1920s Paris.
    H. A young artist who feels at odds with society and finds peace in nature.
    J. A middle-class person traveling Europe to learn more about World War I.

Questions 27–30 ask about both passages.

---

27. Hemingway's "close contact" (lines 24–25) with nature described in Passage A is most closely associated with which consideration addressed in Passage B?
    A. The relationship his characters had with urban life
    B. The "presentation of rural life" (line 70) in his novel
    C. An "intimate connection" (line 64) with the environment
    D. The description of lives of people living in the countryside

28. A similarity between the two passages is that they both:
    F. incorporate facts of Hemingway's life.
    G. examine the techniques Hemingway favored.
    H. reveal the deep-seated issues that drove Hemingway to write.
    J. assert that Hemingway was miscast as a member of the Lost Generation.

29. The information in Passage A supports which assumption about *The Sun Also Rises* as described in Passage B?
    A. The main ideas found in Hemingway's novel were formed from biblical interpretations.
    B. Hemingway's novel suggested that people who live in rural areas attain a better vision of life.
    C. The novel was heavily influenced by Hemingway's connection to nature and the environment.
    D. The symbolism found in the novel is explicitly derived from nature, and avoids any connection to urban life.

30. With which of the following statements would the authors of both passages be most likely to agree?
    F. Hemingway committed suicide.
    G. Hemingway was a passionate writer.
    H. Hemingway published only one book.
    J. Hemingway limited his writing to nature themes.

GO ON TO THE NEXT PAGE.

3   **3**

PASSAGE IV

NATURAL SCIENCE: *Dangerous Visitor*

The huge billboard at the side of the highway is no joke; transporting firewood in certain areas of Michigan and Ohio is a federal crime, punishable by a whopping four thousand dollar fine. The reason? Emerald Ash Borer dis-
5 ease, or EAB disease, a new addition to the long list of dangerous foreign pest infestations on American soil. It was in 2002 when the Emerald Ash Borer beetle was first discovered in southeastern lower Michigan. Not long after, the pest was found in Toledo, Ohio. Originally an Asian
10 insect, this metallic green beetle (*Agrilus planipennis*) probably found its way to North America via a wooden crate or pallet made of ash wood and immediately settled into the bark of a local ash tree. In little time, the species managed to fully establish itself, decimating millions of
15 ash trees as well as a thirty million dollar annual market for this once sought-after landscape choice. To date, over 5,000 square miles of Michigan and Canadian land, as well as several outlying areas in Ohio and Indiana, are officially considered infested, and work is underway to
20 eradicate the disease before ash trees end up in the same category as the elm and chestnut trees, which are all but extinct in many areas.

Ash Borer infestations are particularly troublesome because they are difficult to identify until the ash tree is
25 heavily infested. The larvae of these bugs hide deep within the tree's bark while the adults settle high within the tree's canopy. In addition, other ash trees in the area surround-ing the source will probably also be invaded. This can occur within up to a half mile radius from the source tree,
30 making control and eradication a monumental task, not to mention an extremely costly one.

Researchers are working on a variety of issues related to the control and ultimate elimination of this harmful beetle. For example, it has been discovered that Asian
35 ash trees are not devastated by this native borer as are the ash trees in North America. The presumption is that, over time, Asian ash trees have developed genes resistant to the insect; therein, perhaps, lies the secret to controlling this pest in North American ash trees as well. Insecticide treat-
40 ment is also being explored on several fronts. Research is underway to determine which insecticides are proving to be the most successful. The proper application of the pesticides is being debated as well: directly treating the tree as opposed to injecting the soil, for example. Proper
45 timing of the insecticide application is also an important consideration. And, as always, the benefits of insecticide treatments must be carefully weighed against their poten-tial harm to other plant life and living creatures.

These, however, are all long-range solutions requiring
50 a great deal of study and research. In the meantime, care-ful steps must be taken to prevent the spread of ash tree disease. Methodical identification of infested trees is tak-ing place in all susceptible areas. As questions are raised and research is conducted to answer those questions, the
55 invasive Ash Borer continues to lay its eggs and prey on the nutrients of its host tree. This means that identified trees are being cut down and destroyed, along with the beetle colonies, or "galleries." Ultimately, this puts a huge drain on town and city budgets, as mature tree removal can
60 be extremely expensive. Along with tree removal expenses comes the additional outlay of funds for replacement trees, often an unexpected emergency budget item.

Even though it will be expensive to deal with this problem in the short term, the costs of doing nothing could
65 be far higher, since we could conceivably lose an entire species of tree.

31. Information in the passage suggests that the author of the passage:
   A. is a scientist researching EAB in Canada.
   B. is cautiously optimistic about the success of EAB disease eradication.
   C. is personally involved with the study of EAB dis-ease in Michigan and Ohio.
   D. disagrees with the outrageous fines for transport-ing firewood.

32. The passage indicates that, unlike some other insect infestations, Ash Borer infestations:
   F. can be easily managed.
   G. can be contained in a small area.
   H. can be completely decimated in a short time.
   J. can be difficult to identify and eradicate.

33. As it is used in line 30, the word *monumental* most nearly means:
   A. serving as a monument.
   B. historically significant.
   C. exceptional in scope.
   D. large in stature.

34. The main worry expressed in the first paragraph is:
   F. the cost of EAB infestation to the tree industry.
   G. the transporting of EAB to American soil.
   H. the time period during which the beetles were discovered.
   J. the decimation of ash trees in North America.

35. The author's attitude toward the study of EAB disease is best characterized as one of:
   A. interested concern.
   B. emotional panic.
   C. scholarly interest.
   D. scientific knowledge.

GO ON TO THE NEXT PAGE.

3 ████████████████████████████████████ **3**

36. The passage identifies *Agrilus planipennis* as:
   F. North American ash wood.
   G. pest infestations.
   H. beetle eggs.
   J. Emerald Ash Borer beetle.

37. According to the passage, "galleries" are:
   A. beetle colonies.
   B. places from which to observe the beetles.
   C. insecticide application processes.
   D. infected trees.

38. The passage indicates that EAB beetles might also be correctly identified as:
   F. a North American insect.
   G. a Canadian beetle.
   H. an Asian beetle.
   J. a Dutch elm beetle.

39. The passage states that EAB adults live:
   A. under the tree bark of various local trees.
   B. in the soil of the ash tree.
   C. deep within the tree trunk.
   D. in the upper branches of the ash tree.

40. The passage claims that one of the methods currently being used to control EAB disease is:
   F. budget cuts.
   G. tree removal.
   H. insecticide spray.
   J. tree decimation.

END OF THE READING TEST.
STOP! IF YOU HAVE TIME LEFT OVER, CHECK YOUR WORK ON THIS SECTION ONLY.

SCIENCE TEST

35 Minutes – 40 Questions

DIRECTIONS: There are several passages in this test. Each passage is followed by several questions. You should refer to the passages as often as necessary in order to choose the best answer to each question. Once you have selected your answer, fill in the corresponding bubble on your answer sheet. You may NOT use a calculator on this test.

PASSAGE I

Traditionally, oral drugs in pill or capsule form have been designed to release the dose of medicine in the upper gastrointestinal tract, where drugs are more readily dissolved and absorbed. New research has targeted the colon as an ideal environment for drug absorption to treat certain illnesses. To reach the colon, the drug must first pass through the stomach and small intestine. Table 1 details several drug-delivery systems.

Table 1		
Drug-delivery system	**Mechanics**	**Drawback**
pH	* Dissolves at a higher pH in the small intestine.	Releases early or not at all.
Pressure	* Higher pressure in the colon ruptures capsule. * Capsule size and wall thickness are varied to withstand lower pressures and rupture at higher pressures in the colon.	Food taken with the capsule may alter the pressure enough to disintegrate the capsule in the stomach.
Bacteria	* Synthetic polymer or natural (guar gum) coatings are resistant to bacteria in the stomach and small intestine but arc dissolved by the higher content of bacteria in the colon.	Safety and toxicity guidelines for synthetic polymers have not been established.
Time	* Outer coating dissolves upon entering the small intestine. Inner barrier delays release by settling, eroding, or dissolving.	Transit (movement) is slower in the evening than in the morning. Cannot adapt to an individual's transit time.

The following experiments test two of the drug-delivery systems:

GO ON TO THE NEXT PAGE.

4   **4**

Experiment 1

Bacteria-dependent delivery. This experiment measured the average time it took a coated tablet to travel from the stomach (gastric emptying) through the small intestine (small intestine transit) to arrive in the colon. Twelve healthy men aged 23 to 25 years old and weighing between 55 and 70 kilograms (kg) who had fasted overnight were divided into 3 groups. They each swallowed 1 tablet, which contained a tracer (A or B) and 1 of 2 natural coatings (1 or 2). The location of the tracer was measured every half-hour for 12 hours. The average times are recorded in Table 2.

Table 2						
Group	Gastric emptying (h)	Small intestine transit (h)	Colonic arrival (h)	Tracer	Coating	Target
I	3.3	5.75	9.05	A	1	Colon
II	3.2	5.13	8.33	A	2	Colon
III	3.1	6.25	9.35	B	1	Stomach

Experiment 2

Time-dependent delivery. The methods were the same as those used in Experiment 1, except that the tablets all contained the same tracer and 1 of 2 outer coatings (A or B) and 1 of 2 inner coatings (1 or 2). The average times are recorded in Table 3.

Table 3						
Group	Gastric emptying (h)	Small intestine transit (h)	Colonic arrival (h)	Outer coating	Inner coating	Target
I	3.3	5.65	8.95	A	I	Colon
II	3.2	5.15	8.35	A	2	Colon
III	3.1	5.35	8.45	B	1	Colon

1. Based on Table 1, which drug-delivery system is most affected by food intake?
   A. pH-dependent delivery
   B. Time-dependent delivery
   C. Pressure-dependent delivery
   D. Bacteria-dependent delivery

2. According to Experiment 2, which combination of outer and inner coatings caused the tablet to reach its intended target most quickly?
   F. A and 1
   G. A and 2
   H. B and 1
   J. B and 2

3. The results of Experiment 1 suggest that:
   A. the tracer has no effect on the drug's target destination.
   B. the coating affects colonic arrival time.
   C. the coating affects the drug's target destination more than the tracer does.
   D. the tracer affects gastric emptying time.

4. Which average time is standard for both experiments?
   F. Small intestine transit time
   G. Colonic arrival time
   H. Small intestine transit time and colonic arrival time
   J. Gastric emptying time

5. Which of the following is true about time-dependent delivery?
   A. Synthetic polymers may be unsafe and may disintegrate in the stomach.
   B. Taking food may disintegrate the capsule before it reaches the colon.
   C. Delivery depends on the bacteria in the colon.
   D. An inner barrier delays release of the medicine.

GO ON TO THE NEXT PAGE.

4 ○ ○ ○ ○ ○ ○ ○ ○ 4

PASSAGE II

The process of altering solid rocks by changes in temperature, pressure, and chemistry is called *metamorphism. Foliation* refers to the alternating layers of different mineral compositions. Table 1 lists foliated and nonfoliated rocks. Table 2 shows a source rock and its result after undergoing metamorphism.

Table 1	
Foliated	**Nonfoliated**
Slate	Quartzite
Phyllite	Marble
Schist	Amphibolite
Gneiss	Metacon glomerate
	Hornfels

Table 2	
Source rock	**Result**
Shale	Slate
Slate	Schist
Schist	Gneiss
Rhyolite	Schist
Basalt	Schist
Basalt	Amphibolite
Limestone	Marble
Sandstone	Quartzite

Figure 1 shows the metamorphic intensity of four types of rock.

Figure 1

6. Which source rock's metamorphic result can be either foliated or nonfoliated?
   - F. Shale
   - G. Granite
   - H. Schist
   - J. Basalt

7. According to the passage, the source rock for marble is:
   - A. shale.
   - B. sandstone.
   - C. limestone.
   - D. granite.

8. According to Figure 1, foliation:
   - F. increases as metamorphic intensity increases.
   - G. decreases as metamorphic intensity increases.
   - H. increases as metamorphic intensity decreases.
   - J. is not dependent on metamorphic intensity.

9. Based on the passage, which of the following statements is true?
   - A. Slate and gneiss form at approximately the same intensity.
   - B. Shale forms at a lower intensity than schist.
   - C. Basalt metamorphism results in only foliated rock.
   - D. Schist forms rhyolite at high metamorphic intensity.

10. According to Figure 1 and Table 2, it would be expected that:
    - F. foliation will increase during metamorphism from rhyolite to schist to gneiss.
    - G. foliation will decrease during metamorphism from shale to schist to gneiss.
    - H. metamorphic intensity will decrease from prominent foliation to banding.
    - J. metamorphic intensity will increase from prominent foliation to slaty foliation.

11. According to the passage, schist can result from which of the following source rocks?
    - A. Slate only
    - B. Slate, Shale, and Basalt
    - C. Slate, Rhyolite, and Basalt
    - D. Slate and Basalt only

GO ON TO THE NEXT PAGE.

4   **4**

PASSAGE III

Researchers interested in studying the effect of two different solvents on the rate of *solvation* (chemical process involving the interaction of a solvent and a solute) conducted two experiments. The results are shown below.

A tablet containing 1,285 milligrams (mg) sodium bicarbonate and 1,000 mg citric acid was placed in each of six, 250 milliliter (mL) beakers. The tablets were either whole, crushed into a coarse powder, or crushed into a fine powder. Either 150 mL of water or 150mL of ethanol was added to each beaker. The time it took the tablet to dissolve was recorded.

Experiment 1

Each 250 mL beaker contained a tablet (1,285 mg sodium bicarbonate and 1,000 mg citric acid), which was either whole or crushed. 150 milliliters of water or ethanol was added to each beaker, and the time it took in seconds (s) for the tablet to dissolve was recorded in Table 1.

Table 1			
Beaker	**Tablet form**	**Time (s)**	**Solvent**
1	Whole	35	Water
2	Coarse powder	22	Water
3	Fine powder	17	Water
4	Whole	31	Ethanol
5	Coarse powder	17	Ethanol
6	Fine powder	10	Ethanol

Note: Temperature was held constant at 40°C.

Experiment 2

To each of the 6 beakers, 1 whole tablet (containing 1,285 mg sodium bicarbonate and 1,000 mg citric acid) was added. Fifteen milliliters of water of varying temperatures was added to the beakers, and the time it took in seconds (s) for the tablet to dissolve was recorded in Table 2.

Table 2		
Beaker	**Temperature (°C)**	**Time (s)**
1	10	46
2	20	38
3	40	30
4	60	21
5	80	12
6	90	4

12. In Experiment 1, which of the following scenarios caused the tablet to dissolve the fastest?
    F. Fine powder in water
    G. Coarse powder in ethanol
    H. Fine powder in ethanol
    J. Coarse powder in water

13. In what ways are the methods of Experiments 1 and 2 different?
    A. The solvent was varied in Experiment 1 but held constant in Experiment 2.
    B. The temperature was varied in Experiment 1 but held constant in Experiment 2.
    C. The tablet type was varied in Experiment 2 but held constant in Experiment 1.
    D. The solvent was varied in Experiment 2 but held constant in Experiment 1.

14. What observation can be made from the data in Table 1?
    F. Crushing the tablet does not affect dissolution time.
    G. Solvents do not affect dissolution time.
    H. Crushing the tablet results in slower dissolution time.
    J. Crushing the tablet results in faster dissolution time.

15. What would the result most likely be if 150 mL of 80°C water was added to a beaker containing a finely crushed tablet?
    A. The dissolution rate would be slower than 17 seconds.
    B. The dissolution rate would be faster than 12 seconds.
    C. The dissolution rate would be slower than 12 seconds.
    D. Crushing the tablet would have no effect on dissolution rate.

16. Based on the experiments, what can be done to slow the dissolution rate?
    F. Increase the water temperature
    G. Crush the tablet
    H. Use ethanol to dissolve the tablet
    J. Decrease the water temperature

17. Based on the experiments, which method resulted in the slowest dissolution rate?
    A. Whole tablet dissolved in 10°C water
    B. Finely crushed tablet dissolved in 25°C water
    C. Finely crushed tablet dissolved in ethanol
    D. Whole tablet in 80°C water

GO ON TO THE NEXT PAGE.

4   **4**

PASSAGE IV

A biologist wanted to test the effects of nutrition on the growth of young rats. Two experiments were conducted using different feeds and vitamin supplements. For both experiments, 4 groups of 20 rats each were given a different type of feed over a 6-week period. The rats were measured and weighed weekly. The rats in each group had an average starting weight of 200 grams (g) and an average starting length of 10 centimeters (cm).

Experiment 1

- Group 1 was fed a high-protein feed (Feed W).
- Group 2 was fed a grain-based feed with vitamin supplements (Feed X).
- Group 3 (control group) was fed a grain-based feed without supplements (Feed Y).
- Group 4 was fed a grain-based feed without supplements plus fruits and vegetables (Feed Z).

The results and average measurements are recorded in Table 1.

Table 1

Group	Average weight after 6 weeks (g)	Average length after 6 weeks (cm)
1	350	16.25
2	347	18.00
3	343	14.50
4	343	17.00

Experiment 2

- Group 5 was fed a high-protein feed plus fruits and vegetables (Feed M).
- Group 6 was fed a grain-based feed with vitamin supplements plus fruits and vegetables (Feed N).
- Group 7 (control group) was fed a grain-based feed without supplements (Feed O).
- Group 8 was fed a grain-based feed without supplements plus fruits and vegetables (Feed P).

The results and average measurements are recorded in Table 2 below.

Table 2

Group	Average weight after 6 weeks (g)	Average length after 6 weeks (cm)
5	352	17.00
6	349	18.25
7	342	14.25
8	344	15.75

18. Based on the results of both experiments, the rats in which group increased the most in average length?
    F. Group 6
    G. Group 2
    H. Group 7
    J. Group 4

19. Based on the results of Experiment 2, which feed resulted in the greatest weight gain?
    A. Feed M
    B. Feed N
    C. Feed O
    D. Feed P

20. Based on the results of both experiments, the rats in which of the following groups gained the least amount of weight?
    F. Group 1
    G. Group 3
    H. Group 5
    J. Group 7

21. If the biologist added vitamin supplements to Feed M for a new group (Group 9), what might the result be after 6 weeks?
    A. Group 9 would weigh less than Group 2.
    B. Group 9 would weigh less than Group 6.
    C. Group 9 would have a greater length than Group 5.
    D. Group 9 would have a shorter average length than Group 5.

22. Which of the following statements is true, according to Table 2?
    F. Feed N produces rats that are almost twice as long as those in the control group.
    G. Feed M produces rats that weigh 3 times as much as those in the control group.
    H. Feed P produces rats with the greatest average length.
    J. Feed O produces rats similar to those produced by Feed P.

GO ON TO THE NEXT PAGE.

4 ○ ○ ○ ○ ○ ○ ○ ○ **4**

PASSAGE V

Igneous rocks are formed by the cooling and solidification of molten magma either above ground, when magma, or lava, reaches the Earth's surface and cools, or deep below the surface of the Earth, when magma gets trapped in small pockets and cools. Table 1 lists rock textures and cooling characteristics of igneous rocks. Figure 1 shows the cooling rate and associated grain size of igneous rock textures. Table 2 lists igneous rocks and their respective textures.

Table 1		
Rock texture	**Description**	**Cooling characteristics**
Glassy	No distinct visible grains.	Cools rapidly and above the temperature for crystals to form.
Aphanitic	Minerals arc too small to be seen without a microscope.	Cools quickly but more slowly than glassy-textured rocks.
Phaneritic	Interlocking grains form a mosaic pattern; can be seen without a microscope.	Cools very slowly at a uniform rate.
Porphyritic	Has two grain sizes.	Undergoes two stages of cooling: usually cools slowly first then rapidly.

Table 2	
Rock	**Texture**
Rhyolite	Aphanitic
Andesite	Aphanitic
Basalt	Aphanitic
Granite	Phanerilic
Diorile	Phanerilic
Gabbro	Phanerilic

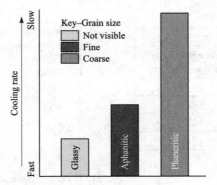

Figure 1

23. Which of the following is true about granite?
    A. It is fine-grained and cools slowly.
    B. It is fine-grained and cools quickly.
    C. It is coarse-grained and cools quickly.
    D. It is coarse-grained and cools slowly.

24. Rhyolite and andesite have which of the following in common?
    F. They cool very slowly at a uniform rate.
    G. They are phaneritic.
    H. They cool quickly but more slowly than glassy rocks.
    J. They are coarse-grained.

25. Using the data in Table 1 and Figure 1, what conclusion can be made about (crystal) grain size?
    A. The slower a rock cools, the larger the crystals will be.
    B. The faster a rock cools, the larger the crystals will be.
    C. Glassy rocks have large crystals.
    D. The slower a rock cools, the smaller the crystals will be.

26. Which rock texture is formed by rapid cooling from a high temperature?
    F. Porphyritic
    G. Glassy
    H. Phaneritic
    J. Aphanitic

27. Based on information in the passage, which rocks cooled quickly?
    A. Rhyolite, granite, and diorite
    B. Granite, gabbro, and peridotite
    C. Rhyolite, andesite, and basalt
    D. Andesite, basalt, and granite

28. Peridotite is an igneous rock with interlocking grains that can be seen without a microscope. What are the likely cooling characteristics of peridotite?
    F. It cools quickly.
    G. It cools at a very slow and uniform rate.
    H. It cools slowly at first, and then speeds up.
    J. It cools at a rapid, constant rate.

GO ON TO THE NEXT PAGE.

4 ◯ ◯ ◯ ◯ ◯ ◯ ◯ ◯ 4

PASSAGE VI

Stars can be classified according to color, surface temperature, mass, radius, and luminosity. Table 1 shows the spectral classification of star types. Figure 1 is a cluster diagram plotting stars near the sun by temperature and luminosity (total brightness). Main sequence stars are young stars shown in Figure 1 as the central band.

Table 1					
Star type	Color	Surface temperature (K)	Mass (solar mass)	Radius (solar radius)	Luminosity (solar units)
O	Blue	28,000–60,000	60	15	1,400,000
B	Blue	10,000–28,000	18	7	20,000
A	Blue	7,500–10,000	3.2	2.5	80
F	Blue to white	6,000–7,500	1.7	1.3	6
G	While to yellow	5,000–6,000	1.1	1.1	1.2
K	Orange to red	3,500–5,000	0.8	0.9	0.4
M	Red	<3,500	0.3	0.4	0.04 (very faint)

Notes: Mass, radius, and luminosity are averages. The sun has the following spectral classifications: mass = 1; radius = 1; luminosity = 1.

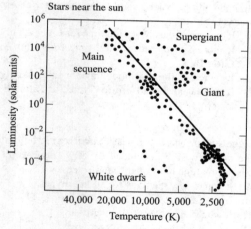

Figure 1

29. According to Table 1, which type of star has a mass 18 times that of the sun?
A. O
B. B
C. F
D. K

30. What color are stars with an approximate surface temperature of 2,500 K?
F. Blue
G. White
H. Yellow
J. Red

31. What is most likely the color range of the giant stars shown on Figure 1?
A. Orange to red
B. Blue to white
C. White to yellow
D. Blue to orange

32. The main sequence stars in Figure 1 represent all the star types EXCEPT:
F. M.
G. A.
H. O.
J. K.

33. A new star with a temperature of 15,000K and luminosity of 10^{-4} solar units is plotted in Figure 1. Based on the passage, what category of star is it?
A. Main sequence
B. White dwarf
C. Supergiant
D. Giant

GO ON TO THE NEXT PAGE.

4   **4**

PASSAGE VII

A student wanted to test the absorbency of several brands of cat litter to determine which absorbed water the fastest. The student conducted two experiments to test the litters.

Experiment 1

The student filled nine 12-inch × 9-inch glass pans 2 inches deep with 1 of 3 types of cat litter (A, B, or C). The student placed each type of litter in 3 areas with different relative humidity levels. The student then poured 100 milliliters (mL) of water into each pan. The student recorded the time it took for each pan of litter to absorb the water. Results are shown in Table 1.

Table 1			
Relative humidity (%)	Time for A (hr)	Time for B (hr)	Time for C (hr)
40	4	2	1
60	7	5	3
80	16	9	5

Experiment 2

The student repeated the previous experiment but used only 3 pans (one of each litter) and added 4 ounces of baking soda (sodium bicarbonate) to each pan. The student mixed the litter and baking soda thoroughly before adding 100 mL of water to each pan. The room had a constant relative humidity of 40% during the experiment. Results are shown in Table 2.

Table 2	
Litter	Time (hr)
A	3.5
B	2.0
C	1.5

34. Based on the experiments, which type of litter absorbs water fastest at 40% relative humidity?
- **F.** Litter A + baking soda
- **G.** Litter C
- **H.** Litter B
- **J.** Litter C + baking soda

35. If the relative humidity was increased to 90%, how long might Litter B take to absorb all of the water?
- **A.** 5 hours
- **B.** 7 hours
- **C.** 9 hours
- **D.** >9 hours

36. Based on the results of Experiment 1, which of the following is true of Litter A?
- **F.** It took almost twice as long as Litter B and more than 3 times as long as Litter C to absorb the water at 80% relative humidity.
- **G.** It absorbed the water almost twice as fast as Litter B and almost 3 times as fast as Litter C at 80% humidity.
- **H.** It absorbed the water faster than both Litter B and Litter C.
- **J.** It absorbed the water faster than Litter B at 60% relative humidity.

37. How does Experiment 1 differ from Experiment 2?
- **A.** Baking soda was added to the litter in Experiment 1.
- **B.** The amount of water varied in Experiment 2.
- **C.** Relative humidity is constant in Experiment 2 but varies in Experiment 1.
- **D.** Relative humidity is constant in Experiment 1 but varies in Experiment 2.

38. How did adding baking soda affect the water absorption times of the litter?
- **F.** It decreased the absorption time for Litter A only.
- **G.** It increased the absorption time for Litter A and Litter B.
- **H.** It decreased the absorption time for Litter B only.
- **J.** It increased the absorption time for Litter B and Litter C.

39. If the student were to repeat Experiment 2, but reduced the quantity of water added by 50%, how would the absorption time most likely be affected?
- **A.** It would stay the same for all litter types.
- **B.** It would decrease for Litter A only.
- **C.** It would increase for all litter types.
- **D.** It would decrease for all litter types.

40. According to the results of the experiments, which of the following conclusions can be reached?
- **F.** Relative humidity levels have no effect on absorption rates.
- **G.** Absorption time will decrease at higher relative humidity levels for all litter types.
- **H.** The type of litter has the greatest effect on absorption rates at all relative humidity levels.
- **J.** Adding baking soda to cat litter increases the absorption rate for all litter types.

END OF THE SCIENCE TEST.
STOP! IF YOU HAVE TIME LEFT OVER, CHECK YOUR WORK ON THIS SECTION ONLY.

WRITING TEST

DIRECTIONS: This test is designed to assess your writing skills. You have forty (40) minutes to plan and write an essay based on the stimulus provided. Be sure to take a position on the issue and support your position using logical reasoning and relevant examples. Organize your ideas in a focused and logical way, and use the English language to clearly and effectively express your position.

When you have finished writing, refer to the Scoring Rubrics discussed in Chapter 7 to estimate your score.

Note: On the actual ACT you will receive approximately 2.5 pages of scratch paper on which to develop your essay, and approximately 4 pages of notebook paper on which to write your essay. We recommend that you limit yourself to this number of pages when you write your practice essays.

Early Childhood Technology Use

Electronic devices with viewing screens are ubiquitous in modern society. Most people have smartphones with them at all times and many also carry laptop computers or tablets with them nearly everywhere. Almost every desk has a computer on it, and televisions are everywhere in homes and public spaces. Nearly from birth, children are exposed to screens that attract their attention and focus. There is much discussion among parents and child development experts regarding the impact of this electronic revolution on young children.

PERSPECTIVE ONE	PERSPECTIVE TWO	PERSPECTIVE THREE
Electronic devices are a fact of life and will certainly be important in the future. Children who adapt to them early will have an advantage later in life. Not only should children become comfortable with screened devices, they should be taught keyboard skills and even basic coding as part of their early-childhood language development.	Children place many demands on their parents' time and energy. Young children need constant supervision and stimulation. So long as parents are responsible about content, it is understandable when they use television and other devices as a means to focus their children and keep them still and quiet for reasonable periods of time.	Children who view electronic screens at a young age often exhibit negative traits, such as inability to focus for appreciable periods of time, near sightedness, and decreased ability to recognize emotions in other human beings. They also tend to be less physically active and more obese. Parents often fail to adequately monitor children's use of technology, leading to elevated stress and even thought disorders.

Essay Task

Write a unified, coherent essay in which you evaluate multiple perspectives on the implications of early childhood technology use. In your essay, be sure to:

- analyze and evaluate the perspectives given
- state and develop your own perspective on the issue
- explain the relationship between your perspective and those given

Your perspective may be in full agreement with any of the others, in partial agreement, or wholly different. Whatever the case, support your ideas with logical reasoning and detailed, persuasive examples.

ANSWER KEY

English Test

1. A	21. C	41. B	61. D
2. F	22. J	42. J	62. H
3. C	23. A	43. C	63. D
4. G	24. J	44. F	64. F
5. A	25. D	45. D	65. A
6. F	26. H	46. F	66. G
7. C	27. A	47. B	67. D
8. H	28. J	48. G	68. G
9. D	29. B	49. C	69. C
10. H	30. F	50. H	70. F
11. B	31. C	51. D	71. D
12. F	32. F	52. F	72. H
13. A	33. B	53. B	73. C
14. H	34. J	54. F	74. G
15. D	35. A	55. C	75. D
16. H	36. G	56. H	
17. B	37. B	57. A	
18. G	38. J	58. F	
19. C	39. C	59. C	
20. J	40. G	60. H	

Mathematics Test

1. D	21. B	41. D
2. H	22. H	42. F
3. E	23. D	43. A
4. H	24. J	44. H
5. D	25. D	45. D
6. F	26. K	46. H
7. B	27. B	47. D
8. J	28. H	48. F
9. C	29. A	49. E
10. K	30. K	50. F
11. D	31. D	51. E
12. G	32. F	52. K
13. A	33. B	53. A
14. J	34. K	54. G
15. B	35. B	55. E
16. H	36. K	56. F
17. D	37. D	57. C
18. G	38. G	58. F
19. A	39. A	59. E
20. K	40. H	60. H

Reading Test

1. B	21. D
2. G	22. J
3. A	23. D
4. J	24. J
5. A	25. C
6. F	26. H
7. C	27. C
8. J	28. H
9. A	29. C
10. J	30. G
11. D	31. B
12. G	32. J
13. A	33. C
14. H	34. J
15. B	35. A
16. H	36. J
17. C	37. A
18. F	38. H
19. D	39. D
20. F	40. G

Science Test

1. C	21. C
2. G	22. J
3. B	23. D
4. J	24. H
5. D	25. A
6. J	26. G
7. C	27. C
8. F	28. G
9. B	29. B
10. F	30. J
11. C	31. A
12. H	32. H
13. A	33. B
14. J	34. G
15. B	35. D
16. J	36. F
17. A	37. C
18. F	38. F
19. A	39. D
20. J	40. H

SCORING GUIDE

Your final reported score is your COMPOSITE SCORE. Your COMPOSITE SCORE is the average of all of your SCALE SCORES.

Your SCALE SCORES for the four multiple-choice sections are derived from the Scoring Worksheet on the next page. Use your RAW SCORE, or the number of questions that you answered correctly for each section, to determine your SCALE SCORE. If you got a RAW SCORE of 60 on the English Test, for example, you correctly answered 60 out of 75 questions.

Step 1 Determine your RAW SCORE for each of the four multiple-choice sections:

English   _____

Mathematics   _____

Reading   _____

Science   _____

The following Raw Score Table shows the total possible points for each section:

RAW SCORE TABLE	
KNOWLEDGE AND SKILL AREAS	RAW SCORES
ENGLISH	75
MATHEMATICS	60
READING	40
SCIENCE	40

Step 2 Determine your SCALE SCORE for each of the four multiple-choice sections using the following Scale Score Conversion Table.

SCALE SCORE	RAW SCORE			
	ENGLISH	MATHEMATICS	READING	SCIENCE
36	75	60	40	39–40
35	74	59	—	38
34	73	57–58	39	37
33	71–72	56	38	36
32	70	55	37	—
31	69	54	—	35
30	68	53	36	34
29	67	52	35	33
28	65–66	51–50	34	32
27	64	48–49	33	31
26	62–63	46–47	32	29–30
25	60–61	44–45	31	27–28
24	58–59	41–43	30	25–26
23	56–57	38–40	29	23–24
22	54–55	35–37	27–28	21–22
21	51–52	31–34	26	20
20	49–50	28–30	24–25	18–19
19	46–48	27	22–23	17
18	43–45	24–26	21	15–16
17	40–42	20–23	19–20	14
16	36–39	16–19	17–18	12–13
15	33–35	12–15	15–16	11
14	30–32	10–11	13–14	10
13	27–29	8–9	11–12	9
12	24–26	6–7	9–10	8
11	21–23	5	8	7
10	19–20	4	6–7	6
9	15–18	—	—	5
8	13–14	3	5	4
7	11–12	—	4	3
6	9–10	2	3	—
5	7–8	—	—	2
4	5–6	1	2	—
3	4	—	—	1
2	2–3	—	1	—
1	0–1	0	0	0

NOTE: Each actual ACT is scaled slightly differently based on a large amount of information gathered from the millions of tests ACT, Inc. scores each year. This scale will give you a fairly good idea of where you are in your preparation process. However, it should not be read as an absolute predictor of your actual ACT score. In fact, on practice tests, the scores are much less important than what you learn from analyzing your results.

   If you take the optional Writing Test, you should refer to Chapter 7 for guidelines on scoring your Writing Test Essay.

Step 3 Determine your COMPOSITE SCORE by finding the sum of all your SCALE SCORES for each of the four sections: English, Mathematics, Reading, and Science, and divide by 4 to find the average. Round your COMPOSITE SCORE according to normal rules. For example, 31.2 ≈ 31 and 31.5 ≈ 32.

$$\frac{}{\text{ENGLISH} \atop \text{SCALE SCORE}} + \frac{}{\text{MATHEMATICS} \atop \text{SCALE SCORE}} + \frac{}{\text{READING} \atop \text{SCALE SCORE}} + \frac{}{\text{SCIENCE} \atop \text{SCALE SCORE}} = \frac{}{\text{SCALE SCORE} \atop \text{TOTAL}}$$

$$\frac{}{\text{SCALE SCORE TOTAL}} \div \ \mathbf{4} \ = \frac{}{\text{COMPOSITE SCORE}}$$

ANSWERS AND EXPLANATIONS

English Test Explanations

PASSAGE I

1. **The best answer is A.** The underlined portion is clear and concise and written in active voice. Answer choices B and D are awkward and not grammatically correct. Answer choice C is written in the passive voice.

2. **The best answer is F.** This question requires you to punctuate the underlined portion correctly. Because the adverb *perfectly* directly modifies the adjective *erect*, you should not separate the words with a comma. Eliminate answer choice H. You should, however, use a comma to separate the two clauses in the sentence.

3. **The best answer is C.** In order to maintain parallel structure in the paragraph, verb forms must match. The verbs *watch, remains,* and *curls* are all in the simple present tense. The subject is the third-person, singular pronoun *he.* Therefore, you should use the third-person, singular, simple present tense verb *appears,* answer choice C.

4. **The best answer is G.** The subordinate clause that introduces this sentence refers to the age of the dog. The appropriate subordinating conjunction to use with time is *when,* answer choice G. Careful reading of the other answer choices within the sentence reveals that they do not make sense.

5. **The best answer is A.** As it is written, the underlined portion provides detailed information about what the mother and her son would find in the nursery. The other answer choices are some-what vague and nonspecific.

6. **The best answer is F.** The singular verb *was* follows the singular pronoun *he*; this sentence is grammatically correct as it is written.

7. **The best answer is C.** This question requires you to determine the correct punctuation. Eliminate answer choice D because it creates an incomplete sentence. A semicolon should be followed by an independent clause, so eliminate answer choice B. To separate independent clauses linked by a coordinating conjunction such as *and,* a comma must precede the coordinating conjunction. In addition, no comma should come between the conjunction and the subject of the second clause. Eliminate answer choice A.

8. **The best answer is H.** The verb *are* in this sentence takes a conjoined predicate. Therefore, in this case, the forms of the adjectives on either side of the

conjunction *and* must be parallel. *Held* is an adjective and a past participle. *Raising,* from answer choice F, is a gerund, so eliminate it. Answer choice G has *risen,* which is the past participle of *rise,* a different verb. With the auxiliary verb *have,* it is awkward in the sentence. Eliminate answer choice G. Eliminate answer choice J because the paragraph is in the present tense.

9. **The best answer is D.** The paragraph is in the present tense, so references to completed actions in the past (like this one about training the dog) should be made in the simple past tense.

10. **The best answer is H.** The best way to answer this question is to try the answer choices in the sentence. The only one that does not make sense and is, therefore, NOT a good alternative, is answer choice H. It is not idiomatic.

11. **The best answer is B.** At this point (after a subordinate clause and a comma), you may be tempted to begin the main clause with a subject and a verb. Notice, however, that the main clause is already present in the underlined portion for Question 12. Therefore, eliminate answer choice D. Eliminate answer choice C because it contains the third-person, singular verb form *marvels,* which has no clear subject. Eliminate answer choice A for the same reason. Answer choice B is best because a gerund phrase is appropriate before the main clause.

12. **The best answer is F.** The underlined portion makes the most sense where it is. Placing it anywhere else in the sentence would create confusion as to who is doing the *watching* and *marveling.*

13. **The best answer is A.** The context of the paragraph indicates that the dog is excited and happy to be returning to its owner. The phrase that best conveys that idea is *races back,* which is the original version. The other answer choices are not supported by the context of the paragraph.

14. **The best answer is H.** The underlined portion, "happy to be alive," indicates the dog's perceived attitude toward returning to its owner. If this part of the sentence were deleted, the sentence would lose its description of the dog's attitude. Therefore, answer choice H is best.

15. **The best answer is D.** This question requires you to determine the main idea of the passage. The passage is primarily about the writer's experience with her dog, not about training her dog to hunt. You can eliminate answer choices A and B. There is nothing in the passage that encourages readers not to train dogs to hunt, so eliminate answer choice C.

PASSAGE II

16. **The best answer is H.** First, no comma should separate the prepositional phrase *of the fence* from the noun it modifies, *issue*. Second, no comma should separate the preposition *of* from its object, *the fence*.

17. **The best answer is B.** This choice contains a comma splice. You cannot separate two independent clauses with a comma. The remaining answer choices are grammatically correct.

18. **The best answer is G.** This paragraph is written in the simple present tense. Therefore, to maintain parallelism among the verbs, the simple present form *dictates* is appropriate here.

19. **The best answer is C.** In this sentence, the *privacy* belongs to the subject *people*. (The possessive determiner *their* before *privacy* has *people* as its antecedent.) The context of the passage supports the idea people *value* their own privacy.

20. **The best answer is J.** The underlined portion is unnecessary and should be omitted.

21. **The best answer is C.** The first step in answering this question is to decide whether to use *then* or *than*. The word *then* indicates the passage of time, which is not appropriate here. Eliminate answer choices A and D. Now look at the punctuation. It is not necessary to include a comma after the word *rather*, so eliminate answer choice B.

22. **The best answer is J.** This question requires you to determine the correct use of commas. It is necessary to set off each item in a list with a comma. Therefore, you should place a comma after *trees, shrubs, vines,* answer choice **J.**

23. **The best answer is A.** The phrase *which lose their foliage* includes important information regarding deciduous trees. Because the foliage belongs to the trees, use the plural possessive pronoun *their*, not the contraction of *they are*. It is also necessary to use *which* to set off the restrictive clause, *lose their foliage.*

24. **The best answer is J.** This question requires you to choose the best preposition. The best one to use with the noun *protection* (or the verb *protect,* which is its root) is *against*. Answer choices F and G can be eliminated because they indicate that the *prying eyes and perked ears* are the ones being ineffectively protected. Answer choice H, *toward,* is a preposition with meanings related to directional motion, so it is not appropriate here.

25. **The best answer is D.** The preceding sentence states that *deciduous trees...prove to be ineffective...* The next sentence presents the better alternative, *evergreen trees*. The function of this sentence is clear, so it is wordy to refer to deciduous trees again.

26. **The best answer is H.** This question requires you to determine the correct use of commas. An intercepting phrase such as *for example* needs to be set off with commas. That is, you should place a comma before and after the phrase, as in answer choice H.

27. **The best answer is A.** The main point of the passage is that fences can provide *privacy and security*. The other answer choices are not supported by the context of the passage.

28. **The best answer is J.** Because the word *carefully* is used in the sentence and is not part of the underlined portion, you should not use words such as *cautious* and *cautiously,* or phrases like *take care*. Answer choices F, G, and H create redundancy.

29. **The best answer is B.** Adding an *s* forms the plural form of *neighbor.* The sentence does not indicate any possession, so eliminate answer choices A and C. It is generally not appropriate to add *s's* to create plural possession, so answer choice D should never be a credited response.

30. **The best answer is F.** First, you can eliminate answer choice G because *full of cost* is not idiomatic. Among answer choices F, H, and J, answer choice F conveys that idea most simply. (Note that *costly* is an adjective and not an adverb, despite the suffix —*ly*.)

PASSAGE III

31. **The best answer is C.** It is necessary to separate all of the items in the list with commas.

32. **The best answer is F.** The word *aptly* means "appropriately." Use the context to determine that the phrases describing Maya Angelou are fitting.

33. **The best answer is B.** This question requires you to express the idea clearly and simply. Answer choice B is clear and concise.

34. **The best answer is J.** The word "booming" does not fit the context of the sentence.

35. **The best answer is A.** The sentence indicates that, after a certain *traumatic incident,* Maya did not speak for five years. It is important to have some explanation for her behavior. If that phrase were deleted, you would not have a clear picture of why Maya *spent the next five years in total and utter silence.*

36. **The best answer is G.** *Different* can be deleted because it is redundant with *variety*. The other words have important roles in the sentence.

37. The best answer is B. When two verb phrases are conjoined as they are here with *and,* no comma is needed. Note that there is no separate subject for the second verb phrase, in which case a comma would be needed. Furthermore, *civil rights movement* is a noun phrase that should not be punctuated, so answer choices C and D can be eliminated.

38. The best answer is J. This paragraph mentions Angelou's professional accomplishments. The new sentence is about salary, which distracts from the author's intent to dignify the poet. It adds little interest to the passage.

39. The best answer is C. The President's name is irrelevant and does not add any necessary information to the passage.

40. The best answer is G. You would either *listen to* or *watch.* You would not watch *to,* so eliminate answer choices F and J. Answer choice J also includes an unnecessary comma. You would not watch *with,* so eliminate answer choice H.

41. The best answer is B. It is important to maintain parallel structure within the sentence. Since the cannons are *deafening,* the flowers must be *blossoming,* answer choice B.

42. The best answer is J. This question tests your ability to express an idea clearly and simply. Maya Angelou *instills* the sense of wonder and joy, so that phrase should directly follow her name in the sentence. She does not *sense* the wonder and joy, so eliminate answer choice F. Answer choices G and H are awkward and should be eliminated as well.

43. The best answer is C. This question requires you to select the correct verb form. The sentence as written does not clearly indicate what Angelou has the ability to do, so eliminate answer choice A. The prepositions *for* and *with* do not complement the noun *ability,* so their meaning is unclear. Eliminate answer choices B and D. One way to complement *ability* appropriately is with a verb in the infinitive form, as in answer choice C.

44. The best answer is F. The sentence does not specify one particular listener, but instead refers to anyone who listens to Maya Angelou. Answer choice H is wordy and awkward, and should also be eliminated. If you omit the underlined portion, the relative pronoun *that* becomes ambiguous.

45. The best answer is D. This question requires you to determine the main idea of the essay. While the essay mentions that Maya Angelou had a difficult childhood, it in no way focuses on southern poverty, so eliminate answer choices A and B. The main focus of the passage is Maya Angelou's life in general.

PASSAGE IV

46. The best answer is F. Answer choices G and J are wordy and can be eliminated. Answer choice H is awkward and can be eliminated because it seems to repeat what has already been stated in the sentence.

47. The best answer is B. The prepositional phrase *to the nearest shopping center* is a complement of the verb *go.* Therefore, no punctuation is needed in the underlined portion.

48. The best answer is G. Because this essay is a reflection of past events, you should use the past-tense verb *seemed;* eliminate answer choices F, H, and J.

49. The best answer is C. Sentence 4 introduces the idea that the writer's mother would receive the fabric. Sentence 5 then indicates that much of the material would be turned into the writer's school clothes. It makes the most sense to place the new sentence between Sentences 4 and 5.

50. The best answer is H. The preposition *because* implies that one thing happened as the result of another. In this sentence, the result of the writer spending most of her time with her grandmother is that she really remembers the *brief moments* that she shared with her grandfather. The other answer choices are not supported by the context of the essay.

51. The best answer is D. Answer choice D is NOT acceptable because it lacks an action verb. All other answer choices have the verb *are.*

52. The best answer is F. The writer indicates that her grandfather *always seemed to be in and out, but mostly out.* This suggests that he was gone much of the time. The other answer choices are not supported by the context of the essay.

53. The best answer is B. Since the subject *the chair and ottoman,* is a plural subject, you must use a plural verb. Eliminate answer choice A. Also, like the rest of the passage, a past-tense form of the verb should be used. Eliminate answer choices C and D.

54. The best answer is F. This question tests your ability to express an idea clearly and simply. The sentence makes it clear that when the writer's grandfather was away on a fishing trip, the chair and ottoman were still forbidden. While answer choice H is grammatically correct, it is too wordy and awkward, and is, therefore, not the best choice.

55. The best answer is C. Answer choice A has a dangling modifier; the phrase *even as a child* should refer to the author, not *Grandpa.* Eliminate answer choice A. Answer choice B contains awkward word order, so eliminate it. Answer choices C and D are both grammatically correct, but answer choice C is made clearer with the subject pronoun *I* and by its standard word order.

56. **The best answer is H.** This question requires you to express an idea clearly and simply. Since a *king* by definition is *royal*, you do not need to use both words in the same phrase. Eliminate answer choices F and J. It is not correct to say *a royalty* in this case, so eliminate answer choice G.

57. **The best answer is A.** The underlined portion effectively describes the conditions under which the writer's grandpa made his fishing lures. Placing the phrase elsewhere in the sentence would create awkwardness.

58. **The best answer is F.** In order to maintain parallel structure within this sentence, the verbs should match. Since the writer says that her grandfather *would invite* her to the garage, the sentence should say that he *would show* her how to tie the fishing lure together, answer choice F. Eliminate answer choice G because it creates a comma splice.

59. **The best answer is C.** Although the answer choices seem to indicate that this is a pronoun/antecedent agreement question, it is more a question about tense. The introductory phrase *by then* triggers the past perfect tense because it points to a time in the past before another time of reference in the past. (The move to the country occurred before the summer visits ended.) Therefore, answer choice C, with *had*, is best. Answer choice A has passive voice, which is rarely the best choice. Answer choice B creates the simple past tense, which is not correct. The pronoun *it* in answer choice D is ambiguous, so eliminate it.

60. **The best answer is H.** This question requires you to determine the main idea of the essay. The essay is primarily about the writer's experiences at her grandparents' house. It does not mention the relationship that her grandparents had with each other, so eliminate answer choices F and G. While it is true that the writer spent more time with her grandmother, this is off-topic and does not effectively answer the question.

PASSAGE V

61. **The best answer is D.** This question requires you to recognize redundancy. Because *jointly, with each other*, and *together* all have the same meaning, it is not necessary to use more than one of them in the sentence. Eliminate answer choices A, B, and C.

62. **The best answer is H.** The passage includes information about the importance of the electric motor, so the most appropriate word choice would be *important*. The other answer choices are not supported by the context of the passage.

63. **The best answer is D.** The sentence as written contains a split infinitive. (The adverbial phrase *more efficiently* falls between the particle *to* and the base-form verb *separate*.) Eliminate answer choice A. Eliminate answer choice B because it uses the gerund form incorrectly. Eliminate answer choice C because it contains the singular verb *separates* instead of the bare form *separate* to form the infinitive with *to*.

64. **The best answer is F.** It is correct to use the simple past tense to match the context of the paragraph.

65. **The best answer is A.** This question requires you to determine the correct use of commas and other punctuation. Because the phrase *who witnessed much of their work* could be omitted without affecting the overall meaning of the sentence, it is considered a nonrestrictive clause, which must be set off by commas. Answer choice B can be eliminated because semicolons do not introduce quotations.

66. **The best answer is G.** This choice clearly and specifically describes what the electromagnetic core would look like. The other answer choices are vague and do not provide a vivid description.

67. **The best answer is D.** The noun phrase *silk wedding dress* is a compound that should not be punctuated. Eliminate answer choice A. Second, no punctuation is needed between the two verb phrases (*sacrificed her silk wedding dress and tore it into strips*) in the sentence or within the second verb phrase. Eliminate answer choices B and C.

68. **The best answer is G.** This question requires you to express an idea clearly and simply. Since the previous sentence states that the strips were torn from Emily's silk wedding dress, it is not necessary to repeat that statement in this sentence.

69. **The best answer is C.** The underlined portion refers to the electromagnet and how it could be *used* to spin a wheel. The other answer choices either do not fit the context or are awkward and not grammatical.

70. **The best answer is F.** The pronoun *those* correctly refers to the specific, matching magnets on the wheel.

71. **The best answer is D.** The act of trying occurred in the past and is completed. Therefore, the simple past tense is required. Answer choice B can be eliminated because *could of* is a common misrepresentation of *could have*.

72. **The best answer is H.** Sentence 2 states that Thomas *grew very frustrated*. It makes sense that something

would cause that frustration. Sentence 1 does not include any information that would suggest a reason for Thomas' frustration, so eliminate answer choice F. The best place for Sentence 2 is between Sentences 5 and 6, because Sentence 2 makes it clear what they *tried* in Sentence 6.

73. **The best answer is C.** First, determine the topic of the paragraph. Information in the paragraph indicates that Thomas *finally received a patent*, so it would make sense that a sentence introducing this paragraph would include some mention of patents. Answer choice C does this best. Answer choice D is irrelevant to the passage.

74. **The best answer is G.** This sentence begins with a subordinate clause headed by *although* which must be set off from the rest of the sentence with a comma. The sentence as it is written does not include any punctuation, so eliminate answer choice F. Answer choices H and J awkwardly conjoin the two clauses with *and*.

75. **The best answer is D.** As the topic of the essay is Davenport's electric motor research, it makes sense that the author would mention the current widespread use of motors to make Davenport's work seem very important. Answer choices A, B, and C, while perhaps true, are specific and unrelated to the main idea of the passage.

Mathematics Test Explanations

1. **The correct answer is D**. According to information in the problem, a vehicle must be *at most* 1,500 pounds to cross the bridge. This means that a vehicle can weigh 1,500 pounds, but it cannot weigh more than 1,500 pounds. Express this mathematically as follows: weight $(w) \leq 1,500$.

2. **The correct answer is H**. This problem requires you to find the smallest number into which 2, 6, and 9 all go. Eliminate answer choice G, because 17 is an odd number and cannot be a multiple of 2. Next, because you are asked to find the smallest multiple, try the remaining answer choices in order from smallest to largest:

    9 does not go into 12, so eliminate answer choice F.

    $2 \times 9 = 18$, and $6 \times 3 = 18$, so 18 is the smallest positive integer that is a multiple of 2, 6, and 9.

3. **The correct answer is E**. Anytime that you have zero in the denominator, the expression is undefined. Therefore, one number that CANNOT be zero is u, which is in the denominator. Likewise, when you multiply any number by 0, the result is 0, so z CANNOT be zero.

4. **The correct answer is H**. The first step in solving this problem is to calculate the percentage of residents who DO have a white house. Set up a proportion:

    648 is to 2,160 as $x\%$ is to 100%

    $$\frac{648}{2,160} = \frac{x}{100}$$

    Cross-multiply and solve for x:

    $$2,160x = 64,800$$

    $$x = 30$$

    30% of the residents have a white house. Therefore, 100%–30%, or 70% of the residents DO NOT have a white house.

5. **The correct answer is D**. To solve this problem, substitute –1 for q and 3 for s wherever those variables appear in the expression:

    $$\frac{(q-s)}{3q}$$

    $$= \frac{(-1-3)}{3(-1)}$$

    $$= \frac{-4}{-3} = \frac{4}{3}$$

6. **The correct answer is F**. You can factor 6 out of $(6p+60)$ so that it is equal to $6(p+10)$. Dividing $6(p+10)$ by 6 results in $p + 10$.

7. **The correct answer is B**. Line s is a transversal that cuts the parallel lines, p and q. When a transversal cuts 2 parallel lines, all corresponding angles created have the same measurement. $\angle m$ corresponds with $\angle n$, because they are alternate interior angles, they have the same measurement. Since you are given that $m + n = 230°$, both $\angle m$ and $\angle n$ must equal $230° \div 2$, or 115°. There are 180° in a straight line. Therefore, if $\angle m$ is 115°, then $\angle o$ must be $180° - 115°$, or 65°.

8. **The correct answer is J**. You are given the equation for the volume of a cylinder, and you are given the lengths of the 2 variables. Simply plug these values into the equation and solve:

    Volume $= \pi r^2 h$

    Volume $= \pi (4)^2 (5)$

    Volume $= \pi (16)(5)$

    Volume $= \pi 80$, or 80π

9. **The correct answer is C**. The absolute value of a number is the numerical value of a real number without regard to its sign. In order to solve this problem, you must first substitute the number 7 for the x in $|4 - x|$, so that you get $|4 - 7|$. Then, perform the operation within the vertical lines, so that you get $|-3|$. Since you must disregard the negative sign in order to determine absolute value, you know that the absolute value of $|-3|$ is 3.

10. **The correct answer is K**. The first step in solving this problem is to recognize that the angles adjacent to the 110° and 135° angles are complementary to 110° and 135°. This means that, when added together, 110° and the angle adjacent to it must equal 180°, and 135° and the angle adjacent to it must equal 180°. So, the angle adjacent to 110° must equal 70°, and the angle adjacent to 135° must equal 45°. Fill in the measurements on the diagram as shown:

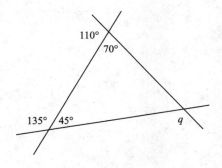

The sum of the interior angles of any triangle is 180°. So, 70° + 45° + the measure of the third angle x = 180°. Solve for the measure of the third angle:

$$70 + 45 + x = 180$$

$$11 + x = 180$$

$$x = 65$$

The angle adjacent to angle q is 65°, which means that angle q must be 180° − 65°, or 115°.

11. The correct answer is D. Use the FOIL method to solve this equation. Multiply the First terms, then the Outside terms, then the Inside terms, then the Last terms, as follows:

$$(\sqrt{2} - 6)(\sqrt{2} - 4) =$$

First terms: $(\sqrt{2})(\sqrt{2}) = 2$

Outside terms: $(\sqrt{2})(-4) = -4\sqrt{2}$

Inside terms: $(\sqrt{2})(-6) = -6\sqrt{2}$

Last terms: $(-6)(-4) = 24$

Now, add like terms together:

$$2 + 24 + (-4\sqrt{2}) + (-6\sqrt{2})$$

$$26 - 10\sqrt{2}$$

12. The correct answer is G. Use the FOIL method to solve this equation. Multiply the First terms, then the Outside terms, then the Inside terms, then the Last terms, as follows:

$$(x - 3y)^2 = (x - 3y)(x - 3y)$$

First terms: $(x)(x) = x^2$

Outside terms: $(x)(-3y) = -3xy$

Inside terms: $(-3y)(x) = -3xy$

Last terms: $(-3y)(-3y) = 9y^2$

Now, add like terms together:

$$x^2 + (-3xy) + (-3xy) + 9y^2$$

$$x^2 - 6xy + 9y^2$$

13. The correct answer is A. Because you are looking for an odd integer, a good way to solve this problem is to pick a value for x, and try the answer choices to see which one yields an odd integer. You are given that x is an odd integer greater than 5, pick 7 as your substitute:

> **Answer choice A:** $x + 2 = 7 + 2 = 9$; $x + 2$ yields an odd integer, so answer choice A could be correct.

Answer choice B: $x + 3 = 7 + 3 = 10$; eliminate answer choice B.

Answer choice C: $x + 5 = 7 + 5 = 12$; eliminate answer choice C.

Answer choice D: $3x = 3(7) = 21$; while this is an odd integer, 21 is greater than 9, so answer choice D is not correct (remember, you're looking for the next greater odd integer).

Answer choice E: $x^2 = 7^2 = 49$; again, while this is an odd integer, it is greater than 9, which means that answer choice A must be correct.

If you remembered that the sum of an even and an odd number is always odd, you could have quickly recognized that answer choice A is correct.

14. The correct answer is J. In order to solve this problem, you must put the equations into the standard form, $y = mx + b$. The equation in the problem is equivalent to $y = \dfrac{-x}{8} + \dfrac{3}{8}$

Convert the answer choices into the standard form:

F. $3x + 11y = 6; 11y = -3x + 6; y = \dfrac{-3}{11}x + \dfrac{6}{11}$

G. $2x + 10y = 5; 10y = -2x + 5;$

$y = \dfrac{-2}{10}x + \dfrac{5}{10}; y = \dfrac{-1}{5} + 2$

H. $3x + y = 8; y = -3x + 8$

J. $3x + 24y = 9; \quad 24y = -3x + 9; \quad y = \dfrac{-3x}{24} + \dfrac{9}{24};$

$y = \dfrac{-1}{8}x + \dfrac{3}{8}$

Answer choice J, when simplified, is the same equation as the one given in the problem, so this choice is correct.

15. The correct answer is B. To solve this problem, set up an equation. The combined age is 24, which means that Anne's age plus Kyle's age equals 24. Solve for Anne's age:

Anne + Kyle = 24

Anne = 3 (Kyle)

3(Kyle) + Kyle = 24

4(Kyle) = 24

Kyle $= \dfrac{24}{4} = 6$

Anne is 6×3, or 18 year old.

16. The correct answer is H. Lines $\overline{PQ}$ and $\overline{ST}$ are 2 parallel lines cut by transversals. This means that the angles created have special relationships. For example, opposite interior angles are congruent that is, they have the same measurement. So, angle P is congruent to angle T, which means that the measure of angle T must also be 65°, answer choice H.

17. **The correct answer is D.** If Carrie has seven dollars less than her brother, who has d dollars, then Carrie has $d - 7$ dollars. If she does not spend any money and earns three dollars, Carrie then has $d - 7 + 3$ dollars, or $d - 4$ dollars.

18. **The correct answer is G.** Solve for a by isolating a on the left side of the equation. Be careful to line up the decimal points:

$$0.2a + 1.8 = a - 2.2$$
$$0.2a - a = -2.2 - 1.8$$

a is equivalent to $1.0\,a$; $1.0 - 0.2 = .8$

$$-0.8a = -4.0$$
$$a = -\frac{-4.0}{-0.8} = 5$$

19. **The correct answer is A.** The best way to solve this problem is to substitute the answer choices for x and solve until you get a negative number. Since the question asks you for the smallest integer, start with the smallest answer choice:

$$-\sqrt{8+2} = -\sqrt{4} \times \sqrt{2} + 2 = -2\sqrt{2} + 2$$
$$-2(1.41) + 2 = -2.82 + 2 = -0.82$$

The smallest integer, x, that will result in a negative value is 2, answer choice A. Test this by trying the remaining choices.

20. **The correct answer is K.** To solve this problem, you could recognize that, if the ratio of the pieces is 2:3, then the larger piece will be equal to $\frac{3}{5}$ of the total length. This is true because the part to part ratio is 2:3, so the part to whole ratios must be equal to 2:5 and 3:5. Solve for $\frac{3}{5}$ of 30:

$$30 \times \frac{3}{5} = x$$
$$30 \times 3 = 5x$$
$$90 = 5x$$
$$18 = x$$

21. **The correct answer is B.** The formula for the area of a circle is πr^2. Since the area is given as 49π, r^2 must equal 49, and r must equal 7. The diameter is equal to twice the radius, so the diameter equals 2(7), or 14.

22. **The correct answer is H.** The first step in solving this problem is to recognize that the figure is made up of a right triangle and a rectangle. Calculate the area

of each separate figure, then add the results to get the area of the entire figure:

$$\text{Area of a triangle} = \frac{1}{2}(bh)$$
$$\text{Area} = \frac{1}{2}(3 \times 4)$$
$$\text{Area} = \frac{1}{2}(12) = 6$$

The area of the triangle is 6.

$$\text{Area of a rectangle} = l \times w$$
$$\text{Area} = 7 \times 4 = 28$$

The area of the rectangle is 28. Therefore, the area of the figure shown is 6 + 28, or 34.

23. **The correct answer is D.** The question asks you to reduce the equation into simpler terms. Since there are 3 variables, a, b, and c, begin simplifying the as first, then the bs, and finally the cs. When multiplying like coefficients with exponents, add the exponents. When dividing like coefficients with exponents, subtract the exponents. Consider the following:

$$\frac{3a^2b^{-4}c^2}{2^{-2}ac^{-2}} = \frac{3ab^{-4}c^2}{2^{-2}c^{-2}} = \frac{3ab^{-4}c^2}{\left(\frac{1}{2^2}\right)\left(\frac{1}{c^2}\right)}$$
$$\frac{3ab^{-4}c^4}{\frac{1}{4}} = 4(3ab^{-4}c^4)$$
$$4\left(\frac{3ac^4}{b^4}\right) = \frac{12ac^4}{b^4}$$

24. **The correct answer is J.** To solve this problem, cross-multiply and solve for x, as follows:

$$\left(\frac{3\sqrt{7}}{7}\right) = \left(\frac{3\sqrt{7}}{x\sqrt{7}}\right)$$
$$21\sqrt{7} = 3x(7)$$
$$21\sqrt{7} = 21x$$
$$\sqrt{7} = x$$

25. **The correct answer is D.** The first step in solving this problem is to rearrange the terms and set the equation equal to 0:

$$3x^2 - 4x = 0$$

The next step is to factor the common value, x, from each of the terms:

$$x(3x - 4) = 0$$

$x = 0$, and $3x - 4 = 0$; solve for x.

$$3x = 4$$
$$x = \frac{4}{3}$$

Therefore, the solutions for x are 0 or $\frac{4}{3}$.

26. The correct answer is K. The slope of a line measures the steepness of a line, and can be calculated $\frac{y_1 - y_2}{x_1 - x_2}$. Two points on the line are given: (3, –8) and (4, 7). The y values are –8 and 7, so the change in y is –8 –7, or –15. The x values are 3 and 4, so the change in x is 3 – 4, or –1. The slope is –15 over –1, or 15.

27. The correct answer is B. A circle centered at (a, b) with a radius r has the equation $(x-a)^2 + (y-b)^2 = r^2$. Plug the information given in the question into the equation:

$$(x-2)^2 + (y-(7))^2 = 5^2$$
$$(x-2)^2 + (y+7)^2 = 25$$

28. The correct answer is H. The key to solving this problem is to recognize that $8x^2 - 8x - 6$ can be factored, as follows:

$$8x^2 - 8x - 6$$
$$= (2x-3)(4x+2)$$

So, $(2x-3)(4x+2) = (ax-3)(4x+a)$. Therefore, a must equal 2.

29. The correct answer is A. The slope-intercept form of a line is $y = mx + b$, where m is the slope and b is the y-intercept. By definition, a line perpendicular to any given line will have a slope equal to the negative reciprocal of the given line. Since the slope of the given line is $-\left(\frac{1}{4}\right)$, a line perpendicular to the given line will have a slope of 4. Eliminate answer choices B, D, and E, because they do not have a slope of 4. You are given that another point on the line is (0, –5). This means, that when $x = 0, y = -5$; by definition, therefore, – 5 is the y-intercept. So the slope-intercept form of the line in the question is $y = 4x - 5$.

30. The correct answer is K. To solve this problem, set up a proportion showing the relationship between the quantity of flour and the number of cookies.

24 cookies is to 60 cookies as 2 cups of flour is to x cups of flour.

$\frac{24}{60} = \frac{2}{x}$; solve for x

$24x = 120$

$x = 5$

31. The correct answer is D. One way to solve this problem is to substitute in the answer choices for the first p-value and solve the equation. Start with the answer

choice in the middle, answer choice C. Since you are multiplying by a decimal, if substituting answer choice C into the equation yields a result that is too small, you can eliminate any answer choices that are greater than answer choice C:

$0.1(800 + 1,800) =$

$0.1(2,600) = 260; 260$ is smaller than 800.

Now you can eliminate answer choices A, B, and C. Try answer choice D:

$0.1(200 + 1,800) = 200; 200 = 200$, so answer choice D is correct.

32. The correct answer is F. The formula of a circle is $(x-a)^2 + (y-b)^2 = r^2$, where (a, b) is the center of the circle, and r is the radius. The diagram shows one edge of the circle at (6,0), and the other at (0,0). The midpoint between 0 and 6 is 3, so the radius is 3 and the center of the circle is at point (3,0). Plug these values into the formula for a and b and the radius, 3, for r:

$$(x-3)^2 + (y-0)^2 = 3^2$$
$$(x-3)^2 + y^2 = 9$$

33. The correct answer is B. To find the solution for the given inequality, isolate x on the left side of the inequality:

$$x + 2(5-x) \le 2x + 3$$
$$x + 10 - 2x \le 2x + 3$$
$$-x + 10 \le 2x + 3$$
$$-3x \le -7$$

Now, you need to divide both sides of the inequality by –3; remember to reverse the inequality sign:

$$x \ge \frac{7}{3}$$

34. The correct answer is K. Remember that when you raise an exponent to another exponent, you must multiply the exponents. Therefore, the correct answer will include a^{16}. Only answer choice K includes the correct exponent value, so it must be correct. The complete mathematical solution is shown next:

$$(4a^4)^4 = 4^4 a^{4\times4} = 256a^{16}$$

35. The correct answer is B. The formula for the area of a parallelogram is base × height. You will need to calculate the height by applying the Pythagorean

Theorem: $a^2 + b^2 = c^2$. The unshaded region is a right triangle, so plug the given values into the Pythagorean Theorem:

$$3^2 + b^2 = 5^2$$
$$9 + b^2 = 25$$
$$b^2 = 16$$
$$b = 4$$

The height of the parallelogram is 4. The base is given as 8, so the area of the parallelogram is 4×8, or 32. Now, calculate the area of the unshaded triangle and subtract it from the total area of the parallelogram. The area of a triangle is $\frac{1}{2}(bh)$, where b is the base, and h is the height:

$$\frac{1}{2}(3 \times 4) =$$
$$\frac{1}{2}(12) = 6$$
$$32 - 6 = 26$$

36. The correct answer is K. This problem requires you to solve for x. Isolate x on the left side of the equation:

$$\frac{3}{4}x - \frac{3}{8} = \frac{1}{4} + \frac{5}{8}x$$
$$\frac{3}{4}x - \frac{5}{8}x = \frac{1}{4} + \frac{3}{8}$$

Now, find the lowest common denominator so that you can add and subtract the fractions. Since both 4 and 8 go into 8, 8 is the lowest common denominator:

$$\frac{3}{4}x = \frac{6}{8}x; \frac{1}{4} = \frac{2}{8}$$
$$\frac{6}{8}x - \frac{5}{8}x = \frac{2}{8} + \frac{3}{8}$$
$$\frac{1}{8}x = \frac{5}{8}$$
$$x = 8\left(\frac{5}{8}\right)$$
$$x = 5$$

37. The correct answer is D. By definition, a right isosceles triangle has 2 sides of equal length and the hypotenuse is equal to $\sqrt{2}$ times the length of either of the sides. Therefore, the smaller isosceles triangle with a hypotenuse of $2\sqrt{2}$ cm has 2 sides with lengths both equal to 2 cm. To answer this question, you must recognize that similar triangles have the same shape and the same proportions. You are given that the larger, similar triangle has a perimeter 2 times the perimeter of the smaller triangle. Therefore, each side in the larger triangle must be 2 times the length of the corresponding side in the smaller triangle. Since the 2 equal sides of the smaller triangle are each 2 cm, the 2 equal sides of the larger triangle are each 4 cm.

38. The correct answer is G. To solve this problem, you should calculate the area of the parallelogram and the area of the triangle, then add the results. The area of a parallelogram is equivalent to the base times the height. The area of a triangle is equivalent to $\frac{1}{2}(bh)$, where b is the base and h is the height. You will need to use the Pythagorean Theorem to calculate the height, which will be the same for both the parallelogram and the triangle.

$$a^2 + b^2 = c^2$$
$$6^2 + b^2 = 10^2$$
$$36 + b^2 = 100$$
$$b^2 = 64$$
$$b = 8$$

Now, plug the appropriate values into the equations:

Parallelogram $= (b)(h) = (13)(8) = 104$.

Triangle $= \frac{1}{2}(b)(h) = \frac{1}{2}(6)(8) = \frac{1}{2}(48) = 24$.

$$104 + 24 = 128$$

39. The correct answer is A. By definition, the sine of any acute angle is calculated by dividing the length of the side opposite the acute angle by the hypotenuse $\left(\sin = \frac{\text{opp}}{\text{hyp}}\right)$. The length of the side opposite angle a is 3, and the length of the hypotenuse is 5. Therefore, $\sin a = \frac{3}{5}$.

40. The correct answer is H. The first step in solving this problem is to solve each element of the equation for x.

$$(x + m) = 0$$
$$x = -m$$
$$(x + n) = 0$$
$$x = -n$$

Now, substitute the value of the solutions given in the equation for x in order to get the values for m and n:

$$x = -m; -3 = -m, \text{ so } m = 3$$
$$x = -n; 5 = -n, \text{ so } n = -5$$

Now add $m(3)$ to $n(-5)$:

$$3 + -5 = -2$$

41. The correct answer is D. The slope-intercept form of the equation for a line is $y = mx + b$, where m is the slope and b is the y-intercept. You can determine the slope of the line with the 2 points given in the question: $(-2, -1)$ and $(2, 2)$. By definition, the slope is equal to $\frac{y_1 - y_2}{x_1 - x_2}$:

$$\frac{-1 - 2}{-2 - 2} = \frac{-3}{-4} = \frac{3}{4}$$

The slope of the line is $\frac{3}{4}$. Use this value as m and 1 of the 2 points given in the question as x and y in the equation for a line. Solve for b:

$$2 = \frac{3}{4}(2) + b$$

$$2 = \frac{3}{2} + b$$

$$b = \frac{1}{2}$$

The equation of this line is $y = \frac{3}{4}x + \frac{1}{2}$. The question asks you to determine what the value of x is when $y = 5$, so substitute 5 for y in the equation of the line and solve for x:

$$5 = \frac{3}{4}x + \frac{1}{2}$$

$$4\frac{1}{2} = \frac{3}{4}x$$

$$x = 6$$

When $y = 5$, $x = 6$.

42. The correct answer is F. By definition, the tangent of any acute angle is $\frac{\sin}{\cos}$. Sin B is given as $\frac{8}{17}$ and cos B is given as $\frac{15}{17}$. Therefore, tan $B = \frac{8}{17} \div \frac{15}{17}$. To divide fractions, multiply the numerator by the reciprocal of the denominator: $\frac{8}{17} \cdot \frac{17}{15}$; the 17s will cancel each other out, so tangent $B = \frac{8}{15}$.

43. The correct answer is A. The first step in solving this problem is to recognize that you are looking for the equation of a line in the slope-intercept form, $y = mx + b$, where m is the slope and b is the y-intercept. Since the line shown intersects the y-axis at 5, the y-intercept must be 5. Eliminate answer

choices C, D, and E. Since the line shown has a positive slope, answer choice A must be correct. You can calculate the slope as the change in y-values over the change in x-values:

$$\frac{5 - 0}{0 - (-3)} = \frac{5}{3}$$

44. The correct answer is H. Two adjacent angles have one common ray. As in the picture below, the non-common rays form a straight angle (a line) which has a measure of 180°.

Given that the measure of one angle is twice $(2x)$ that of the other angle (x), the total degree measure of the angles can be found by setting 180° equal to $3x$ $(180 = 3x)$. Solve for x (the measure of the smaller angle) to get 60°.

45. The correct answer is D. One way to solve this problem is to recognize that each of the 6 letters can be involved in 20 different 3-letter combinations. For example, when P is in the first position, and O is in the second position, there are 4 possible 3-letter combinations (PON, POI, POE, and POS). Likewise, when P is in the first position, and N is in the second position, there are an additional 4 possible 3-letter combinations (PNO, PNI, PNE, and PNS). Therefore, because you cannot repeat a letter, each letter can be included in $5 \times 4 = 20$ different combinations; a total of 120 (6×20) 3-letter orderings can be made.

46. The correct answer is H. The volume of a cube is calculated by multiplying the length by the width by the height $(l)(w)(h)$. You are given that each side has a length of 5 centimeters, so the volume would be equivalent to $5 \cdot 5 \cdot 5$, or 5^3.

47. The correct answer is D. To answer this question, you should know that complex numbers are the sum of a real and an imaginary number, represented as $a + bi$. Using the complex plane, you can plot complex numbers similar to how you plot a coordinate on the (x,y) coordinate plane. To graph a complex number, $a + bi$, locate the real part, a, on the real axis (the x-axis), and move up or down to locate b, from the imaginary part, on the imaginary axis (the y-axis). Likewise, you can apply the Distance Formula to calculate the distance between two given points:

$$\sqrt{([x_2 - x_1]^2 + [y_2 - y_1]^2)}$$

You are given $3 + 6i$ and $-2 + 3i$, where the 3 and the -2 correspond to the values on the x-axis, and $6i$ and $3i$ correspond to values on the y-axis. Plug those points into the Distance Formula:

$$\sqrt{\left([-2-3]^2 + [3i-6i]^2\right)} = \sqrt{\left([-5]^2 + [-3i]^2\right)} = \sqrt{\left(25 - 9i^2\right)}$$

Now, you need to recognize that $i^2 = -1$ and use substitution:

$$\sqrt{(25 - 9(-1))} = \sqrt{(25 + 9)} = \sqrt{34}$$

48. The correct answer is F. By definition, in a perfect square trinomial the first and last terms are perfect squares, and the middle term is twice the product of the square roots of the first and last terms. Eliminate answer choices G and J because the last terms are not perfect squares. Eliminate choice H because the first term is not a perfect square. Look at the middle term in answer choices F and K; $12 = 2(2 \cdot 3)$, so answer choice F is a perfect square trinomial:

$$4x^2 + 12x + 9 = (2x + 3)(2x + 3)$$

49. The correct answer is E. By definition, a rational number can be expressed as a ratio of 2 integers. Whole numbers are rational numbers, as are fractions and most decimal numbers. Since you are given that both p and q are negative integers, all of the operations represented by the roman numerals will result in rational numbers. Negative numbers can be rational; pick numbers that solve the equation given, to check this theory:

$$p = 2q$$

$$-6 = 2(-3) \,;\, p = -6 \text{ and } q = -3$$

Now try the given operations using these values:

$p + q = -6 + -3 = -9$; this is a rational number.

$\dfrac{p}{q} - \dfrac{-6}{-3} = 2$; this is a rational number.

$\dfrac{q}{p} - \dfrac{-3}{-6} = \dfrac{1}{2}$; this is a rational number.

50. The correct answer is F. To solve this problem, first recognize the relationship between the exponents: $6b = 3(2b)$. Since $a^{2b} = 3$, then $a^{3(2b)}$ must equal 3^3, which is 27.

51. The correct answer is E. For this problem, the best approach is to use the given equation and test the answer choices to see which yields the greatest value. Replace r with each of the values in the answer choices and solve the equations:

A: $s = 19 - (5 + 19)^3$

$s = 19 - (24)^3$

$s = 19 - 13,824$

$s = -13,805$

B: $s = 19 - (5 + 5)^3$

$s = 19 - (10)^3$

$s = 19 - 1,000$

$s = -981$

C: $s = 19 - (5 + 1)^3$

$s = 19 - (6)^3$

$s = 19 - 216$

$s = -197$

D: $s = 19 - (5 + -5)^3$

$s = 19 - (0)^3$

$s = 19 - 0$

$s = 19$

E: $s = 19 - (5 + -19)^3$

$s = 19 - (-14)^3$

$s = 19 - (-2,774)$

$s = 2,793$

Answer choice E yields the greatest, or maximum value.

52. The correct answer is K. The sum of the interior angles of a regular octagon is $6(180°)$, or $1,080°$. Since all of the angles are the same, each interior angle is $\dfrac{1,080°}{8} = 135°$.

53. The correct answer is A. According to the rules of exponents, $x^0 = 1$, when x does not equal 0. Therefore, the exponent $x^2 + 1$ must equal 0, and x^2 must equal -1.

54. The correct answer is G. To solve this problem, extend the transversals so that they cross the parallel lines again, as shown below:

Apply the rules regarding parallel lines cut by a transversal to fill in the angle measures. Because the total measure of the other 2 angles of the triangle created by extending the transversals is 135, the measure of angle x must be 45.

55. The correct answer is E. This question tests your ability to recognize and apply the distributive property. According to the distributive property, for any numbers a, b, and c, $c(a+b) = ca + cb$. According to the distributive property, $a(b+c) =$

$ab + ac$ is equivalent to $ca + ba$, so roman numeral I is correct; eliminate answer choices B and C.

$ab + ac$, so roman numeral II is correct; eliminate answer choice A.

$(b+c)a$, so roman numeral III is also correct, eliminate answer choice D.

Since all of the operations are equivalent to $a(b+c)$, answer choice E is correct.

56. The correct answer is F. By definition, the tangent of any angle is $\frac{\sin}{\cos}$. Therefore, $\frac{(\tan x)}{(\sin x \cos x)}$, simplified as $(\tan x) \cdot \left(\frac{1}{\sin x \cos x} \right)$ is equal to $\frac{\sin}{\cos} \cdot \left(\frac{1}{\sin x \cos x} \right)$. Multiply the fractions, first canceling the $\sin x$ from the numerator and denominator to get:

$$\frac{1}{\cos^2 x}$$

57. The correct answer is C. The absolute value is always positive, so in order for the absolute value of x^3 to equal $-x^3$, x must be either a negative number or 0, answer choice C. If you cube a negative number, the result is always negative. So, if x were equal to -1, for example, the absolute value of x^3 would be $(-1)(-1)(-1)$, or 1. The value of $-x^3$ would also be 1,

because $-(-1)^3$ is equivalent to 1^3. Zero is an option as well, since 0 is neither negative nor positive, and 0 raised to any power is still 0.

58. The correct answer is F. The best way to solve this problem is to substitute in the answer choices for c and factor the equation:

$$3x^2 + 2x - 1 = 0$$
$$(3x - 1)(x + 1) = 0$$
$$3x - 1 = 0; \ 3x = 1; \ x = \frac{1}{3}$$
$$x + 1 = 0; \ x = -1$$

Answer choice F gives you 2 real solutions for x. Testing the other answer choices will yield 2 distinct complex roots, not real roots.

59. The correct answer is E. To answer this question, substitute the given values of x and y into the equation, as follows:

$$y = -2x^2 - 4$$
$$3a = -2(2)^2 - 4$$

Now solve for a:

$$3a = -2(2)^2 - 4$$
$$3a = -8 - 4$$
$$3a = -12$$
$$a = -4$$

60. The correct answer is H. Let $x =$ the number of 2-person tables and $y =$ the number of 4-person tables. You are given that a total of 202 people attended the party and that there were 60 tables. This information can be expressed in the following system of equations:

$$x + y = 60$$
$$2x + 4y = 202$$

Because you are asked to solve for the number of 2-person tables (x), multiply the first equation by 4:

$$4(x + y) = 4(60)$$
$$4x + 4y = 240$$

Next, subtract the second equation from the first equation. This will eliminate y, and you will be able to solve for x:

$$4x + 4y = 240$$
$$2x + 4y = 202$$
$$\overline{2x + 0 \ = 38, \text{ and } x = 19.}$$

Reading Test Explanations

PASSAGE I

1. **The best answer is B.** Paragraph 2 states that the narrator "had fancied it was down nearer the Circus," which suggests that he is not sure where the Magic Shop is, and had only "imagined" its location. The other answer choices are not supported by the context of the passage.

2. **The best answer is G.** In the first paragraph, the narrator states that, "I had not even been sure that the place was there, to tell the truth," and later in the second paragraph that, "I had fancied it was down nearer the Circus, or round the corner in Oxford Street, or even in Holborn; always over the way and a little inaccessible it had been, with something of the mirage in its position." Both of these statements support the idea that the shop's location was not where the narrator expected it to be. This is best represented by answer choice G. Answer choice F is most nearly the opposite, and answer choices H and J describe the shop itself, not its location.

3. **The best answer is A.** The first paragraph indicates that the narrator "had seen the Magic Shop from afar several times; I had passed it once or twice;" this suggests that he first learned of the Magic Shop when he had passed by it before, answer choice A. The other answer choices are not supported by details in the passage.

4. **The best answer is J.** The context in which that statement was made suggests that Gip was a polite child, answer choice J. The passage indicates that Gip "inherits his mother's breeding," but not that he was worried about his mother, so eliminate answer choice F. The other answer choices are not supported by the passage.

5. **The best answer is A.** Paragraph 4 indicates that the narrator found the clerk's action "unexpected," which means the same as "surprising." This best supports answer choice A.

6. **The best answer is F.** Based on the last two paragraphs, Gip's reaction to the shopman's trick can best be described as quietly astonished. Gip does not speak either during or after the trick, and after taking the glass balls he "resumed [the narrator's] reassuring finger, and nerved himself for the next event." The other answer choices are not supported by the passage.

7. **The best answer is C.** In the third paragraph, the narrator is taking his son into the magic shop to buy him some tricks for his birthday.

Throughout the rest of the passage, it becomes clear that they are enjoying themselves, and that the narrator wants to have fun. "Anything amusing?" is how the narrator requests the type of tricks that they are looking for. The passage as a whole supports the idea that the relationship between narrator and son is one of enjoyment, answer choice C. Although the narrator does show patience in the magic shop, that is not the primary focus of his relationship with his son, so answer choice D is not best. Likewise, the other answer choices are not supported by the passage.

8. **The best answer is J.** The passage indicates that Gip is excited about entering the Magic Shop. He "hauled [the narrator] by my finger right up to the window" and went on to describe each of the items in the window. The other answer choices are not supported by the passage.

9. **The best answer is A.** Paragraph 4 suggests that the narrator and his son were surprised to find the shopman suddenly behind the counter; "and so with a start we were aware of him." It is likely that this surprise caused them to stop laughing together, since this is what they were doing just before the surprise. The other answer choices are not supported by the passage.

10. **The best answer is J.** The last sentence in the passage states that Gip "nerved himself for the next event." This suggests that, although he may have been a bit uncertain, he was ready to see the next trick, answer choice J.

PASSAGE II

11. **The best answer is D.** The passage focuses on the difficulties that Alaska and her inhabitants encountered on the way to achieving statehood. In fact, according to the passage, it "took almost 100 years from beginning to end." This best supports answer choice D.

12. **The best answer is G.** The word *enigma* refers to a riddle, or anything that is puzzling. Since, according to Paragraph 1, the author doesn't know a lot about Alaska (at least as compared to Hawaii) it makes sense that *enigma* would mean "mystery," answer choice G.

13. **The best answer is A.** Paragraph 1 states that the author was "a ten-year-old girl" when Alaska became a state. The paragraph goes on to state that "nearly fifty years later,. . . Alaska remains an enigma." It is safe to conclude, then, that the author must be almost sixty years old, answer choice A.

14. The best answer is H. According to the passage, Alaska was a remote, unpopulated area that held little interest for most Americans. "Many people marveled at the stupidity" of Seward's plan to purchase Alaska in 1867. However, when gold was discovered, people began to realize that Alaska had some value.

15. The best answer is B. The passage emphasizes Alaska's struggle for statehood. You can infer that the reason the author posed the question is to introduce the main topic of the passage and follow it up with supporting information.

16. The best answer is H. While the author does offer some personal information, she does not make an emotional appeal, nor does she describe her childhood. Eliminate answer choice F. It is made clear in the passage that the author has never visited Alaska, so eliminate answer choice G. The bulk of the passage contains historical background information on Alaska's progression to statehood, which best supports answer choice H.

17. The best answer is C. The statement that "Alaska's own natural wealth was being stripped for the benefit of a handful of outside entrepreneurs" suggests that Alaskans were not reaping the benefits of their own land's resources, answer choice C.

18. The best answer is F. Paragraph 4 states that "the bombing of Pearl Harbor ... propelled Congress to provide Alaska with billions of dollars for defense spending," which suggests that Congress was motivated to give Alaska money due to the onset of World War II.

19. The best answer is D. The only reason that the author contrasts Alaska and Hawaii throughout the passage is to emphasize her personal impressions of each state, answer choice D. The other answer choices are not supported by the passage.

20. The best answer is F. The final sentence in Paragraph 4 states that "Alaska finally gained its statehood on January 3, 1959, due primarily to growing and organized public and political pressure." This best supports answer choice F.

PASSAGE III

21. The best answer is D. The passage states that "Ernest Hemingway is one of those rare authors most people know about, whether they have read him or not, because of his sensational publicity and personal invective. He has the distinction of being one of the most famous twentieth-century American writers with his image of ruggedness, confidence, virility,

and bravery. He has been regarded less as a writer dedicated to his craft than as a man of action who happened to be afflicted with genius." These details best support answer choice D.

22. The best answer is J. According to the passage, "He acquired his expertise through well-reported acts of participation as well as observation: by going to all of the wars of his time, hunting and fishing for great beasts. . . ." These details contradict answer choice J, which makes it the best option.

23. The best answer is D. Details in the passage show that Hemingway was an outdoorsman who "rejected out of hand the role of the indoor esthete." Additionally, the passage states that "Hemingway assuredly took some amusement in confounding public expectations of how a writer should look and conduct himself."

24. The best answer is J. The passage states that, "Hemingway described the novel as less about the life of postwar expatriates than about the rhythms of nature as an expression of eternity." Likewise, according to the author, "The novel pushes the limits of pastoral convention by testing its vision, acknowledging its enduring attraction, and questioning its very construct." This information best supports answer choice J.

25. The best answer is C. Only "ecological values" and "traditional pastoral conventions" are mentioned in the passage as ways in which Hemingway's novel has been interpreted.

26. The best answer is H. According to the passage, *The Sun Also Rises*, has frequently been treated as a novel of the Lost Generation—a group of young American expatriate writers living in Paris who came of age during World War I and established their reputations in the 1920's. They considered themselves "lost" because their inherited values could not operate in the postwar world, and they felt spiritually alienated from a country that they considered hopelessly provincial and emotionally barren." This best matches answer choice H.

27. The best answer is C. Passage A presents Hemingway as an outdoorsman and naturalist who "pursued the hunting and fishing sports that he had learned from his father." This is a reflection of the "meaning and value in cultivating a more intimate connection with the natural environment" desired by the characters in his novel.

28. The best answer is H. A main focus in both passages is Hemingway's connection to nature and how that connection shaped his writing.

29. **The best answer is C.** According to Passage A, Hemingway "wrote about what he knew best: traveling, bullfights, libations, women, wars, big game hunting, deep-sea fishing, and courage. He acquired his expertise through well-reported acts of participation as well as observation: by going to all of the wars of his time, hunting and fishing for great beasts, marrying four times, occasionally getting into fistfights, and drinking to excess." Details in Passage B show that Hemingway's novel "criticizes conventional depictions of nature and calls for a literature that offers a more complex picture of the connection between humanity and the natural world. It invokes the central elements of pastoral convention: the presentation of city life as complex and of city people as corrupt, the presentation of rural life (and of nature) as somehow more "real" and more simple than life in the city, and the presentation of rural folk as more honest, direct, and virtuous than city dwellers."

30. **The best answer is G.** Hemingway's passion and genius are established to some extent in both passages. Therefore, it is logical to believe that both authors viewed Hemingway as a passionate writer.

PASSAGE IV

31. **The best answer is B.** Throughout the passage the author discusses several options for eradicating EAB disease. The author also indicates that some of these options have not been proven (insecticide treatment), while others can be costly (cutting down and destroying infested trees). This suggests that the author believes EAB disease can possibly be controlled or eradicated, but it may take a lot of time and money. Answer choice B is best supported by information in the passage.

32. **The best answer is J.** The passage states that, "Ash Borer infestations are particularly troublesome because they are difficult to identify until the ash tree is heavily infested." Additional details throughout the passage indicate that Ash Borer infestation eradication is costly and time-consuming.

33. **The best answer is C.** The passage indicates that the task of controlling and eradicating the Ash Borer will be very difficult and expensive. Because infestations are generally well underway before they are identified, the scope of the task is considered exceptional.

34. **The best answer is J.** The primary focus of the first paragraph is the destruction of millions of trees and the infestation of "over 5,000 square miles of Michigan and Canadian land," which suggests that the main worry expressed is the decimation (extensive destruction) of ash trees in North America, answer choice J.

35. **The best answer is A.** Clearly the author is interested in the study of EAB disease. In addition, the author expresses a concern for the spread of the disease, as well as for the quantity of time and money that most likely will be needed to study EAB disease. The other answer choices are not supported by details in the passage.

36. **The best answer is J.** According to the passage, *Agrilus planipennis* is the scientific name for the Emerald Ash Borer beetle, answer choice J.

37. **The best answer is A.** The passage states that infested trees are being "cut down and destroyed, along with the beetle colonies, or galleries." The other answer choices are not supported by the passage.

38. **The best answer is H.** The passage clearly states that the EAB beetle is native to Asia, answer choice H.

39. **The best answer is D.** Paragraph 2 states that, "the adults settle high within the tree's canopy." The "canopy" refers to the upper branches of the ash tree, answer choice D.

40. **The best answer is G.** According to the passage, "identification of infested trees is taking place in all susceptible areas," and that "identified trees are being cut down and destroyed." While insecticide spray is being considered as a method of control, the passage does not indicate that it is currently being used. Eliminate answer choice H. The other answer choices are not supported by details in the passage.

SCIENCE TEST EXPLANATIONS

PASSAGE I

1. **The correct answer is C.** To answer this question, look at the list of drawbacks for each drug-delivery system. According to Table 1, in the Pressure drug-delivery system, "food taken with the capsule may alter the pressure enough to disintegrate the capsule in the stomach."

2. **The correct answer is G.** The passage states that "new research has targeted the colon as an ideal environment for drug absorption to treat certain illnesses." This suggests that the intended target in these experiments is the colon. According to the results of Experiment 2 (found in Table 3) the tablet with the "A" outer coating and the "2" inner coating reached the colon in the shortest amount of time.

3. **The correct answer is B.** The results of Experiment 1 are shown in Table 2. Both Group I and Group II included tablets with Tracer A, but the tablets in each group had different coatings. Therefore, it is most likely that the coating, not the tracer would have a greater impact on either gastric emptying time or colonic arrival; eliminate answer choices A and D. Since the target is the same for all groups (the colon) the drug's target destination will not be affected; eliminate answer choice C. You can see that with Coating 2, the colonic arrival time is faster than with Coating 1, which best supports answer choice B.

4. **The correct answer is J.** According to the results of both experiments, across all groups, the time that remained standard, or constant, was the gastric emptying time, answer choice J.

5. **The correct answer is D.** Table 1 provides details about each drug-delivery system. When you locate Time-dependent delivery, you see that the mechanics of the delivery include an inner barrier that delays release, answer choice D. The other answer choices are not associated with time-dependent delivery.

PASSAGE II

6. **The correct answer is J.** To answer this question you need to consider the data in both Table 1 and Table 2. According to Table 2, the source rock basalt results in either schist or amphibolite. Table 1 indicates that schist is a foliated rock, and amphibolite is a non-foliated rock. Therefore, the metamorphic results of basalt can be either foliated or nonfoliated.

7. **The correct answer is C.** Look at Table 2 and find marble in the second column. The source rock is listed directly to the left, in the first column. Based on Table 2, limestone is the source rock for marble.

8. **The correct answer is F.** Figure 1 indicates that at low levels of metamorphic intensity there is little to no foliation. As metamorphic intensity increases, so does foliation. This best supports answer choice F.

9. **The correct answer is B.** According to Figure 1, shale is at the far left of the metamorphic intensity scale. This corresponds to a low level of intensity. Schist forms at a higher level of metamorphic intensity, as shown in Figure 1. This data best supports answer choice B.

10. **The correct answer is F.** According to Table 2, rhyolite is the source rock for schist. This means that, at a certain level of intensity, rhyolite becomes schist. Schist is the source rock for gneiss. It would be logical to conclude that levels of metamorphic intensity increase as one type of rock changes into another, as Figure 1 indicates. Figure 1 also shows that, as metamorphic activity increases, foliation increases. This information best supports answer choice F.

11. **The correct answer is C.** To answer this question, first find schist in Column 2 (Result) of Table 2. It appears 3 times, and is the result of 3 different source rocks: slate, rhyolite, and basalt, answer choice C.

PASSAGE III

12. **The correct answer is H.** The results of Experiment 1 are shown in Table 1. According to these results, the fastest dissolution time was recorded when the tablet was in fine-powder form, dissolved in ethanol, answer choice H.

13. **The correct answer is A.** According to the passage, the tablets were only dissolved in water in Experiment 2, whereas both water and ethanol were used as solvents in Experiment 1. This best supports answer choice A.

14. **The correct answer is J.** Based on Table 1, the dissolution time was always faster when the tablet was crushed, answer choice J. The other answer choices are not supported by the passage.

15. **The correct answer is B.** The temperature was varied in Experiment 2, so look at Table 2 first to answer this question. At 80°, it took 12 seconds for a whole tablet to dissolve. According to Experiment 1, crushing the tablet resulted in faster dissolution times. Therefore, you can conclude that the dissolution time would be faster than 12 seconds, answer choice B.

16. **The correct answer is J.** The results of Experiment 1 reveal that crushing the tablet increases the dissolution

rate, as does dissolving the tablet in ethanol. Eliminate answer choices G and H. Table 2 indicates that lower temperatures result in slower dissolution times. This best supports answer choice J.

17. **The correct answer is A.** The results of Experiment 1 indicate that crushing the tablet increases the dissolution rate, so eliminate answer choices B and C. According to Table 2, lower temperatures result in slower dissolution times, so dissolving a whole tablet in 10°C water would be slower than dissolving a whole tablet in 80°C water.

PASSAGE IV

18. **The correct answer is F.** The passage states that the average starting length of the rats in each group was 10 cm. Beginning with answer choice F, calculate the difference between the starting length and the average length after 6 weeks for each group:

    Group 6: 18.25 – 10.00 = 8.25 cm

    Group 2: 18.00 – 10.00 = 8.00 cm

    Group 7: 14.25 – 10.00 = 4.25 cm

    Group 4: 17.00 – 10.00 = 7.00 cm

    The rats in Group 6 increased the most in average length, answer choice F.

19. **The correct answer is A.** The passage states that the average starting weight of the rats in each group was 200 grams. Find the corresponding group on Table 2 for each feed-type listed, and calculate the difference between the starting weight and the average weight after 6 weeks for each group:

    Feed M = Group 5: 352 – 200 =152 g

    Feed N = Group 6: 349 – 200 = 149 g

    Feed O = Group 7: 342 – 200 = 142 g

    Feed P = Group 8: 344 – 200 = 144 g

    Feed M resulted in the greatest weight gain, answer choice A.

20. **The correct answer is J.** The passage states that the rats in each group weighed an average of 200 grams at the start of the experiments. Starting with answer choice F, calculate the difference between the starting weight and the average weight after 6 weeks for all groups:

    Group 1: 350 – 200 =150 g

    Group 3: 343 – 200 = 143 g

    Group 5: 352 – 200 =152 g

    Group 7: 342 – 200 =142 g

The rats in Group 7 gained the least amount of weight, answer choice J.

21. **The correct answer is C.** According to the question, Group 9 would receive Feed M (the same as Group 5) and a vitamin supplement (like Group 6). According to Table 1 and the information in the passage, the rats in Group 6 had a greater average length than did Group 5 after 6 weeks. Therefore, if Group 9 is fed vitamin supplements, the rats will most likely have a greater average length than the rats in Group 5, answer choice C.

22. **The correct answer is J.** The best way to answer this question is to examine each of the answer choices, and eliminate those that are not supported by the data in Table 2. Group 7 is the control group. Group 6 was fed Feed N. It is not true that the rats in Group 6 were twice as long as the rats in Group 7, so eliminate answer choice F. Group 5 was fed Feed M. It is not true that the rats in Group 5 weighed 3 times more than the rats in Group 7, so eliminate answer choice G. Group 8 was fed Feed P; rats in this group did not have the greatest average length, so eliminate answer choice H. Answer choice J is correct, because it is true that the rats in Group 7 are similar in both weight and length to the rats in Group 8.

PASSAGE V

23. **The correct answer is D.** According to Table 2, granite is phaneritic in texture. Table 1 indicates that phaneritic rocks cool slowly, and Figure 1 indicates that phaneritic rocks have coarse grains. This information best supports answer choice D.

24. **The correct answer is H.** According to Table 2, both rhyolite and andesite are aphanitic in texture. Table 1 indicates that aphanitic rocks cool "quickly but more slowly than glassy textured rocks," answer choice H.

25. **The correct answer is A.** Figure 1 indicates that phaneritic rocks have a slower cooling rate and coarser grain size than either glassy or aphanitic rocks. According to Table 1, the grains in phaneritic rocks can be seen without a microscope, so they are larger than the grains of both glassy and aphanitic rocks. This information best supports answer choice A.

26. **The correct answer is G.** To answer this question, look at the cooling characteristics listed in Table 1. Glassy rock "cools rapidly and above the temperature for crystals to form." This information best supports answer choice G.

27. **The correct answer is C.** Table 1 indicates that aphanitic rocks cool quickly. Table 2 lists rhyolite, andesite, and basalt as aphanitic rocks. The other

answer choices are not supported by information in the passage.

28. **The correct answer is G.** According to Table 1, rocks with interlocking grains that can be seen without a microscope are classified as phaneritic rocks. The cooling characteristics of phaneritic rocks indicate that the rocks "cool very slowly at a uniform rate," answer choice G.

PASSAGE VI

29. **The correct answer is B.** The passage states that the sun has a mass of 1. Therefore, star type B, with a mass of 18, has a mass 18 times that of the sun.

30. **The correct answer is J.** To answer this question, find the column for surface temperature in Table 1. Stars with a surface temperature less than 3,500 K are red in color, answer choice J.

31. **The correct answer is A.** The giant stars shown in Figure 1 have a surface temperature ranging from about 5,000 K to about 2,500 K. According to Table 1, stars at these temperatures will range from orange to red, answer choice A.

32. **The correct answer is H.** This question requires you to look at both Figure 1 and Table 1. The main sequence stars in Figure 1 have a temperature range from about 20,000 K down to about 2,500 K. According to Table 1, star type O has a surface temperature that ranges from 28,000 K to 60,000 K. Star type O, therefore, is NOT a main sequence star.

33. **The correct answer is B.** To answer this question, look at Figure 1. A star with a temperature of 15,000 K and a luminosity of 10^{-4} would most likely be a white dwarf, answer choice B.

PASSAGE VII

34. **The correct answer G.** To answer this question look at both Table 1 and Table 2. The data presented in each table indicate that, at 40% relative humidity, Litter C absorbs water faster than either Litter A or Litter B.

35. **The correct answer is D.** According to Table 1, at 80% relative humidity, Litter B absorbs water in about 9 hours. It makes sense that at a higher relative humidity level, it would take longer to absorb water, so answer choice D is correct.

36. **The correct answer is F.** To answer this question, compare the answer choices with the data presented in Table 1. Based on Table 1, Litter A took 16 hours to absorb water at a relative humidity level of 80%, Litter B took 9 hours, and Litter C took 5 hours. This information best supports answer choice F.

37. **The correct answer is C.** In Experiment 1, the relative humidity levels were varied from 40% to 80%, while in Experiment 2, the relative humidity level was held constant at 40%. The other answer choices are not supported by the passage.

38. **The correct answer is F.** According to the results of both experiments, adding baking soda to the litter decreased the absorption time for Litter A only, answer choice F.

39. **The correct answer is D.** It makes sense that decreasing the quantity of water added to all of the litter types would also decrease the absorption time. The other answer choices are not supported by the passage.

40. **The correct answer is H.** The results of the experiments indicate that the different litter types had different absorption rates. This best supports answer choice H. The other answer choices are not supported by the results of the experiments.

ACT PRACTICE TEST 4
Answer Sheet

ENGLISH

1 (A) (B) (C) (D)
2 (F) (G) (H) (J)
3 (A) (B) (C) (D)
4 (F) (G) (H) (J)
5 (A) (B) (C) (D)
6 (F) (G) (H) (J)
7 (A) (B) (C) (D)
8 (F) (G) (H) (J)
9 (A) (B) (C) (D)
10 (F) (G) (H) (J)
11 (A) (B) (C) (D)
12 (F) (G) (H) (J)
13 (A) (B) (C) (D)
14 (F) (G) (H) (J)
15 (A) (B) (C) (D)
16 (F) (G) (H) (J)
17 (A) (B) (C) (D)
18 (F) (G) (H) (J)
19 (A) (B) (C) (D)
20 (F) (G) (H) (J)

21 (A) (B) (C) (D)
22 (F) (G) (H) (J)
23 (A) (B) (C) (D)
24 (F) (G) (H) (J)
25 (A) (B) (C) (D)
26 (F) (G) (H) (J)
27 (A) (B) (C) (D)
28 (F) (G) (H) (J)
29 (A) (B) (C) (D)
30 (F) (G) (H) (J)
31 (A) (B) (C) (D)
32 (F) (G) (H) (J)
33 (A) (B) (C) (D)
34 (F) (G) (H) (J)
35 (A) (B) (C) (D)
36 (F) (G) (H) (J)
37 (A) (B) (C) (D)
38 (F) (G) (H) (J)
39 (A) (B) (C) (D)
40 (F) (G) (H) (J)

41 (A) (B) (C) (D)
42 (F) (G) (H) (J)
43 (A) (B) (C) (D)
44 (F) (G) (H) (J)
45 (A) (B) (C) (D)
46 (F) (G) (H) (J)
47 (A) (B) (C) (D)
48 (F) (G) (H) (J)
49 (A) (B) (C) (D)
50 (F) (G) (H) (J)
51 (A) (B) (C) (D)
52 (F) (G) (H) (J)
53 (A) (B) (C) (D)
54 (F) (G) (H) (J)
55 (A) (B) (C) (D)
56 (F) (G) (H) (J)
57 (A) (B) (C) (D)
58 (F) (G) (H) (J)
59 (A) (B) (C) (D)
60 (F) (G) (H) (J)

61 (A) (B) (C) (D)
62 (F) (G) (H) (J)
63 (A) (B) (C) (D)
64 (F) (G) (H) (J)
65 (A) (B) (C) (D)
66 (F) (G) (H) (J)
67 (A) (B) (C) (D)
68 (F) (G) (H) (J)
69 (A) (B) (C) (D)
70 (F) (G) (H) (J)
71 (A) (B) (C) (D)
72 (F) (G) (H) (J)
73 (A) (B) (C) (D)
74 (F) (G) (H) (J)
75 (A) (B) (C) (D)

MATHEMATICS

1 (A) (B) (C) (D) (E)
2 (F) (G) (H) (J) (K)
3 (A) (B) (C) (D) (E)
4 (F) (G) (H) (J) (K)
5 (A) (B) (C) (D) (E)
6 (F) (G) (H) (J) (K)
7 (A) (B) (C) (D) (E)
8 (F) (G) (H) (J) (K)
9 (A) (B) (C) (D) (E)
10 (F) (G) (H) (J) (K)
11 (A) (B) (C) (D) (E)
12 (F) (G) (H) (J) (K)
13 (A) (B) (C) (D) (E)
14 (F) (G) (H) (J) (K)
15 (A) (B) (C) (D) (E)

16 (F) (G) (H) (J) (K)
17 (A) (B) (C) (D) (E)
18 (F) (G) (H) (J) (K)
19 (A) (B) (C) (D) (E)
20 (F) (G) (H) (J) (K)
21 (A) (B) (C) (D) (E)
22 (F) (G) (H) (J) (K)
23 (A) (B) (C) (D) (E)
24 (F) (G) (H) (J) (K)
25 (A) (B) (C) (D) (E)
26 (F) (G) (H) (J) (K)
27 (A) (B) (C) (D) (E)
28 (F) (G) (H) (J) (K)
29 (A) (B) (C) (D) (E)
30 (F) (G) (H) (J) (K)

31 (A) (B) (C) (D) (E)
32 (F) (G) (H) (J) (K)
33 (A) (B) (C) (D) (E)
34 (F) (G) (H) (J) (K)
35 (A) (B) (C) (D) (E)
36 (F) (G) (H) (J) (K)
37 (A) (B) (C) (D) (E)
38 (F) (G) (H) (J) (K)
39 (A) (B) (C) (D) (E)
40 (F) (G) (H) (J) (K)
41 (A) (B) (C) (D) (E)
42 (F) (G) (H) (J) (K)
43 (A) (B) (C) (D) (E)
44 (F) (G) (H) (J) (K)
45 (A) (B) (C) (D) (E)

46 (F) (G) (H) (J) (K)
47 (A) (B) (C) (D) (E)
48 (F) (G) (H) (J) (K)
49 (A) (B) (C) (D) (E)
50 (F) (G) (H) (J) (K)
51 (A) (B) (C) (D) (E)
52 (F) (G) (H) (J) (K)
53 (A) (B) (C) (D) (E)
54 (F) (G) (H) (J) (K)
55 (A) (B) (C) (D) (E)
56 (F) (G) (H) (J) (K)
57 (A) (B) (C) (D) (E)
58 (F) (G) (H) (J) (K)
59 (A) (B) (C) (D) (E)
60 (F) (G) (H) (J) (K)

READING

1 Ⓐ Ⓑ Ⓒ Ⓓ	11 Ⓐ Ⓑ Ⓒ Ⓓ	21 Ⓐ Ⓑ Ⓒ Ⓓ	31 Ⓐ Ⓑ Ⓒ Ⓓ
2 Ⓕ Ⓖ Ⓗ Ⓙ	12 Ⓕ Ⓖ Ⓗ Ⓙ	22 Ⓕ Ⓖ Ⓗ Ⓙ	32 Ⓕ Ⓖ Ⓗ Ⓙ
3 Ⓐ Ⓑ Ⓒ Ⓓ	13 Ⓐ Ⓑ Ⓒ Ⓓ	23 Ⓐ Ⓑ Ⓒ Ⓓ	33 Ⓐ Ⓑ Ⓒ Ⓓ
4 Ⓕ Ⓖ Ⓗ Ⓙ	14 Ⓕ Ⓖ Ⓗ Ⓙ	24 Ⓕ Ⓖ Ⓗ Ⓙ	34 Ⓕ Ⓖ Ⓗ Ⓙ
5 Ⓐ Ⓑ Ⓒ Ⓓ	15 Ⓐ Ⓑ Ⓒ Ⓓ	25 Ⓐ Ⓑ Ⓒ Ⓓ	35 Ⓐ Ⓑ Ⓒ Ⓓ
6 Ⓕ Ⓖ Ⓗ Ⓙ	16 Ⓕ Ⓖ Ⓗ Ⓙ	26 Ⓕ Ⓖ Ⓗ Ⓙ	36 Ⓕ Ⓖ Ⓗ Ⓙ
7 Ⓐ Ⓑ Ⓒ Ⓓ	17 Ⓐ Ⓑ Ⓒ Ⓓ	27 Ⓐ Ⓑ Ⓒ Ⓓ	37 Ⓐ Ⓑ Ⓒ Ⓓ
8 Ⓕ Ⓖ Ⓗ Ⓙ	18 Ⓕ Ⓖ Ⓗ Ⓙ	28 Ⓕ Ⓖ Ⓗ Ⓙ	38 Ⓕ Ⓖ Ⓗ Ⓙ
9 Ⓐ Ⓑ Ⓒ Ⓓ	19 Ⓐ Ⓑ Ⓒ Ⓓ	29 Ⓐ Ⓑ Ⓒ Ⓓ	39 Ⓐ Ⓑ Ⓒ Ⓓ
10 Ⓕ Ⓖ Ⓗ Ⓙ	20 Ⓕ Ⓖ Ⓗ Ⓙ	30 Ⓕ Ⓖ Ⓗ Ⓙ	40 Ⓕ Ⓖ Ⓗ Ⓙ

SCIENCE

1 Ⓐ Ⓑ Ⓒ Ⓓ	11 Ⓐ Ⓑ Ⓒ Ⓓ	21 Ⓐ Ⓑ Ⓒ Ⓓ	31 Ⓐ Ⓑ Ⓒ Ⓓ
2 Ⓕ Ⓖ Ⓗ Ⓙ	12 Ⓕ Ⓖ Ⓗ Ⓙ	22 Ⓕ Ⓖ Ⓗ Ⓙ	32 Ⓕ Ⓖ Ⓗ Ⓙ
3 Ⓐ Ⓑ Ⓒ Ⓓ	13 Ⓐ Ⓑ Ⓒ Ⓓ	23 Ⓐ Ⓑ Ⓒ Ⓓ	33 Ⓐ Ⓑ Ⓒ Ⓓ
4 Ⓕ Ⓖ Ⓗ Ⓙ	14 Ⓕ Ⓖ Ⓗ Ⓙ	24 Ⓕ Ⓖ Ⓗ Ⓙ	34 Ⓕ Ⓖ Ⓗ Ⓙ
5 Ⓐ Ⓑ Ⓒ Ⓓ	15 Ⓐ Ⓑ Ⓒ Ⓓ	25 Ⓐ Ⓑ Ⓒ Ⓓ	35 Ⓐ Ⓑ Ⓒ Ⓓ
6 Ⓕ Ⓖ Ⓗ Ⓙ	16 Ⓕ Ⓖ Ⓗ Ⓙ	26 Ⓕ Ⓖ Ⓗ Ⓙ	36 Ⓕ Ⓖ Ⓗ Ⓙ
7 Ⓐ Ⓑ Ⓒ Ⓓ	17 Ⓐ Ⓑ Ⓒ Ⓓ	27 Ⓐ Ⓑ Ⓒ Ⓓ	37 Ⓐ Ⓑ Ⓒ Ⓓ
8 Ⓕ Ⓖ Ⓗ Ⓙ	18 Ⓕ Ⓖ Ⓗ Ⓙ	28 Ⓕ Ⓖ Ⓗ Ⓙ	38 Ⓕ Ⓖ Ⓗ Ⓙ
9 Ⓐ Ⓑ Ⓒ Ⓓ	19 Ⓐ Ⓑ Ⓒ Ⓓ	29 Ⓐ Ⓑ Ⓒ Ⓓ	39 Ⓐ Ⓑ Ⓒ Ⓓ
10 Ⓕ Ⓖ Ⓗ Ⓙ	20 Ⓕ Ⓖ Ⓗ Ⓙ	30 Ⓕ Ⓖ Ⓗ Ⓙ	40 Ⓕ Ⓖ Ⓗ Ⓙ

You may wish to remove these sample answer document pages to respond to the practice ACT Writing Test.

Begin WRITING TEST here.

_____

_____

_____

_____

_____

_____

_____

_____

_____

_____

_____

_____

_____

_____

_____

_____

_____

_____

_____

_____

_____

_____

_____

_____

_____

_____

_____

Cut Here

1

If you need more space, please continue on the next page.

WRITING TEST

If you need more space, please continue on the back of this page.

2

WRITING TEST

If you need more space, please continue on the next page.

3

WRITING TEST

_____

_____

_____

_____

_____

_____

_____

_____

_____

_____

_____

_____

_____

_____

_____

_____

_____

_____

_____

_____

_____

_____

_____

_____

_____

Cut Here

END OF THE WRITING TEST.
STOP! IF YOU HAVE TIME LEFT OVER, CHECK YOUR WORK ON THIS SECTION ONLY.

4

1 ■ ■ ■ ■ ■ ■ ■ ■ 1

ENGLISH TEST

45 Minutes – 75 Questions

DIRECTIONS: In the passages that follow, some words and phrases are underlined and numbered. In the answer column, you will find alternatives for the words and phrases that are underlined. Choose the alternative that you think is best and fill in the corresponding bubble on your answer sheet. If you think that the original version is best, choose "NO CHANGE," which will always be either answer choice A or F. You will also find questions about a particular section of the passage, or about the entire passage. These questions will be identified by either an underlined portion or by a number in a box. Look for the answer that clearly expresses the idea, is consistent with the style and tone of the passage, and makes the correct use of standard written English. Read the passage through once before answering the questions. For some questions, you should read beyond the indicated portion before you answer.

PASSAGE I

The following paragraphs may or may not be in the most logical order. You may be asked questions about the logical order of the paragraphs, as well as where to place sentences logically within any given paragraph.

Rubber Cement

[1]

[1] The next time you should see one of those huge
                          ———————
                              1

cement trucks moving down the road take a closer look.
                                        ————————
                                            2
[2] You may find that the truck is labeled "rubber cement" as

opposed to "concrete." [3] When I was in grade school I used

rubber cement, the kind with the little brush attached to the

underside of the jar's lid. ⬚3

[2]

[1] Of course, these huge rubber cement trucks are not

making deliveries of glue to the local elementary schools

for students to use at their desks. [2] In fact, they may be on

their way to a high school's athletic facilities to pour out a
                    ——————————
                         4
thick layer of rubber cement for a tennis or basketball court.

[3] Rubber cement surfaces are also being used on athletic

tracks.

1. **A.** NO CHANGE
   B. have seen
   C. ought to see
   D. see

2. **F.** NO CHANGE
   G. road, take
   H. road; take
   J. road. Take

3. At this point, the writer would like to extend the discussion of her personal experience with rubber cement. Which of the following sentences (assuming all are true), if added here, would most successfully achieve this effect?
   A. We decided to have our driveway paved with rubber cement instead of concrete.
   B. I remember that I found it difficult to keep the glue from dripping all over the place.
   C. We also used paste in elementary school.
   D. Today, glue sticks make it much easier to do craft projects.

4. **F.** NO CHANGE
   G. high school
   H. high schools
   J. high schools'

GO ON TO THE NEXT PAGE.

1 ■ ■ ■ ■ ■ ■ ■ ■ 1

[3]

5 [1] Experts find that the pliability of a rubber cement surface adds to the comfort level of walkers and runners.

[2] It provides a bit of bounce preferred to the hardness
    6

of concrete. [3] This bounciness also tends to cause lesser
                                                        7
injuries to knees and ankles. [4] A rubber cement surface also

helps athletes to reduce the dangers of falling and is easier to
                                                        8
maintain than traditional cement.

[4]

[1] Many consumers are taking into consideration
                                        9

rubber cement for their patios and driveways. [2] Cities also
                10

sometimes use it for sidewalks. [3] Another advantage, of
                                                11
rubber cement surfacing is the ease of repairing it. [4] Cracks

or etchings can be more easily taken out of rubber cement
              12
by using a blowtorch. [5] In spite of its normally excellent

performance record, however, rubber cement is not the

best choice for surfaces everywhere. [6] Some regions of

the country experience weather conditions less suitable for
                                                13
rubber cement surfacing. [7] It is worth the time to inquire

5. Which of the following sentences (assuming all are true), if added here, would best introduce the new subject of Paragraph 3?
   A. There are many reasons why rubber cement is winning out over other traditional surfacing materials.
   B. Use of athletic tracks is increasing.
   C. Rubber cement is still useful as an adhesive.
   D. Rubber cement trucks are often even larger than traditional cement trucks.

6. F. NO CHANGE
   G. It will
   H. They
   J. Such a surface

7. A. NO CHANGE
   B. less
   C. least
   D. fewer

8. F. NO CHANGE
   G. are easier
   H. is made easier
   J. are to be easier

9. A. NO CHANGE
   B. Taking into consideration are many consumers
   C. Many consumers consider
   D. Considering many consumers choose

10. F. NO CHANGE
    G. there
    H. they're
    J. those

11. A. NO CHANGE
    B. advantage of
    C. advantage in
    D. advantage:

12. F. NO CHANGE
    G. are most easily removed out of
    H. can be removed or taken easily out of
    J. are easily removed from

13. Which of the following alternatives to the underlined portion would be LEAST acceptable?
    A. that aren't suitable for
    B. not as suitable for
    C. least suitable with
    D. that don't suit

GO ON TO THE NEXT PAGE.

locally <u>about</u> rubber cement surfacing before embarking on a
major flooring, patio, or driveway installation.

14. F. NO CHANGE
    G. with
    H. to
    J. on

> Question 15 asks about the preceding passage as a whole.

15. In reviewing notes, the writer discovers that the following information has been left out of the essay:

> For example, a great deal of sunshine may cause rubber cement surfaces to crack, yellow, and peel.

If added to the essay, the sentence would most logically be placed after Sentence:
    A. 3 in Paragraph 4.
    B. 6 in Paragraph 4.
    C. 2 in Paragraph 3.
    D. 3 in Paragraph 1.

PASSAGE II

Rosalind Franklin, Pioneer Scientist

Nearly every student of science learns about James Watson and Francis Crick, the scientists who discovered the structure of DNA, but probably not as many have learned about other scientists whose work <u>began after</u> the discovery.
16

16. The writer wants to emphasize that Watson and Crick did not arrive at their conclusions about DNA alone. Which choice does that best?
    F. NO CHANGE
    G. resulted from
    H. laid the foundation for
    J. was eclipsed by

17. Which of the following sentences, if inserted here, would best connect the idea that Rosalind Franklin was one of the scientists whose work is referred to in the first paragraph?
    A. Rosalind Franklin was a pioneering and brilliant scientist.
    B. Rosalind Franklin was one of the most well-known female scientists of her time.
    C. One of these lesser-known scientists was Rosalind Franklin.
    D. Watson and Crick used the work of a prominent scientist named Rosalind Franklin to make their discovery.

[17] Franklin graduated from Cambridge in 1941 and then began work on her doctorate.

<u>This advanced degree focused on, using coal and</u>
18
charcoal efficiently, which was very important during World War II. After earning her Ph.D., Franklin spent some time

18. F. NO CHANGE
    G. This research, focused on using
    H. This advanced degree, on using her research for
    J. Her research focused on using

GO ON TO THE NEXT PAGE.

1 ■ ■ ■ ■ ■ ■ ■ ■ 1

in France learning x-ray diffraction techniques that later
became essential to her work with DNA. She later returned
                                                    19

to England to further her scientific career, and accepting
                                                    20
an offer to work with a team of scientists studying DNA

at King's College in the early 1950s. At this time, there
                                          21

was a race among scientists to find the structure of DNA.
                22
The leader of Franklin's team assigned her to work with a

graduate student—Maurice Wilkins, on a DNA project. Either
                                    23
due to a miscommunication or to bad management on the

part of the team leader, Wilkins thought that Franklin was
                                        24
there to assist him, while Franklin correctly assumed they
                                        24
were equals.
      24
        Despite the tension between Wilkins and herself,

Franklin still performed meticulous research on DNA. This
                                                    25
was not easy being a woman in a man's world. She utilized
                    25
x-ray diffraction technology to photograph DNA strands. In

fact, one of these photographs is what ultimately gave them
                                                    26
the definitive edge in the DNA race. Wilkins showed the

photograph to Watson without Franklins' permission, and
                                27
Watson realized it was a crucial piece of the puzzle in the

19. **A.** NO CHANGE
    B. later returning
    C. returning lately
    D. later return

20. **F.** NO CHANGE
    G. accepted
    H. was accepting
    J. accepts

21. Which of the following alternatives to the underlined portion would NOT be acceptable?
    A. 1950s; at this time,
    B. 1950s at this time
    C. 1950s, when
    D. 1950s, at a time when

22. **F.** NO CHANGE
    G. within
    H. between
    J. to

23. **A.** NO CHANGE
    B. student, Maurice Wilkins, on
    C. student Maurice Wilkins on
    D. student Maurice Wilkins; on

24. Given that all of them are true, which choice most specifically illustrates the result of the miscommunication?
    F. NO CHANGE
    G. Wilkins and Franklin continued to have problems with their work relationship.
    H. Wilkins and Franklin were still excellent scientists.
    J. Wilkins and Franklin were able to work together on DNA anyway.

25. **A.** NO CHANGE
    B. DNA.
    C. DNA—this was not easy being a woman in a man's world!
    D. DNA, which all scientists would probably do as well.

26. **F.** NO CHANGE
    G. it
    H. Watson and Crick
    J. the DNA strands

27. **A.** NO CHANGE
    B. Franklins's
    C. Franklins
    D. Franklin's

GO ON TO THE NEXT PAGE.

1 ▪ ▪ ▪ ▪ ▪ ▪ ▪ ▪ 1

search to uncover the structure of DNA. Very soon thereafter,
⎯⎯⎯
28

in 1953, Watson and Crick published the now-famous article

revealing the structure of DNA.

    It was only in later years that the full truth about

Franklin's contribution come to light; unfortunately, much of
⎯⎯⎯
29

the credit came after her death from ovarian cancer at the age

of thirty-seven. ☐30

28. F. NO CHANGE
   G. for uncovering
   H. uncovering for
   J. where they would uncover

29. A. NO CHANGE
   B. will come
   C. was coming
   D. came

> Question 30 asks about the preceding passage as a whole.

30. The writer wants the final sentence of the last paragraph to reflect the main idea of the whole essay. Given that all of the following sentences are true, which one, if inserted here, would do that best?
   F. Soon after the DNA incident, Franklin left King's College and continued to perform other work and research at Birkbeck College.
   G. The DNA race was an exciting time in the history of science.
   H. Although her life was extinguished early, Franklin survived through the indelible mark she left on biological science.
   J. The discovery of the structure of DNA proved to be a crucial scientific breakthrough, and Watson, Crick, and Wilkins were later awarded the Nobel Prize for their work.

PASSAGE III

Family Remodel

    We managed to raise five children in our home, mostly
⎯⎯⎯
31

by moving the master bedroom to the finished basement.

At the time, the move made sense, the kids had the upstairs
⎯⎯⎯⎯⎯⎯⎯⎯
32

(ground level) and we had a nice big room downstairs.

    As our youngest child neared high school graduation, the
⎯⎯⎯⎯⎯⎯⎯⎯⎯⎯⎯⎯⎯⎯⎯⎯⎯⎯⎯⎯⎯⎯⎯
33

time came to consider moving back upstairs. At this point,

however, a move back into the original master bedroom

31. Which choice would most precisely sharpen the focus of this paragraph?
   A. NO CHANGE
   B. brick home
   C. three-bedroom ranch home
   D. ranch home

32. F. NO CHANGE
   G. sense, and the kids
   H. sense the kids
   J. sense; the kids

33. Which choice best specifies the basis on which the writer was ready to move back upstairs?
   A. NO CHANGE
   B. While the children were young
   C. As the bedrooms filled up
   D. When guests would come for a visit

GO ON TO THE NEXT PAGE.

1 ■ ■ ■ ■ ■ ■ ■ ■ **1**

would have reduced <u>some space</u> by over half; in fact, our
bedroom furniture would not even fit up there! Add to that

a hopeful future <u>with</u> grandchildren, and we came to the
conclusion that it was time to expand our little ranch home.

Due to the limited size of our lot, <u>the only way to go was up.</u>

We began formulating our building plans, <u>and including</u>
cathedral ceilings, an open second-floor walkway, a huge
master bedroom, a good-sized office, and a nursery. The
concepts and ideas flowed endlessly <u>creative</u> from our
imaginations.

The first sign that our major remodeling project
would have its ups and downs was when the contractor
announced his bottom-line price to cover all those wondrous
plans; it became <u>immediately clear right away</u> that a scale-
back was necessary. For the sake of maintaining our
enthusiasm for the project, my husband and I sat right down
and began discussing those items <u>that</u> could easily give

<u>up; some of them</u> now actually seemed extravagant and silly.
After reducing the contractor's original bid by a significant

<u>amount we</u> finally had a feasible plan, and work soon began.
A major remodeling job is fraught with intense anxiety.

<u>Nevertheless,</u> the absolute strangers who begin invading your
home quickly become like members of your family. They
regularly use your bathroom facilities, observe you in your

34. F. NO CHANGE
 G. its space
 H. our space
 J. their space

35. A. NO CHANGE
 B. of
 C. for
 D. among

36. F. NO CHANGE
 G. our house was too small.
 H. all of the children would soon be gone.
 J. we were able to turn the backyard into a sunroom.

37. A. NO CHANGE
 B. which included
 C. by inclusion of
 D. so included

38. The best placement for the underlined portion would be:
 F. where it is now.
 G. after the word *ideas*.
 H. after the word *our*.
 J. after the word *imaginations*.

39. A. NO CHANGE
 B. right away immediately clear
 C. immediately clear instantly
 D. immediately clear

40. F. NO CHANGE
 G. they
 H. I
 J. we

41. A. NO CHANGE
 B. up, so some of them
 C. up, some of them
 D. up; some of them,

42. F. NO CHANGE
 G. amount, then we
 H. amount, we
 J. amount because we

43. A. NO CHANGE
 B. Before,
 C. Once,
 D. Suddenly,

GO ON TO THE NEXT PAGE.

1 ■ ■ ■ ■ ■ ■ ■ ■ 1

<u>bathrobe and spend</u> entire days with you for the next several
44
months. And, as with family, your emotions range from

hating these people to not being able to live without them.

Be prepared for a lot of change if you

<u>should ever want to decide</u> to remodel your home in a major
45
way. Just as with each of our children as he or she left home,

we were elated to see our beloved workers leave when the

project was finished, but we mourned their loss for a solid

two months afterward.

44. F. NO CHANGE
   G. bathrobe, and spend
   H. bathrobe; and spend
   J. bathrobe. And spend

45. A. NO CHANGE
   B. should be deciding
   C. should ever have to decide
   D. decide

PASSAGE IV

"Weathering" the Climate

Visitors to the United States should <u>take care</u> when
46
describing the United States and its climate to family and

friends. Due to the vast size of the United States and the huge

<u>differences in temperatures and weather patterns</u> across the
47
regions, it is neither appropriate nor accurate to describe the

country's climate as anything but diverse <u>and varied.</u> In the
48
United States, the climate varies drastically depending on

where you are. 49

46. F. NO CHANGE
   G. care
   H. make observations
   J. be descriptive

47. A. NO CHANGE
   B. temperature differences and weather patterns
   C. differing weather patterns and temperature differences
   D. difference in temperature weather patterns

48. F. NO CHANGE
   G. or different depending on where you are
   H. and geographically variable
   J. DELETE the underlined portion.

49. The writer would like to link the information already
   presented about climate to her personal experiences
   regarding weather in the United States. Assuming all are
   true, which of the following sentences, if added here, best
   achieves this effect?
   A. I have spoken to people across the country about vari-
      ations in climate, and they agree that the United States
      is very large.
   B. I have lived in the Northwest most of my life, and,
      while I enjoy the mild winters, the abundance of rain-
      fall in the summer is quite tiresome.
   C. I have seen people struggle through bad weather con-
      ditions, and often suggest that they relocate.
   D. Many people enjoy the different climates that exist in
      the United States.

GO ON TO THE NEXT PAGE.

1 ■ ■ ■ ■ ■ ■ ■ ■ **1**

Two of my sisters live in the Southwest—one in
                                          50
Phoenix, Arizona, and the other in Las Vegas, Nevada.

Both of these two cities are known for their constant
       51

sunshine, and soaring summer temperatures. To my sisters,
          52
a "partly cloudy" weather report generally signifies

a few light, puffy clouds here and there. "Mostly cloudy" still
                              53
allows for the sun to peek out almost all day long. Local

newspapers and meteorologists are constantly challenged

to come up with new phrases to describe yet another sunny

day. Basically, the only real topic of conversation regarding

the weather in either Phoenix or Las Vegas is the monsoon

season; which is a two- to three-week period of intermittent
             54
rain. One of my sisters loves to go to her vacation home on

the Pacific Ocean, because "they have weather there; a nice

fog rolls by every morning."
        55
By contrast, many northern U.S. inhabitants are ecstatic

when the sun pokes through the seemingly constant clouds,

even if for only a few moments in a twenty-four hour period.

A "mostly cloudy" forecast means there will be a heavy layer

of grayish clouds and no sun visible for the entire day. A

so-called "cloudy" day means that it will probably continue
                              56
for at least three days!

50. **F.** NO CHANGE
    G. Southwest one
    H. Southwest, the one
    J. Southwest. One

51. **A.** NO CHANGE
    B. Because both of the
    C. Some of these
    D. Some

52. **F.** NO CHANGE
    G. sunshine and, soaring
    H. sunshine and soaring
    J. sunshine and soaring,

53. **A.** NO CHANGE
    B. here and there, a few light, puffy clouds
    C. light, puffy clouds, here and there, a few
    D. a few, here and there, light, puffy clouds

54. **F.** NO CHANGE
    G. season. A
    H. season, which is a
    J. season a

55. **A.** NO CHANGE
    B. rolled in
    C. rolls in
    D. rolled by

56. **F.** NO CHANGE
    G. they
    H. this condition
    J. that

GO ON TO THE NEXT PAGE.

[57] Surviving days and months of bad weather truly does

build character. First, you make a stronger, tougher person
whose survival skills have been tested. Second, you can

enhance great your vocabulary as you attempt to find at least
one positive description of the weather each day. This winter,
the positives on my list include "crystalline," "deafeningly
silent," and "rugged." I may make it through this winter
after all!

57. Which of the following choices, if inserted here, provides the most effective introductory sentence to the essay's concluding paragraph?
   A. Good weather can often enhance your mood.
   B. It is healthier to live in areas of predominant sunshine and warm temperatures.
   C. A poor climate can be extremely detrimental to human survival.
   D. There are advantages to living in more severe climates.

58. F. NO CHANGE
   G. come to be
   H. get to be
   J. become

59. A. NO CHANGE
   B. greatly enhance
   C. be greatly enhancing
   D. enhance the greatness of

Question 60 asks about the preceding passage as a whole.

60. Suppose the writer had been assigned to write a brief essay illustrating all of the differences in climate across the entire country. Would this essay fulfill the assignment?
   F. Yes, because the essay focuses on climate differences between some regions of the country.
   G. Yes, because the writer has had personal experience living in the Northwest.
   H. No, because the essay limits its comparison to the Southwest and the Northwest.
   J. No, because the essay is primarily focused on descriptive words for different weather conditions.

PASSAGE V

The following paragraphs may or may not be in the most logical order. You may be asked questions about the logical order of the paragraphs, as well as where to place sentences logically within any given paragraph.

Trip to Turkey

[1]

I was incredibly jet-lagged from the long plane flight I

had just been enduring, but that could scarcely dampen my
enthusiasm when I arrived in Istanbul, Turkey. Our tour guide

61. A. NO CHANGE
   B. happened to endure
   C. finished enduring
   D. endured

GO ON TO THE NEXT PAGE.

knew that we would be hungry and would like to relax. So he
took us to a restaurant in a tourist area. We sat down on rugs
around a low table and were served the very popular Turkish
drink chai (caffeinated tea) and delicious Turkish food. We
enjoyed a traditional Turkish band and were surprised to see
a local woman get up and begin to dance!

[2]

Because of the copious amounts of chai I drank at the
restaurant, I was still able to fall asleep easily as soon as I got
to my hotel room in Istanbul. I woke up the next day ready to
experience this major cosmopolitan city. As we walked, I was
struck by how the city was similar to large American cities
in many ways, yet also very different. For example, people
in business clothes, rushing about and talking on their cell
phones was a common sight.

On the other hand, the calls to prayer five times daily were a
new experience for me.

[3]

The first stop on our tour of Istanbul was the world-
famous Hagia Sophia. Being that I had studied a bit of its
history on the Internet, I knew that it had been a church for
nearly 1,000 years, and then a mosque for over 500 years. The
photos I had looked at on the Internet did not compare to the

actual sights you could get of this magnificent building.

62. F. NO CHANGE
G. relax; so
H. relax, so
J. relax,

63. Given that all the choices are true, which one most
specifically and vividly describes the food?
A. NO CHANGE
B. a delicious meal consisting of a variety of meats and
vegetables, along with rice, salad, and pastries for
dessert.
C. some tasty Turkish food, including dessert.
D. a lot of food typically found in Turkey.

64. F. NO CHANGE
G. Despite
H. In lieu of
J. However,

65. A. NO CHANGE
B. People rushing about talking on their cell phones was
a common sight in their business clothes, for example.
C. For example, rushing about wearing business clothes,
people were a common sight talking on their cell
phones.
D. Talking on their cell phones, for example, people were
a common sight rushing about in business clothes.

66. F. NO CHANGE
G. By the way
H. Nonetheless
J. In addition

67. A. NO CHANGE
B. I knew that it had been a church for nearly 1,000
years, and then a mosque for over 500 years; I had
studied a bit of its history on the Internet.
C. I knew that it had been a church for nearly 1,000 years
because I had studied a bit of its history on the Internet, and then a mosque for over 500 years.
D. From studying a bit of its history on the Internet, I
knew that it had been a church for nearly 1,000 years
and then a mosque for over 500 years.

68. F. NO CHANGE
G. magnificent building and the actual sights
H. actual sight of this magnificent building
J. the actual magnificent building

GO ON TO THE NEXT PAGE.

1 ■ ■ ■ ■ ■ ■ ■ 1

The central dome soared high above us. Near every surface
69
was covered in beautiful Turkish designs. Ancient mosaics

spoke of superb craftsmanship from an era very different

from our own. 70

[4]

[1] After leaving the Hagia Sophia, we headed to the

"Grand Bazaar." [2] It is a huge, covered market, where

thousands of vendors sell jewelry, spices, rugs, alabaster; and,
71
various other Turkish crafts. [3] As I walked through the

Bazaar, I was held captive because of the merchants calling
72
out in German, French, Spanish, English, and Japanese,

trying to appeal to as many tourists as possible. [4] As we

headed back to the hotel, I relished the memories of a day

full of exotic cultural experiences. 73

69. A. NO CHANGE
  B. (Begin new paragraph) Near
  C. (Do NOT begin new paragraph) On near
  D. (Do NOT begin new paragraph) Nearly

70. At this point, the writer would like to convey a sense of
  wonder about the Hagia Sophia. Which of the following
  sentences, if added here, would most effectively
  accomplish this?
  F. I couldn't help but wish that modern buildings could
    be as breathtaking as the Hagia Sophia.
  G. The restaurant where we ate the night before couldn't
    compare to the Hagia Sophia.
  H. I am glad that I took the time to do some Internet
    research.
  J. It occurred to me that perhaps I should take a course
    in architecture next semester, in order to learn more
    about the Hagia Sophia.

71. A. NO CHANGE
  B. alabaster;
  C. alabaster, and
  C. alabaster—and

72. F. NO CHANGE
  G. captivated by
  H. a captive of many of
  J. in captivity of

73. The writer would like to add the following sentence to the
  final paragraph:

  > After almost two overwhelming hours in the Bazaar,
  > our tour group was ready to rest.

  Where is the best place to put it?
  A. After Sentence 1.
  B. After Sentence 2.
  C. After Sentence 3.
  D. After Sentence 4.

GO ON TO THE NEXT PAGE.

1 ■ ■ ■ ■ ■ ■ ■ ■ **1**

Questions 74 and 75 ask about the preceding passage as a whole.

74. The writer is considering adding the following sentence to the essay in order to emphasize his interest in the blending of cultures:

> It was intriguing to observe firsthand some of the effects of cross-cultural exchange.

If added, this new sentence would best be placed:
F. at the end of Paragraph 1.
G. at the end of Paragraph 2.
H. at the end of Paragraph 3.
J. at the beginning of Paragraph 4.

75. Suppose the writer had been assigned to write a short essay about the Hagia Sophia for an art history class. Would this essay successfully fulfill that assignment?
A. Yes, because the essay describes several of the key artistic features of the Hagia Sophia.
B. Yes, because the essay is scholarly in form.
C. No, because the essay makes a brief mention of the religious history of the Hagia Sophia.
D. No, because the essay is primarily focused on a description of a visit to Istanbul.

END OF THE ENGLISH TEST.
STOP! IF YOU HAVE TIME LEFT OVER, CHECK YOUR WORK ON THIS SECTION ONLY.

MATHEMATICS TEST

60 Minutes – 60 Questions

DIRECTIONS: Solve each of the problems in the time allowed, then fill in the corresponding bubble on your answer sheet. Do not spend too much time on any one problem; skip the more difficult problems and go back to them later. You may use a calculator on this test. For this test you should assume that figures are NOT necessarily drawn to scale, that all geometric figures lie in a plane, and that the word *line* is used to indicate a straight line.

DO YOUR FIGURING HERE.

1. Amanda ate lunch at a restaurant, where her bill was $27.60. She tipped 15%. What was the amount of Amanda's tip?
   A. $4.14
   B. $12.60
   C. $15.00
   D. $23.46
   E. $31.74

2. What is the fourth term of the arithmetic sequence 3, 7, 11, ___, 19?
   F. 5
   G. 9
   H. 12
   J. 13
   K. 15

3. A library contains 1,274 books. Of these books, 524 are paperback. Approximately what percentage of the books at the library are paperback?
   A. 37.4%
   B. 41.1%
   C. 52.4%
   D. 58.8%
   E. 74.8%

4. If $5x + 4 = 7(x - 2)$, then $x = ?$
   F. 4
   G. 5
   H. 7
   J. 9
   K. 18

5. What is the least common denominator when adding the fractions $\frac{f}{3}, \frac{g}{4}, \frac{h}{8},$ and $\frac{j}{12}$?
   A. 24
   B. 48
   C. 64
   D. 96
   E. 288

GO ON TO THE NEXT PAGE.

2   **2**

6. If $x = -4$, then $21 - 3(x - 2) = ?$
   F. 3
   G. 11
   H. 15
   J. 27
   K. 39

7. What is the value of $x^2y + 2x - 3y$ if $x = -4$ and $y = 2$?
   A. −9
   B. 0
   C. 18
   D. 30
   E. 32

8. Randall is scheduling his classes for next term. He has a choice of 3 different science classes, 4 different math classes, and 5 different humanities classes. How many different class schedules can Randall create if he must take 1 science class, 1 math class, and 1 humanities class?
   F. 14
   G. 23
   H. 30
   J. 45
   K. 60

9. Michelle expects to get 85% of the questions correct on her 120-question math test. If Michelle gets 10 more questions correct than she expects, approximately what percentage of questions will she get correct on the test?
   A. 75%
   B. 80%
   C. 93%
   D. 95%
   E. 100%

   Use the following information to answer questions 10–11.

The table below shows Energy Consumption by Source for a certain area within the United States during one calendar year.

Energy Source					
Petroleum	Natural gas	Coal	Nuclear power	Hydroelectric power	Geothermal power
Consumption in million btu's 32.5	20.2	18.8	6.5	6.8	0.2

GO ON TO THE NEXT PAGE.

2 △ △ △ △ △ △ △ △ **2**

10. The consumption of nuclear power comprised approximately what percent of total energy consumption in million btu's?
- **F.** 6.5%
- **G.** 7.6%
- **H.** 23.1%
- **J.** 65%
- **K.** 93.5%

11. If the information in the table were converted into a circle graph (pie chart), then the central angle of the sector for petroleum would measure about how many degrees?
- **A.** 32.5°
- **B.** 71.3°
- **C.** 75.0°
- **D.** 137.6°
- **E.** 327.5°

---

12. What is the area of a circle with a circumference of 8π?
- **F.** 2π
- **G.** 4π
- **H.** 8π
- **J.** 16π
- **K.** 32π

13. What is the smallest integer that divides evenly into 36 and 72, but not into 21?
- **A.** 3
- **B.** 4
- **C.** 5
- **D.** 6
- **E.** 8

14. What is the value of $f(3)$ if $f(x) = x^3 - 3x + 3$?
- **F.** 3
- **G.** 6
- **H.** 15
- **J.** 21
- **K.** 27

15. Of 36 students in the Chess Club, 14 are new members. If 1 of the 36 students is chosen at random to design the club logo, what is the probability that the student chosen will be a new member?
- **A.** $\dfrac{1}{36}$
- **B.** $\dfrac{1}{4}$
- **C.** $\dfrac{7}{18}$
- **D.** $\dfrac{18}{25}$
- **E.** $\dfrac{7}{25}$

DO YOUR FIGURING HERE.

GO ON TO THE NEXT PAGE.

2   **2**

DO YOUR FIGURING HERE.

16. If the hypotenuse of a right triangle measures 10 cm and one of the legs measures 8 cm, what is the length, in centimeters, of the third leg of the triangle?
    F. 6
    G. $4\sqrt{41}$
    H. $\sqrt{10}$
    J. $2\sqrt{2}$
    K. 9

17. In the standard (x,y) coordinate plane, what is the y-intercept of the line $\frac{1}{2}y = x - \frac{1}{5}$?
    A. 5
    B. 1
    C. 15
    D. −15
    E. −1

18. For all x, $\sqrt{(x+2)(x-2)}$ is equivalent to:
    F. $x^2 - 4$
    G. $x - 2$
    H. $\sqrt{x^2 - 4}$
    J. $|x^2 - 4|$
    K. $x + 2$

19. If the area of a rectangle is equal to $9w^2 - 1$ and the width is equal to $3w + 1$, which of the following is an expression of the length of the rectangle?

    A. $\dfrac{9w^2 - 1}{3w - 1}$
    B. $3w - 1$
    C. $\dfrac{3w + 1}{9w^2 - 1}$
    D. $3w + 1$
    E. $9w^2 + 3w$

20. If $x > 40$ and $y < 50$, then the sum of x and y:
    F. is always zero.
    G. is always positive.
    H. is always negative.
    J. can be any real number.
    K. cannot be zero, but can be any other real number.

21. Which of the following is a polynomial factor of $3x^2 + 3x - 18$?
    A. $(3x + 3)$
    B. $3(x + 6)$
    C. $(x + 3)$
    D. $(x - 3)$
    E. $3x(x + 2)$

GO ON TO THE NEXT PAGE.

2   **2**

22. What is the sum of the two solutions of the equation $x^2 + 7x - 18 = 0$?

F. 9
G. 7
H. 2
J. 0
K. −7

DO YOUR FIGURING HERE.

23. If the lengths of the sides of one triangle are 3 inches, 5 inches, and 7 inches, respectively, and the shortest leg of a similar triangle is 6 inches, what is the perimeter of the second triangle, in inches?

A. 14
B. 18
C. 30
D. 36
E. 56

24. When asked her age, the college student answered "If you square my age, then subtract 18 times my age, the result is 40." How old is she?

F. 58
G. 36
H. 22
J. 20
K. 18

25. Which of the following is equivalent to $\dfrac{4x - \sqrt{2}}{\sqrt{2}}$?

A. $4\sqrt{2x} - 2\sqrt{2}$

B. $2\sqrt{2x}$

C. $\dfrac{x - 2}{2}$

D. $4\sqrt{2} - 2x$

E. $2x\sqrt{2} - 1$

26. Allen makes a fixed amount of money for every calendar that he sells. If Allen makes $84.00 when he sells 24 calendars, how much would he make if he sold 10 more calendars?

F. $119.00
G. $108.00
H. $94.00
J. $74.00
K. $49.00

27. What is the sum of 0.375 and $\dfrac{1}{4}$?

A. 0.0125
B. 0.093
C. 0.40
D. 0.625
E. 1.5

GO ON TO THE NEXT PAGE.

2   **2**

28. In △RUV below, S lies on line segment $\overline{RV}$; T lies on line segment $\overline{RU}$; and a, b, c, and d are angle measures, in degrees. The measure of ∠R is 35°. What is $a + b + c + d$?

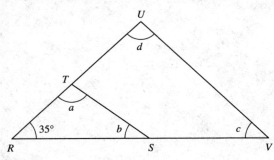

DO YOUR FIGURING HERE.

   F. 115°
   G. 145°
   H. 245°
   J. 290°
   K. 325°

29. $\dfrac{(1.181+0.019)}{3(1.155)-5(0.533)} = ?$
   A. 0.80
   B. 0.96
   C. 1.20
   D. 1.33
   E. 1.50

30. If $22 - 2(3 + x) = x + 4$, then $x = ?$
   F. 3
   G. 4
   H. 6
   J. 9
   K. 10

31. The following sketch shows a parking lot. What is the total surface area of the parking lot in square feet?

   A. 2,600
   B. 2,800
   C. 3,000
   D. 3,400
   E. 5,525

GO ON TO THE NEXT PAGE.

2   △ **2**

32. What is the slope of a line that is parallel to the line with the equation $4y - 3x = 8$?

- **F.** 2
- **G.** $\frac{3}{4}$
- **H.** 12
- **J.** −43
- **K.** −83

DO YOUR FIGURING HERE.

33. In the standard (x, y) coordinate plane, what is the midpoint of the line segment that has endpoints $(−2, −1)$ and $(3, 4)$?

- **A.** $\left(\dfrac{-5}{2}, \dfrac{-3}{2}\right)$
- **B.** $\left(\dfrac{1}{2}, 2\right)$
- **C.** $\left(\dfrac{1}{2}, \dfrac{3}{2}\right)$
- **D.** $(1, 3)$
- **E.** $(5, 5)$

34. A certain perfect square has exactly 4 digits (it is an integer between 1,000 and 9,999). The positive square root must have how many digits?

- **F.** 4
- **G.** 3
- **H.** 2
- **J.** 1
- **K.** Cannot be determined from the given information

35. If $a = bc − 2$ and $b \neq 0$, which of the following equations expresses c in terms of b and a?

- **A.** $c = \dfrac{b-2}{a}$
- **B.** $c = \dfrac{a}{2b}$
- **C.** $c = \dfrac{b}{a-2}$
- **D.** $c = \dfrac{a}{b+2}$
- **E.** $c = \dfrac{a+2}{b}$

GO ON TO THE NEXT PAGE.

2   **2**

36. In the right triangle shown below, which of the following statements is true about ∠x?

DO YOUR FIGURING HERE.

F. $\tan x = \dfrac{13}{12}$

G. $\cos x = \dfrac{12}{13}$

H. $\sin x = \dfrac{12}{13}$

J. $\cos x = \dfrac{13}{12}$

K. $\tan x = \dfrac{12}{13}$

37. The solution set of $\sqrt{(x+1)} < 4$ is the set of all real numbers x such that:
   A. $x < 16$
   B. $-1 < x < 15$
   C. $x > 4$
   D. $x > 3$
   E. $x = 4$

38. What is the area, in square centimeters, of a trapezoid with a height of 16 centimeters and parallel bases of 13 centimeters and 11 centimeters, respectively?
   F. 160
   G. 175
   H. 192
   J. 228
   K. 256

39. In the standard (x, y) coordinate plane, if the x-coordinate of each point on a line is 3 less than twice its y-coordinate, what is the y-intercept of the line?
   A. 3
   B. $\dfrac{3}{2}$
   C. 1
   D. $-\dfrac{1}{2}$
   E. $-\dfrac{3}{2}$

GO ON TO THE NEXT PAGE.

2   **2**

40. Casey's average bowling score after 5 games was 126. Her score in the 6th game was 142. If all 6 scores were equally weighted, which of the following is closest to Casey's bowling average after 6 games?

F. 125
G. 129
H. 133
J. 137
K. 142

DO YOUR FIGURING HERE.

41. The lengths of the sides of a right triangle are shown in the figure below. What is the sine of the larger of the unknown angles?

A. $\dfrac{25}{65}$

B. $\dfrac{65}{60}$

C. $\dfrac{25}{60}$

D. $\dfrac{60}{65}$

E. $\dfrac{60}{25}$

42. If a and b are positive integers such that the greatest common factor of a^2b^2 and ab^3 is 45, then which of the following could b equal?

F. 3
G. 5
H. 9
J. 15
K. 45

GO ON TO THE NEXT PAGE.

2   **2**

43. In the figure below, an equilateral triangle *ABC* is circumscribed by a circle with a radius of 3 inches. What is the length of arc *AC*?

DO YOUR FIGURING HERE.

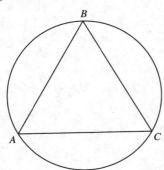

A. $\dfrac{1}{3}\pi$

B. $\dfrac{1}{2}\pi$

C. 2π

D. 3π

E. 6π

44. For the 2 functions $f(x)$ and $g(x)$, tables of values are shown below. What is the value of $g(f(2))$?

f(x)	x	g(x)	x
3	2	3	−5
1	3	2	−3
−2	−5	1	−1
−5	7	−2	3

F. −3

G. −2

H. 1

J. 2

K. 3

45. Which of the following are the solutions to $x^2 + \dfrac{5}{4}x = 0$?

A. 1 and $\dfrac{4}{5}$

B. 0 and $\dfrac{5}{4}$

C. $-\dfrac{5}{4}$ and $-\dfrac{4}{5}$

D. $-\dfrac{4}{5}$ and $\dfrac{4}{5}$

E. 0 and $-\dfrac{5}{4}$

GO ON TO THE NEXT PAGE.

2   **2**

46. A sound wave travels at approximately 761.18 miles per hour at sea level. About how many miles will a sound wave travel at sea level in 4 hours?

F. 3.04×10^3
G. 3.04×10^5
H. 3.04×10^6
J. 7.61×10^4
K. 19.03×10^4

47. The sides of a triangle are 5, $5\sqrt{3}$, and 10 inches long. What is the measure of the angle between the shortest side and the longest side?

A. 15°
B. 30°
C. 45°
D. 60°
E. 90°

48. In the figure below, the lengths of the sides are given in inches. What is the total area of pentagon *RSTUV*, in square inches?

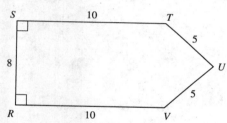

F. 38
G. 50
H. 80
J. 92
K. 106

49. In the standard (x, y) coordinate plane, what is the equation of a circle with a center at (4, 3) that passes through point (0, 3)?

A. $(x - 4)^2 + (y - 3)^2 = 16$
B. $(x - 3)^2 + (y - 3)^2 = 16$
C. $(x - 4)^2 + (y - 3)^2 = 9$
D. $(x + 4)^2 - (y + 3)^2 = 16$
E. $(x + 4)^2 + (y + 3)^2 = 9$

50. In the standard (x, y) coordinate plane, at which point do the lines $y = -\dfrac{1}{2}x + 5$ and $y = 2x - 10$ intersect?

F. The lines do not intersect
G. (2, 6)
H. (6, 3)
J. (6, 2)
K. (2, −1)

DO YOUR FIGURING HERE.

GO ON TO THE NEXT PAGE.

2   **2**

51. The radius of a circle is $\dfrac{34}{\pi}$ centimeters. How many centimeters long is its circumference?

   A. 68π
   B. 34
   C. 17
   D. 68
   E. 340π

DO YOUR FIGURING HERE.

52. One of the graphs below is that of $y = C\sin\theta$ for θ between 0 and 6.28 radians, where C is a constant. Which graph?

   F.

   G.

   H.

   J.

   K.

GO ON TO THE NEXT PAGE.

2   **2**

53. If $x = 3a + 7$ and $y = 6 + a$, which of the following expresses y in terms of x?

A. $y = 6x + 21$

B. $y = 4x + 13$

C. $y = 2x - 1$

D. $y = \dfrac{6x}{21}$

E. $y = \dfrac{11 + x}{3}$

DO YOUR FIGURING HERE.

54. A small cube has edges that are $\dfrac{1}{2}$ the length of those of a large cube. The volume of the large cube is 64. What is the volume of the small cube?

F. 4

G. 8

H. 16

J. 32

K. 128

55. What is the supplementary acute angle to a 110° angle?

A. 20°

B. 30°

C. 40°

D. 70°

E. 90°

56. In the figure below, $\sin \alpha = ?$

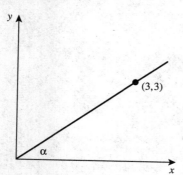

F. $\dfrac{1}{3}$

G. $\dfrac{3}{3\sqrt{2}}$

H. 1

J. $\dfrac{3\sqrt{2}}{3}$

K. $3\sqrt{2}$

GO ON TO THE NEXT PAGE.

2 △ △ △ △ △ △ △ △ **2**

57. For all real integers, which of the following is *always* an odd number?

> I. x^3
> II. $x + 1$
> III. $2x + 1$

   A. I only
   B. II only
   C. III only
   D. I and II only
   E. II and III only

58. Jenny has an empty container and puts in 4 red chips. She now wants to put in enough white chips so that the probability of drawing a red chip at random from the container is $\frac{1}{5}$. How many white chips should she put in?

   F. 1
   G. 5
   H. 9
   J. 16
   K. 20

59. In the standard (x, y) coordinate plane, the graphs of the three equations $x - 1 = 0$, $y + 2 = 0$, and $x + y = 4$ form the boundary of a triangle. What is the area of this triangle, expressed in square coordinate units?

   A. $\frac{49}{2}$
   B. $\frac{25}{2}$
   C. 8
   D. $\frac{9}{2}$
   E. $\frac{1}{2}$

60. For any real number a, $|x - a| = 9$. On a number line, how far apart are the two solutions for x in terms of a?

   F. a
   G. $9 + a$
   H. $9a$
   J. 18
   K. $3\sqrt{a}$

DO YOUR FIGURING HERE.

END OF THE MATHEMATICS TEST.
STOP! IF YOU HAVE TIME LEFT OVER, CHECK YOUR WORK ON THIS SECTION ONLY.

3   3

READING TEST

35 Minutes – 40 Questions

DIRECTIONS: This test includes four passages, each followed by ten questions. Read the passages and choose the best answer to each question. After you have selected your answer, fill in the corresponding bubble on your answer sheet. You should refer to the passages as often as necessary when answering the questions.

PASSAGE I

LITERARY NARRATIVE: *This passage is adapted from "Paul Prescott's Charge" by Horatio Alger, published in 1865.*

"HANNAH!"

The speaker was a tall, pompous-looking man, whose age appeared to verge close upon fifty. He was sitting bolt upright in a high-backed chair and looked as if it would be
5 quite impossible to deviate from his position of unbending rigidity.

Squire Benjamin Newcome, as he was called, in the right of his position as Justice of the Peace, Chairman of the Selectmen, and wealthiest resident of Wrenville,
10 was a man of rule and measure. He was measured in his walk, measured in his utterance, and measured in all his transactions. He might be called a dignified machine. He had a very exalted conception of his own position, and the respect which he felt to be his due, not only from his
15 own household, but from all who approached him. If the President of the United States had called upon him, Squire Newcome would very probably have felt that he himself was the party who conferred distinction, and not received it.
20 Squire Newcome was a widower. His wife, who was as different from him as could well be conceived, did not live long after marriage. She was chilled to death, as it was thought, by the dignified iceberg of whose establishment she had become a part. She had left, however, a child, who
25 had now grown to be a boy of twelve. This boy was a thorn in the side of his father, who had endeavored in vain to mould him according to his idea of propriety. But Ben was gifted with a spirit of fun, sometimes running into mischief, which was constantly bursting out in new directions,
30 in spite of his father's numerous and rather prosy lectures.

"Han-nah!" again called Squire Newcome, separating the two syllables by a pause of deliberation, and strongly accenting the last syllable—a habit of his with all proper names. Hannah was the Irish servant of all work,
35 who was just then engaged in mixing up bread in the room adjoining, which was the kitchen.

Feeling a natural reluctance to appear before her employer with her hands covered with dough, she hastily washed them. All this, however, took time, and before she
40 responded to the first summons, the second "Han-nah!" delivered with a little sharp emphasis, had been uttered. At length she appeared at the door of the sitting-room.

"Han-nah!" said Squire Newcome, fixing his cold gray eye upon her, "when you hear my voice a calling you,
45 it is your duty to answer the summons IMMEJIATELY."

I have endeavored to represent the Squire's pronunciation of the last word.

"So I would have come IMMEJOUSLY," said Hannah, displaying a most reprehensible ignorance, "but me
50 hands were all covered with flour."

"That makes no difference," interrupted the Squire. "Flour is an accidental circumstance."

"What's that?" thought Hannah, opening her eyes in amazement.
55 "And should not be allowed to interpose an obstacle to an IMMEJIATE answer to my summons."

"Sir," said Hannah, who guessed at the meaning though she did not understand the words, "you wouldn't have me dirty the door-handle with me doughy hands?"
60 "That could easily be remedied by ablution."

"There ain't any ablution in the house," said the mystified Hannah.

"I mean," Squire Newcome condescended to explain, "the application of water—in short, washing."
65 "Shure," said Hannah, as light broke in upon her mind, "I never knew that was what they called it before."

"Is Ben-ja-min at home?"

"Yes, sir. He was out playin' in the yard a minute ago. I guess you can see him from the winder." So saying she
70 stepped forward, and looking out, all at once gave a shrill scream, and rushed from the room, leaving her employer in his bolt-upright attitude gazing after her with as much astonishment as he was capable of.

1. The passage suggests that one of the concerns Squire Newcome had about his son was that:
A. the boy lacked a sense of humor.
B. the boy was too pompous.
C. the boy was undisciplined.
D. the boy received gifts from his servant.

GO ON TO THE NEXT PAGE.

3 ████████████████████████████████████ **3**

2. Information in the passage as a whole best supports which of the following statements about Squire Newcome?
   F. Squire Newcome was well liked both within the community and within his own household.
   G. Squire Newcome thought very highly of himself and his position within the community.
   H. Squire Newcome was overjoyed by his son's sense of humor and adventure.
   J. Squire Newcome showed great respect for the servants that he employed.

3. The passage indicates that Hannah was delayed in answering Squire Newcome's calls because:
   A. she intentionally ignored them.
   B. she had to wash her hands.
   C. she had to finish baking the bread.
   D. she was looking for Benjamin.

4. As she is presented in the passage, Hannah can best be described as:
   F. hardworking and uneducated.
   G. well educated and cultured.
   H. condescending and pompous.
   J. uneducated and lazy.

5. It is implied in the third paragraph (lines 20–30) that Squire Newcome's wife died because:
   A. the house in which they lived was too cold.
   B. she stepped on a thorn shortly after she was married and was poisoned.
   C. childbirth was too difficult.
   D. her husband cared more about his position than he did about her.

6. As it is used in the passage (line 13) the word *exalted* most nearly means:
   F. elevated.
   G. extended.
   H. humble.
   J. ordinary.

7. It can be inferred from the last paragraph (lines 68–73) that:
   A. Squire Newcome was very astonished by Hannah's attitude and subsequent behavior.
   B. Hannah was frightened by something Squire Newcome had said.
   C. Hannah was greatly alarmed by something she saw when she looked out the window.
   D. Benjamin was not allowed to play out in the yard under any circumstances.

8. In the fourth paragraph (lines 31–36) the phrase "a habit of his with all proper names" contributes to the passage's depiction of Squire Newcome as someone who is:
   F. mischievous and happy.
   G. rigid and formal.
   H. ignorant and distinguished.
   J. wealthy and solemn.

9. The passage indicates that Hannah's remark "So I would have come IMMEJOUSLY" is an attempt to:
   A. disrespect her employer.
   B. intentionally mispronounce a word.
   C. copy her employer's language.
   D. show her employer that she is more intelligent than he is.

10. It can be reasonably inferred that Ben's attitude toward his father was one of:
    F. great admiration.
    G. disdain.
    H. deep respect.
    J. indifference.

GO ON TO THE NEXT PAGE.

3   **3**

PASSAGE II

SOCIAL SCIENCE: *Marcus Garvey, Man of Action*

Marcus Garvey wrote in his book *Philosophy and Opinions*, "Where is the black man's government? Where is his king and his kingdom? Where is his president, his country and his ambassador, his army, his navy, his men of big
5   affairs?" These questions posed by Garvey clearly enumerated his goals and dreams. Garvey was a famous Black Nationalist leader, poet, writer, orator, businessman, entrepreneur, political candidate, and philosopher. His fiery speeches and strong opinions made him many enemies,
10 but his beliefs and achievements continue to make him a prominent figure in American history. To fully understand where Garvey's anger and radical agenda stemmed from, the social environment of the early 1900s must be examined. World War I had ended. Many African American
15 soldiers had fought in the war and died for their country. However, when the surviving African American soldiers returned to the United States, they found themselves facing discrimination and prejudice. There was an enormous amount of racial tension in America. Bloody incidents like
20 the East St. Louis race riots and the Red Summer broke out across the country. Despite these tense conditions, the Negro Era began to emerge and the Harlem Renaissance started to gain national recognition. It was amidst these changes that Garvey came to America and began a move-
25 ment that would forever change American society.

Garvey had many bold ideas for African Americans. He admired the Black Power and Black Pride movements. He also greatly supported the legendary "Back to Africa" movement known as Black Nationalism. He wanted to
30 colonize Africa and make a new homeland in Libya for all displaced Africans. Garvey believed that the races could never mix and live together in harmony. Garvey despised integration and believed African Americans should own their own businesses and churches, and live in nations
35 separate from other races.

Garvey's platform, entitled "Negro World," had eight main goals. These lofty aspirations encouraged pride and autonomy for black people around the world.

Garvey's radical ideas were far from universally pop-
40 ular. Garvey's most powerful enemies came from his controversial stance against the National Association for the Advancement of Colored People (NAACP) and the peaceful civil rights movement. Garvey argued that the NAACP only supported and helped certain members of the African
45 American population. His harsh comments against the peaceful NAACP and the civil rights movement turned many important people against him. In addition, Garvey's refusal to accept mainstream America's help or support made many people angry.
50 Despite his overly simplistic philosophy and blunt

behavior, Garvey did many things to inspire his race. He organized the Universal Negro Improvement Association (UNIA) in Harlem and started many African American-
55 owned businesses and industries. The UNIA was very impressive, numbering one thousand divisions around the world, with thousands of members. Garvey also organized a thirty-one-day conclave in Madison Square Garden, which resulted in the Back to Africa movement and the
60 Declaration of Black Rights. Garvey even wrote poems and books that provided encouragement and praise for the African race.

Garvey's life was a notable one. He came from Jamaica as an immigrant without connections, friends, or
65 money. Garvey went on to create a small empire. Although his plan for a colony in Africa was mostly a failure, his ability to instill pride in his race was remarkable. In a period of history when African Americans were continually told that they were inferior, Garvey reminded them
70 that success and happiness were possible.

Although Garvey did some imprudent things in his career, it must be remembered that he devoted his life to a cause he believed in. Garvey's views never wavered even when he was harshly criticized. Today, there is a United
75 Negro Improvement Association that promotes many of the same values that Garvey preached back in the 1920s. Marcus Garvey is dead, but his pride and goals live on in today's dreamers, and his writing continues to inspire leaders around the world.

---

11. The primary purpose of the passage is to:
    A. give a description of Garvey's platform, entitled "Negro World," and contrast it to earlier programs that supported African Americans.
    B. explain his affiliation with the Universal Negro Improvement Association.
    C. show how Garvey's radical ideas were both harmful and unproductive.
    D. illustrate Garvey's mark on history by detailing the ways in which Garvey's ideas had a lasting impact on the lives of African Americans.

12. From the information given in the passage, the work of Marcus Garvey can best be summarized as being about:
    F. becoming an important literary figure.
    G. political and social change.
    H. attacking prominent African American organizations.
    J. inciting race riots in East St. Louis.

GO ON TO THE NEXT PAGE.

3   **3**

13. According to the information presented in the passage, which of the following best describes the relationship between Marcus Garvey and the NAACP?

   A. A partnership, because both groups had the same goals and strategies.

   B. Competitive, because African Americans were equally divided in support of these two rivals.

   C. Antagonistic, because of Garvey's opinion of the NAACP.

   D. Indifferent, because Garvey and the NAACP were interested in different aspects of African American life.

14. According to the passage, African Americans in the early 1900s were angry because:

   F. many of them had died in World War I.

   G. there were race riots in East St. Louis and other cities in America.

   H. despite having fought for America in World War I, they were still subject to unfair treatment.

   J. they felt that the NAACP and W.E.B. Du Bois only fought for the interests of certain groups of African Americans.

15. As it is used in line 38, the word *lofty* most closely means:

   A. lengthy.

   B. upper-class.

   C. idealistic.

   D. superior.

16. As it is depicted in the passage, the UNIA can best be described as:

   F. secretive and selective.

   G. diverse and international.

   H. controversial and discriminatory.

   J. inactive and poorly organized.

17. It can be inferred that the word *empire*, as it is used in the sixth paragraph, primarily refers to Garvey's:

   A. plan to create a colony in Libya.

   B. feelings about the NAACP's status in America.

   C. achievements in many areas of society.

   D. creation of the UNIA.

18. According to the passage, all of these things were occurring around the time Marcus Garvey came to America EXCEPT:

   F. riots in East St. Louis.

   G. the Negro Era.

   H. the Harlem Renaissance.

   J. the Back to Africa Movement.

19. According to the passage, all of the following words could be used to describe Marcus Garvey EXCEPT:

   A. direct.

   B. ambitious.

   C. timid.

   D. multifaceted.

20. According to the passage, which of the following is true of the UNIA?

   F. The UNIA ceased to exist after Marcus Garvey died and reemerged during the late twentieth century.

   G. The UNIA had almost one hundred divisions around the world.

   H. The UNIA was criticized by the NAACP and W.E.B. Du Bois.

   J. The UNIA had thousands of members.

GO ON TO THE NEXT PAGE.

3 ⬛⬛⬛⬛⬛⬛⬛⬛⬛⬛⬛⬛⬛⬛⬛⬛⬛⬛⬛⬛ **3**

PASSAGE III

HUMANITIES: *Surviving the Great Depression: One Woman's Courage*

How did people in the 1930s manage to survive the Great Depression when unemployment skyrocketed, land and homes were repossessed, and proud women and men had to stand in long lines to receive government aid to feed
5 their families? The freedom to work, to provide for a family, and to live the American Dream did not exist during what my grandmother remembers as the most devastating time in her life. Imagine if you can, an entire family standing in the yard after a police officer and banker
10 told them that they were homeless because they could not make their mortgage payments. To get some idea of what things were like, listen to the stories of the Great Depression's survivors and read the works of American authors like John Steinbeck, who hoped to immortalize this brave
15 generation.

In the early 1920s, life had never been better in America. The stock market was booming, people were becoming fabulously wealthy, and carefree flappers danced the night away listening to a new wave of music fresh from
20 Harlem. However, all of this changed when the stock market crashed in 1929. Overnight, millionaires became paupers and the whole nation began to crumble. In 1932, my grandmother was fifteen years old. Within three years of the stock market crashing, she and her family had lost their
25 car, farm, and dreams.

After her family was forced to move into town, my grandmother cleaned a rich woman's house for twenty-five cents a week to help feed her eight brothers and sisters. She helped patch and resew the only two dresses she
30 owned. During these hardships, my grandmother managed to finish high school. She knew that an education could one day allow her to have a job that did not involve scrubbing or mopping.

During her teenage years, my grandmother did not
35 spend her time giggling with friends at slumber parties or going to the movies. Her day began early in the morning as she caught the streetcar and rode it to school. After school was out for the day, my grandmother rushed home to clean the rich woman's house. When she was done, there was
40 still homework and helping around her own house. There was never a moment for her to rest or be carefree. The secret dreams and fantasies so common to teenage girls today were absent from my grandmother's life, as she focused on earning money to continue her education and
45 to help her family.

But what, you will ask, did my hardworking grandmother have to show for her sacrifices and struggle?

Her reward came in her late twenties when a shy car salesman looked beyond her work-roughened hands and
50 tired face and saw the woman of his dreams. After they were married, my grandmother cared for my grandfather

and their two children through good times and bad. When my grandfather suffered a stroke, my grandmother learned to drive at the age of sixty and faithfully shuttled her hus-
55 band back and forth between endless doctor's appointments and hospital visits. The grace, determination, and work ethic she had acquired in her teenage years during the Great Depression served her well as she faced the many challenges of married life.

60 During my teenage years, I went in search of my grandmother's past. She was always so stern and hardworking. There was nothing frivolous or extravagant about her. She was a frugal and thrifty woman who used coupons, recycled plastic margarine containers, and drove a
65 fifteen-year-old Chevy. Her social life revolved around her many church activities, where she was known among the congregation as the most virtuous and pious of women. My grandmother also busied herself with numerous charitable activities and always managed to spare both time and
70 money to help those less fortunate.

Although my grandmother never did move back to a farm, the seeds of goodness and virtue she planted in the big city sprouted and flourished. With strength, determination, and a spirit that refused to be muzzled, my
75 grandmother, along with the other survivors of the Great Depression, showed the next generations of Americans what it really takes to achieve the American Dream.

21. The passage suggests that the narrator's grandmother, as a young girl, was different from most teenage girls because:

A. most teenage girls do not work, while the narrator's grandmother did.

B. the narrator's grandmother did not attend school like most teenage girls because of the Great Depression.

C. the narrator's grandmother did not have time to spend doing some of the activities that modern teenage girls enjoy.

D. most teenage girls seem to be callous about the needs of their families and concentrate solely on their own dreams and fantasies.

22. It can be reasonably inferred from the sixth paragraph that the narrator's grandmother:

F. was often bitter because of her struggle to raise two children and care for a sick husband.

G. was willing to learn new things if she needed to in order to help her family.

H. married the shy car salesman in order to have comfort and security.

J. had more difficulties as an adult than she did as a teenager during the Great Depression.

3 ■ **3**

23. The passage primarily emphasizes the idea that the narrator's grandmother:
 A. was braver and more hardworking than subsequent generations of women.
 B. was poor and forced to work hard her whole life in order for her family to survive.
 C. was involved in charity work and church activities because of her own hardships and poverty.
 D. was a woman who used the character traits developed earlier in her life to overcome challenges in adulthood.

24. As it is used in line 74, the word *muzzled* most nearly means:
 F. sustained.
 G. nurtured.
 H. suppressed.
 J. matured.

25 The passage begins by asking a question that the rest of the passage:
 A. investigates.
 B. modifies.
 C. disregards.
 D. reiterates.

26. In the context of the passage, the phrase "With strength, determination, and a spirit that refused to be muzzled, my grandmother, and all of the other survivors of the Great Depression, showed the next generations of Americans what it really takes to achieve the American Dream" (lines 73–77) suggests that:
 F. without surviving a crisis like the Great Depression, the American Dream is unlikely to be achieved.
 G. despite facing poverty and hardship, everyone will achieve the American Dream.
 H. the American Dream can be achieved by emulating the qualities of the narrator's grandmother and other Great Depression survivors.
 J. it is unlikely that people before the Great Depression truly achieved the American Dream.

27. It can reasonably be inferred from the passage that the narrator uses the example of her grandmother learning to drive a car at age sixty to:
 A. illustrate the grit and determination of the narrator in the face of adversity.
 B. show that her grandmother's bravery was undiminished throughout her life.
 C. prove that only through hardship will people conquer their fears and learn new skills.
 D. show that the narrator's grandmother used her hard-won education to earn more money later in life.

28. The passage indicates that all of these are true of the narrator's grandmother EXCEPT:
 F. she was involved in activities outside of her home during adulthood.
 G. she planted and grew seeds in a garden at her city home.
 H. she was not prone to excess or a lavish lifestyle.
 J. she was devoted to her family and the less fortunate.

29. The narrator indicates that life in the early 1920s:
 A. had no effect on her grandmother because her grandmother was too young to remember that time period.
 B. caused her grandmother to reject the lavish and extravagant lifestyle of the early 1920s.
 C. could be compared to her grandmother's early childhood that was carefree and marked by wealth.
 D. was associated with the wealth and lightheartedness that became foreign to her grandmother in the 1930s.

30. It can reasonably be inferred from the passage's last sentence that when the author thinks of her grandmother, the memory of her grandmother's life makes her feel:
 F. pained over the loss of a loved one.
 G. proud of her grandmother's accomplishments and character.
 H. eager to have the same experiences that her grandmother did.
 J. anxious that today's society is not dedicated to the same principles of discipline and hard work.

GO ON TO THE NEXT PAGE.

3 ████████████████████████████████████ **3**

PASSAGE IV

NATURAL SCIENCE: *The following passages address the weather phenomenon known as El Niño.*

PASSAGE A

El Niño is the name given to a periodic disturbance of the normal ocean and atmospheric system in the tropical Pacific that causes severe weather around the world. In ordinary years, the trade winds blow west across the
5 tropical Pacific. These trade winds then build up warm surface water in the west Pacific. This results in Indonesia having a sea surface about a half meter higher than Ecuador. The surface temperature of the ocean is about eight degrees higher in the west Pacific. An upwelling of cold
10 water from deeper levels leads to cooler temperatures near South America. This cold water is full of nutrients that are essential for maintaining the marine ecosystems and fishing industries of the region.

    In El Niño years, the trade winds become calmer
15 in the central and western Pacific. This reduction in air movement leads to fewer temperature changes in the deep waters of the eastern Pacific Ocean, and greater temperature changes in the deep waters of the western Pacific Ocean. This change decreases the ability of upwelling to
20 cool the surface water. By reducing the upwelling, the supply of cooler water to the euphotic zone (the surface layer of the ocean) is greatly decreased. This results in warmer sea surface temperature and a severe decline in the population of organisms such as phytoplankton. This reduction of
25 lower-food-chain organisms harms the higher levels of the food chain, including fish.

    During El Niño, the easterly trade winds weaken. Rain follows the warm water eastward. This rain causes flooding in Peru and drought in Australia and neighboring
30 countries. Professionals define El Niño as including continual heavy precipitation near parts of the equator, with excessively warm ocean surface temperatures that reach from the International Date Line to the South American coast. El Niño occurs on an average of every four to five
35 years, and can last up to a year and a half, often dramatically affecting global weather and climate. The initial sign of an impending El Niño is unusually warm water in the tropical Pacific Ocean. This provides more rising warm air, which can change the air pressure patterns.

PASSAGE B

40 The weather disturbance known as El Niño can affect climate worldwide. Some common impacts on the United States, for example, include fewer tropical storms in the Atlantic region; a dry monsoon around Texas, Arizona, and New Mexico; an especially dry fall and winter around
45 Oregon and Washington; an extremely wet winter in the Gulf Coast; and a warmer-than-average fall and winter in many Midwestern states.

    Industries directly affected by weather or climate compose almost 10 percent of the Gross Domestic Product (GDP)
50 in the United States. Weather and climate also impact insurance industries, services, retail and wholesale trade, and manufacturing. Nearly 25 percent of the GDP may be directly or indirectly affected by weather and climate.

    Unusual weather can lead to both gains and losses in
55 different regions and industries. For instance, department store sales went up by 5 to 15 percent during an El Niño winter in the Midwest. However, snowmobile and ski sales were down drastically during that same period. During an El Niño year, the ski industry was unusually profitable in
60 the West, but the unusually warm Midwest saw a decrease in skiing. Households and businesses saved a total of two to seven billion dollars in heating costs during an El Niño year, while the energy industry lost money from sales.

    In addition, El Niño can cause severe economic loss
65 when storms ravage property or crops fail. These losses are not usually offset by other gains and are also largely unpreventable. An average El Niño results in agricultural losses of almost two billion dollars worldwide. In recent years, El Niño disturbances have caused damages reaching
70 almost three billion dollars worldwide.

    Within the agriculture industry, many things can be adjusted to reduce susceptibility to El Niño weather conditions. The water industry and hydroelectric power companies can make storage and production decisions that
75 take into account the large rainfall of El Niño years. The natural gas and fuel industries can adjust their production and distribution levels to decrease losses when warm El Niño winter conditions are expected. Homeowners and the public can also make appropriate plans to safeguard their
80 homes or offices against dangerous storms.

Questions 31 – 33 ask about Passage A.

---

31. The passage suggests that:
- **A.** the decrease of phytoplankton and similar creatures may affect the fishing industry.
- **B.** phytoplankton are not essential to maintaining marine ecosystems.
- **C.** once phytoplankton populations decrease, they will only reemerge during subsequent El Niño episodes.
- **D.** phytoplankton prefer the warmer sea temperatures that an El Niño year can bring to their region.

32. As it is used in Paragraph 1, the word *disturbances* refers to all of these mentioned in the passage EXCEPT:
- **F.** flooding in certain regions.
- **G.** excess rainfall in the Gulf Coast.
- **H.** unusual drought near and in Mexico.
- **J.** decreased temperatures and increased snowfall in the Midwest.

GO ON TO THE NEXT PAGE.

3 ▬▬▬▬▬▬▬▬▬▬▬▬▬▬▬▬▬▬▬▬▬▬▬▬ **3**

33. The description of an El Niño given in the first paragraph does all of the following EXCEPT:
   A. provide information on sea levels in Indonesia and Ecuador.
   B. explain the behavior of trade winds during non-El Niño years.
   C. explain a consequence of abnormal trade wind activity.
   D. indicate what El Niño is.

> **Questions 34 – 37 ask about Passage B.**

34. The passage states that El Niños:
   F. occur roughly every year and a half and last about four to five months.
   G. occur approximately every four to five years and never last for more than one year.
   H. occur about every four to five years and last up to a year and a half.
   J. occur roughly every four to six years and normally last about two years.

35. The suggestions made in the last paragraph are used in this passage to support the idea that:
   A. the effects of El Niño can be completely eliminated by taking specific precautions.
   B. El Niños are predictable and therefore pose less of a danger than other weather occurrences.
   C. El Niños can cause many problems to different industries, but precautions may help alleviate some of the hardship caused by the effects of this phenomenon.
   D. any attempts to prepare for El Niños are useless because it is impossible to gauge how long a particular El Niño will last.

36. The author refers to the effects of El Niño on the GDP primarily to underscore the idea that:
   F. El Niños merely harm very specific weather-sensitive industries, like fishing and skiing.
   G. steps need to be taken to ensure that El Niños do not occur because they cause severe economic hardship.
   H. El Niño weather affects a wide range of businesses and industries, and it can harm the overall economic health of a region.
   J. all negative effects of El Niño weather are compensated for in other economic gains.

37. As it is used in line 65, the word *ravage* most nearly means:
   A. to offset a gain or loss.
   B. to severely damage or injure.
   C. to lose meaning or essential features.
   D. to reconstruct or rebuild.

> **Questions 38 – 40 ask about both passages.**

38. Based on the passages, the authors' presentation of the material is similar in that both authors:
   F. use personal anecdotes to highlight their expertise.
   G. provide evidence to support their claims.
   H. suggest that essential scientific data is missing.
   J. want to portray themselves in a flattering way.

39. Which of the following elements is most clearly similar in the two passages:
   A. The details regarding crop failure to the El Niño
   B. The significance of the economic impacts of El Niño
   C. The statements regarding the global effects of El Niño
   D. The description of the atmospheric systems created by El Niño

40. An element of Passage A that is not present in Passage B is a reference to what aspect of El Niño?
   F. Duration of El Niño
   G. Climate impact of El Niño
   H. Economics
   J. Loss mitigation

END OF THE READING TEST.
STOP! IF YOU HAVE TIME LEFT OVER, CHECK YOUR WORK ON THIS SECTION ONLY.

4 ◯ ◯ ◯ ◯ ◯ ◯ ◯ 4

SCIENCE TEST

35 Minutes – 40 Questions

DIRECTIONS: There are several passages in this test. Each passage is followed by several questions. You should refer to the passages as often as necessary in order to choose the best answer to each question. Once you have selected your answer, fill in the corresponding bubble on your answer sheet. You may NOT use a calculator on this test.

PASSAGE I

The Earth's *lithosphere*, or crust, consists of tectonic plates that move. It is believed that at one point in the past, all of the continents comprised one large landmass. Over time, the tectonic plates shifted to form the continents as we know them today. There is not a consensus in the scientific community about why the tectonic plates move. Two scientists discuss their viewpoints.

Scientist 1

The tectonic plates are constantly moving, causing earthquakes and volcanic eruptions. A large burst of energy along with this movement is what created the separate continents on the Earth. The tectonic plates move as a result of convection currents within the fluid, lower layer of the Earth's crust, the asthenosphere. The plates rest on top of this hot, plastic substance of the mantle. The asthenosphere moves in a circular motion, causing the plates to collide with each other on all sides. This circular motion is evidenced by the multiple locations along each plate's boundary where earthquakes and volcanic eruptions occur.

Scientist 2

The tectonic plates only move with sudden bursts of lithospheric motion. Otherwise they are stationary. The creation of the individual continents is the first evidence of this theory. There was originally one large landmass. A sudden burst of energy caused the plates to move apart and form the continents. Since that time there has not been much plate movement. The little movement that does occur releases small bursts of energy in only one direction along a fault line. This is apparent when looking at historical data and the fact that there are certain areas that are more affected by earthquakes than others.

1. Which of the following phrases best describes the main point that the two scientists have in common?
   A. The movement of the tectonic plates created the continents.
   B. The tectonic plates are constantly moving.
   C. The tectonic plates are not linked to earthquakes.
   D. The movement of the tectonic plates is circular.

2. You can infer from Scientist 1's viewpoint that which of the following could cause an earthquake?
   F. A volcanic eruption
   G. Tectonic plate collision
   H. A small burst of energy
   J. Stationary fault lines

3. Scientist 1's viewpoint indicates that the material in the asthenosphere is:
   A. liquid.
   B. solid.
   C. gaseous.
   D. stationary.

4. Which of the following statements best describes how Scientist 2 would explain the occurrence of many small earthquakes?
   F. Constant tectonic plate movement creates large bursts of energy along the plates' boundaries.
   G. Convection currents within the asthenosphere move the tectonic plates against each other.
   H. Volcanic eruptions along the fault lines move in only one direction.
   K. Limited tectonic plate movement releases small bursts of energy along the fault line.

5. According to the passage, the lower layer of the Earth's crust is called the:
   A. continental shift.
   B. asthenosphere.
   C. fault line.
   D. lithosphere.

6. Which of the following statements would both scientists most likely use to explain the creation of the continents? The tectonic plates experienced:
   F. a large burst of energy.
   G. little movement.
   H. many small energy bursts.
   K. slow, gradual motion.

GO ON TO THE NEXT PAGE.

7. Scientist 1's viewpoint would be *weakened* by which of the following statements about tectonic plates, if true?

   A. The tectonic plates rest on the rigid upper crust.
   B. The tectonic plates experience constant motion.
   C. The tectonic plates cause multiple earthquakes.
   D. The tectonic plates experience large bursts of motion.

GO ON TO THE NEXT PAGE.

4 ○ ○ ○ ○ ○ ○ ○ **4**

PASSAGE II

Fire is the result of a chemical reaction between oxygen and a fuel, such as wood or gasoline, that has been heated to its ignition temperature (the temperature that a fuel must reach before combustion can begin). Once a fuel has been heated, it begins *thermal degradation*. Thermal degradation is a process by which materials in the fuel are broken down into several by-products. Wood, for example, breaks down into charred wood, ash, and a volatile gas (smoke). The actual burning of wood will begin once the volatile gas has reached a high enough temperature. In this case, the volatile gas must reach approximately 260°C before the wood will actually begin to burn.

A study was conducted to investigate the use of flame retardants in treating plywood samples to reduce the risk of fire damage. Flame retardants reduce fire damage by interfering with the combustive actions of fuels. In order to work, the flame retardant must suppress or slow down the combustion process. Flame retardants can be used to suppress combustion at many different stages in the process. This study focused on protective coatings that act as an insulator to protect against fire damage during the beginning stages of combustion: thermal degradation and heat transfer.

Blocks of untreated pine plywood were tested at various temperatures in a controlled environment. Three different types of fire retardant (inorganic salts) were used to treat several other identical blocks of pine plywood that were tested at the same temperatures as the untreated plywood. The percentage loss of mass was recorded for both the untreated and treated plywood samples after being exposed to various temperatures, as shown in Figure 1 below.

Figure 1

8. At approximately 375°C, wood begins to break down into char and smoke. According to the passage, this is called:
   F. the combustion phase.
   G. thermal degradation.
   H. the ignition temperature.
   J. the insulation point.

9. According to the passage, flame-retardant protective coating on wood is used to:
   A. protect against the breakdown of the materials in the wood.
   B. transform the volatile gases released into noncombustible material.
   C. protect against the heat transferred during the final stages of combustion.
   D. destroy any ash that was produced during combustion.

10. According to Figure 1, the untreated wood loses mass most quickly:
    F. between 200° and 260°C.
    G. between 260° and 400°C.
    H. between 400° and 600°C.
    K. between 600° and 700°C.

11. Which of the following is true of the plywood treated with Fire retardant 3, as compared to the other samples of plywood used in the study?
    A. Fire retardant 3 suppresses combustion more effectively than either Fire retardant 1 or Fire retardant 2.
    B. Fire retardant 3 only protects from the loss of mass at lower temperatures.
    C. Fire retardant 3 is the least effective at temperatures above 600°C.
    D. Fire retardant 3 is more effective than untreated wood, but less effective than Fire retardant 2.

12. According to the passage, at about which temperature do Fire retardant 1 and Fire retardant 2 experience the same percent of mass loss?
    F. 250°C
    G. 425°C
    H. 550°C
    K. 625°C

GO ON TO THE NEXT PAGE.

4   **4**

PASSAGE III

All scientists agree that carbon dioxide (CO_2) is used by trees during photosynthesis. Trees and other plants that undergo photosynthesis are often called carbon sinks because they absorb large amounts of atmospheric carbon dioxide. It seems logical that planting more trees and cutting down fewer trees would be the best solution to removing excess carbon dioxide from the atmosphere. Excess carbon dioxide in the atmosphere is blamed for the greenhouse effect that may be leading to global climate change.

Two scientists present their views on planting and preserving trees as a solution to eliminating excess carbon dioxide in the atmosphere.

Scientist 1

Planting new trees and preserving existing trees is not a good long-term solution to eliminate excess carbon dioxide in the atmosphere. As the world's population increases, forests will need to be converted into farms on which to grow food and raise livestock. In addition, planting more trees or preserving trees may give people the impression that no other measures are needed to reduce carbon dioxide emissions. Car pooling, conservation of electricity, and creation of cars that do not emit carbon dioxide are necessary for long-term reduction of carbon dioxide in the atmosphere. Furthermore, dead and decomposing trees emit carbon dioxide. Forest fires and droughts are just two forces that kill off large numbers of trees and cause a rapid release of carbon dioxide into the atmosphere. In addition, planting trees also accelerates climate change in snow-covered areas by reducing the amount of sunlight energy that is directed back into space.

Scientist 2

Planting and preserving trees is a great long-term solution for reducing the levels of carbon dioxide in the atmosphere. Planting and preserving trees can help reduce the destruction of the world's forests and protect biodiversity. Trees and forests are the largest carbon sinks on earth. In fact, 458 tons of carbon dioxide are absorbed and stored in one hectare of mature forest. Although some carbon dioxide is released when the leaves decompose, planting or preserving trees is still an effective means by which to greatly reduce the carbon dioxide levels in the atmosphere.

13. If Scientist 1 is correct, which of the following generalizations about carbon dioxide levels is most accurate?
    A. Planting trees is the only known way to decrease the levels of carbon dioxide in the atmosphere.
    B. Young forests do not store as much carbon dioxide as older forests.
    C. It will not be possible to both reduce carbon dioxide levels and feed the growing population.
    D. It will take more than one measure to effectively reduce carbon dioxide levels in the atmosphere in the long run.

14. There have been periods of increased carbon dioxide levels in the atmosphere during hot, dry summers. Scientist 1 would probably explain this by saying that:
    F. hot and dry summers often lead to droughts and forest fires that kill large numbers of trees. These dying trees release stored carbon dioxide into the air.
    G. hot and dry summers most likely accelerate climate change because leaves grow smaller and create less shade. This leads to the ground absorbing more sunlight than usual.
    H. trees planted during hot and dry summers are less likely to flourish. They will grow to be smaller than normal and absorb less carbon dioxide.
    J. cool and wet weather allows trees to absorb more carbon dioxide because there is more carbon dioxide present in the atmosphere.

15. In 2004, people reported that they believed the number one way to reduce CO^2 levels in the atmosphere was to plant or preserve trees. According to Scientist 2, what other benefits could new and preserved forest areas provide?
    A. Increased economic stability for people who harvest trees for furniture and lumber
    B. Increased climate change as the trees absorb carbon dioxide from the atmosphere
    C. Reduction in the destruction of forest areas and protection of biodiversity
    D. Increased interest in decreasing the levels of carbon dioxide in the atmosphere

16. Which of the following is NOT mentioned by Scientist 1 as a solution to reducing CO^2 in the atmosphere?
    F. Car pooling
    G. Conservation of electricity
    H. Solar power
    K. Low-emission vehicles

17. According to the information presented in the passage, Scientists 1 and 2 disagree about:
    A. whether car pooling can reduce carbon dioxide levels in the atmosphere more than conservation of electricity will.
    B. whether planting and preserving trees is a good long-term solution to reducing the levels of carbon dioxide in the atmosphere.
    C. whether decomposing trees and leaves release carbon dioxide.
    D. whether excess carbon dioxide can lead to global climate change.

GO ON TO THE NEXT PAGE.

18. An increase in newly planted trees in snow-covered areas has not accelerated climate change. How might Scientist 1 account for this?

F. The newly planted trees have not yet grown large enough to reduce the amount of sunlight energy directed back into space.

G. The newly planted trees are not absorbing as much carbon dioxide as mature trees.

H. The newly planted trees are not compensating for other practices that are increasing the carbon dioxide levels in the atmosphere.

J. There has been an overall reduction in carbon dioxide levels from droughts and forest fires.

19. Which of the following findings, if true, would *weaken* the arguments of Scientist 2?

A. Cities that encourage car pooling have lower levels of carbon dioxide in their atmospheres than cities that do not encourage carpooling.

B. Decomposing leaves reemit 99% of the carbon dioxide that a tree absorbs.

C. Sales of cars that emit less carbon dioxide are rapidly growing in areas with snow-covered terrain.

D. Planting trees in areas that receive little or no snow has not been found to accelerate climate change.

GO ON TO THE NEXT PAGE.

4   **4**

PASSAGE IV

The color of a leaf results from an interaction of different pigments (colored substances) produced by the plant. The main pigment classes responsible for leaf color are *porphyrins*, *carotenoids*, and *flavonoids*. The leaf color that we see depends on the amount and types of the pigments present.

The primary porphyrin in leaves is a green pigment called *chlorophyll*. Chlorophyll is produced in response to sunlight. As the seasons change and the amount of sunlight decreases, less chlorophyll is produced by the leaves, and the leaves appear less green. Chlorophyll is broken down at a constant rate, so green leaf color will gradually fade as chlorophyll production slows or stops.

Light is not needed in order for a plant to produce carotenoids; therefore, these pigments are always present in a living plant. One of the flavonoids, *anthocyanin*, provides a natural sunscreen for plants.

Chlorophyll masks the other pigment colors, so when it is present, leaves will appear green. Anthocyanins, in turn, mask carotenoids. As summer turns to autumn, decreasing light levels cause chlorophyll production to slow. At the same time, anthocyanin production in leaves increases. Leaves containing primarily anthocyanins will appear red. Leaves with large amounts of both anthocyanins and carotenoids will appear orange. Leaves with carotenoids but little or no anthocyanins will appear yellow.

Table 1 shows the three main pigment classes, the compounds that make up the pigments, and the leaf colors that they produce.

Table 1

Pigment class	Compound type	Resulting colors
Porphyrin	Chlorophyll	Green
Carotenoid	Carotene and lycopene	Yellow, orange, red
Flavonoid	Xanthopyll Flavone Flavonol Anthocyanin	Yellow Yellow Yellow Red, blue, purple

20. According to the passage, chlorophyll production:
- **F.** increases the amount of carotenoids.
- **G.** is dependent upon sunlight.
- **H.** slows down in the summer.
- **J.** decreases the amount of pigment.

21. Based on Table 1, the presence of which of the following compounds produces yellow leaves?
- **A.** Lycopene only
- **B.** Chlorophyll only
- **C.** Lycopene and anthocyanin
- **D.** Lycopene, flavone, and carotene

22. Is the statement "decreased light levels have little to no effect on color changes in leaves" supported by information presented in the passage, and why?
- **F.** Yes, because light is not needed for a plant to produce flavonol, which causes leaves to change from green to yellow.
- **G.** Yes, because chlorophyll breaks down at a constant rate.
- **H.** No, because chlorophyll is produced in response to sunlight, and decreasing light levels slow chlorophyll production.
- **J.** No, because anthocyanin provides a natural sunscreen for plants.

23. According to the passage, leaves with more anthocyanins than carotenoids will:
- **A.** retain their green color.
- **B.** appear red.
- **C.** appear yellow.
- **D.** not produce chlorophyll.

24. According to the passage, of the main pigment classes, which has the most color variety?
- **F.** Porphyrin
- **G.** Chlorophyll
- **H.** Flavonoid
- **J.** Carotenoid

GO ON TO THE NEXT PAGE.

4   **4**

PASSAGE V

The meerkat is a member of the mongoose family that lives on the African grasslands. Unlike other mongooses, meerkats live in large social communities of up to 30 members. These groups are called "mobs" or "gangs." Often at sunrise, all of the members of a gang will gather together, stand up, and turn their bellies to the sun, soaking up the sunlight.

In addition to being social, meerkats are very territorial, and they will fiercely defend their homes against other meerkat gangs, as well as against all other intruders. Meerkat "sentries" can often be seen scanning the horizon for predators, standing up on their hind legs and using their tails for balance. When a predator or other intruder appears, a sentry will make an alarm call, alerting the other members of its gang to possible danger. Known meerkat predators include eagles and jackals.

Meerkats feed on small mammals, birds, and reptiles, as well as eggs and the roots of some plants. Scorpions are considered a special treat for meerkats; the scorpion's stinger is quickly bitten off before the rest of the animal is consumed. It is thought that meerkats use specialized vocalizations to alert the gang to the presence of food.

Zoologists have been studying meerkat alarm calls to determine whether they have special meanings. A gang of meerkats was observed for several days. The observer noted the type of call that was made, the time of day that the call was made, and the possible reason for the alarm call (approaching predator, etc.). The aggregate results of these observations are presented in Table 1.

Table 1

Meerkat alarm call	Time of day	Possible alarm call cue
One quick "chirp"	Sunset or sunrise only	None observed
Series of repeating quick "chirps"	Throughout the day	Individual meerkat from another gang; small group of meerkats from another gang
Constant loud "chattering"	Throughout the day	Jackal, eagle, large snake
Three quick "chirps" followed by a short pause and three more "chirps"	Throughout the day	Meerkat from the sentry's gang

25. Based on Table 1, when a meerkat sentry begins to chatter constantly, it is most likely signaling:
- **A.** the end of the day.
- **B.** the approach of a meerkat from another gang.
- **C.** the approach of a predator.
- **D.** the presence of a food source.

26. Meerkats have been called the "Solar Panel of the Animal World." The most likely reason for this is:
- **F.** the meerkats' natural habitat on the African grasslands.
- **G.** the meerkats' habit of soaking up the morning sun.
- **H.** the meerkats' ability to make specialized alarm calls.
- **J.** the meerkats' ability to stand up on their hind legs.

27. According to the passage, as compared to other mongooses, meerkats:
- **A.** eat small mammals and birds.
- **B.** live in Africa.
- **C.** do not live in large social groups.
- **D.** live in large social groups.

28. Which of the following statements is most consistent with the results shown in Table 1?
- **F.** Meerkats vocalize for reasons other than to warn each other of possible danger.
- **G.** Meerkats will only vocalize when predators are close by.
- **H.** Meerkats have specialized alarm calls for each type of predator.
- **J.** Meerkats will not vocalize if a member of a rival gang approaches.

29. Which of the following assumptions about meerkat alarm calls was made before the observations were noted?
- **A.** None of the meerkats in rival gangs would be able to hear the alarm calls made by the sentries.
- **B.** All of the meerkats in a certain gang will recognize and understand the different alarm calls made by the sentries.
- **C.** Only the alarm calls made after sunrise would be considered important.
- **D.** Meerkat predators may be able to mimic the alarm calls made by the sentries.

30. Which of the following, if it had occurred, would NOT support the theory that meerkat alarm calls have special meanings?
- **F.** The sentries repeated the same alarm call to indicate the presence of both predators and members of rival gangs.
- **G.** The sentries varied the alarm calls depending on what type of predator was approaching.
- **H.** Different alarm calls were made depending on the direction from which the predator was approaching.
- **J.** The sentries altered the alarm call to indicate the proximity of the approaching rival gang.

GO ON TO THE NEXT PAGE.

4 ◯ ◯ ◯ ◯ ◯ ◯ ◯ **4**

PASSAGE VI

The oceans of the world contain millions of creatures and animals, and more are being discovered each day. Every animal found in the ocean has special characteristics that define its living conditions, or, more specifically, the different zones of the ocean in which each animal will best survive. Figure 1 shows the different zones of the ocean, beginning at the surface and continuing to the sea floor, which can extend as far as 11,000 meters (m) in some locations.

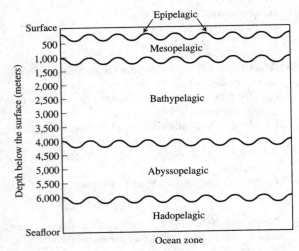

Figure 1

In the midwater zone (200 m–2,000 m) of the ocean, many fish must adapt to the scarce food supply. The debris that falls from more shallow waters and the other animals that live there make up the available food supply. Most of these animals have relatively low levels of protein in their muscles, making them very weak. Most likely, these characteristics are adaptations to the low-energy environment. To compensate, the animals have unique mechanisms to ensure survival even though feedings are infrequent: mouths that expand to two times the size of their bodies, large stomachs, and large teeth to maximize the size of prey that they can consume, as well as large eyes and photophores (organs that produce light), which make it possible to survive in an environment with little to no light. Table 1 shows several animals that live at various depths of the ocean. Although most animals generally stay within a certain range of depths, some are found in much deeper zones.

Table 1		
Animal	**Found at depths (m)**	**Max depth (m)**
Snipe Eel	40–550	2,000
Crested Bigscale	600–2,100	3,200
Eelpout	2,500–5,000	5,000
Cuskeel	1,975–5,200	5,200
Stout Blacksmelt	225–1,400	6,700

Some midwater species are vertical migrators that travel up to 1,500 feet each day. At night, they travel closer to the surface (at the uppermost part of their range of depth) to feed in areas where more food is available, and then travel back down during the day (to the lowermost part of their range of depth). These creatures travel at night to reduce the chances of being seen and preyed upon.

31. Based on information in the passage, which of the following is the most likely reason for the expandable mouth of a midwater species? The expandable mouth is used:
    A. to catch and consume available prey that may be larger in size.
    B. to absorb more carbon dioxide from the deep sea waters.
    C. to make use of the sensory pores inside the mouth.
    D. to communicate with other animals.

32. According to the passage, the midwater zone includes which of the following ocean zones?
    F. Epipelagic and mesopelagic
    G. Mesopelagic and bathypelagic
    H. Bathypelagic and abyssopelagic
    J. Abyssopelagic and hadopelagic

33. According to the passage, the snipe eel may be found in which ocean zones?
    A. Epipelagic only
    B. Epipelagic and mesopelagic
    C. Mesopelagic only
    D. Epipelagic, mesopelagic, and bathypelagic

34. According to the passage, if eelpouts are vertical migrators, to which depth might they travel at night?
    F. 225 m below the surface.
    G. 1,400 m below the surface.
    H. 2,500 m below the surface.
    J. 5,000 m below the surface.

35. The worldwide average temperature of the ocean from the surface down to 400 m below the surface is 22°C. From 400 to 800 m, the temperature drops drastically, and the temperatures range from 0°C to 4°C from this point down to the sea floor. According to Table 1 and the information given, which of the following animals would best survive at any temperature from the surface to the deep sea?
    A. Cuskeel
    B. Crested bigscale
    C. Stout blacksmelt
    D. Eelpout

GO ON TO THE NEXT PAGE.

PASSAGE VII

When two female snakes of a certain species encounter each other, there is often a threat display. The dominant snake usually forces the submissive snake to coil. A biologist conducted two experiments to determine the rank in aggression of female snakes. In the experiments described below, 5 adult female snakes were placed together in a cage and their interactions were observed and recorded.

Experiment 1

To determine what factors might affect aggressiveness, the biologists recorded the sequence in which the snakes were placed in the cage, their length, their ages, and the number of hisses each snake made during the experiment. In addition, the snakes were ranked according to their aggressiveness toward one another, from most aggressive (1) to least aggressive (5). The results are shown in Table 1.

Table 1					
Snake	Sequence	Length (cm)	Age in years	Number of hisses	Aggression (rank)
A	1st	50	3	26	2
B	2nd	30	5	10	5
C	3rd	40	2	31	1
D	4th	60	4	20	3
E	5th	20	1	17	4

Experiment 2

The snakes were placed back into the cage in the same sequence as in Experiment 1. The results of all aggressive encounters between pairs of snakes were recorded. A snake was declared a "winner" if it forced the other snake, the "loser," to coil. Table 2 shows the results of the interactions between the snakes. There were no draws, or ties, observed.

Table 2					
Winning snake	A	B	C	D	E
A	-	0	30	20	10
B	0	-	0	10	5
C	15	20	-	20	20
D	35	5	5	-	10
E	0	10	15	15	-

Table 3 summarizes the results of all the encounters for each snake.

Table 3			
Snake	Wins	Losses	Encounters
A	60	50	110
B	15	35	50
C	75	50	125
D	55	65	120
E	40	45	85

36. Which of the following generalizations about the relationship between snake length and rank is consistent with the experimental results?
   F. The longest snake will be the most dominant.
   G. The longest snake will be the most submissive.
   H. Length has no effect on rank.
   J. The shortest snake will be the most dominant.

37. It was suggested that the more dominant a female snake was, the safer her eggs were. Accordingly, one would predict, based on win-loss records, that the snake with the safest eggs would be:
   A. Snake B
   B. Snake D
   C. Snake C
   D. Snake A

38. A sixth snake, whose length was 55 centimeters and whose age was 3 years, was added to the experimental cage. It was observed that the snake hissed a total of 21 times during the experiment. Based on the results of Experiment 1, what would be the rank of the sixth snake in terms of its aggressiveness?
   F. 1
   G. 3
   H. 4
   J. 5

39. According to the results of Experiments 1 and 2, which of the following factors is (are) related to the number of hisses the snake will make?
   I. Age
   II. Length
   III. Aggressiveness

   A. I and II only
   B. I and III only
   C. II only
   D. III only

GO ON TO THE NEXT PAGE.

4 ◯ ◯ ◯ ◯ ◯ ◯ ◯ ◯ **4**

40. One can conclude from the results of Experiment 2 that Snake C and Snake A had a total of how many encounters with each other?
   F. 15
   G. 35
   H. 45
   J. 75

END OF THE SCIENCE TEST.
STOP! IF YOU HAVE TIME LEFT OVER, CHECK YOUR WORK ON THIS SECTION ONLY.

WRITING TEST

DIRECTIONS: This test is designed to assess your writing skills. You have forty (40) minutes to plan and write an essay based on the stimulus provided. Be sure to take a position on the issue and support your position using logical reasoning and relevant examples. Organize your ideas in a focused and logical way, and use the English language to clearly and effectively express your position.

When you have finished writing, refer to the Scoring Rubrics discussed in Chapter 7 to estimate your score.

Note: On the actual ACT you will receive approximately 2.5 pages of scratch paper on which to develop your essay, and approximately 4 pages of notebook paper on which to write your essay. We recommend that you limit yourself to this number of pages when you write your practice essays.

Surveillance Technology

The data technology revolution has brought a surveillance revolution. Government agencies and private companies have access to unprecedented amounts of information about citizens. Smartphones have become commonplace, and information about exactly how they are used is stored on telecommunications companies' servers. At the same time, cameras are used to capture images of people and vehicles in densely populated areas. Huge databases consisting of images of license plates and facial recognition technology combine to mean that many citizens are under constant surveillance. Is this a positive development? Given the prevalence of surveillance technology, it is worth examining the implications and meaning of its presence in our lives.

PERSPECTIVE ONE	PERSPECTIVE TWO	PERSPECTIVE THREE
The world has become a dangerous place. There are active, violent groups dedicated to the destruction of our way of life. Surveillance technology can be used to protect citizens from these threats. Government needs tools that are relevant to the current technological environment in order to prevent tragic loss of life.	Mass surveillance is an important investigatory tool for solving ordinary crime. Police and prosecutors can mine the collected data for evidence that might lead to arrest and prosecution of criminals involved in violence or fraud and theft. Without these databases, many online criminals, who only leave electronic traces rather than physical evidence, might go unpunished.	Surveillance technology is eroding our fundamental right to privacy. Citizens who use technology, or simply travel through areas under the watch of security cameras, are routinely being treated as criminal suspects, even when there is no evidence that they are involved in crime or terrorism.

Essay Task

Write a unified, coherent essay in which you evaluate multiple perspectives on the implications of surveillance technology. In your essay, be sure to:

- analyze and evaluate the perspectives given
- state and develop your own perspective on the issue
- explain the relationship between your perspective and those given

Your perspective may be in full agreement with any of the others, in partial agreement, or wholly different. Whatever the case, support your ideas with logical reasoning and detailed, persuasive examples.

ANSWER KEY

English Test

1. D	21. B	41. A	61. D
2. G	22. F	42. H	62. H
3. B	23. B	43. A	63. B
4. F	24. F	44. G	64. G
5. A	25. B	45. D	65. A
6. J	26. H	46. F	66. F
7. D	27. D	47. A	67. D
8. F	28. F	48. J	68. J
9. C	29. D	49. B	69. D
10. F	30. H	50. F	70. F
11. B	31. C	51. B	71. C
12. J	32. J	52. H	72. G
13. C	33. A	53. A	73. C
14. F	34. H	54. H	74. G
15. B	35. A	55. C	75. D
16. H	36. F	56. H	
17. C	37. B	57. D	
18. J	38. H	58. J	
19. A	39. D	59. B	
20. G	40. J	60. H	

Mathematics Test

1. A	21. C	41. D
2. K	22. K	42. F
3. B	23. C	43. C
4. J	24. J	44. G
5. A	25. E	45. E
6. K	26. F	46. F
7. C	27. D	47. D
8. K	28. J	48. J
9. C	29. E	49. A
10. G	30. G	50. J
11. D	31. B	51. D
12. J	32. G	52. F
13. B	33. C	53. E
14. J	34. H	54. G
15. C	35. E	55. D
16. F	36. H	56. G
17. E	37. B	57. C
18. H	38. H	58. J
19. B	39. B	59. B
20. J	40. G	60. J

Reading Test

1. C	21. C
2. G	22. G
3. B	23. D
4. F	24. H
5. D	25. A
6. F	26. H
7. C	27. B
8. G	28. G
9. C	29. D
10. J	30. G
11. D	31. A
12. G	32. J
13. C	33. C
14. H	34. H
15. C	35. C
16. G	36. H
17. C	37. B
18. J	38. G
19. C	39. C
20. J	40. F

Science Test

1. A	21. D
2. G	22. H
3. A	23. B
4. K	24. H
5. B	25. C
6. F	26. G
7. A	27. D
8. G	28. F
9. A	29. B
10. G	30. F
11. A	31. A
12. K	32. G
13. D	33. D
14. F	34. H
15. C	35. C
16. H	36. H
17. B	37. C
18. F	38. G
19. B	39. D
20. G	40. H

SCORING GUIDE

Your final reported score is your COMPOSITE SCORE. Your COMPOSITE SCORE is the average of all of your SCALE SCORES.

Your SCALE SCORES for the four multiple-choice sections are derived from the Scoring Worksheet on the next page. Use your RAW SCORE, or the number of questions that you answered correctly for each section, to determine your SCALE SCORE. If you got a RAW SCORE of 60 on the English Test, for example, you correctly answered 60 out of 75 questions.

Step 1 Determine your RAW SCORE for each of the four multiple-choice sections:

English   _____

Mathematics   _____

Reading   _____

Science   _____

The following Raw Score Table shows the total possible points for each section:

RAW SCORE TABLE	
KNOWLEDGE AND SKILL AREAS	RAW SCORES
ENGLISH	75
MATHEMATICS	60
READING	40
SCIENCE	40

Step 2   Determine your SCALE SCORE for each of the four multiple-choice sections using the following Scale Score Conversion Table.

SCALE SCORE	RAW SCORE			
	ENGLISH	MATHEMATICS	READING	SCIENCE
36	75	60	40	39–40
35	74	59	—	38
34	73	57–58	39	37
33	71–72	56	38	36
32	70	55	37	—
31	69	54	—	35
30	68	53	36	34
29	67	52	35	33
28	65–66	51–50	34	32
27	64	48–49	33	31
26	62–63	46–47	32	29–30
25	60–61	44–45	31	27–28
24	58–59	41–43	30	25–26
23	56–57	38–40	29	23–24
22	54–55	35–37	27–28	21–22
21	51–52	31–34	26	20
20	49–50	28–30	24–25	18–19
19	46–48	27	22–23	17
18	43–45	24–26	21	15–16
17	40–42	20–23	19–20	14
16	36–39	16–19	17–18	12–13
15	33–35	12–15	15–16	11
14	30–32	10–11	13–14	10
13	27–29	8–9	11–12	9
12	24–26	6–7	9–10	8
11	21–23	5	8	7
10	19–20	4	6–7	6
9	15–18	—	—	5
8	13–14	3	5	4
7	11–12	—	4	3
6	9–10	2	3	—
5	7–8	—	—	2
4	5–6	1	2	—
3	4	—	—	1
2	2–3	—	1	—
1	0–1	0	0	0

NOTE: Each actual ACT is scaled slightly differently based on a large amount of information gathered from the millions of tests ACT, Inc. scores each year. This scale will give you a fairly good idea of where you are in your preparation process. However, it should not be read as an absolute predictor of your actual ACT score. In fact, on practice tests, the scores are much less important than what you learn from analyzing your results.

   If you take the optional Writing Test, you should refer to Chapter 7 for guidelines on scoring your Writing Test Essay.

Step 3 Determine your COMPOSITE SCORE by finding the sum of all your SCALE SCORES for each of the four sections: English, Mathematics, Reading, and Science, and divide by 4 to find the average. Round your COMPOSITE SCORE according to normal rules. For example, $31.2 \approx 31$ and $31.5 \approx 32$.

$$\frac{}{\substack{\text{ENGLISH}\\ \text{SCALE SCORE}}} + \frac{}{\substack{\text{MATHEMATICS}\\ \text{SCALE SCORE}}} + \frac{}{\substack{\text{READING}\\ \text{SCALE SCORE}}} + \frac{}{\substack{\text{SCIENCE}\\ \text{SCALE SCORE}}} = \frac{}{\substack{\text{SCALE SCORE}\\ \text{TOTAL}}}$$

$$\frac{}{\text{SCALE SCORE TOTAL}} \div \mathbf{4} = \frac{}{\text{COMPOSITE SCORE}}$$

ANSWERS AND EXPLANATIONS

English Test Explanations

PASSAGE I

1. **The best answer is D.** All that is needed in this position is a simple present tense verb, which is the clearest and most concise of the answer choices. Answer choices A, B, and C complicate the sentence by adding auxiliary verbs.

2. **The best answer is G.** The main clause of this sentence is *take a closer look*. It is a command in which the subject *you* is implied. Introductory material, especially as lengthy as it is here, must be separated from the main clause with a comma.

3. **The best answer is B.** Since the question asks for the answer that extends the discussion of the writer's personal experience with rubber cement, answer choice B is the only real possibility here. The other choices either discuss other subjects or are not necessarily about the writer's experiences.

4. **The best answer is F.** The sentence indicates that the *athletic facilities* belong to *a high school*. Therefore, the singular possessive form is correct.

5. **The best answer is A.** The new subject of Paragraph 3 is the various uses to which rubber cement can be put. Answer choice A effectively introduces this topic. The other answer choices are focused on either narrow details or irrelevant information, and they should be eliminated.

6. **The best answer is J.** The logical subject of this sentence is *a rubber cement surface*, which is singular. Eliminate answer choice H, which is plural. Eliminate answer choice G because the auxiliary *will* is used with the bare form of a verb, which *provides* is not. Although the sentence is grammatically correct as written, the pronoun *it* has an unclear antecedent. The singular noun immediately preceding it is *comfort level*, not *a rubber cement surface*, so the full subject must be expressed. Answer choice J is a good alternative to repeating the subject word for word.

7. **The best answer is D.** It is correct to use *fewer* to modify a noun that can be counted, such as *injuries*. Use *less* to modify a quantity or a noun that cannot be counted.

8. **The best answer is F.** The form of the verb within this phrase depends on its subject. The subject is *a rubber cement surface*, which is singular. Eliminate answer choices G and J, which are plural. Answer choice H can be eliminated because the verb *made* is unnecessary and distracting.

9. **The best answer is C.** This sentence should parallel the next sentence, which is in simple present tense (*Cities also sometimes use it . . .*). Answer choice C is in simple present tense and is the most concise of the answer choices. Furthermore, answer choice B is awkward, and answer choice D would create a sentence fragment.

10. **The best answer is F.** This question requires you to differentiate among homonyms. The underlined portion immediately precedes the conjoined nouns *patios* and *driveways*, which are possessed by *consumers*, a plural noun. Therefore, the plural possessive determiner *their* is appropriate.

11. **The best answer is B.** The prepositional phrase *of rubber cement surfacing* is a complement to the noun *advantage*, so the two should not be separated by a comma. Eliminate answer choice A. Eliminate answer choice D because the colon awkwardly breaks up the complete sentence. Eliminate answer choice C because the preposition *in* is not idiomatic with *advantage*.

12. **The best answer is J.** Answer choices F and G are awkward because they use the comparative *more* and superlative *most*, respectively, although there is no clear basis for comparison. *Remove* and *take out* are synonyms; therefore, answer choice H is redundant and can be eliminated. Answer choice J expresses the idea clearly and simply.

13. **The best answer is C.** Answer choices A, B, and D are all idiomatic and grammatically correct. Therefore, answer choice C is the LEAST acceptable.

14. **The best answer is F.** Idiomatically, one inquires *about* something, just as one asks *about* something. The other answer choices are not idiomatic and can be eliminated.

15. **The best answer is B.** The new sentence gives a specific example of conditions experienced in some parts of the country that may create problems with rubber cement surfaces. It makes the most sense to place this sentence after Sentence 6 in Paragraph 4. Clear writing generally involves placing specific examples immediately after general statements or assertions.

PASSAGE II

16. **The best answer is H.** The question asks you to choose the revision that gives credit to other people besides Watson and Crick. Only answer choice H emphasizes the contributions of others.

17. **The best answer is C.** Answer choice C ties the introduction of Rosalind Franklin to the ideas that precede it. In particular, the demonstrative determiner *these* marking *lesser-known scientists* points to the *other scientists* mentioned in the first sentence. This specifically responds to the question, which asks you to tie Franklin to the first paragraph.

18. **The best answer is J.** This question tests your ability to express an idea clearly and simply. Answer choices F, G, and H all refer to "this advanced degree," apparently referring back to the "doctorate" mentioned in the previous sentence. In addition, answer choices F and G can be eliminated for incorrect comma usage. Answer choice H can be eliminated because it is very awkward.

19. **The best answer is A.** It is correct to use the simple past tense to match the context of the paragraph. Additionally, the adverb *later* correctly modifies the verb *returned*.

20. **The best answer is G.** Franklin's acceptance of the offer occurred in the past (the early 1950s specifically, according to the sentence). Therefore, a simple past tense verb is required.

21. **The best answer is B.** It is necessary to join independent clauses within a compound sentence with some sort of punctuation. Answer choice B creates a run-on sentence, so it is not acceptable.

22. **The best answer is F.** It is correct to use *among* because the context implies that more than two scientists were engaged in the race to find the structure of DNA.

23. **The best answer is B.** Appositives (restatements of nouns) must be set apart with commas. The name *Maurice Wilkins* renames the noun that precedes it, *graduate student.*

24. **The best answer is F.** Only answer choice F explains precisely the nature of Wilkins and Franklin's miscommunication. Answer choice G is vague, and answer choices H and J do not specify any problem.

25. **The best answer is B.** This question tests your ability to express an idea clearly and simply. The information following the period in the underlined portion does not contribute anything meaningful to the essay. It is distracting and off-topic. Therefore, it should not be included. It is best to end the sentence after *DNA*.

26. **The best answer is H.** It is not clear to whom or what the pronoun *them* refers, so eliminate answer choice F. In order to maintain clarity in the sentence, it is best to identify who received *the definitive edge in the DNA race*. It does not make sense that the DNA strands received the *definitive edge*, so eliminate

answer choice J. It is clear from the first paragraph that Watson and Crick discovered the structure of DNA, although there were other important yet uncredited scientists, like Rosalind Franklin and graduate student Maurice Wilkins, behind the scenes, so answer choice H is best.

27. **The best answer is D.** The first step in answering this question is to recognize that Franklin is one person. You should, therefore, use the singular possessive form with apostrophe plus *s*. Eliminate answer choices A and C because they are not possessive. Answer choice B includes an extra *s*, so eliminate it.

28. **The best answer is F.** Answer choices G, H, and J are each awkward and can be eliminated. Given four answer choices, it is important to strongly consider the simplest answer choice. With verbs, such as *uncover*, the simplest form is generally short and stands alone. Answer choice G embeds the verb in a prepositional phrase. Answer choice H seems to begin a gerund phrase that ends up making little sense. Answer choice J embeds the verb in a relative clause, which is also awkward. Answer choice F is the infinitive form, and it fits the sentence well.

29. **The best answer is D.** The action took place in the past, so you should use the simple past-tense verb *came*. Answer choice B is the past perfect tense, and answer choice C is the past progressive tense. Both are used to reference when another action took place in the past. As this is not the case here, eliminate answer choices B and C.

30. **The best answer is H.** This question requires you to determine the main idea of the last paragraph. The paragraph consists of one sentence that discusses Franklin's contribution to the discovery of the structure of DNA. It would make sense to insert a sentence that includes additional information about both Franklin and the discovery of the structure of DNA. Only answer choice H does this. The other answer choices are either too broad or irrelevant. The final paragraph begins by mentioning Franklin's death, so it doesn't make sense to bring up her last research work. Eliminate answer choice F. Answer choice G doesn't reference Franklin, so eliminate it. Answer choice J refers to other scientists besides Franklin, so eliminate it.

PASSAGE III

31. **The best answer is C.** The best way to sharpen the focus of the first paragraph would be to include a better description of the home in which the writer raised her family. The first sentence implies that it was difficult to raise five children in the home, primarily

because it was too small. The phrase *three-bedroom ranch home* is a better, more detailed description of the home's size.

32. **The best answer is J.** The sentence as written is a comma splice, a run-on formed by joining independent clauses with a comma. Eliminate answer choice F. Some other punctuation is needed. Eliminate answer choice H. The clauses are very closely related; in fact, the second and third clauses directly explain the statement made by the first clause. For this reason, a semicolon (answer choice J) would tie the first and second clauses together better than a comma and conjunction (answer choice G) would.

33. **The best answer is A.** The context of the passage implies that, because the kids no longer needed the master bedroom, it was time for the writer and her husband to move back upstairs. The sentence is correct as written because it best identifies the reason behind the writer's decision to move back upstairs. The other answer choices are not supported by the context of the passage.

34. **The best answer is H.** This question tests your ability to express an idea clearly and simply. In the sentence as it is written, there is no clear sense of which space is being discussed. The context of the passage indicates that the writer's space will be reduced if she and her husband move from their current bedroom (in the basement) back into the master bedroom. Therefore, you should use the first-person, plural possessive determiner *our*. Answer choices G and J contain ambiguous pronouns. Answer choice F uses the definite article *the*, which seems to indicate that the master bedroom space would be reduced by half, which is not the correct meaning.

35. **The best answer is A.** The author is hoping to have a future that includes grandchildren, so *with* is the correct word to use here.

36. **The best answer is F.** The paragraph discusses the topic of the house being too small and the need to expand. Answer choices G and H do not make sense based on the context of the paragraph. The phrase *the only way to go was up* indicates that the ranch home would most likely have to be turned into a two-story home, which is supported by the statement that the lot was small. Answer choice J, while a possible way to remodel a home, is not possible in this case because the sentence specifically mentions the *limited size of our lot*. This indicates that the house could not be expanded horizontally, but must be expanded vertically.

37. **The best answer is B.** The underlined portion introduces some of the plans that the writer had for the expansion of her home. Idiomatically, when a form of

include is used to modify a noun phrase (*our building plans*), it takes the gerund form (*including*) without a conjunction (*and*) or a simple past (*included*) or present (*include* or *includes*) form after a relative pronoun such as *which* or *that*. Therefore, answer choices A, C, and D are awkward.

38. **The best answer is H.** In this sentence, the adjective *creative* is best placed after the possessive pronoun *our* to correctly modify the noun *imaginations*. Placing it elsewhere in the sentence disrupts the natural flow and creates awkwardness.

39. **The best answer is D.** This question requires you to express the idea clearly and simply. Because *right away*, *instantly*, and *immediately* all have the same meaning, it would be redundant to use more than one of them in the sentence. Eliminate answer choices A, B, and C.

40. **The best answer is J.** The sentence makes it clear that both the writer and her husband are discussing the remodeling project (*our enthusiasm*). Therefore, use the first-person, subject plural pronoun *we*.

41. **The best answer is A.** A semicolon is used to separate two independent clauses within a sentence, so the sentence is correct as it is written. You should not use a comma to separate main clauses; this is called a comma splice. Eliminate answer choice C. There should not be a comma between the subject of a phrase (*some of them*) and the modified verb (*seemed*), so eliminate answer choice D.

42. **The best answer is H.** This question requires you to punctuate the underlined portion correctly. The sentence begins with a prepositional phrase, so a comma should be used to separate it from the main clause as in answer choice H. The addition of the transition words *then* and *because* does not help with the clarity of the sentence, so eliminate answer choices G and J.

43. **The best answer is A.** The preceding sentence mentions the *anxiety* associated with home renovations. The sentence beginning with this underlined portion indicates that *absolute strangers . . . invading your home* eventually *become like . . . family*. This is a contradiction to the *anxiety* mentioned previously. Answer choice A, *nevertheless*, is the best adverb to express this contradiction.

44. **The best answer is G.** A comma must separate each item in a series of three or more elements. In this sentence, the elements are verb phrases: *use your bathroom facilities, observe you in your bathrobe,* and *spend entire days with you.*

45. **The best answer is D.** This question requires you to express the idea clearly and simply. The sentence as it is written is awkward and wordy, so eliminate answer

choice A. Eliminate answer choice C for the same reason.

PASSAGE IV

46. **The best answer is F.** This question requires you to express the idea clearly and simply. The implication in the paragraph is that visitors can sometimes give inaccurate descriptions of the climate in the United States if they only visit one region. So, it makes sense that the writer would advise them to *take care* when giving descriptions. Answer choice G makes the sentence very awkward. Answer choice H is vague. Answer choice J is redundant.

47. **The best answer is A.** This question requires you to express the idea clearly and simply. *Temperatures* and *weather patterns* are two distinct things. The sentence as it is written makes this clear. Answer choice B suggests that the *weather patterns*, not the *differences in weather patterns*, are huge. This does not make sense, so eliminate answer choice B. Eliminate answer choice C because using any form of *differ* twice in one phrase is redundant. Answer choice D should be eliminated because the phrase *temperature weather patterns* is unclear.

48. **The best answer is J.** The underlined portion and answer choices G and H are wordy and redundant. The adjective *diverse* already in the sentence captures the meaning that the climate is different depending on the area of the country.

49. **The best answer is B.** The question requires you to select the sentence that links information already presented with information about the writer's *personal experiences*. Eliminate answer choices A, C, and D because they discuss other people, not the writer. Answer choice B is the only selection that introduces a personal experience of the writer.

50. **The best answer is F.** Choice G is wrong because it lacks any punctuation to set off the appositive phrase. Choice H is not idiomatic. Choice J creates a sentence fragment.

51. **The best answer is B.** The rest of the paragraph proves that the topic is specifically the cities of Phoenix and Las Vegas. Between answer choices A and B, choose the more concise, which is answer choice B.

52. **The best answer is H.** This question requires you to punctuate the underlined portion correctly. The phrase *constant sunshine and soaring summer temperatures* is a noun phrase composed of two noun phrases conjoined with *and*. You do not need to separate the elements of that phrase with a comma. No punctuation is necessary.

53. **The best answer is A.** For the sake of clarity, the verb *signifies* should be followed by the noun phrase that is its object. Of the answer choices, the best one places the elements of the noun phrase in standard order. Answer choice A has clear, standard word order: *a* (indefinite article) *few* (adjective) *light*, (adjective) *fluffy* (adjective) *clouds* (noun) *here and there* (idiom acting as an adverb). The only comma needed comes between *light* and *fluffy*, which are coordinate adjectives, meaning they modify *clouds* in the same way.

54. **The best answer is H.** This question requires you to punctuate the underlined portion correctly. The relative pronoun *which* should be preceded by a comma, not a semicolon, so eliminate answer choice F. Eliminate answer choice G because it creates an incomplete sentence, and eliminate answer choice J because it creates a run-on sentence.

55. **The best answer is C.** The semicolon in the quotation indicates that each half of the sentence must be an independent clause. The idiom uses *in* rather than *by*, so eliminate answer choices A and D. Furthermore, the expression of time *every day* indicates that the *nice fog* rolls in on a regular basis, so eliminate choice B. This case calls for the simple present tense, answer choice C.

56. **The best answer is H.** To maintain clarity, it is best to restate the antecedent. The pronouns *it*, *they*, and *that* are ambiguous.

57. **The best answer is D.** This question requires you to determine the topic of the paragraph. Since the paragraph is a discussion of enduring severe weather, it makes sense that the introductory sentence would mention some aspect of living in severe weather conditions. Eliminate answer choices A and B, which include information on good weather conditions. The paragraph discusses some character-building aspects of good weather. Eliminate answer choice C because it is too negative.

58. **The best answer is J.** The meaning of *make* in the sentence as written is unclear. Eliminate answer choice F. Of the remaining answer choices, answer choice J is the most concise and specific. One precise word is always better than conveying the same meaning with several small, common words.

59. **The best answer is B.** Because the underlined portion follows the auxiliary *can*, only a verb in the bare form can be used. Eliminate answer choice C. Eliminate answer choice A because an adjective (*great*)

cannot modify a verb (*enhance*). Between answer choices B and D, answer choice B is most concise.

60. **The best answer is H.** This question requires you to determine the main idea of the passage. Because the passage focuses on only two regions of the United States, it would not fulfill the assignment. Eliminate answer choices F and G. Eliminate answer choice J because the primary focus of the passage is not the descriptive words for different weather conditions.

PASSAGE V

61. **The best answer is D.** The fact that all the answer choices are grammatically correct indicates that you must choose the clearest and most concise answer. This is answer choice D, which simply uses the past participle *endured* to complete the past perfect construction with *had*.

62. **The best answer is H.** Dependent clauses (like this one beginning with *so*) should be set apart from the main clause using a comma. Using a period or semicolon makes the dependent clause become a sentence fragment. Eliminate answer choices F and G. Answer choice J creates a comma splice.

63. **The best answer is B.** This choice most vividly describes the meal served to the author and the other tourists in her group. The other answer choices are not as specific.

64. **The best answer is G.** The underlined portion immediately precedes the long noun phrase *the copious amounts of chai I drank at the restaurant*. The implication of the sentence is that *chai*, which was previously defined as tea, contains a stimulant, probably caffeine, that the writer supposed would keep him awake. The main clause of the sentence indicates that he succeeded in sleeping anyway. The appropriate word to signal that the *chai* drinking should have worked against attempts to sleep is *despite*.

65. **The best answer is A.** The best answer choice places all the phrases in the correct order based on what they modify. First, an introductory phrase like *for example* is best placed at the beginning of a sentence. Second, the phrase *business clothes* should not be very distant from the noun *people* that it modifies. Therefore, eliminate answer choices B and D. Eliminate answer choice C because it is ambiguous whether all people wear business clothes and whether all people have cell phones. The writer wants to convey that the people rushing about and talking on their cell phones are the ones in business clothes. This is the meaning conveyed by the sentence as written.

66. **The best answer is F.** The preceding sentence and this one are parallel to the sentence immediately before them. That one reads: *similar to large American cities in many ways, yet also very different*. Therefore, the next sentence presents a similarity, and the one beginning with the underlined portion presents a difference. Among the answer choices, the best introductory phrase for an opposite or contrasting idea is F, *on the other hand*.

67. **The best answer is D.** Eliminate answer choice A because it unnecessarily nests the first clause beginning *I had studied* inside a gerund phrase (*being that*). Eliminate answer choice B because it is unnecessarily complicated by the semicolon. Eliminate answer choice C because of its awkward phrase order. Answer choice D is clear, with a prepositional phrase set apart from the main clause with a comma.

68. **The best answer is J.** This question requires you to express the idea clearly and simply. Therefore, eliminate answer choices F, G, and H because they are wordy and confusing.

69. **The best answer is D.** It is not necessary to begin a new paragraph because this sentence directly relates to the sentence preceding it. Eliminate answer choice B. The appropriate word is the adverb *nearly*, which can modify the adjective *every*. Here, it means the same as *almost*, meaning that all surfaces with few exceptions were *covered in beautiful Turkish designs*.

70. **The best answer is F.** The best way to convey a sense of wonder is to use words such as *breathtaking*, as answer choice F does. The other answer choices are not effective.

71. **The best answer is C.** This underlined portion is within a list of five elements which must all be separated by commas. In addition, the last element should be preceded by *and*. It is not appropriate to use a semicolon or dash in this instance.

72. **The best answer is G.** This question requires you to express the idea clearly and simply. It does not make sense that the writer was *held captive because of* or was *a captive of* the merchants, so eliminate answer choices F and H. Likewise, she was not *in captivity*, so eliminate answer choice J. *Captivated* means *enchanted*, which suits the meaning of the sentence, so choose answer G.

73. **The best answer is C.** The last sentence (Sentence 4) of the paragraph indicates that the tour group was heading back to the hotel. It would make sense that the sentence before the last sentence would include a reason for the group to head back to the hotel. The

new sentence does just that, so it should be placed between Sentence 3 and Sentence 4.

74. **The best answer is G.** Paragraph 2 includes a discussion of the similarities and differences between Istanbul and American cities. This implies the *cross-cultural exchange* mentioned in the new sentence. Therefore, the new sentence would be a good concluding statement for Paragraph 2.

75. **The best answer is D.** This question requires you to determine the main idea of the passage. The passage mentions the Hagia Sophia, but the focus of the passage is the writer's visit to Istanbul. Therefore, answer choice D is best.

Mathematics Test Explanations

1. **The correct answer is A.** To solve this problem, calculate 15% of $27.60. Multiply $27.60 by 0.15, the decimal equivalent of 15%: $27.60(0.15) = $4.14

2. **The correct answer is K.** By definition, an arithmetic sequence has a constant that is added to the previous number to get the next number, and so on. The first step in solving this problem is to calculate the constant in the sequence. To find the constant, find the difference between each of the terms. The difference between 3 and 7 is 4, and the difference between 7 and 11 is 4. Since the difference in the terms is 4, the missing number must be 15.

3. **The correct answer is B.** This problem requires you to determine the percent of 1,274 that is equivalent to 524. Set up a proportion, as follows:

   524 books is to 1,274 books as x% is to 100%

   $\frac{524}{1,274} = \frac{100}{x}$; solve for x

   $5241,274 = 100x$; solve for x

   $1,274x = 52,400$

   $x = 41.13$, or approximately 41.1%

4. **The correct answer is J.** This problem requires you to solve for x. Isolate x on the left side of the equation:

   $5x + 4 = 7(x - 2)$

   $5x + 4 = 7x - 14$

   $-2x = -18$

   $x = 9$

5. **The correct answer is A.** The first step in finding the least common denominator is to calculate the least common multiple of the fractions given. In other words, what is the smallest number into which all of the denominators will divide evenly? The denominators are 3, 4, 8, and 12. The smallest number into which all of those numbers divide evenly is 24. Therefore, the least (smallest) common denominator is 24.

6. **The correct answer is K.** The best way to solve this problem is to substitute −4 for x where it appears in the equation, and solve the equation. Remember to keep track of the negative signs!

   $21 - 3(-4 - 2)$

   $21 - 3(-6)$

   $21 - (-18)$

   $21 + 18 = 39$

7. **The correct answer is C.** To solve this problem, substitute −4 for x and 2 for y wherever they appear in the equation, and solve the equation. Remember to keep track of the negative signs!

   $x^2y + 2x - 3y =$

   $(-4)^2(2) + 2(-4) - 3(2) =$

   $16(2) + (-8) - 6 =$

   $32 - 8 - 6 = 18$

8. **The correct answer is K.** To answer this question, you need to multiply the number of choices of science, math, and humanities classes together to determine the total number of combinations. The question states that there are 3 science class choices, 4 math class choices, and 5 humanities class choices, so you have $3 \times 4 \times 5 = 60$ total class options. For every science class choice, you have 4 math class choices. Given 4 math class choices, you have $(3)(4) = 12$ science and math class choices. For every science and math class combination, you have 5 humanities class choices. Given 12 math and science class choices, you have $(12)(5) = 60$ total class options.

9. **The correct answer is C.** The first step in solving this problem is to calculate 85% of 120. Multiply 120 by 0.85, the decimal equivalent of 85%:

   $120 \times 0.85 = 102$

   Michelle expects to get 102 questions correct. If she gets 10 more questions correct, she will get 112 questions correct on the test. Calculate the percent of 120 that is equivalent to 112. Set up a proportion, as follows:

   112 is to 120 as x% is to 100%

   $\frac{112}{120} = \frac{x}{100}$; solve for x

   $120x = 11,200$

   $x = 93.33\%$, or 93%

10. **The correct answer is G.** The first step in solving this problem is to calculate the total energy consumption in million btu's:

$$32.5 + 20.2 + 18.8 + 6.5 + 6.8 + 0.2 = 85$$

Next, set up a proportion to calculate the percentage comprised by nuclear power: Nuclear power (6.5) is to total energy (85) as x is to 100%

$$\frac{6.5}{85} = \frac{x}{100}$$

$$85x = 650$$

$$x = 7.6471\%, \text{ or approximately } 7.6\%.$$

11. **The correct answer is D.** The first step in solving this problem is to calculate the total energy consumption in million btu's:

$$32.5 + 20.2 + 18.8 + 6.5 + 6.8 + 0.2 = 85$$

Next, find the fraction represented by petroleum and multiply by 360 (the number of degrees in a circle):

$$\frac{32.5}{85} \times 360°$$

$$= 0.382329 \times 360°$$

$$= 137.64706, \text{ or approximately } 137.6°$$

12. **The correct answer is J.** The circumference of a circle is calculated by using the formula $2\pi r$. You are given that the circumference is 8π, so $2r$ must be equal to 8, and r must be equal to 4. The area of a circle is calculated by using the formula πr^2. Substitute 4 for r:

$$\pi r^2 =$$

$$\pi(4)^2 = \pi 16, \text{ or } 16\pi.$$

13. **The correct answer is B.** Since the question asks you to find the smallest integer that divides evenly into 36 and 72, but not into 21, try the answer choices in order from smallest to greatest:

Answer choice A: The integer 3 divides evenly into 36 (3 × 12 = 36), 72 (3 × 24 = 72), and 21 (3 × 7 = 21), so eliminate answer choice A.

Answer choice B: The integer 4 divides evenly into 36 (4 × 9 = 36) and 72 (4 × 18 = 72). However, 4 does not divide evenly into 21, so answer choice B is the correct answer.

Answer choices C, D, and E can be eliminated because they are greater than 4.

14. **The correct answer is J.** $f(x)$ is function notation that means "f of x" and indicates that you should solve the equation by substituting a number for x. The question states that x is 3.

To solve this problem, substitute 3 for x wherever it appears in the expression:

$$f(3) = 3^3 - 3(3) + 3$$

$$f(3) = 27 - 9 + 3$$

$$f(3) = 21$$

15. **The correct answer is C.** Since 14 of the members are new and there are a total of 36 members, the probability, or chance, that the member chosen to design the logo is a new member is $\frac{14}{36}$, which can be reduced to $\frac{7}{18}$.

16. **The correct answer is F.** To solve this problem, use the Pythagorean Theorem, which says that $a^2 + b^2 = c^2$, where c is the hypotenuse.

$$8^2 + b^2 = 10^2$$

$$64 + b^2 = 100$$

$$b^2 = 36$$

$$b = 6$$

17. **The correct answer is E.** The first step in solving this problem is to put the equation in the slope intercept form of a line, $y = mx + b$, where b is the y-intercept:

$$\frac{1}{5}y = x - \frac{1}{5}$$

$$y = 5x - 1$$

The y-intercept is -1.

18. **The correct answer is H.** The best way to solve this problem is to perform the operation under the square root sign, using the FOIL method:

$$(x + 2)(x - 2)$$

Multiply the first terms: $(x)(x) = x^2$

Multiply the outside terms: $(x)(-2) = -2x$

Multiply the inside terms: $(x)(2) = 2x$

Multiply the last terms: $(2)(-2) = -4$

Now, add the like terms.

$$x^2 + -2x + 2x - 4 = x^2 - 4$$

This value should be under the square root sign, $\sqrt{x^2 - 4}$.

19. **The correct answer is B.** The area of a rectangle is calculated by multiplying the length by the width. You are given that the area is $9w^2 - 1$ and the width is $3w + 1$. Substitute these values into the formula Area = length × width:

$$9w^2 - 1 = \text{length}(3w + 1)$$

$$\frac{9w^2 - 1}{3w + 1} = \text{length}$$

Factoring $9w^2 - 1$ gives you $(3w + 1)(3w - 1)$.

Canceling the $(3w + 1)$ from the numerator and denominator leaves you with $3w - 1$.

20. **The correct answer is J.** To solve this problem, first recognize that to get the sum of two numbers, you add the numbers $(x + y)$. Next, pick some numbers for x and y and try the answer choices:

Answer choice F: $x + y$ is not always 0, because x could be -1 and y could be 2, making $x + y = -1 + 2 = 1$.

Answer choice G: $x + y$ is not always positive, because x could be -2 and y could be 1, making $x + y = -2 + 1 = -1$.

Answer choice H: $x + y$ is not always negative; you just determined that it could be 1.

Answer choice J: it is possible for $x + y$ to be any real number (which includes 0).

Answer choice K: $x + y$ can be 0, because x could be -1 and y could be 1, making $x + y = -1 + 1 = 0$.

21. **The correct answer is C.** To solve this problem, you need to factor $3x^2 + 3x - 18$.

$$3x^2 + 3x - 18 = 0$$

Divide by 3 to simplify: $x^2 + x - 6 = 0$

$$(x + \underline{\quad})(x - \underline{\quad}) = 0$$

Find two numbers that when added together give you 1, and that when multiplied together give you -6. The only numbers that will work are 3 and -2. $(x + 3)$ and $(x - 2)$ are factors of $3x^2 + 3x - 18$, but only $(x + 3)$ is an answer choice.

22. **The correct answer is K.** To find the sum of the two solutions, you must first find the solutions. Solutions to equations are found by factoring. Because the last value in the equation is negative (-18), you know that the solution sets will be "x plus some number" and "x minus some number." Next, find two numbers that when multiplied together give you -18, and when added together give you 7. The only numbers

that work are 9 and -2. So, your solution sets become $(x + 9)$ and $(x - 2)$. To find the solutions, set each of those sets equal to zero, and solve for x:

$$(x + 9) = 0; x = -9$$

$$(x - 2) = 0; x = 2$$

The sum of 2 and -9 is -7.

23. **The correct answer is C.** Since the two triangles are similar, the ratio of the sides is the same. If the shortest leg on the smaller triangle is 3 and the shortest leg on the larger triangle is 6, then the lengths of the other two sides of the larger triangle are twice the lengths of the sides of the smaller triangle. The lengths of the larger triangle are 6, 10, and 14. To find the perimeter, add the lengths of all of the sides.

$$6 + 10 + 14 = 30$$

24. **The correct answer is J.** Translate this word problem into an equation. Since you are solving for the student's age, let the variable x represent her age.

Square her age: x^2

Subtract 18 times her age: $x^2 - 18x$

Set it equal to 40: $x^2 - 18x = 40$

Subtract 40 from both sides and factor the equation using the FOIL method:

$$x^2 - 18x - 40 = 0$$

$$(x - 20)(x + 2) = 0$$

$$x - 20 = 0 \text{ so } x = 20$$

$$x + 2 = 0 \text{ so } x = -2$$

Because an age cannot be negative, the student must be 20 years old.

25. **The correct answer is E.** The question asks you to reduce the equation to simpler terms. First, remove $\sqrt{2}$ from the denominator by multiplying the numerator and denominator by $\sqrt{2}$:

$$\frac{\left(4x - \sqrt{2}\right)}{\sqrt{2}} \times \frac{\sqrt{2}}{\sqrt{2}}$$

$$\frac{\sqrt{2}\left(4x - \sqrt{2}\right)}{\sqrt{2}\left(\sqrt{2}\right)}$$

Distribute $\sqrt{2}$ as follows:

$$\frac{4x\sqrt{2} - 2}{2}$$

Now, factor out the 2:

$$\frac{4x\sqrt{2}-2}{2}=\frac{2\left(2x\sqrt{2}-1\right)}{2}$$

The twos will cancel each other out to leave you with $2x\sqrt{2}-1$.

26. **The correct answer is F.** To solve this problem, set up a proportion: $84.00 is to x as 24 calendars is to (24 + 10) calendars.

$$\frac{84}{x}=\frac{24}{34};\text{ solve for }x$$

$$24x = 2,856$$

$$x = 119$$

Allen would make $119.00.

27. **The correct answer is D.** Since the answer choices are all decimals, convert 14 into its decimal equivalent, which is 0.25. Now add 0.25 to 0.375, remembering to align the decimal points:

$$\begin{array}{r}0.375\\+\ 0.250\\\hline 0.625\end{array}$$

28. **The correct answer is J.** The degree measure of any triangle is 180°. $\angle R$ is part of both $\triangle RTS$ and $\triangle RUV$. The three angles in each triangle must add up to 180°; $a + b + 35° = 180°$. Therefore, both $a + b$ and $c + d = 145°$. If each pair of angles is equal to 145°, then the four angles together are equal to twice that, or 290°.

29. **The correct answer is E.** To solve this problem, perform the operations that follow:

$$(1.181 + 0.019) = 1.2$$

$$3(1.155) - 5(.533) =$$

$$3.465 - 2.665 = 0.8$$

Now you are left with $\frac{1.2}{0.8}$. Divide 1.2 by 0.8 (1.2 ÷ 0.8) to get 1.5.

30. **The correct answer is G.** This problem requires you to perform the operations in the correct order and then solve for x:

$$22 - 2(3 + x) = (x + 4)$$

$$22 - 6 - 2x = x + 4$$

$$16 - 2x = x + 4$$

$$16 - 4 = x + 2x$$

$$12 = 3x$$

$$4 = x$$

31. **The correct answer is B.** To calculate the surface area of the figure shown, break it down into a rectangle and a right triangle, as shown below.

Calculate the area of the rectangle (l × w):

$$65 \times 40 = 2,600$$

Because the length of the top side is 75, and the length of the bottom side is 65, the length of the short side, or base, of the triangle must be 10.

Calculate the area of the triangle

$12(b)(h)$, where b is the base and h is the height:

$$\frac{1}{2}(10)(40) =$$

$$\frac{1}{2}(400) = 200$$

Now, add the area of the rectangle (2,600) to the area of the triangle (200) to get a total surface area of 2,800.

32. **The correct answer is G.** The first step in solving this problem is to put the given equation into the slope-intercept form, $y = mx + b$, where m is the slope:

$$4y - 3x = 8$$

$$4y = 3x + 8$$

$$y = \frac{3}{4}x + 2$$

The slope of this line is $\frac{3}{4}$. By definition, parallel lines have the same slope.

33. **The correct answer is C.** If you are given two points on a line, you can find the midpoint by applying the following: $\frac{(x_1 + x_2)}{2}$ and $\frac{(y_1 + y_2)}{2}$

Plug in the given points, (−2, −1) and (3, 4), and solve:

$$x = \frac{(-2+3)}{2} = \frac{1}{2}$$

$$y = \frac{(-1+4)}{2} = \frac{3}{2}$$

The midpoint of the line segment is $\left(\frac{1}{2}, \frac{3}{2}\right)$.

34. The correct answer is H. A good approach to answering this question is to look first at the high end of the interval. You know that $100^2 = 10,000$, which is not in the interval. Therefore, the largest perfect square in the interval must be 99, which has 2 digits. Eliminate answer choices F and G. Use common sense and trial and error to find the smallest perfect square in the interval:

Start with 30 (an easy number to work with):

$30^2 = 900$, which is not in the interval.

Try 31: $31^2 = 961$, which is not in the interval.

Try 32: $32^2 = 1,024$, which is in the interval.

So, the perfect squares range from 32 to 99, which means that the positive square root of any number in the given interval must have 2 digits.

35. The correct answer is E. The question asks you to solve for c, so isolate c on the left side of the equation:

$$a = bc - 2$$
$$a - bc = -2$$
$$-bc = -a - 2$$
$$bc = a + 2$$
$$c = \frac{a+2}{b}$$

36. The correct answer is H. Because the question asks about angle x, and the answer choices include sin, cos, and tan, the best approach to answering the question is to determine sin, cos, and tan of angle x:

$$\sin x = \frac{\text{opp}}{\text{hyp}} = \frac{12}{13}.$$

This is choice H.

37. The correct answer is B. Solve the inequality for x as follows:

$$\sqrt{(x+1)} < 4$$

Square both sides:

$$x + 1 < 16$$
$$x < 15$$

Also, when $x < -1$, $x + 1$ will be negative. You cannot take the square root of a negative number, so $x \geq -1$. Therefore, the correct answer is $-1 \leq x < 15$.

38. The correct answer is H. The formula for the area of a trapezoid with parallel bases is $\frac{(h)(b_1+b_2)}{2}$, where b_1 and b_2 are the bases and h is the height.

This can be seen as the average of the bases multiplied by the height of the figure, as follows:

$$\frac{(16)(24)}{2} = \frac{384}{2} = 192$$

39. The correct answer is B. If the x-coordinate is 3 less than twice the y-coordinate, then $x = 2y - 3$. Put this equation into the slope-intercept form of a line, $y = mx + b$, where m is the slope, and b is the y-intercept:

$$x = 2y - 3$$
$$-2y = -x - 3$$
$$y = \frac{1}{2}x + \frac{3}{2}$$

The y-intercept is $\frac{3}{2}$.

40. The correct answer is G. When dealing with averages where all elements are weighted equally, you can consider each element to be equal to the average. This means that if Casey's average after five games was 126, each of her five scores can be seen as 126, and the total of her scores is 5×126, or 630. Add her 6th score to the total and divide by 6 to get her new average:

$$\frac{630+142}{6} = \frac{772}{6} = 128.66, \text{ which is closest to } 129.$$

41. The correct answer is D. By definition, the longer side will be opposite the larger angle. So, the angle opposite the side with a length of 60 is the larger of the unknown angles. (The measure of the angle opposite the hypotenuse is 90.) The sine of any acute angle is calculated by dividing the length of the side opposite to the acute angle by the hypotenuse ($\sin = \frac{\text{opp}}{\text{hyp}}$). This means that the sine of the larger of the unknown angles is $\frac{60}{65}$.

42. The correct answer is F. First, notice that ab^2 is the greatest common factor of a^2b^2 and ab^3. Therefore, ab^2 must be equal to 45. The question asks you to solve for b, so set ab^2 equal to 45 and substitute the answer choices for b. The answer choice that correctly solves the equation could be a value of b:

Answer Choice F: When $b = 3$, then $a = 5$ because $ab^2 = a \times 3^2 = 5 \times 9 = 45$.

Therefore, b could equal 3. Since this answer choice works, it is the correct answer.

43. The correct answer is C. The formula for arc length is $\left(\dfrac{n}{360}\right) \times 2\pi r$, where n is the measure of the degree of the arc, which is always twice the measure of the inscribed angle. Since the inscribed angle of B is 60 degrees, the measure of the degree of the arc is 120 degrees. The radius is given as 3 inches, so the length of arc AC is

$$\left(\frac{120}{360}\right) \times 2\pi(3), \text{ or } \frac{1}{3} \times 6\pi, \text{ which is } 2\pi.$$

44. The correct answer is G. To solve this problem, first locate the value of $f(2)$ in the first table.

According to the table, $f(2) = 3$, so $g(f(2)) = g(3)$.

Now, locate the value of $g(3)$ on the second table: $g(3) = -2$.

45. The correct answer is E. To answer this question, you need to factor the equation and set each group equal to 0:

$$x^2 + \frac{5}{4}x = 0$$

$$x\left(x + \frac{5}{4}\right) = 0$$

$$x = 0, \text{ and}$$

$$x + \frac{5}{4} = 0$$

$$x = -\frac{5}{4}$$

The solutions to this equation are $x = 0$ and $x = -\dfrac{5}{4}$.

46. The correct answer is F. The first step in solving this problem is to multiply 761.18 by 4:

$$761.18 \times 4 = 3,044.72$$

Next, to find the correct scientific notation, count the number of places that the decimal point moves from 3,044.72, to 3.04.

$$3 \quad 0 \quad 4 \quad 4.72 \rightarrow 3.04$$
$$\underset{3 \quad 2 \quad 1}{\underline{\lfloor \quad \lfloor \quad \lfloor \quad \rfloor}}$$

The decimal point moved 3 places to the left, so 3,044.72 is approximately equal to 3.04×10^3.

47. The correct answer is D. The triangle described is a special right triangle, where the measures of the angles are 90°, 60°, and 30°. Since the shortest side is opposite the smallest angle, and the hypotenuse is the longest side, the angle adjacent to both the shortest side and the hypotenuse must be 60°. Test this by drawing a diagram:

48. The correct answer is J. The best way to solve this problem is to divide the pentagon into a triangle and a rectangle, as shown below:

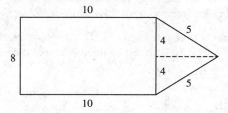

Calculate the area (lw) of the rectangle: $108 \times 80 = 80$.

Since the pentagon will have a larger area than the rectangle, eliminate answer choices F, G, and H. The area of the triangle is calculated by using the formula $\dfrac{1}{2}(b)(h)$, where b is the base and h is the height. You know that the base is 8. Determine the height by using the Pythagorean Theorem, which says that $a^2 + b^2 = c^2$, where c is the hypotenuse:

$$a^2 + b^2 = c^2$$

$$4^2 + b^2 = 5^2$$

$$16 + b^2 = 25$$

$$b^2 = 9$$

$$b = 3$$

The area of the triangle is $\dfrac{1}{2}(8)(3)$ or $\dfrac{1}{2}(24)$, which is 12. Add this to the area of the rectangle $(80 + 12)$ to get 92.

49. The correct answer is A. The formula for a circle is $(x-a)^2 + (y-b)^2 = r^2$, where (a, b) is the center of the circle and r is the radius of the circle. The first step is to determine the radius of the circle. The question gives you the center of the circle as $(4, 3)$ and another point on the circle as $(0, 3)$. Since the y is constant, these two points form a straight line from the center to the edge of the circle, or the radius. Point $(0, 3)$ is 4 units away from $(4, 3)$ on the x-axis, so the radius is 4. Use the points given for the center of the circle, $(4, 3)$, and the radius in the formula:

$$(x-4)^2 + (y-3)^2 = 4^2$$
$$(x-4)^2 + (y-3)^2 = 16$$

50. The correct answer is J. Based on the given slopes, the lines are perpendicular, so eliminate answer choice F. To determine the point where the two lines intersect, you need to find the values of x and y that make the equations equal to each other. Set the equations equal to each other and solve for x first:

$$2x - 10 = -\frac{1}{2}x + 5$$
$$2\frac{1}{2}x = 15$$
$$x = 6$$

Now that you know the value of $x = 6$, substitute 6 into one of the equations to solve for y:

$$y = -\frac{1}{2}(6) + 5$$
$$y = -3 + 5$$
$$y = 2$$

The point where the two lines intersect is $(6, 2)$, answer choice J. Note that you can eliminate answer choices G and K because they do not have an x-coordinate equal to 6.

51. The correct answer is D. The formula for the circumference of a circle is $2\pi r$, where r is the radius of the circle. If the radius of this circle is equal to $\frac{34}{\pi}$, then the circumference would be $2\pi\left(\frac{34}{\pi}\right)$. You can cancel out the π, and multiply $2(34)$ to get 68.

52. The correct answer is F. To answer this question, recall that 3.14 radians $= \pi$; therefore, 6.28 radians $= 2\pi$, which is equivalent to one cycle of a sine curve, as shown in answer choice F. Also, sine starts at 0, so you can eliminate answer choices G, J, and K.

53. The correct answer is E. The first step in solving this problem is to solve $x = 3a + 7$ for a:

$$x = 3a + 7$$
$$x - 7 = 3a$$
$$\frac{x-7}{3} = a$$

Now you can substitute $\frac{x-7}{3} = a$ for a in the second equation, and solve for y:

$$y = 6 + a$$
$$y = 6 + \frac{x-7}{3}$$
$$y = \frac{18}{3} + \frac{x-7}{3}$$
$$y = \frac{11+x}{3}$$

54. The correct answer is G. To solve this problem, first calculate the length of each edge of the large cube:

$$\text{Volume} = \text{edge, or side(s) cubed}$$
$$64 = s^3$$
$$4 = s$$

You are given that the small cube has edges that are $\frac{1}{2}$ the length of those of the large cube, so the small cube has edges equal to 2. The volume of the small cube is 2^3, or 8.

55. The correct answer is D. By definition, the sum of supplementary angles is 180°. Therefore, the supplementary acute angle to a 110° angle must be 70°.

56. The correct answer is G. The sine of any acute angle is calculated by dividing the length of the side opposite to the acute angle by the hypotenuse ($\sin = \frac{\text{opp}}{\text{hyp}}$). It may help you to draw a diagram to solve this problem:

Use the Pythagorean Theorem to calculate the length of the hypotenuse:

$$a^2 + b^2 = c^2$$

$$3^2 + 3^2 = c^2$$

$$9 + 9 = c^2$$

$$18 = c^2$$

$$\sqrt{18} = c; \ \sqrt{9}\sqrt{2} = c; \ 3\sqrt{2} = c$$

So, the sine of angle α is $\dfrac{3}{3\sqrt{2}}$.

57. **The correct answer is C.** Integers can be even or odd, and positive or negative. Pick real numbers to substitute into the expressions in each roman numeral, then eliminate any roman numerals that do not always yield an odd number.

Roman numeral I: x^3: substitute 1, 2, –1, and –2 for x:

$1^3 = 1$; $2^3 = 8$, which is not an odd number, so stop here and eliminate answer choices A and D.

Roman numeral II: $x + 1$; substitute 1, 2, –1, and –2 for x:

$1 + 1 = 2$, which is not an odd number, so stop here and eliminate answer choices B and E.

This means that answer choice C must be correct. Whenever you multiply any integer by 2, the result will be even; when you then add 1, the result will always be odd.

58. **The correct answer is J.** Probability refers to the likelihood of something happening. How many white chips should Jenny put into the container so that she is likely to draw a red chip on every fifth draw? Try the answer choices.

F: If she puts in 1 white chip, then the probability of drawing a red chip is 4 (red chips) out of 5 (total chips). Eliminate answer choice F.

G: If she puts in 5 white chips, then the probability of drawing a red chip is 4 (red chips) out of 9 (total chips). Eliminate answer choice G.

H: If she puts in 9 white chips, then the probability of drawing a red chip is 4 (red chips) out of 13 (total chips). Eliminate answer choice H.

J: If she puts in 16 white chips, then the probability of drawing a red chip is 4 (red chips) out of 20 (total chips), which is equivalent to 1 out of 5, or $\dfrac{1}{5}$.

She should add 16 white chips.

59. **The correct answer is B.** To solve this problem, it might be helpful to draw the given lines in the (x, y) coordinate plane, as shown here:

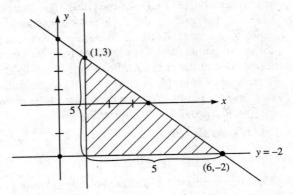

You are given that $x - 1 = 0$, so $x = 1$ will be represented by a vertical line that crosses the x-axis at 1. You are also given that $y + 2 = 0$, so $y = -2$ will be represented by a horizontal line that crosses the y-axis at –2. Finally, you are given that $x + y = 4$, so $y = -x + 4$ will be a line that crosses the y-axis at 4, and has a slope of –1.

You can see from the figure that the area of the triangle will be $\dfrac{1}{2}(5 \times 5) = \dfrac{25}{2}$.

60. **The correct answer is J.** Because this is an absolute value question, remember that x will have two distinct values—one positive, the other negative. Solve for both values of x in terms of a as follows:

$$x - a = 9 \text{ and } -x - a = 9$$

$$x = 9 + a \text{ and } -x = 9 - a$$

$$x = a + 9 \text{ and } x = a - 9$$

These equations can be represented on the number line as shown:

| –9 | $x = a - 9$ | a | $x = a + 9$ | 9 |

The distance on the number line from –9 to 9 is 18.

Reading Test Explanations

PASSAGE I

1. **The best answer is C.** The passage states that Squire Newcome's son "was a thorn in the side of his father, who had endeavored in vain to mould him according to his idea of propriety." This suggests that Squire Newcome had some trouble disciplining his son, which best supports answer choice C. The other answer choices are not supported by the passage.

2. **The best answer is G.** The second paragraph states that Squire Newcome had "a very exalted conception of his own position, and the respect which he felt to be his due, not only from his own household, but from all who approached him." This statement, along with other information in the passage, best supports answer choice G.

3. **The best answer is B.** According to the passage, "Feeling a natural reluctance to appear before her employer with her hands covered with dough, she hastily washed them." This took time, however, so she was delayed. The other answer choices are not supported by the passage.

4. **The best answer is F.** The conversation between Hannah and Squire Newcome suggests that Hannah was not very well educated, so eliminate answer choice G. The words *condescending* and *pompous* can be used to describe Squire Newcome, not Hannah, so eliminate answer choice H. Nothing in the passage suggests that Hannah was lazy, so eliminate answer choice J.

5. **The best answer is D.** The third paragraph states that Squire Newcome's wife "did not live long after marriage." The paragraph goes on to suggest that the reason for this is that she found her husband and her marriage to be cold. Based on the description of Squire Newcome, you can infer that this coldness was the result of his preoccupation with his position in the community, and that he cared more about that relationship than he did about his marriage. The other answer choices are not supported by the passage.

6. **The best answer is F.** The context of the passage makes it clear that Squire Newcome thought very highly of himself, so it makes sense that he would have an "exalted," or "elevated" conception of his own position. The other answer choices are not supported by the context of the passage.

7. **The best answer is C.** According to the last paragraph, Hannah stepped toward the window, looked out, and immediately "gave a shrill scream." This suggests that she was greatly alarmed or surprised by something she saw. The other answer choices are not supported by the passage.

8. **The best answer is G.** Squire Newcome is depicted in the passage as being rigid, as mentioned in the first paragraph, and dignified, as mentioned in the second paragraph. The statement supports this depiction by suggesting another way in which the Squire is rigid and dignified, or formal. While Squire Newcome may be wealthy and solemn, the phrase does not contribute to this depiction of him. The other answer choices are not supported by the passage.

9. **The best answer is C.** The passage indicates that Squire Newcome's use of the word *IMMEJIATELY* is an attempt to place importance and emphasis on the word *immediately*. It is clear that Hannah did not recognize that attempt, and simply copied her employer's use of the language. The other answer choices are not supported by the passage.

10. **The best answer is J.** According to the passage, it was more important to Ben to have fun than to listen to his father. The passage states that Ben "was constantly bursting out in new directions, in spite of his father's numerous and rather prosy lectures." This best supports the idea that Ben was *indifferent* to his father's instructions on how he was to behave. There is nothing in the passage to indicate that Ben felt "great admiration" or "deep respect" for his father, so eliminate answer choices F and H. *Disdain* means "hatred" or "contempt," which are too strong based on the context of the passage, so eliminate answer choice G.

PASSAGE II

11. **The best answer is D.** The passage gives a brief biographical outline of the work done by Marcus Garvey, and repeatedly states how he "did many things to inspire his race." The passage also speaks of how "Today, there is a United Negro Improvement Association that promotes many of the same values that Garvey preached back in the 1920s." Answer choice D most clearly exhibits the lasting influence of Garvey's work and correctly encompasses the main idea and primary purpose of the passage.

12. **The best answer is G.** The passage mentions Garvey's work to advance African Americans both politically and socially. An example of Garvey's work for social advancement is his organization of "the Universal Negro Improvement Association in Harlem" and "many African American-owned businesses and industries." An example of Garvey's work for political advancement is his organization of "a thirty-one-day conclave in Madison Square Garden,

which resulted in the Back to Africa Movement and the Declaration of Black Rights."

13. **The best answer is C.** The passage states, "Garvey's most powerful enemies came from his controversial stance against the National Association for the Advancement of Colored People and the peaceful civil rights movement. Garvey argued that the NAACP only supported and helped certain members of the African American population. His harsh comments against the peaceful NAACP and the civil rights movement turned many important people against him." This best supports answer choice C.

14. **The best answer is H.** The passage states, "World War I had ended. Many African American soldiers had fought in the war and died for their country. However, when the surviving African American soldiers returned to the United States, they still found themselves facing discrimination and prejudice." This best supports answer choice H.

15. **The best answer is C.** The word "lofty" is often used to indicate that a person has "high," or idealistic goals. The context of the paragraph best supports answer choice C.

16. **The best answer is G.** The passage states, "The UNIA was very impressive, numbering one thousand divisions around the world, with thousands of members." This best supports answer choice G.

17. **The best answer is C.** The passage states that Garvey achieved success in literary, financial, political, social, and academic fields. This far-reaching influence allowed Garvey to control many aspects of those fields because he was so successful.

18. **The best answer is J.** The passage states that the following events were occurring when Garvey arrived in America: "Bloody incidents like the *East St. Louis race riots* and the Red Summer broke out across the country. Despite these tense conditions, the *Negro Era* began to emerge and the *Harlem Renaissance* started to gain national recognition." Garvey supported the Back to Africa Movement, which occurred after his arrival.

19. **The best answer is C.** Garvey's behavior was described as "blunt" and he had "bold ideas." He would not be described as "timid." He was also very ambitious and successful in many areas.

20. **The best answer is J.** The passage states, "The UNIA was very impressive, numbering one thousand divisions around the world, with thousands of members." The other answer choices are not supported by details in the passage.

21. **The best answer is C.** The passage states that "during her teenage years, my grandmother did not spend her time giggling with friends at slumber parties or going to the movies." In addition, the passage reveals, "The secret dreams and fantasies so common to teenage girls today were absent from my grandmother's life as she focused on earning money to continue her education and to help her family." This best supports answer choice C.

22. **The best answer is G.** The passage states, "When my grandfather suffered a stroke, my grandmother learned to drive at the age of sixty and faithfully shuttled her husband back and forth between endless doctor's appointments and hospital visits." Therefore, we know that the grandmother learned to drive late in life in order to take her husband to doctor's appointments. This best supports answer choice G.

23. **The best answer is D.** The passage states, "The grace, determination, and work ethic she had acquired in her teenage years during the Great Depression served her well as she faced the many challenges of married life." The beginning of the passage talks about how and why the grandmother acquired her personality traits. The rest of the passage speaks about how the grandmother used these personality traits throughout her life.

24. **The best answer is H.** Based on the context of the paragraph, *muzzled* is another word for *suppressed*. The narrator is telling us that her grandmother's spirit prevailed and would not be suppressed even though the grandmother faced great hardship throughout her life. The other answer choices are not supported by the passage.

25. **The best answer is A.** The passage begins by asking the question, "How did people in the 1930s manage to survive the Great Depression when unemployment skyrocketed, land and homes were repossessed, and proud women and men had to stand in long lines to receive government aid to feed their families?" The rest of the passage explains how one woman survived the Great Depression and used what she learned during that period to succeed in life. This best supports answer choice A.

26. **The best answer is H.** Strength, determination, and spirit were qualities that the narrator's grandmother and her fellow survivors had. The narrator suggests that having these qualities was what helped the "Great Depression generation" achieve the American Dream, and also that having these qualities could help others achieve their dreams.

27. **The best answer is B.** The narrator is pointing out that it took bravery and determination to learn how to drive so late in life, and that her grandmother's bravery had not diminished over the years.

28. **The best answer is G.** The passage states, "Although my grandmother never did move back to a farm, the seeds of goodness and virtue she planted in the big city sprouted and flourished." These seeds were not planted in a garden at a city home. These seeds were a metaphor for the grandmother's ability to grow and spread goodness and virtue during her life.

29. **The best answer is D.** The passage states, "In the early 1920s, life had never been better in America. The stock market was booming, people were becoming fabulously wealthy, and carefree flappers danced the night away listening to a new wave of music fresh from Harlem. However, all of this changed when the stock market crashed in 1929. Overnight, millionaires became paupers and the whole nation began to crumble. In 1932, my grandmother was fifteen years old. Within three years of the stock market crashing, she and her family had lost their car, farm, and dreams." The narrator is pointing out that the wealth and light-heartedness of the 1920s is in sharp contrast to the hardships of the 1930s.

30. **The best answer is G.** The narrator expresses pride in her grandmother and her grandmother's accomplishments by telling about the trials and adversities that her grandmother overcame throughout her life. The narrator also speaks about her grandmother's strong work ethic, goodness, and strength. This best supports answer choice G.

PASSAGE IV

31. **The best answer is A.** The passage suggests that, because phytoplankton are among the organisms harmed when the upwelling decreases the supply of cooler water to the euphotic zone, the fish that eat phytoplankton would see a decrease in their food supply. This would, in turn, harm the fishing industry. The other answer choices are not supported by the passage.

32. **The best answer is J.** The passage states that "some common impacts on the United States include fewer tropical storms in the Atlantic region; a dry monsoon around Texas, Arizona, and New Mexico; an especially dry fall and winter around Oregon and Washington; an extremely wet winter in the Gulf Coast; and a warmer-than-average fall and winter in many Midwestern States." Additionally, the passage states that El Niño caused flooding in Peru.

33. **The best answer is C.** The first paragraph compares the sea levels of Indonesia and Ecuador, explains the behavior of trade winds during normal, or non-El Niño, years and indicates what El Niño is. It does not explain a consequence of abnormal trade wind activity.

34. **The best answer is H.** The passage states that "El Niño occurs on an average of every four to five years, and can last up to a year and a half."

35. **The best answer is C.** The end of the passage details the problems El Niño might cause certain industries, but it also gives advice about how the different industries can help prevent some of the disastrous effects. For instance, the passage states, "The natural gas and fuel industries can adjust their production and distribution levels to decrease losses when warm El Niño winter conditions are expected." This best supports answer choice C.

36. **The best answer is H.** The passage states, "Industries directly affected by weather or climate compose almost 10 percent of the Gross Domestic Product (GDP) in the United States. Weather and climate also impact insurance industries, services, retail and wholesale trade, and manufacturing. Nearly 25 percent of the GDP may be directly or indirectly somehow affected by weather and climate." These statements inform the reader that almost all of the industries can be impacted by El Niño and that a significant percent of the GDP could be affected.

37. **The best answer is B.** The word *ravage* is used in this passage to describe the damage that storms cause to crops and property. The other answer choices are not supported by the passage.

38. **The best answer is G.** The authors of both passages make several claims regarding the formation and impacts of El Niño and support these claims by providing evidence and examples.

39. **The best answer is C.** Since both passages discuss the global effects of El Niño, answer choice C is correct. The other answer choices are elements found in either Passage A or Passage B, but not both.

40. **The best answer is F.** According to Passage A, "El Niño occurs on an average of every four to five years, and can last up to a year and a half …" Information regarding the duration of El Niño is not mentioned in Passage B.

SCIENCE TEST EXPLANATIONS

PASSAGE I

1. **The best answer is A.** Both scientists directly state that the movement of tectonic plates created the continents. None of the other answer choices are supported by information the passage.

2. **The best answer is G.** Scientist 1 states that circular motion of the asthenosphere causes "the plates to collide with each other." The passage goes on to say that earthquakes occur in the same location as the circular motion, implying that where circular motion occurs, earthquakes also occur. The other answer choices are not supported by the passage.

3. **The best answer is A.** The passage states that tectonic plates move "within the fluid, lower layer of Earth's crust, the asthenosphere." This best supports answer choice A.

4. **The best answer is K.** Scientist 2 states that, since the formation of the continents, there has been little movement of the tectonic plates. The movement that does occur is released in "small bursts . . . along a fault line." It is also "apparent . . . [in] the fact that there are certain areas that are more affected by earthquakes than others." In other words, Scientist 2 claims that the small bursts of energy that occur on fault lines cause earthquakes, answer choice K. The other answer choices are not supported by the passage.

5. **The best answer is B.** The passage directly states that the "fluid, lower layer of the Earth's crust" is the asthenosphere, answer choice B.

6. **The best answer is F.** Scientist 1 states that a "large burst of energy . . . is what created the separate continents." Scientist 2 states that the continents were formed from "a sudden burst of energy" and that now only "small bursts of energy" occur, causing earthquakes. You can assume from this statement that Scientist 2 believes that a large burst of energy must have caused the separation of the continents. The other answer choices are contradictory to the statements made by both scientists.

7. **The best answer is A.** Scientist 1 states that the "tectonic plates are constantly moving." Therefore, if the tectonic plates did not move, Scientist 1's viewpoint would be weakened. If the tectonic plates rested on the "rigid upper crust," they would not be "constantly moving."

PASSAGE II

8. **The best answer is G.** The passage states that the breakdown of wood into charred wood, ash, and volatile gas occurs during thermal degradation, answer choice G. While the ignition temperature must be reached before thermal degradation can begin, the ignition temperature is not the process in which the breakdown of wood occurs, so you can eliminate answer choice H. The other answer choices are not supported by information in the passage.

9. **The best answer is A.** According to the passage, the study focused on protective coatings that "act as an insulator to protect against fire damage during . . . thermal degradation." Thermal degradation is the process in which the materials of a fuel (wood) break down into several byproducts, including char and smoke. The other answer choices are not supported by information in the passage.

10. **The best answer is G.** The question requires you to look at the line that represents untreated wood in Figure 1 and find the part of the line where a small increase in temperature results in the greatest decrease in mass loss %. This part of the line will represent the temperatures at which the untreated wood lost the greatest percent of mass. As you can see in Figure 1, the line that represents untreated wood slowly declines at first (between 200° and 260°C), rapidly declines at temperatures between 260° and 400°C, and levels off to a more gradual decrease in mass after 400°. Therefore, the greatest amount of mass is lost between 260° and 400°C, answer choice G.

11. **The best answer is A.** Figure 1 shows the amount of mass that is lost as the temperature that the plywood was exposed to is increased. At each of the temperatures tested, Fire retardant 3 consistently had the greatest amount of mass remaining. According to the passage, a fire retardant is more effective when it reduces the amount of damage caused by combustion. Therefore, Fire retardant 3 is most effective at suppressing combustion. The other answer choices are not supported by the passage.

12. **The best answer is K.** To answer this question, you must find the point on Figure 1 where the line representing Fire retardant 1 meets the line representing Fire retardant 2. This point represents the moment when both fire retardant wood samples (1 and 2) experience the same percent of mass loss. Once you have found the point where the two lines meet, follow it down to determine the temperature at this point. According to Figure 1, the two lines meet at approximately 625°C, answer choice K.

PASSAGE III

13. **The best answer is D.** Scientist 1 claims that "Planting new trees and preserving existing trees is not a good long-term solution" and "may give people the impression that no other measures are needed to reduce carbon dioxide emissions." Scientist 1 goes on to list many ways in which carbon dioxide emissions can be reduced. Based on this information, answer choice D is best. Answer choices A, B, and C can be eliminated because they are not supported by the passage.

14. **The best answer is F.** The question requires you to determine what might cause increased carbon dioxide levels during a hot, dry summer. Common sense tells you that hot, dry summers are related to the occurrence of drought and forest fires. The passage states that forest fires and droughts rapidly increase carbon dioxide levels. Based on this information, you can assume that answer choice F is correct. The remaining answer choices cannot be supported by information in the passage.

15. **The best answer is C.** Scientist 2 directly states that planting and preserving trees "can help reduce the destruction of the world's forests and protect biodiversity." The other answer choices are not supported by the passage.

16. **The best answer is H.** All of the other answer choices are mentioned in the passage. While "sunlight energy" is mentioned, it is not the same thing as "solar power," usually heat or electricity, that is created from the sun's radiation.

17. **The best answer is B.** According to the passage, Scientist 1 believes that planting and preserving trees is "not a good long-term solution" and Scientist 2 believes that it is a "great long-term solution" to reducing the levels of carbon dioxide in the atmosphere. This best supports answer choice B.

18. **The best answer is F.** Scientist 1 claims that "planting trees . . . accelerates climate change in snow-covered areas by reducing the amount of sunlight energy that is directed back into space." You can assume that this occurs because the leaves and branches reduce the amount of sunlight that can be reflected off the snow. If it is found that newly planted trees in snow-covered areas have not accelerated climate change, then Scientist 1 would most likely say that the leaves and branches were not large enough to block sunlight and cause a change in climate.

19. **The best answer is B.** Scientist 2 says that "although some carbon dioxide is released when the leaves decompose, planting or preserving trees is still an effective means by which to greatly reduce the carbon dioxide levels in the atmosphere." If most of the carbon dioxide was emitted when a plant decomposed, planting or preserving trees would not be a great way to help reduce the carbon dioxide levels.

PASSAGE IV

20. **The best answer is G.** The passage states that "chlorophyll is produced in response to sunlight," which best supports answer choice G. The other answer choices are not supported by details in the passage.

21. **The best answer is D.** To answer this question, locate yellow in the Resulting Colors column of Table 1. Next, move to the left to see which compound type corresponds with yellow. The information in Table 1 indicates that the presence of lycopene, flavone, and carotene will result in yellow leaves.

22. **The best answer is H.** The first step in answering this question is to answer either yes or no. It is clear in the passage that light levels do affect color change, so eliminate answer choices F and G. The passage states that "chlorophyll is produced in response to sunlight" and "decreasing light levels cause chlorophyll production to slow." Chlorophyll is responsible for the green color of leaves; answer choice H is correct.

23. **The best answer is B.** The passage states that leaves "containing primarily anthocyanins will appear red," answer choice B.

24. **The best answer is H.** To answer this question, look at Table 1, and find the column for Pigment Class. You will see that porphyrin yields only green leaves, so eliminate answer choice F. Chlorophyll is not a pigment class—it is a compound type—so eliminate answer choice G. Based on Table 2, flavonoid yields yellow, red, blue, and purple, so it has the most color variety.

PASSAGE V

25. **The best answer is C.** According to the passage, meerkat predators include eagles and jackals. Table 1 indicates that a constant loud chattering is produced when the sentry sees a jackal, eagle, or large snake. This information best supports answer choice C.

26. **The best answer is G.** The passage states that meerkats "will gather together, stand up, and turn their bellies to the sun, soaking up the sunlight." Since a solar panel also soaks up the sunlight, it makes sense that meerkats would be called the "Solar Panel of the Animal World" due to their habit of soaking up the morning sun, answer choice G.

27. **The best answer is D.** The passage states that "unlike other mongooses, meerkats live in large social communities," answer choice D.

28. **The best answer is F.** The results shown in Table 1 indicate that meerkat sentries will make one quick "chirp" at sunrise and sunset, when no possible alarm cue is observed. This suggests that meerkats vocalize for other reasons, and not just to warn each other of danger. The other answer choices are not supported by the results shown in Table 1.

29. **The best answer is B.** The observers must have assumed that the meerkats would recognize and understand what the different alarm calls meant, otherwise the study would have been pointless.

30. **The best answer is F.** The theory that alarm calls have special meanings would NOT be supported if the same alarm call was made to indicate more than one thing. The other answer choices all indicate different alarm calls being made to signal specific events, which, if they had occurred, would support the theory.

PASSAGE VI

31. **The best answer is A.** According to the passage, the animals have "mouths that expand to two times the size of their bodies . . . to maximize the size of prey that they can consume." This best supports answer choice A.

32. **The best answer is G.** The passage states that the midwater zone extends from 200 m to 2,000 m. According to Figure 1, this range includes the mesopelagic zone (that extends from 200 m to 1,000 m) and a portion of the bathypelagic zone (that extends from 1,000 m to 4,000 m).

33. **The best answer is D.** To answer this question, look at Table 1. The table shows that the snipe eel can be found in the ocean from depths of 40 to 550 m and at a maximum of 2,000 m. Now look at Figure 1. Since the snipe eel can be found anywhere between 40 and 2,000 m, determine which of the ocean zones fall within this range: a portion of the epipelagic zone, the entire mesopelagic zone, and a portion of the bathypelagic, answer choice D.

34. **The best answer is H.** The passage states that vertical migrators travel toward the surface at night, to "the uppermost part of their range of depth." According to Table 1, the Eelpout is found at depths ranging from 2,500 m to 5,000 m. The uppermost part of this range is 2,500 m, so that depth is most likely where the eelpouts would travel up to at night if they were vertical migrators.

35. **The best answer is C.** The question requires you to determine which species could survive at the broad range of temperatures that exist from the ocean's surface down to the sea floor. The temperature of the ocean water depends on the depth. The stout blacksmelt is normally found at depths of 225 m to 1,400 m, but it can also be found at depths of 6,700 m. This is the broadest range of any of the species listed, so answer choice C is correct.

36. **The best answer is H.** The best approach to solving this problem is process of elimination. All of the answer choices refer to snake length, so look at Table 1. Snake D is the longest snake, but it ranks 3rd in aggression, so eliminate answer choice F. By the same token, eliminate answer choice G. It does not appear that length has any effect on rank, so answer choice H is correct.

37. **The best answer is C.** Table 3 shows win-loss records for all of the snakes. You can logically conclude that the more dominant snake would have more wins. Therefore, the snake with the most wins would also have the safest eggs. According to Table 3, Snake C had the most wins.

38. **The best answer is G.** To solve this problem, compare the values given with the values listed in Table 1. Based on those values, the sixth snake is most similar to Snake D, which had an aggression rank of 3, and Snake A, which had an aggression rank of 2. Of the answer choices, G is best.

39. **The best answer is D.** To solve this problem, look at each roman numeral and decide if it answers the question. According to Table 1, there is not a direct relationship between age and the number of hisses. Therefore, roman numeral I does not meet the requirements stated in the question. Eliminate answer choices A and B, because they include roman numeral I. Table 1 also indicates that length is not directly related to the number of hisses. Eliminate answer choice C—this leaves you with answer choice D.

40. **The best answer is H.** The results of Experiment 2 are shown in Table 2. When Snake A encountered Snake C, Snake A won 15 times, and Snake C won 30 times. Therefore, they must have had a total of 45 encounters with each other.

215

EXTRA CHALLENGING ACT QUESTIONS EVERY TOP-SCORING STUDENT SHOULD KNOW

Introduction

Welcome to *215 Extra Challenging ACT Questions!* The questions in this section have been chosen because they are especially challenging for many test-takers. Your experience may vary. These questions are representative of the most difficult questions found on the ACT. Don't get discouraged if you struggle with them. Learn from your experience, and work toward maximizing your test score.

There are several different ways that the test-makers can create more difficult questions on the various sections. One of the more common is to simply make the questions more time-consuming. Since time is the limited resource when testing, questions that take longer to solve create stress. Of course, the subject matter may be advanced as well. For example, the Reading Test passages often include obscure vocabulary and complicated sentence structure. The question stems may be misleading and the distractor answer choices may often contain words from the passage or true statements that are not responsive to the question. But don't panic! The questions in this section can help you to identify subject matter that you need to review or learn before your real ACT.

Keep in mind that the only difficulty level that really matters is your subjective difficulty level. Even if the test-makers consider any given question to be an easier one, if you don't know the subject matter or don't recognize exactly what a given question is looking for, it will be difficult for you.

You will score significantly higher on your ACT if you take time to get to know all of the question types and how you respond to them, regardless of the objective difficulty level assigned by the test-makers. Use the questions in this section to identify any weak areas or gaps in your knowledge, and then work through the chapters and practice tests in the book. Even if you do well on these questions, you should still practice doing timed, in-format sections and full-length tests to sharpen your skills for test day. Endurance is especially important and can only be improved through practice.

Good luck!

ENGLISH

PASSAGE I

Return of the San Juan Capistrano Swallows

Whenever I think of springtime, I remember the return of the swallows to San Juan Capistrano in southern California. <u>When I was, growing up, my family</u> would
1
visit Capistrano every March to celebrate the Festival of the Swallows <u>with thousands</u> of other tourists.
2

This special event <u>honoring</u> the return of flocks of cliff
3
swallows from their winter habitat in Argentina, 7,500 miles away.

　　The Festival is a major affair. For three months, the town residents offer activities focused around their summer visitors. ▢4 My sister loved the extensive parade

and exciting <u>dances; my</u> brother could not get enough of
5

1. **A.** NO CHANGE
   B. When I was growing up, my family
   C. When, I was growing up, my family
   D. When I, was growing up, my family

2. **F.** NO CHANGE
   G. for thousands
   H. to thousands
   J. between thousands

3. **A.** NO CHANGE
   B. honors
   C. will have honored
   D. would of honored

4. At this point, the writer is considering adding the following true information:

   There are many other interesting festivals taking place in California this time of year.

   Would this be a relevant addition to make here?
   F. Yes, because the paragraph focuses on festivals in general.
   G. Yes, because the following sentences expand on the new information.
   H. No, because the paragraph focuses only on the Festival of the Swallows.
   J. No, because the Festival of the Swallows is the only interesting festival.

5. Which of the following alternatives to the underlined portion would NOT be acceptable?
   A. dances. My
   B. dances, and my
   C. dances, my
   D. dances, while my

GO ON TO THE NEXT PAGE.

the special food. My mom would spend hours <u>browsing</u>
                                            6
the local craft booths, while my dad and I would place

private bets about who would win the competitions and

contests. It was no surprise to learn that the "Festival

of the Swallows" <u>has become</u> Capistrano's primary
                  7
focus: a time to boost the town's economy, showcase the

<u>resident's offerings</u>, encourage community involvement,
      8
and increase cultural pride.

    <u>Of course</u>, we would always tour the historic
     9
Catholic

mission itself. <u>Once they arrive in</u>

<u>Capistrano, their nests many of the swallows make</u>
                          10
<u>there.</u> The celebration of the swallows' return is not only

sanctioned by the Church, it is heightened by its overlap

with the feast day of St. Joseph on March 19. My pious

mother would tell us that by roughly coinciding with St.

Joseph's Day and Easter, the arrival of the birds served

as a double reminder of hope and rebirth.

    For us kids, the Festival always meant the <u>reproach</u>
                                                 11
of summer vacation, and we couldn't wait to see the swal-

lows return. However, during a period of rebuilding for

earthquake protection in the early 1990s, <u>they</u> started
                                           12
worrying when the swallows bypassed the Capistrano

mission.

6. Which of the following alternatives to the under-
   lined portion would be LEAST acceptable?
   F. visiting
   G. surveying
   H. perusing
   J. reading

7. A. NO CHANGE
   B. in becoming
   C. has became
   D. will become

8. F. NO CHANGE
   G. residents' offerings
   H. residents' offering's
   J. resident's offering's

9. A. NO CHANGE
   B. In doing so
   C. Since
   D. For example

10. F. NO CHANGE
    G. Once they arrive in Capistrano, the swallows
       make many of their nests there.
    H. The swallows, once they arrive in Capistrano,
       make many of their nests there.
    J. Once the swallows, they arrive in Capistrano,
       make many of their nests there.

11. A. NO CHANGE
    B. censure
    C. approach
    D. delivery

12. F. NO CHANGE
    G. one
    H. it
    J. people

GO ON TO THE NEXT PAGE.

The scaffolding surrounding the buildings of San Juan Capistrano scared off the little birds, threatening the town's <u>reliance for</u> summer tourism and my family's
13
first vacation of the year.

Fortunately, the building fortification projects were completed in record time, and the swallows soon returned to their usual patterns.

<u>Despite</u> their local significance, the swallows of
14
Capistrano were only popularized among the general public when songwriter Leon Rene romanticized the event in a song. Written in 1939, the tune "When the Swallows Come Back to Capistrano" has been recorded by numerous artists. My father would play the song in the car as we drove back home <u>to remind us that we, too, would return the next year to San Juan Capistrano.</u>
15

13. **A.** NO CHANGE
    B. reliance about
    C. reliance into
    D. reliance on

14. **F.** NO CHANGE
    G. Due to
    H. Because of
    J. In light of

15. Given that all of the choices are accurate, which one best concludes the essay by referring back to the first paragraph?
    A. NO CHANGE
    B. from San Juan Capistrano.
    C. after seeing the swallows in San Juan Capistrano.
    D. listening to the song about the swallows of San Juan Capistrano.

PASSAGE II

Robin Hood: Fact or Fiction?

People <u>who</u> know of Robin Hood only through
₁₆
Hollywood movies might be a little surprised to

discover that the original stories are markedly more

complicated. Robin Hood may

have robbed from the rich, <u>as they were the ones with</u>

<u>the money,</u> but did he give to the poor? Not necessarily.
₁₇
There are other differences to reconcile as well.

    <u>Despite this</u>, the first records of Robin Hood are
₁₈
from the early thirteenth century, a few years after the

reign of King John (called "Prince John" in the legends).

While it is possible that there was a real historical figure

at the heart of the Robin Hood stories, many historians

believe <u>its</u>
₁₉

existence was unlikely. By 1261, "Robin Hood" became

just a generic term used to describe thieves and other

common criminals. By the fourteenth century, more-

detailed legends were being written down. Since then,

Robin has been portrayed in various <u>lights: as</u> a relent-
₂₀
less do-gooder, a pious gentleman, and even a treason-

ous murderer. Some of these later legends borrowed

events from the lives of documented historical

figures, but only beginning in the nineteenth century

does Robin Hood <u>take to</u> the role of savior of the poor
₂₁
and defender of righteousness.

16. **F.** NO CHANGE
    G. whom
    H. they
    J. we

17. **A.** NO CHANGE
    B. while they were in their expensive houses,
    C. who made up the wealthy people in medieval England,
    D. DELETE the underlined portion.

18. **F.** NO CHANGE
    G. For example
    H. Similarly
    J. Therefore

19. **A.** NO CHANGE
    B. their
    C. his
    D. it's

20. **F.** NO CHANGE
    G. lights, as
    H. lights, and as
    J. lights as:

21. **A.** NO CHANGE
    B. take from
    C. take upon
    D. take on

GO ON TO THE NEXT PAGE.

Robin Hood's companions were not always who we would expect, either. Even though such characters <u>like</u> Will Scarlet and Little John appear early, a female companion would not have been

22

socially <u>exceptable,</u> considering Robin Hood's outlaw lifestyle. Consequently, Robin Hood

23

had no romantic interest in the original tales. Maid Marian did not appear with him until the sixteenth century. Marian, derived from a very old legend in which she is a shepherdess, was a late borrowing from the May Day festivals. Robin Hood and his men celebrated the day, as did Maid Marian in works of <u>disparate</u> literature. This notion of Robin Hood sustaining an inclusive, nearly democratic society friendly to the poor and

24

women is an <u>adaptation before</u> modern times.

25

By the time Marian entered the legend, the character of Robin Hood had already changed dramatically. He gained an aristocratic title, Earl of Huntingdon, and <u>begun</u> to represent

26

legitimate kingship battling tyrannical despotism with a good measure of violence. Over generations, however, the <u>savagery</u> was shed, and what resulted was

27

the charmingly charismatic outlaw so popular today. Robin Hood is, after all, a literary creation, so the reader must accept him and his exploits as fiction.

Considering the real history of the Middle Ages, <u>resist</u> the ruling class would have been

28

22. F. NO CHANGE
G. as
H. being
J. DELETE the underlined portion.

23. A. NO CHANGE
B. acceptable
C. exceptionable
D. exceptional

24. The best place for the underlined portion would be:
F. where it is now.
G. after the word *as.*
H. before the word *works.*
J. after the word *literature.*

25. A. NO CHANGE
B. adaption from
C. adaptation to
D. adaptation about

26. F. NO CHANGE
G. beginning
H. began
J. had began

27. Which choice would most clearly indicate the contrast between Robin Hood's early image and how he is currently viewed in literature?
A. NO CHANGE
B. appeal
C. boyishness
D. intensity

28. F. NO CHANGE
G. resisting
H. resists of
J. resisted

GO ON TO THE NEXT PAGE.

forbiddingly difficult and bloody, and certainly not fodder for children's stories. [29]

29. Given that all are true, which of the following sentences, if inserted here, would best conclude this paragraph?
   A. Robin Hood has always been a popular character.
   B. Robin Hood's stories have had a lasting impact on English literature.
   C. While critics, citing the plots' predictability, have not always valued Robin Hood's legends, the character remains a staple of English culture.
   D. In reality, Robin Hood's best modern incarnations retain many of his fearsome qualities found in early legends.

Question 30 asks about the preceding passage as a whole.

---

30. Suppose the writer's goal had been to write a brief descriptive essay about the evolution of the Robin Hood tales. Would this essay fulfill that goal?

   F. No, because the essay focuses on how Robin Hood may never have existed.
   G. No, because the essay focuses on how literature in general has adapted over many centuries.
   H. Yes, because the essay objectively describes how changing times affect the plot and characterization of the Robin Hood tales.
   J. Yes, because the essay fails to show whether Robin Hood actually stole from the rich to give to the poor.

PASSAGE III

Marian Anderson: Soulful Songstress

(1)

When Marian Anderson was born in Philadelphia in 1897, no one, <u>could of</u> predicted
₃₁
the artistic success the world-famous contralto would achieve in her lifetime, or the many barriers she would overcome. <u>While</u> she is remembered both for her mag-
₃₂
nificent singing voice and for her struggle on behalf of African American civil rights.

31. **A.** NO CHANGE
    B. could have
    C. would of
    D. could

32. **F.** NO CHANGE
    G. Even though
    H. Until
    J. Today

(2)

Anderson developed a love of singing early in her life. As a child, she and her family often <u>were gathering</u> to sing spirituals and other beloved songs.
₃₃
Anderson gave her first public

concert at the age of six, <u>where she</u> was an ardent
₃₄
member of her church choir. The singer received a lot of help from her church and community as she developed her vocal skills. Many people contributed money for her education in Philadelphia, and Anderson studied with several accomplished opera singers.

33. **A.** NO CHANGE
    B. gather
    C. seemed to gather
    D. gathered

34. **F.** NO CHANGE
    G. if she
    H. and she
    J. she

(3)

Anderson's manager found it difficult to book singing engagements for her in the United States. <u>Because of</u> her enormous talent, many venues refused to
₃₅
hold concerts with her because

35. **A.** NO CHANGE
    B. Despite
    C. Since
    D. In light of

GO ON TO THE NEXT PAGE.

of strict racial barriers. 36 As a result, Anderson traveled to Europe, where she was able to perform and refine her skills more freely. In 1939, Anderson was barred from performing in a concert at Washington's Constitution Hall by the hall's owners, the Daughters of the American Revolution. In response, Eleanor Roosevelt issued a personal invitation to Anderson to perform from the front steps of the Lincoln Memorial in Washington, D.C. <u>That personal invitation was eventually shared with 75,000 other people who attended the</u>
           37
<u>concert as an audience.</u>

(4)

Anderson worked hard to train her voice, and she entered a competition <u>sponsored by</u> the
                                                  38

New York Philharmonic Society. <u>Since</u> hundreds of
                                      39
vocalists competed, she was declared the winner. Her prize was a featured appearance with the prestigious New York Philharmonic Orchestra. Her performance was so stirring that the manager of the orchestra offered her a contract <u>continuing to sing</u> professionally.
                       40

36. At this point, the writer is considering adding the following true statement:

    Other African American musicians and athletes suffered under the same constraints.

    Should the statement be added here?

    F. Yes, because Marion Anderson was a popular African American musician.
    G. Yes, because African American athletes were prevented from competing in certain events.
    H. No, because Marion Anderson was not constrained by her ethnicity.
    J. No, because the statement disrupts the flow of the essay, which is about one African American musician.

37. Which of the alternatives provides the most logical and succinct conclusion for Paragraph 3?
    A. NO CHANGE
    B. That concert drew an audience of over 75,000 people.
    C. Eleanor Roosevelt knew a good thing when she heard it; the concert drew a crowd of over 75,000 people.
    D. 75,000 people crowded the area in front of the Memorial in order to hear Anderson singing her songs.

38. F. NO CHANGE
    G. sponsored for
    H. sponsored with
    J. sponsored to

39. A. NO CHANGE
    B. In the end
    C. Although
    D. However

40. F. NO CHANGE
    G. by continuing to sing
    H. to continue that song
    J. to continue singing

GO ON TO THE NEXT PAGE.

(5)

Anderson did not let the racial prejudices of the time keep her from entertaining her fans. Her talent which forced others to recognize her abilities. In 1943, she gave a concert in the same
<u>41</u>

Constitution Hall where she had been rejected four years earlier. In 1955, she became the first African American performer to appear onstage at the Metropolitan Opera House in New York City. She also received the Presidential Medal of Freedom in 1963. Anderson gave her last

public concert in 1965, but her legacy as a <u>courageous and groundbreaking</u> woman and
<u>42</u>

performer remains. Two years before her death in 1993, Anderson was given a Grammy Lifetime

Achievement Award <u>in honor of her own ability and her own determination</u>.
<u>43</u>

41. A. NO CHANGE
B. that
C. as
D. DELETE the underlined portion.

42. Which choice most clearly conveys the significance of Anderson's accomplishments?
F. NO CHANGE
G. popular
H. well-known African American
J. talented and important

43. A. NO CHANGE
B. honoring her ability and its determination
C. to honor her ability and determination
D. honoring her own ability for being determined

GO ON TO THE NEXT PAGE.

Questions 44 and 45 ask about the preceding passage as a whole.

44. The writer wishes to add the following sentence to the essay:

By the age of 20, she had performed in many public concerts and was giving solo performances.

If added, this sentence would best support and most logically be placed:

F. after the last sentence of Paragraph 2.
G. before the first sentence of Paragraph 3.
H. before the first sentence of Paragraph 4.
J. before the first sentence of Paragraph 5.

45. The writer has been asked to write an essay assessing the effectiveness of the civil rights movement in bettering social conditions for African Americans. Would this essay fulfill that assignment?

A. Yes; the writer focuses exclusively on the struggles and successes of an African American singer before and after the civil rights movement.
B. Yes; the writer focuses on the necessity of the civil rights movement to achieve equal opportunities for African Americans.
C. No; the writer focuses on the struggles of just one person and only tangentially refers to the civil rights movement.
D. No; the writer focuses narrowly on the struggles of vocalists and not on those of African Americans in general.

PASSAGE IV

Appaloosa: Horse of the Nez Perce Tribe

Throughout the centuries, one particular breed of horse

has stood out from all the others,
                              46

the Appaloosa, or spotted horse. While it is

unique and beautifully colored, this breed of horse was
                47
at one time the pride and joy of the Nez Perce Indian

tribe. The Nez Perce was a tribe

of the Pacific Northwest: and the Appaloosa was inte-
                  48
gral to the tribe's success.

   While historians dispute the manner in which the

Nez Perce Indians originally acquired their horses,

there is no doubt that the Nez Perce people were well-

respected for their breeding knowledge and the quality

of their horses. 49 As Meriwether Lewis wrote in 1806

after

staying for the Nez Perce for a time, "Their horses
      50
appear to be an excellent race; they are

46. F. NO CHANGE
  G. others
  H. others:
  J. others, which include:

47. Which of the choices would be most appropriate
  here?
  A. NO CHANGE
  B. Despite being unique and beautifully colored,
  C. Although it is unique and often beautifully
       colored,
  D. Often unique and beautifully colored,

48. F. NO CHANGE
  G. Northwest, and
  H. Northwest and,
  J. Northwest and

49. Which of the following sentences, if added here,
  would best introduce the breadth of public awareness
  of Nez Perce skill with Appaloosa horses?
  A. Many people knew about Nez Perce and their
       horses.
  B. Breeding knowledge was especially important to
       the local community.
  C. Appaloosa horses were owned by a surprising
       number of people.
  D. This respect was expressed by other tribes and
       even traveling Europeans.

50. F. NO CHANGE
  G. staying with
  H. staying upon
  J. staying against

GO ON TO THE NEXT PAGE.

lofty, and would make a figure in any country." 51

The Appaloosa described by Lewis gave the Nez Perce the opportunity to travel across many miles in order to visit other tribes, to obtain food, and to sell surplus horses. Because the tribe had so many of these fine horses, the Nez Perce soon became a wealthy and self-sufficient community. By the mid-1800s, the Nez Perce had the <u>mobility</u>
52

and resources <u>to aid</u> other tribes and even European
53
missionaries. For example, Chief Lawyer traveled back and forth from his own land of Kamiah in Oregon to Whitman Mission in Washington State, where he eventually helped resolve a conflict between Rev. Marcus Whitman and Rev. Asa Smith. Likewise, Chief Looking Glass traveled from Oregon to Wyoming, where he followed the buffalo and, in 1873, helped the Montana Crow <u>end a dispute</u> with the Sioux.
54

In 1877, after years of discussion and compromise, the U.S. Army ordered the Nez Perce to leave Oregon and to settle on a reservation in

Idaho. 55 They attempted to flee to Canada. Unfortunately, a final battle took place, scattering their nearly 2,000 finely bred

51. The writer wishes to add information here that will explain and further support the point made in the preceding sentence. Which of the following sentences will do that best?
  A. The description is all the more impressive given Lewis's knowledge of horses.
  B. The description is significant because Lewis was a well-known animal lover.
  C. English horses were considered to be very good.
  D. The description by Lewis was made public back east.

52. Which of the following alternatives to the underlined portion would be LEAST acceptable?
  F. tendency
  G. flexibility
  H. maneuverability
  J. movability

53. A. NO CHANGE
  B. which would aid
  C. for aiding
  D. for the aiding of

54. Which choice provides the most intense description of Chief Looking Glass's involvement with the Crow?
  F. NO CHANGE
  G. negotiate a hard-won truce
  H. finish an argument
  J. stop fighting

55. The writer wants to describe why the tribe attempts to flee to Canada, as mentioned in the next sentence. Which of the following sentences, if added here, will do that best?
  A. This was a long and difficult journey.
  B. This was not acceptable to the tribe because they had already seen several broken treaties.
  C. Idaho was not far from Oregon.
  D. The tribe had never been to Oregon with their horses.

GO ON TO THE NEXT PAGE.

Appaloosa <u>horses. Which the</u> horses were never
56
recovered.

     Today, attempts are being made <u>to reestablish,</u>
57
<u>between the Appaloosa and the present-day Nez Perce</u>
57
<u>tribe, the connection</u> in Idaho. Horse breeders there
57
have created a new breed by crossing the Appaloosa

with a rare central Asian breed

called "Akhal-teke." <u>Because this</u> new horse has many
58
of the same characteristics as the original Nez Perce

horse: sleek and lean, muscular and <u>strong, and usually</u>
59
sporting a beautiful spotted coat. As one member of the

Nez Perce tribe stated, "The loss of the horses was like

the loss of a good friend…It's similar to taking away

our braids, our strength; with the horses, we have our

strength back."

---

56. F. NO CHANGE
    G. horses the
    H. horses, the
    J. horses: the

57. A. NO CHANGE
    B. to reestablish the connection between the
       Appaloosa and the present-day Nez Perce tribe
    C. through the connection, to re-establish the
       Appaloosa and the present-day Nez Perce tribe
    D. by reestablishing the connection, between the
       Appaloosa and the present-day Nez Perce tribe.

58. F. NO CHANGE
    G. Although this
    H. Seeing as this
    J. This

59. A. NO CHANGE
    B. strong and, usually
    C. strong, and, usually,
    D. strong and usually,

Question 60 asks about the preceding passage as a
whole.

60. Suppose the writer's primary purpose had been to document the relationship between the Nez Perce Tribe and the Appaloosa horse. Would this essay accomplish that purpose?
    If added, this sentence would best support and most logically be placed:
    F. Yes, because the essay focuses on how the Appaloosa horse helped the Nez Perce become a thriving tribe.
    G. Yes, because the Appaloosa horse is a unique and beautiful breed of horse.
    H. No, because the essay describes the role of the horse in general across the Pacific Northwest.
    J. No, because the Nez Perce were ordered to leave their horses behind in Oregon.

PASSAGE V

The Detroit Tigers: from Tiger Stadium to Comerica Park

"Out with the old, in with the new!" More than a decade later, some Detroit Tigers fans are still disappointed by this notion when it comes to their beloved Tiger Stadium. Today,

Tiger Stadium is no more. Only a photograph or memory preserves its existence, despite that

90% of the structure itself will eventually be recycled being needed elsewhere.

Their extremely happy with the new and improved Comerica Park, mainly because of its comfort, entertainment value, and multiple

amenities. The new park was designed by which every seat in the house got a clear view of the action, even if it was relatively far off in the distance. There are rides for the children, displays of baseball history, and a slew of choices to slate both hunger and thirst. Finally, a grand production of fountain fireworks explodes for every

61. A. NO CHANGE
B. disappointed unto
C. disappointed for
D. disappointed besides

62. F. NO CHANGE
G. existence, because
H. existence, although
J. existence, where

63. A. NO CHANGE
B. for other uses.
C. and put to use in another way.
D. DELETE the underlined portion.

64. F. NO CHANGE
G. There
H. They're
J. Most fans are

65. A. NO CHANGE
B. in which
C. despite that
D. so that

66. Which of the following alternatives to the underlined portion would NOT be acceptable?
F. quench
G. satisfy
H. pacify
J. appease

GO ON TO THE NEXT PAGE.

home run, <u>delighting</u> the crowd every time.
67

    Clearly, Comerica Park is a huge improvement over the ancient Tiger Stadium. 68 Fans who continue to lament Tiger Stadium's demise complain most about Comerica Park's large size. In the old stadium, spectators sat so

close to <u>them</u>, they felt they could almost touch
69

their idols. At the very least, fans could see their <u>favorite players'</u> facial expressions, observe their physi-
70
cal techniques, and, at dramatic moments, almost feel their emotions. It was easier to make a connection with the guys on the field back then, and now it is difficult at times to determine who is actually on base or at bat.

    Other criticisms of the Tigers' new home include the angle at which it was <u>built. Which</u>
71

67. A. NO CHANGE
B. it is a delight for
C. causing delight to
D. which will have delighted

68. At this point, the writer is considering adding the following sentence:

    "Huge," however, is the operative word.

Should the writer make this addition?

F. No, because it causes unnecessary confusion regarding the size of the new stadium.
G. No, because it adds information that blurs the focus of the information that follows regarding the new stadium.
H. Yes, because it makes a connection between the perceived value of the new stadium and its actual size.
J. Yes, because it captures the emotion of the builders who worked on the new stadium.

69. A. NO CHANGE
B. the players
C. it
D. some

70. F. NO CHANGE
G. favorite player's
H. favorite players
J. favorite player

71. A. NO CHANGE
B. built; which
C. built, which
D. built which

GO ON TO THE NEXT PAGE.

causes spectators to be blinded by the setting sun during evening games. Also, while the upper

deck seats are certainly cheap enough, those ticket-holders might as well have stayed home to watch the game on television. Spectators are seated so far away from the game <u>with the result being</u> they feel they are watching
₇₂
little white dots moving on a green background.

However, the bottom line is that Tiger Stadium was literally falling apart. 73

Its infrastructure was no longer safe for its thousands of visitors, and even its restrooms were way <u>past by</u> being
₇₄
acceptable. Spending several hours watching a baseball game requires a certain amount of comfort, cleanliness, and convenience for it to be an enjoyable experience. Comerica Park is more than just a baseball diamond surrounded by rows and tiers of comfortable seats. For $360 million, the <u>densely populated</u> city of Detroit now
₇₅
boasted one of the finest baseball parks in the world, while offering the best baseball experience a fan could imagine.

72. F. NO CHANGE
G. causing the result to be that
H. and then
J. that

73. The way in which the phrase "literally falling apart" functions in the preceding sentence might best be described as being:
A. accuracy intended to support the writer's thesis.
B. understatement acting to restrict the essay's dramatic impact.
C. exaggeration intended to highlight the writer's disillusionment with the old Tiger Stadium.
D. nonsense working to further the writer's strongly impassioned style.

74. F. NO CHANGE
G. in passing
H. past
J. passed

75. Which choice most clearly conveys the notion that Detroit was in desperate need of a new and improved baseball stadium?
A. NO CHANGE
B. large
C. beleaguered
D. sports-loving

MATHEMATICS

76.

If $\dfrac{4x + 4x + 4x + 4x}{4} = 4$, what is the value of $4x$?

F. $\dfrac{1}{4}$

G. 1

H. 4

J. 16

K. 24

77.

How many irrational numbers are there between 8 and 12?

A. 1

B. 2

C. 3

D. 4

E. Infinitely many

78.

If c and d are any integers such that $d < 7$ and $3c + d = 18$, which of the following is the solution set for c?

F. $c \geq 4$

G. $c \geq 3$

H. $c \leq 0$

J. $c \leq 3$

K. $c \leq 4$

79.

For $i^2 = -1$, $(3 + i)^2 = ?$

A. 8

B. 10

C. $8 + 3i$

D. $8 + 6i$

E. $9 + 3i$

80.

If 4 more than twice n is a negative number and 6 more than n is a positive number, which of the following *could* be the value of n?

F. -8

G. -6

H. -4

J. -2

K. 0

81.

For the function $g(x) = ax^2 + 24$, a is a constant and $g(4) = 8$. What is the value of $g(-4)$?

A. 8

B. 0

C. -1

D. -8

E. -16

82.

For real numbers x and y, when is the inequality $|x + y| < |x - y|$ true?

F. Always

G. Only when $x = y$

H. Only when $x < 0$ and $y < 0$

J. Only when $x < 0$ and $y > 0$

K. Never

83.

If the average (arithmetic mean) of two numbers is 16 and one of the numbers is x, what is the other number in terms of x?

A. $16 - x$

B. $16 - 2x$

C. $16 + x$

D. $32 - x$

E. $32 - 2x$

84.

For what value of a would the following system of equations have an infinite number of solutions?

$$2x - y = 8$$
$$6x - 3y = 2a$$

F. 2

G. 8

H. 12

J. 16

K. 24

85.

How many whole numbers less than 14 are also prime numbers?

(Note: The first prime number is 2.)

A. 2

B. 3

C. 4

D. 6

E. 7

86.

For what value of p does $|p - 1| + 1 = 0$?

F. 0

G. 1

H. 2

J. 3

K. There is no such value of p.

87.

If the statement "If a pepper is ripe, then it is red" were true, which of the following statements would also have to be true?

A. "If a pepper is red, then it is ripe."

B. "If a pepper is not red, then it is ripe."

C. "If a pepper is not red, then it is not ripe."

D. "If a pepper is not ripe, then it is not red."

E. "If a pepper is not ripe, then it is red."

88.

Which of the following expressions is equivalent to $(4 + x)^{-100}$?

F. $-4^{100} - x^{100}$

G. $-400 - 100x$

H. $\dfrac{1}{4^{100}} + \dfrac{1}{x^{100}}$

J. $\dfrac{1}{(4x)^{100}}$

K. $\dfrac{1}{(4 + x)^{100}}$

89.

What is the determinant of the matrix shown below?

$$\begin{pmatrix} 4 & 8 \\ 2 & 5 \end{pmatrix}$$

A. 0

B. 4

C. 14

D. 25

E. 48

90.

Consider the graph of the equation $y = \dfrac{2x - 12}{3x - 6}$ in the standard (x, y) coordinate plane.

Which of the following equations represents the *vertical* asymptote of the graph?

F. $x = 2$

G. $x = 3$

H. $x = 4$

J. $x = 6$

K. $x = 12$

91.

An integer is *abundant* if its positive integer factors, excluding the integer itself, have a sum that is greater than the integer. How many of the integers 8, 10, 12, and 15 are abundant?

A. 0

B. 1

C. 2

D. 3

E. 4

92.

When the average of a list of course grades is multiplied by the number of courses, the result is n. What does n represent?

F. Half the number of courses

G. Half the sum of the course grades

H. The number of courses

J. The average of the course grades

K. The sum of the course grades

93.

Which of the following trigonometric functions is equivalent to the function $h(x) = \sec x \sin x$?
(Note: $\sec x = \dfrac{1}{\cos x}$)

A. $f(x) = \tan x$

B. $f(x) = \cot x$

C. $f(x) = \csc x$

D. $f(x) = \sin x$

E. $f(x) = \cos x$

94.

If the degree measures of the angles of a triangle are in the ratio 2:3:4, what is the degree measure of the smallest angle?

F. 15°

G. 20°

H. 40°

J. 45°

K. Cannot be determined from the given information.

95.

Which of the following is an irrational number that is a solution to the equation $|n^2 - 12| - 4 = 0$?

A. $2\sqrt{3}$

B. $4\sqrt{2}$

C. $2\sqrt{2}$

D. $\sqrt{2}$

E. 4

96.

Which of the following graphs best shows a strong *negative* relationship between a and b?

F.

G.

H.

J.

K.

97.

The number of students who joined the Math Club last year is twice the number of students who joined this year. If 30 students joined the Math Club last year and x students joined this year, which of the following equations is true?

A. $30x = 2$

B. $2x = 30$

C. $x^2 = 30$

D. $x + 30 = 2$

E. $30 + 2 = x$

98.

If a circle in the (x,y) coordinate plane has the equation $x^2 + y^2 + 4x - 2y = -1$, what is the radius of the circle?

F. 2

G. 3

H. 4

J. 9

K. 16

Use the following information to answer questions 99–101.

The table below shows the weekly sales totals (in thousands of dollars) for 4 salespeople who work for Square One Furniture Sales during the 5 most recent weeks. Data is missing due to a computer error. The data in the table has been verified as being accurate.

Salesperson	Week number				
	1	2	3	4	5
April	5	6	6	5	4
Ben	3				
Carrie	1	2	2	3	
Dillon	4	5		4	4

99.

Which of the following is closest to the percent increase in April's sales from Week 1 to Week 2?

A. 5%

B. 15%

C. 20%

D. 25%

E. 56%

100.

Ben recalls that his sales increased at a very high rate during the 5 weeks due to a personal goal that he set. He says that for each week from Week 2 to Week 5, his sales increased 20% from the previous week. Which of the following values, in thousands of dollars, is closest to Ben's sales for Week 5?

F. 3.2

G. 4.3

H. 5.8

J. 6.2

K. 7.0

101.

Prior to Week 3, April set a goal for her sales to average $6,000 per week from the beginning of Week 3 to the end of Week 6. To meet this goal, what must be her minimum sales for Week 6, in thousands of dollars?

A. 4

B. 5

C. 6

D. 7

E. 9

102.

What real number a satisfies $(2^a)(4) = 8^3$?

F. 2

G. 3

H. 4

J. 6

K. 7

103.

If the inequality $|x| > |y|$ is true, then which of the following *must* be true?

A. $x > 0$

B. $x > y$

C. $x < y$

D. $x \neq y$

E. $x = y$

104.

The ratio of *m* to *n* is 1:2, and ratio of *p* to *n* is 3:4. What is the ratio of *m* to *p*?

F. 1:1

G. 3:1

H. 2:3

J. 3:8

K. 6:1

105.

Which of the following is equal to $\frac{1}{4}$ of 0.1 percent?

A. 0.000025

B. 0.00025

C. 0.0025

D. 0.025

E. 0.25

106.

For every pair of real numbers a and b such that $ab = 0$ and $\dfrac{a}{b} = 0$, which of the following statements is true?

F. $a = 0$ and $b = 0$

G. $a \neq 0$ and $b = 0$

H. $a = 0$ and $b \neq 0$

J. $a \neq 0$ and $b \neq 0$

K. None of the statements is true for every such pair of real numbers a and b.

107.

Suppose that x will be randomly selected from the set $\{-3, -2, -1, 0, 1\}$ and that y will be randomly selected from the set $\{-2, -1, 0, 1\}$. What is the probability that $xy > 0$?

A. $\dfrac{3}{200}$

B. $\dfrac{1}{20}$

C. $\dfrac{3}{10}$

D. $\dfrac{7}{20}$

E. $\dfrac{3}{5}$

108.

Which of the following is closest to $\sqrt[4]{80}$?

F. 5

G. 4

H. 3

J. 2

K. 1

109.

If the average (arithmetic mean) of 7 consecutive integers is 16, what is the sum of the least and greatest of the 7 integers?

A. 13

B. 14

C. 16

D. 32

E. Cannot be determined from the given information.

110.

In parallelogram *WXYZ*, *WY* is perpendicular to *YZ* and the measure of angle *WZY* is 72°. What is the measure of angle *XYW*?

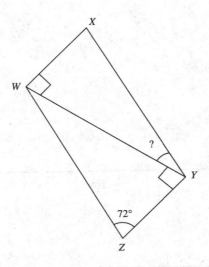

F. 12°

G. 18°

H. 36°

J. 58°

K. 72°

111.

Which of the following expressions, if any, are equal for all real numbers n?

$$\text{I.} \quad \sqrt{(-n)^2}$$

$$\text{II.} \quad |-n|$$

$$\text{III.} \quad -|n|$$

A. I and II only

B. I and III only

C. II and III only

D. I, II, and III

E. None of the expressions are equivalent.

112.

In the figure below, AB is a line segment. What is the value of $\dfrac{(y-x)}{(y+x)}$?

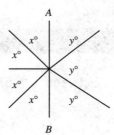

F. $\dfrac{1}{3}$

G. $\dfrac{1}{4}$

H. $\dfrac{1}{5}$

J. $\dfrac{1}{7}$

K. Cannot be determined from the given information.

113.

Whenever a and b are positive integers such that $\left(\sqrt{3}\right)^a = 27^b$, what is the value of $\dfrac{a}{b}$?

A. 6

B. 4

C. 3

D. $\dfrac{3}{2}$

E. $\dfrac{1}{6}$

114.

What is the distance, in coordinate units, between $3 + 6i$ and $-2 + 3i$ in the complex plane?

F. 5

G. 9

H. $\sqrt{13}$

J. $\sqrt{34}$

K. $\sqrt{65}$

115.

The fraction $\frac{1}{13}$ is equivalent to $0.\overline{076923}$. What is the digit in the 801st decimal place of $0.\overline{076923}$? (Note: The digit in the 4th decimal place of $0.\overline{076923}$ is 9.)

A. 2

B. 3

C. 6

D. 7

E. 9

116.

The average weight of 10 girls is 110.0 pounds. If the oldest girl is excluded, the average weight of the 9 remaining girls is 112.0 pounds. What is the weight, in pounds, of the oldest girl?

F. 90

G. 92

H. 109

J. 111

K. 122

117.

Each of the variables f, g, h, j, and k represents a different *positive* real number. Given the equations below, which of the four variables g, h, j, and k necessarily has the greatest value?

$$1.23g = f$$
$$1.01h = f$$
$$0.99j = f$$
$$0.23k = f$$

A. g

B. h

C. j

D. k

E. Cannot be determined from the given information.

118.

What is the x-intercept of the graph of $y = x^2 - 4x + 4$?

F. 2

G. 1

H. 0

J. −1

K. −2

119.

Katrina went into Downtown Digital to price cameras. All cameras were discounted 21% off the marked price. Which of the following is an expression for the discounted price on a marked price of d dollars?

A. $0.21d$

B. $d - 21$

C. $d - 21d$

D. $d - 0.21$

E. $d - 0.21d$

120.

For all positive integers n, what is the greatest common factor of the two numbers $273n^3$ and $189n^2$?

F. $21n^2$

G. $21n$

H. 42

J. 13

K. 7

121.

Two angles are supplementary. The measure of one angle is 4 times the measure of the other angle. What is the measure of the larger angle?

A. 288

B. 144

C. 72

D. 36

E. 18

122.

When $af - g = x$ and $f \neq 0$, $a = ?$

F. $x + g - f$

G. $\dfrac{(g + f)}{x}$

H. $x - g - f$

J. $\dfrac{(x - g)}{f}$

K. $\dfrac{(x + g)}{f}$

123.

Every graph in one of the following categories has a vertical line of symmetry regardless of how it is oriented in the standard (x, y) coordinate plane. Which one?

A. Squares

B. Rectangles

C. Circles

D. Triangles

E. Ellipses

124.

If $0° \leq x° \leq 90°$ and $\tan x - 1 = 0$, then $x° = ?$

F. 0

G. 15

H. 30

J. 45

K. 60

Use the following information to answer questions 125–126.

In the figure below, R and Q are on SP and L and M are on SN. The measurements given are in centimeters. Both $LMQR$ and $MNPQ$ are trapezoids. The area, A, of a trapezoid is given by $A = \frac{1}{2}h(b_1 + b2)$, where h is the height and b_1 and b_2 are the lengths of the 2 parallel sides.

125.

What is the area of $LMQR$, in square centimeters?

A. 1,750

B. 3,712

C. 4,900

D. 5,462

E. 9,800

126.

What is the radius, in centimeters, of the largest circle that can be drawn so that no point of the circle is outside of $MNPQ$?

F. 35

G. 45

H. 55

J. 65

K. 75

127.

The median of a set of data containing 5 items was found. Six data items were added to the set. Three of these items were greater than the original median, and the other 3 items were less than the original median. Which of the following statements *must* be true about the median of the new data set?

A. It is the average of the 2 new lower values.

B. It is the same as the original median.

C. It is the average of the 2 new higher values.

D. It is greater than the original median.

E. It is less than the original median.

128.

The fixed costs of manufacturing tennis rackets in a factory are $1,600.00 per day. The variable costs are $7.25 per tennis racket. Which of the following expressions can be used to model the cost of manufacturing t tennis rackets in 1 day?

F. $1,607.25$t$

G. 7.25t$ − $1,600.00

H. $1,600.00$t$ + $7.25

J. $1,600.00 − 7.25t$

K. $1,600.00 + 7.25t$

129.

A triangle, $\triangle RST$, is reflected across the x-axis to have the image $\triangle R'S'T'$, in the standard (x, y) coordinate plane; thus R reflects to R'. The coordinates of point R are $(-a, b)$. What are the coordinates of point R'?

A. $(-a,-b)$

B. $(a,-b)$

C. (a, b)

D. $(b,-a)$

E. Cannot be determined from the given information.

130.

If $d > c$, then $|c - d|$ is equivalent to which of the following?

F. $c + d$

G. $-(c + d)$

H. $\sqrt{(c - d)}$

J. $d - c$

K. $c - d$

131.

Which of the following defines the solution set for the system of inequalities below?

$$x \leq 4$$
$$9 + 3x \geq 0$$

A. $x \geq -3$

B. $x \leq 4$

C. $-18 \leq x \leq 4$

D. $-3 \leq x \leq 4$

E. $3 \leq x \leq 4$

132.

The graph of the solution set for the system of linear equations below is a single line in the standard (x, y) coordinate plane.

$$28x - 36y = 76$$
$$7x + by = 19$$

What must be the value of b?

F. -9

G. -7

H. $\dfrac{1}{4}$

J. 4

K. 9

133.

For all real numbers g and h such that the product of h and 5 is g, which of the following expressions represents the sum of h and 5 in terms of g?

A. $g + 5$

B. $5g + 5$

C. $5(g + 5)$

D. $\dfrac{g + 5}{5}$

E. $\dfrac{g}{5} + 5$

134.

The probability of Jane being chosen to bat first in the lineup for her softball team is $\dfrac{1}{9}$. What are the odds in favor of Jane being chosen to bat first?

(Note: The odds in favor of an event are defined as the ratio of the probability that the event will happen to the probability that the event will NOT happen.)

F. $\dfrac{9}{1}$

G. $\dfrac{8}{1}$

H. $\dfrac{1}{10}$

J. $\dfrac{1}{9}$

K. $\dfrac{1}{8}$

135.

As shown in the (x, y, z) coordinate space below, the cube with vertices P through W has edges that are 2 coordinate units long. The coordinates of U are $(0, 0, 0)$, and V is on the positive y-axis. What are the coordinates of S?

A. $(0, 2, 2)$

B. $(0, \sqrt{8}, 0)$

C. $(0, \sqrt{8}, 2)$

D. $(2, 2, \sqrt{8})$

E. $(2, 2, 2)$

READING

PASSAGE 1 – LITERARY NARRATIVE

The following passage is adapted from Jack London's story *"Burning Daylight,"* © 1910.

Line   No time was lost. Hines and Finn, with the dogs, already on short rations, were two days in pulling down. At noon of the third day Elijah arrived, reporting no signs of moose. That night
5   Daylight came in with a similar report. As fast as they arrived, the men had started careful panning of the snow all around the cache. It was a large task, for they found stray beans fully a hundred yards from the cache. One more day all
10   the men toiled. The result was pitiful, and the four showed their caliber in the division of the few pounds of food that had been recovered. Little as it was, the lion's share was left with Daylight and Elijah. The men who pulled on with the
15   dogs, one up the Stewart River and one down, would come more quickly to grub. The two who remained would have to last out till the others returned. Furthermore, while the dogs, on several ounces each of beans a day, would travel slowly,
20   nevertheless, the men who traveled with them, on a pinch, would have the dogs themselves to eat. But the men who remained, when the pinch came, would have no dogs. It was for this reason that Daylight and Elijah took the more desper-
25   ate chance. They could not do less, nor did they care to do less. The days passed, and the winter began merging imperceptibly into the Northland spring that comes like a thunderbolt of sudden-ness. It was the spring of 1896 that was prepar-
30   ing. Each day the sun rose farther east of south, remained longer in the sky, and set farther to the west. March ended and April began, and Daylight and Elijah, lean and hungry, wondered what had become of their two comrades. Granting every
35   delay, and throwing in generous margins for good measure, the time was long since passed when they should have returned. Without doubt they had met with disaster. The party had considered the possibility of disaster for one man, and that
40   had been the principal reason for dispatching

the two in different directions. But that disaster should have come to both of them was the final blow.

In the meantime, hoping against hope,
45   Daylight and Elijah eked out a meager existence. The thaw had not yet begun, so they were able to gather the snow about the ruined cache and melt it in pots and pails and gold pans. Allowed to stand for a while, when poured off, a thin deposit
50   of slime was found on the bottoms of the vessels. This was the flour, the infinitesimal trace of it scattered through thousands of cubic yards of snow. Also, in this slime occurred at intervals a water-soaked tealeaf or coffee-ground, and there
55   were in it fragments of earth and litter. But the farther they worked away from the site of the cache, the thinner became the trace of flour, the smaller the deposit of slime.

Elijah was the older man, and he weakened
60   first, so that he came to lie up most of the time in his furs. An occasional tree squirrel kept them alive. The hunting fell upon Daylight, and it was hard work. With but thirty rounds of ammunition, he dared not risk a miss; and, since his rifle
65   was a 45-90, he was compelled to shoot the small creatures through the head. There were very few of them, and days went by without seeing one. When he did see one, he took infinite precautions. He would stalk it for hours. A score of times, with
70   arms that shook from weakness, he would draw a sight on the animal and refrain from pulling the trigger. His inhibition was a thing of iron. He was the master. Not until absolute certitude was his did he shoot. No matter how sharp the pangs
75   of hunger and desire for that palpitating morsel of chattering life, he refused to take the slightest risk of a miss. He, born gambler, was gambling in the bigger way. His life was the stake, his cards were the cartridges, and he played as only a big
80   gambler could play, with infinite precaution, with infinite consideration. Each shot meant a squirrel, and though days elapsed between shots, it never changed his method of play.

136.

Which of the following statements best characterizes Daylight in this passage?

F. Brave and patient

G. Angry and bitter

H. Nervous and scared

J. Smart but reckless

137.

It can be reasonably inferred from the passage that the two men traveled in different directions along the river in order to:

A. emphasize that they did not know where they were going.

B. prove that they could not agree on a plan of action.

C. improve the chances that at least one of them would find help.

D. suggest that they needed additional time to locate food.

138.

In the passage, what is Elijah and Daylight's response when it becomes clear that Hines and Finn are lost (lines 32–43)?

F. Desperate hope and a strong will to survive the difficult situation

G. Despair that starvation seems inevitable

H. Fruitless anger at the failure of Hines and Finn

J. Relief that there are now fewer mouths to feed

139.

As presented in the first paragraph, what is Elijah and Daylight's response to the movement of the sun in the spring of 1896?

A. Relief that the long winter was almost over and Finn and Hines would soon be back at camp

B. Happiness that the weather was gradually warming and they could finally hunt again

C. Concern, as the sun's movement reinforced the long passage of time since the departure of Finn and Hines

D. Renewed hope that they would soon be rescued by other hunters

140.

The last paragraph (lines 59–83) primarily reinforces the author's:

F. horror over the suffering of the two men.

G. admiration of Daylight's inner strength.

H. love for the northern wilderness.

J. confusion regarding Daylight's lack of success.

141.

As used in line 27, the word "imperceptibly" means:

A. quickly.

B. surprisingly.

C. quietly.

D. gradually.

142.

The passage implies that a 45-90 rifle is:

F. inaccurate.

G. powerful.

H. small.

J. expensive.

143.

According to the passage, the dogs are valuable to the men as:

A. a sign of prestige.

B. a means of communication.

C. a reserve food source.

D. a source of entertainment and joy.

144.

In the passage, the author makes it clear that, compared to Daylight, Elijah was:

F. stronger.

G. a better hunter.

H. a born gambler.

J. weaker.

145.

The phrase "They could not do less, nor did they care to do less" (lines 25–26) mainly serves to emphasize that:

A. Daylight and Elijah were unconcerned about the other men.

B. Daylight and Elijah were allowed to share their food with the dogs.

C. Daylight and Elijah were concerned about not having enough to eat.

D. Daylight and Elijah were determined to outlast the other men.

PASSAGE 2 – SOCIAL SCIENCE

In this passage, the legal concept of eminent domain is introduced and further discussed.

Line   Eminent domain is the power of a government to take, or condemn, privately owned
property. This condemnation power is part of
the fundamental authority of a governmental
5   entity. Indeed, in 1879, in *Boom Co v Patterson*,
the United States Supreme Court explained that
eminent domain is "an attribute of sovereignty."
However, this power is not without its limitations.
        The Fifth Amendment to the United States
10 Constitution provides that the federal government
may not take private property unless it is done for
a public use and the owner is reimbursed with just
compensation. Just compensation is a monetary
amount that will make the owner whole again for
15 his loss and is generally measured in relation to
the fair market value of the property, which is the
amount of money a reasonable purchaser would
pay for the property. Almost all state constitutions
contain similar clauses requiring just compensa-
20 tion when a state governmental agency takes
private property for public use. Some states, like
Alabama, Oklahoma, and South Carolina, allow
property to be taken for private use if the owner
consents. Arizona, Washington, and Wyoming
25 even allow their governments to take private
property for specific, limited private uses.
        "Public use" has traditionally meant that
the government could only take private land if it
could demonstrate that the land was necessary to
30 develop a project that had a valid public purpose,
that being that it would be used by the public.
The most common example of such a use is a new
road or highway. Other examples include public
utilities, public buildings, public parks, railroads,
35 and bridges. In 1954, in *Berman v Parker*, the
United States Supreme Court expanded the

scope of the government's taking power when it
affirmed the taking of a blighted area, or slum, for
redevelopment by a private enterprise. The Court
40 reasoned that the redeveloped property would be
beneficial to the public welfare of the community.
        In June 2005, the United States Supreme
Court broadened even further the scope of what
type of use constitutes a "public use." In *Kelo v
45 New London*, the Court held that private land can
be taken for the purpose of economic development even when the land taken does not qualify
as blighted but merely economically depressed.
In that case, private homes and businesses in
50 a desirable waterfront locale were taken for
the development of new residences, hotels, and
retail and office space, which the city contended
would create new jobs and increase tax revenues.
Opponents of such acquisitions argue that merely
55 incidental benefits to the state are not enough
to justify the exercise the power of condemnation. They are troubled by the potential abuses
that may result from interpreting "public use"
so broadly. For instance, as Justice Sandra Day
60 O'Connor suggested in her dissenting opinion,
the power would very likely be most beneficial
to those citizens "with disproportionate influence and power in the political process" to the
detriment of residents of poorer sectors of the
65 community or neighborhoods inhabited primarily
by minorities. But supporters of the *Kelo* decision
emphasize the potential appreciable benefit to the
community at large, citing that the needs of the
many often outweigh the needs of the few. They
70 also point out that Justice Paul Stevens expressly
recommended that the states are free to impose
limitations on the use of such power by local
governmental authorities.

146.

The second and third sentences (lines 3–7) are characterized, respectively, by:

F. warning and justification.

G. assertion and confirmation.

H. invocation and definition.

J. authority and reverence.

147.

According to the passage, eminent domain does all of the following, EXCEPT:

A. allows for condemnation of private property.

B. provides for just compensation, which is usually based on fair market value.

C. prevents local governments from limiting its power.

D. allows for redevelopment of blighted areas.

148.

The passage suggests that those who disapprove of the *Kelo* ruling and those who support it differ the most in:

F. their level of respect for the United States Supreme Court.

G. their belief in the free enterprise system.

H. their views regarding the definition of public use.

J. their confidence in the public's ability to decide what purposes to support.

149.

The author suggests which of the following about "a new road or highway" (lines 32–33)?

A. It would be planned to avoid taking private property.

B. It is an exemplary public use of land.

C. Private ownership rights outweigh government's rights to seize land on which to build it.

D. Private landowners would not benefit from its construction.

150.

The author included discussion of two Supreme Court justices' opinions (lines 59–73) in order to:

F. suggest that the Supreme Court maintains unlimited control over eminent domain rights.

G. assert that the debate over eminent domain is fractious.

H. claim that eminent domain rights are fundamentally wrong for democracy.

J. show that expansion of eminent domain rights is executed in a balanced manner.

151.

As used in the passage, the word "sovereignty" most likely means:

A. capital expenditures.

B. royal lines of succession.

C. inherent attribute of government.

D. English dominion.

152.

The passage serves primarily to:

F. introduce a topic in real estate law.

G. define Latin terms used in law.

H. describe a feud between Supreme Court justices.

J. advocate for the abolition of eminent domain.

153.

It can be reasonably inferred from the passage that, according to the Supreme Court, eminent domain is:

A. a nuisance.

B. impractical.

C. likely to be abused.

D. necessary.

154.

The author of the passage would most probably agree with which of the following statements?

F. All private property is sovereign.

G. Eminent domain powers have evolved over time.

H. Some states are not required to adhere to the Constitution.

J. Justice O'Connor opposed all uses of eminent domain.

155.

Justice Stevens's recommendation was most likely included in order to:

A. provide an example of flawed reasoning.

B. illustrate a mechanism for preventing governmental abuse of power.

C. prove that Justice O'Connor was in error.

D. refute an argument put forth by supporters of the *Kelo* decision.

PASSAGE 3 – HUMANITIES

In the following passage, the origin of and some of the variations in individual languages are examined.

Line The history of human language is as much a story of human expansion and interaction as it is one of political turmoil and cultural oppression. Careful analysis of language variation must seek evi-
5 dence not just in the flow of people and information across physical barriers such as oceans and mountain ranges, but also across political barriers such as borders, battlefields, and occupied lands. Too often are the natural, peaceful integration
10 and disintegration of cultures emphasized over the oppression and racism in human history that molds what we call individual languages today. This begs the question: What is the difference between a language and a dialect or vernacular?
15 For better or worse, the answer lies in the seemingly unshakeable tendency of humans to assert the dominance of their own culture over those of other people less capable of resistance.

So what the first assumption that must be made
20 is that the concept of individual languages—English, French, Spanish, and so on—is commonly misunderstood. In countries with a dominant national language, children are taught to speak and write in a standard way. This is
25 called *prescriptive language instruction*, meaning teaching a standard usage of the language. In England, people refer to this standard usage as The King's English; in the United States, many terms exist to describe this idealized form of the
30 English language, such as Standard American English, standard written English, or even Newscaster English, after the accent and grammar achieved by major national broadcasters who strive to remove the regional markers in their
35 mother tongue. Speakers of the prescriptive norm are often perceived to be well educated, intelligent, or of the upper classes.

So what does this reveal about language in general? First, the idea of well-defined languages
40 is false and stems from the tradition of teaching a prescriptive grammar. Linguists avoid making value judgments based on these differences; there is no such thing as American English, but rather an indeterminable number of varied speech
45 patterns that resemble each other closely enough to be considered part of a common group. We call this a language. For example, though many prominent journalists come from the American South, the typical listener would be shocked to
50 hear these professionals use *y'all* instead of the standard pronoun *you*. The common response to an example like this is rejection of *y'all* as "correct" English. The question has little merit, since again it presupposes a higher value placed
55 on Standard American English. One can narrow down the divisions of such languages into groups called dialects, though this term is controversial. What separates dialects from languages and languages from each other is better defined in
60 political history.

A clear example of the problem of labeling speech is in the Romance Languages, a term describing those forms of speech descended from Vulgar Latin, the language of the soldiers,
65 slaves, and commoners in the Roman Empire. As the Empire fell and its far-reaching possessions became more fractured and independent, Vulgar Latin took on unique traits in every separate area of Europe where it was spoken. With enough
70 time, clear differences emerged within different groups' usage of Vulgar Latin. Today, Portuguese, French, Spanish, Italian, and Romanian are treated as separate languages, though Occitan, Catalan, Sardinian, and other lesser-known lan-
75 guages are often called dialects. The key features that separate each of these are not in the grammar or lexicon, but instead in the political history behind them. Only recently have efforts been made to preserve what language diversity Western
80 Europe has left. It is a case study in minority discrimination, clearly manifest in a mistaken view of language.

156.

The purpose of lines 3–12 ("Careful . . . today") is to:

F.   defend diverse perspectives on language change.

G.   support the views held by professional linguists.

H.   introduce a topic of interest to most speakers of English.

J.   object to certain conceptions of language change.

157.

The rhetorical question in lines 13–14 ("What . . . vernacular") is used to:

A.   characterize the challenges faced by learners of a second language.

B.   illustrate the connection between social injustice and language learning.

C.   identify an ambiguity in defining languages.

D.   suggest the way that terminology can help clarify a difficult distinction.

158.

The author suggests that the method of "prescriptive language instruction" described in lines 26–35 ("In . . . tongue") is one of:

F.   deliberate racism.

G.   genuine empathy.

H.   uncommon effectiveness.

J.   traditional ethnocentrism.

159.

One can reasonably infer from the passage that the explanation for "Newscaster English" (line 32) shows the:

A. concern over the intelligibility of regional vernaculars.

B. resistance that most people exhibit toward rural dialects.

C. fear that most people feel about not speaking well in public.

D. importance of appearing intelligent and, therefore, credible.

160.

The example of "*y'all*," described in the third paragraph, emphasizes:

F. social discrimination.

G. mutual respect.

H. journalistic ethics.

J. audience expectations.

161.

The passage implies that:

A. some modern languages derive from the Latin spoken by the lower classes of Ancient Rome.

B. all Romance languages have several dialects.

C. prescriptive language instruction is only imposed on children in England and America.

D. Western European language diversity is beyond salvation.

162.

The passage could best be described as which of the following?

F. A call to action

G. A challenge to a commonly held belief

H. A history of oppression and racism

J. An examination of political language

163.

The author's attitude toward linguists can best be described as:

A. approving.

B. skeptical.

C. frustrated.

D. controversial.

164.

As used throughout the passage, the word, "lexicon" most likely means:

F. structure.

G. dialect.

H. vocabulary.

J. location.

165.

This passage is most likely directed toward:

A. experienced military translators.

B. Western European broadcasters.

C. American historians.

D. unsophisticated linguists.

PASSAGE 4 – NATURAL SCIENCE

The following passage is an adaptation from a report about the neurological disorder called synesthesia.

Line   Thousands, perhaps even millions, of people around the world are afflicted with a neurological condition called *synesthesia*. The word *synesthesia* comes from the Greek words *syn*, which
5   means "together," and *aisthesis*, which means "perception or sensation." Those affected by the disorder experience an involuntary, simultaneous joining of two senses; for example, some synesthetes—people with *synesthesia* —
10   perceive words or numbers as colors. These people might visualize the number "4" as red, or the letter "a" as blue when they hear or read numbers or words. Researchers do not know the causes of *synesthesia*, nor do they fully under-
15   stand the mechanisms of the disorder. However, some scientists believe that *synesthesia* results from crossed connections in the brain; synapses that are traditionally associated with one sensory system have somehow crossed over into another
20   sensory system, which leads to a juxtaposition of two, typically unrelated senses.

        Another theory postulates that *synesthesia* results from a perception breakdown. Researchers espouse the idea that, up until about four months
25   of age, infants experience undifferentiated sensory stimuli; most sounds also result in visual and tactile sensations. As infants continue to develop, the sensory process becomes modularized. *Synesthesia* occurs when this differentiation of
30   the senses is incomplete.

        Synesthetic perceptions are idiosyncratic and are as varied as the perceivers themselves. Theoretically, the number of types of *synesthesia* is bound only by the sensory pairings themselves,

35   such as the color/auditory pairing mentioned previously. Researchers estimate that there could be as many as 35 different broad pairings—sound/touch, taste/hearing, and so on—each characterized by many permutations and unique features.
40   Indeed the variations could be endless, with each synesthete perceiving a slightly different color or sensation, for example. Although the perceptions vary among individuals, according to Dr. Richard Cytowic, a leading *synesthesia* expert, no matter
45   what senses are joined in a given *synesthete*, the lifelong intersensory associations of the synesthetes remain stable. In other words, if the word "horse" is dark green, it is always perceived as such by the individual.

50   Despite the potential diversity in the manifestation of *synesthesia*, the actual known number of people with the disorder is relatively small. This is due, in part, to the probability that many people have the condition but do not realize what
55   it is. Most synesthetes are of normal or above normal intelligence and show no outward signs of an aberrant mental condition. In addition, standard neurological exams indicate no difference between a synesthete's brain activity and the
60   brain activity of a so-called non-synesthete. As a result, most people with *synesthesia* do not know that what they are experiencing is any different from what their friends and family perceive. It is also quite common for a synesthete, once he or
65   she realizes any anomaly, to remain silent for fear of being shunned or misunderstood.

        Currently, there is no officially established criterion or method for diagnosing *synesthesia*; researchers customarily must rely on an indi-
70   vidual recognizing his or her perceptual differences and then seeking answers from medical or psychological professionals.

166.

The passage can primarily be described as:

F. a personal account leading to a universal theory.

G. a description of a particular phenomenon.

H. an introduction to a firmly established ideal.

J. a story of how one individual inspired others.

167.

In line 20, "juxtaposition" most nearly means:

A. positioning close together.

B. crossing over.

C. disconnecting two closely related things.

D. associating based on tradition.

168.

The purpose of the second paragraph (lines 22–30) is to:

F. present a basis for questioning the existence of synesthesia.

G. advance an alternative explanation for a certain neurological condition.

H. question the motives of synesthetes who seek treatment.

J. develop a general theory from evidence of a specific condition

169.

The author uses the term "idiosyncratic" (line 31) in order to:

A. convey the difficulty of diagnosing synesthesia.

B. contrast normal sensory development with abnormal sensory development.

C. evoke a sense of mystery regarding synesthetic perceptions.

D. suggest that synesthetic perceptions are unique to the perceiver.

170.

Why does the author use the phrase "standard neurological exams" in line 58?

F. To dispel the notion that synesthetes undergo normal sensory development

G. To illustrate the point that synesthetes often suffer from aberrant mental conditions

H. To establish the fact that regular medical testing shows no difference between synesthetes and nonsynesthetes

J. To suggest that synesthetes are often subjected to unwarranted medical tests in order to diagnose their condition

171.

As used in line 28, "modularized" most likely means:

A. defective.

B. normal.

C. separate.

D. infantile.

172.

The author of the passage would most likely agree with which of the following?

A. All humans experience synesthesia at some point in their lives.

B. Synesthesia will eventually be cured.

C. The rate of synesthesia in the human population is often overestimated.

D. Synesthesia is difficult to diagnose.

173.

This passage most likely appeared in which of the following?

A. A children's book about the human body.

B. A college textbook used in an anatomy course.

C. An introductory text on brain science.

D. A hospital's direct mail fund-raising campaign.

174.

The passage states that the precise number of synesthetes is:

F. well-documented.

G. larger than expected.

H. relatively small.

J. growing exponentially.

175.

The author mentions a dark-green horse in line 48 primarily to:

A. illustrate a possible sensory association a synesthete may perceive.

B. challenge a common misconception about synesthesia.

C. show an error committed by researchers.

D. provide an example of a diagnostic criterion.

SCIENCE

PASSAGE I

The destruction of the coral reefs along coastlines worldwide presents a scientific challenge. Researchers have postulated various theories to explain it. Two scientists discuss competing theories that have found support among some members of the scientific community. Oceanographers are not unanimous in supporting either one.

Scientist 1

Coral bleaching is a phenomenon that occurs when coral has lost its symbiotic algae, *zooxanthellae*, which live within the coral's tissue. As the phenomenon's name suggests, bleaching causes the coral to lose its color, becoming either lighter or completely white. When coral is stressed, the *zooxanthellae* (which are responsible for giving the coral its color in the first place) will be expelled. Many factors can stress coral, not the least of which are water temperature changes. Also, changes in the ocean's acidity, overfishing, pathogens present in the water, and contaminated runoff can produce situations that affect the growth of the coral's necessary algae. Coral can survive this bleaching occurrence and may eventually be recolonized either by the same *zooxanthellae* species as before or by a new species. Generally, coral bleaching affects an entire colony of coral at one time. Scientists continue to study coral bleaching in an effort to understand its cause.

Scientist 2

White syndrome is a disease among coral that leaves these beautiful sea creatures completely colorless and often lifeless as well. Some scientists believe that white syndrome is triggered within the coral itself and is not representative of an attack from an outside enemy. For some unknown reason, the infected coral's immune system attacks not only the pathogenic cells that cause the disease but destroys healthy cells as well. Curiously, studies have shown that very dense populations of coral colonies are more susceptible to this disease than are more isolated groupings. Additionally, the white syndrome pathogens seem to move from one coral to the next, attacking healthy coral colonies in methodical strips, similar to humans passing cold or flu germs from one person to the next. Attempts at understanding this coral killer point to global changes in ocean temperature in combination with high coral density.

176.

Oceanographers who subscribe to the two theories above would most likely agree that:

F. loss of color in coral reefs is the result of pathogens.

G. coral reefs that have lost their color will bounce back once conditions return to normal.

H. fluctuations in ocean temperature are likely to affect coral adversely.

J. a concerted effort can reverse the effects of global warming on ocean temperatures.

177.

According to Scientist 1, healthy coral tissue will expel *zooxanthellae* when:

A. the algae becomes acidic.

B. the coral turns white.

C. the coral is under stress.

D. the algae attacks the coral.

178.

Which of the scientists would be most likely to agree that algae has a positive impact on coral growth?

F. Scientist 1 only

G. Scientist 2 only

H. Both Scientist 1 and Scientist 2

J. Neither Scientist 1 nor Scientist 2

179.

According to Scientist 2, pathogens methodically attack coral reefs, moving from one coral to another. Which of the following findings, if true, could be used to *counter* this argument?

A. Dense populations of coral are frequently attacked by known pathogens.

B. Isolated groups of coral are less healthy than dense populations of coral.

C. Global changes in ocean temperatures adversely impact large groups of healthy coral.

D. Healthy coral are found thriving next to completely colorless and lifeless coral.

180.

Suppose that an offshore oil drilling platform was constructed at a site thousands of miles from a coral reef. How would this most likely affect the scientists' viewpoints, if at all?

F. It would strengthen Scientist 1's viewpoint only.

G. It would weaken Scientist 2's viewpoint only.

H. It would strengthen both scientists' viewpoints.

J. It would have no effect on either scientists' viewpoint.

181.

Which of the following would Scientist 1 suggest leads to the destruction of coral reefs?

A. Infection of healthy cells in the immune system

B. Expulsion of symbiotic algae due to stress

C. Attack from an unknown predator

D. Passing of pathogens from one coral to another

182.

Which of the following best illustrates the major difference between the two scientists' opinions?

F. Scientist 1 points to an external cause, while Scientist 2 suggests an internal cause.

G. Scientist 1 proves a definitive cause, whereas Scientist 2 indicates that more research is necessary.

H. Scientist 1 examines a well-known problem, while Scientist 2 brings new information to light.

J. Scientist 1 relies on anecdotal evidence, whereas Scientist 2 adheres to scientific fact.

PASSAGE II

Benzene gas is carcinogenic; it has been linked to causing certain cancers, such as leukemia and lymphoma. Cars are a major source of atmospheric benzene gas in urban areas. A group of researchers hypothesize that cars emit more benzene gas at colder temperatures, compared to warmer temperatures, during the first 15 minutes after a car engine has been started. The following experiments were designed to test this hypothesis.

Experiment 1

To collect car exhaust, researchers attached a hose from the tailpipe of a car to a plastic bag. The engine was started, and researchers used a syringe to extract 1 mL samples of exhaust at 2-minute intervals. The samples were injected in a *gas chromatograph*, an instrument used to separate a mixture of gases into individual components. Researchers determined the percent by volume of benzene in the exhaust by comparing the exhaust with mixtures of known benzene concentrations. Samples of exhaust were taken from four cars tested at an external temperature of −10°F. The results were recorded in Table 1.

	Table 1			
Time after starting (min)	Percent of benzene in the exhaust at −10°F:			
	1976 Model A	1976 Model B	1995 Model A	1995 Model B
1	1.7	1.6	0.6	0.1
3	2.0	1.9	0.5	0.6
5	4.3	3.8	0.7	1.2
7	1.8	5.0	0.5	1.5
9	1.6	4.5	0.3	1.3
11	1.5	4.0	0.3	1.0
13	1.4	3.5	0.3	1.0
15	1.2	3.5	0.2	0.9

GO ON TO THE NEXT PAGE.

Experiment 2

The procedure from Experiment 1 was repeated at an external temperature of 20°F. The results were recorded in Table 2.

Table 2				
Time after starting (min)	Percent of benzene in the exhaust at 20°F:			
	1976 Model A	1976 Model B	1995 Model A	1995 Model B
1	1.0	0.4	0.1	0.1
3	1.4	1.0	0.2	0.5
5	1.7	3.0	0.3	0.7
7	0.8	3.5	0.1	0.4
9	0.7	3.5	0.1	0.3
11	0.5	3.2	0.1	0.2
13	0.5	2.5	0.1	0.1
15	0.4	2.4	0.1	0.1

183.

In the experiments, which of the following was an independent variable?

A. The temperature at which the engine was started

B. The percent of benzene in the exhaust

C. The volume of exhaust that was collected

D. The method of collecting samples

184.

Do the results of Experiment 1 support the hypothesis that, at a given time and temperature, the exhaust of newer cars contains less benzene gas than the exhaust of older cars?

F. Yes; the highest percent of benzene was in the exhaust of the 1995 Model B.

G. Yes; each of the 1995 models had a lower percent of benzene than either of the 1976 models.

H. No; the highest percent of benzene was in the exhaust of the 1976 Model B.

J. No; each of the 1976 models had a lower percent of benzene than either of the 1995 models.

185.

Based on the results of the experiments and the information in the table below, cars in which of the following cities would most likely contribute the greatest amount of benzene to the atmosphere in January? (Assume that the types, numbers, and ages of cars used in each city are approximately equal.)

City	Avg. temperature (°F) in January
Detroit	22.2
Chicago	28.9
Denver	39.8
Pasadena	67.5

A. Detroit

B. Chicago

C. Denver

D. Pasadena

186.

Experiment 1 and Experiment 2 differ in that in Experiment 1:

F. older cars were used.

G. the temperature was lower.

H. the starting times were adjusted.

J. more exhaust was collected.

187.

Many states require annual testing of cars to determine the levels of benzene and other gases in their exhaust emissions. Based on the experiments, in order to determine the maximum percent of benzene found in a car's exhaust, during which of the following times after starting a car would it be best to sample the exhaust?

A. 1–3 min

B. 5–7 min

C. 11–13 min

D. 13 min or longer

PASSAGE III

A physics class studied the frictional forces of moving objects. Students performed three experiments using their physics book as the moving object. The book was either wrapped in paper or left unwrapped. To pull the book, students tied a twine around the book and attached it to a spring scale, as shown in Figure 1.

Figure 1

The spring scale measured the amount of force, in newtons (N), required to move the book across the table at a constant speed, which is equal to the amount of frictional force between the book and the tabletop.

(Note: All physics books were pulled at a constant low speed, unless stated otherwise.)

Experiment 1

Four physics books were wrapped in a different type of paper and then pulled across the table. The measured forces are provided in Table 1.

Table 1	
Type of paper	**Force (N)**
Wrapping paper	5.7
Notebook paper	5.3
Waxed paper	4.9
Newspaper	4.1

GO ON TO THE NEXT PAGE.

Experiment 2

Students pulled an unwrapped physics book across the table. The process was then repeated with 1, 2, 3, or 4 identical unwrapped physics books stacked on top of the first book (see Table 2).

Table 2	
Number of physics books pulled across the table at one time	**Force (N)**
1	3.4
2	6.9
3	10.2
4	13.7
5	17.0

Experiment 3

A physics book wrapped in wrapping paper was pulled in order for it to move at a medium speed. Then it was pulled in order for the book to move at a high speed (see Table 3).

Table 3	
Speed	**Force (N)**
Medium	5.7
High	5.7

188.

Which of the following ranks the different types of paper used to wrap the physics books in order from the paper that presented the greatest resistance to sliding to the paper that presented the least resistance to sliding?

F. Newspaper, waxed paper, notebook paper, wrapping paper

G. Notebook paper, wrapping paper, waxed paper, newspaper

H. Wrapping paper, notebook paper, waxed paper, newspaper

J. Wrapping paper, waxed paper, newspaper, notebook paper

189.

In Experiment 1, students wrapped physics books in different types of paper to vary the amount of frictional force between:

A. wrapped books and the tabletop.

B. stacked books, so that the books would not slide over each other when pulled across the table.

C. wrapped books and the twine used to pull the books.

D. types of papers and the books.

190.

If Experiment 3 was repeated with a stack of 6 unwrapped physics books, the reading on the spring scale would be closest to which of the following?

F. 8.6 N

G. 9.9 N

H. 13.8 N

J. 20.6 N

191.

The students conducted a fifth experiment, in which they took the 4 wrapped physics books from Experiment 1 and pushed them in such a way that the books slid across the table at similar initial speeds. Based on results from Experiment 1, the physics book wrapped in which paper would most likely have taken the *longest* amount of time to come to a complete stop?

A. Wrapping paper

B. Notebook paper

C. Waxed paper

D. Newspaper

192.

Based on the results of Experiments 1 and 3, which of the following correctly describes the effect of a book's speed on the amount of frictional force on the physics book?

F. As speed increased, the amount of frictional force always decreased.

G. As speed increased, the amount of frictional force always increased.

H. As speed increased, the amount of frictional force increased and then decreased.

J. The speed did not affect the amount of frictional force on the physics book.

193.

What was the main purpose of Experiment 2?

A. To determine the relationship between frictional force and the mass of a wrapped physics book

B. To determine the relationship between frictional force and the weight of a stack of physics books

C. To determine the relationship between frictional force and the speed of the moving physics books

D. To determine the relationship between frictional force and the type of paper used to wrap the physics book

PASSAGE IV

Amino acids are the building blocks of proteins. They are formed together based on DNA and its interaction with RNA. The process first starts with *transcription*, where the base sequence DNA is copied to form messenger RNA (mRNA). It then travels to a ribosome, where transfer RNA (tRNA) finds and delivers amino acids that match the base sequence of the mRNA, a process called *translation*. The amino acids then bond together to form peptide strands. These strands fold and bond together to form proteins. This process is depicted in Figure 1.

Figure 1

Each 3-base unit on the mRNA forms a *codon*, which corresponds to a specific amino acid. Table 1 displays the 64 codons scientists have identified, along with the amino acids specified by each codon.

GO ON TO THE NEXT PAGE.

Table 1							
AAU AAC	Asparagine	CAU CAC	Histidine	GAU GAC	Aspartic acid	UAU UAC	Tyrosine
AAA AAG	Lysine	CAA CAG	Glutamine	GAA GAG	Glutamic acid	UAA UAG	**Stop
ACU ACC ACA ACG	Threonine	CCU CCC CCA CCG	Proline	GCU GCC GCA GCG	Alanine	UCU UCC UCA UCG	Serine
AGU AGC	Serine	CGU CGC CGA CGG	Arginine	GGU GGC GGA GGG	Glycine	UGU UGC	Cysteine
AGA AGG	Arginine					UGA	**Stop
						UGG	Tryptophan
AUU AUC AUA	Isoleucine	CUU CUC CUA CUG	Leucine	GUU GUC GUA GUG	Valine	UUU UUC	Phenylalanine
AUG	Methionine					UUA UUG	Leucine

**Stop codons specify the end of the polypeptide chain.

194.

According to Table 1, the mRNA strand shown below, when read from left to right, encodes for which amino acids?

C U G A G A U G G

F. Arginine, glutamic acid, methionine

G. Leucine, arginine, tryptophan

H. Leucine, serine, cysteine

J. Lysine, isoleucine, tyrosine

195.

Based on the information in Table 1, all of the following codons encode for the same amino acid EXCEPT:

A. AGA.

B. AGG.

C. AGU.

D. CGU.

196.

If the codon labeled A, shown below in a mRNA strand, was changed to CCA, what would the effect be on the translation of this mRNA strand?

F. The amino acid specified by codon A would be the only variation.

G. The amino acid specified by codon A and the amino acids specified by the following codons would be altered.

H. The original polypeptide strand would be identical to the new polypeptide strand.

J. Translation would stop because CCA is a stop codon.

197.

According to the passage, the correct order for the synthesis of proteins is which of the following?

A. DNA, RNA, proteins, polypeptides

B. DNA, tRNA, mRNA, polypeptides, proteins

C. RNA, DNA, tRNA, polypeptides, proteins

D. DNA, mRNA, tRNA, polypeptides, proteins

198.

Based on the information in Table 1, all of the following codons *must* appear at the end of a polypeptide chain EXCEPT:

F. UGA.

G. UAG.

H. AGU.

J. UAA.

PASSAGE V

Nitrates are substances that occur naturally in the environment at low concentrations in water (including drinking water), plants, and the soil. In nature, nitrates are relatively nontoxic and are not likely to be a health hazard. In higher concentrations, however, nitrates can be potentially threatening contaminants.

Human activities can be responsible for increased levels of nitrates in groundwater. The most common sources of nitrates produced by human activity can be traced to industrial pollution, human waste septic systems, and agricultural processes. Industrial wastewaters and refuse dumps contaminate the soil and can contribute to excess nitrate levels if pollutants seep into groundwater supplies. Nitrogen fertilizers, widely used to promote the growth of plants, wash into rivers and streams and seep into the groundwater when it rains. Septic systems, if poorly constructed or leaky, also allow contaminants to seep into the soil and eventually into the groundwater.

Figure 1 shows the nitrate concentration (in milligrams per liter) for each of four locations (1, 2, 3, and 4) of drinking water supplies in a township. Figure 1 also shows the water quality standard (set by officials in this particular township) and the Maximum Contaminant Level (MCL) set by the Environmental Protection Agency (EPA). Any drinking water source that exceeds the MCL is considered unsafe for human consumption.

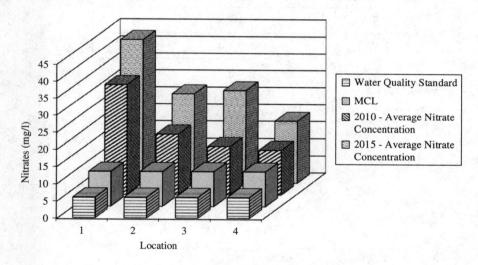

Figure 1

GO ON TO THE NEXT PAGE.

Concerned with the high level of nitrates in Location 1, several scientists attempt to determine the source of nitrate pollution in a lake within Location 1. Table 1 shows the nitrate concentration of water samples collected from three different streams that empty into the lake at Location 1. The streams chosen for the study collect runoff from nitrogen fertilizers used at a nearby farm. Two samples were collected from each stream, one in the early summer (S) and one in early winter before the water froze (W).

Table 1	
	Nitrates (mg/l)
Stream A	
S	26.5
W	35.7
Stream B	
S	8.9
W	15.4
Stream C	
S	19.8
W	23.4

199.

According to Figure 1, at Location 1, the average nitrate concentration in 2010 was:

A. lower than the average nitrate concentration in 2015.

B. higher than the average nitrate concentration in 2015.

C. the same as the average nitrate concentration in 2015.

D. not measured.

200.

According to Figure 1, water with a nitrate concentration below the MCL is most likely:

F. contaminated by human waste.

G. considered safe for human consumption.

H. considered unsafe for human consumption.

J. contaminated by fertilizer runoff.

201.

According to Figure 1, all of the following are most likely true, EXCEPT:

A. the water quality standard is the same at all locations.

B. the MCL is the same at all locations.

C. the average nitrate concentration in 2010 is the same at all locations.

D. the average nitrate concentration in 2015 is different at all locations.

202.

Based on Table 1, compared to the nitrate levels in early summer, the nitrate levels in early winter are:

F. always lower.

G. always higher.

H. sometimes lower, sometimes higher.

J. constant for all streams.

203.

According to the passage, which of the following contributes most to the pollution of the lake within Location 1?

A. Stream A in early summer

B. Stream B in early summer

C. Stream A in early winter

D. Stream B in early winter

204.

Suppose that in 2012, the septic systems of several homes in an older subdivision near the lake in Location 1 began leaking. Does this information support the data presented in Figure 1?

F. Yes, because the nitrate levels in Location 1 decreased between 2010 and 2015.

G. Yes, because the nitrate levels in Location 1 increased between 2010 and 2015.

H. No, because the high nitrate levels in Location 1 were due solely to fertilizer runoff.

J. No, because the nitrate levels in Location 1 were higher than those in Location 2 in 2015.

PASSAGE VI

Certain caterpillars have been observed eating specific crops, thereby reducing the total harvest of the crops. Table 1 is a key for identifying caterpillars commonly found across the United States.

	Table 1		
Step	Trait	Appearance	Result
1	Hair thickness	Dense	Go to Step 2.
		Thin	Go to Step 5.
2	Length of hair	Long (>3 cm)	Go to Step 3.
		Short (<3 cm)	Go to Step 4.
3	Color	Yellow	*Spilosoma virginica*
		Green	*Automeris io*
4	Stripe color	Orange	*Pieris rapae*
		Pink	*Colias eurytheme*
5	Hornlike projections	Present	Go to Step 6.
		Absent	Go to Step 8.
6	Position of hornike projection	Behind the head	*Papilio polyxenes*
		Posterior end	Go to Step 7.
7	Color of hornlike projection	Blue	*Manduca quinquemaculata*
		Red	*Manduca sexta*
8	Spots on head	Present	Go to Step 10.
		Absent	Go to Step 9.
9	Skin texture	Wrinkled	*Melittia cucurbitae*
		Rough	*Helicoverpa zea*
10	Color of spots	Brown	*Plutella xylostella*
		White	*Spodoptera ornithogalli*

GO ON TO THE NEXT PAGE.

A farmer tending to his fields discovered four caterpillars. The characteristics of each caterpillar are listed in Table 2.

Table 2	
Caterpillar	**Traits**
A	• Dense hair • Long hair • Green
B	• Thin hair • Hornlike projections on posterior end • Blue hornlike projections
C	• Thin hair • No projections • Head solid color • Skin is wrinkled
D	• Dense hair • Short hair • Pink stripe

205.

Table 1 is used to identify organisms that belong to which kingdom?

A. Animal

B. Protozoa

C. Plant

D. Fungus

206.

According to Table 1, which of the following traits will a caterpillar have if it is closely related to *Colias eurytheme*?

F. Yellow body

G. Pink stripe

H. Rough skin

J. White spots

207.

According to Tables 1 and 2, which trait of Caterpillar C distinguishes it from *Spodoptera ornithogalli*?

A. Thin hair

B. No hornlike projections

C. Head is a solid color

D. Skin is wrinkled

208.

Caterpillar B and Caterpillar C diverge at which of the steps listed in Table 1?

F. Step 2

G. Step 3

H. Step 4

J. Step 5

209.

According to Tables 1 and 2, Caterpillar A is most likely a:

A. *Spilosoma virginica.*

B. *Automeris io.*

C. *Papilio polyxenes.*

D. *Manduca sexta.*

PASSAGE VII

To investigate cricket chirps, high school biology students developed the following field studies.

Study 1

Students placed tape recorders at outdoor sites to record cricket chirps for 1 hour on 1 day. Students used the recordings to estimate the cricket population and the chirp rate (chirps/minute) of individual crickets. Students then ranked the volume of each chirp on a scale of 1 to 10 (1 signifying a very soft chirp and a 10 signifying a very loud chirp). The results are displayed in Table 1.

Table 1		
Population size	Average chirp rate (chirps/minute)	Average chirp volume
<10	28.3	3.4
10–15	20.9	3.5
16–20	32.4	3.7
>20	39.1	3.3

Study 2

For 4 hours, cricket populations with greater than 20 crickets were studied following the procedure described in Study 1. Average chirp rates and chirp volumes are displayed in Table 2. Figure 2 displays the average call rates, broken down into 15 minute increments.

Table 2		
Time of day (P.M.)	Average chirp rate (chirps/minute)	Average chirp volume
7–8	24.3	3.2
8–9	38.4	3.5
9–10	38.9	3.7
10–11	38.9	3.9

GO ON TO THE NEXT PAGE.

Figure 2

Study 3

Students studied populations of greater than 20 crickets, using the same procedure as in Study 1. Chirps were record between 9 and 10 P.M. for 30 days. Air temperatures were also recorded. The results are displayed in Table 3.

Table 3		
Air temperature (°C)	**Average chirp rate (chirps/minute)**	**Average chirp volume**
15–17	0.0	0.0
18–20	5.1	0.5
21–23	16.3	2.1
24–26	39.7	3.4

210.

Study 3 was designed to investigate how average chirp rate and average chirp volume vary with respect to which of the following factors?

F. Time of day

G. Population size

H. Air temperature

J. Predator presence

211.

Based on the results of Studies 1 and 3, one would predict that crickets exposed to which of the following sets of conditions would chirp most frequently?

A. A cricket population of 10 and an air temperature of 15°C

B. A cricket population of 10 and an air temperature of 19°C

C. A cricket population 20 and an air temperature of 21°C

D. A cricket population of 20 and an air temperature of 25°C

212.

After further research, the students learned that in the species studied, only male crickets chirp. Based on this finding, the students should reevaluate which of the following conclusions from data?

F. The time during which crickets are most likely to chirp

G. The number of crickets in each population

H. The temperature at which crickets are most likely to chirp

J. The volume at which crickets generally chirp

213.

Based on the data in Table 3, one would conclude that at 8:30 P.M. on the day that study 2 was performed the air temperature at the study sites was approximately:

A. 16°C.

B. 19°C.

C. 22°C.

D. 24°C.

214.

Do the data support the hypothesis that crickets in small populations chirp more frequently than crickets in large populations?

F. No; the data in Table 1 contradict this hypothesis.

G. No; the data in Table 2 contradict this hypothesis.

H. Yes; the data in Table 1 support this hypothesis.

J. Yes; the data in Table 2 support this hypothesis.

215.

Based on Studies 1, 2, and 3, the average volume of cricket chirps is most strongly affected by which of the following factors?

A. Air temperature

B. Time of day

C. Average chirp rate

D. Population size

ANSWERS AND EXPLANATIONS

ENGLISH

1. **The best answer is B.**   This is a punctuation question. According to Standard Written English, a comma should be used to join a dependent and an independent clause. In this case, the dependent clause is the introductory clause, "When I was growing up." This clause is considered dependent because it does not contain a main verb and is therefore dependent on the rest of the sentence to provide the main verb. The rest of the sentence can stand alone as an independent clause because it contains a subject and a verb: "My family (subject) would visit (verb)."

2. **The best answer is F.**   The ACT often tests idiom, the common usage of a word or phrase, with prepositions. Prepositions are short words used to show position, location, direction, and time. You need to pay attention to the context of the sentence and rely upon your knowledge of how the English language works. In this sentence, the prepositional phrase "with thousands" correctly shows the location of the author's family: *with* thousands of other tourists at the festival.

3. **The best answer is B.**   This question tests verb tense. Verbs indicate the action taking place in the sentence, and a verb's tense tells you *when* the action took place. In this case, the simple present tense verb *honors* is used to show that the festival is something that takes place regularly or repeatedly.

4. **The best answer is H.**   This ACT question tests your ability to determine whether information is relevant. The question tells you that the statement is true, so you have to decide whether, as a reader, you care about the information. In other words, is it relevant? If it doesn't add something to the topic being discussed or it distracts the reader from the topic, it is not relevant and should not be added to the essay. In this case, while the fact that California has many other festivals might be interesting, it is not relevant. The essay focuses on only one such festival.

5. **The best answer is C.**   This is an example of a NOT question, which requires a slight shift in your question-answering paradigm. You are mostly required to identify the correct answer to each question. However, NOT and EXCEPT questions require you to identify the choice that doesn't work. You can assume that the underlined portion is correct, so your job is to eliminate any of the answer choices that do the same thing as the underlined portion. In this case, you want to look at the punctuation being used. The underlined portion uses a semicolon to join two independent clauses. Since a period does the same thing, answer choice A can be eliminated. Answer choice B correctly uses a comma and a coordinating conjunction to join two independent clauses, so it can also be eliminated. Answer choice C, however, contains a comma splice, wherein a comma is used to join two independent clauses, which it can never do alone. Therefore, answer choice C would NOT be acceptable.

6. **The best answer is J.**   This is a question that tests your ability to use the correct word in context. If you have a strong vocabulary, you will likely answer these questions with ease. You can assume that the underlined portion is acceptable, so a good way to answer this kind of question is to plug the answer choices into the sentence in place of the underlined word. The choice that least fits the context is the best answer. Even though *perusing* and *reading* can be synonymous, the context does not support the word *reading*.

7. **The best answer is A.** This question tests verb tense. Verbs indicate the action taking place in the sentence, and a verb's tense tells you *when* the action took place. The present perfect simple tense, *has become*, is used here because the consequences of past actions are important in the present.

8. **The best answer is G.** Here we have a punctuation question. Many students are confused about the difference between an apostrophe before the *s* and an apostrophe after the *s*. According to Standard Written English, the apostrophe comes before the *s* at the end of a noun when the noun shows singular possession, and after the *s* at the end of the noun when the noun shows plural possession. In this case, we know that there are many residents, so the noun is plural. This means that you can eliminate answer choices F and J, which indicate singular possession (the apostrophe comes before the *s*). Next, focus on the word *offerings*. Does it show possession, or is it just a plural noun? Because it is just a plural noun (nothing "belongs to" the possessions; the possessions "belong to" the residents), only answer choice G works.

9. **The best answer is A.** This question tests your ability to recognize the correct transitional word or phrase to use in context. Because the previous paragraph discusses some of the specific things the family enjoyed during the festival, it makes sense that they might also enjoy visiting one of the town's historical sites. The phrase "Of course" suggests the obvious nature of the family's interest in all aspects of the Festival. Additionally, this paragraph goes on to tell you that the author's mother was devout in her Catholic faith, so the transition makes even more sense as written. Answer choice C creates an incomplete sentence—always be careful not to introduce additional errors on the English test.

10. **The best answer is G.** The ACT will always reward the most clear and concise expression of the idea. Look for opportunities to use active over passive voice, fix misplaced modifiers, and avoid awkward sentence construction. Only answer choice G makes it clear that it is the swallows who make their nests in Capistrano.

11. **The best answer is C.**   This is a question that tests your ability to use the correct word in context. If you have a strong vocabulary, you will likely answer these questions with ease. If vocabulary is not your strong suit, plug the answer choices back into the sentence and check to see if they "sound" right. Use the process of elimination to get rid of answer choices that just don't fit the context of the sentence. For example, it doesn't make sense that a summer vacation would be delivered, so eliminate answer choice D. And although *reproach* and *approach* sound similar, when you read each word in the sentence, it should become clear that *approach* conveys the intended idea and is the right word to use.

12. **The best answer is J.**   When faced with a question about pronouns, always make sure that the pronoun has a clear antecedent. In other words, does the reader know who *it* is or who *they* are? If the answer to that question is not evident, it's usually best to use a noun instead of a pronoun. Remember that the antecedent (the noun to which the pronoun refers) should be close enough to the pronoun to eliminate any ambiguity.

13. **The best answer is D.**   The ACT often tests idiom, the common usage of a word or phrase, with prepositions. Prepositions are short words used to show position, location, direction, and time. You need to pay attention to the context of the sentence and rely upon your knowledge of how the English language works. In this sentence, the town relies *on* summer tourism; it does not rely *about*, *into*, or *aside* summer tourism.

14. **The best answer is F.**   This is a transitional language question. The word *despite* suggests a contrast. The fact that the swallows are locally significant but only became popular because of a song provides the contrast that *despite* introduces. The other answer choices do not fit the context.

15. **The best answer is A.**   This type of question asks you to make connections in the text. Look back at the first paragraph: it introduces the Festival of the Swallows and mentions that the writer and her family visit San Juan Capistrano to celebrate the return of the swallows. The best answer will reference the return of the family to San Juan Capistrano, mimicking the return of the swallows.

16. **The best answer is F.**   This is a pronoun question. Pronouns replace the antecedent, or the noun that comes before the pronoun. Here, that noun is *people*, and the word *people* also happens to be the subject of the sentence. Therefore, *people* should be replaced with the subjective pronoun, *who*.

17. **The best answer is D.**   This is a classic ACT redundancy question. Because being rich implies wealth, it's not necessary to include any further information about money or wealth. Always remember to read the sentence in its entirety and eliminate any redundant statements.

18. **The best answer is G.**   Here is a transitional language question. In this case, you want to look for the best way to lead the reader from the last sentence of the first paragraph to the topic of the second paragraph. Because the last sentence of the first paragraph mentions "other differences," it makes sense that the next paragraph would provide an example of some of those differences.

19. **The best answer is C.**   The ACT is notorious for tricky questions, and this is no exception. Often when pronouns are being tested, the ACT will include the word *its'* among the answer choices. Remember that the apostrophe after the *s* indicates plural possession. Since *it* is a singular pronoun, it can never take plural possession. Therefore, you can always eliminate any answer choice that includes the word *its'*. Your next task here is to determine whether the antecedent is singular or plural—in other words, whose existence are we talking about? The noun phrase in this sentence is "a real historical figure," which refers to Robin Hood. The pronoun *his* is the most precise and fits best here.

20. **The best answer is F.**   This is a verb question. Remember when choosing a verb to pay specific attention to who or what performs the action and when the action takes place. In this case, the helping verbs *has been* indicate present perfect continuous tense. This form is used to refer to an action that started in the past and is still continuing in the present or expected to continue in the future. Therefore, the correct active verb to use here is *portrayed*.

21. **The best answer is D.**   The ACT often tests idiom, the common usage of a word or phrase, with prepositions. Prepositions are short words used to show position, location, direction, and time. You need to pay attention to the context of the sentence and rely upon your knowledge of how the English language works. The context here indicates that Robin Hood is the savior of the poor—he "takes on" this role.

22. **The best answer is G.**   In Standard Written English, *like* is used as a preposition to show the relationship between words in a sentence, and *as* is used as a conjunction to connect ideas. The author intends to make the connection that the characters in question are Will Scarlet and Little John, so it is appropriate to use the word *as*.

23. **The best answer is B.**   This is a question that tests your ability to use the correct word in context. If you have a strong vocabulary, you will likely answer these questions with ease. If vocabulary is not your strong suit, plug the answer choices back into the sentence and check to see if they "sound" right. Use the process of elimination to get rid of answer choices that just don't fit the context of the sentence. The word *except* means to exclude, while the word *accept* means to agree to something. Therefore, *acceptable* is the best choice here.

24. **The best answer is H.**   This question tests your ability to understand sentence structure and flow of ideas. The best approach to this type of question is to try the underlined portion in the spots indicated in each answer choice, and listen to the sentence. In this case, the word *disparate* is an adjective modifying the noun *works*, so it is best placed before the word *works*.

25. **The best answer is B.**   The ACT often tests idiom, the common usage of a word or phrase, with prepositions. Prepositions are short words used to show position, location, direction, and time. You need to pay attention to the context of the sentence and rely upon your knowledge of how the English language works. In this sentence, the notion of "Robin Hood sustaining an inclusive, nearly democratic society friendly to the poor and women" is a modern ideal, so it is an *adaption to* modern times.

26. **The best answer is H.**   This is a verb question, so take a look at the action represented in the sentence. The sentence implies that once Robin Hood became the Earl of Huntingdon, he started to represent legitimate kingship. In other words, the action (representing) *began* when Robin became an earl. Standard Written English requires the use of a helping verb with *begun*, but NOT with *began*. The word *beginning* is used as a participle and not a main verb, so answer choice G creates an incomplete sentence.

27. **The best answer is A.**   To answer this question, you have to look closely at the context. Because the sentence includes the word *however*, you know that the Robin Hood's early image is in contrast to his current image. The sentence states that today Robin Hood is considered a popular and charming outlaw. The word that most clearly indicates a contrast to popular and charming is *savagery*.

28. **The best answer is G.**   This is a verb question, so take a look at the action represented in the sentence. Consider the modal verb *would have been*, which is useful for expressing your present feelings about a past action. You can simplify the action to help make sense of the verbs: "Resisting the ruling class would have been difficult due to the real history of the Middle Ages." The other verb forms would not work in this restructuring of the sentence.

29. **The best answer is D.**   To answer this question, look back at the paragraph to determine the main idea or topic. The paragraph is mostly about comparing the fictional character Robin Hood to the reality of the Middle Ages. Only answer choice D combines both of the primary ideas discussed in the paragraph, making it the best concluding sentence.

30. **The best answer is H.**   To answer this question, you must consider the overall topic of the passage. Rephrase the question as follows: Is this a brief descriptive essay about the evolution of the Robin Hood tales? Next, look at the title, the introductory paragraph, and the first sentences of a few of the body paragraphs. You will quickly see that the answer to the question is yes, this is a brief descriptive essay about the evolution of the Robin Hood tales, because the essay provides examples of how the character of Robin Hood is perceived differently now than it was in the early thirteenth century.

31. **The best answer is B.**   This is a classic ACT verb question. Notice that the underlined portion, *could of*, and answer choice C, *would of*, incorrectly use the preposition *of* instead of the auxiliary verb *have*. The modal verb *could have* suggests that something was possible in the past, but it didn't happen, which fits the context perfectly.

32. **The best answer is J.**   To answer this transitional language question, read the sentence in its entirety to let your brain "hear" it. Answer choices F, G, and H create incomplete sentences, whereas answer choice J maintains both the flow of information and the correct sentence structure.

33. **The best answer is D.**   This is a verb question. Remember when choosing a verb to pay specific attention to who or what performs the action and when the action takes place. It is also important to maintain parallel structure—in other words, make sure the verb forms match. The paragraph is written in the simple past tense, so the simple past tense verb *gathered* is correct.

34. **The best answer is H.**   To correctly answer this question, notice that the sentence is giving you two pieces of information—she gave a concert and she was a member of the church choir. There is nothing conditional about those two pieces of information, so you should join them with the coordinating conjunction *and*.

35. **The best answer is B.**   To answer this transitional language question, read the sentence in its entirety to let your brain "hear" it. Pay attention to the context. This sentence indicates a contrast—even though she was talented, venues refused to allow her to perform because of her race. The transitional word that represents a contrast is *despite*.

36. **The best answer is J.**   This ACT question tests your ability to determine whether information is relevant. The question tells you that the statement is true, so you have to decide whether, as a reader, you care about the information. In other words, is it relevant? If it doesn't add something to the topic being discussed or it distracts the reader from the topic, it is not relevant and should not be added to the essay. This statement is distracting and disrupts the flow of the essay, which is only about Marion Anderson's struggles.

37. **The best answer is B.**   The ACT tests Standard Written English, so the intended idea should be expressed clearly and concisely. In addition, the question asks for the most succinct answer. Answer choice B gives the reader the necessary information and maintains the tone of the essay. The other answer choices are grammatically correct but too wordy.

38. **The best answer is F.**   The ACT often tests idiom, the common usage of a word or phrase, with prepositions. Prepositions are short words used to show position, location, direction, and time. You need to pay attention to the context of the sentence and rely upon your knowledge of how the English language works. In Standard Written English, it is customary to say that the competition was *sponsored by* the New York Philharmonic Society, because the Society made it possible for the competition to take place.

39. **The best answer is C.**   To answer this transitional language question, read the sentence in its entirety to let your brain "hear" it. Pay attention to the context. This sentence indicates a contrast—even though hundreds of vocalists competed, she was still able to win. Both *although* and *however* indicated a contrast, but *however* would be more logically placed before the word *she*.

40. **The best answer is J.**   This is a verb question. Remember when choosing a verb to pay specific attention to who or what performs the action and when the action takes place. In this sentence, the orchestra manager offered Anderson a contract *to continue singing*, as she had already been singing. Answer choice J creates the most clear and concise sentence.

41. **The best answer is D.**   Several ACT English Test questions will offer "DELETE the underlined portion" as the last of four answer options. Generally, this type of question will ask you to avoid redundancy, create a concise sentence, or eliminate an unnecessary word or two from the sentence. In this case, if you remove the word *which* from the sentence and read the sentence back, you will see that a simple, complete sentence remains. The other answer choices, including the underlined portion, create incomplete or nonsense sentences.

42. **The best answer is F.**   To select the best answer to this question, look for clues in the question stem. The question asks for the choice that clearly conveys the significance of Anderson's accomplishments, so look for strong, positive words that describe how important her accomplishments were. This question is tricky because all of the answer choices indicate some level of achievement, but the underlined portion includes the most descriptive and powerful language, so it is the best option.

43. **The best answer is C.**   The ACT will always reward the most clear and concise expression of the idea. Look for opportunities to use active over passive voice, fix misplaced modifiers, and avoid awkward sentence construction. Answer choice C includes an active main verb and most clearly and succinctly conveys the intended idea.

44. **The best answer is F.**   To answer this question, try the sentence in each location indicated in the answer choices. Because Paragraph 2 includes a chronology of Anderson's singing, it makes sense to put a sentence that talks about her age at the end of this paragraph. None of the other locations is appropriate, and putting the sentence anywhere else would disrupt the flow of the essay.

45. **The best answer is C.** To answer this question, you must consider the overall topic of the passage. Rephrase the question as follows: Is this an essay about assessing the effectiveness of the civil rights movement in bettering social conditions for African Americans? Next, look at the title, the introductory paragraph, and the first sentences of a few of the body paragraphs. You will quickly see that the answer to the question is no; this is, in fact, an essay about the struggles of one African American woman. The civil rights movement is only mentioned in regard to Marion Anderson's struggles and successes.

46. **The best answer is H.** This question is asking you to look at the correct way to punctuate the sentence. Since you need to join an independent clause with a related, dependent clause, the best choice is a colon.

47. **The best answer is D.** To answer this question, you must consider the context of the entire sentence and determine the writer's intended idea. The transitional language in answer choices A, B, and C suggest a contrast that is not supported by the sentence. Only answer choice D correctly conveys the notion that the unique and beautiful coloring of the horse was the reason for it being the pride and joy of the Nez Perce tribe.

48. **The best answer is G.** This is a punctuation question. According to Standard Written English, a comma should be used along with a coordinating conjunction to join two independent clauses. The phrase "The Nez Perce was a tribe of the Pacific Northwest" and the phrase "the Appaloosa was integral to the tribe's success" each contain a subject and a main verb, so they are both independent clauses.

49. **The best answer is D.** The key to correctly answering this question is to find the clues in the question stem. The word *breadth* suggests that the public awareness is widespread. Additionally, pay attention to the context. The previous sentence mentions that the Nez Perce were respected for their horses. The best answer choice will consider both of these elements.

50. **The best answer is G.** The ACT often tests idiom, the common usage of a word or phrase, with prepositions. Prepositions are short words used to show position, location, direction, and time. You need to pay attention to the context of the sentence and rely upon your knowledge of how the English language works. In Standard Written English, it is customary to *stay with* someone.

51. **The best answer is A.** The first step in finding the best answer to this question is to determine the point made in the preceding sentence. According to the sentence, Meriwether Lewis wrote something positive about the Appaloosa horse after having spent some time presumably observing the horse and its relationship to the Nez Perce. The best answer will include information about both Meriwether Lewis and horses, so answer choice A makes the most sense.

52. **The best answer is F.** This is a question that tests your ability to use the correct word in context. If you have a strong vocabulary, you will likely answer these questions with ease. If vocabulary is not your strong suit, plug the answer choices back into the sentence and check to see if they "sound" right. For this question, use the process of elimination to get rid of answer choices that DO fit the context of the sentence. The word *tendency* is not appropriate based on the context.

53. **The best answer is A.** For this ACT verb question, the best choice will clearly and concisely show the action taking place in the sentence. It is generally best to avoid *–ing* words because they are usually not main verbs. While answer choice B sounds pretty good, you would need to have a comma before *which*; additionally, answer choice A is more concise, so it is the better option.

54. **The best answer is G.** The key to correctly answering this question is to find the clues in the question stem. The word *intense* is best reflected in the phrase *negotiate a hard-won truce*. The other choices convey the intended meaning, but not as intensely.

55. **The best answer is B.** This type of question asks you to make connections in the text. Context clues will tell you why the tribe attempted to flee. The previous sentence mentions "years of discussion and compromise," which provides support for answer choice B over the other options.

56. **The best answer is J.** This is both a punctuation and sentence structure question. Look for the best way to join the two clauses. As it's written, the underlined portion creates an incomplete sentence. Answer choices G and H create run-on sentences. Only answer choice J uses the correct punctuation to join the two related ideas.

57. **The best answer is B.** The ACT will always reward the most clear and concise expression of the idea. Look for opportunities to use active over passive voice, fix misplaced modifiers, and avoid awkward sentence construction. Answer choice B includes an active main verb and most clearly and succinctly conveys the intended idea.

58. **The best answer is J.** Remember that the best way to approach the ACT English Test is to read the essay and "listen" to the underlined portions. In this case, the underlined portion creates an incomplete sentence. In fact, the use of any transitional language will cause the same problem. You need a clear subject—*this new horse*—to create the independent clause that precedes the colon introducing the list of characteristics.

59. **The best answer is A.** This is a punctuation question. According to Standard Written English, a comma should be used to separate items in a list or series. The characteristics listed are *sleek and lean, muscular and strong, sporting a beautiful spotted coat.*

60. **The best answer is F.** To answer this question, you must consider the overall topic of the passage. Rephrase the question as follows: Is this an essay about the relationship between the Nez Perce Tribe and the Appaloosa horse? Next, look at the title, the introductory paragraph, and the first sentences of a few of the body paragraphs. You will quickly see that the answer to the question is yes, because the essay focuses on how the Appaloosa horse helped the Nez Perce becoming a thriving tribe.

61. **The best answer is A.** The ACT often tests idiom, the common usage of a word or phrase, with prepositions. Prepositions are short words used to show position, location, direction, and time. You need to pay attention to the context of the sentence and rely upon your knowledge of how the English language works. In this context, it is customary to say *disappointed by* because the idea caused disappointment.

62. **The best answer is H.** To answer this transitional language question, read the sentence in its entirety to let your brain "hear" it. Pay attention to the context. This sentence indicates a contrast. Even though the phrase *despite that* shows contrast, it is awkward and wordy. A better way to express the idea of contrast is with the word *although.*

63. **The best answer is D.** Several ACT English Test questions will offer "DELETE the underlined portion" as the last of four answer options. Generally, this type of question will ask you to avoid redundancy, create a concise sentence, or eliminate an unnecessary word or two from the sentence. Because *recycled* implies another use for the materials, you can delete the underlined portion without losing any essential information from the sentence.

64. **The best answer is J.** This sentence is looking for the correct subject. Eliminate answer choices F and G because neither *there* nor *their* work in this context. *They're* is the contraction of *they are*, which would generally work in this situation. However, a better choice would be *Most fans are* because it provides the sentence with a clear, unambiguous subject.

65. **The best answer is D.** The ACT will always reward the most clear and concise expression of the idea. Look for opportunities to use active over passive voice, fix misplaced modifiers, and avoid awkward sentence construction. This sentence intends to inform the reader that the design was the reason for the clear view. The phrase *so that* most clearly conveys that meaning.

66. **The best answer is H.** This is a question that tests your ability to use the correct word in context. If you have a strong vocabulary, you will likely answer these questions with ease. If vocabulary is not your strong suit, plug the answer choices back into the sentence and check to see if they "sound" right. For this question, use the process of elimination to get rid of answer choices that DO fit the context of the sentence. The word *pacify* is not appropriate based on the context.

67. **The best answer is A.** For this ACT verb question, the best choice will clearly and concisely show the action taking place in the sentence. This sentence correctly uses the present participle *delighting* as part of the continuous form of a verb—each time the fireworks explode, the crowd is delighted.

68. **The best answer is H.** This ACT question tests your ability to determine whether information is relevant. You have to decide whether, as a reader, you care about the information. In other words, is it relevant? If it doesn't add something to the topic being discussed or it distracts the reader from the topic, it is not relevant and should not be added to the essay. In this case, the sentence adds a useful connection between the perceived value of the new stadium and its actual size.

69. **The best answer is B.** When faced with a question about pronouns, always make sure that the pronoun has a clear antecedent. In other words, does the reader know who *it* is or who *they* are? If the answer to that question is not evident, it's usually best to use a noun instead of a pronoun. Remember that the antecedent (the noun to which the pronoun refers) should be close enough to the pronoun to eliminate any ambiguity.

70. **The best answer is F.** Here we have a punctuation question. Many students are confused about the difference between an apostrophe before the *s* and an apostrophe after the *s*. According to Standard Written English, the apostrophe comes before the *s* at the end of a noun when the noun shows singular possession, and after the *s* at the end of the noun when the noun shows plural possession. Because the context indicates more than one player and the facial expressions "belong" to the players, the plural possessive form *players'* is correct.

71. **The best answer is C.** This is a punctuation question. According to Standard Written English, a comma should be used to join an independent and a restrictive clause. In this case, the independent clause is "Other criticisms of the Tigers' new home include the angle at which it was built." This clause is considered independent because it contains a subject and a verb. The rest of the sentence is considered a restrictive clause because it provides information essential to the meaning of the sentence.

72. **The best answer is J.** The ACT will always reward the most clear and concise expression of the idea. Look for opportunities to use active over passive voice, fix misplaced modifiers, and avoid awkward sentence construction. This sentence intends to give the reader information regarding the distance of the seats from the playing field. The word *that* most clearly and simply conveys the intended meaning.

73. **The best answer is A.** Based on the context of the essay and this particular paragraph, it is clear that the old stadium was in disrepair and was actually falling apart. The phrase "literally falling apart" is intended to provide accurate information regarding the condition of the old stadium and support the main idea of the essay—the transition from old stadium to new stadium.

74. **The best answer is H.** This question tests homonyms, which are words that sound alike but have different meanings. The phrase *past being acceptable* is used here to modify the noun *restrooms*. It shows that they were no longer acceptable.

75. **The best answer is C.** The key to correctly answering this question is to find the clues in the question stem. The word *desperate* is best reflected in the word *beleaguered*, which means "in a very difficult situation." The other choices could be used to describe the city of Detroit, but they do not convey any sense of desperation.

MATHEMATICS

76. **The correct answer is H.** This may, at first glance, seem like an easy question. However, it is the kind of question that many students often miss because they fail to pay attention to the details. Notice that the question asks for the value of $4x$, not x, but that the value of x is among the answer choices. If you rush through a question like this, you will likely choose the wrong answer. The first step in solving a problem like this is to actually write down $4x = ?$; then you will remember exactly what value you need to find and will be less likely to make a careless error. Next, do the math on the left side of the original equation: $4(4x) = 16x$, and $16x$ divided by 4 equals $4x$. You can see that the value of $4x = 4$, answer choice H.

77. **The correct answer is E.** This question is considered a more challenging concept question and does require some knowledge of irrational numbers. An irrational number cannot be expressed as a ratio of two integers and cannot be written as a fraction. Therefore, numbers like 8.13 and 11.27, etc. would be considered irrational numbers, and there are infinitely many such numbers between 8 and 12.

78. **The correct answer is F.**   Many students get stuck on a problem like this because of how the information is presented. When you encounter a problem that contains more than one variable, look for opportunities to select a value for one of the variables. Also, let the answer choices guide you—what should my answer look like? You see that each of the answer choices sets c either greater than or equal to some number. Therefore, you should try to find a value for d and substitute that value into the inequality $3c + d = 18$. You are given that d must be less than 7, so set d equal to 6. When $d = 6$, $3c = 12$, and $c = 4$. Now check the answer choices. Both answer choices F and H are still contenders. But answer choice G says that c must be less than or equal to 3, so switch tactics and set $c =$ to 3 and solve the original equation for d: $3(3) + d = 18$; $9 + d = 18$; $d = 9$. Since the question tells you that d must be less than 7, eliminate answer choice G.

79. **The correct answer is D.**   At first glance, this might seem like an imaginary number question, but it's actually just a factoring and substitution question. The first step is to FOIL $(3 + i)^2$, as follows:

$$(3 + i)(3 + i) = 9 + 6i + i^2$$

Next, substitute -1 in place of i^2: $9 + 6i - 1 = 8 + 6i$, answer choice J.

   If you encounter a question that looks like it might test a concept you don't understand, always consider what you DO know. If the question had asked about $(3 + x)^2$, you would likely have immediately thought to apply the FOIL method.

80. **The correct answer is H.** To solve this problem, first translate the words into their mathematical equivalents:

4 more than twice n translates to $4 + 2n$. You are given that this quantity is a negative number, which translates to $4 + 2n < 0$.

6 more than n translates to $6 + n$. You are given that this quantity is a positive number, which translates to $6 + n > 0$.

Solve each inequality as follows:

$$4 + 2n < 0$$
$$n < -2$$
$$6 + n > 0$$
$$n > -6$$

So, n could be any number less than -2 and greater than -6. Only -4, answer choice H, is greater than -6 and less than -2.

81. **The correct answer is A.**   Many students struggle with questions that reference a constant. But this is really just a function question that requires a little extra attention to detail. First, you are given that $g(4) = 8$. Substitute 4 in place of x in the first equation—the one that contains the constant. Now set the equation equal to 8. This gives you the opportunity to solve for a:

$$a(4)^2 + 24 = 8$$
$$a16 = 8 - 24$$
$$a16 = -16$$
$$a = -1$$

Remember that the question asks you to find $g(-4)$, so simply substitute -4 for x and -1 for a in the original equation and solve:

$$-1(-4)^2 + 24 =$$

$$-1(16) + 24 =$$

$$-16 + 24 = 8, \text{ answer choice A.}$$

82. **The correct answer is J.**   Don't be intimidated by the fact that you have two variables in the question. Because you are given parameters regarding those variables, and you have the same variables in the answer choices, simply choose values for x and y, and evaluate the answer choices. Since x and y can be any real numbers, remember to choose both positive and negative values; first, set both x and y equal to 2 and plug the values into the given inequality:

$$|2 + 2| < |2 - 2|$$

Perform the operations inside the absolute value signs, then compare the results:

$$|4| < |0|$$

Because the absolute value of positive 4 is NOT less than the absolute value of 0, you can eliminate both answer choices F and G. Now let the answer choices guide you. Answer choice H says that the inequality is true only when $x < 0$ and $y < 0$. Make $x = -2$ and $y = -2$:

$$|2 + 2)| < |2 + - 2|$$

Perform the operations inside the absolute value signs, and then compare the results:

$$|0| < |0|$$

This is not a true statement, so eliminate answer choice H. Now try D, which says that the inequality is true only when $x < 0$ and $y > 0$. Make $x = -2$ and $y = 2$:

$$|-2 + 2)| < |-2 - 2|$$

Perform the operations inside the absolute value signs, then compare the results:

$$|0| < |-4|$$

This statement is true because the absolute value of -4 is 4, and 0 is less than 4.

83. **The correct answer is D.** This is a great example of a question in which you should "name" the missing number. You are given that the average of two numbers, x and some other number is 16. Set the other number equal to y and solve:

$$\frac{(x + y)}{2} = 16 .$$ Thus $x + y = 32$ and $y = 32 - x$.

84. **The correct answer is H.** The trick to solving this problem is to recognize that a system of equations will have an infinite number of solutions when the equations are equal. The most direct route to finding the value of a that makes the equations equal is to make the other variables, x and y, equal to each other. Notice that the second equation is 3 times greater than the first equation. Multiply the first equation by 3 and solve for a:

$$2x - y = 8 \rightarrow 3(2x - y) = 3(8) \rightarrow 6x - 3y = 24$$

Now, the two equations are $6x - 3y = 24$ and $6x - 3y = 2a$

$$6x = 6x$$
$$3y = 3y$$
$$24 = 2a, \text{ and } a = 12.$$

85. **The correct answer is D.**   Clearly, the best way to answer this question is to list all of the prime numbers less than 14, starting with the number 2. Be very careful not to rush and make a careless error; for example, assuming that all odd numbers are prime.

> Prime numbers less than 14: 2, 3, 5, 7, 11, 13. There are six such numbers.

86. **The correct answer is K.**   This can be a fairly straightforward question if you don't rush through it or forget a critical step. The most logical first step is to subtract 1 from both sides of the equation, so that $|p - 1| = -1$. You might be tempted at this point to assume that $p = 0$. However, take note that the absolute value of any number is always positive. Therefore, the absolute value of $p - 1$ can never be -1, and there is no such value of p that satisfies the equation.

87. **The correct answer is C.**   To answer this question, you need to apply some rules of logic. Statements in the form of "If X, then Y" are known as *conditionals*; if X occurs, Y is certain to occur. You know then, that if a pepper is ripe, it is certain to be red. If we reverse the position of the terms and negate both terms, we arrive at a statement that always has exactly the same truth-value as the original statement. This is known as the *contrapositive*. The contrapositive of the original statement is, "If a pepper is NOT red, then it is NOT ripe." Among the answer choices, this is the only true statement.

88. **The correct answer is K.** This question tests your knowledge of the rules of exponents, one of which states that $x^{-m} = \dfrac{1}{x^m}$. Therefore, $(4 + x)^{-100}$ is equivalent to $\dfrac{1}{(4 + x)^{100}}$.

89. **The correct answer is B.** You are likely to see at least one matrix question on your ACT, so if you are not familiar with the concept, review the Math chapter in this book. To answer this question, you must know that the determinant (A) of a matrix can be calculated using the following formula:

$$A = ad - bc \begin{bmatrix} a & b \\ c & d \end{bmatrix}$$

Therefore, the determinant of the given matrix is $(4)(5) - (8)(2) = 20 - 16 = 4$.

90. **The correct answer is F.** A vertical asymptote is a vertical line which corresponds to the zero of the denominator of a rational function. In other words, it is the value of x that makes the denominator equal to 0. In this question, the denominator is $3x - 6$. Therefore, the vertical asymptote must be $x = 2$.

91. **The correct answer is B.**   This is a classic ACT Math question designed to make you think that you can't answer it because you have never heard of a term mentioned in the question. However, the term is defined for you, so all you have to do is apply the given definition to the actual question—How many of the integers 8, 10, 12, and 15 are abundant? List each of the integers and write down all of the factors, excluding the integer itself. Based on the definition of abundant, if the sum of the factors is greater than the integer itself, the integer is abundant.

Integer:	8	10	12	15
Factors:	1, 2, 4	1, 2, 5	1, 2, 3, 4, 6	1, 3, 5
Sum of factors:	7	8	**16**	9

According to the given definition, only the integer 12 is abundant.

92. **The correct answer is K.**   You are given that the product of the average of a list of course grades and the total number of courses is n. Recall that average, A, is equal to the sum of the course grades, G, divided by the number of courses, C; thus $A = \dfrac{G}{C}$. Because n is the product of the number of courses, C, and the average of the course grades, A, $n = AC$. Further, because $A = \dfrac{G}{C}$, multiplying both sides by C yields $G = AC$. Finally because $n = AC$ and $G = AC$, it follows that $n = G$. Thus n is the sum of the course grades.

93. **The correct answer is A.**   The ACT Math test will often include questions with a "Note." Very critical information is included therein, so make sure you pay attention. In this case, the Note tells you that $\sec x = \dfrac{1}{\cos x}$. Your first step should be to substitute $\dfrac{1}{\cos x}$ in place of $\sec x$ in the given function:

$$f(x) = (\sec x)(\sin x)$$
$$f(x) = \left(\frac{1}{\cos x}\right)(\sin x)$$

Now just do the math:

$$f(x) = \frac{\sin x}{\cos x}, \text{ which is equal to } \tan x.$$

94. **The correct answer is H.**   You are given that the degree measures of the angles of a triangle are in the ratio 2:3:4. This is a part to whole ratio, so the smallest angle will constitute $\dfrac{2}{(2+3+4)}$, or $\dfrac{2}{9}$ of the sum of the three angles of the triangle. Because all triangles are composed of three angles whose sum is 180°, the degree measure of the smallest angle is $\dfrac{2}{9}$ of 180°. A shortcut to finding the correct answer is to first find $\dfrac{1}{9}$ of 180°: $180° \div 9 = 20°$, so $\dfrac{2}{9}$ of 180° must equal 40°.

95. **The correct answer is C.**   Remember that an irrational number cannot be expressed as a ratio of two integers and cannot be written as a fraction. Based on this information, you can quickly eliminate answer choice E because 4 is a rational number. Next, begin to solve the equation:

$$|n^2 - 12| - 4 = 0$$

$$|n^2 - 12| = 4$$

You should recall that absolute value refers to the value of a number without regard for its sign. Therefore, the quantity $(n^2 - 12)$ is equal to both positive 4 AND negative 4.

When $n^2 - 12 = 4$, $n^2 = 16$, and $n = 4$. Since 4 is a rational number and you've already eliminated 4 as a possible answer, solve the next equation for n:

When $n^2 - 12 = -4$, $n^2 = 8$, and $n = \sqrt{8}$, which $= 2\sqrt{2}$.

96. **The correct answer is J.**   This question requires you to consider graphs in the answer choices. Don't let this intimidate you! It's not necessary to perform any calculations or know the values of a and b. You just need to determine the relationship between values on the b-axis and values on the a-axis. A negative relationship will be represented by a line with a negative slope. Because lines with negative slopes go "down and to the right," answer choice J becomes obvious. When faced with a question that looks challenging, always start with "things you know." The ACT Math test rewards this kind of problem-solving skill.

97. **The correct answer is B.**   To solve this problem, you first need to translate the English into Math. You are given that the number of students who joined the Math Club last year is twice the number of students who joined this year. Therefore, Last Year = 2(This Year). You are also given that the number of students who joined last year is 30 and the number who joined this year is x. Therefore, $30 = 2x$, which is the same as $2x = 30$.

98. **The correct answer is F.**   Recall that the equation of a circle with center (h,k) and radius r is $(x - h)^2 + (y - k)^2 = r^2$. Your first step is to put the given equation into the standard form of the equation of a circle. To do this, you must complete the square, as follows:

$$x^2 + y^2 + 4x - 2y = -1$$

$$(x^2 + 4x) + (y^2 - 2y) = -1$$

$$(x^2 + 4x + 4) - 4 + (y^2 - 2y + 1) - 1 = -1$$

$$(x + 2)^2 + (y - 1)^2 = 4, \text{ which means the radius must equal 2.}$$

99. **The correct answer is C.**   To correctly answer this question, you need to know that Percent Increase = (New Amount − Original Amount) ÷ Original Amount × 100%. Because the question asks for April's percent change from Week 1 to Week 2, find that information on the table, and substitute it into the equation (New Amount − Original Amount) ÷ Original Amount × 100%:

$$\text{Percent Increase} = (6 - 5) \div 5 \times 100\%$$

$$\text{Percent Increase} = 1 \div 5 \times 100\%$$

$$\text{Percent Increase} = .2 \times 100\% = 20\%$$

100. **The correct answer is J.**   Your first task is to notice that the only information you have for Ben is his Week 1 sales: $3,000. According to the question, Ben's sales increased 20% EACH week. Let's calculate his sales for each week using the decimal equivalent of 20%, which is .2:

$$\text{Week 1} = \$3,000$$

$$\text{Week 2} = \$3,000 + \$3,000(.2) = \$3,000 + \$600 = \$3,600$$

$$\text{Week 3} = \$3,600 + \$3,600(.2) = \$3,600 + \$720 = \$4,320$$

$$\text{WEEK 4} = \$4,320 + \$4,320(.2) = \$4,320 + \$864 = \$5,184$$

$$\text{Week 5} = \$5,184 + \$5,184(.2) = \$5,184 + \$1,036.8 = \$6,220.8$$

The question asks for the amount, in thousands of dollars, that is closest to Ben's sales for Week 5. Simply divide $6,220.8 by $1,000 and round: $6,220 ÷ $1,000 = 6.22, which is closest to 6.2.

101. **The correct answer is E.**   This question asks you to solve for an unknown number, so make that number equal to x. Remember that to calculate the average of a data set, you just add up all of the values in the set, and then divide that total by the number of values in the set:

$$\text{Week } 3 = 6$$

$$\text{Week } 4 = 5$$

$$\text{Week } 5 = 4$$

$$\text{Week } 6 = x$$

According to the question, she wants her average to be \$6,000, or 6 (the question asks for the sales in thousands of dollars):

$$6 = \frac{6+5+4+x}{4}$$

$$6 = \frac{15+x}{4}$$

$$24 = 15 + x$$

$$9 = x$$

102. **The correct answer is K.** Because this question involves exponents, you should think about the relationship between bases and exponents. Notice that all of the bases are powers of 2:

$$(2^a)(4) = 8^3$$

$$(2^a)(2^2) = (2^3)^3$$

Apply the rules of exponents: $(2^a)(2^2) = 2^{a+2}$ and $(2^3)^3 = 2^9$

Therefore, $2^{a+2} = 2^9$, and $a + 2 = 9$, so $a = 7$. The ACT tests exponents frequently, so be sure to review all of the rules. If you cannot recall the rules of exponents, notice that, in this question, you could simply try the answer choices in place of a. This process of elimination takes time, but it is a very useful strategy!

103. **The correct answer is D.** To solve this problem, you need to know the difference between *must* and *could* as you evaluate the answer choices. For example, x *could* be greater than 0 to satisfy the given inequality. However, because the inequality includes the absolute value of x and y, x *could* also be less than 0. Likewise, the inequality *could* be satisfied if x were either less than or greater than y. Clearly, if $x = y$, the inequality will not be satisfied. Only the statement $x \neq y$ *must* always be true to satisfy the inequality.

104. **The correct answer is H.**   The trick to answering this question correctly is to keep track of everything. While the math behind this question may not be too complicated for most test-takers, it is included here because it's the kind of question many students miss due to a careless error. First, recall that a ratio is a numerical comparison of 2 or more quantities which indicates their relative sizes. Next, write down all of the given ratios:

$$m{:}n = 1{:}2$$

$$p{:}n = 3{:}4$$

$$m{:}p = ?$$

Remember that ratios are expressed as fractions because they can be a way of comparing numbers by division, so you need to find the lowest common denominator:

$$m{:}n = 1{:}2 = \frac{1}{2} = \frac{2}{4} = 2{:}4$$

$$p{:}n = 3{:}4$$

$$m{:}p = ?$$

Now you can substitute the values for m and p into the ratio you've been asked to find:

$$m{:}p = 2{:}3$$

105. **The correct answer is B.**   To solve this problem, remember that $\frac{1}{4}$ is equivalent to .25, and that 0.1 percent is equivalent to 0.001. Therefore, $\frac{1}{4}$, or .25 of 0.001 = 0.00025; do not get confused and simply find $\frac{1}{4}$ of 0.1, (0.025) because the question asks for $\frac{1}{4}$ of 0.1 *percent*.

106. **The correct answer is H.**   The first thing to notice here is that, if $ab = 0$, either a or b or both a and b must equal 0. The next thing to notice is that $\dfrac{a}{b} = 0$. Since a fraction with 0 in the denominator is undefined, b cannot equal 0; therefore, a must equal 0.

107. **The correct answer is D.**   Probability refers to the likelihood of something happening. In other words, what is the chance that the product of x and y will be greater than 0? Because you're multiplying, x and y must either both be positive or both be negative in order for the product of xy to be positive (greater than 0). There are a total of 20 total chances, since you have 5 values for x in the first set and 4 values for y in the second set ($5 \times 4 = 20$). Evaluate all of the possible combinations of xy that will yield a positive result:

$$x = -3$$
$$y = -2 \qquad -1, \text{ which gives you 2 chances for } xy > 0.$$

$$x = -2$$
$$y = -2 \qquad -1, \text{ which gives you 2 more chances for } xy > 0.$$

$$x = -1$$
$$y = -2 \qquad -1, \text{ which gives you 2 more chances for } xy > 0.$$

$$x = 1 \text{ and } y = 1, \text{ which gives you 1 final chance for } xy > 0.$$

Therefore, there are $2 + 2 + 2 + 1 = 7$ chances out of 20 that xy will be greater than 0.

108. **The correct answer is H.**   To easily solve this problem, recognize that $\sqrt[4]{81}$ (the fourth root of 81) is equivalent to 3, since $3^4 = 81$. Therefore, of the choices given, 3 is closest to $\sqrt[4]{80}$. You could have eliminated answer choice K, because 1 raised to any power will always be 1.

109. **The correct answer is D.**   This is a classic ACT Math problem designed to make you think that there is no way to solve it based on the given information. However, you can determine a pattern by assigning variables. First, set the least of the seven integers to x. When the least of the seven integers is x, the remaining numbers are $x + 1, x + 2, x + 3, x + 4, x + 5$, and $x + 6$, because the numbers are consecutive. You are given that the average of the seven numbers is 16, so $[x + (x + 1) + (x + 2) + (x + 3) + (x + 4) + (x + 5) + (x + 6)]$ divided by 7 = 16. Solve for x:

$$\frac{(7x + 21)}{7} = 16$$
$$7x + 21 = 112$$
$$7x = 91$$
$$x = 13$$

The smallest number, x, is 13, and the largest number is $x + 6$. Therefore the largest number is equal to $13 + 6$, or 19, and the sum of these two numbers is $13 + 19$, or 32.

110. **The correct answer is G.** To answer this question, keep in mind the relationship of angles in triangles and angles formed by parallel lines cut by a transversal. According to the figure, angle *WZY* is 72°. Note that angle *WYZ* is 90°, which means that angle *ZWY* must be 18° (180 − 72 − 90 = 18). Therefore, because the angle in question is vertical to (opposite of) angle *ZWY*, its measure must also be 18°.

111. **The correct answer is A.** The best way to solve this problem is to pick a value for *n* and evaluate each of the Roman numeral statements. Set *n* equal to 2 because it is an easy number to work with:

I. When $n = 2$, $\sqrt{(-n)^2} = \sqrt{(-2)^2} = \sqrt{4} = 2$.

II. When $n = 2$, $|-n| = |-2| = 2$.

III. When $n = 2$, $-|n| = -|2| = -2$.

Only Roman numeral statements I and II are equal.

112. **The correct answer is J.**   The first step in answering this question is to solve for x and y. Because there are 180 degrees in a straight line, the sum of the four angles with value x must be 180, and the sum of the three angles with value y must be 180:

$$4x = 180 \text{ so } x = 45$$

$$3y = 180 \text{ so } y = 60$$

Thus, $\dfrac{(y - x)}{(y + x)} = \dfrac{(60 - 45)}{(60 + 45)}$, which is equivalent to $\dfrac{15}{105}$, or $\dfrac{1}{7}$.

113. **The correct answer is A.**   Because this question involves exponents, you should think about the relationship between bases and exponents, as well as the rules regarding exponents. First, notice that $27 = 3^3$, so $27^{b} = (3^3)^b$.

Next, because $\left(\sqrt{3}\right)^{a} = \left(3^{\frac{1}{2}}\right)^{a} = 3^{\frac{a}{2}}$, you can rewrite the given equation as $3^{\frac{a}{2}} = 3^{3b}$. Set the exponents equal to each other and solve for $\dfrac{a}{b}$:

$$\frac{a}{2} = 3b$$

$$a = 2(3b)$$

$$a = 6b$$

$$\frac{a}{b} = 6$$

114. **The correct answer is J.** To answer this question, you should know that complex numbers are the sum of a real and an imaginary number, represented as $a + bi$. Using the complex plane, you can plot complex numbers similar to how you plot a coordinate on the (x,y) coordinate plane. To graph a complex number, $a + bi$, locate the real part, a, on the real axis (the x-axis), and move up or down to locate b, from the imaginary part, on the imaginary axis (the y-axis). Likewise, you can apply the Distance Formula to calculate the distance between two given points:

$$\sqrt{([x_2 - x_1]^2 + [y_2 - y_1]^2)}$$

You are given $3 + 6i$ and $-2 + 3i$, where the 3 and the -2 correspond to the values on the x-axis, and $6i$ and $3i$ correspond to values on the y-axis. Plug those points into the distance formula:

$$\sqrt{([-2 - 3]^2 + [3i - 6i]^2)} = \sqrt{([-5]^2 + [-3i]^2)} = \sqrt{(25 - 9i^2)}$$

Now, you need to recognize that $i^2 = -1$ and use substitution:

$$\sqrt{(25 - 9(-1))} = \sqrt{(25 + 9)} = \sqrt{34}$$

115. **The correct answer is A.** The ACT Math test will often include questions with a "Note." Very critical information is included therein, so make sure you pay attention. Because both the question and the Note include information regarding the repeating decimal, you can simply disregard the fraction. Its primary purpose is to distract you. Next, look for the pattern in the repeating decimal. You are told that the digit in the 4th decimal place is 9; therefore, because 4 is a divisor of 800, you can assume that the 800th decimal place is also 9, which means that the 801st decimal place must be the digit that comes after 9 in the repeating decimal.

116. **The correct answer is G.** To solve this problem, first calculate the total weight of the 10 girls: $10 \times 110 = 1,100$. Next, recognize that the total weight of the 9 remaining girls must be $1,100 - x$ (the weight of the oldest girl). Finally, solve for x, as follows:

$$112 \text{ (given new average weight)} = \frac{1,000 - x}{9}$$

$$9(112) = 1,100 - x$$
$$1,008 - 1,100 = -x$$
$$-92 = -x$$
$$92 = x$$

117. **The correct answer is D.** To answer this question, solve each of the given equations for f:

$$g = f/1.23 \approx 0.81f$$

$$h = f/1.01 \approx 0.99f$$

$$j = f/0.99 \approx 1.01f$$

$$k = f/0.23 \approx 4.35f$$

Since the value of f is fixed, $4.35f$ yields the largest number, so k will have the greatest value.

118. **The correct answer is F.**   The ACT Math Test is primarily a problem-solving test, so look for the most direct and logical way to arrive at the correct answer. One way to find the x-intercept is to replace y with 0 and solve for x. If $0 = x^2 - 4x + 4$, then $(x - 2)^2 = 0$, and $x = 2$.

119. **The correct answer is E.**   Apply some logic and common sense to solve this problem. First, since the cameras were discounted off the marked price, d, the discounted price must be something *less than* d. Therefore, you can quickly eliminate answer choices A and B. Next, you are given that the discount is 21% of d, and since the decimal equivalent of 21% is 0.21, only answer choice E will work. Another approach to quickly solving percent problems is to assign a dollar value of $100 to the original marked price. Then set up an equation:

$$\text{Marked price} = \$100$$

$$\text{Discounted price} = \$100 - 0.21(\$100)$$

120. **The correct answer is F.**   This is a good example of letting the answer choices guide you to the correct answer. You are asked for the greatest common factor of the two numbers, which is simply the things that they have in common. A close look at the numbers will reveal that they both have n^2 in common, and only answer choice F includes n^2, so it must be correct. Sometimes it pays to look at the answer choices each time you make a decision about the question to save you from doing too much math.

121. **The correct answer is B.**   Remember that supplementary angles add up to 180°. If one angle is 4 times the measure of the other angle, then the smaller angle can be x and the larger angle can be $4x$.

$$4x + x = 180$$

$$5x = 180$$

$$x = 36$$

Don't forget that the question asks for the value of the larger angle, which must 4(36), or 144.

122. **The correct answer is K.**   Don't be intimidated by variables—they act the same way that numbers do. This question is simply asking you to solve the given equation for a:

$$af - g = x$$

$$af = x + g$$

$$a = \frac{x + g}{f}$$

123. **The correct answer is C.**   To solve this problem, you should remember that a line of symmetry is a line along which we can fold an image and have both halves match exactly. Imagine orienting a circle anywhere in the standard (x, y) coordinate plane and drawing a line through the middle of the circle parallel to the y-axis. Because a circle has an infinite number of lines of symmetry, it will have a vertical line of symmetry regardless of its orientation within the coordinate plane.

124. **The correct answer is J.** If $\tan x - 1 = 0$, then $\tan x = 1$. Since $\tan 45 = 1$, $x = 45$. Likewise, since $\tan = \dfrac{\text{opposite}}{\text{adjacent}}$, then $\dfrac{\text{opposite}}{\text{adjacent}} = 1$, which means that the opposite and adjacent sides are congruent and $x = 45$.

125. **The correct answer is C.** The question is asking you to find the area of the right trapezoid in the middle of the triangle. If you don't know the formula for the area of a trapezoid, turn the trapezoid into a rectangle and a triangle by dropping a vertical line down from R to MQ. When you do that, you create a rectangle that has side lengths of 45 and 70, so its area is $45 \times 70 = 3{,}150$. Eliminate answer choice A because it is too small and answer choice E because it is too big. Next, calculate the area of the triangle, whose base must be 50 ($95 - 45$) and whose height must be 70: Area $= \frac{1}{2}(b)(h) = \frac{1}{2}(50)(70) = \frac{1}{2}(3{,}500) = 1{,}750$. Now, simply add the two areas together: $3{,}150 + 1{,}750 = 4{,}900$.

126. **The correct answer is F.** A good approach to solving this problem is to draw a circle inside trapezoid $MNPQ$. You will see that you are limited by the shortest side of the trapezoid, which is 70 centimeters. Therefore, the largest circle you can draw will have a diameter of 70 centimeters and a radius of 35 centimeters.

127. **The correct answer is B.** The median is the middle value of the ordered data set. Visualize the problem by drawing five blanks to represent the five items in the set:

___ ___ X ___ ___

The median is the third blank. You are told that six new items are added to the set—three of the items are greater than the original median, and three of the items are less than the original median. Because you are adding three blanks at the beginning and three blanks at the end, the original median will not move:

___ ___ ___ ___ ___ X ___ ___ ___ ___ ___

128. **The correct answer is K.** Cost is determined by adding the fixed costs to the variable costs. You are given that the fixed costs are $1,600 and the variable costs are $7.25 for each tennis racket, t. The variable costs can be represented by $7.25t$. The total cost of manufacturing, then, is $1,600 + $7.25t$.

129. **The correct answer is A.** Because you are reflecting the triangle across the x-axis, the x-coordinate values will stay the same, but the y-coordinate values will become negative. Therefore, if R has coordinates $(-a, b)$, R' will have coordinates $(-a, -b)$.

130. **The correct answer is J.** A good strategy for solving problems with variables in the question and the answer choices is to pick values for the given variables. You are told that $d > c$, so set $d = 3$ and $c = 2$. When $d = 3$ and $c = 2$, $|c - d| = |2 - 3| = |-1| = 1$. Now plug your values into the answer choices to see which one is equivalent to 1. Only answer choice J works.

131. **The correct answer is D.** To answer this question, solve the second inequality:

$$9 + 3x \geq 0$$

$$3x \geq -9$$

$$x \geq -3$$

Note that you do not have to reverse the sign because you are dividing both sides by 3, NOT –3. Therefore, the solution set for the inequalities is defined by $x \leq 4$ and $x \geq -3$.

132. **The correct answer is F.** You are given a system of linear equations, so the first step is to convert the equations into the standard form, $y = mx + b$:

$$28x - 36y = 76 \qquad \qquad 7x + by = 19$$

$$-36y = 28x + 76 \qquad \qquad by = -7x + 19$$

$$y = \frac{28}{36}x - \frac{76}{36} \qquad \qquad y = -\frac{7}{b}x + \frac{19}{b}$$

Since the graph of the solution set is a single line, you can set the y-intercepts equal to each other and solve for b:

$$\frac{-76}{36} = \frac{19}{b}$$

$$-76b = (36)(19)$$

$$-76b = 684$$

$$b = \frac{684}{-76} = -9$$

133. **The correct answer is E.** The trick to solving this problem is to convert the question into math. The phrase "the product of h and 5 is g" translates into $5h = g$. The phrase "the sum of h and 5" translates into $h + 5$. Now solve the first equation for h: $5h = g$; $h = \dfrac{g}{5}$. Finally, substitute $\dfrac{g}{5}$ in place of h in the second equation: $h + 5$; $\dfrac{g}{5} + 5$.

134. **The correct answer is K.** It is very common for the ACT Math Test to include notes at the end of questions. Always read the notes because they generally tell you exactly how to solve the problem! In this case, you should first determine that the probability Jane WILL be chosen is $\dfrac{1}{9}$. Therefore, the probability she WILL NOT be chosen is $\dfrac{8}{9}$. According to the note, the odds in favor of Jane being chosen is the ratio of $\dfrac{1}{9}$ (will happen): $\dfrac{8}{9}$ (will not happen). Since ratios can be expressed as fractions, the odds in favor of Jane being chosen is equivalent to $\dfrac{\frac{1}{9}}{\frac{8}{9}}$, which is equivalent to $\dfrac{1}{9} \times \dfrac{9}{8}$; $\dfrac{1}{9} \times \dfrac{9}{8} = \dfrac{9}{72} = \dfrac{1}{8}$.

135. **The correct answer is E.** This question may appear very challenging, which is why we've included it here, but if you focus on one coordinate at a time, the question becomes much more manageable. You are given that each edge of the cube is 2 coordinates long. Therefore, vertices P, S, T, and W must each be 2 coordinate units along the x-axis. Likewise, vertices R, S, V, and W must each be 2 coordinate units along the y-axis. Eliminate answer choices A, B, and C because both the x-coordinate and the y-coordinate of vertex S must be 2. Now you can see that S must also be 2 coordinates along the z-axis, which means answer choice E is correct.

READING

136. **The best answer is F.**   This is both an Inference and a Tone question. Look for evidence in the passage that supports one answer choice over the others. Statements in the passage such as, "But the men who remained, when the pinch came, would have no dogs. It was for this reason that Daylight and Elijah took the more desperate chance. They could not do less, nor did they care to do less," and "he took infinite precautions. He would stalk it for hours," support the notion that Daylight was both brave and patient.

137. **The best answer is C.**   This is clearly an Inference question, so look for evidence in the passage to support one answer choice over the others. For example, according to the passage, "Little as it was, the lion's share was left with Daylight and Elijah. The men who pulled on with the dogs, one up the Stewart River and one down, would come more quickly to grub," and "Granting every delay, and throwing in generous margins for good measure, the time was long since passed when they should have returned. Without doubt they had met with disaster. The party had considered the possibility of disaster for one man, and that had been the principal reason for dispatching the two in different directions." These statements best support answer choice C.

138. **The best answer is F.**   This is both an Inference and a Tone question. Look for evidence in the passage that supports one answer choice over the others. Statements in the passage such as, "Daylight and Elijah, lean and hungry, wondered what had become of their two comrades. Granting every delay, and throwing in generous margins for good measure, the time was long since passed when they should have returned. Without doubt they had met with disaster," and "In the meantime, hoping against hope, Daylight and Elijah eked out a meager existence," as well as "No matter how sharp the pangs of hunger and desire for that palpitating morsel of chattering life, he refused to take the slightest risk of a miss," suggest that, while their situation was grim, the men remained hopeful and did whatever it took to stay alive.

139. **The best answer is C.**   For this question, you can locate the area in the passage that should contain the answer by skimming the passage for the year 1896. Take advantage of this kind of clue in the question to make your job easier. According to the passage, "It was the spring of 1896 that was preparing. Each day the sun rose farther east of south, remained longer in the sky, and set farther to the west. March ended and April began, and Daylight and Elijah, lean and hungry, wondered what had become of their two comrades. Granting every delay, and throwing in generous margins for good measure, the time was long since passed when they should have returned." This shows that Elijah and Daylight were concerned about the safety of their comrades.

140. **The best answer is G.** This question would likely be considered an Inference question, which requires you to find evidence in the passage that supports one answer choice over the others. In the last paragraph, the author describes Daylight's hunting prowess: "The hunting fell upon Daylight, and it was hard work," and "and days went by without seeing one. When he did see one, he took infinite precautions. He would stalk it for hours. A score of times, with arms that shook from weakness, he would draw a sight on the animal and refrain from pulling the trigger. His inhibition was a thing of iron. He was the master. Not until absolute certitude was his did he shoot." These statements reinforce the author's admiration for Daylight's inner strength.

141. **The best answer is D.** This is a Vocabulary in Context question. Inserting the word "gradually" in place of "imperceptibly" changes the meaning of sentence the least. "Quickly" (answer choice F), and "surprisingly" (answer choice G) are so similar in meaning that they must both be incorrect since there can be only one correct answer. If you chose either of them, you were probably confused by the word "suddenness" at the end of the sentence. While "quietly" is similar to "imperceptibly," it does not fit the context.

142. **The best answer is G.** This is an Inference question. The passage states that Daylight took great care to shoot the squirrels through the head, "Since his rifle was a 45-90..." This would be done so that the large bullet wouldn't ruin any edible meat on the animal. It is also stated in the second sentence of the passage–that the men were hoping for a moose. Moose are large animals, so this sentence provides more evidence for answer choice B.

143. **The best answer is C.**   This is an Explicit Detail question. According to the passage, "…the men who traveled with them, in a pinch, would have the dogs themselves to eat." None of the other answer choices are supported by evidence from the passage.

144. **The best answer is J.**   This is an Inference question. According to the passage, "Elijah was the older man, and he weakened first, so that he came to lie up most of the time in his furs. An occasional tree squirrel kept them alive. The hunting fell upon Daylight, and it was hard work."

145. **The best answer is C.**   This is an Inference question. According to the passage, "But the men who remained, when the pinch came, would have no dogs. It was for this reason that Daylight and Elijah took the more desperate chance. They could not do less, nor did they care to do less." This suggests that the men were concerned about not having enough to eat, so they took desperate measures in order to survive.

146. **The best answer is G.**   This is a Tone question. Pay attention to the language the author uses in the sentences. An "assertion" is a statement. The word "indeed" is a word of confirmation. This language best supports answer choice G.

147. **The best answer is C.**   Because this is an EXCEPT question, you must select the answer choice that is NOT supported by evidence in the passage. Questions that begin with "According to" are generally Specific Detail questions, so you can often use the process of elimination. Turn the answer choices into Yes or No questions:

Answer choice A: Does eminent domain allow for condemnation of private property? Yes. According to the passage, "Eminent domain is the power of a government to take, or condemn, privately owned property." Eliminate answer choice A.

Answer choice B: Does eminent domain provide for just compensation? Yes. According to the passage, "The Fifth Amendment to the United States Constitution provides that the federal government may not take private property unless it is done for a public use and the owner is reimbursed with just compensation." Eliminate answer choice B.

Answer choice C: Does eminent domain prevent local governments from limiting its power? No. According to the passage, "Justice Paul Stevens expressly recommended that the states are free to impose limitations on the use of such power by local governmental authorities." Answer choice C is the best answer.

148. **The best answer is H.**   This is an Inference question, so look for evidence that supports one answer choice over the others. According to the passage, "Opponents of such acquisitions argue that merely incidental benefits to the state are not enough to justify the exercise the power of condemnation. They are troubled by the potential abuses that may result from interpreting 'public use' so broadly." This information best supports answer choice H.

149. **The best answer is B.**   This is an Inference question, so look for evidence that supports one answer choice over the others. Locate the lines given in the question and read for context. The passage states that, "'Public use' has traditionally meant that the government could only take private land if it could demonstrate that the land was necessary to develop a project that had a valid public purpose, that being that it would be used by the public. The most common example of such a use is a new road or highway." This evidence supports the idea that roads and highways are an exemplary public use of land.

150. **The best answer is G.**   This is an Author's Purpose question. Locate the lines mentioned in the question to determine why the author included them. According to the passage, "Opponents of such acquisitions . . . are troubled by the potential abuses that may result from interpreting 'public use' so broadly . . . But supporters of the *Kelo* decision emphasize the potential appreciable benefit to the community at large, citing that the needs of the many often outweigh the needs of the few." The word *fractious* refers to conflict. The author mentions the two opinions that are in conflict with each other in order to show the arguments on both sides of this issue.

151. **The best answer is C.**   This is an Explicit Detail question. The passage uses the phrase, "…fundamental authority of a governmental entity" and "attribute of sovereignty." The other choices are all incorrect even though they use words and concepts that are similar to other parts of the passage.

152. **The best answer is F.** This is a Main Idea or Purpose question. The passage is clearly meant to provide information to the reader about a topic in real estate law. It is probably meant to introduce the topic, as evidenced by the fact that terms are defined. So, we can deduce that the passage is not meant for experts on the subject. Each of the incorrect choices is exaggerated in a way that is not supported by the content or tone of the passage.

153. **The best answer is D.** This is an Inference question. According to the passage, "In 1954, in *Berman v Parker*, the United States Supreme Court expanded the scope of the government's taking power when it affirmed the taking of a blighted area, or slum, for redevelopment by a private enterprise. The Court reasoned that the redeveloped property would be beneficial to the public welfare of the community."

154. **The best answer is G.** This is an Inference or Conclusion question. The passage moves in chronological order from the 1879 case *Boom v Patterson* at the beginning to the *Kelo* case from 2005. At each stage, some change is mentioned. So, "evolve over time" in answer choice G is supported. The word "all" in answer choices F and J is an indicator that they are less likely to be correct. Categorical (absolute) phrasing means that a sentence is more susceptible to challenge than answer choices that are phrased more carefully.

155. **The best answer is B.** This is an Extrapolation question. The passage indicates that Justice O'Connor pointed out a potential abuse of government power "...to the detriment of residents of poorer sectors. . . ." Justice Stevens's recommendation is brought up as a counterpoint used by "supporters of the Kelo decision. . . ."

156. **The best answer is J.**   This is an Author's Purpose question. Locate the lines mentioned in the question to determine why the author included them. The author is arguing for a deeper understanding of the development of language. The implication here is that the common understanding is insufficient.

157. **The best answer is C.**   This is an Author's Purpose question. Locate the lines mentioned in the question to determine why the author included them. The author is showing that there is not a clear line between language, dialect, and vernacular. The word *ambiguity* means "less than perfectly clear."

158. **The best answer is J.**   This is both an Author's Purpose and an Inference question, so look for evidence that supports one answer choice over the others. Locate the lines given in the question and read for context to determine why the author included them. The word *ethnocentrism* refers to remaining focused on one's own culture and not seeing things from the perspective of members of other cultures.

159. **The best answer is D.**   This is an Inference question, so look for evidence that supports one answer choice over the others. The passage states that, "Speakers of the prescriptive norm are often perceived to be well educated, intelligent, or of the upper classes." This best supports answer choice D.

160. **The best answer is J.** This is both a Vocabulary in Context and an Inference question. Skim for evidence that supports one answer choice over the others. According to the passage, ". . . the typical listener would be shocked to hear these professionals use *y'all* as 'correct' English." Based on the context, you can assume that the word *listener* is synonymous with the word *audience*.

161. **The best answer is A.** This is an Inference question. The last paragraph mentions "Vulgar Latin" and then lists those who spoke that form of Latin: "...soldiers, slaves, and commoners..." and the modern languages that grew from it and are spoken "Today": "...Portuguese, French, Spanish, Italian, and Romanian..." Each of the remaining choices is exaggerated such that they are not supported by the passage.

162. **The best answer is G.** This is a Main Idea question. The passage states, "Too often are the natural, peaceful integration and disintegration of cultures emphasized over the oppression and racism in human history that molds what we call individual languages today." This sentence reveals the main idea and structure of the passage as a whole. Both answer choices H and J are too broad and would describe much longer works than this passage. Answer choice F would only be appropriate if the passage urged the reader to do something specific.

163. **The best answer is A.** This is a Tone questions. The author is setting out to correct a common misconception. "Linguists" are cited more than once as the source of correct ideas that contrast with the common misconception that the passage is correcting. The only choice with a positive emotional charge is A. The other choices are either negative (B and C) or neutral (D).

164. **The best answer is H.** This is a Vocabulary in Context question. "Lexicon" means "dictionary." The choice closest in meaning is "vocabulary." The other choices are similar to other concepts mentioned in the passage. However, substituting "vocabulary" in for "lexicon" in the passage best preserves the meaning of the passage.

165. **The best answer is D.** This is a Main Idea and Author's Purpose question. The passage is clearly meant as an introductory piece. It defines its terms. So, it is not meant for advanced experts on the topic. While "battlefields" are mentioned in the first paragraph, answer choice A is too specific for the tone and content of the passage and the word "experienced" in A is not appropriate. The regional/national designations in B and C are likewise too specific for this passage.

166. **The best answer is G.** This is a Main Idea question. It is usually best to answer these questions last, which gives you a chance to learn about the passage while answering the more direct questions. You could also read the passage description, as well as the first sentence of each paragraph to get a general sense of the topic. This is clearly a passage about *synesthesia*. When you read the word *phenomenon* in answer choice G, you can replace it with the word *thing*. So, answer choice G would read: "a description of a particular thing." The *thing* in this case is *synesthesia*.

167. **The best answer is A.** This is a Vocabulary in Context question. Sometimes, if you know the definition of the word in the question, you can check the answer choices and find the one that best matches the definition. If you don't know the definition of the word, find the line referenced in the question, and read for context. Remember to start reading several lines before the line mentioned. The passage states that, "Those affected by the disorder experience an involuntary, simultaneous joining of two senses." It later indicates that those suffering from *synesthesia* experience "a juxtaposition of two, typically unrelated senses." These details best match answer choice A.

168. **The best answer is G.** This is an Author's Purpose question. Locate the lines mentioned in the question to determine why the author included them. The passage states that "Another theory postulates," which refers to an alternative explanation.

169. **The best answer is D.** This is both a Vocabulary in Context and an Author's Purpose question. Locate the lines mentioned in the question to determine why the author included them, and be sure to read the information surrounding the line referenced in the question to understand the context. According to the passage, "Synesthetic perceptions are idiosyncratic and are as varied as the perceivers themselves." If you know that idiosyncratic means unique, or specific to an individual, answer choice D is clear. However, you could take a clue from this statement that is found a few sentences later: "Indeed the variations could be endless, with each *synesthete* perceiving a slightly different color or sensation, for example." Among the answer choices, only D makes sense.

170. **The best answer is H.** This is an Author's Purpose question. Locate the lines mentioned in the question to determine why the author included them. As it is used in the passage, the word *standard* refers to the exams or tests that most individuals would ordinarily be subjected to. Because *standard* and *regular* are synonyms, answer choice H makes the most sense.

171. **The best answer is C.**   This is a Vocabulary in Context question. The passage states, "Synesthesia occurs when **this differentiation** process is incomplete," referring back to the word "modularization" in the preceding sentence. "Differentiation" is very similar in meaning to "separate" in answer choice C.

172. **The best answer is J.**   This is an Inference or Conclusion question. The last sentence of the passage makes clear that synesthetes can only be diagnosed if they come forward on their own because there is a lack of methods and standards for general diagnosis. Answer choice F is far too broad because of the inclusion of the word "all." Answer choice G is incorrect because there is no mention of "curing" synesthesia anywhere in the passage. Answer choice H states the opposite of what is strongly implied in the passage.

173. **The best answer is C.**   This is an Extrapolation question. The passage is clearly about brain science and does not require extensive prior knowledge to understand. Specific terms are defined for the reader, and the passage is aimed at beginners in this field. Answer choices A and B are too broad. Answer choice D is incorrect because there is no call for donations in the passage.

174. **The best answer is H.**   This is an Explicit Detail question. According to the passage, "Despite the potential diversity in the manifestation of *synesthesia*, the actual known number of people with the disorder is relatively small."

175. **The best answer is A.**   This is an Explicit Detail question. The "dark-green horse" is used and an example of the sort of crossed connection between the senses that characterize synesthesia. None of the other answer choices are supported by the passage.

SCIENCE

176. **The best answer is F.**   Because this question asks you to consider both theories, the best answer choice will contain information supported by both Scientist 1 and Scientist 2. Evaluate the answer choices as Yes or No questions, and look at the viewpoints to determine the answer:

Is it true that oceanographers who subscribe to both theories would agree that the loss of color in coral reefs is the result of pathogens? Yes, both Scientist 1 and Scientist 2 mention pathogens as a potential cause of loss of color in coral reefs.

This answer choice is very clearly supported by evidence presented by both scientists, so you don't have to check the remaining choices.

177. **The best answer is C.**   This is a Detail question, the answer to which is found directly stated in the passage: "When coral is stressed, the *zooxanthellae* . . . will be expelled." The question asks only about Scientist 1's viewpoint, so simply skim that paragraph for a form of the word "expel" to find your answer.

178. **The best answer is F.**   This question asks about both scientists, so start with Scientist 1's viewpoint, and skim the paragraph for a discussion of algae. The first sentence mentions that coral bleaching occurs when "coral has lost its symbiotic algae." *Symbiosis* suggests a relationship between the coral and the alga that benefits both organisms. This is a term that is often tested on the ACT, so it would be a good one to add to your vocabulary list. Scientist 2 doesn't mention algae at all.

179. **The best answer is D.** The way to counter an argument is to find one instance in which the argument does not hold true. Since Scientist 2 argues that the pathogens move from one coral to another, finding a healthy coral next to a diseased coral would counter, or contradict, Scientist 2's argument.

180. **The best answer is J.** To answer this question, it is necessary to extrapolate from the given information. A quick skim of Scientist 1's viewpoint reveals that Scientist 1 believes that "pathogens present in the water and contaminated runoff can produce situations that affect the growth of the coral's necessary algae." Therefore, you might be tempted to say that constructing an oil drilling platform would strengthen Scientist 1's viewpoint. However, the question indicates that the platform is thousands of miles from a coral reef. Additionally, the question provides no information regarding whether the oil drilling platform is contaminating the water. Scientist 2 believes that the bleaching is "triggered within the coral itself." So, this new information has no impact on either of the viewpoints.

181. **The best answer is B.** According to Scientist 1, "Coral bleaching is a phenomenon that occurs when coral has lost its symbiotic algae, *zooxanthellae*, which live within the coral's tissue." Scientist 1 goes on to say, "When coral is stressed, the *zooxanthellae* (which are responsible for giving the coral its color in the first place) will be expelled."

182. **The best answer is F.** Scientist 1 states that "Many factors can stress coral, not the least of which is water temperature changes. Also, changes in the ocean's acidity, overfishing, pathogens present in the water, and contaminated run-off can produce situations that affect the growth of the coral's necessary algae." This suggests that bleaching results from external causes. Scientist 2 states that "Some scientists believe that white syndrome is triggered within the coral itself and is not representative of an attack from an outside enemy. For some unknown reason, the infected coral's immune system attacks not only the pathogenic cells that cause the disease but destroys healthy cells as well." This suggests an internal cause.

183. **The best answer is A.**   An *independent variable* is one that is under the control of the experimenter. As the experimenter changes or manipulates the independent variable, it is hoped that the *dependent variable*, the thing being observed, will be affected in some way. Because the two experiments were conducted at different temperatures in order to determine the effect of temperature on benzene concentrations, the temperature was the independent variable.

184. **The best answer is G.**   To answer this question, you need to compare the benzene concentrations for each car model and year. Because the question mentions Experiment 1, you only need to consider Table 1. According to Table 1, both the 1995 models (A and B) had lower benzene concentrations than the 1976 models. Make sure you compare A to A and B to B for each year. You can predict that the answer is yes, the results do support the hypothesis because the benzene concentrations were lower in the newer cars. Look for your predicted answer among the choices—answer choice G matches.

185. **The best answer is A.**   The first step in answering this question is to compare the temperatures of each city in the table. Based on the table, Detroit has the lowest average temperature. Now you need to make a connection between this information and the data in the passage. The results of the experiments show that, at −10°F, the percent of benzene in the exhaust was higher than the percent of benzene in the exhaust at 20°F. Based on this evidence, you can conclude that cars in the city with the lowest average temperature, Detroit, would likely have more benzene in their exhaust than cars in cities with higher average temperatures.

186. **The best answer is G.**   This question requires you to find a difference between the experiments. Note that the question asks about Experiment 1, so turn the answer choices into yes-or-no questions about Experiment 1:

Is it true that in Experiment 1, older cars were used? No, both experiments used cars from 1976 and 1995. Eliminate answer choice F.

Is it true that in Experiment 1, the temperature was lower? Yes, the temperature in Experiment 1 was $-10°F$, while the temperature in Experiment 2 was $20°F$. Answer choice G is correct.

187. **The best answer is B.**   Since the question asks about the best time to determine the maximum percent of benzene in a car's exhaust, it would make sense to test the car's exhaust when the greatest amount of benzene is present. According to both Table 1 and Table 2, the greatest amount of benzene was present between approximately 5–7 minutes after the car's engine was started.

188. **The best answer is H.**   Based on the passage, the paper that presented the greatest resistance to sliding is the paper that required the greatest frictional force. According to Table 1, wrapping paper had the highest measured force, followed by notebook paper, waxed paper, and newspaper.

189. **The best answer is A.**   Because the students were pulling the wrapped physics books across the tabletop, it makes sense that they were varying the amount of frictional force between the wrapped books and the tabletop.

190. **The best answer is J.**   Data presented in Table 2 indicate that, as the number of books in the stack increases by 1 book, the force (N) increases by roughly 3.5. Therefore, because a stack of 5 books required a force of 17.0 N, you can assume that a stack of 6 books will require a force of approximately 20.6 N.

191. **The best answer is D.**   Logic tells you that the book wrapped in the paper with the *lowest* amount of frictional force would take the *longest* amount of time to come to a complete stop. According to Table 1, newspaper has the lowest N value.

192. **The best answer is J.**   According to both Experiment 1 and Experiment 3, a book wrapped in wrapping paper had a measured frictional force of 5.7 regardless of the speed at which the book was pulled across the table.

193. **The best answer is B.**   To determine the purpose of an experiment, look at how the experiment was designed as well as the results that were obtained. In Experiment 2, the students stacked unwrapped books on top of one another and pulled them across the tabletop. The students then recorded the measured frictional force in Table 2. Therefore, the purpose of the experiment must have been to determine the relationship between frictional force and the weight of a stack of physics books.

194. **The best answer is G.**   This passage might seem intimidating at first, but the goal with answering the Science Test questions is to keep it simple! In this case, just let the answer choices guide you. Whenever you're asked to put things in order, always start with the first position. Notice that the terms in the answer choices are found in Table 1 and that they all seem to be associated with a group of three letters. The "strand" shown in the question also includes the letters, so just break the strand into groups of three letters. The first group is CUG. Find CUG on the table—it matches up with Leucine. Check the answer choices and notice that only choices G and H put Leucine in the first position. Move on to the next group of three letters—AGA. Find AGA on the table—it matches up with Arginine, so answer choice G must be correct. Don't worry about the fact that Arginine matches up with other letters. Just focus on the information in the question.

195. **The best answer is C.**   Don't be intimidated by the passage—just notice that the three letter groups appear on Table 1 and that they correspond to specific amino acids. Evaluate each of the answer choices, and write down the corresponding amino acids:

AGA—Arginine

AGG—Arginine

AGU—Serine

CGU—Arginine

The only one that doesn't match up with Arginine is AGU.

196. **The best answer is G.**   This question requires some attention to detail as well as the ability to make connections among the data. First, make note of the codon labeled in the given figure: ACC. Next, find ACC in Table 1. You will see that ACC codes for the amino acid Threonine. Next, find CCA in Table 1. You will see that CCA codes for the amino acid Proline. Apply some logic to your interpretation of the data to determine that, if you alter the codon in this way, you will most certainly change both the amino acid specified by the new codon and the amino acids that come next.

197. **The best answer is D.**   The best approach to this question is to find where in the passage the terms in the answer choices are found. And, because this is an ordering question, let's start with the first position. You can spot the terms in the answer choices in both the introductory paragraph and Figure 1. According to Figure 1, DNA most definitely comes first. Confirm this assumption by looking at the introductory paragraph, which states "The process first starts with transcription, where the base sequence DNA is copied to form messenger RNA (mRNA)." This sentence actually tells you the first and second positions—first DNA, then mRNA. Only answer choice D puts those terms in the proper positions, so it must be the correct answer.

198. **The best answer is H.**   You might need to do a little digging to find the correct answer to this question. The first step should be to locate in Table 1 the codons in each answer choice. Write down the corresponding amino acid next to each codon:

UGA = **Stop
There is no amino acid listed! But notice that, below the table, **Stop is defined as a codon that specifies the end of the polypeptide chain. Try the next answer choice.

UAG = **Stop
At this point, common sense should kick in and tell you that the stop codons *must* come at the end of the polypeptide chain, so the exception will be the codon that is *not* a stop codon. Look at the next answer choice.

AGU = Serine.

Since this is *not* a stop codon, it is the exception, and answer choice H is correct.

199. **The best answer is A.**   Figure 1 is a bar graph, so look at the relationship between the height of each bar on the graph. According to the graph, at Location 1, the bar for average nitrate concentration in 2010 is shorter than the bar for average nitrate concentration in 2015. Therefore, the average nitrate concentration in 2010 was lower than the average nitrate concentration in 2015.

200. **The best answer is G.**   The passage states that "Any drinking water source that exceeds the MCL is considered unsafe for human consumption." You can assume that if the nitrate concentration is below the MCL, the water would be considered safe for human consumption.

201. **The best answer is C.** Because the bars in Figure 1 representing the average nitrate concentration in 2010 are different heights at the different locations, those concentrations must NOT be the same.

202. **The best answer is G.** You can quickly answer this question by just looking at the numbers in Table 1. All of the values that correspond to W (winter) are higher than all of the values that correspond to S (summer). Therefore, the nitrate levels in early winter are always higher than the levels in early summer.

203. **The best answer is C.** You can quickly answer this question by just looking at the numbers in Table 1. Higher nitrate values indicate higher contamination. Therefore, the stream that contributes most to the pollution of the lake within Location 1 will have the highest nitrate values. Stream A in early winter has a nitrate level of 35.7, which is the highest value in the table.

204. **The best answer is G.** According to the passage, "In higher concentrations, however, nitrates can be potentially threatening contaminants. Human activities can be responsible for increased levels of nitrates in groundwater. The most common sources of nitrates produced by human activity can be traced to industrial pollution, human waste septic systems, and agricultural processes." Therefore, it makes sense that potential contamination from leaking septic systems would increase the nitrate levels in the lake.

205. **The best answer is A.** The ACT Science Test will include some common knowledge questions. This is such a question. According to the passage, the characteristics of certain caterpillars are listed in Table 1. Caterpillars belong to the Animal kingdom.

206. **The best answer is G.**   To answer this question, locate *Colias eurytheme* on Table 1, then analyze the answer choices. Because "yellow body" ends at Step 3 with *Spilosoma virginica* and *Colias eurytheme* is found in Step 4, you can eliminate answer choice F. Step 4 indicates that a caterpillar with a pink stripe is a *Colias eurytheme*, so answer choice G must be correct.

207. **The best answer is C.**   The trait that distinguishes one caterpillar from another is a trait that they DO NOT share. According to Table 2, Caterpillar C has a solid head color, while, according to Table 1, *Spodoptera ornithogalli* has spots on its head.

208. **The best answer is J.**   To answer this question, you can evaluate each of the answer choices and compare the traits of Caterpillar B and Caterpillar C. According to Table 1, Step 2 involves the length of hair. Length of hair is not listed in Table 2 for either Caterpillar B or Caterpillar C, so eliminate answer choice F. Likewise, body color is not listed for either caterpillar, so eliminate answer choice G. Again, because strip color is not listed in Table 2 for either caterpillar, eliminate answer choice H. Because Step 5 mentions the presence or absence of hornlike projections and Caterpillar C has no projections while Caterpillar B has blue hornlike projections, this is the step at which the caterpillars diverge.

209. **The best answer is B.**   To answer this question, first look at the traits listed in Table 2 for Caterpillar A. Then compare that data to Table 1. Because Caterpillar A has long, dense hair and a green body, it is most likely an *Automeris io*, which also has those traits.

210. **The best answer is H.**   Because Study 3 included data regarding temperature, it's likely the study was designed to investigate how average chirp rate and average chirp volume vary with respect to temperature. None of the other answer choices is supported by the data.

211. **The best answer is D.**   A quick way to solve problems like this is to start with one of the conditions and eliminate answer choices. According to Study 1, a population size greater than 20 yielded the highest average chirp rate, so eliminate answer choices B and C. Study 3 shows a higher than average chirp rate associated with temperatures between 24°C and 26°C, so eliminate answer choice A.

212. **The best answer is G.**   You can assume that initially, based on the design of the studies, the students included both male and female crickets when collecting data. Since the further research indicates that only male crickets chirp, the observations regarding the number of crickets in each population would need to be reevaluated because the female crickets should no longer be counted.

213. **The best answer is D.**   According to Figure 2, at 8:15 P.M. the average chirp rate was around 40 chirps per minute. Table 3 shows a chirp rate of 39.7 between 24°C and 26°C. This data best supports answer choice D.

214. **The best answer is F.**   To answer this question, refer to Table 1, which shows that *larger* populations have a higher average chirp rate. This data contradicts the hypothesis.

215. **The best answer is A.**   This question asks you to compare data from each study. According to Study 1, the average chirp volume did not vary much among population sizes. The results of Study 2 show a greater variation in average chirp volume depending on time of day. However, the data from Study 3 show the greatest variation in average chirp volume across different air temperatures—from 0.0 to 3.4.

PART V

APPENDIXES

APPENDIX 1

What's Next?

APPENDIX 2

Grammar and Punctuation Rules

APPENDIX 3

ACT Vocabulary List

What's Next?

Once you have successfully tackled the ACT exam, you will still need to deal with the rest of the admissions process. This appendix is meant to provide some useful hints and suggestions to help you make the best decisions about what colleges and programs to apply to, as well as how to maximize your chances of getting into the college and program of your choice.

CHOOSING THE BEST COLLEGE OR UNIVERSITY FOR YOU

There are many resources out there that include lists of the "best" schools. The truth is that there may be several "best" schools for you as an individual and you may not be a good fit for any of the so-called top schools that appear on those lists. There are positive and negative features of all colleges, and the final decision is up to you and your parents. Our goal here is to provide some food for thought as you make your decision. The following are some factors to consider when choosing a school. As you will see, there are many areas where the factors overlap.

Size

The largest university campuses are in the 35,000 to 50,000 student range. They are small cities unto themselves with their own fire departments and police forces and their own streets and power plants. At the other end of the spectrum are small colleges with just a few hundred students, which are smaller than many high schools. Of course, there are campuses of every size in between.

It is possible to make some generalizations about large versus small campuses. Large campuses tend to have more interesting activities and a wider variety of resources such as libraries and museums. There will be people from all walks of life and from many different places in the world. Large campuses are just more exciting for students than most smaller schools are. On the negative side, large campuses typically have terrible parking problems. For example, one large Midwestern school takes in over one million dollars every year just in parking ticket fines. There also can be more serious crime issues with large schools. Predators of every sort are sometimes drawn to places where there are many young people who may be less vigilant about personal security and theft prevention than they should be.

Another negative is the fact that many students at large schools find that it is increasingly difficult to graduate within the traditional four years. Graduation times for a first bachelor's degree are closer to five years than four at many schools. This means one extra year of tuition, and room and board expenses, and one year fewer of making money working in your chosen field.

Location

Many students want to stay close to the support system of their parents' homes. They like the idea of visiting on weekends and of short travel times back and forth. Other students like the idea of striking out on their own and becoming self-reliant. One of the negatives of being far away can be the expense and inconvenience of travel during holiday breaks and other time off. Also, there is the issue of residency to consider. At most state-supported colleges and universities, nonresidents pay a much higher rate for tuition than do residents. The difference in cost can make a state school just as expensive as any private school.

Climate is another factor that falls within the general topic of location. If you are used to surf and sun, think twice before you enroll at a school where summer is defined as "three months of bad sledding."

Another way to look at location is to realize that there are three general types of campuses: rural, suburban, and urban. Each has its own advantages and disadvantages, which you should carefully consider before selecting a campus where you will probably be spending much of your early adulthood.

Cost

Several financial factors need to be considered. For some students, at some campuses, tuition is not the most important financial factor to consider; housing is. There are some college towns where a student can expect to pay an amount each month for housing and parking that is equal to his or her parents' house payment back home. In many such places, it is simply cost prohibitive for a student to own a car. In fact, some campuses are so short on parking that they actually forbid undergraduates from having cars on campus. Make sure that you can afford the rent at the college that you select so that you don't end up living on toast sandwiches, oatmeal, and ramen noodles for four years.

There is also the issue of financial aid, which is a significant question for many students. Make sure that you contact the financial aid office at all of the schools that you are seriously considering to find out about loans, scholarships, and grants that might be available. Do not assume that your family is too well off for you to qualify for aid. Some scholarships are not need-based and can be awarded to students based solely on other factors such as academic performance or standardized test scores.

Reputation

A school's reputation is the most subjective factor to consider. Some schools are so famous that everyone has heard of them. Many more are known only to specialists in a specific field or industry or to people in a certain geographic area. Maybe one of this latter group of schools is just the place for you. Although there may be some correlation between the school you attend and your starting pay or the opportunities that are available to you right after graduation, those correlations tend to break down as time progresses and you build a career and résumé of your own.

The reputation of an institution can be affected by factors that are completely nonrelated to what you will experience as a student. For example, schools that win big national athletic championships tend to be well known; many people assume that they are academically superior to other schools, even though there may be no connection at all between those two aspects of a university.

Resources

If you plan to study physics, you should probably look for a school that has some advanced physics equipment. If you want to study large-animal veterinary medicine, you should probably look for a school that has a farm where you can care for horses and cows. This may seem like common sense. But, as Voltaire pointed out, "Common sense is not so common." We have seen many students who were disappointed by the actual facilities available for their chosen majors at various campuses.

Athletics

There are two major aspects to athletics at the college level: participation and observation. Do you want a school where you can be an athlete or a fan? Are there scholarship dollars available for your sport? Is your sport a varsity sport or a club sport at the schools in which you are interested? Does your sport even exist at all of the colleges on your list? If you are interested in being a fan, the good news is that even the big powerhouse athletic departments are good about setting aside a fair number of tickets just for students.

Instructors

Some schools, usually the larger ones, have a high proportion of classes that are taught by graduate students, usually called TAs (Teaching Assistants) or GAs (Graduate Assistants). Like most college professors, they probably have had little or no instruction on how to be a teacher. They are underpaid and often sleep deprived. Some of them have a tenuous grasp of the English language. But, there are also some gems. Some of these people are bound to be among the best teachers that you have ever had. However, some students and their families feel that it is worth going out of their way to be certain that they have access to professors and that the class sizes are manageable. Some classes at some colleges can have hundreds of students in a large, amphitheatre-like lecture hall, leaving little opportunity for meaningful interaction.

Some professors are famous. You may decide that it is worth going out of your way just to sit in a large crowd being lectured to by a particular person of note in his or her chosen field. Some students are, frankly, more comfortable in an environment where it is easy to blend in and they don't have to worry about being called on to answer in class.

Many professors and instructors are focused on delivering quality education to their students, and some colleges go out of their way to arrange for frequent and high-quality interaction between students and instructors.

Social Environment

Everyone is aware that part of the college experience is social interaction. Some schools are single-sex and some are co-ed. Some dorms are segregated by sex also. The male–female ratio can vary from one school to the next. Some schools have reputations for being "party schools." Some schools that are not known as "party schools" actually have some issues with things getting out of control from time to time.

Generally, smaller schools tend to be more socially homogeneous. Students tend to act, dress, and think more like one another. Larger schools tend to consist of a wider variety of perspectives and subcultures. Your comfort level with the social circumstances at your school can have an impact on your college success. Think about your personal social needs carefully when choosing a college.

Diversity

To most people, diversity usually means racial diversity. However, there are other aspects to diversity, particularly when considering college: diversity of opinion, socioeconomic background, gender, majors, and countries of origin. All of these are factors on many college campuses. Some students feel that they will learn best in an environment where they are surrounded by people like themselves. Others are interested in experiencing more diversity and learning from people from different backgrounds.

The best way to get the true picture of most of these factors is to visit the campuses about which you are serious. You can do some preliminary research on the Internet, but you should remember that websites set up by the schools are essentially sales brochures. They have a significant financial interest in getting you to attend. You should be a wise consumer and take some of the sales pitches that you receive with a grain of salt. In fact, it is not a bad idea to try to meet some "real" students if you do a campus visit. Chances are that the school will match you up with a "campus guide," who is a student with training in salesmanship. He or she will tell you about all of the wonderful aspects of life on campus. You probably won't hear any complaints from your campus guide. It might be worth getting out on campus on your own for a while.

APPLYING TO COLLEGE

The general rule of thumb is that you should get all of your application materials into the colleges to which you are applying by the holiday break of your senior year. This means that you will have to have all of your personal statements finished, your applications filled out, your letters of recommendation and résumé sent in, and your test scores available to the admissions departments by New Year's Day if you want to be ahead of most of the applicants, some of whom will often actually wait until near the final deadlines to turn in their applications.

Don't "shotgun" your applications; be selective when choosing colleges. Many applications contain a question asking you to list all other colleges to which you are applying. The admissions office will review the answer to this question in order to gauge how realistic you are and whether you actually think that you have a shot at their school.

A good average number of schools to which to apply is about five. Choose one or two "backup" schools that you will attend only if something goes horribly wrong with your applications to your other choices. Two or three should be the schools that are realistic choices for you in terms of your GPA, ACT score, and other factors. One or two should be "reach" or "stretch" schools that might be long shots but where you have some chance at getting in and you will certainly attend if you are selected.

Applications

Applications are usually available as paper documents or as online forms on the schools' websites. They vary in length (from two to ten pages, usually three or four pages) and in the type of information that they request. Fees and deadlines also vary. Don't send in an application too early. Candid discussions with admissions professionals reveal that they appreciate promptness and neatness and don't mind a reasonable amount of follow-up. What they do NOT like is sloppiness, an apparent inability to follow directions (sending a five-page personal statement when there is a two-page limit), aggressive and/or annoying follow-up, last-minute applications, or applications that come in before the department is ready for the year's avalanche of incoming documents.

If you call an admissions department with a specific question or two, be focused. Write down your question ahead of time and keep your call polite, professional, and short. Do not expect anyone in the department to tell you that you can get in or definitely cannot get in. They have a procedure for making those decisions and they simply cannot make exceptions. You should listen for "code words" when you talk to admissions professionals. If they say, "we recommend . . . " they mean, "Do it." If they say, "we discourage . . . " they mean, "Don't do it."

Personal Statements

Many schools require you to write an essay or two. Some schools are very general in their requirements. They simply ask you to write an essay explaining why you would be a valuable addition to the school. Other institutions give very specific assignments. You should follow the directions and guidance that they give. Don't write on a topic of your own choosing. Don't go over the page limits given. Don't turn in more essays than requested. Do make sure that the essays that you turn in are your own work. There is nothing wrong with asking a family member, teacher, or other professional for a little guidance and editing assistance. However, if you actually let someone else write your statements for you, it will be fairly simple for an experienced admissions professional to spot your fraud.

The best way to come up with a solid personal statement is to start early. Brainstorm a bit at the beginning of the process. List all of the topics and points that you want to include. Create a few different outlines. Get input from friends, family, teachers, and other professionals. Then do first drafts of the two or three best ideas. Put them aside for a week or two, then take them back out and read them again. We all have a tendency to fall in love with our own ideas and our own writing at first. If the idea still looks solid when you review it days later, it is probably worth finishing. Plan to go through several drafts and to get feedback from people who you trust along the way. The personal statement is usually your only chance to get the admissions committee to see you as a human being rather than just a set of numbers or a resumé.

The best personal statements are more than just mere résumé information. They are also more than just the all-too-common "kiss up" letter. You should definitely avoid the standard format of "You guys are soooo cool! [Here are some details that I looked up to prove it.] And, I'm cool too! [Here are some wonderful things about me.] Therefore, let me in!"

Instead, you should try to tell a story about yourself that illustrates a positive characteristic about which you want the admissions committee to know. A narrative format with a beginning, a middle, and a conclusion is far more effective than simply pasting in some information about the school that you probably learned from its website and that they probably already know. If the story illustrates something unique about you, or a hardship that you have overcome, that is fine. But make sure that you avoid the whiny tone that turns readers off. There is a big difference between explaining a legitimate reason for a temporary dip in your Grade Point Average and trying to gain admission through sympathy for your plight. The latter almost never works.

Letters of Recommendation

Most colleges have some famous alumni. They are not likely to be overly impressed if you get a recommendation letter from someone who is famous or powerful, unless that person actually knows you well and can honestly praise you effusively and in great detail. Be careful about the choice of people you ask to recommend you. Make sure that they are people who know you well and can speak about your academic strengths and/or strength of character. Give them plenty of time and don't be afraid to follow up to be certain that your letters are ready or went out to the schools on time. Provide them with a pre-addressed, stamped envelope if the letter is to be sent via U.S. Postal Service. Offer to provide them with a copy of your résumé, or work that you did in their class, or a list of bullet points that you hope that they will include in your letter.

Be sensitive to "code words" in this situation also. If you hear, "I'm not sure that I'd be the best person for this," or, "I'm not 100 percent comfortable . . . , " or, "Maybe you should ask someone who knows you better," run, don't walk, to find someone else to write your letter. If you persist, some folks are too polite to refuse outright but they may end up doing something that is fairly well known in the admissions game, called "damning with faint praise." If a letter of recommendation is lukewarm in its descriptions of your abilities and positive attributes, the admissions committee reads it as saying, "I couldn't get out of this gracefully but I can't really recommend this candidate wholeheartedly."

Résumé

You may not have ever had a reason to put together a résumé before. Most colleges will either ask you for one or accept one if you include it with your application. There are many great sources of information regarding how to format your résumé. The best advice is to keep it simple and straightforward. Don't play games with fonts, colors, and so on. Just lay out the information in an easy-to-read format so that the busy person who will be looking at it can quickly find what he or she needs. Don't include information that might be construed as negative. For instance, if you volunteered for a political candidate, you might think twice about putting that information on your résumé for application purposes. The people reading your résumé might have political ideals that are directly opposed to "your" candidate's ideals and they might let their feelings about politics start to influence their decisions about your application.

SUGGESTED HIGH SCHOOL COURSES

We are including a discussion of the courses that you should probably take to help with your ACT score and to help you get ready for college. Not surprisingly, most of the courses that help with ACT preparation also help with college preparation. Actual course names vary by high school so we are listing the course content that you should try to get in if there is still time.

Mathematics: Algebra, Geometry, Trigonometry, Precalculus

Basic, intermediate, and some advanced algebra concepts will be tested on the ACT. There won't be any geometry proofs, but there will be plenty of circles and triangles, and at least one diagram that will include two parallel lines crossed by a transversal. There won't be any more than four trigonometry questions, so it is probably not worth taking a whole trigonometry course just to do better on the ACT. But, it will probably come in handy as preparation for college math. Similarly, precalculus will help with a very limited number of ACT math problems but is an important part of a College Prep curriculum.

English: Writing/Composition Courses

Reading and discussing literature can be an enlightening experience and is certainly part of a good education. However, the English courses that help most with the ACT are the ones that focus on writing skills. Creative Writing course instructors can sometimes be too easy on mechanics and clarity of expression. The more rigorous the course, the better it will prepare you for the ACT and for college-level work.

Science: Biology, Chemistry, Physics

The Science Test does not test your memory of the concepts that you learn in high school science courses. It does, however, assume that you have some background knowledge and a clear understanding of how scientific experiments and studies are conducted. If you have written up a few lab reports of your own, you will have a much easier time reading and understanding the information on the Science Test.

Languages: Latin, Spanish, Italian, French

Most English vocabulary comes from Latin. If you study Latin, or one of the modern versions of Latin that is spoken today, you'll have a much easier time with English vocabulary. It is also true that many native English-speaking students learn much more about English grammar by studying a foreign language than those students who take only English courses.

Good Luck!

If you have followed our advice and worked through all of the material in this book, you should give yourself a hearty "Well done!" and remember that you have put in plenty of effort to ensure your ACT success. Thanks for letting us help you get ready for the ACT. Good luck with your exam and with college!

Grammar and Punctuation Rules

Punctuation Rules

> **Punctuation:** *Standard marks and signs in writing and printing to separate words into sentences, clauses, and phrases in order to clarify meaning.*

A properly punctuated sentence will help the reader understand the organization of the writer's ideas. The ACT English Test includes questions that address both the rules and usage of punctuation. You should be able to identify and correct errors involving the following punctuation marks:

1. Commas
2. Apostrophes
3. Colons and Semicolons
4. Parentheses and Dashes
5. Periods, Question Marks, and Exclamation Points

Commas

A comma is used to indicate a separation of ideas or elements within a sentence.

Use a comma with a coordinating conjunction to separate independent clauses within a sentence.

A coordinating conjunction connects words, phrases, or clauses that are of equal importance in the sentence.

Jenny sings in the choir, *and* she plays the guitar in a rock band.
Amanda enjoys her job, *but* she is looking forward to her vacation.
His mother doesn't eat meat, *nor* does she eat dairy products.
Jordan will be playing football this year, *for* he made the team.
Frank earned a promotion, *so* we decided to celebrate.
I just completed my workout, *yet* I'm not tired.

Use a comma to separate elements that introduce and modify a sentence.

Yesterday, I painted the entire garage.
Before deciding on a major at college, Rana discussed her options with her parents.

Use commas before and after a parenthetical expression.

A parenthetical expression is a phrase that is inserted into the writer's train of thought. Parenthetical expressions are most often set off with commas.

Stephanie's decision, in my opinion, was not in her best interest.
The new park, of course, is a popular tourist destination.

Use commas before and after an appositive.

An appositive is a noun or phrase that renames the noun that precedes it.

My brother, a well-respected scientist, made an important discovery.
Mr. Smith, the fifth-grade math teacher, was a favorite among the students.

Use a comma to set off an interjection.

Well, it's about time that you got here!
Say, did you pass your history test?

Use commas to separate coordinate adjectives.

If two adjectives modify a noun in the same way, they are called coordinate adjectives. Coordinate adjectives can also be joined with *and* (without a comma).

We walked the long, dusty road to the abandoned farm.
OR—We walked the long and dusty road to the abandoned farm.
My cousin received a dedicated, signed copy of her favorite book.
OR—My cousin received a dedicated and signed copy of her favorite book.

Use commas to set off a nonrestrictive phrase or clause.

A nonrestrictive phrase or clause is one that can be omitted from the sentence without changing the meaning of the sentence. Nonrestrictive clauses are useful because they serve to further describe the nouns that they follow.

My sister's dog, forever annoying, barks at me whenever I visit.
Katie celebrated her birthday, which was in June, with a party and a chocolate cake.

Use a comma to separate items in a list or series.

Jill decided to purchase a leash, a collar, and a water dish for her dog.
Skippy packed his suitcase, put on his jacket, and left the house.
Please bring the following items to camp: pillow, blanket, toothbrush, and other personal hygiene products.

The so-called *serial comma*, the one preceding *and* or *or* before the last item in a series of three or more items, is considered standard for ACT English purposes. Nevertheless, this remains a disputed usage in the United States. The ACT uses the serial comma in every case that warrants it.

Use commas in dates, addresses, place names, numbers, and quotations.

Commas generally separate a quotation from its source.

> Mary is leaving for Jamaica on January 7, 2004.
> The Library of Congress is located at 101 Independence Avenue, Washington, D.C.
> Annual tuition is currently $42,500.
> ''My sister is a nurse,'' Becky said proudly.

Do <u>not</u> use a comma:

-to separate a subject from a verb.

> The police officer walked down to the corner.
> *NOT*—The police officer, walked down to the corner.

-to separate an adjective from the word it modifies.

> The pretty girl sat in front of me on the bus.
> *NOT*—The pretty, girl sat in front of me on the bus.

-before a coordinate conjunction and a phrase (NOT an independent clause with its own subject and a verb).

> Jeff likes to relax on his couch and listen to music.
> *NOT*—Jeff likes to relax on his couch, and listen to music.

-to separate two independent clauses; this is known as a comma splice.

> I plan to attend a liberal arts college. My parents want me to get a well-rounded education.
> *NOT*—I plan to attend a liberal arts college, my parents want me to get a well-rounded education.

Apostrophes

An apostrophe is used to form possessives of nouns, to show the omission of letters in contractions, and to form plurals of letters and numbers with "s."

Add an apostrophe and an "s" to form the possessive of singular nouns, plural nouns, or indefinite pronouns that do not end in "s."

> My friend's house is at the end of the street.
> The Women's Society meets every Thursday at the high school.
> Someone's bicycle is leaning against the building.

Add an apostrophe to form the possessive of plural nouns ending in "s."

> The horses' stalls were filled with straw.
> I did not enjoy the two brothers' rendition of my favorite song.

Add an apostrophe to the last noun to indicate joint possession.

> Frank and Ruth's anniversary is in September.

Add an apostrophe to all nouns to indicate individual possession.

Brian's, Jason's, and Michael's computers were all stolen.

Add an apostrophe to indicate contractions.

It's raining outside again.
We're running against each other in the election.
If you're going to the movie with me, we should leave now.
My cousin should've taken the bus.
Didn't Kevin know that classes had begun?

Add an apostrophe to form the plural of letters and numbers.

Did you dot your i's and cross your t's?
There are a total of four 7's in my phone number.

Do __not__ use an apostrophe with a possessive pronoun.

The car with the flat tire is ours.
NOT —The car with the flat tire is our's.
Yours is the dog that barks all night.
NOT—Your's is the dog that barks all night.

Colons and Semicolons

A colon is used before a list or after an independent clause that is followed by information that directly modifies or adds to the clause. An independent clause can stand alone as a complete sentence. A semicolon is used to join closely related independent clauses when a coordinate conjunction is not used, with conjunctive adverbs to join main clauses, to separate items in a series that contains commas, and to separate coordinate clauses when they are joined by transitional words or phrases.

Use a colon before a list.

We are required to bring the following items to camp: a sleeping bag,
a pillow, an alarm clock, clothes, and personal-care items.

Use a colon after an independent clause that is followed by information that directly modifies or adds to the clause.

Jennifer encountered a problem that she had not anticipated: a broken
Internet link.
My sister suggested a great location: the park down the street from our house.

Colons may also precede direct quotations and should be used in business salutations and titles.

Captain John Paul Jones said: "I have not yet begun to fight."
Dear Mr. Smith:
Blaze: A Story of Courage

Use a semicolon to join closely related independent clauses when a coordinate conjunction is not used.

> Jane starts a new job today; she is very excited.
> I don't understand the directions; my teacher must explain them to me.

Use a semicolon with conjunctive adverbs to join independent clauses.

> Skippy is interested in taking the class; however, it does not fit in his schedule.
> My brother seems short compared to his friends; nevertheless, he is the tallest person in our family.

Use a semicolon to separate items that contain commas and are arranged in series.

> The art museum contained some beautiful, classically designed furniture; bronze, plaster, and marble statues; and colorful, abstract modern art pieces.
> My first meal at college consisted of cold, dry toast; runny, undercooked eggs; and very strong, acidic coffee.

Use a semicolon to separate coordinate clauses when they are joined by transitional words or phrases.

When a sentence contains more than one clause, each of which is considered equally as important as the other, the clauses are called "coordinate clauses." They are typically joined by a coordinating conjunction, such as *and*, *but*, *or*, *so*. When a coordinating conjunction is not used, a semicolon should be.

> My sister and I enjoyed the play; afterward, we stopped for an ice cream cone.
> *OR*—My sister and I enjoyed the play, and afterward, we stopped for an ice cream cone.
> Betty often misplaces her keys; perhaps she should get a key locator.
> *OR*—Betty often misplaces her keys, so perhaps she should get a key locator.

Parentheses and Dashes

Parentheses are used to enclose supplemental information that is not essential to the meaning of the sentence. Dashes are used to place special emphasis on a certain word or phrase within a sentence.

Use parentheses to enclose explanatory or secondary supporting details.

> In addition to serving as Class Treasurer (during her junior year), she was also a National Merit Scholar.
> Alan visited the Football Hall of Fame (on a guided tour) during his summer vacation.

Use dashes in place of parentheses to place special emphasis on certain words or phrases.

> Dr. Evans—a noted scientist and educator—spoke at our commencement ceremony.
> The Homecoming float—cobbled together with wire and nails—teetered dangerously down the street.

Periods, Question Marks, and Exclamation Points

Periods, question marks, and exclamation points are considered "end punctuation" and should be used at the end of a sentence.

Use a period to end most sentences.

Scott enrolled in classes at the university.

Use a question mark to end a direct question.

Do you think it will rain today?

Use an exclamation point to end an emphatic statement.

Please don't leave your vehicle unattended!

Grammar Rules

> **Grammar:** *The study and application of combining words to form sentences.*

A well-formed sentence contains a subject and a verb and expresses a complete thought. The ACT English Test includes questions that will test your ability to identify and correct poorly written sentences. You should have a firm grasp of the following concepts:

Subject/Verb Agreement
Nouns and Pronouns
Verbs and Verb Forms

Subject/Verb Agreement

A sentence has two essential parts: a subject and a verb. The subject is who or what the sentence is about. The verb tells you what the subject is doing, what is being done to the subject, or something about the state of being of the subject. The subject and verb must agree; that is, they must share the same *person*, *number*, and *voice*. In addition, verbs in successive clauses and sentences normally must match in *voice* and *tense*.

Person

A verb must have the same person as the subject.

1st person: *I am* eating lunch.
2nd person: *You are* eating lunch.
3rd person: *She is* eating lunch.

In addition to person, subject and verb must agree in number, which is either singular or plural.

Number

1st person, singular: *I have* a headache today.
2nd person, singular: *You are* my best friend in the entire world!
3rd person, singular: *It/He/She was* interesting today.
1st person, plural: *We make* amazing barbecue.
2nd person, plural: *You are* going to work in pairs for this assignment.
3rd person, plural: *They enjoy* suspense novels.

Voice

Active voice means that the subject is acting. In the following sentence, *dog* is the subject.

The *dog licked* my brother.

The ACT English Test is more likely to reward answer choices that are in the active voice. The graders on the Writing Test are also more likely to award points to essays that are in the active voice.

Passive voice means that the subject is being acted upon. In the following sentence, *my brother* is the subject.

My brother was licked by the dog.

Although some situations demand the passive voice, the vast majority of passive sentences can be effectively reworded to have active voice.

Tense

Verb tense provides you with information about when the action took place. Actions take place in the present, in the past, or in the future. The ACT English Test will not require you to recall the names of the tenses, but it will require you to recognize correct and incorrect uses of verb tense. While there are many classifications of verb tense, for the purpose of preparing for the ACT, you should remember the following tenses:

Simple past—the action took place in the past and is completed: *Jenny worked* a double shift at the mall yesterday.

Past progressive—the action was taking place in the past when some other action took place: *Jenny was working* at the mall last night when the fire alarm sounded.

Past perfect—the action took place before another specified point in time or action in the past: *Jenny had worked* at the mall before she went to college.

Simple present—the action takes place regularly or repeatedly: *Jenny works* at the mall after school. (She works there repeatedly.)

Present progressive—the action is taking place now: *Jenny is working* at the mall until 9 o'clock tonight.

Present perfect—the action began in the past and is ongoing: *Jenny has worked* at the mall for the last two years.

Future—the action will take place in the future: *Jenny will work* more hours at the mall next summer.

Future progressive—the action will be taking place in the future when some other action will take place: *Jenny will be working* at the mall when her friends begin gathering for her surprise party.

Future perfect—the action took place before another specified action or point in time in the future: *Jenny will have worked* over 3 years at the mall when she graduates next spring.

Some special verb tenses:

Habitual actions in the past using *would* and *used to*—the action took place on a regular basis in the past:

When I was a boy, *I would buy* a root beer float every chance I could.
OR When I was a boy, *I used to buy* a root beer float every chance I could.

Near future with progressive tenses of *go*—the action is upcoming relative to past or present:

I was going to call you, but I could not find my phone.
The girls are going to have dinner before the movie tonight.

Nouns and Pronouns

The English language contains two forms of nouns: *proper nouns*, which name a specific person, place, or object, and *common nouns*, which name a nonspecific person, place, or object. Proper nouns begin with an uppercase letter, and common nouns do not. *Pronouns* take the place of either a proper or a common noun. Generally, a pronoun begins with an uppercase letter only if the pronoun begins a sentence. The one notable exception is the personal pronoun *I*, which is always capitalized. A pronoun should be placed so that it clearly refers to a specific noun. One of the errors that the ACT commonly tests is a pronoun with an unclear antecedent. You should be able to select pronouns from the appropriate set, as follows:

Personal Pronouns

Personal pronouns come in several forms, including *subject pronouns, possessive determiners, possessive pronouns, object pronouns*, and *reflexive pronouns*. Each of these pronouns is discussed next.

Subject pronouns (renames nouns in subject position)

Singular
    1st person: I
    2nd person: you
    3rd person:
        Masculine (names males): he
        Feminine (names females): she
        Neuter (names nouns without gender): it

Plural
>   1st person: we
>   2nd person: you
>   3rd person: they

Consider the following example:

>   *Mandy* (singular, 3rd person, feminine) recently graduated from college; *she* (singular, 3rd person, feminine) now has a degree in nursing.

Possessive determiners (assigns possession)

These can also be called *possessive adjectives.*
>   Singular
>>   1st person: my
>>   2nd person: your
>>   3rd person:
>>>   Masculine: his
>>>   Feminine: her
>>>   Neuter: its
>   Plural
>>   1st person: our
>>   2nd person: your
>>   3rd person: their

Consider the following example:

>   That piece of paper is *my* boarding pass. (The boarding pass belongs to the speaker, who is singular and 1st person.)

Possessive pronouns (replace nouns and show possession)

These do not mark nouns, as the possessive determiners do; rather, they replace nouns.

>   Singular
>>   1st person: mine
>>   2nd person: yours
>>   3rd person:
>>>   Masculine: his
>>>   Feminine: hers
>>>   Neuter does not exist.
>   Plural
>>   1st person: ours
>>   2nd person: yours
>>   3rd person: theirs

Take note that no apostrophes are used in these pronouns, even though they indicate possession.

Consider the following example:

>   That boarding pass is *hers.* (The boarding pass belongs to a singular, 3rd person, female.)

Object pronouns (rename nouns in object position)

These are used as indirect and direct objects in verb phrases and as objects of prepositions.

Singular
1st person: me
2nd person: you
3rd person:
Masculine: him
Feminine: her
Neuter: it

Plural
1st person: us
2nd person: you
3rd person: them

Consider the following example:

John (singular, 3rd person, masculine) wondered why everyone kept staring at *him* (singular, 3rd person, masculine) during dinner. (The pronoun is the object of the preposition *at*.)

Reflexive pronouns (rename the subject in object position)

These are used when the subject is also the object of the verb.

Singular
1st person: myself
2nd person: yourself
3rd person:
Masculine: himself
Feminine: herself
Neuter: itself

Plural
1st person: ourselves
2nd person: yourselves
3rd person: themselves

Consider the following example:

If *we* (plural, 1st person) don't win this game, boys, we'll be kicking *ourselves* (plural, 1st person) tomorrow. (The subject group of boys represented by *we* is kicking the same group of boys.)

In addition, the ACT requires that you distinguish among the preceding personal pronouns, as well as *relative* and *indefinite* pronouns.

Common traps with personal pronouns

Following is a description of some common mistakes of pronoun use. Be especially cautious of these traps on the ACT.

Use subject pronouns in compound subjects (subjects with more than one noun)
Paul, *you*, and *I* will be Team A.
    NOT: Paul, *you*, and *me*. . .
She and Mark have been dating for years.
    NOT: Mark and *her*. . .

Use subject pronouns as subjects of clauses in comparative constructions (more . . . than, less . . . than, as . . . as, etc.) when the clause is not repeated. Add the missing clause back to reveal the subject position of the pronoun.

No one in the classroom was as surprised as *I* (was).
    NOT: . . . as *me*.
He worked longer today than *she* (worked).
    NOT: . . . than *her*.

Use possessive determiners before gerunds (-ing verb forms)

Her singing has often been admired.
The class was shocked by *his* studying for the exam.

Relative Pronouns

These are used to identify nouns at the beginning of relative clauses.

Subject
    Non-human: which/that
        Bob loves dogs *that* can catch Frisbees. (*Dogs* can catch Frisbees.)
    Human: who
        Jenny is looking for a mechanic *who* has experience with carburetors. (Some *mechanic* has experience with carburetors.)
Object
    Non-human: which/that
        I finally got back the DVD *that* John borrowed. (John borrowed *the DVD*.)
    Human: whom
        Traci has not yet been paid by the client *whom* she billed last week. (Traci billed *the client*.)
Possessive
    Non-human or human: whose
        Mrs. Peters loves Edgar Allan Poe, *whose* poems and stories give her chills. (*Edgar Allan Poe's* poems and stories give her chills.)

Indefinite Pronouns

Indefinite pronouns are used to represent an indefinite number of persons, places, or things. Following are some examples of indefinite pronouns:

1. *Everyone* gather around the campfire!
2. There will be a prize for *each* of the children.
3. *One* of my sisters always volunteers to drive me to school.

Be sure to maintain consistency in pronoun person and number.

It is not grammatically correct to use the plural pronoun *their* to represent neutral gender with singular nouns. This is an example of a major difference between standard written English and the English that we ordinarily use when speaking.

> A *small child* should always be with *his or her* parent or guardian.
> *NOT*—A *small child* should always be with *their* parent or guardian.

Verbs and Verb Forms

A *verb* describes the action that is taking place in the sentence. All verbs have four principle forms:

Simple Present: write
Simple Past: wrote
Present Participle: writing
Past Participle: written

Simple Past vs. Past Participle

The simple past and past participle forms of verbs can sometimes be confusing. Most past tenses are formed by adding *-ed* to the word.

> Simple Present Tense—We *move* often.
> Simple Past Tense—We *moved* again this year.

Some verbs have irregular past tense forms.

> Simple Present Tense—I *see* my best friend every day.
> Simple Past Tense—I *saw* my best friend yesterday.
> Simple Present Tense—My little sister *eats* her breakfast quickly.
> Simple Past Tense—My little sister *ate* her breakfast quickly.

Remember that the perfect tenses include a form of *have*, a so-called *auxiliary verb*, and a past participle.

> Past Participle—I *had seen* my best friend the day before.
> *NOT*—I *had saw* my best friend the day before.
> Past Participle—My little sister *has eaten* her breakfast quickly.
> *NOT*—My little sister *has ate* her breakfast quickly.

In most cases, be sure to maintain parallel verb forms throughout a sentence.

We *rode* to school on the bus and *started* our first class at 9:00 A.M.
NOT—We *ride* to school on the bus and *started* our first class at 9:00 a.m.
His brother *walks* to school and often *arrives* ahead of us.
NOT—His brother *walks* to school and often *arrived* ahead of us.

Some sentences follow a specific sequence of tenses. The order of the clauses is normally interchangeable.

Hypothetical/Conditional: These sentences usually use a clause with *if* and a subjunctive verb phrase (*were to walk*, for example) in one clause, and a conditional (*would*) verb construction in the second clause.

If I *were to buy* tickets for the game, *would* you *go* with me?
Mike *would* be shocked if he *were to discover* the truth.
If I *were* you, *I'd* get out of town as fast as you can.
(Notice the contraction *I'd* from *I would*.)

Simple past/past progressive

The accident *occurred* while the traffic light *was changing*.

Simple past/past perfect

The children *had drunk* all their milk before Ms. Thompson *dismissed* them for recess.

Simple past/simple present

In a recent poll, 7% of teens *thought* that Vietnam *is* in North America.

Simple present/future progressive

I *will be cleaning* the house when you *return* from work.

Simple present/future perfect

By the time you *awaken*, Dr. Smythe *will have finished* stitching the incision.

Simple present/present progressive (suggests the future)

I *am watching* a movie when John leaves the *living* room.

Simple present/present perfect

Martha *knows* that she *has earned* all of her promotions.

Future/simple past

Susie *will cry* if you lost her teddy bear.

Future/simple present

I *will buy* you both lunch if you *wash* my car.

Future/present perfect

Sammy's Pizza *will close* this week if quarterly profits *have* not *improved*.

Future perfect/present perfect (equivalent to future perfect/simple present)

Our cows *will have moved* toward the barn by the time the bobcat *has entered* the pasture.

Sentence Structure Rules

> **Sentence Structure:** *The grammatical arrangement of words and phrases in sentences.*

It is important that a sentence be arranged so that the idea is expressed completely and clearly. The ACT will test your ability to recognize and correct errors involving the following:

Run-on Sentences
Sentence Fragments
Misplaced Modifiers
Parallelism

Run-on Sentences

A run-on sentence is a sentence that is composed of more than one main idea and that does not use proper punctuation or connectors. The ACT requires you to recognize run-on sentences, as well as avoid creating run-on sentences. The following are examples of run-on sentences along with suggested corrections:

Run-on Sentence—Jill is an actress she often appears in major network television shows.
Correct Sentence—Jill is an actress who often appears in major network television shows.
Run-on Sentence—My nephew loves to play football you can find him on the practice field almost every day.
Correct Sentences—My nephew loves to play football. You can find him on the practice field almost every day.

Run-on sentences are often created by substituting a comma for a semicolon or a period. This is called a *comma splice*, and it is incorrect. Following are examples of comma splices along with suggested corrections:

Comma Splice—Yesterday my mother prepared my favorite dinner, she even baked a cake.
Correct Sentence—Yesterday my mother prepared my favorite dinner; she even baked a cake.
Comma Splice—History is my favorite subject in school, I always get the highest grade.
Correct Sentences—History is my favorite subject in school. I always get the highest grade.

Sentence Fragments

A sentence fragment is a *dependent clause*, which must function as part of a complete sentence and cannot stand alone. (Fragments often lack a subject or a verb with tense. Sentence fragments are incorrectly punctuated as if they were complete sentences.) The following are examples of sentence fragments along with suggested corrections:

Sentence Fragment—My car is difficult to start in the winter. Because of the cold weather.

Correct Sentence—Because of the cold weather, my car is difficult to start in the winter.

Sentence Fragment—Michigan State University offers a variety of courses. Such as Psychology, Biology, Physics, and Music.

Correct Sentence—Michigan State University offers a variety of courses, such as Psychology, Biology, Physics, and Music.

Misplaced Modifiers

Modifiers are words, phrases, or clauses that provide description in sentences. Typically, a modifier is placed near the word or phrase that it modifies. A misplaced modifier creates confusion because it appears to modify some word or phrase other than the word or phrase it was intended to modify. The following are examples of misplaced modifiers along with suggested corrections:

1. Misplaced Modifier—Josh had trouble deciding which college to attend *at first*. (Does he plan to attend more than one college?)
2. Correct Sentence—*At first*, Josh had trouble deciding which college to attend.
3. Misplaced Modifier—The young girl was walking her dog *in a raincoat*. (Was her dog in a raincoat?)
4. Correct Sentence—The young girl *in a raincoat* was walking her dog.

Parallelism

Parallelism, or parallel construction, enables you to show order and clarity in a sentence or a paragraph by putting grammatical elements that have the same function in the same form. For example, when two adjectives modify the same noun, the adjectives should have similar forms. When providing a list, each element of the list should have the same form. Also, when the first half of a sentence has a certain structure, the second half should maintain that structure. Following are examples of faulty parallel construction along with suggested corrections:

1. Faulty Parallel Construction—Amy enjoyed *running* and *to ride* horses.
2. Correct Sentence—Amy enjoyed *running* and horseback *riding*.
3. Faulty Parallel Construction—Our field trip included *a visit to the art museum, talking to a local artist*, and *a workshop on oil-painting techniques*.
4. Correct Sentence—Our field trip included *visiting the art museum, talking to a local artist*, and *attending a workshop on oil-painting techniques*.

COMMONLY MISUSED WORDS

There are certain words and phrases in the English language that are often misused and that often show up on the ACT English Test. We've included a list of commonly misused words here, along with definitions and examples of the proper use of the words.

Accept, Except

Accept is a verb that means "to agree to receive something."
Example: Jenny did not **accept** my invitation to dinner.
Except is usually a preposition that means "excluding," or more rarely a verb meaning "to omit or leave out."
Example: The entire family **except** for my sister Jill attended the reunion.

Affect, Effect

Affect is usually a verb meaning "to influence."
Example: His opinion will **affect** my decision.
Effect is usually a noun meaning "result" or "force."
Example: His opinion had a great **effect** on my decision.

All ready, Already

All ready means "completely ready" or "everyone is ready."
Example: The instructor asked the climber if he was **all ready** to begin.
Already means "by or before a specified time."
Example: The students were **already** late for the bus.

Among, Between

Among is used with more than two items.
Example: The scientist is living **among** a group of native people.
Between is used with two items.
Example: The race **between** Amy and Jenny was very close.

Amount, Number

Amount is used to denote a quantity of something that cannot be divided into separate units.
Example: There was a small **amount** of water in the glass.
Number is used when the objects involved are discrete or can be counted.
Example: A large **number** of students participated in the festivities.

Assure, Ensure, Insure

Assure means "to convince," or "to guarantee" and usually takes a direct object.
Example: I **assure** you that I will not be late.
Ensure means "to make certain."
Example: **Ensure** that the door is locked when you leave.
Insure means "to guard against loss."
Example: Please **insure** this package for $100.

Bring, Take

Bring should be used in situations where something is being moved toward you.
Example: Please **bring** me the book.
Take should be used in situations where something is being moved away from you.
Example: Did you **take** my book with you when you left?

Capital, Capitol

Capital refers to "the official seat of government of a state or nation."
Example: The **capital** of Michigan is Lansing.
Capital can also be used to mean "wealth or money."
Example: He needed to raise investment **capital** to start his company.
Capital, when used as an adjective, means "foremost," or "excellent."
Example: "That is a **capital** idea," Steve said.
Capitol refers to the "building where government meets, or when capitalized, refers to the building in which the U.S. Congress is housed."
Example: Some members of the legislature have their offices in the **capitol** building downtown.

Compare to, Compare with

Compare to means "assert a likeness."
Example: My grandmother often **compares** me *to* my mother.
Compare with means "analyze for similarities and differences."
Example: The detective **compared** the photograph *with* the drawing.

Complement, Compliment

Complement is a noun or verb that implies "something that completes or adds to" something else.
Example: The dessert was a tasty **complement** to my meal.
Compliment is a noun or verb that implies "flattery or praise."
Example: Pam appreciated Mike's **compliment** on her high test scores.

Eager, Anxious

Eager implies "an intense desire" and usually has a positive connotation.
Example: Carrie was **eager** to begin her new job.
Anxious indicates "worry or apprehension" and has a negative connotation.
Example: Fred waited **anxiously** for the plane to take off.

Farther, Further

Farther refers to distance.
Example: Matt traveled **farther** than all of the others.
Further indicates "additional degree, time, or quantity."
Example: The airline representative told us to expect **further** delays.

Fewer, Less

Fewer refers to units or individuals.
Example: **Fewer** students went on the class trip this year.
Example: I weigh **fewer** pounds this year than I did last year.
Less refers to mass or bulk.
Example: There is **less** air in my bicycle's front tire than in its rear tire.
Example: I weigh **less** this year than I did last year.

Imply, Infer

Imply means "to suggest." The speaker or author "implies."
Example: His pants and shirt colors **imply** that he is color blind.
Infer means "to deduce," "to guess," or "to conclude." The listener or reader "infers."
Example: He is not color blind, so we can **infer** that he simply has bad taste in clothes.

Its, It's

The possessive form of *it* is **its**.
Example: The dog lost **its** collar.
The contraction of *it is* is **it's**.
Example: **It's** too bad that your dog ran away.

Lay, Lie

Lay means "to put" or "to place," and takes a direct object.
Example: Please **lay** your scarf on the back of the chair.
Lie means "to recline, rest, or stay," or "to take a position of rest." This verb does not take a direct object.
Example: Carrie likes to **lie** down when she gets home from school.

Learn, Teach

Learn means to "gain knowledge."
Example: I have always wanted to **learn** how to cook.
Teach means to "impart, or give knowledge."
Example: My uncle agreed to **teach** me to cook.

Lend, Borrow

Lend means to "give or loan something" to someone else.
Example: Will you **lend** me your jacket for the evening?
Borrow means to "obtain or receive something temporarily" from someone else.
Example: May I **borrow** your jacket for the evening?

Precede, Proceed

Precede means "to go before."
Example: Katie **preceded** Kahla as an intern at the law office.
Proceed means "to move forward."
Example: Please **proceed** to the testing center in an orderly fashion.

Principal, Principle

Principal is a noun meaning "the head of a school or an organization."
Example: Mr. Smith is the **principal** of our high school.
Principal can also mean "a sum of money."
Example: Only part of the payment will be applied to the **principal** amount of the loan.
Principal can also be used as an adjective to mean "first," or "leading."
Example: Betty's **principal** concern was that Gary would be late.
Principle is a noun meaning "a basic truth or law."
Example: We learned the **principles** of democracy in class today.

Set, Sit

The verb **set** takes a direct object, while the verb **sit** does not.
Example: Please **set** the glass down on the table.
Example: Please **sit** in the chair next to mine.

Than, Then

Than is a conjunction used in comparative constructions.
Example: Jill would rather eat fruit **than** eat chocolate.
Then is an adverb denoting time.
Example: First, I will go for a run, **then** I will do my homework.

That, Which

That is used to introduce an essential clause in a sentence. Commas are not normally used before the word *that*.
Example: This is the book **that** Jenny recommended I read.
Which is best used to introduce a clause containing nonessential and descriptive information. Commas are required before the word *which*.
Example: That book, **which** is old and tattered, is a favorite of mine.

There, Their, They're

There indicates location.
Example: My car is parked over **there**.
Their is a possessive determiner.
Example: **Their** car is parked next to mine.
They're is a contraction of *they are*.
Example: **They're** afraid of getting a ticket if the car is not moved.

To, Too, Two

To is a preposition.
Example: Send the check **to** my office.
Too is an adverb, and means *also, excessively*, or *prohibitively*.
Example: It is important that you read the textbook, **too**.
Example: John has been **too** sick to work this week.
Example: That silk scarf is **too** expensive for me to buy right now.
Two is a number.
Example: There are only **two** tickets remaining for the game.

Your, You're

Your is a possessive determiner.
Example: **Your** brother is going to be late for school.
You're is a contraction of *you are*.
Example: **You're** going to be late as well.

ACT Vocabulary List

While this is not a comprehensive list, all of these words have been used on past ACTs. Some of them are included because former students asked about them. Some are included here because they have been selected by experienced ACT instructors as representative of the vocabulary level that is expected on the ACT. We have also included some math and science terms with which you should be familiar.

A

Abound:	to be well supplied; to have great quantities
Absence:	being away or lacking something; inattentiveness
Absurd:	extremely ridiculous or completely lacking reason
Abundance:	having considerably more than is necessary or adequate; more than plenty
Acceleration:	the rate of change of velocity
Accommodate:	to adapt or adjust in a way that makes someone else comfortable; to make room
Accusation:	a statement blaming someone for a crime or error
Acidic:	having a pH less than 7 (contrast with *alkalinity*, which is having a pH greater than 7)
Acrid:	harsh or bitter taste or smell
Acute:	(adj.) refers to an angle that is less than 90 degrees; (adj.) refers to a triangle with angles that are all less than 90 degrees; sharp; quick and precise; intense
Adapt:	to change or modify to suit a particular purpose
Adjacent:	in the nearest position; next to
Adolescence:	the stage of development between puberty and maturity
Aerobic respiration:	the breakdown of glucose in the body of an animal to supply muscles with oxygen
Aerosol:	solid or liquid particles suspended in gas
Aesthetic:	appeals to the senses because it is beautiful
Affiliation:	a connection between groups of people, organizations, or establishments
Agility:	the quality of being quick and nimble

Agronomist:	a soil management and field-crop production expert
Alienate:	to isolate oneself from others or another person from oneself
Align:	to adjust parts so that they fit together correctly, usually in a straight line
Alkalinity:	having a pH greater than 7 (contrast with *acidic*, which is having a pH less than 7)
Allegiance:	loyalty to a person, group, country, or cause
Altitude:	elevation above a level of reference, usually given in feet above sea level
Ambiguous:	unclear or capable of having more than one meaning
Amino acids:	various organic compounds that link together to form proteins
Ample:	a more-than-sufficient amount; roomy
Analogous:	items that are similar and comparable in some way; serving a similar function
Analogy:	a comparison of similarities between two or more things
Anatomical:	related to the structure of an organism
Ancestral:	relating to or inherited from an ancestor
Anew:	starting again in a new or different way
Anomaly:	something that is different from the norm
Anticipate:	to look forward to or to expect
Antigen:	a substance such as a toxin or enzyme capable of eliciting an immune response
Antitoxin:	an antibody created for and capable of neutralizing a toxin
Apathy:	lack of any emotion or concern
Aperture:	an opening or hole, usually in an optical instrument, such as a camera, that limits the amount of light passing through a lens
Apocalypse:	great or total devastation; approximating the end of the world
Apparatus:	a material or device used for a specific purpose
Appealing:	attractive or inviting; the act of making a request for a decision or help
Arisen:	the state of being up after sitting or lying
Aristocratic:	having the qualities of the elite, ruling class
Articulate:	(v.) to clearly explain; (adj.) the quality of being able to speak clearly
Aspect:	a certain part of something; the side of an object that faces a certain direction
Assert:	to demonstrate power; to defend a statement as true
Assumption:	something believed to be true without proof; unsupported evidence
Asteroid:	small celestial body that revolves around the sun, with a diameter between a few and several hundred kilometers
Asthenosphere:	a lower layer of the Earth's crust

Astonishing:	amazing or bewildering
Atrium:	an area of a building, usually a courtyard, that is skylighted or open to the sky and that often contains plants

B

Bacteria:	single-celled microorganisms
Banish:	to force to leave; to exile
Banyan:	East Indian tree that has aerial shoots growing down into the soil and forming additional trunks; loose jacket worn in India
Basalt:	solidified lava; a dense, gray, fine-grained igneous rock
Bemoan:	to express grief; to deplore
Beneficiary:	recipient of benefits, for example, funds or property from an insurance policy or will
Binge:	a duration of excessive and uncontrolled self-indulgence
Biomass:	total mass of all the living matter within a given area
Biosynthesis:	the production of a chemical compound within the body
Boiling point:	the temperature a liquid must be to change states from liquid to gas
Brood:	(v.) to dwell over past misfortune; (n.) a group of offspring
Buoyant:	tending to float; lighthearted
Bureaucrat:	an official in government; a term usually used in an insulting manner
By-products:	products made in the process of making something else, sometimes unexpected

C

Calamity:	horrible event that results in extreme loss
Calligraphy:	elegant lettering; the art of producing such writing
Capacity:	maximum amount that an object or area can hold; mental ability
Capillary:	a very slim tube; one of a network of extremely small blood vessels
Carbohydrate:	sugars and starches that serve as a major energy source for animals
Catalogue:	a systematic list of things, such as books in a library or items for sale at a store
Catalyst:	an agent that causes or speeds up a chemical reaction
Celestial:	relating to the sky; divine or heavenly
Celsius:	a temperature scale in which the freezing point of water is 0 degrees and the boiling point is 100 degrees under normal atmospheric conditions

Cerebral edema: brain swelling

Cesarean: relating to the medical procedure of surgical abdominal birth, referred to as a *cesarean section*

Chaos: a state of complete disarray

Characteristics: distinguishing attributes or qualities of a person or thing

Chlorophyll: a green pigment produced in response to sunlight during photosynthesis

Cholesterol: a soft, waxy compound found in the body and in the food we eat

Chronology: a list of events arranged by time of occurrence

Circumscribe: to enclose a shape with lines or curves, so that every vertex of the enclosed object touches part of the enclosing configuration

Coherent: the quality of being logical and clear

Cohesiveness: the quality of sticking together

Coincidental: occurring by chance

Collinear: passing through or lying on the same straight line

Colloid: a gelatinous material

Comet: a celestial body, having an elongated, curved vapor tail, which is seen only in that part of its orbit that is relatively close to the sun

Commendable: worthy of praise

Common difference: the equal distance between one number in an arithmetic sequence and the next (for example, the common difference between 4, 6, and 8 is 2)

Common ratio: the ratio of one term and the next in a geometric sequence (for example, the common ratio between 2, 4, and 8 is $\frac{4}{2}$ and $\frac{8}{4}$, or 2)

Comparison: a description of similarities or differences between two things

Compatriot: someone from one's own country; a colleague

Competence: the quality of having adequate skill, knowledge, and experience

Compose: to form by placing parts or elements together; to bring oneself to a state of calm

Comprehensive: all-inclusive

Compressibility: the ease with which pressure can alter the volume of matter

Concede: to admit or reluctantly yield; to surrender

Concentration: the amount of one substance contained within another; intense mental effort or focus

Concentric: having a common center

Concerto: composition for an orchestra and one or more solo instruments, typically in three movements

Concoct:	to prepare by mixing ingredients together; devise a plan
Condense:	to become more compact; to change from a vapor to a liquid
Conducive:	tending to cause or bring about
Congruent:	corresponding; equal in length or measure
Conjure:	to bring to mind; to produce as if by magic
Conscience:	the mental sense that guides moral decisions
Consecutive:	uninterrupted sequence
Consent:	(n.) permission; (v.) to agree to
Consequence:	result of an action
Conservatory:	a fine arts school; a greenhouse of plants aesthetically arranged
Constant:	the quality of being unchanging; marked by firm resolution or loyalty
Constituency:	a group of citizens who have the power to elect an official; an electoral district
Contemplate:	to carefully consider
Contemporary:	person or thing of the same era or age; current, modern
Context:	text or spoken words that surround a word or passage and help determine meaning; circumstances that surround an event
Contradict:	to assert the opposite
Contrive:	to clearly plan; to cleverly devise
Controversial:	characterized by dispute; debatable
Cordial:	sincere; courteous
Correlate:	to have corresponding characteristics
Cos:	abbreviation of cosine
Cosine:	in a right triangle, the ratio of the length of the side adjacent to the acute angle divided by the hypotenuse $\left(\cos = \dfrac{adj}{hyp}\right)$
Credulity:	a tendency to trust too easily
Crimson:	a deep red color
Criterion:	requirement on which judgment can be based
Crucial:	extremely important
Cryopreservation:	preservation (as of cells) by very low temperatures
Cube:	a term raised to the third power; a regular solid having six congruent faces
Cubic inch:	the volume of a cube with edges that all measure one inch
Cuisine:	the food prepared by a style of cooking, for example, "Italian cuisine"
Cylindrical:	having the shape of a cylinder, or a solid with circular ends and straight sides

D

Decipher:	to interpret the meaning, usually of a code or hard-to-read handwriting
Decompose:	to disintegrate into components
De-emphasize:	to minimize the importance
Defection:	withdrawing one's support; to escape or become a traitor
Deform:	to disfigure; to ruin the shape of an object
Degree:	one in a series of steps in a process or scale; a unit of measurement
Delegate:	(v.) to transfer responsibilities to another; (n.) a personal representative
Deliberate:	(adj.) carefully planned out; (v.) to consider carefully
Delve:	to deeply and thoroughly search
Demean:	to reduce in worth
Demise:	the end of existence
Demur:	to express opposition
Derive:	to infer certain knowledge; to trace the origin or development of something
Descend:	to come from a particular origin; to move down from a higher point
Descendant:	a person, animal, or plant that can be traced back to a certain origin; future or subsequent generations
Deter:	to prevent from taking a particular course of action
Determinant:	the difference between multiplied terms in a matrix
Deviation:	a divergence from a certain path; in mathematics: the difference, especially the absolute difference, between one number in a set and the mean of the set
Devise:	(v.) to design or create; often confused with the noun *device*, which means "tool that fulfills a certain purpose"
Diagonal:	a line segment joining two nonadjacent vertices of a polygon or solid (polyhedron)
Diffusion time:	the time that it takes for a material to spread from one area to another
Diligent:	continuously putting in great effort
Dilute:	to weaken the strength of a solution
Diminish:	to make smaller, decrease, or lessen
Directly proportional:	increasing or decreasing together or with the same ratio
Disavow:	to deny knowledge of, responsibility for, or association with
Discern:	to differentiate or distinguish; to perceive
Discomforting:	embarrassing
Disconcerting:	unsettling

Discriminatory: showing a bias

Disdainful: scornful and sneering

Dispel: to rid one's mind of; to drive out

Disperse: to scatter or spread out everywhere

Disquieting: lacking peace of mind; mental unrest

Dissolution: the process of dissolving or disintegrating

Dissolve: to pass into or become part of; to terminate

Distinct: easily distinguishable from others

Dominant: the most prominent; exuding authority

Dowry: in certain cultures, the money, goods, and so on, that a woman brings to a marriage

Drag force: the frictional force that resists or slows down motion through a medium such as air

Drastic: extreme

Durable: resistant to wear

Durable goods: in economics, goods that are not depleted with use, such as household appliances or cars

E

Ecology: the field of science that concentrates on relationships between organisms and their environments

Elaborate: (adj.) rich with detail and well developed; (v.) to expand on the idea of something

Electorate: the body of all of the people who possess the right to vote

Eloquent: very clear and precise; quality of being skilled in clear and precise speech

Emanant: something such as a gas or odor coming forth and off of a source

Embalm: to maintain a dead body by treating it with chemical preservatives

Embittered: possessing bitter feelings

Embrace: to enclose in one's arms; become accepting of other ideas or people

Emigration: leaving one country and traveling to live in another

Emissions: things that are discharged (often gases into the air)

Emit: to release particles such as light, heat, gases

Empowered: possessing the necessary abilities for a particular task; given power or authority

Emulate: to follow an admirable example; imitate

Emulsion: a state in which one liquid is suspended in another because the liquids will not dissolve in one another

Endorsement:	a guarantee to support; a signature on a document such as a check
Endow:	to give a positive trait; to provide monetary funds by donation
Endpoints:	what defines the beginning and end of a line segment
Endure:	to continue despite difficulty; to tolerate
Enrich:	to improve
Enshrine:	to enclose in a shrine or place of devotion
Entangle:	to twist and tie up in a complicated manner
Enumerate:	to state things in a list
Envision:	to picture a mental image
Eon:	duration of time, so long it cannot be measured
Epic:	(n.) widely celebrated literary work that has survived a long period of time; (adj.) very impressive and extraordinary
Epicanthic fold:	a fold of skin of the upper eyelid that only partly covers the eye's inner corner
Equilibrium:	a state of balance
Erosion:	the wearing away of an object by outside forces, like wind or water
Error:	a mistake; the difference between a computed value and the correct value
Escapist:	one who mentally leaves the real world for a world of fantasy
Essence:	important characteristics that help differentiate something; the key element of an idea; something spiritual; a scent
Essential:	(adj.) the quality of being indispensable or necessary
Essentially:	at the very core
Establish:	to create a foundation
Ethical:	in line with what is right and wrong
Ethnicity:	cultural and racial association
Evaporate:	to draw away moisture and convert into vapor
Exceed:	to go far beyond a limit; excel
Exceptional:	rare due to uncommonly great qualities
Exhibit:	(v.) to display; (n.) something that is displayed; (n.) a piece of evidence submitted to a court during a trial
Expatriate:	(v.) to banish someone; (v.) to move from one's native land; (n.) one who lives in a foreign country
Experimental variables:	elements of an experiment that are changed (distinguished from the *constant*, which is held the same in order to produce significant results)
Expertise:	skill or knowledge in a certain area
Exquisite:	characterized by great beauty and intricacy

Extensive:	detailed and far-reaching
Extinct:	no longer existing
Extrapolate:	to guess by inferring from known information
Extravagant:	lavish beyond the norm
Exultant:	gleeful because of success

F

Fahrenheit:	a temperature scale that measures the boiling point of water at 212 degrees and the freezing point at 32 degrees
Feign:	to fabricate or deceive
Fermentation:	the chemical process of breaking down an organic substance into simpler substances such as the fermentation of sugar to alcohol
Fickle:	constantly changing one's mind
Fjord:	an inlet lined by steep slopes that is long, narrow, and deep
Fledgling:	a young bird that has just acquired feathers; also used to describe an inexperienced newcomer
Flourish:	(v.) to prosper; (v.) to thrive; (n.) a dramatic gesture; (n.) a written embellishment
Foil:	(n.) a character whose traits exemplify the opposite traits of another character when they are compared; (v.) to prevent an action, often by ruining a plan; (n.) a weapon used in the sport of fencing
Foliation:	the alternating layers of different mineral compositions within solid rocks
Forecast:	to predict future events, such as the weather
Foresee:	to know beforehand
Foreshadow:	to suggest or hint at future occurrences
Forgo:	to refrain from doing something previously planned
Formalize:	to make something official or valid
Franchise:	a right given to an individual or group to operate a branch of a business and sell the business' products; the right to vote
Frenzied:	in a temporary crazed state
Friction:	the force resistant to motion
Frivolous:	unnecessary and silly

G

Gable:	the triangular section of a wall that fills the space between the two slopes of a roof
Galvanism:	a direct electrical current produced by chemical reactions

Gas:	a fluid (such as air) that is not independent in shape or volume but tends to expand
Gas chromatograph:	a device used to detect the composition of an unknown material
Gastric emptying:	the movement from the stomach to the small intestine, and finally into the colon
Gaudy:	tastelessly flashy
Glacial:	relating to a glacier; callous and cold; extremely slow
Glib:	doing something with ease and slickness, but lacking sincerity
Gravity:	the force of attraction between two bodies of mass
Gypsum:	a yellowish-white mineral used to make plaster

H

Haggle:	to bargain in an annoying manner; to harass
Halitosis:	the condition of having breath with a foul odor
Harbinger:	a sign that foreshadows upcoming events
Herbivorous:	a plant-eating organism
Hindu:	(adj.) relating to the religion of Hinduism, which originated in India; (n.) a person who practices Hinduism
Hoist:	to lift up
Homeric epic:	a classic Greek tale of heroism written by the ninth-century B.C. Greek author, Homer
Hue:	color
Humidity:	a measure of how damp the air is
Hydraulic:	operated by using water or fluid pressure
Hydrogen bonding:	the chemical bonding of a hydrogen atom with another electronegative atom
Hypotenuse:	the longest side of a right-angle triangle, which is always the side opposite the right angle

I

Ideological:	relating to the fundamental ideas of an individual or group
Idiosyncrasy:	a peculiar characteristic
Igneous rock:	rock that is formed by the cooling and solidification of molten magma
Ignition temperature:	the temperature that a fuel must reach before combustion can begin
Immerse:	to completely submerge
Imminent:	close to happening; impending
Imply:	to indirectly suggest, often confused with *infer*, which means "to conclude"

Improvise: to do or perform without preparation; to create something only from readily available materials

Inalienable: impossible to take away

Inauguration: a formal initiation or induction

Incarcerate: to imprison

Incinerate: to set fire to and burn something until it is reduced to ashes

Inclined: disposed to a certain path of thought; sloping

Inconstant: not following a pattern; varying

Incorporate: to bring two things or certain aspects of two things together

Indifference: total lack of concern or interest

Indigenous: native to or naturally existing in a certain area

Indignation: anger due to unfairness

Indulge: to freely partake in; to yield to the wish or desire of oneself or others

Inevitable: bound to happen; unavoidable

Inexhaustible: plentiful; impossible to use up completely

Inexplicable: impossible to give the reason for; unexplainable

Infer: to deduce from evidence, often confused with *imply*

Infirmary: a small hospital, often in an institution, used to provide care for the sick

Infrared: light energy having a wavelength below the visible range; it is experienced as heat

Infuse: for one substance to penetrate into another (for example, steak infused with garlic flavor)

Ingenious: brilliant and clever

Inherent: naturally occurring, permanent element or attribute

Inscribe: to write or engrave words on a surface; to write one's name on something

Insinuate: to subtly imply

Institute: (v.) to enact or establish; (n.) an organization

Institution: an establishment; a pillar of society (for example, the institution of marriage)

Interior angle: an angle inside of a shape (that is, all of the interior angles in a triangle add up to 180 degrees)

Intern: one who is confined during wartime against his or her will; a student or recent graduate working as an apprentice in a certain professional field

Interpret: to translate or explain a concept

Interpretation: a personal explanation for another's creation, such as a play or poem

Interstitial: (n.) fluid outside of cells; (adj.) occupying the small spaces between objects; (adj.) occurring during the short time periods between events

Intracellular: within a cell or cells

Intricacy: a detail of something complex

Invaluable: priceless

Involuntary: an action done without one's consent or free will

Irony: use of words to express a meaning that is the opposite of the real meaning; similar to and often confused with *sarcasm*, which means "words used to insult or scorn"

Irreconcilable: impossible to adjust or compromise

Irrelevant: not relevant or pertinent; outside the scope of a discussion or argument

Irrevocable: impossible to reverse

Isosceles triangle: a triangle with two congruent sides and two congruent angles

Isotopes: two or more atoms with an identical atomic number and differing in number of neutrons

J

Juxtaposition: an act of placing things next to each other, usually for comparing or contrasting

K

Kelvin: a unit of temperature where 0 K is absolute zero, the freezing point of water is 273 K, and the boiling point of water is 373 K

L

Languish: to become weak; to become disenchanted

Lavish: (adj.) elaborate and luxurious; (v.) to freely and boundlessly bestow

Law of Sines: the relationship among the angles and the sides of a triangle (the sine of the angles is equal to the lengths of the sides)

Least Common Denominator (LCD): the smallest number (other than 0) that is a multiple of a set of denominators (for example, the LCD of $\frac{1}{4}$ and $\frac{1}{6}$ is 12)

Least Common Multiple (LCM): the smallest number that is a multiple of a set of numbers (for example, the LCM of 6 and 9 is 18)

Liberally: done in a manner that is generous (for example, liberally applying sunscreen)

Limbo: a precarious state; in Roman Catholicism, the otherworldly place for unbaptized but good people

Linear:	relating to a line
Lipid:	an oily/waxy organic compound that cannot be dissolved in water
Liquid:	(n.) a substance that is neither a solid nor a gas; (adj.) flowing freely
Lithosphere:	the outer part of the Earth that includes the crust and upper mantle
Log:	abbreviation of *logarithm*. Logarithms are used to indicate exponents of certain numbers called bases. By definition, $\log_a b = c$ if $a^c = b$ (for example, $\log_x 36 = 2$ if $x^2 = 36$. In this case, $x = 6$).
Lumbering:	lethargically walking around with clumsiness

M

Macrophages:	protective cells
Manifest:	(adj.) clearly recognizable; (v.) to make clear; (n.) a list of transported goods or passengers used for record keeping
Manometer:	a device that measures the pressure of liquids and gases
Marine:	(adj.) relating to the sea; (n.) a member of the U.S. Marine Corps
Matrix:	rows and columns of elements arranged in a rectangle
Mean (also *arithmetic mean*):	average; found by adding all the terms in a set and dividing by the number of terms
Median:	the middle value in a set of ordered numbers
Mediocre:	lacking any special qualities, even inferior
Melancholy:	glumness; deep contemplative thought
Melting point:	the temperature at which a solid softens into a liquid
Mere:	small; (adv. merely) nothing more
Mesosphere:	a layer of the atmosphere fifty to eighty kilometers above the Earth's surface
Metamorphism:	the process of altering solid rock by changing its temperature, pressure, and chemistry
Meteorite:	a meteor that reaches the surface of the Earth before it is entirely vaporized
Meticulous:	devoting a high amount of attention to detail
Microorganism:	an organism of microscopic or very small size
Midpoint:	the point that divides a line segment into two equal segments
Minuscule:	extremely small; unimportant
Mole:	a unit of measurement for the molecular weight of a substance
Molecular weight:	the weight of all of the atoms in a molecule
Molten:	turned to liquid because of heat

Moral:	(adj.) based on standards of good and bad; (n.) a rule of proper behavior
Morale:	mental well-being; mood
Mortar:	a bowl in which substances are ground; a mixture, usually cement and water, used to bond bricks or stones; a military weapon similar to portable artillery
Mutability:	the ability to transform

N

Nanometer:	one billionth of a meter
Negligible:	meaningless and insignificant
Neural:	relating to the nervous system
Neurological:	relating to neurology, the study of the nervous system
Newton:	the amount of force needed to accelerate a one-kilogram mass at a rate of one meter per second, per second
Nostalgia:	sentimental yearning for the past
Notion:	a belief, sometimes without much conviction
Numerous:	existing in great numbers of units or persons

O

Oblong:	deviating from a square, circular, or spherical form by being slightly longer in one area
Obtuse:	an angle that is larger than a right angle
Offal:	wasted trimmings of an animal carcass; trash or rubbish
Onus:	a burden of responsibility
Opus:	a creative composition, usually musical
Oracle:	a shrine devoted to a future-telling deity or the deity himself; a prophet
Organic matter:	matter that is derived from living organisms
Organism:	a living thing, either plant or animal
Overt:	obvious and clearly shown

P

Paradox:	a statement that seems contradictory but is actually true
Paragon:	an example of excellence
Parallel:	lines in the same plane that do not intersect each other; in a coordinate plane, non-collinear lines or segments having the same slope as one another

Parallelogram:	a quadrilateral (a figure that has four sides) with opposite sides that are parallel and congruent
Parenthetical:	an explanatory statement that is set off by parentheses
Pathetic:	deserves pity or sympathy
Peculiarity:	unusual quality or characteristic
Pendulum:	a device that is suspended in such a way as to allow it to swing back and forth using gravity
Perceive:	the act of becoming aware of something, usually through the senses
Percolate:	to slowly pass through a porous substance
Perfunctorily:	in a manner that suggests little interest or attention; a routine duty
Perimeter:	the boundary of a figure; in math, the distance from one point around the figure to the same point
Periphery:	the outermost boundary of an area
Perpendicular:	lines that intersect and form 90-degree angles
pH:	a scale that measures how acidic or basic a substance is on a scale of 0 to 14. Lower numbers indicate an increasing acidity and higher numbers indicate increasing basicity
Phantom:	exists only in the mind (an illusion); a ghost
Phenomenon:	an event or circumstance that is significant or extraordinary
Photophores:	organs that produce light
Photosynthesis:	the process by which plants turn carbon dioxide and water into energy with the aid of sunlight
Pigmentation:	coloration
Plagiarism:	an act of fraud consisting of copying another's work and pretending that it is original
Point-slope formula:	the formula used to calculate the slope of a line: $\dfrac{(y_1 - y_2)}{(x_1 - x_2)}$
Positive slope:	the incline of a line that slants upward (from left to right)
Pow-wow:	a meeting or gathering
Preceding:	coming before
Precipitate:	to cause something to happen very suddenly
Precipitation:	falling products of condensation in the atmosphere (such as rain)
Predominant:	having superior strength, paramount
Preliminary:	precedes or comes prior to

Prerequisite:	required beforehand
Prestigious:	having honor or respect from others
Prevail:	to triumph or come out on top
Prevalent:	commonly used or occurring
Prime number:	a positive integer that can only be evenly divided by 1 and itself
Primordial:	happening first or very early
Protagonist:	the main character of a story or tale
Protein:	a compound that consists of amino acids and plays various structural, mechanical, and nutritional roles within organisms
Prototype:	an original form of something
Protract:	to lengthen or prolong
Prowess:	great skill in something
Pseudoscience:	irrational or unfounded beliefs masquerading as science (for example, astrology)
Psychologizing:	explaining something in psychological terms
Pyrotechnics:	a display of fireworks

Q

Quadrant:	one part of a larger object that has been divided into four parts
Quadratic equation:	an equation in the form of $ax^2 + bx + c = 0$, where $a \neq 0$, and has only two solutions for x
Quasi:	resembles to some degree
Quintessential:	considered the perfect form

R

Radian:	a unit of angle measure within a circle
Radiate:	to emit energy or light that extends from a single source
Radii:	the plural form of radius
Radioactive decay:	a natural process by which an atom of a radioactive isotope spontaneously decays into another element
Radius:	a line segment with endpoints at the center of the circle and on the perimeter of the circle, equal to one-half the length of the diameter
Rapid:	moving very quickly
Rapt:	being completely occupied by, or focused on, something

Ratio:	a comparison between two quantities (for example, the ratio of girls to boys in the class is 1:2)
Real number line:	an infinite line of real numbers represented on a one-dimensional graph
Real numbers:	numbers that can be associated with points on a number line
Recount:	to describe the facts or details of a past event; to retell a story or repeat testimony
Rectangular:	having the shape of a rectangle (a parallelogram with four right angles)
Recurrent:	taking place over and over
Redeem:	to pay off a debt or fulfill an obligation; to make good
Redirect:	to alter the course or direction
Rediscover:	to learn about or see something as though for the first time
Regular hexagon:	a six-sided figure with congruent sides and angles
Relevant:	logically connected; pertinent
Reluctant:	unwilling and resistant
Reparation:	compensation given to make amends
Resonate:	to produce or amplify vibrations
Respectively:	in the order given
Retention:	the ability to hold things in or retain
Rifling:	(v.) to search through, looking for something to steal; (n.) the spiral grooves on the inside of a gun barrel
Rift:	a split or a break
Rotate vs. Revolve:	rotate: to turn about a fixed point; revolve: to turn on an axis
Rudimentary:	very basic or not fully developed

S

Sacrilege:	to misuse something that is sacred
Sanctuary:	a sacred place; a refuge
Saplings:	young trees
Saturation:	a state of being completely full or soaked
Sauropod:	a type of plant-eating dinosaur, for example, the brontosaur
Scientific inquiry:	based on experiment and observation and the application of the Scientific Method; examination into facts or principles
Scrutiny:	very close examination
Sediment:	solid materials that sink to the bottom of a liquid

Seedling: a young plant grown from seed

Seminal: forms the basis for future development; at the beginning; original

Simultaneously: happening or existing at the same time

Skepticism: an attitude of doubt or disbelief

Social rituals: specific gestures and behaviors that are observed by members of a community

Solace: comfort; safety

Solid: neither gas nor liquid; of definite shape and volume

Solute: a dissolved substance

Solution: a mixture of two or more substances

Solution set: the set of values that make an equation true

Sovereign: (adj.) having supreme power; (n.) ruler or king

Span: distance between two things

Specific gravity: the ratio of the density of one substance to the density of another substance

Speculators: people who form theories based on uncertain evidence; those who purchase something with the hope of reselling it later at a profit

Sphere: a solid, round figure where all points on the surface are the same distance from the center (for example, a basketball)

Spleen: a vascular, ductless organ that is located in the left abdominal region close to the stomach

Stagnant: not moving or changing; stale

Standard (x, y) coordinate plane: a plane that is formed by a horizontal x-axis and a vertical y-axis that meet at point (0,0) (also known as the *Cartesian Coordinate Plane*)

Steerage passenger: someone who rides in the least expensive section of a ship

Straddle: having one leg on each side of something

Stratosphere: a layer of the atmosphere between the troposphere and mesosphere

Subcontractor: someone who agrees to perform one part of a larger commitment or contract

Subjective: dependent on a person's attitudes or opinions

Subsequent: to come next or later

Subtropical: near the tropical areas of the world; extremely humid and hot climate

Sucrose: a simple sugar

Summary: (n.) a statement that has condensed a larger body of work; (adj.) conducted without trial

Supercooled: below freezing but remaining liquid

Suspension:	the state of a substance when its particles are combined together but have not been dissolved in a fluid or solid
Sustenance:	things that provide nourishment for survival
Synchronized:	occurring at the same time and at the same rate
Synthesis:	combining separate elements to form a whole
Synthetic polymer:	a human-made, repeating chain of atoms

T

Tenet:	a belief that is held to be true by a certain group
Terrestrial:	relating to dry land as opposed to water; relating to the Earth as opposed to other planets
Territorial:	the protective behavior that is displayed when an animal is defending its area
Thermal degradation:	a process of combustion where materials in a fuel are broken down into several by-products
Thermosphere:	the outermost layer of the atmosphere
Toxins:	poisons
Transcend:	to go above and beyond; to rise above
Translucent:	allowing light to pass through but clouded or frosted in such a way that objects on the other side are not clearly visible; often confused with *transparent*, which means "clear"
Transversal:	a line that cuts through two or more lines
Trapezoid:	a quadrilateral (a figure with four sides) with only two parallel lines
Treason:	a betrayal of loyalty
Triannual:	lasting three years or occurring every three years
Tropical area:	an area near the equator that has a frost-free climate with high temperatures that can support year-round vegetation
Troposphere:	the lowest part of the Earth's atmosphere
Tyranny:	absolute power exercised by an oppressive ruler

U

Ultraviolet:	situated beyond the visible spectrum
Unemotional:	devoid of sentiment or emotion
Uniform:	(adj.) continuing to be the same or consistent; (n.) identical clothing worn by members of a certain group

Unilaterally: related to or occurring on one side only

Unparalleled: without an equal or comparison

Unprecedented: having no previous example

Unsolicited: unwanted

V

Vapor pressure: the pressure exerted by the molecules of a vapor

Vaporize: to change into a cloud of diffused matter

Various: of differing kinds

Velocity: speed of motion

Vertical migrators: marine species that travel toward the surface of the ocean to feed

Vertices: the plural form of vertex, which is a point of intersection

Vindication: the act of clearing someone or something from blame

Virtually: in almost all instances; simulated as by a computer

Virus: organism that causes infection

Viscosity: a fluid's resistance to flow

Visionary: (adj.) characterized by dreams or illusions; (n.) a person with vision or foresight

Voltage: a measure of the energy of an electric current

W–Z

Wavelength: the distance between repeating peaks or crests of waves

x-intercept: the point where a line on a graph crosses the x-axis

y-intercept: the point where a line on a graph crosses the y-axis

Practice Test Question Index

Use this index to locate the different question types on the Diagnostic Test and each of the Practice Tests in the book. Please note that there is some overlap in the question types because some questions test more than one concept.

English

Adjectives and Adverbs	p.17, Question 17	p.20, Question 32	p.304, Question 20
	p.383, Question 29		
Nouns and Pronouns	p.16, Question 10	p.310, Question 62	p.466, Question 70
	p.18, Question 21	p.311, Question 64	p.534, Question 6
	p.22, Question 52	p.380, Question 6	p.534, Question 10
	p.26, Question 75	p.381, Question 13	p.536, Question 26
	p.304, Question 21	p.389, Question 66	p.538, Question 34
	p.304, Question 28	p.460, Question 23	p.538, Question 40
	p.305, Question 33	p.464, Question 59	p.540, Question 56

Organization	**Introductory and Concluding Paragraphs and Sentences:**		
	p.15, Question 4	p.303, Question 15	p.387, Question 54
	p.18, Question 26	p.304, Question 30	p.390, Question 73
	p.23, Question 57	p.309, Question 58	p.467, Question 73
	p.25, Question 70	p.311, Question 72	p.541, Question 57
	Main Idea:		
	p.17, Question 15	p.385, Question 45	p.465, Question 60
	p.23, Question 60	p.388, Question 60	p.537, Question 30
	p.307, Question 45	p.392, Question 75	p.541, Question 60
	p.310, Question 60	p.459, Question 15	p.544, Question 75
	p.312, Question 75	p.462, Question 45	
	Ranking/Ordering Paragraphs, Sentences, and Words:		
	p.19, Question 3	p.389, Question 72	p.535, Question 15
	p.25, Question 68	p.458, Question 12	p.538, Question 38
	p.307, Question 43	p.464, Question 57	p.543, Question 73
	p.312, Question 73	p.466, Question 72	p.544, Question 74
Punctuation	**Apostrophes:**		
	p.16, Question 6	p.304, Question 28	p.460, Question 29
	p.16, Question 13	p.389, Question 66	p.533, Question 4
	p.26, Question 73	p.459, Question 17	p.536, Question 27
	Colons, Semicolons, and Dashes:		
	p.16, Question 11	p.21, Question 45	p.304, Question 21
	p.17, Question 19	p.22, Question 53	p.304, Question 25
	p.18, Question 21	p.301, Question 3	p.305, Question 34
	p.18, Question 24	p.302, Question 8	p.306, Question 37
	p.21, Question 43	p.302, Question 9	p.306, Question 40
	p.21, Question 44	p.303, Question 18	p.311, Question 67

p.379, Question 2

p.380, Question 10

p.384, Question 34

p.385, Question 42

p.386, Question 51

p.388, Question 59

p.389, Question 68

p.458, Question 7

p.459, Question 17

p.460, Question 47

p.461, Question 31

p.465, Question 65

p.466, Question 67

p.533, Question 2

p.534, Question 11

p.536, Question 21

p.536, Question 23

p.537, Question 32

p.538, Question 41

p.539, Question 44

p.540, Question 50

p.540, Question 54

p.542, Question 62

p.543, Question 71

Commas:

p.15, Question 2

p.16, Question 6

p.16, Question 11

p.16, Question 13

p.17, Question 19

p.18, Question 21

p.18, Question 24

p.20, Question 37

p.21, Question 43

p.21, Question 44

p.21, Question 45

p.21, Question 46

p.22, Question 53

p.26, Question 73

p.301, Question 1

p.301, Question 2

p.301, Question 3

p.302, Question 8

p.302, Question 9

p.303, Question 18

p.304, Question 21

p.304, Question 25

p.305, Question 34

p.306, Question 37

p.306, Question 40

p.308, Question 46

p.308, Question 48

p.309, Question 55

p.311, Question 67

p.311, Question 71

p.379, Question 2

p.379, Question 5

p.380, Question 10

p.381, Question 16

p.384, Question 34

p.385, Question 40

p.385, Question 42

p.386, Question 51

p.387, Question 53

p.388, Question 59

p.389, Question 68

p.389, Question 70

p.457, Question 2

p.458, Question 7

p.459, Question 16

	p.459, Question 17	p.466, Question 67	p.538, Question 42
	p.459, Question 21	p.467, Question 74	p.539, Question 44
	p.460, Question 22	p.533, Question 2	p.540, Question 50
	p.460, Question 26	p.536, Question 21	p.540, Question 52
	p.461, Question 31	p.536, Question 23	p.540, Question 54
	p.461, Question 37	p.537, Question 32	p.542, Question 62
	p.463, Question 47	p.538, Question 41	p.543, Question 71
	p.465, Question 65		
Strategy	**Add/Delete Information:**		
	p.22, Question 49	p.381, Question 15	p.463, Question 49
	p.24, Question 64	p.382, Question 17	p.463, Question 52
	p.25, Question 70	p.384, Question 33	p.533, Question 3
	p.303, Question 17	p.390, Question 74	p.534, Question 5
	p.307, Question 42	p.458, Question 14	p.535, Question 17
	p.310, Question 59	p.461, Question 35	p.539, Question 49
	p.312, Question 74	p.462, Question 38	p.543, Question 70
	p.380, Question 7		
	Flow of Ideas/Function/Relevance:		
	p.19, Question 29	p.309, Question 54	p.464, Question 59
	p.20, Question 33	p.311, Question 65	p.467, Question 75
	p.20, Question 36	p.380, Question 9	p.535, Question 16
	p.24, Question 64	p.384, Question 36	p.536, Question 24
	p.25, Question 71	p.387, Question 56	p.537, Question 33
	p.303, Question 16	p.457, Question 4	p.538, Question 36
	p.304, Question 24	p.462, Question 39	p.543, Question 69
	p.306, Question 35		

Sentence Structure/Misplaced Modifiers:

p.15, Question 5	p.26, Question 74	p.462, Question 42
p.16, Question 8	p.302, Question 11	p.463, Question 51
p.16, Question 9	p.306, Question 41	p.464, Question 55
p.18, Question 22	p.308, Question 47	p.534, Question 9
p.19, Question 27	p.309, Question 51	p.538, Question 42
p.20, Question 46	p.311, Question 66	p.539, Question 47
p.20, Question 47	p.379, Question 1	p.540, Question 53
p.22, Question 50	p.382, Question 19	p.542, Question 65
p.22, Question 54	p.383, Question 28	p.542, Question 67
p.23, Question 58	p.386, Question 46	p.542, Question 68
p.23, Question 59	p.389, Question 67	p.543, Question 72

Transitional Language:

p.16, Question 14	p.308, Question 49	p.538, Question 43
p.21, Question 42	p.382, Question 25	p.542, Question 64
p.26, Question 72	p.463, Question 50	p.542, Question 66
p.302, Question 12		

Word Choice:

p.19, Question 31	p.386, Question 49	p.460, Question 27
p.24, Question 64	p.388, Question 61	p.461, Question 32
p.24, Question 65	p.388, Question 62	p.461, Question 34
p.25, Question 67	p.389, Question 64	p.461, Question 36
p.25, Question 71	p.389, Question 69	p.465, Question 62
p.301, Question 4	p.457, Question 5	p.466, Question 66
p.304, Question 22	p.458, Question 13	p.534, Question 7
p.309, Question 53	p.459, Question 19	p.537, Question 31
p.380, Question 11	p.459, Question 20	p.542, Question 63
p.385, Question 43	p.459, Question 21	

Style	**Clear Expression:**		
	p.20, Question 34	p.384, Question 35	p.462, Question 40
	p.20, Question 35	p.385, Question 39	p.462, Question 41
	p.20, Question 40	p.385, Question 41	p.462, Question 44
	p.24, Question 63	p.386, Question 47	p.464, Question 54
	p.25, Question 66	p.386, Question 48	p.465, Question 63
	p.25, Question 71	p.386, Question 50	p.466, Question 66
	p.301, Question 6	p.387, Question 57	p.466, Question 69
	p.302, Question 14	p.387, Question 58	p.533, Question 4
	p.303, Question 19	p.388, Question 62	p.534, Question 12
	p.305, Question 32	p.388, Question 63	p.534, Question 13
	p.307, Question 44	p.389, Question 69	p.535, Question 18
	p.309, Question 57	p.457, Question 1	p.537, Question 28
	p.311, Question 63	p.458, Question 11	p.537, Question 31
	p.311, Question 69	p.459, Question 20	p.539, Question 45
	p.311, Question 70	p.460, Question 23	p.539, Question 46
	p.381, Question 13	p.460, Question 27	p.540, Question 51
	p.381, Question 16	p.461, Question 33	p.541, Question 58
	p.383, Question 32		

Idiom:

p.16, Question 7	p.311, Question 68	p.462, Question 43
p.22, Question 48	p.380, Question 8	p.534, Question 11
p.302, Question 7	p.382, Question 22	p.535, Question 14
p.305, Question 31	p.383, Question 27	p.536, Question 22
p.306, Question 36	p.384, Question 38	p.538, Question 35
p.309, Question 5	p.458, Question 10	p.540, Question 55
p.310, Question 61	p.460, Question 24	

Redundancy:

p.15, Question 3	p.304, Question 26	p.460, Question 28
p.17, Question 16	p.309, Question 52	p.464, Question 56
p.18, Question 23	p.379, Question 4	p.465, Question 61
p.20, Question 39	p.382, Question 18	p.536, Question 25
p.21, Question 41	p.382, Question 20	p.538, Question 39
p.22, Question 51	p.382, Question 24	p.539, Question 48
p.24, Question 61	p.385, Question 41	p.540, Question 51
p.25, Question 69	p.460, Question 25	

Verb Usage:

p.15, Question 1	p.302, Question 10	p.381, Question 12
p.16, Question 10	p.302, Question 13	p.381, Question 14
p.16, Question 12	p.304, Question 23	p.382, Question 21
p.17, Question 18	p.304, Question 27	p.382, Question 23
p.18, Question 20	p.305, Question 29	p.383, Question 26
p.18, Question 25	p.306, Question 36	p.383, Question 30
p.19, Question 28	p.306, Question 38	p.383, Question 31
p.20, Question 38	p.306, Question 39	p.384, Question 37
p.23, Question 56	p.310, Question 62	p.385, Question 39
p.24, Question 62	p.379, Question 1	p.385, Question 44
p.301, Question 5	p.379, Question 3	p.387, Question 52
p.301, Question 6	p.380, Question 6	p.387, Question 55
p.388, Question 63	p.462, Question 44	p.536, Question 19
p.389, Question 71	p.463, Question 48	p.536, Question 20
p.457, Question 3	p.464, Question 53	p.537, Question 28
p.458, Question 6	p.464, Question 58	p.537, Question 29
p.458, Question 8	p.465, Question 64	p.538, Question 37
p.458, Question 9	p.466, Question 71	p.540, Question 55

p.458, Question 11   p.533, Question 1   p.541, Question 58

p.459, Question 18   p.534, Question 8   p.541, Question 61

p.462, Question 43

Wordiness:

p.20, Question 34   p.309, Question 56   p.463, Question 46

p.20, Question 35   p.389, Question 65   p.466, Question 68

p.20, Question 40   p.460, Question 30   p.540, Question 61

p.22, Question 55

Mathematics

Absolute Value:

p.314, Question 9   p.479, Question 57   p.558, Question 60
p.470, Question 9

Angles, Parallel Lines, and Perpendicular Lines:

p.28, Question 7   p.397, Question 32   p.471, Question 16
p.34, Question 32   p.403, Question 58   p.477, Question 44
p.37, Question 44   p.469, Question 7   p.479, Question 54
p.314, Question 7   p.470, Question 10   p.557, Question 55

Coordinates:

p.30, Question 14   p.401, Question 51   p.480, Question 59
p.36, Question 39   p.476, Question 41   p.552, Question 39
p.394, Question 17

Complex/Imaginary Numbers and Radical/Rational Expressions:

p.31, Question 21   p.470, Question 11   p.478, Question 50
p.32, Question 27   p.471, Question 19   p.479, Question 53
p.35, Question 36   p.472, Question 24   p.548, Question 18
p.40, Question 57   p.477, Question 47   p.549, Question 25
p.319, Question 36   p.478, Question 49

Data Interpretation:

p.315, Question 14   p.400, Question 45   p.547, Question 11
p.400, Question 44   p.547, Question 10

Equation of a Circle:

p.33, Question 29   p.325, Question 59   p.474, Question 32
p.318, Question 29   p.473, Question 27   p.555, Question 49

Equation of a Line:

p.33, Question 28	p.393, Question 13	p.548, Question 17
p.39, Question 54	p.398, Question 39	p.551, Question 33
p.41, Question 59	p.470, Question 14	p.552, Question 39
p.319, Question 33	p.473, Question 29	p.555, Question 50
p.320, Question 39	p.477, Question 43	p.558, Question 59
p.321, Question 44		

Exponents:

p.32, Question 26	p.317, Question 25	p.468, Question 3
p.33, Question 31	p.317, Question 26	p.472, Question 23
p.37, Question 42	p.318, Question 31	p.474, Question 34
p.39, Question 52	p.323, Question 52	p.478, Question 50
p.314, Question 6	p.392, Question 6	p.479, Question 53
p.315, Question 11	p.395, Question 20	p.479, Question 57
p.316, Question 20	p.396, Question 26	p.553, Question 42

Functions:

p.30, Question 17	p.313, Question 4	p.547, Question 14
p.36, Question 41	p.396, Question 25	p.554, Question 44

Inequalities:

p.321, Question 42	p.396, Question 27	p.474, Question 33
p.394, Question 19	p.468, Question 1	p.552, Question 37
p.395, Question 21		

Linear Equations:

p.27, Question 1	p.313, Question 1	p.391, Question 1
p.28, Question 5	p.316, Question 16	p.545, Question 4
p.28, Question 8	p.324, Question 56	p.557, Question 53
p.29, Question 11		

Logarithms:

p.38, Question 47   p.317, Question 27

Logic:

p.27, Question 2	p.398, Question 37	p.479, Question 55
p.40, Question 56	p.399, Question 42	p.549, Question 24
p.313, Question 2	p.402, Question 51	
p.314, Question 6	p.478, Question 51	

Matrices:

p.32, Question 23   p.401, Question 48

Mean, Median, and Mode:

p.28, Question 9	p.398, Question 36	p.403, Question 60
p.315, Question 14	p.399, Question 41	p.553, Question 40
p.391, Question 4	p.402, Question 54	

Number Line:

p.34, Question 34	p.319, Question 34	p.398, Question 34
p.38, Question 50	p.323, Question 50	

Operations Using Whole Numbers, Decimals, and Fractions:

p.29, Question 10	p.316, Question 21	p.393, Question 15
p.29, Question 12	p.317, Question 22	p.394, Question 16
p.30, Question 18	p.317, Question 24	p.395, Question 20
p.31, Question 20	p.318, Question 31	p.395, Question 24
p.33, Question 31	p.320, Question 37	p.396, Question 28
p.35, Question 37	p.322, Question 47	p.396, Question 29
p.40, Question 56	p.323, Question 54	p.397, Question 31
p.41, Question 60	p.391, Question 2	p.398, Question 37
p.313, Question 3	p.392, Question 5	p.399, Question 42
p.315, Question 12	p.392, Question 10	p.400, Question 46

p.403, Question 59   p.472, Question 23   p.549, Question 25

p.468, Question 2   p.473, Question 31   p.549, Question 27

p.468, Question 3   p.473, Question 31   p.550, Question 29

p.468, Question 5   p.475, Question 36   p.558, Question 57

p.469, Question 6   p.545, Question 5

p.471, Question 15   p.548, Question 13

p.471, Question 18   p.548, Question 20

Percent, Percent Change:

p.27, Question 3   p.325, Question 60   p.545, Question 3

p.316, Question 17   p.468, Question 4   p.546, Question 9

p.316, Question 19   p.545, Question 1

Perimeter, Area, and Volume:

p.31, Question 22   p.392, Question 7   p.474, Question 35

p.34, Question 33   p.392, Question 9   p.475, Question 38

p.37, Question 43   p.395, Question 22   p.477, Question 46

p.37, Question 45   p.399, Question 43   p.547, Question 12

p.38, Question 49   p.401, Question 49   p.548, Question 19

p.319, Question 35   p.469, Question 8   p.552, Question 38

p.321, Question 43   p.472, Question 21   p.557, Question 54

p.321, Question 45   p.472, Question 22   p.558, Question 59

Polynomial Operations and Factoring:

p.30, Question 15   p.315, Question 15   p.472, Question 25

p.32, Question 24   p.392, Question 8   p.473, Question 28

p.36, Question 41   p.393, Question 15   p.478, Question 48

p.314, Question 8   p.470, Question 12   p.546, Question 7

Properties and Relations of Figures:

p.29, Question 13   p.398, Question 35   p.547, Question 12

p.35, Question 35   p.401, Question 51   p.548, Question 16

p.39, Question 51   p.402, Question 55   p.548, Question 19

p.315, Question 13   p.403, Question 57   p.549, Question 23

p.318, Question 32   p.472, Question 21   p.550, Question 28

p.322, Question 49   p.472, Question 22   p.554, Question 43

p.323, Question 51   p.475, Question 37   p.555, Question 47

p.393, Question 14   p.475, Question 38   p.555, Question 48

p.395, Question 23   p.478, Question 52   p.556, Question 51

Properties of Integer Exponents and Square Roots:

p.400, Question 46   p.551, Question 33   p.552, Question 37

Radians:

p.397, Question 33   p.556, Question 52

Ratios and Proportions:

p.27, Question 4   p.402, Question 56   p.473, Question 30

p.321, Question 41   p.471, Question 20

Roots of Polynomials and Factoring:

p.315, Question 15   p.548, Question 21   p.554, Question 45

p.476, Question 40   p.549, Question 22

Scientific Notation:

p.555, Question 46

Sequences:

p.39, Question 53   p.391, Question 3   p.545, Question 2

p.323, Question 53   p.477, Question 45

Simple Probability, Permutations, and Standard Deviation:

p.40, Question 58   p.402, Question 53   p.547, Question 15

p.324, Question 57   p.546, Question 8   p.558, Question 58

p.325, Question 58

Slope, Distance, and Midpoint:

p.35, Question 38   p.320, Question 38   p.473, Question 26

p.317, Question 23   p.398, Question 38   p.480, Question 60

p.317, Question 28   p.402, Question 50   p.551, Question 32

Systems of Equations:

p.37, Question 46   p.322, Question 46

Trigonometry:

p.33, Question 30   p.322, Question 48   p.476, Question 42

p.36, Question 40   p.324, Question 55   p.479, Question 56

p.38, Question 48   p.397, Question 30   p.552, Question 36

p.40, Question 55   p.399, Question 40   p.553, Question 41

p.318, Question 30   p.476, Question 39   p.557, Question 56

p.320, Question 40

Variables:

p.28, Question 5   p.320, Question 37   p.479, Question 55

p.28, Question 6   p.391, Question 2   p.480, Question 60

p.29, Question 10   p.392, Question 10   p.545, Question 5

p.30, Question 16   p.394, Question 16   p.546, Question 6

p.32, Question 25   p.395, Question 24   p.550, Question 30

p.37, Question 42   p.469, Question 6   p.551, Question 35

p.314, Question 10   p.473, Question 31   p.553, Question 42

p.316, Question 16   p.478, Question 51

Vertices:

p.401, Question 49   p.480, Question 59

Word Problems:

p.27, Question 4	p.324, Question 56	p.473, Question 30
p.29, Question 13	p.324, Question 57	p.480, Question 60
p.30, Question 16	p.325, Question 60	p.545, Question 1
p.30, Question 18	p.391, Question 4	p.545, Question 3
p.31, Question 19	p.391, Question 7	p.546, Question 8
p.31, Question 22	p.392, Question 5	p.546, Question 9
p.32, Question 23	p.393, Question 11	p.547, Question 15
p.35, Question 37	p.394, Question 18	p.548, Question 16
p.38, Question 48	p.395, Question 23	p.548, Question 19
p.313, Question 4	p.396, Question 25	p.549, Question 23
p.314, Question 5	p.396, Question 27	p.549, Question 24
p.315, Question 14	p.400, Question 45	p.550, Question 26
p.316, Question 18	p.403, Question 57	p.550, Question 31
p.316, Question 19	p.403, Question 58	p.551, Question 34
p.321, Question 41	p.468, Question 1	p.552, Question 38
p.321, Question 45	p.468, Question 4	p.553, Question 40
p.322, Question 49	p.469, Question 8	p.553, Question 42
p.323, Question 50	p.471, Question 15	p.555, Question 46
p.323, Question 53	p.471, Question 17	p.558, Question 58
p.323, Question 54	p.471, Question 20	

Reading

Compare/Contrast:

p.45, Question 17	p.407, Question 18	p.486, Question 29
p.45, Question 20	p.407, Question 19	p.486, Question 30
p.333, Question 38	p.407, Question 20	p.566, Question 38
p.333, Question 39	p.486, Question 27	p.566, Question 39
p.333, Question 40	p.486, Question 28	p.566, Question 40

Conclusion/Inference:

p.43, Question 1	p.330, Question 22	p.484, Question 17
p.43, Question 4	p.330, Question 25	p.484, Question 19
p.43, Question 9	p.330, Question 26	p.485, Question 21
p.44, Question 11	p.331, Question 27	p.487, Question 32
p.45, Question 17	p.332, Question 33	p.559, Question 1
p.47, Question 25	p.333, Question 39	p.560, Question 3
p.47, Question 26	p.405, Question 2	p.560, Question 5
p.48, Question 34	p.405, Question 3	p.560, Question 7
p.48, Question 39	p.405, Question 5	p.560, Question 9
p.327, Question 2	p.405, Question 7	p.560, Question 10
p.327, Question 5	p.405, Question 8	p.562, Question 17
p.327, Question 7	p.407, Question 16	p.563, Question 21
p.327, Question 8	p.409, Question 25	p.563, Question 22
p.327, Question 9	p.409, Question 26	p.564, Question 27
p.328, Question 12	p.482, Question 2	p.564, Question 30
p.329, Question 16	p.482, Question 3	p.566, Question 33
p.329, Question 17	p.482, Question 7	p.566, Question 35
p.329, Question 18	p.482, Question 8	p.566, Question 36
p.329, Question 20	p.483, Question 13	
p.330, Question 21	p.484, Question 15	

Extrapolation:

p.43, Question 3	p.405, Question 6	p.484, Question 14
p.44, Question 12	p.405, Question 10	p.484, Question 20
p.44, Question 14	p.407, Question 12	p.486, Question 23
p.45, Question 16	p.407, Question 13	p.486, Question 26
p.45, Question 19	p.407, Question 17	p.486, Question 27
p.46, Question 23	p.409, Question 28	p.486, Question 29
p.326, Question 1	p.410, Question 32	p.560, Question 2
p.327, Question 3	p.410, Question 34	p.560, Question 4
p.327, Question 6	p.411, Question 36	p.560, Question 8
p.328, Question 13	p.411, Question 38	p.562, Question 16
p.330, Question 24	p.411, Question 39	p.564, Question 26
p.331, Question 29	p.482, Question 4	p.564, Question 29
p.333, Question 34	p.482, Question 5	p.565, Question 31
p.333, Question 36	p.482, Question 6	p.565, Question 32
p.333, Question 37	p.482, Question 9	
p.405, Question 1	p.483, Question 11	

Main Idea/Point of View/Structure/Tone:

p.43, Question 7	p.405, Question 9	p.487, Question 35
p.45, Question 18	p.407, Question 20	p.560, Question 8
p.46, Question 21	p.408, Question 21	p.561, Question 11
p.46, Question 24	p.408, Question 23	p.561, Question 12
p.47, Question 28	p.410, Question 31	p.562, Question 13
p.327, Question 10	p.411, Question 37	p.564, Question 23
p.330, Question 23	p.484, Question 16	p.564, Question 25
p.331, Question 30	p.486, Question 24	
p.333, Question 38	p.487, Question 31	
p.333, Question 40	p.487, Question 34	

Specific Detail:

p.43, Question 5	p.48, Question 40	p.411, Question 40
p.43, Question 6	p.328, Question 11	p.482, Question 10
p.43, Question 8	p.329, Question 14	p.485, Question 22
p.43, Question 10	p.329, Question 19	p.486, Question 25
p.45, Question 15	p.331, Question 28	p.486, Question 30
p.46, Question 22	p.407, Question 15	p.488, Question 36
p.47, Question 27	p.407, Question 18	p.488, Question 37
p.47, Question 29	p.407, Question 19	p.562, Question 14
p.47, Question 30	p.408, Question 22	p.562, Question 18
p.48, Question 31	p.409, Question 27	p.562, Question 19
p.48, Question 32	p.409, Question 29	p.562, Question 20
p.48, Question 33	p.409, Question 30	p.564, Question 28
p.48, Question 35	p.410, Question 33	p.566, Question 34
p.48, Question 36	p.411, Question 35	
p.48, Question 38		

Vocabulary in Context:

p.43, Question 2	p.407, Question 11	p.488, Question 39
p.44, Question 13	p.407, Question 14	p.488, Question 39
p.48, Question 37	p.409, Question 24	p.488, Question 40
p.327, Question 4	p.482, Question 1	p.560, Question 6
p.329, Question 15	p.483, Question 12	p.562, Question 15
p.332, Question 31	p.484, Question 18	p.564, Question 24
p.332, Question 32	p.487, Question 33	p.566, Question 37
p.333, Question 35	p.488, Question 37	
p.405, Question 4		

Science

Common Knowledge:

p.54, Question 20   p.424, Question 39

Compare/Contrast:

p.52, Question 9   p.413, Question 5   p.567, Question 1
p.52, Question 11   p.492, Question 13   p.567, Question 6
p.52, Question 12   p.494, Question 24   p.570, Question 17
p.336, Question 7   p.496, Question 37   p.573, Question 27
p.337, Question 12

Conclusion/Inference:

p.51, Question 4   p.415, Question 13   p.496, Question 36
p.52, Question 6   p.415, Question 15   p.496, Question 38
p.52, Question 12   p.416, Question 17   p.567, Question 2
p.57, Question 33   p.419, Question 31   p.567, Question 6
p.59, Question 35   p.419, Question 33   p.569, Question 11
p.335, Question 3   p.419, Question 34   p.573, Question 25
p.336, Question 9   p.490, Question 3   p.573, Question 26
p.339, Question 22   p.491, Question 9   p.574, Question 31
p.343, Question 37   p.494, Question 25   p.576, Question 40
p.414, Question 11

Data Trends and Relationships:

p.50, Question 1   p.54, Question 22   p.335, Question 5
p.51, Question 3   p.56, Question 24   p.339, Question 23
p.53, Question 14   p.56, Question 27   p.339, Question 24
p.53, Question 17   p.57, Question 28   p.340, Question 25
p.54, Question 19   p.57, Question 30   p.340, Question 28
p.54, Question 21   p.58, Question 34   p.340, Question 29

p.342, Question 35

p.342, Question 36

p.343, Question 40

p.413, Question 1

p.413, Question 4

p.414, Question 8

p.414, Question 8

p.414, Question 12

p.415, Question 14

p.416, Question 16

p.416, Question 17

p.417, Question 20

p.418, Question 25

p.418, Question 28

p.419, Question 32

p.420, Question 37

p.420, Question 38

p.491, Question 8

p.491, Question 10

p.492, Question 16

p.493, Question 22

p.496, Question 35

p.572, Question 22

p.574, Question 34

p.575, Question 36

Experimental Design:

p.52, Question 10

p.57, Question 29

p.335, Question 4

p.335, Question 6

p.338, Question 15

p.338, Question 18

p.343, Question 39

p.413, Question 7

p.490, Question 4

Extrapolation:

p.51, Question 5

p.52, Question 7

p.52, Question 8

p.52, Question 9

p.53, Question 16

p.54, Question 18

p.56, Question 26

p.57, Question 31

p.59, Question 38

p.59, Question 40

p.335, Question 1

p.335, Question 5

p.336, Question 7

p.336, Question 10

p.336, Question 11

p.337, Question 12

p.338, Question 14

p.338, Question 17

p.338, Question 19

p.339, Question 20

p.339, Question 21

p.340, Question 26

p.341, Question 31

p.341, Question 33

p.341, Question 34

p.343, Question 38

p.413, Question 2

p.413, Question 3

p.413, Question 4

p.414, Question 10

p.417, Question 19

p.418, Question 26

p.421, Question 39

p.490, Question 5

p.492, Question 14

p.492, Question 15

p.493, Question 21

p.494, Question 28

p.495, Question 33

p.496, Question 39

p.496, Question 40

p.567, Question 4

p.570, Question 13   p.571, Question 18   p.575, Question 37

p.570, Question 14   p.573, Question 28   p.575, Question 38

p.570, Question 15   p.574, Question 35

Logic:

p.52, Question 8   p.338, Question 17   p.571, Question 19

p.52, Question 11   p.417, Question 21   p.573, Question 29

p.337, Question 13   p.568, Question 7   p.573, Question 30

p.338, Question 15

Specific Detail:

p.50, Question 2   p.418, Question 27   p.495, Question 29

p.51, Question 3   p.419, Question 29   p.495, Question 30

p.53, Question 13   p.419, Question 30   p.495, Question 31

p.53, Question 15   p.419, Question 35   p.495, Question 32

p.54, Question 19   p.420, Question 36   p.496, Question 34

p.56, Question 23   p.421, Question 40   p.567, Question 3

p.56, Question 25   p.490, Question 1   p.567, Question 5

p.57, Question 32   p.490, Question 2   p.569, Question 8

p.59, Question 37   p.491, Question 6   p.569, Question 9

p.59, Question 39   p.491, Question 7   p.569, Question 10

p.335, Question 2   p.491, Question 11   p.569, Question 12

p.336, Question 8   p.492, Question 12   p.570, Question 16

p.340, Question 27   p.492, Question 17   p.572, Question 20

p.341, Question 30   p.493, Question 18   p.572, Question 21

p.341, Question 32   p.493, Question 19   p.572, Question 23

p.413, Question 6   p.493, Question 20   p.572, Question 24

p.417, Question 18   p.494, Question 23   p.574, Question 32

p.417, Question 22   p.494, Question 26   p.572, Question 33

p.418, Question 23   p.494, Question 27   p.576, Question 39

p.418, Question 24

Notes

Notes

Notes

Notes

Notes

Notes

Notes

Notes

Notes

Notes

Notes

Notes

The Cross-Platform Prep Course

McGraw-Hill Education's multi-platform course gives you a variety of tools to help you raise your test scores. Whether you're studying at home, in the library, or on-the-go, you can find practice content in the format you need—print, online, or mobile.

Print Book

This print book gives you the tools you need to ace the test. In its pages you'll find smart test-taking strategies, in-depth reviews of key topics, and ample practice questions and tests. See the Welcome section of your book for a step-by-step guide to its features.

Online Platform

The Cross-Platform Prep Course gives you additional study and practice content that you can access *anytime, anywhere.* You can create a personalized study plan based on your test date that sets daily goals to keep you on track. Integrated lessons provide important review of key topics. Practice questions, exams, and flashcards give you the practice you need to build test-taking confidence. The game center is filled with challenging games that allow you to practice your new skills in a fun and engaging way. And, you can even interact with other test-takers in the discussion section and gain valuable peer support.

Getting Started

To get started, open your account on the online platform:

Go to www.xplatform.mhprofessional.com

↓

Enter your access code, which you can find on the inside back cover of your book

↓

Provide your name and e-mail address to open your account and create a password

↓

Click "Start Studying" to enter the platform

It's as simple as that. You're ready to start studying online.

Your Personalized Study Plan

First, select your test date on the calendar, and you'll be on your way to creating your personalized study plan. Your study plan will help you stay organized and on track and will guide you through the course in the most efficient way. It is tailored to *your* schedule and features daily tasks that are broken down into manageable goals. You can adjust your test date at any time and your daily tasks will be reorganized into an updated plan.

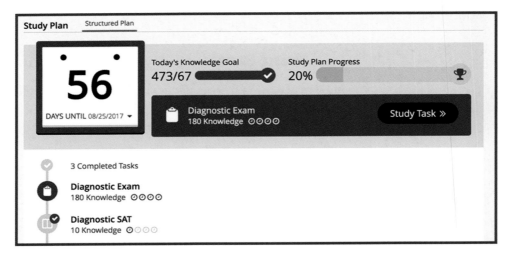

You can track your progress in real time on the Study Plan Dashboard. The "Today's Knowledge Goal" progress bar gives you up-to-the minute feedback on your daily goal. Fulfilling this every time you log on is the most efficient way to work through the entire course. You always get an instant view of where you stand in the entire course with the Study Plan Progress bar.

If you need to exit the program before completing a task, you can return to the Study Plan Dashboard at any time. Just click the Study Task icon and you can automatically pick up where you left off.

Practice Tests

One of the first tasks in your personalized study plan is to take the Diagnostic Test. At the end of the test, a detailed evaluation of your strengths and weaknesses shows the areas where you need the most focus. You can review your practice test results either by the question category to see broad trends or question-by-question for a more in-depth look.

The full-length tests are designed to simulate the real thing. Try to simulate actual testing conditions and be sure you set aside enough time to complete the full-length test. You'll learn to pace yourself so that you can work toward the best possible score on test day.

Lessons

The lessons in the online platform are divided into manageable pieces that let you build knowledge and confidence in a progressive way. They cover the full range of topics that you're likely to see on your test.

After you complete a lesson, mark your confidence level. (You must indicate a confidence level in order to count your progress and move on to the next task.) You can also filter the lessons by confidence levels to see the areas you have mastered and those that you might need to revisit.

> *Use the bookmark feature to easily refer back to a concept or leave a note to remember your thoughts or questions about a particular topic.*

Practice Questions

All of the practice questions are reflective of actual exams and simulate the test-taking experience. The "Review Answer" button gives you immediate feedback on your answer. Each question includes a rationale that explains why the correct answer is right and the others are wrong. To explore any topic further, you can find detailed explanations by clicking the "Help me learn about this topic" link.

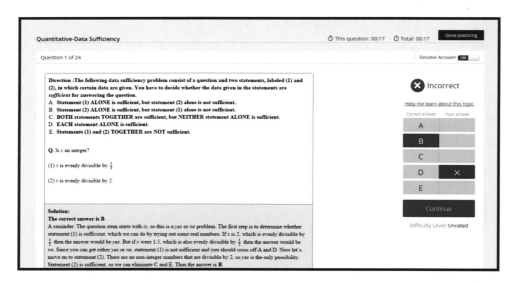

You can go to the Practice Dashboard to find an overview of your performance in the different categories and sub-categories.

Dashboard

The dashboard is constantly updating to reflect your progress and performance. The Percentile Rank icon shows your position relative to all the other students enrolled in the course. You can also find information on your average scores in practice questions and exams.

A detailed overview of your strengths and weaknesses shows your proficiency in a category based on your answers and difficulty of the questions. By viewing your strengths and weaknesses, you can focus your study on areas where you need the most help.

Flashcards

The hundreds of flashcards are perfect for learning key terms quickly, and the interactive format gives you immediate feedback. You can filter the cards by category and confidence level for a more organized approach. Or, you can shuffle them up for a more general challenge.

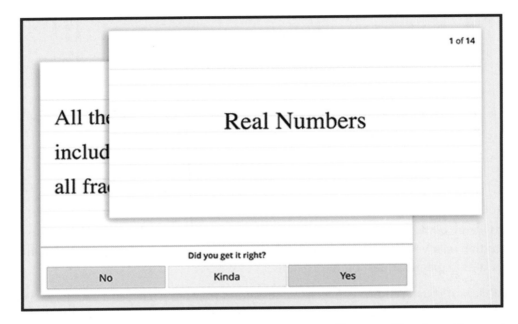

Another way to customize the flashcards is to create your own sets. You can either keep these private or share or them with the public. Subscribe to Community Sets to access sets from other students preparing for the same exam.

Game Center

Play a game in the Game Center to test your knowledge of key concepts in a challenging but fun environment. Increase the difficulty level and complete the games quickly to build your highest score. Be sure to check the leaderboard to see who's on top!

Social Community

Interact with other students who are preparing for the same test. Start a discussion, reply to a post, or even upload files to share. You can search the archives for common topics or start your own private discussion with friends.

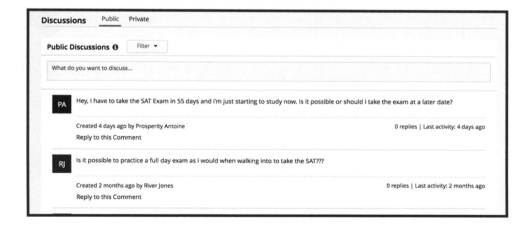

Mobile App

The companion mobile app lets you toggle between the online platform and your mobile device without missing a beat. Whether you access the course online or from your smartphone or tablet, you'll pick up exactly where you left off.

Go to the iTunes or Google Play stores and search "McGraw-Hill Education Cross-Platform App" to download the companion iOS or Android app. Enter your e-mail address and the same password you created for the online platform to open your account.

Now, let's get started!